To my dear wife Elisabeth,
who stood by me when my life was threatened
and insisted that I better die as a martyr than stop preaching,

and to our daughter Dorothy,
who grew up in the atmosphere of martyrdom
and of joy unspeakable and full of glory.

SUFFERING, MARTYRDOM, AND REWARDS IN HEAVEN

Josef Ton

Lanham • New York • Oxford

First Edition Copyright © 1997

Reprint, Copyright © 2000 by
The Romanian Missionary Society
1415 Hill Avenue
Wheaton, Illinois 60187

ISBN 0-7618-0832-9 (cloth:alk.ppr.)
ISBN 0-7618-0833-7 (pbk:alk.ppr)

Acknowledgments

The author gratefully acknowledges the following publishers' permission to reprint portions of the publications listed below:

"The Conception of Reward in the Teaching of Jesus," by G. de Ru, in *Novum Testamentum* 8 (1966): 202-222. Used by permission of Brill Academic Publishers, Leiden, The Netherlands.

"Degrees of Glory: Protestant Doctrine and the Concept of Rewards Hereafter," by Emma Disley, in the *Journal of Theological Studies* 42, part 1 (April 1991): 77-105. Used by permission of Oxford University Press, Oxford, England.

"The Monk and the Martyr," by Edward E. Malone, in *Studia Anselmiana* 38 (1956): 201-228. Used by permission of Centro Studi S'Anselmo, Rome, Italy.

Excerpts taken from the 1,157-page book, *The Bloody Theater or Martyrs' Mirror of the Defenseless Christians*, by Thielemann J. van Braght, are reprinted by permission of Herald Press, Scottdale, PA 15683.

What Luther Says, copyright 1959, 1987 Concordia Publishing House, St. Louis MO. Used by permission. All rights reserved.

v

Contents

Part Four: A Survey of Christian Thought on Suffering, Martyrdom, and Rewards in Heaven

Preface

In the spring of 1972, I was completing my undergraduate studies in theology at the University of Oxford, England. As I was making plans to return to Romania, I received different warnings that after I returned there I might be arrested, imprisoned or even killed. I knew that God wanted me back in my own country, and I was determined to obey Him, whatever the cost. Yet I wanted to understand exactly what my Heavenly Father's purpose could be in sending me to a place where I would most likely be killed. Precisely this question launched me into two decades of in-depth study on the issue of martyrdom.

One of the most popular professors of Bible in Oxford at that time was G. B. Caird. I loved to sit in his classes and to absorb his commentaries on different books of the New Testament. My deep appreciation for his lectures motivating me, I picked up his commentary on the book of Revelation. It was this book that introduced me to the Biblical teaching on martyrdom. It was there that I saw how God always conquers by a love that is self-giving and self-sacrificing. It was there that I understood God's method of sending His Lamb into the world, followed by many thousands of other lambs, to overcome the world by proclaiming the love of God and by dying for the sake of their proclamation.

This astonishing biblical principle that God always conquers through people who will preach the gospel and then die for it helped me immeasurably to be able to go back to Romania. It gave me the solid rationale I needed for the dangerous return home. Buttressed by this teaching, I preached, lectured, and wrote for nearly a decade, ready to be martyred for what I was doing, yet knowing that death would be my supreme weapon of conquest and my road to the highest glory in heaven.

Since I wanted to broaden and deepen my understanding of the theology of martyrdom, I began a serious search for bibliography on this issue. It was not long before I realized, however, that Protestant theologians unfortunately have never articulated a systematic and universal investigation of suffering and martyrdom.

In 1981, I was exiled from Romania with my wife Elisabeth and our daughter Dorothy. Upon arriving in America, we settled in Wheaton, Illinois. Two years later I was asked to teach a course at Wheaton College entitled "Theological Issues in Eastern Europe." I was given complete freedom to determine exactly what were the theological issues facing the Eastern European Christian Church under communist persecution and which of those I should include in my lectures. Among the many issues that I determined should be discussed in my course, the most important for me was the issue of being ready to die for Christ and His gospel; in other words, the issue of utmost significance for me was that of martyrdom. It was not surprising, then, that I ended up devoting half of my lectures to an exposition of the biblical view of persecution and martyrdom.

Consequently, I have Wheaton College and that course to thank for obligating me to commence a comprehensive review of the history of the concept of martyrdom. I also found it necessary to begin a new and fresh examination of all that the Bible has to say about persecution, suffering, and martyrdom.

As my research progressed, I came to see that whenever the Bible talks about persecution, suffering, and martyrdom, these discussions are always accompanied by promises of great rewards in heaven. I also discovered that the vision of heaven, together with the hope of heavenly rewards, has always been one of the greatest motivations for people facing persecution and martyrdom. I was forced, therefore, to investigate the question of rewards in heaven, as well. Soon it became clear to me that the issue of rewards in heaven was organically linked with suffering and martyrdom. One cannot adequately understand the scriptural teaching on suffering and martyrdom in isolation from the

Bible's pronouncement of God's final purpose with mankind in His heavenly kingdom and in the new heaven and the new earth.

If we seriously believe that God's final purpose with men and women is to give them dominion, that is, functions of ruling with responsibility over the entire created universe, and if we truly believe what Jesus taught us about ranks in the kingdom of heaven based on the way people have discharged their God-given duties in this present life, then we will be able to discern the process by which men and women are prepared, educated, trained, and tested, through hardship, sufferings, trials, temptations, and calls to self-sacrifice, for that final destiny of reigning with Christ.

As these concepts took shape and matured in my mind, I was led to the realization that I needed to develop and articulate a biblical theology in the following areas:

1. A theology of good works consistent with the Protestant theology of grace (Protestant theologians have had difficulty integrating these two doctrines into a coherent system);

2. A theology of character development and its importance for the eternal destiny of persons;

3. A theology of the judgment seat of Christ for believers based on works, issuing in a verdict that determines a person's position in the eternal kingdom of God;

4. A theology of functions, positions of authority, ranks, and relationships in the kingdom of heaven.

Only when we resolve these numerous theological problems can we attain a proper understanding and a proper theology of suffering and martyrdom.

As I was working out these themes, I detected two main stumbling blocks that have caused Protestant theologians either to completely reject the issues of martyrdom and rewards in heaven or to merely pay lip service to them with pious devotional comments, with which, in fact, they have conveniently spiritualized these issues and have effectively explained them away.

The first stumbling block originated in the third century A.D., when the martyrs came to be so highly esteemed and valued that they were raised to the rank of saints. Eventually, the death of these martyrs was considered to have the same atoning value as the death of Christ. They were said to have the same power to forgive sins and to mediate between individuals and God. The veneration of the martyrs, transformed into the adoration of the saints, began in earnest in the fourth century A.D.

While the Reformers continued to value martyrdom because they had to face it themselves, they had the difficult task of purging the meaning of martyrdom of all its pagan accretions annexed from the fourth century to the fifteenth century. The job turned out to be troublesome, indeed, and the easiest way out of the predicament eventually proved to be to ignore the subject altogether. This is why the Protestants have never integrated a theology of martyrdom into their systematic theology as a whole.

The second problem of Protestant theologians has had to do with the issue of rewards. In our minds, when we speak of rewards we immediately think of having to earn them; we think of merit and, ultimately, of boasting and pride. On the contrary, the Bible is very clear that:

a) you cannot earn anything from God (Lk.17:5-10; Rom.4:1-5);

b) you cannot obtain anything from God based on "merit," because everything He gives you has already been predestined from before the foundation of the world;

c) you will never be able to boast by saying "I did it," because He gives you both the willing and the achieving (Phil 2:13).

Hence, Protestants have perpetually questioned how one can coherently talk of rewards. If everything is given by God by grace, then speaking about rewards seems to be nonsense. I struggled with this issue for many years, but when I looked deeper into the *content* of the rewards, the answers emerged. A thorough analysis of the biblical concepts of dominion, of reigning, and of inheriting with Christ, as well as an examination of the scriptural concepts of worthiness and of being trained and tested for trustworthiness, helped me to see that, yes, we *can* speak about rewards consistently *without* entailing any ideas of earning, of meriting or of prideful boasting.

Today, the book market is overflowing with volumes on suffering. A plethora of new books on this subject has been published in the last few decades. As I went through many of them, I came to see that a large number of them have one thing in common: they are all inward-looking. They ask only one question: What does suffering do to the sufferer? Most of them are correct in showing that suffering builds character and perfects the sufferer. This is a biblical question and a biblical answer. But it is not *all* that the Bible has to say about suffering. We have to enlarge our horizons. Our attention has to be drawn away from ourselves. We have to ask many other questions, including the following: What are the purposes of God in suffering and martyrdom beyond those directed toward the sufferers themselves? What does our suffering do for others, for the conversion of the lost, for the building up of the body of Christ, for the defeat of Satan, and for the triumph of God's truth on the earth?

Suffering and martyrdom have many functions in God's strategy. We have to explore all of them. Only then can we understand why suffering, self-denial, and self-sacrifice are so undeniably central to the teaching of the entire Word of God.

These are the issues raised by my study of the concept of martyrdom. I should also say a few words now about the structure of my presentation. There are three books in the Old Testament that deal specifically with the functions of the suffering and death of the just in God's overall plan and strategy; these are the Books of Job, Isaiah, and Daniel. I will start with an exposition of these three, because the basic ideas that should make up our theology of martyrdom have already been outlined in these three books. Next I will present the ideas about suffering, martyrdom, and rewards in heaven formulated in the intertestamental literature. I will follow this up by making an extended study of the teaching of the New Testament on these topics, from which I will draw some preliminary conclusions about a theology of suffering, martyrdom, and rewards in heaven.

At the same time, I believe that we should not neglect what Christians have thought and taught about these issues over the centuries. In fact, there were two creative epochs in which the subjects of suffering and martyrdom received great attention, namely, the first four centuries of the Christian era and the time of the Reformation (the sixteenth and seventeenth centuries). Accordingly, in the last part of this book, I will present a survey of the main ideas that were conceived and articulated in those two epochs.

I have carefully reviewed all the modern publications on martyrdom that I could find in the English language. However, I did not find any *new* ideas. But I did find an abundance of secondary sources on the books of the Bible discussed in the chapters to follow, on the intertestamental period, and on the two epochs of Christian history that I mentioned. Because these secondary sources greatly aided my understanding of the thinking of the past, I considered them very useful resources; yet I did not think it necessary to write a special chapter addressing the thinking of the last two centuries on suffering and martyrdom. Whatever was of importance from what was produced in the modern era, I incorporated into my presentation of the previous epochs. What follows, then, in this book, is "an inventory of ideas." Based on the historical ideas inventoried, I will attempt in the end to build what I consider to be a biblical theology of suffering, martyrdom, and rewards in heaven.

One more word of explanation is needed. My objectives have led me to a very extensive investigation, from the Book of Job to the texts and events of the seventeenth century A.D., and I have touched upon very many themes and issues. Many times I have felt that a certain epoch or theme deserved a much larger treatment than I was able to give it. However, in the interest of space and time, I have had to compress and summarize much of the rich material that I have gathered; I have had to restrict myself to an abridged and sketchy panoramic survey, including only those basic things which have ultimately assisted me in constructing my own systematic theology of suffering, martyrdom, and rewards in heaven.

As I indicated at the beginning of this introduction, my research was born out of my own confrontation with the possibility of physical death for the cause of Christ and of His gospel. What made me able to face this possibility with peace and joy was the understanding that martyrdom is a very essential part of the way God chooses to tackle the evil of this world. Suffering and self-sacrifice are, first of all, God's selected methods for His own involvement in history and for the accomplishment of His purposes with mankind. When He chooses human instruments, therefore, to achieve His purposes through them, God uses the same methods He employed with His Son.

When I started on this road with Christ in 1972, I first explained to my dear wife Elisabeth about God's method of conquest in the world. I asked her to give me to the Lord for this kind of battle to which He has called me. She not only released me to this battle but offered herself to fight and, if need be, to die for the same. I must confess here that at crucial points in our clashes with the Romanian secret police, my wife was the strongest of the two, and she was the one who kept me going. Furthermore, all the way through my long investigation of this subject, as well as through my writing of this dissertation, she has been my beloved partner and secretary. My gratitude to her is beyond my capacity of verbal expression.

Our daughter, Dorothy, shared with us as a little child in the tribulations we faced under the communists. She was there when the police searched and ransacked our house, she witnessed the arrests, and at four years of age was even taken to the secret police station with her mother. Now, I want to extend my special recognition and gratitude to her for thoroughly proofreading and editing this book and for checking the accuracy of all my quotes and Greek terms. I also thank her for making the indexes and for preparing the whole manuscript for printing.

In 1985, while I was searching for more writings on martyrdom at the Wheaton College and Billy Graham Center libraries, somebody gave me a typed paper entitled "Martyrdom: Gateway to Heaven," written by Professor Dr. Peter Beyerhaus of Tübingen University in Germany. The paper was presented in 1983, in Vancouver, Canada, at a meeting dedicated to the persecuted church in the communist world.[1] That paper made me aware of the fact that Dr. Beyerhaus was a man who was seriously interested in the issue of martyrdom and one who had given it extensive theological consideration. In 1992, I decided to work my Ph.D. dissertation on the theology of martyrdom at the Evangelical Faculty of Theology in Heverlee, Belgium. To my delight, I heard that Dr. Beyerhaus served as professor at this school, as well. I got in touch with him, telling him of my intention, and he graciously invited me to go to Tubingen to discuss the subject with him. I went with six folders of notes. Dr. Beyerhaus gave me two days of his precious time to listen to my findings and to my ideas. At the end, he simply said, "I believe that you have an important contribution to make to theology, and that your message must be heard. You have enough material in those six folders for a doctorate. Go ahead and write the dissertation." Well, it took me another three and a half years, including one year and a half as a research scholar at the Billy Graham Center in Wheaton, to finish this dissertation. My gratitude to Dr. Beyerhaus for being my promoter is very great indeed.

I also have to express my gratitude to Dr. Peter Wagner, at that time the Dean of the Evangelical Faculty of Theology in Belgium, and now Professor of Missiology at the Golden Gate Seminary in California, for taking the time to carefully read the last draft of this dissertation and for giving me valuable suggestions and guidance.

I am also grateful to my second reader, Dr. Philip Roberts, professor at Southeastern Baptist Seminary in Wake Forest, North Carolina. A good friend for more than twenty years, he has stood by me in all my times of struggle, battle, and hardship in Romania, thereby contributing much to the development of my theology of martyrdom.

Likewise, I have to include a special word of thanks to another exceptional friend, Dr. R. T. Kendall, pastor of the Westminster Chapel in London, England. In the early eighties, we spent many days together in his home discussing the theological issues of rewards and merit. When I argued with him that one had to accept some idea of merit if one spoke of rewards, he was adamant in maintaining that the moment I introduced the concept of merit, I was finished as a Protestant theologian. In desperation, I replied, "But then, how can I speak about rewards, as the Bible speaks so much about them, and nevertheless exclude all notions of merit?" At that point, R. T. Kendall turned to me and said, "Josef, I have no idea what the solution to this problem is; but I do have a hunch that if you took some time to study the concept of 'being worthy,' you just might find your clue there." Picking up a Greek concordance of the Bible, he then showed me how many times this word appears in the New Testament. Yes, indeed, as I studied the concept of worthiness, it turned out to be the doorway to my understanding of the concepts of inheritance and of the training and testing of God's children for positions of ruling in heaven.

Furthermore, I am especially grateful to the Trustees of the Romanian Missionary Society of Wheaton, Illinois, for giving me a sabbatical leave for a year and a half, and for creating for my wife and I all the conditions needed to write this dissertation in Wheaton, Illinois. I also thank the Billy Graham Center of Wheaton, Illinois, for offering me the status of Scholar-in-Residence, in order to enable me to do the necessary research for the completion of this work.

Most of all, I thank my Lord and Master for calling me to the wonderful partnership of suffering with Him and for showing me all the riches that are hidden in this amazing partnership.

PART ONE

Suffering, Witness, and Martyrdom in the Old Testament

Introduction

Suffering, pain, and death are the ever-present, undesired, and hated side of human existence. They are a part of the history of man, and no one can escape them. They are the starting point of man's search for meaning, and the stuff of man's poetry, drama, and philosophy.

The Old Testament is full of stories of disaster, calamity, tragedy, and all kinds of other sufferings. Naturally, many of its authors commented on these sufferings, offering some explanation for their existence. Of course, the basic explanation is that suffering has come into the life of mankind as a result of the disobedience of Adam and Eve. Book after book in the Old Testament shows us the tragic consequences of breaking God's commandments. It is most illuminating to see these consequences as they are described in the curses pronounced by God through Moses in Leviticus 26:14-39 and in Deuteronomy 28:15-68. The consequences of disobedience are also systematically illustrated in the stories of the unfaithfulness of Israel and Judah presented in the Books of Chronicles. The results of their disobedience culminate in the destruction of Israel and in the Babylonian exile of Judah.

However, the most disturbing and most painful phenomenon is the suffering of the innocent, of the just and the upright. Time and time again, we watch calamities come over people who have been faithful to

God, and these men and women see no reason why God has apparently deserted them or has even acted against them. In contrast, we see the unjust and the wicked prospering and enjoying good lives. Psalms 44 and 73 are just two examples of the literature that deals with this problem which tempts even the most faithful to lose their hope in the Almighty God.

Yet when these anguished individuals meditate on the *cause* of their suffering, they eventually begin to see that at least some of the *effects* of their suffering are not detrimental after all. On the contrary, they are led to acknowledge that suffering produces good in the life of the one who patiently and graciously accepts it. This is the insight of the author of Psalm 119:

> Before I was afflicted I went astray, but now I keep Thy word. . . .
> It is good for me that I was afflicted, that I may learn Thy statutes.
> . . . I know, O Lord, that Thy judgments are righteous, and that in
> faithfulness Thou hast afflicted me. O may Thy lovingkindness
> comfort me, according to Thy word to Thy servant. (Ps. 119:67,
> 71, 75-76, NASB)[1]

The author of the Book of Lamentations comes close to the same understanding:

> It is good for a man that he should bear the yoke in his youth. Let
> him sit alone and be silent since He has laid it on him. Let him put
> his mouth in the dust, perhaps there is hope. Let him give his
> cheek to the smiter; let him be filled with reproach. For the Lord
> will not reject forever, for if He causes grief, then He will have
> compassion according to His abundant lovingkindness. For He
> does not afflict willingly, or grieve the sons of men. (Lam. 3:27-
> 33)

The writer of Deuteronomy goes one step further to explain that God acts toward us like a father disciplining a son: "Thus you are to know in your heart that the Lord your God was disciplining you just as a man disciplines his son" (Deut. 8:5). This idea is developed even more in the Book of Proverbs: "For whom the Lord loves He reproves, even as a father, the son in whom he delights" (Prov. 3:12).

When one becomes aware of the fact that sufferings may come from the hand of a loving God and that they can be His instruments in one's life, it then becomes easier to accept sufferings and to go through them.

However, there are some Old Testament authors who venture even beyond this realization. They do not stop at merely seeing suffering as an instrument of God *acting in the one who suffers*. They come to see suffering as an instrument by which the one who suffers *carries out God's purposes in other people, in history, or even above history, in the spiritual realm*. When one comes to see that even God Himself is involved in this kind of suffering, one has reached the pinnacle of understanding.

There are three books in the Old Testament which see suffering as an experience undertaken and endured for others, for the fulfillment of God's purposes in history and in the spiritual realm. These are the Book of Job, the Book of Isaiah (chapters 40-66), and the Book of Daniel. Chronologically, Job comes first. Nevertheless, it serves our purposes best to begin with Isaiah, to follow his prophecy with that of Daniel, and finally, to bring in the Book of Job, which presents the culminating, cosmic dimension of the impact of human suffering.

Chapter 1

The Book of Isaiah

Who can describe all the devastation and pain of a people whose country has been conquered, pillaged, and burned by a brutal and savage enemy? Who can describe the agony and despair of the remnant of that nation, taken captive and deported to a distant country, bound to live in a foreign and pagan land as hated and despised strangers? Individuals may yet endure and may find a way to live and cope with this calamity, but nations do not survive such a disaster.

The sermons contained in Isaiah 40-66 are meant to achieve the unheard of and extraordinary purpose of giving the exiled nation of Israel a new hope, a new vision, and a new purpose for living in a strange and foreign land as a very distinct people.

In order to achieve this, the author presents a breathtaking description of the greatness and power of Yahweh, the God of Israel. God is portrayed as absolutely sovereign over all creation and over all the nations. Human history in its entirety is planned by Him, and nothing can thwart His plans. The fact that His own people are in exile is itself a part of His sovereign rule! The good news is that this sovereign God, who allowed His own people to be taken into exile, will act again and will deliver His people. He still has a special plan with His people, and He will accomplish it soon.

More than this, God's concern is for *all* the nations, for *all* the peoples of the world. When God will descend to rescue His own people, He will do it with the purpose of reaching out to the whole of mankind, and He will provide the solution to the problem of every human being. The end result will be a new heaven and a new earth in which suffering and pain and death will have completely disappeared.

The strange paradox is that God's method of solving the human problem of suffering, of pain, and of death *is* by suffering and pain and self-sacrifice to the point of death. God's special Servant will execute this plan, but this Servant of the Lord will be only the initiator, the spearhead, and the trailblazer, because the remnant of God's people are called to follow the Servant, to imitate Him, and to continue His ministry using the same method of suffering and of self-sacrifice.

Before we start exploring how this peculiar message is developed in chapters 40 through 66 of the prophecy of Isaiah, we must be aware of the literary technique used by the author throughout the book. It is best described by Allan MacRae:

> The construction of this part of Isaiah is somewhat like a symphony. A theme is presented and briefly discussed. Then, a second theme is introduced which, in turn, may lead into a third. Again there is a felt need for reiteration of the first theme, and perhaps of the third again, and then of the second. Thus certain basic ideas are presented, repeated, and stressed, not merely to state the ideas they contain, important as this is, but to make a profound effect upon the hearts and minds of people who are already in their imagination suffering the horrors of the Babylonian exile.[1]

It is crucial to make a mental note of this literary technique, since we will discover it being used in some of the other books of the Bible we will discuss, particularly in the Book of Daniel and in Revelation.

Isaiah sees the origin of the plight of mankind in the sin of Adam and Eve. It was man's sin that put a barrier between God and human beings (Isa. 59:1-2). The original sin of Adam and Eve resulted in the blindness of the human mind, in idolatry, and in immorality. Isaiah goes out of his way to show that the alienation of men and women from God resulted in an intellectual blindness that manifests itself in the stupidity of idol worship: "They do not know, nor do they understand, for He has smeared over their eyes so that they cannot see and their hearts so that they cannot comprehend. And no one recalls, nor is there knowledge and understanding; . . . And he cannot deliver himself, nor say, 'Is there not a lie in my right hand?' " (44:18-20). Men and women estranged from God live as though in a dark prison; they "dwell in darkness" (42:7). Or, switching metaphors, they are trapped in a cave from which they cannot see the true reality (42:22). Their whole life is a groping in darkness: "We grope along the wall like blind men, we grope like those who have no eyes; we stumble at midday, as in the twilight" (59:10). Deep darkness covers the whole earth and all the nations that are in it (60:2).

In the midst of this situation, God Himself calls out to His created beings: "Hear, you deaf! And look, you blind, that you may see" (42:18). But God's saving action has a purpose: "that they may *see* and *recognize*, and *consider* and *gain insight* as well" (41:20, italics mine). When the role and the mission of the Servant of the Lord are defined, salvation and enlightenment are placed side by side: "I will also make You a light of the nations, so that My salvation may reach to the ends of the earth" (49:6); the Servant will do this by "saying to those who are bound, 'Go forth,' [and] to those who are in darkness, 'Show yourselves' " (49:9). As the Father has done, so the Servant also calls the one "that walks in darkness and has no light" to come forth and trust in God (50:10). God will set His justice to be "a light of the peoples" (51:4).

How can the nations come to the saving knowledge of God? Their predicament is complicated by the fact that the God of Israel, the Savior and only true God, is a God who hides Himself (45:15). People cannot see Him directly. They must see Him in the things that He does. Isaiah shows us four places where people can see the reality of God: in creation, in prophecy, in the history of Israel, and in a very special way, in the story of the Servant of the Lord. For our purposes, it is necessary to analyze only the last two ways in which God reveals Himself to humankind.

We must see how God has demonstrated His power and His redeeming love in the life of the nation of Israel, and how He intends to use Israel as His witness, His missionary, to bring the rest of the nations to a knowledge of Himself. In addition, we will need to examine how God uses His special Servant as a witness and as the Agent that will redeem the world and bring it back to God. These two themes, the mission of Israel and the mission of the Servant, are woven together by Isaiah. He presents them in this way because they *are* organically linked; most of the functions of the Servant are also the functions of the people of God. When we see this link in Isaiah, it becomes much easier for us to see it in the rest of Scripture.

We properly begin with the fact that God hides Himself, and that He can only be seen indirectly, in His works and in His actions. Hence, one way God reveals Himself to all the nations of the world is through His people, Israel. In fact, this is precisely God's purpose in forming the nation of Israel: "The people whom I formed for Myself will declare My praise" (43:21); and, "You are My Servant, Israel, in Whom I will show My glory" (49:3). In the context of God's central purpose with the people of Israel, Isaiah introduces the concept of the "witness."

Isaiah tells the story in the form of the following drama. The sovereign God has summoned the nations to court to participate in a debate. The dispute is about their gods. Yahweh intends to convince the pagan nations that their gods are not real but false. For this purpose, He draws their attention to history. He asks the assembly before Him, "Who leads history? Certainly the one who leads it knows what is going to happen in the future and therefore is able to foretell the events of the future. Now, can the gods of the pagans make any prophecies?" The nations are then invited to call in their witnesses so that "they may be justified" (43:9). But they have none, and this fact serves as evidence that their gods are not real. After the nations have been proven wrong, God points them to the history of Israel and to the utterances of her prophets. They have seen that the God of Israel plans and leads history. Consequently, He can also foretell it. It is at this point in the debate that God bids His chosen people to step forward as His witnesses:

> "You are my witnesses," declares the Lord, "and My servant whom I have chosen, in order that you may know and believe Me, and understand that I am He. Before Me there was no God formed, and there will be none after Me. I, even I, am the Lord; and there is no savior besides Me. It is I who have declared and saved and proclaimed, and there was no strange god among you; so you are My witnesses," declares the Lord, "and I am God." (43:10-12)

As J. Muilenburg comments, "Israel does not exist for herself. She has a mission, and that mission is to be God's witness and elect servant. She exists to fulfill His purposes and to do His will."[2] And God's purpose is that through her service as a witness, all the nations should come to know that Yahweh is the only and true God.

After a thorough analysis of these Isaianic texts, Allison Trites draws this most important conclusion concerning the concept of the witness: "It is the task of the witness not only to attest the facts *but also to convince the opposite side of the truth of them.* "[3]

This is evidently an enormous task, and Israel is small and weak. Yet the Lord knows her desperate need for encouragement and therefore says to Israel, "Do not tremble and do not be afraid; have I not long since announced it to you and declared it? And you are my witnesses. Is there any God besides Me, or is there any other Rock? I know of none" (44:8). It is not Israel but the pagan nations that should tremble, because their own witnesses have failed, putting the nations to shame (44:9-11).

Two other important things should be noticed in these texts. The first is that the task of being God's witness is given both to the Servant of the Lord and to Israel (43:10). Secondly, Israel is referred to as both a witness and a servant (41:8; 43:1; 44:21). So far, then, the functions of the two are identical.

I should inform the reader that in the New Testament, the word "witness" (in the Greek, μάρτυς) will gradually develop a second meaning, namely, that of "martyr." This will take place because the Christians who "witness" that Jesus Christ is Lord are sentenced to death and are cruelly executed. However, the word "witness" already carries the import of suffering and of self-sacrifice even as early as the Book of Isaiah.

The Servant of the Lord as a distinct person appears for the first time in the forty-second chapter of Isaiah. He appears again in chapters 49 and 50, and once more in chapter 52, verse 13, through chapter 53, verse 12. Right from the start, Isaiah makes it clear that the Servant is God's main agent in human history. He is sent to a world covered by darkness to be a light to the nations. In a world of evil and injustice, He will bring forth justice to all the nations and will establish righteousness upon the earth. He will open the eyes of the blind and will release the prisoners from their dungeons. Yet He will accomplish all of these things in ways that will be totally contrary to our expectations. He will not make a riotous display of His power, but will act quietly, modestly, even secretly. He will have only one weapon: the sword of His Word. This sword, however, will be a very sharp sword.

We have already seen that the Servant of the Lord is God's witness. His mission is to be God's mouthpiece, to declare God's truth.

He must announce the good news of God's solution for the problem of mankind. The problem is the darkness caused by the lie and the blindness produced by Satan's deception. Hence, the goal is to bring mankind to *see*, to *understand*, to *comprehend*, to *believe*, and to *know* the *God of truth* (a phrase repeated twice in 65:16; see also 44:18; 45:6; 45:23-24). In order to achieve this goal, Satan's lie must be destroyed by the sword of truth, and therefore, the Servant's words will cut deeply through the darkness. They will penetrate deep, and they will hurt, producing great pain. This is because in a world overshadowed by the lie, the truth always hurts and disturbs.

Not surprisingly, then, the penetrating incisiveness of the Servant's words gives rise to a violent reaction upon the earth. This idea is further developed in 50:4-7; there the Servant tells us that the Lord has given Him a tongue able "to sustain the weary one with a word." Yet not everybody accepts the Servant's words. Some oppose them violently. It is at this point that the concept of the Servant's suffering appears. Due to the fact that the deceived and darkened world is pierced and wounded by the sword of truth, the world retaliates with violence. Although the words of the Servant are ultimately meant to bring comfort, the world still feels the sharp pain caused by His truth; recoiling in anger then, the world strikes out at the one who has wielded the sword.

The most surprising and unexpected development in this book is the way in which the Servant of the Lord accepts suffering, and the way in which He solves the problem of this dark world through suffering and dying. His behavior certainly has no precedent. In the Old Testament, we find many worshipers of God lamenting and protesting against the maltreatment and persecution they must endure (cf. Ps. 143:3-4). In sharp contrast to them, the Servant of the Lord willingly offers His back to the ones who strike Him and His cheeks to those who pluck out His beard; He does not shield His face from their spitting and derision.

Why this unprotesting acceptance of humiliation and suffering? Isaiah gives us the reason in the well-known fifty-third chapter of his book. Isaiah has just finished telling us that the problem of the world is its sin. Man's revolt against God and his subsequent alienation from God have resulted in the darkening of his mind, in idolatry, and in immorality. The solution to this predicament is beyond human powers. But the *good news*—Isaiah uses this exact term in 52:7—is that God has taken the initiative and has found the solution. God's solution is exactly this: the suffering and death of His Servant. God Himself "was pleased to crush Him, putting Him to grief" (53:10); yet God will raise Him up, and the Servant will then see "the result of the anguish of His soul" in the fact that He "will justify the many" (53:11).

Let us recall what we stated earlier about the concept of suffering in the Old Testament. Throughout the history of mankind, people have asked, "Why does suffering exist?" In the Old Testament, before the prophetic activity of Isaiah, one of the following three answers was offered in response to this question. In the first place, suffering exists as a punishment for sin. The Book of Genesis shows us that the origin of suffering is in man's sin; even so, this answer does not exhaust the meaning of suffering. The friends of Job limited themselves to this answer, and God condemned them for it. The second response, adding to the first, is that suffering comes as a consequence of the sins of one's parents. Exodus 20:5 tells us that God visits the iniquity of the fathers on their children to the third and fourth generations. Lastly, the third explanation for suffering maintains that suffering comes upon a person with the purpose of training and educating, for "the rod and reproof give wisdom" (Prov. 29:15).

The Book of Isaiah brings a new dimension to the concept of suffering. Not always does it have a punitive or educational purpose. Sometimes it has a positive function in God's purposes. In Isaiah's account, we meet a Person who has been called to live a life of suffering and humility; He has been called to die not for His own sins—for He has none—but for the sins of other people, for the salvation of others from the dreadful consequences of their sins. The Servant has been called to voluntarily accept suffering and death for others, being assured that He will have a great reward in seeing "the result of the anguish of His soul" (53:11); He will also be exalted by God to the position of highest honor.

Isaiah's revelation about suffering as a method used by God, as His way of tackling and solving the most fundamental problem of humanity, becomes the most important and the most essential idea of the Judeo-Christian religion. Indeed, as the heavens are higher than the earth, so are His ways higher than our ways (55:9). The essence of the Christian religion is this: God's plan for the salvation of the human race from its sin and from sin's catastrophic consequences was fulfilled through the suffering and death of His Son, Jesus Christ. However, God's plan does not stop there. In order for salvation to reach the nations, other servants have to step in and do their part; hence, their mission involves them in suffering, too.

We have already seen that the functions of the Servant of the Lord and of Israel tend to overlap. In some places, the two are identical (cf. 49:3); both are called "servants," and both are to be God's witnesses. We have also learned that the function of the witnesses is to convince the nations of the truth of God and to bring the nations to Him. Now we turn to Isaiah's teaching that suffering is God's decided *method* for fulfilling His purposes with both the nation of Israel and with the Servant.

In 50:6-7, Isaiah announces for the first time that the Servant of the Lord will go through reproach and suffering. Immediately after that, the author addresses the ones who "fear the Lord" and who "obey the voice of the Servant" (50:10). *All* that follows, up to the point where the words are addressed again to the Servant in 52:13, is a message to the people of God, to the ones who have been called to be His "servants." The reason I emphasize *all* is because most commentators are uncomfortable with some of the things that are said to God's servants and would rather assume that they were addressed to God's enemies. This refers especially to the text in 50:11, "This you shall have from My hand: You shall lie down in torment" (NKJV). There is no need to consider this an interpolation addressed to somebody else in the course of a speech that is clearly addressed to the people of God. The entire speech makes sense as it stands, directed to the servants of the Lord. In this address, the servants are given their orders for action, parallel with and in continuation to the actions of the Servant of the Lord. In fact, the whole passage and all that is said from here to the end of the book make sense only if we do not cut the text into pieces to fit our own tastes, but rather leave it as it is and simply listen to *all* that it has to say to the servants of God.

Having established the identity of the addressee, we must now seek to understand the message itself. Until this moment, the servants have all been in darkness, but now they have kindled a fire and have encircled themselves with firebrands (50:11). The command they receive from the Lord is to walk in the light of their own fire. Accompanying this command, however, is a warning: kindling a fire and walking in its light in the midst of a world full of darkness will surely result in "torment" for them. Even more than that, the servants' engagement in suffering comes to them from the hand of God Himself

(50:10-11)! Exactly the same is said with respect to the Servant: "But the Lord was pleased to crush Him, putting Him to grief" (53:10).

What follows in chapter 51 is simply the continuation of the address begun in the previous chapter. The servants have just been told to be the light of the world, and that this action will most certainly involve them in suffering. It is not difficult to understand their surprise at this news, as well as their reservations and objections to such a task. After all, they are few in number, they are weak, and they are in the midst of a very hostile world. How can they be expected to be the light of the world? The answer to this question can only be grasped by the servants if they first understand how God generally accomplishes His purposes. An excellent model to look at is the way in which God used Abraham and Sarah. They were just two people, but God made them a multitude. The lesson to be learned here by the servants is this: instead of focusing on the weakness of the instruments, they should look rather at the power of God to transform weakness into strength; they should look at His power to turn the wilderness into a fertile land. It is *He* who will establish His Law "as the light of the peoples" (51:4). The servants of the Lord have the Law of God in their own hearts (51:7). Yes, it is true that their status as God's agents makes them targets for hostile treatment, yet in spite of this frightening reality, the comforting words of God are: "Do not fear the reproach of man, neither be dismayed at their revilings" (51:7). It is important to remember that just before God gives this message to His servants, the Servant Himself declared that He did not shrink back from the beatings or from the shame and humiliation. Now it is the servants' turn to go through the same kind of treatment for the same kind of ministry.

Chapter 53 represents the culmination of the Servant of the Lord's ministry of bringing about the redemption of the world through His suffering and death. However, it also shows the Servant alive to see the results of the travail of His soul (53:11). But how will His redemption reach the whole world? The portion of Isaiah from chapter 54 to the end of the book answers this question. It is the task of the servants of God to spread His salvation to all the nations of the world. The chapter begins with an explosion of joy. Israel is told that even though she was barren in the past, she is presently going to have very many children. Therefore, she is instructed to enlarge her tent, because soon she will need to "spread abroad" to reach all the nations (54:1-3). Again, Israel is told not to fear; her gaze is directed once more toward the power and sovereignty of God over creation and over history.

The missionary theme continues to the end of the book. In chapter 55, all who are thirsty are called to drink from the new source of satisfying water. This news of God's salvation must be heard by all, in order that all may live. For this purpose, David, who certainly represents Israel, is made "a witness to the peoples," in order to call many nations, of which they had never heard or known, to come to "the Holy One of Israel" (55:1-7). This statement relates back to chapters 43 and 44, where both the Servant and Israel are called to be God's witnesses; they both have the task of convincing the nations that Yahweh is the true God. After He has given His Servant to be a ransom for many, all that God is prepared to do for the salvation of the world is to send out His messengers as witnesses. This strategy may sound strange, but God informs us that His ways are not our ways, and His thoughts are not our thoughts. He thinks in a totally different way from us, and His ways are totally different from our ways (55:8-9). "His way" is simply the witness of His servants. Moreover, He assures us that His word, which is the content of His servants' witness, will not return to Him empty (55:10-11).

The Lord's exhortations to the nation of Israel continue, earnestly urging her to go forth and carry out her mission as a witness. In 57:14, Israel is assured that the way will be prepared for her; God will command every obstacle to be removed from her way. A very important explanation follows: "For thus says the high and exalted One who lives forever, whose name is Holy, 'I dwell on a high and holy place, and also with the contrite and lowly of spirit in order to revive the spirit of the lowly and to revive the heart of the contrite' " (57:15). The description of the people with whom God "dwells," that is, through whom He accomplishes His purposes in the world, is similar (naturally!) to the description of the Servant. For the explication of the Hebrew text, A. J. Motyer is helpful: "**Contrite/** 'crushed' is used in 53:5, 10 of the Servant 'crushed' by suffering. Here it refers to those crushed by life's burdens and batterings."[4]

When we read that God will prepare the way of His people and will remove all barriers from their way, we tend to conclude that there will be no more problems. Yet we have just been told that God's ways are so radically different from ours. This is demonstrated by the fact that when He prepares the way for His people, He announces crushing and humiliation! This is so because God has decided not to use any other method but the one He used with His Servant/Son. When we become His agents, we have to be prepared for Him to apply the same formula with us as with His Servant; God has no other formula but that of self-giving and self-sacrifice.

A new and impressive call to the people of God to be the light of the world is issued in 60:1-3: "Arise, shine; for your light has come, and the glory of the Lord has risen upon you. For behold, darkness will cover the earth, and deep darkness the peoples; but the Lord will rise upon you, and His glory will appear upon you. And nations will come to your light, and kings to the brightness of your rising." The mission to all the nations of the world culminates with the creation of a new heaven and a new earth (65:17). The prophet had previously mentioned in 51:16 that the servants' work of evangelism was somehow directly implicated in God's creation of a new heaven and earth: "And I have put My words in your mouth, and have covered you with the shadow of My hand, to establish the heavens, to found the earth." This amazing statement is followed shortly afterwards by a hymn about the beauty of the one who brings the "good news" (52:7).

The last chapter of the book concludes the prophet's portrayal of the witness's ministry as an evangelist to all the nations. Chapter 66 starts with a declaration of the greatness of God: "Thus says the Lord, 'Heaven is My throne, and the earth is My footstool' " (66:1). Now, if God is so great, what could people do for Him? Human beings are so lowly and insignificant! God's answer to this question is simply that men and women are nevertheless His chosen instruments for carrying out His work: "But to this one I will look, to him who is humble and contrite of spirit, and who trembles at My word" (66:2). The description in this verse reminds the reader of the character of the Servant of the Lord, who is also "humble and contrite of spirit."

God is expressly looking for men and women who will accept to suffer with Him the pain of this world's apostasy and who will dedicate themselves to work for the nations' return to God. The "contrite of spirit" are those who make the sufferings of this world their sufferings, who understand the tragedy of a world eclipsed by the darkness of alienation from God, and who accept in their spirit to bear the burden that God Himself bears: namely, the burden for the salvation of those who walk on the road to eternal damnation. The one who "trembles" at God's Word is the one who accepts God's plans and His method, who makes God's ways his own ways, and who *obeys* God's commands implicitly.

It is a simple fact that God's purposes cannot be accomplished without sufferings, just as a birth cannot be accomplished without birth pangs. Israel had hoped that she could bear children without birth pangs, but that is not what God had determined in His plans for her. Using the following analogies in order to help the reader understand, Isaiah says that a country cannot be born in one day, and neither can a nation be formed instantly. The achievement of such things requires much time and much suffering (66:7-8).

The final chapter of the Book of Isaiah continues with a promise to those who have accepted to mourn over Jerusalem, the city which represents the kingdom of God. Those who have accepted the way of suffering will one day delight in the fullness of the glory of the City of God (66:10-11).

Isaiah ends appropriately with the fulfillment of the plan of God with mankind: "The time is coming to gather all nations and tongues. And they shall come and see My glory" (66:18). How will this be achieved? The very next verse speaks about the "survivors." Isaiah spoke of them earlier in 45:20, where "the fugitives (or survivors) of the nations" are invited to partake of the salvation of the Lord: "Turn to Me, and be saved, all the ends of the earth" (45:22). Incidentally, this is a good example of a rhetorical technique used regularly by Isaiah; he announces one idea briefly and only later develops it fully. He resumes the idea of this portion of chapter 45 right at the end of chapter 66. The "survivors from the nations" are now designated as God's ambassadors, His missionaries sent into all the world to bring people "from all the nations as a grain offering to the Lord" (66:19-20). Regarding these missionaries, C. Westermann's comment is fitting and illuminating:

> This is the first sure and certain mention of mission as we today employ the term—the sending of individuals to distant peoples in order to proclaim God's glory among them. This completely corresponds to the mission of the apostles when the church first began. One is amazed at it: here, just as the Old Testament is coming to its end, God's way is already seen as leading from the narrow confines of the chosen people out into the wide, whole world.[5]

Westermann continues his argument by stating that the interpretation of the "survivors" to mean the gentile converts corresponds not only to Isaiah 45:20-25:

> . . . it also agrees with the places in the Servant songs where the Servant is appointed to be the light to the Gentiles, and is destined to bring God's justice to them. There can be no doubt about it: the

people who tell the tidings of God's glory are also characterized as witnesses. As those saved from the catastrophe (the 'survivors') and, as saved, having experienced that Yahweh is God, they go to those who have not seen or heard. As His witnesses they can be made into people who proclaim His glory among the nations.[6]

Verse 21 of chapter 66 completes the vision of the final triumph of the gospel with the declaration that some of the converts from the nations will be made "priests and Levites." Westermann rightly observes that orthodox Jews had never dreamed of the admission of the heathen into the innermost circles of their priesthood. Notwithstanding, Isaiah clearly states that the witnesses from among the nations, together with their converts, are so integrally a part of the chosen people that they even qualify to be servants of the holy place.[7] The prophecy of Isaiah comes to its triumphant conclusion with a vision of the new heaven and the new earth and of the whole human race worshipping God.

The message of Isaiah is eminently clear. God is sovereign over His creation and over history. Confronted with a humanity that has turned its back to Him and that consequently lives in darkness and misery, God did not choose to use force or a dazzling manifestation of His glory in order to compel people to come back to Him. Instead, He has hidden Himself and His glory. Furthermore, the method He has chosen to manifest Himself to the world is in and through His Son, the Lord's Servant, together with His human servants; they are the ones who joyfully accept self-giving and self-sacrifice for others, thereby revealing the heart of God to the world. The purpose of God is to bring all the nations under His authority and rule; yet He does not do this by force, but by the sacrifice and suffering of His chosen servants.

It has become evident in the unfolding of Isaiah's prophecy that in this book suffering gains both a redemptive dimension and a missionary purpose. First, the Servant has been called to suffer and to die for the redemption of the sins of the world; following in His footsteps, the other servants chosen by the Lord have also been called to suffer in order that they may proclaim and manifest the redemption of God, conquering the lost world for God.

It is also significant that in Isaiah the purpose of one's election entails mission or witnessing. God says this about Israel: "This people I formed for Myself: They shall declare My praise," (43:21, NKJV) and "You are My Servant, Israel, in Whom I will show My glory" (49:3). Of the Servant, God says that He formed Him from the womb to bring Israel back to Himself and to be the light of the world, so that salvation should reach to the ends of the earth (49:5-7). Israel is also repeatedly told that her mission is directed to all the nations of the earth. Then, in the New Testament, when Peter depicts the nature of the new people of God, his account includes the purpose of their election: "that you may proclaim the excellencies of Him who has called you out of darkness into His marvelous light" (1 Peter 2:9).

Nonetheless, the nation of Israel has continually refused to fulfill her mission. As a direct result, the Lord pronounced the following sentence over her: "Therefore I say to you, the kingdom of God will be taken away from you, and be given to a nation producing the fruit of it" (Matt. 21:43).

Verily, this is the rule with God: He elects in order to bestow an obligation, and He gives a blessing in order that it be passed on to others. The one who refuses to fulfill the obligation also loses the blessing.

Chapter 2

The Book of Daniel

Next to the Book of Revelation, the Book of Daniel is the most controversial book in the Bible, having been given the most diverse interpretations. In what follows, I will try to explain the reasons for this controversy and the reasons for the diversity of the book's interpretations.

The book relates a series of stories from the life of Daniel dating from the beginning of the reign of Nebuchadnezzar in Babylon (605 B.C.) to the third year of the reign of Cyrus (536 B.C.). It also portrays a number of visions that Daniel had had regarding four empires, the Babylonian, the Median, the Persian, and the Grecian, a history that can be identified approximately to the year 165 B.C., and that contains predictive elements beyond that date.

The first controversy is between liberal and conservative theologians. The liberals, rejecting the possibility of prophecy, suppose that the author lived and wrote the book in 165 B.C., but that the author attributed his work to a person who lived 400 years before him, in order to give the book scriptural authority. Liberal scholars argue that the author made mistakes when writing about the events in Babylon, Media, and Persia, and that he showed more detailed knowledge regarding the time of Alexander the Great and of the empires formed after Alexander's death.

Conservative scholars, who believe in prophecy, maintain that the book was written by Daniel, close to the end of his life, approximately in the year 536 B.C. They accept as proof of this fact the archeological discoveries of the last decades which confirm what Daniel says about Babylon, Media, and Persia. The position I adhere to and uphold in these pages is the conservative one.

It is important to know that many liberal scholars agree with the conservative position on the unity of the book. Even though the first chapters contain short stories from the lives of Daniel and his colleagues in exile and the last six chapters contain visions of the future, and even though a part of the book is written in Hebrew and the other in Aramaic, a careful reading of the entire book is sufficient to convince the reader that the author has thought through his material very well, and that he has systematically developed his ideas to form a coherent and unified whole.

The conservative commentators are divided when it comes to the interpretation of Daniel's prophecies. Many different answers have been advanced for the following questions: Which prophecies refer to the historical period from the time of Daniel up to 165 A.D.? Which of them refer to the person and work of Jesus Christ? Which of them refer to the second coming of Christ? There is no end to the eschatological plots devised by theologians on the basis of this book.

The prophetic interpretation of the Book of Daniel is made difficult by the fact that the author covers the same future events *five times*. With each new representation, he employs different symbols, adding new aspects and new ideas to the themes that he evidently wants to develop all the way through the repeated visions. The five visions are as follows:

1. In chapter two, Nebuchadnezzar sees in a dream a great statue with the head made of gold, the breast made of silver, the belly and the thighs made of bronze, and the feet made of iron and clay. A stone was cut out "without hands" (2:34), and it crushed the feet of the statue. Daniel interprets this first vision telling the king that his empire is represented by the golden head, after which three other empires will follow, and the stone that will crush them is representative of an eternal kingdom to be established by God.

2. In chapter seven, Daniel has a vision in which he sees four beasts that come out of the sea: a lion, a bear, a leopard, and a beast with ten horns. It appears that the beasts stand for the same empires as the ones represented by the statue in chapter two, due to the fact that the vision ends once more with God establishing an eternal kingdom

which He will give to the "one like a Son of Man" (7:13) and to "the saints of the Highest One" (7:18, 22, 27).

3. In chapter eight, Daniel has the vision of a ram who dominates for some time. Then, a male goat appears and destroys the ram. The large horn of the male goat is broken, but four horns replace it, while a smaller horn grows to becomes exceedingly great. This horn fights with the "host of heaven" and conquers them. He removes the regular sacrifice from the sanctuary (8:11-13). This time the angel Gabriel tells Daniel that the ram with its two horns symbolizes the empires of the Medes and of the Persians, and that the male goat represents the empire of the Greeks. The horns represent different kings, and the last one "will be broken without human agency" (8:25), a reference to the stone of 2:34, which is symbolic of the eternal kingdom that God will establish.

4. As an answer to Daniel's fast and to his yearning for an understanding of God's plan in history, in chapter nine the angel Gabriel comes to him again and reveals to him that "seventy weeks are determined for your people and for your holy city, to finish the transgression, to make an end to sins, to make reconciliation for iniquity, to bring an everlasting righteousness, to seal up vision and prophecy, and to anoint the Most Holy" (9:24, NKJV). This interval of 70 weeks is then divided into 7 weeks, 62 weeks and 1 week. Regarding the interpretation of these "weeks" we can only say that the theories available are without number.

5. Lastly, in chapter eleven, Daniel has a new vision in which the angel Gabriel gives him a further and more detailed description of the events that will take place during the time of the Greek empire, including the persecution and the martyrdom of God's people as well as the purpose for these events. Finally, Gabriel tells him about the time of the end: the resurrection of some to eternal life, of the others to eternal punishment, and the establishment of the eternal kingdom.

How are these visions to be interpreted? On the one hand, those who believe that the author wrote the book in 165 B.C. try to match up the different animals and horns with different persons in history, from Nebuchadnezzar to Antiochus Epiphanes; then, they go back to check if the author relates the historical facts accurately. Their goal in this attempt is to decipher the message that the author wanted to convey through his stories.

The conservative commentators, on the other hand, believing that Daniel wrote sometime between 550 and 536 B.C., truly prophesying future events, have a triple problem. First, to fulfill their intended goal, they must identify each symbol with some person in history; second, they must show that Daniel correctly prophesied the future events; and third, they must determine which prophesies refer to the period of time up to Antiochus Epiphanes, which ones refer to the time of Jesus of Nazareth, and which ones refer to the events at the end of history. Only in passing do most of them study the actual message that the author desires to convey through his stories and visions.

Liberal and conservative commentators meet in the belief that the main preoccupation of the author was to give us a faithful depiction of history, either as prophecy or as a history *post factum*. I take the liberty to differ from both camps. I do not believe that Daniel's main concern was to give us a history or a calendar of future events. Daniel does indeed offer us a history of mankind until the establishment of the kingdom of God. But this is just the frame into which he places his main purpose, which is to show why "the saints of the Most High" undergo sufferings and martyrdom and to show what purposes of God are accomplished through these sufferings and martyrdoms.

The events that Daniel selects to include in his book are not intended to form a complete account of history. They are chosen for their illustrative value; they make vivid the ideas that the author wants to convey, and that is the only purpose they serve. They are parables with the same design and purpose as the parable of Jesus about the nobleman who "went to a distant country to receive the kingdom for himself, and then return" (Luke 19:12). It is common knowledge that behind this parable stands the historical fact of the journey to Rome made by one of Herod the Great's sons in order to convince the Roman authorities to give him the kingship after his father's death. It is also known that the Jews sent a delegation to Rome to tell the Roman authorities that they did not want this man to rule over them, exactly as in the parable. The point is this: Who will be interested to analyze whether Jesus told exactly all the details of that story? The historical accuracy of the parable is not important here; rather, the purpose of the parable is to illustrate the fact that the man who leaves for a while in order to receive his kingdom in another place has entrusted his possessions for administration to some of his servants. The parable paints a picture of the fact that when the man came back, he asked his servants to give an account of how they administered what had been entrusted to them. Everybody who reads the parable will easily recognize Jesus as the nobleman who leaves in order to receive His kingdom, and His followers as the servants to whom He entrusted His business for administration. Readers do not ask if the parable is history or not, and neither do they scrutinize whether the details of the parable do or do not correspond with the actual historical record. Instead, they rightly inquire what teaching Jesus wanted to communicate by means of this parable.

The Book of Daniel must be approached exactly as we approach Jesus' parable of the minas. In order to understand Daniel, we must try to capture the specific teaching that he wants to impart through the stories he relates from his own life and through selective visions of the future, spanning the period of time from the present up to the establishment of the kingdom of God.

For an accurate comprehension of the message of the Book of Daniel, we have to start by asking another question: Why does Daniel choose to speak five times in five different ways about the same epoch? Can we find the source of his literary method? The second question should prompt us to think back to the Book of Isaiah. In Isaiah's prophecy, we observed how the author repeated the same themes many times, adding to them new elements with each repetition. In order to understand one particular theme, we had to pursue it as it evolved in each block of material. Even more importantly, however, Daniel is indebted to Isaiah not only for his literary technique but also for his theological content. In fact, the main theological ideas in Daniel are a further development of the ideas found in Isaiah. We now turn to the central concepts of the Book of Daniel.

For a long time the prophets of Jerusalem had warned the people to give up their idolatrous practices and turn back to Yahweh with their whole hearts, for otherwise destruction will surely come over them, their city and their land. But they did not heed the prophetic message, and the calamity came over them in the form of the Babylonian exile.

Daniel and his friends, Hannaniah, Mishael, and Azariah, were part of the first group of exiles who went to Babylon in 605 B.C. Right from the beginning of their stay in Babylon, they were faced with the inevitable necessity of making fundamental decisions: Would they adapt to the culture and religion of their new country or would they remain faithful to the religion of their parents and to the Law of their God, risking their own lives in the process? In fact, they decided that, whatever the cost, even if it cost them their lives, they would remain faithful to their God and to His Law.

The first test of their convictions occurred at the royal school, where they decided that they would not eat the food forbidden by the Mosaic Law. On this occasion, they saw for the first time that God saves those who remain faithful to His covenant. God honored their faithfulness with wisdom and with the promotion to positions at the highest level; they were elevated higher than they could ever have dreamed possible. Later on, Daniel's three friends preferred to be thrown into the fiery furnace rather than worship the image of the king. God again proved faithful to them and miraculously saved them from the flaming furnace.

Tests such as these were theirs all their lives long. Even at an old age, Daniel was forced to choose whether he would obey the new law that prohibited him to pray to his own God or be faced with the punishment of being thrown to the lions. Once again, Daniel publicly demonstrated his faithfulness to God, and without fail, God miraculously saved him from danger, closing the lions' mouths.

Daniel was raised up to the highest governmental positions under Nebuchadnezzar, and continued to serve in these positions during the reigns of Belshazzar, of Darius, and even during the first years of Cyrus. As early as the time of Nebuchadnezzar's rule, Daniel was called to interpret the king's dream about the succession of empires that would rise and fall in the coming centuries. He saw that in all the turbulent times to follow, the small remnant of the people of God were going to be continuously oppressed and crushed. It was normal, then, for Daniel to meditate deeply on the profound meaning of history, on the purpose of those empires, and on the reasons why God would let His own people be persecuted and crushed under the oppressors' feet.

From his study of the prophets, Daniel learned that Israel's exile was a punishment from God for her continuous and persistent idolatry and moral corruption: "Indeed all Israel has transgressed Thy law and turned aside, not obeying Thy voice; so the curse has been poured out on us" (9:11). For this reason, Daniel fasts and intercedes for his nation (9:1-19; 10:1-3). As Daniel is fasting and praying, the angel Gabriel comes to him and announces that because Daniel has set his heart on understanding God's purposes and on humbling himself before His God, he, Gabriel, was sent to give him understanding of what will happen to his people in the future (10:11-14).

The most shocking thing in all the visions Daniel receives about the future is the fact that history will be terribly brutal with the children of God. Daniel says that his "natural color turned to a deathly pallor" (10:8), and he tells the angel: "O my lord, as a result of the vision anguish has come upon me, and I have retained no strength" (10:16; cf. 7:15, 28; 8:8).

One thing was perfectly clear to Daniel: God was able to save His people from trouble. He himself had been rescued from the lions, and his friends had been rescued from the fiery furnace. But now Daniel is told that the best of God's people "will fall by sword and by flame, by captivity and by plunder for many days" (11:33); even more, their enemies will "finish shattering the power of the holy people" (12:7).

Why will it be like this? What will God accomplish through *such* events? This is the fundamental question of the Book of Daniel. The answer that is given to it will become evident as we gather together all the ideas that Daniel develops step by step through all his stories and through all his visions. Let us briefly review them.

The first idea that dominates the whole book is the fact of the sovereignty of God over the universe and in history. It should be underlined here that it is normal for the people of God to ask themselves whether God is in command whenever their enemies rush over them with arrogance and brutality, whenever their enemies persecute and kill the faithful ones. They may even ask themselves if God has not perhaps already lost the battle. Nothing is more important for believers in times of distress than to know that God *is* in command and that He fulfills His glorious purposes with His children even through the calamities they experience. Precisely because in a hostile environment there is a need for such an understanding of God, Daniel never tires of repeating it again and again in different forms in his stories and visions.

Right at the beginning of his book, Daniel tells us that when Nebuchadnezzar went down to besiege Jerusalem, "God gave Jehoiakim king of Judah into his hand, along with some of the vessels of the house of God" (1:2). It was God who caused Daniel to receive favor from the commander of the officials that he might not defile himself (1:8-9), and it was God again who gave the four young Jews "knowledge and intelligence in every branch of literature and wisdom" and to Daniel even the understanding of all kinds of visions and dreams (1:17). Listen to the way Daniel describes the sovereignty of God to Nebuchadnezzar: "For wisdom and power belong to Him. And it is He who changes the times and the epochs; He removes kings and establishes kings; He gives wisdom to wise men, and knowledge to men of understanding. It is He who reveals the profound and hidden things; He knows what is in the darkness" (2:20-22). The fact that

Nebuchadnezzar is king is due solely to the will of God: "You, O king, are the king of kings, to whom the God of heaven has given the kingdom, the power, the strength, and the glory" (2:37).

Chapters four and five in particular can be called the chapters of the sovereignty of God. In chapter four, we see Nebuchadnezzar at the apex of his power and arrogance, in a moment when he believed that all he had achieved had come about by his own powers. In that instant, the decision was taken in heaven that the king's mind would be darkened, and that he would go mad, believing himself to be an animal. The judgment was given "in order that the living may know that the Most High is ruler over the realm of mankind, and bestows it on whom He wishes, and sets over it the lowliest of men" (4:17). Daniel tells the king, "Your dwelling place [will] be with the beasts of the field, . . . until you recognize that the Most High is ruler over the realm of mankind, and bestows it on whomever He wishes" (4:25). The king's sanity would be restored only after he recognized "that it is Heaven that rules" (4:26).

Nebuchadnezzar did not turn away from his pride and arrogance, and just as Daniel had promised, madness engulfed his mind and body. However, the king's insanity was effective in bringing about the required result. In due time, Nebuchadnezzar lifted his head towards heaven and recognized the sovereignty of God. In due course, his reason was returned to him. The king finally acknowledged that God "does according to His will in the host of heaven and among the inhabitants of earth" (4:35). He then proclaimed: "Now I Nebuchadnezzar praise, exalt, and honor the King of heaven, for all His works are true and His ways just, and He is able to humble those who walk in pride" (4:37).

In chapter five, we watch Belshazzar, the son of Nebuchadnezzar, exhibiting the same kind of arrogance that reduced his father to madness. His guilt is even greater than that of his father, since Belshazzar witnessed what had happened to his father as a result of his self-exalting pride, and the son should have learned his lesson. Instead, Belshazzar stubbornly raises himself against the Lord of heaven. As a direct result, his kingdom is taken away from him and is given to the Medes and the Persians.

In the prophetic chapters of Daniel, chapters seven through twelve, the visions of the successive empires that rise and fall give us the same general impression that all events are decided beforehand by God. It is even clearer in these chapters that God has a plan to fulfill through these empires. After He is finished with them, they will be crushed "without human agency" (8:25; 2:34, 45). The afflictions that come over the people of God are also decided from above: "even to the end there will be war; desolations are determined" (9:26). The "one that is decreed" will bring "complete destruction" (9:27). The same idea is expressed by the following pronouncement: "the end is still to come at the appointed time" (11:27, 35).

In most cases, Daniel refers to the sovereignty of God as His "rule," a term that can also be replaced by "authority." The second important idea in the Book of Daniel is that God wants to share His authority with man. The development of this idea in Daniel can be pursued step by step as it develops throughout the whole book, but in order to fully grasp it in its wider perspective, we shall start with it in the Creation story.

We read in Genesis that man was created in the image of God in order to "rule" over the rest of creation. The man and the woman receive this command from God, and it signifies His purpose for creating them: "Be fruitful and multiply, and fill the earth, and subdue it; and rule over the fish of the sea and over the birds of the sky, and over every living thing that moves on the earth" (Gen. 1:28). David, meditating upon the first chapter of Genesis and upon the reason for God's creation of man, writes: "Thou hast made him a little lower than God, and dost crown him with glory and majesty! Thou dost make him to rule over the works of Thy hands; Thou hast put all things under his feet" (Ps. 8:5-6).

Picking up this concept of the authority that God intends to entrust to man, Daniel develops it further. It is interesting to notice, first of all, how authority was entrusted to Nebuchadnezzar in words that seem to be taken directly from the first chapter of Genesis and from the eighth Psalm. Here are Daniel's words to the king: "You, O king, are the king of kings, to whom the God of heaven has given the kingdom, the power, the strength, and the glory; and wherever the sons of men dwell, or the beasts of the field, or the birds of the sky, He has given them into your hand and has caused you to rule over them all" (2:37-38).

Some time later, God punishes Nebuchadnezzar by taking away his authority, power, strength, and glory. Moreover, God humiliates him by lowering him to the level of the animals. God's reason for punishing him in this manner is obvious; the king did not want to recognize the authority or the rule of God over himself. In no uncertain terms, Nebuchadnezzar's experience demonstrates that God entrusts authority, the function of ruling over other created beings, on a trial basis only, in order to see if the one to whom the authority is entrusted will himself continue to submit to the authority of God. To be proud means to believe that your authority springs out of your own self, and that no one else rules over you. To be proud means to fail the test of authority, of power, of wealth, and of glory. Consequently, Nebuchadnezzar felt in his flesh that God humbles "those who walk in pride" (4:37); for "pride goes before destruction, and a haughty spirit before stumbling" (Prov. 16:18), and *vice versa*, "before honor comes humility" (Prov. 15:33). Being humble means that however much authority and power and glory God gives you, you remain under His authority and rule, and always give Him all the praise and all the glory.

The purpose of God, then, is to find people who are capable of handling authority and to whom, in the end, He can entrust the jobs of ruling over His creation, not merely as a trial run, but for all eternity. The vision of Daniel recorded in chapter seven clearly denotes this truth:

> I kept looking in the night visions, and behold, with the clouds of heaven one like a Son of Man was coming, and He came up to the Ancient of Days and was presented before Him. And to Him was given dominion, glory and a kingdom, that all the peoples, nations, and men of every language might serve Him. His dominion is an everlasting dominion which will not pass away; and His kingdom is one which will not be destroyed. (7:13-14)

We know that Jesus applied these words to Himself in Matthew 26:67 and that He identified Himself as the Son of Man. Of utmost importance for our study is to observe that immediately after it is stated that the authority and the kingdom are given to the "Son of Man," Daniel is informed that the kingdom—the authority or the function of ruling—will also be given to "the saints of the Highest One." We find this in verse 18, in verses 21 and 22, and finally in these words of verse 27: "Then the sovereignty, the dominion, and the greatness of all the kingdoms under the whole heaven will be given to the people of the saints of the Highest One." The saints are the ones who will never usurp the authority of the King. To make this certainty of the saints' submission distinctly clear, we are immediately told that "all the dominions will serve and obey Him" (7:27).

In these verses, we discover that the sovereignty and dominion, the authority and the function of ruling, will be given to the saints of God. This discovery is directly followed by the revelation of "*His* kingdom" and of the fact that all the dominions or rulers will do two basic things: they will *serve* God and they will *obey* God. Unquestionably, their authority will be subject to God's authority, and their rule will be exercised under His rule.

Yet, we may ask, what is the nature of the relationship between the Son of Man and the saints of the Most High? The kingdom, authority, and dominion will be given to both. Previously, the prophet Isaiah had revealed the similarities between the functions of the Servant of the Lord and the functions of His chosen servants from the nations. The Servant of the Lord by His sufferings and self-sacrifice will justify the many; in their turn, the servants of the Lord will take that salvation to all the nations of the earth by their sufferings and self-sacrifice. In the end, God will make a new heaven and a new earth for His servants. Concerning the Lord's Servant, God discloses what He intends to do: "I will allot Him a portion with the great, and He will divide the booty with the strong" (Isa. 53:12); with respect to His other servants, God says, "My chosen ones shall inherit [the land]" (Isa. 65:9), and they shall "be glad and rejoice forever" (65:18).

The same parallelism and continuity are present in the prophecy of Daniel regarding the person called the "one like a Son of Man" (Dan. 7:13) and "the saints of the Highest One" (7:18, 22, 27). I believe that the Son of Man revealed here in chapter seven is the Messiah of 9:24-26. In the second passage, the "Anointed One," or the Messiah, is also called "the Prince," and we are told that He "will be cut off and have nothing" (9:26). There is some controversy here about the translation of these verses. The King James Version puts it this way: "the Messiah shall be cut of, but not for Himself." For our purposes, we will bypass the controversy and simply say that this information in Daniel serves as a reminder of the sufferings and death of the Servant of the Lord foretold in Isaiah 53. Daniel, however, does not extend his statements about this Person, because his main interest lies in the destiny of the "saints"—in the people who, like himself, live under tyrannical and violently hostile empires that persecute and kill the "saints." It is about them that he wants to know more, and it is about them that we shall receive information in the following visions.

In the midst of difficulties, dangers, and persecutions, many will give up their faith and will "forsake the holy covenant" (Dan. 11:30). Nevertheless, there will be others who will accept to die for their faith.

What is revealed to Daniel in this vision is of great import for our study:

> . . . but the people who know their God will display strength and take action. And those who have insight among the people will give understanding to the many; yet they will fall by sword and by flame, by captivity and by plunder, for many days. Now when they fall they will be granted a little help, and many will join with them in hypocrisy. And some of those who have insight will fall, in order to refine, purge, and make them pure, until the end time; because it is still to come at the appointed time. (11:32-35)

This is the key paragraph of the entire Book of Daniel. At last, in this passage, the position of God's people in the course of history is revealed. Daniel is told both *what* will happen to them and *why* it will happen. Here he is also informed about what is expected of the people of God in the course of history.

A closer look at the terminology of these verses will aid our comprehension of them. The discussion is about "the people who know their God." They are also called "those who have insight," or those who "understand." Their wisdom is in the fact that they know God; they know His plans and methods. They are also wise in that they obey God to the end, remaining faithful to Him even at the cost of their lives.

The author intimates, however, that there is hypocrisy in some. Not everyone is sincere, and there are those among them who will merely play the heroes for a while. Persecution, pushed to its furthest limits, will effectively sift these false ones from the true. Yet the metaphors of "refining" and "purging" imply that even those who are genuinely faithful will undergo and endure the hard process of testing.

From what we have seen so far, we can legitimately conclude that in the Book of Daniel, persecution and martyrdom have a dual purpose, namely, the purpose of testing and of purification. The first purpose, that of testing the saints, is a theme pursued through the entire book. It was earlier pointed out that the final purpose of God with man is to confer upon him the position of ruler over the rest of creation. But in order for this purpose to be fulfilled, man must first be put to the test of submission. God wants to be certain that the one He entrusts with authority, with riches, and with glory will accept to remain under His supreme authority; if, on the other hand, the servant fails the test, if he becomes drunk with his power and glory, attributing everything to himself and ignoring the rightful Sovereign, then God will take away his kingdom and will give it to somebody else (5:21-28).

Accordingly, Daniel and his colleagues were put to the test of obedience to the Law of God in a hostile environment (ch. 1) and to the test of faithfulness to the unique God of Israel even at the cost of their lives (ch. 3 and 6). Later on, chapter eleven shows the people of God being tested through calamities and persecutions. The rewards of the faithful ones who pass these tests are revealed in the following chapter, where we are told that they will be entrusted with eternal authority.

The second purpose of suffering, according to Daniel, is the purification of the person enduring it. In chapter eleven we are not told *how* the sufferings purify the sufferer, but in 9:24, the angel told Daniel that seventy weeks had been decreed for his people "to finish the transgression, to make an end of sin, to make atonement for iniquity, to bring in everlasting righteousness." We shall see later that the writers of the intertestamental Maccabean literature would take this idea and develop it into the teaching that the people of God must suffer in order to atone for their own sins, and that the martyrs, by giving their lives, make atonement for the sins of the whole nation. Some commentators see the origin of this teaching in Daniel, especially because 12:3 may be translated to the effect that the wise men "will make righteous the many." But this text can also be understood in the light of 11:33, where we are told that the wise "will give understanding to the many." In this light, the Revised Standard Version is justified in translating 12:3 as "those who lead the many to righteousness."

If Daniel had wanted to attribute to the wise the function of making other people righteous, or even the function of purifying their own sins by their own sufferings, he would have done so in chapter nine in his prayer of confession and intercession for his own sins and for the sins of his people. His prayer reveals that the calamities that have come over God's people were indeed a consequence of their sins (9:16), but Daniel is very clear and explicit in attributing the prerogative of forgiveness exclusively to God (9:17-19). He says nothing to the effect that the sufferings of people might make atonement for their sins. If Daniel had entertained such a belief, this prayer would have been the appropriate place to express it.

Cleansing or purification through sufferings is mentioned in Job 23:10, Psalm 66:10, Isaiah 48:10, and Zechariah 13:9. In each of these cases, it refers to the refining of gold or silver by fire. This is also the case in Daniel 12:10, where Daniel repeats that "many will be purged, purified and refined." Just as the impurities in noble metals are burned off by the fire, the noble person enters the furnace of tribulations, and the flames of suffering destroy all that is bad, selfish, and inferior in him; as a result, the man of God comes out of the furnace more noble, more pure, and closer to the ideal to which the Creator intends to bring him.

One of the principal offices of the wise, of the people who know their God, is to teach others (11:33) and to lead many others in the way of righteousness (12:3). Isaiah has extensively elaborated this as being the role of the servants of the Lord. Daniel shows us the same thing, not primarily by means of direct statements but by means of the stories in the first six chapters of his book. In those chapters we watch the exiles becoming missionaries and evangelists. Daniel himself uses every opportunity to speak to the kings about his own God (2:27-38; 4:19-27; 5:17-28; 6:21-22). Similarly, Daniel's three friends, when threatened with the fiery furnace, use that opportunity to witness about the God they worship and serve (3:17-18). Furthermore, their evangelistic success is emphatically represented. Daniel vividly portrays the wisdom they use in their presentation and the faithfulness they exhibit under threats and in deadly situations. Finally, God's miraculous intervention in saving His servants leads the kings to acknowledge the sovereignty of their God (2:47; 3:28-29; 4:34-37; 6:25-27).

Nevertheless, many of the wise will experience martyrdom, and even the ones who do not die a violent death will not see the establishment of the kingdom of God in their lifetime. In fact, the angel resolutely tells Daniel that "as soon as they finish shattering the power of the holy people, all these events will be completed" (12:7). The people of God will not fully realize the purposes of God until they accept to be completely broken as a consequence of their total dedication and obedience to God. They must learn that with God, one wins by losing.

When and how will the victory and the attainment of the rewards take place? Daniel gives us the answer: the day of resurrection will come, and then "those who have insight will shine brightly like the brightness of the expanse of heaven, and those who lead the many to righteousness, like the stars forever and ever" (12:3). As for Daniel, he is told to continue on his way "to the end," for only "at the end of the age," will he rise to obtain his inheritance and "allotted portion" (12:13).

Now we have the complete picture: God will give the kingdom, the authority, and the power to His saints. However, this will happen only at the end of history, when He will raise them up and will give to each one of them his own inheritance in that kingdom. And the more faithful they were in this life, the more people they led in the way of righteousness, the brighter their glory will be.

It is significant that each time Daniel sees this long road of sufferings and death on the way to the final glory, he loses his power and trembles in fear. Prior to Daniel, another man of God also had this type of experience. The prophet Habakkuk asked the same painful question: Why does God allow the wicked to crush the righteous ones? (Hab. 1:13). Habakkuk was referring specifically to the Assyrians, but God answered him by stating that He will bring even worse invaders, ones who will burn the whole country and will take the people into captivity. When he heard about these calamities, Habakkuk, like Daniel, trembled in horror (3:2, 16).

Habakkuk is not told why these things will happen; instead, he is given a vision of a time in history when "the earth will be filled with the knowledge of the glory of the Lord, as the waters cover the sea" (2:14). By showing him this vision, God lets the prophet understand that He will not abandon His purposes in history and that, in spite of the coming calamities and even by means of these calamities, God will accomplish His plan of establishing His authority on the whole earth.

God tells Habakkuk one other important thing: the righteous man who must endure these terrible times will live "by his faith" (2:4); in other words, he will live by his faith in the God who fulfills His purposes through disasters and calamities. Even though he will be caught in the midst of this brutal history, his faith will help him to remain faithful to God; he will know, by faith, that God will ultimately win the final victory in history. For precisely this reason, Habakkuk was able to conclude his book with the tremendous statement that whatever may happen, he will rejoice in the God of his salvation, even if the entire country was completely devastated and left barren (3:17-19).

Daniel's conclusion is the same, although it is expressed in different words. The righteous will fall and be crushed. In spite of this, they must trust in their God, because He accomplishes His purposes in history exactly through the calamities that seem to be so dreadful and destructive. Moreover, He is a God who raises the dead. Daniel's first prophetic explication of the future succession of evil empires holds the first clue to this reality: "In the days of those kings the God of heaven will set up a kingdom which will never be destroyed; . . . it will crush and put an end to all these kingdoms, but it will itself endure forever" (2:44).

Now, we would expect to read that it will be *at the end* of the evil empires that God will set up His kingdom, but the text is very clear in affirming that God will set up His kingdom *during* the time of these kingdoms. Why will He act in this manner? The answer to this hard question is simply this: it is in the course of this harsh history that God will form His people. Through the challenges presented by these hostile empires, He will test and purify His own; in this way, He will qualify them for the kingdom, for authority, for dominion, and for glory. Precisely when it appears that God's plans have been shattered, God is in fact systematically and consistently accomplishing all that He has purposed from the beginning.

What do we glean from the Book of Daniel for our investigation of suffering, martyrdom, and glory? We learn that God, the sovereign Ruler of history, has the purpose of raising and forming a people to whom He plans to entrust dominion and authority and glory in His eternal kingdom. We learn that in the present history of persecutions, difficulties, and deadly dangers, He educates and tests the individuals who will be able in the end to exercise dominion and authority. Suffering and martyrdom have this dual purpose of probation and purification.

What kind of people is God looking for? What kind of people will be able to handle the authority and glory correctly? Some of their character traits as they emerge from the Book of Daniel are as follows:

1. They are men and women who have taken the fundamental decision that they will obey their God absolutely; they will live according to His laws whatever the cost they may have to pay for it.

2. When confronted by trials, persecutions, and the threat of death, they prove faithful, persevering through all the difficulties, tortures, and even through martyrdom.

3. They are passionate to proclaim the sovereign rule of God and to acknowledge Him in everything, always giving Him all the praise and all the glory, without ever attributing any merit to themselves.

4. They are continually immersed in the task of telling others about their God, leading others to Him, and showing others the way of

righteousness.

5. They have a clear understanding of history knowing that the loss of temporary goods and even of life itself for God's cause is in reality not a loss but a gain. Instead of instant satisfaction here and now, they look forward to their true fulfillment in the eternal future.

Chapter 3

Job and Satan

The suffering of a good and upright person has always been a big problem for those who believe in a just God. How can a just God allow an obedient and faithful person to suffer tragedies and distresses of all kinds?

The Book of Job addresses this question and brings forth a surprising and unexpected answer. The answer is not given in the debate between Job and his friends. While Job stubbornly insists that he is innocent, his friends believe that he must be a sinner because they view his sickness as a punishment from God for his sins. They believe that God always gives health and prosperity to a just and faithful person. The debate ends with each participant maintaining his own original position; neither Job nor his friends succeed in persuading the other side to yield. Hence, we do not obtain our answer from their debate, but from the words of *the author of the book* himself. He responds to the above question in the prologue and in the epilogue of his book.

It is not necessary for our investigation to lay out the various theories about how the Book of Job was written. Suffice it to say that we approach the book as it stands, as an integral whole. We want to listen to what it had to say to the people of the New Testament as well as to those in the centuries to follow, and we will try to hear what it has to say to us today on the brink of the twenty-first century.

The book opens with the presentation of Job, a citizen of the land of Uz, a man who "was blameless, upright, fearing God, and turning away from evil" (1:1). The father of ten children, he was the richest man in the East, but he also feared God above all. Whenever his children gathered for a party, Job afterwards offered sacrifices for them in case they had sinned during the course of the party.

The action at the beginning of the book takes place in heaven, at a meeting of "the sons of God" (1:6). Satan is among them, as well. God asks Satan if he has considered Job, a man whom God himself describes as different from everyone else on earth, "a blameless and upright man, fearing God and turning away from evil" (1:8). Apparently Satan cannot contradict God on the facts of that description, but he raises the issue of Job's *motivation* for being upright and faithful to God. Satan raises the suspicion that Job's blamelessness has been motivated by the many riches God has given him and by the fact that God has shielded him from all kinds of trouble. If God would one day take these riches away from him, Satan suspects that Job would curse God to His face.

Satan's attack on the integrity of Job was at the same time an attack on the honor of God. Before the whole population of heaven, God had declared that Job was His special man on the earth. In order to discredit God, Satan had come forward, in front of the same audience, with the assertion that the godliness of Job was not genuine. Job had been faithful to God not because he really loved God, but because God had given him riches and protection. If Job's godliness was not genuine, and if he was what God had best upon the earth, then who else could God show as His faithful one? Satan insinuated that God bribed people into faithfulness to Him, that He bought their allegiance with riches, and that people worshipped Him merely as a result of the material goods they had obtained from Him, not because He alone is God.

There must have been a great and fearful silence in heaven when this challenge was hurled at the honor of God! It is remarkable enough to notice, however, that God and Satan agreed on one very essential point. They concurred that a righteousness and faithfulness to God based upon and dependent upon the wealth He bestows is not genuine.

By throwing this challenge to the authenticity of Job's godliness and implicitly to the honor of God, Satan created a situation in which the only solution was to submit Job to a test. God Himself had no other solution than to test Job by taking away all his riches so that He could observe Job's behavior in the event of his losing all his possessions. Accordingly, God gave Satan permission to execute the test, and thus Satan caused a series of attacks by hostile peoples and several strong storms that destroyed all of Job's wealth and killed each of his ten children. Inferring from the discussion in heaven, we are entitled to think that at this moment the entire population of the spiritual realm was breathlessly watching to see the reaction of this one man. Will he remain faithful to God? Will he curse God for these dreadful calamities? The very honor of God was at stake in this man's response. Will this man prove that God does indeed have people upon the earth who would still worship Him even after He stripped them of all earthly goods? At this point, Job became a spectacle for the entire cosmos.

As one messenger after another came to tell Job of the disasters and as he realized that all he had owned, as well as his ten children, had perished and been destroyed, Job stood in silence, dazed and bewildered. But then, contrary to Satan's expectations, Job did not lash out at God with protests or with questioning; he simply responded with a plain comment on the common destiny of human beings: "Naked I came from my mother's womb, and naked I shall return there. The Lord gave and the Lord has taken away;" following this, realizing that what was expected in such a situation was a statement displaying his attitude towards this God who gives and takes away as He pleases, Job exclaimed: "Blessed be the name of the Lord" (1:21)! With these words, Job had, in effect, declared: I did not bring these things with me when I came into this world. They were given to me by God and, being His, He has the right to take them away. Regarding my attitude towards God, my praise does not depend on my possession of these material goods. No, I give Him my worship because of who He is, because He alone is God.

Satan had predicted that Job would curse God. Instead, Job had blessed Him. Is it too much to imagine that at the precise moment in which Job uttered, "Blessed be the name of the Lord," all the angels exploded into wild applause and commenced singing hymns of praise to God?

Despite his glaring defeat, Satan did not give up. Addressing himself once more to God, he retorted that Job could still enjoy life because he was healthy. In the pain of a terrible sickness, Job would surely curse God. This was yet another challenge to God's honor, and God accepted to submit Job to a new test.

Doing what he does best, Satan caused an ugly and painful

sickness to come upon Job, making him unspeakably miserable. Apparently he was thrown out of the city. Lying on a heap of ashes, Job rubbed his skin with a piece of broken pottery in order to help ease his pain. His wife was amazed that he still remained faithful to God, and she advised him to curse God, reasoning that God would then kill him, thereby putting an end to his misery. She did not know, of course, that this was exactly what Satan wanted to see happen. Without being aware of it, she had become Satan's accomplice.

Job's friends came to comfort him, but in their limited understanding and shortsightedness, they could only demand that Job confess that it was his sin that had caused his sickness. Despite their tedious lecturing, Job insisted that he was innocent. Although he did not understand why God was treating him in this manner, Job persisted to the end in expressing his faith in God: "Though He slay me, yet I will trust Him" (13:15, NKJV).

There was no further dialogue in heaven between God and Satan, but we may understand that Job gave God a great victory that day, unmistakably defeating Satan and proving him wrong. Job, of course, knew nothing about it; meanwhile, the whole spiritual realm was able to witness that God indeed had a genuinely faithful person on the earth. Satan was put to shame before the entire cosmos, and God's honor was vindicated.

For an understanding of the whole message of the book, it is necessary to read God's discourse to Job in chapters 38 through 41 as well as the epilogue in chapter 42. God's speech is a long list of questions about the mysteries of the universe. Again and again, God asked Job if he had knowledge about or if he could explain these mysteries. Obviously, God wanted to bring Job to the position in which he would admit the complexity of God's universe, and that he, as a limited being, must not expect to know all the answers or to have all the explanations of why things happen as they do. Job had to come to the place where he could affirm that even if the events of his life seemed absurd and devoid of logic, he would still firmly believe that God had His own reasons for what He did. Job had to demonstrate his persistent and childlike trust that God would ultimately fulfill His good intentions with him.

There are a few basic ideas that the Book of Job obviously intends to convey. The first one is that as long as we are on this earth, God does not disclose to us every one of His reasons for what happens in our lives. The second idea is that our suffering may have a cosmic dimension to it. There may be reasons for our suffering that are totally beyond our perception. Our suffering may very well serve to glorify God and to defeat Satan. The third concept is that while suffering is a test of our fidelity to God, the process by which we are tested also changes us for the better. At one point during his terrible sufferings, Job gained the distinct awareness that he was being tested by God. Discerning that God already knew the result of the test even before it took place, Job declared, "But He knows the way I take; when He has tried me, I shall come forth as gold" (23:10). Job did not know what the purpose of God's testing was, but he knew that the testing would transform him, making him "come forth as gold" (Ibid.).

It is in the epilogue that we find Job's account of what he had gained from his sufferings: "I have heard of Thee by the hearing of the ear; but now my eye sees Thee" (42:5). It can be inferred from this statement that before his experience of suffering, Job's knowledge of God was merely theoretical. He had learned about God from his parents, his teachers, etc.; due to their instruction, Job had believed in God and had even feared Him. In his sufferings, however, something strange had happened to Job: his eyes were opened and God became "visible" to him. Only in suffering did God become real to him; only there did Job come to personally experience the presence of God.

I can confirm Job's experience. During the time I was expecting to be crushed by the Romanian secret police interrogators, God became more real to me than ever before or after in my life. It is difficult to put into words the experience I had with God at that time. It was like a rapture into a sweet and total communion with the Beloved. God's test for me then became the pathway to a special knowledge of the reality of God.

PART TWO

Suffering and Martyrdom in the Intertestamental Period

Chapter 4

The Intertestamental Literature

The Old Testament Books of Isaiah, Daniel, and Job have so far given us extensive treatments of the difficult problem regarding the suffering of the just and have offered us deep teachings about the meaning and purpose of this suffering in the process of accomplishing God's plan with mankind. Yet they were not the only writers who dealt with this problem in the Old Testament. From Moses to Ezekiel, all the messengers of God who delivered the oracles of God to Israel were met with opposition, enmity, and violence. In some cases, they had to pay with their lives for their courage in delivering God's message of rebuke, warning, or condemnation. Moses, Jeremiah, and Ezekiel, as well as the composers of the Psalms and the writer of Proverbs, each had something important to say about the suffering of the people of God. We shall explore some of their ideas in this chapter and in our later treatment of this theme.

We turn now to the persecution of the Jews under Antiochus IV, during the period of time between 175 and 164 B.C., and to the literature produced in and after this period. Prompted by the desire to unify his multiethnic empire, the Seleucid king Antiochus IV launched a brutal campaign for the hellenization of all the peoples under his rule. Since the Jews resisted the process of hellenization, Antiochus decided to break their resistance using all possible means. He replaced the high priest Onias III and then sold the high priesthood for an immense sum of money to Onias' brother Jason who was a pro-hellenist collaborationist. After some time, once again for a huge amount of money, Antiochus permitted another Hellenist, Menelaus, to throw Jason out and to take his place as high priest, even though he was not hereditarily qualified for the job. Menelaus plotted the assassination of Onias in 170 B.C., generating in this way the first martyr for the Law.

In 169 B.C., Antiochus IV entered Jerusalem and plundered the Temple. A year later, a revolt broke out in Jerusalem, but Antiochus quickly crushed the revolt, destroying part of the city wall and reducing the city to the status of a village; henceforward, Jerusalem was subject to Syrian military rule. The practice of the Jewish religion was completely forbidden. The keeping of the Sabbath was prohibited, and circumcision was considered a crime punishable by death. On 15 Kislev (6 December) 167 B.C., the Temple was desecrated and transformed into a temple dedicated to Zeus. An "abomination of desolation" was placed in the temple, in the form of an altar dedicated to Zeus on the site of the altar of Yahweh; a statue of Zeus was probably also erected there. On the new altar, pigs were sacrificed, and the Jews were forced to eat pork.

All those who broke the new rules had their property confiscated, and they were either killed or sold into slavery. The opposition of the devout Jews was varied and extraordinary, ranging from non-violent opposition and acceptance of death for the faith to open revolt and the war for national liberation.

These events were of crucial importance for the future development of Judaism and Christianity. They represent the first religious persecution in history, the first epoch of great martyrdoms for one's faith, the first religious war in history, and one of the great victories of the spirit against brute force and intolerant dictatorship. One example of the non-violent actions of the Jews during that time is the decision of a group of a thousand men, women, and children to flee into the wilderness in order to avoid breaking the Sabbath. The Syrian army found them and demanded that they return to their homes on a Sabbath day, an act that would have meant breaking the Sabbath laws. When they refused to obey the order, the Syrians killed them all.[1]

Another instance of Jewish non-violent action was that of a man from the tribe of Levi named Taxo, who called his seven sons to fast for three days in order to purify themselves. Then he and his sons left their dwelling to live in a cave in order to manifest their refusal to break the commandments of the Law. Taxo explained to them the reason for his action: "For if we do this and die, our blood will be avenged before the Lord."[2] The writers of that time also tell us about two mothers who circumcised their newborn boys. After they were discovered, each baby was bound and hung on his mother's neck over her breasts; the women were made to walk like that through the city, and then they were thrown from the wall to the precipice below.[3] Some of the most famous martyrs during this time included an old man named Eleazar and a mother with her seven children. They were forced to eat pork, and because they refused to defile themselves, they were tortured one after another until they all died. Their martyrdom is related in two intertestamental books, 2 Maccabees and 4 Maccabees. We shall come back to them. The revolt led by Mattathias and his sons, the Maccabees, resulting in the liberation of Judea and Jerusalem and in the re-consecration of the Temple on 15 Kislev 164 B.C., also deserves mention.

The experience of persecution and the long war for independence that followed it led many Jewish thinkers to a process of re-evaluation of their views on life and history. They saw that the following burning issues needed further or even new clarification: the meaning of the suffering of the just and the purpose of the death of God's people for their faith; the nature or the character of a God who lets the evil one triumph and the just one suffer and die; the nature of the world and of human life in general; the final plan of God with individuals, with nations, and with the entire cosmos; and lastly, the nature of the conflict between good and evil and the final outcome of this conflict.

Issues so great and so difficult gave birth to a large number of writings, some of them philosophical, some theological, and some apocalyptic. Most of them are known today only by specialists in the field of intertestamental literature, but for the Jews who lived in the century before Christ and for the Jews and Christians who lived in the first centuries after Christ, these books were enormously important. Alongside the writings of the Old Testament, these texts molded the thinking of these centuries. They influenced the writers of the New Testament, and many of these books provided nourishment for the minds of persecuted Christians in the first four centuries, thereby assisting them to form their own view of suffering and martyrdom, as well as of other issues related to them.

Therefore, it is necessary for our present investigation to take a closer look at these books, so that we may consider the ways in which they dealt with the topics of suffering, martyrdom, and the subsequent rewards for them. These are the titles that I have found to be pertinent to our study:

> The Wisdom of Jesus Ben Sirah
> 1 Maccabees
> 2 Maccabees
> 4 Maccabees
> 1 Enoch
> The Book of Jubilees
> The Testament of Abraham
> The Testaments of the Twelve Patriarchs
> The Testament of Moses (or The Assumption of Moses)
> The Wisdom of Solomon
> The Psalms of Solomon
> The Ascension of Isaiah
> The Testament of Judah

From the manuscripts of Qumran, the following are of some interest for our theme:

> The Psalms of Thanksgiving
> The Rule of the Congregation
> The Manual of Discipline

The exact dating of these books is impossible to achieve. Scholarly opinion varies greatly on this question. The case of the dating of 2 Maccabees serves to illustrate the point. Some say that it was written about 120 B.C., while others hold that it was written about the time when Christ was born, and still others speculate that it was written about the year 40 after Christ. This wide variety of opinions is characteristic of most of the books on our list. Nonetheless, what can be held with considerable certainty is that these books were written not earlier than the Syrian persecution and not later than the first half of the first century of the Christian era.

Most of the concepts developed in these books will appear in one way or another in the New Testament literature and thereafter in the Christian literature of the first four hundred years of the Christian era, centuries that deal with the issue of martyrdom in particular and in detail. For this reason, it is important to take an inventory of the ideas that appear in these texts related to our subject.

The primary phenomenon for us to observe is that the authors of these writings typically searched the Scriptures, or in other words, the Old Testament, in order to find answers to their questions about the suffering of the people of God and about their dying as a consequence of their faithfulness to God. During the interval of time between the Old and the New Testaments, the Scriptures became the foundation for Jewish thought. The Jews were thoroughly biblical thinkers. If we keep this in mind, we will not be surprised then to see that the Maccabean martyrs looked to the heroes of the Old Testament as their models. Mattathias, before his death, instructed his sons in this way: "Therefore, my children, be zealous for the Torah, and be ready to give your lives for the covenant of our fathers. Remember the deeds of our ancestors, which they did in their generations, and win for yourselves great glory and undying renown."[4] Mattathias followed this advice by pointing them to the examples of Abraham, Joseph, Phineas, Joshua, Caleb, David, Elijah, Hananiah, Azariah, Mishael, and Daniel, briefly recounting the main heroic action of each of them.

The mother of the seven children who were about to be martyred reminded them of the manner in which their father educated them in the Scriptures:

> He, when he was still with you, taught you the Law and the Prophets. He read to you about Abel, done to death by Cain; of Isaac, offered as a holocaust; and of Joseph in prison. He spoke to you of the zeal of Phineas; and taught you concerning Hananiah, Mishael, and Azariah in the fire. He also glorified Daniel, in the pit of lions, and called him blessed. He admonished you of the Scripture of Isaiah, which declares, "When thou walkest through fire the flame shall not burn thee." He chanted to you the psalm of David which says, "Many are the ills of the righteous." He recited the proverb of Solomon which says, "He is a tree of life to them that do his will." He affirmed the word of Ezekiel, "Shall these dry bones live?" Nor indeed did he forget, in his instruction, the song that Moses taught, which says, "I kill and I make alive; for that is thy life and the length of thy days."[5]

Some of the martyrs are described as fulfilling certain portions of the Scriptures, especially Deuteronomy 32 and Isaiah 55 and 56. In Deuteronomy 32:36, it is written that "the Lord will vindicate His people, and will have compassion on His servants; when He sees that their strength is gone;" verse 43 adds that "He will avenge the blood of His servants, and will render vengeance on His adversaries, and will atone for His land and His people." Holding fast to these prophesies as well as to some of the promises made to the Sabbath keepers in Isaiah, approximately a thousand people who were "seeking Justice and Vindication" went into the wilderness to keep the Sabbath there. Apparently their hope was that either God would act to save them, or that once they died for keeping the Law, the Lord would avenge their blood. He would punish the persecutor and would bring deliverance to the nation. It seems that this was also the hope of Taxo, who called his seven sons to live in a cave because he refused to break the Law. Taxo specifically quotes the promise made in Deuteronomy that God would avenge their blood.[6] 2 Maccabees, when relating the martyrdom of the mother and her seven sons, quotes exactly the same passage of Scripture.[7]

The suffering Servant in the Book of Isaiah was also a model for them; in Him, they were able to find a rationale and an explanation for the suffering and death of God's people. One can observe this influence in their description of the Maccabean martyrs as well as in the presentation of the suffering wise man's destiny in the Wisdom of Solomon 1-6, in the Testament of Moses, and in the Book of Jubilees.[8]

Certain passages in the Old Testament state directly that the prophets of God suffered persecution and death. For example, 2 Chronicles looks back on the history of Israel and Judah, and relates how "the Lord, the God of their fathers, sent word to them again and again by His messengers, . . . but they continually mocked the messengers of God, despised His words and scoffed at His prophets" (2 Chron. 36:15-16). Nehemiah, in his prayer of confession and intercession for the nation, also mentions that they had "killed Thy prophets who had admonished them so that they might return to Thee" (Neh. 9:26). Some of the intertestamental literature develops this theme of the suffering and martyrdom of the prophets.[9]

The prophets suffered because they spoke for God, condemning their generation for its sinfulness. The Maccabean martyrs, likened to the prophets, were also seen as spokesmen for God; they too spoke words of condemnation to the persecutors of God's people. Listen to what one of the martyred brothers declared to the persecuting king:

> But you, who have shown yourself to be the contriver of every
> evil against the Hebrews, shall not escape the hands of God. . . .
> You profane wretch, vilest of all men, be not vainly buoyed up by
> your insolent uncertain hopes, raising your hand against His
> servants. You have not escaped the judgment of the Almighty, all-
> seeing God. . . . you under God's judgment will receive just

punishment for your arrogance.[10]

The first idea that we see in the literature of the intertestamental period is that suffering has always been the lot of the special people of God, from Abel to the end of the line of prophetic history. For one reason or another, God's special people have always been subject to persecution, and many have suffered a violent death.

The second idea that we find in these writings is that suffering is God's way of chastising His people for their own sins. With this in mind, one of the seven brothers told the king: "Through our own fault we are subjected to these sufferings, because we have sinned against our God."[11] Another brother said this: "As for us, we are suffering for our own sins. If our living God has for a short time become angry with us in order to chastise and teach us, He will again become reconciled with His servants."[12] The same view is expressed in the Wisdom of Solomon: "But we are at peace, for though in the sight of men they may be punished, they have a sure hope of immortality; and after a little chastisement they will receive great blessings."[13]

The chastisement is not only a grim penalty applied by a severe Judge. It is a demonstration of the love of God towards His own people. He punishes them in order to teach them something as well as to make them pay for their sins. Furthermore, if they are punished for their sins in this life, they will not have to pay for them throughout eternity. The way the author of 4 Maccabees explains this belief is worth quoting *in extenso*:

> I beg the readers of my book not to be disheartened by the calamities but to bear in mind that chastisements come not in order to destroy our race but in order to teach it. If the ungodly among us are not left long to themselves but speedily incur punishment, it is a sign of God's great goodness to us. With the other nations the Lord waits patiently, staying their punishment until they reach the full measure of their sins. Quite otherwise is His decree for us, in order that He should not have to punish us after we have come to the complete measure of our sins. Consequently, God never lets His mercy depart from us. Rather, though He teaches us by calamity, He never deserts His people.[14]

Having to suffer the punishment of God for their own sins is one way of explaining the calamity that has swept over them. As we previously pointed out, this rationale was given by Daniel, as well, in Daniel 9:3-15. However, both in the Book of Daniel and in the intertestamental literature, the writers quickly move beyond this individualistic explanation of personal sufferings to the larger view that the martyrs' sufferings are, in one way or another, for the benefit of the entire nation.

The would-be-martyrs felt that by means of their deaths, they would exhaust the measure of God's anger which had to come upon the nation: "With me and my brothers may the Almighty put an end to the rightful anger inflicted upon our nation."[15] The writer of 4 Maccabees offers further explanations for the effects of their martyrdom: "because of them our enemies did not prevail over our nation,"[16] and "it was because of them that our nation obtained peace: they renewed the observance of the Law in their country, and lifted their enemies' siege."[17]

We have seen that in the Book of Daniel one of the functions of martyrdom is "to refine, purge, and make [the martyrs] pure" (Dan. 11:35). The idea that suffering cleanses a person of sins appears again in the Psalms of Solomon: "Happy is the man whom the Lord remembers by a reproof . . . that he may be cleansed of sin."[18]

One takes a step further when one considers suffering or martyrdom a solution for somebody else's sin, in addition to being an answer for one's own sin. We discovered earlier in Isaiah 53:5 and 10 that the death of the Servant of the Lord is a guilt offering for the sins of the people. It is significant to observe a similar function being attributed to the suffering of the "elect" people of God in the literature of the Qumran. Thus, in a commentary on Habakkuk 1:12-13, we read that "God will execute the judgment of the nations by the hand of his Elect. And through their chastisement all the wicked of his people shall expiate their guilt who keep the Commandments in their distress."[19] In another place, we read that "they shall preserve the faith in the land with steadfastness and meekness and shall atone for sin by the practice of justice and by the sorrow of affliction."[20]

The notion that the death of the martyrs or the blood of the martyrs is an expiation or an atonement for the sins of the nation is directly and unambiguously taught in the Fourth Book of the Maccabees. In the introduction to the book, the author already mentions the overall effects of the deaths of the martyrs: "By their courage and perseverance . . . they became responsible for the dissolution of the tyranny which oppressed our nation; the tyrant they overcame by their perseverance, so that through them the fatherland was purged (καθαρισθῆναι)."[21] The author builds on this idea in his conclusion, saying that "our land was purified (καθαρισθῆναι) they having become as it were a ransom (ἀντίψυχον) for the sins of the nation. It was through the blood of these righteous ones, and through the expiation (ἰλαστηρίον) of their death that the divine Providence preserved Israel, which had been ill used."[22]

The concept we need to retain from these texts is that an individual's sacrifice is able to atone for the sins of a whole nation, acting as a ransom and thereby procuring its freedom. The First Book of Enoch also teaches that the salvation of a nation can be accomplished by the sacrifice and "blood of the righteous"; thus, the author writes:

> And in those days shall have ascended the prayer of the righteous, and the blood of the righteous from the earth before the Lord of the Spirits. . . . And the hearts of the holy were filled with joy, because the number of the righteous had been offered, and the prayers of the righteous had been heard, and the blood of the righteous been required before the Lord of the Spirits.[23]

In the process of suffering and dying, the martyrs themselves are both refined and tested. Thus, we read in Ecclesiasticus: "Whatsoever is brought upon thee take cheerfully, and be patient when thou art changed to a low estate. For gold is tried in the fire, and acceptable men in the furnace of adversity."[24] In the Wisdom of Solomon, we read that "after a little chastisement they will receive great blessings, because God has tested them and found them worthy to be His. Like gold in a crucible He put them to the proof, and found them acceptable like an offering burnt whole upon the altar."[25]

The attempt of Antiochus IV to eradicate the Jewish religion was perceived as a war against the God of Israel. For this reason, one of the seven sons who would be martyred said to the king, "Do not think that you will go free in thus daring to wage war against God."[26] The language of war is constantly used throughout the writings of this period. The mother of the seven martyred children is eulogized with these words: "Mother, soldier of God through religion, Elder woman! By your constancy you have vanquished even the tyrant."[27] One of the brothers exhorted the others in the following exalted manner: "Imitate me, my brothers; do not desert your post in my trial, do not abjure our brotherhood in nobility. Fight the sacred and noble fight for religion's sake."[28] Another brother drew this grand conclusion: "Holy and seemly is the passion to which we brethren so many have been summoned, a contest of suffering for religion's sake; and we have not been vanquished."[29] In another place, the author calls Eleazar "a noble athlete."[30] This language would become standard for the description of Christian martyrs in the second, third, and fourth centuries A.D.

The martyrs were aware that this war was not merely fought against human enemies. It was a battle against Satan and his agents. This awareness is vividly expressed in the Ascension of Isaiah: "Beliar, the great prince, will come down, the king of this world, who has had dominion over it since it first came into being; he will come down from his abode in the vault of heaven in the form of a man, as a lawless king and matricide."[31] We are told next that "Beliar's anger was roused against Isaiah because of these visions, and he took up his abode in Manasseh's heart; and he sawed Isaiah in two with a wood-saw."[32]

A few more elements in the story of Isaiah's martyrdom should be noted, due to the way they also display the standard mode of speaking about martyrdom. Thus, Isaiah informed Manasseh: "You can take nothing from me but only the skin off my body."[33] Soon afterward Isaiah instructed the prophets who were his disciples to run and take refuge in the region of Tyre and Sidon, "because God has mixed this cup for me alone."[34] Isaiah accepted his martyrdom as the "cup" that God had given him, and because the Holy Spirit was in him, his martyrdom was not painful: "While he was being sawn in two Isaiah neither cried nor wept; but he went on speaking by the Holy Spirit until he was sawn right through."[35]

When brought before pagan kings and courts, the martyrs took advantage of each opportunity to witness about their faith. For instance, one of the seven brothers warned the king: "You shall suffer through the judgment of God the just punishment for your arrogance"; but then he added a prayer for him: "May you through being afflicted and scourged come to acknowledge that He alone is God."[36] Eleazar, when asked under threat of torture and death to eat pork, responded with a speech in which he explained to the king the faith of the Jews and tried to convince the king that their religion was a reasonable and true religion. The mother of the seven instilled in her sons the awareness that they were called to be witnesses in the battle of martyrdom: "My sons, noble is the contest; and since you are summoned to it in order to bear testimony (διαμαρτυρίας) strive zealously on behalf of the Law of our fathers."[37] Clearly, in these writings "martyrdom is a witness with a view to conversion."[38]

Resurrection and Rewards

In times of persecution and martyrdom, men and women are forced to reconsider issues of ultimate concern, particularly with respect to the nature of God and the eternal destiny of man. If God is good and just and almighty, why do His people suffer unjustly? Why must they die the death of criminals? In the literature of the intertestamental period, both of these questions were resolved by the beliefs in immortality and resurrection, in the final judgment, and in the rewards or punishments issued at the last judgment.

The belief in the resurrection of the just was taught both in Isaiah and in Daniel. In the Book of Isaiah, in the context of the prophecy concerning the restoration of Israel, the prophet wrote, "Your dead will live; their corpses will rise. You who lie in the dust, awake and shout for joy, for your dew is as the dew of the dawn, and the earth will give birth to the departed spirits" (26:19). Other prophets, speaking about the restoration, evidently used the language of the resurrection in a symbolic way (e.g., Hosea 5:15-6:3; Ezekiel 37:11-14). Some commentators maintain that Isaiah 26:19 has the same metaphoric nature. However, because in 26:14, Isaiah spoke about the abusive rulers who will not rise, it is clear that Isaiah was referring here to a literal resurrection.[39] Furthermore, in Isaiah 53:11, the prophet announces that the Servant of the Lord, after He has died for the sins of the people, will see the result of the labor of His soul. This certainly indicates a resurrection.

We have already seen what Daniel had to say in the twelfth chapter of his book about the resurrection of the just for eternal life and the resurrection of the unjust for eternal punishment. We have also learned that the great reward of the saints is in the fact that they will be given "the sovereignty, the dominion, and the greatness of all the kingdoms under the whole heaven" (Dan. 7:27).

There are quite a number of texts in the intertestamental literature which expand upon these ideas. To begin with, 2 Maccabees speaks explicitly about the resurrection of the body. Thus, before his death, the second martyred son said to the king, "You accursed wretch, you may release us from our present existence, but the King of the Universe will raise us up to everlasting life because we have died for His laws."[40] The third son also told the king, "Better is it for people to be done to death by men if they have the hopeful expectation that they will again be raised up by God."[41] Previously, their mother had explained to them:

> How you ever appeared in my womb, I do not know. It was not I
> who graced you with breath and life, nor was it I who arranged in
> order within each of you the combination of the elements. It was
> the Creator of the World, who formed the generation of man and
> devised the origin of all things, and He will give life back to you
> in mercy, even as you now take no thought for yourselves on
> account of His laws.[42]

Again, she encouraged one of her sons in the following manner:
"Do not be afraid of this executioner, but show yourself worthy of your
brothers. Accept death, that in God's mercy I may receive you back
again along with your brothers."[43]

In 4 Maccabees, although the narrative is about the same heroes as
in the second book, the author wrote not about the resurrection but
about the immortality of the soul. We are told that old Eleazar stood
heroically under every torture "until he entered the harborage of
deathless victory."[44] One of the brothers defied the king with these
words: "If you have any means of torture, apply it to my body; my soul
you cannot touch, even if you would."[45] Another brother said to the
others: "Let us not fear him who thinks that he kills. . . . When we
have died in such fashion, Abraham and Isaac and Jacob will receive
us, and all the patriarchs will praise us."[46]

The Second and the Fourth Books of the Maccabees tell us that the
strength of the martyrs came from their knowledge that death was not
the end of their existence. Whether it will be through a resurrection or
through the direct passing of the soul into eternity, the martyrs will
obtain a new life. The second book does not tell us anything about
rewards in that resurrected life, but the fourth book does state that the
martyrs will receive praises from the patriarchs. Then, the Assumption
of Moses gives us the following picture:

> And then shall his kingdom appear throughout all his creation;
> And then shall the Devil meet his end,
> And sorrow shall depart with him.
> Then the angel who has been appointed chief shall be consecrated,
> Who will immediately avenge them of their enemies.
> For the Heavenly One will (arise) from his royal throne,
> And go forth from his holy dwelling place
> With wrath and anger because of his sons. . . .
> Then happy will you be, Israel:
> And you will trample upon their necks,

For the time allotted to them will have run its course.
And God will exalt you,
And set you in heaven above the stars,
In the place where he dwells himself.
And you will look from on high and see your enemies on earth (or
in Gehenna).[47]

Interesting features in this text are the destruction of the devil, the exaltation of all Israel to the stars, and the fact that they will be able to view their enemies below them. There is no information about what will happen after their exaltation or after the judgment of their enemies. We see a similar picture in the Book of Jubilees:

> . . . and there will be no Satan nor any evil agent to corrupt them; for all their days will be days of blessing and of healing. And at that time the Lord will heal his servants, and they shall be exalted and prosper greatly; and they shall drive out their adversaries. And the righteous shall see it and be thankful, and rejoice with joy for ever and ever; and they shall see all the punishments and curses that had been their lot falling on their enemies. And their bones shall rest in the earth, and their spirits shall have much joy; and they shall know that the Lord is one who executes judgment, and shows mercy to hundreds, and to tens of thousands, and to all that love him.[48]

In the passage above, we observe the judgment and punishment of the enemies of God's people, and the happy life enjoyed by God's servants after their enemies have been vanquished. While their bones rest in the ground, their spirits are shown to enjoy happiness, presumably in heaven. We are not told when their spirits went to heaven, whether immediately upon death or later at the time of the judgment. Neither is there any mention of a future resurrection of their bodies.

The Testament of Judah, however, does speak about a future resurrection:

> And after this Abraham and Isaac and Jacob will rise to life again.
> . . . And there will be one people of the Lord and one language;
> And there will be no spirit of error of Beliar any more,
> For he will be thrown into the fire for ever.
> And those who have died in grief will rise again in joy. . . .
> And those who have been put to death for the Lord's sake will
> awake to life.[49]

It is not clear from the text if this is a general resurrection or a

selective one. It seems that the latter is the probable case. The ones
who were selected for mention in this resurrection, besides Abraham,
Isaac, and Jacob, are "those who have died in grief," and "those who
have been put to death for the Lord's sake." To die "in grief" means to
die a violent death. It is clear, then, from the context, that the author
was speaking of a death in persecution, of a martyrdom. The
clarification comes in the last line: their death is for the sake of the
Lord.

The Wisdom of Solomon gives us the most extensive picture of the
martyrs' heavenly rewards. It begins by presenting to us the wicked
plotting of a group of godless men against a "poor and honest man."[50]
These godless men mock the poor man when he says that "God is his
father."[51] They try to test his claim by "outrage and torment" and
ultimately, by "a shameful death."[52] But what they do not know is that
through their terrible deeds, they are actually fulfilling "God's hidden
plan."[53] These wicked men had "never expected that holiness of life
would have its recompense; they thought that innocence had no
reward. But God created man for immortality and made him the image
of His own eternal self."[54] The author then explains what happens to
such martyred men of God:

> But the souls of the just are in God's hand, and torment shall not
> touch them. In the eyes of foolish men they seem to be dead; their
> departure was reckoned as defeat, and their going from us a
> disaster. But they are at peace, for though in the sight of men they
> may be punished, they have a sure hope of immortality; and after a
> little chastisement they will receive great blessings, because God
> has tested them and found them worthy to be his. Like gold in a
> crucible he put them to the proof, and found them acceptable like
> an offering burnt whole upon the altar. In the moment of God's
> coming to them they will kindle into flame, like sparks that sweep
> through stubble; they will be judges and rulers over the nations of
> the world, and the Lord shall be their king for ever and ever.[55]

The people of God who pass the test are "found worthy" to belong
to God and to receive "great blessings." At last, we are informed what
their rewards will be: the martyrs "will be judges and rulers over the
nations of the world." However, not only martyrdom will be rewarded;
purity will have its reward, as well. For example, a childless woman
who has lived in purity in this life, "at the great assize of souls . . .
shall find a fruitfulness of her own,"[56] and a eunuch who has led a
pure life "shall receive special favour in return for his faith, and a

place in the Lord's temple to delight his heart the more."[57] These statements are then succeeded by the general remark that "honest work bears glorious fruit."[58]

The unbelievers who plotted and killed the man of God are later enabled to see their victim in glory. Filled with terror, groaning and gasping for breath, they exclaim: "To think that he is now counted as one of the sons of God and assigned a place of his own among God's people!"[59] The ungodly men receive their punishment, and the author gives us one last clue about the heavenly destiny of the children of God: "But the just live forever; their reward is in the Lord's hand, and the Most High has them in His care. Therefore royal splendor shall be theirs, and a fair diadem from the Lord Himself; He will protect them with His right hand and shield them with His arm."[60]

Some of the Psalms of Solomon also express faith in the resurrection, while the First Book of Enoch deals with this subject, as well. However, these books do not add anything of substance to this topic.

From the writings of the intertestamental period, we have learned that God's justice will be witnessed beyond this life at the time of His judgment, when He will punish the wicked and will reward the just. In the present, God is testing His own people in sufferings in order that He may find the ones who are worthy of Himself. The ones who pass the tests will find their true fulfillment in the positions and functions that God will give them in His heavenly realm. Some of these texts show that a soul will reach the heavenly realm through a resurrection, whereas others show that the soul is immortal and passes from this life directly into the next. Whatever the case may be, they all concur in this: the martyrs find the courage to face the tortures in the knowledge that after this short period of suffering and on account of it, the glories of eternal life will surely come.

PART THREE

Suffering, Witness, and Martyrdom in the New Testament

Chapter 5

Jesus and Martyrdom

The principal thesis of our study in the New Testament is that the essentials of the doctrine of suffering, martyrdom, and rewards in heaven are found in the teachings of Jesus. In order to discover these essentials, we have to look at Jesus' teachings in their "*sitz im leben*," that is, we must see them as they were given to His disciples and at times to the multitudes. We must try to understand what *He* meant when He gave them these teachings. Later on, we will have to explore what *the disciples themselves* understood Jesus to mean, and for that we will have to read their own writings, starting with the Book of Acts and ending with the Book of Revelation. Their understanding of the teachings of Jesus will confirm if we rightly understood what Jesus taught them.

In order to arrive at an accurate understanding of Jesus' teaching on these subjects, we have to establish some foundational principles of approach, and we will start with the three that are the most important and the most basic. It is not within the scope of this dissertation to argue and to justify them here; rather, we will assume them as our basic working presuppositions:

1. We believe that the Gospels present an accurate account of what Jesus said and did on the earth. *The sayings of Jesus* are exactly what the Gospels present them to be: they are *His sayings*, not later creations of the church or of the authors of the Gospels.

2. The Gospel of John does not present a different Jesus or a different teaching of Jesus; hence, Jesus' teaching in the Gospel of John should not be presented in isolation from His teaching in the Synoptic Gospels. Consequently, we shall combine the information we find in all four Gospels in order to obtain a total picture of what Jesus taught during His earthly ministry.

3. Jesus did not change His views according to the circumstances that developed in the course of His ministry. When He started His ministry He had a clear and definite conception of who He was and of what His ministry had to be. He knew exactly what His own function and work had to be. He knew what sort of work had to be done after He had finished His own work, and therefore, He knew what sort of people He would need and what kind of training He had to give them.

As we approach the four Gospels with these principles in mind, and as we gather and combine the information given about Jesus, it is necessary to fix in our minds the following seven basic facts about Him. They will serve as the fundamental presuppositions of our study:

1. The man Jesus drew all His information from and based all His conceptions upon the writings of the Scriptures (i.e., the Old Testament). We never find Him using other written sources or appealing to other thinkers. We may assume that He was familiar with the currents of thought of His time but that He chose to reject them, remaining strictly with the Scriptures; however, we do not have any information in this regard.

2. Jesus' chosen method of interpretation of the Scriptures was the one we refer to as "typological." This method starts from the basic premise that God's way of acting in history does not change. God always has the same principles of action. The events, individuals, and nations presented in the Old Testament, including the nation of Israel, are "patterns" or "types" that illustrate how God deals within the human drama. Jesus selected Old Testament events and persons, as well as Israel as a whole, and used them as illustrations of the way God accomplishes His purposes in human history, in and through His Son.

3. Jesus saw Himself as belonging to the line of succession of Old Testament prophets. Thus, when he was rejected in Nazareth, He explained it as something that was common to a prophet's experience: "A prophet is not without honor except in his home town and among his own relatives and in his own household" (Mk. 6:4). When He was warned that Herod might kill Him, Jesus replied that He still had some

work to do in that area, but afterwards He must go to Jerusalem, "for it cannot be that a prophet should perish outside of Jerusalem" (Lk. 13:33).

Jesus' view of Israel's history was that she had always persecuted and killed the prophets God had sent to her. Hence Jesus' lament over Jerusalem: "O, Jerusalem, Jerusalem, the city that kills the prophets and stones those sent to her!" (Lk. 13:34), and His subsequent burst of anger and condemnation:

> You serpents, you brood of vipers, how shall you escape the sentence of hell? Therefore, behold, I am sending you prophets and wise men and scribes; some of them you will kill and crucify, and some of them you will scourge in your synagogues, and persecute from city to city, that upon you may fall the guilt of all the righteous blood shed on earth, from the blood of righteous Abel to the blood of Zechariah, the son of Berechiah, whom you murdered between the temple and the altar. Truly I say to you, all these things shall come upon this generation. (Matt. 23:33-36)

4. Jesus knew from the beginning of His ministry that Israel would reject Him and kill Him. As early as the second chapter of Mark, when asked why His disciples did not fast, He anticipated that "the bridegroom [would be] taken away from them, and then will they fast in that day" (2:20); with this statement, He was obviously referring to His death. In the Gospel of John, the prediction of His death comes as early as verse 29 of the first chapter, when John the Baptist pointed to Jesus and declared, "Behold, the Lamb of God who takes away the sin of the world!" Jesus Himself elaborated upon this in John 3:14-16.

Later in His ministry Jesus repeatedly predicted that He must go to Jerusalem to suffer and be killed (Mk. 8:31; 10:33-34). Again, He saw His rejection and suffering as patterned after the experience of the prophets: "Elijah already came, and they did not recognize him, but did to him whatever they wished. So also the Son of Man is going to suffer at their hands" (Matt. 17:12). Interpreting present events typologically, Jesus discerned the rejection of Elijah recurring in John the Baptist's experience and then in His own. In the parable of the tenants, Jesus again included Himself in the long historical line of God's messengers who have been rejected and killed by the people of Israel, with the difference that He was not one of the "servants" but the "Son" of the Owner of the vineyard (Mk. 12:1-12).

5. Jesus saw Himself portrayed in the most comprehensive way by Isaiah 40-66, as well as by the seventh chapter of Daniel. He saw

Himself as fulfilling the destiny of the suffering Servant of the Lord in Isaiah and the destiny of the Son of Man in Daniel. The debates on this issue have produced an enormous amount of literature. Because it is not within the orbit of this dissertation to go into these debates, I will simply refer to R. T. France's *Jesus and the Old Testament* for an argumentation of the position taken here.[1] In the course of our exposition, Jesus' application of Isaiah and Daniel not only to Himself but also to the role and function of His disciples will become clear.

6. Jesus considered Israel to have failed in fulfilling the mission given to her by God. As a consequence of her failure, Jesus pronounced the following momentous judgment upon her: "Therefore I say to you, the kingdom of God will be taken away from you, and be given to a nation producing the fruit of it" (Matt. 21:43). Because He knew this verdict from the beginning of His public ministry, Jesus chose the twelve disciples in order to train them to be the beginning of the true Israel. It was part of Jesus' overall plan to establish a new people of God, with whom He would institute a new covenant in His own blood (Lk. 20:22).

7. From the very beginning, Jesus had a clear picture of His own mission and of the mission of His disciples. With this in mind, Jesus took them into His school, taught them and trained them systematically, so that they might continue His work after His departure. *It is in this training of the disciples that we find the essentials of Jesus' teaching on suffering, martyrdom, and rewards in heaven.*

Jesus had a great number of disciples. Luke tells us about the seventy disciples whom Jesus sent to preach in the places where He would preach later (Lk. 10:1-24). Out of this larger group, at one point Jesus selected twelve men to be His "apostles." This very name, "the sent ones," shows Jesus' basic intent with them. Mark informs us of the purpose for which they were chosen: "that they might be with Him, and that He might send them out to preach" (Mk. 3:14). Their place in Jesus' overall plan was a very important matter for Jesus, so important that He spent a whole night in prayer before making His selection (Lk. 6:12-13).

Jesus gave special attention to the training of His disciples. His last prayer in the upper room, recorded in John 17, shows how seriously Jesus handled this task. In this prayer, the Son reported to His Father that He had finished the work given to Him (17:4).[2] His detailed recounting of the work He had completed testifies to the fact that *the training of the twelve was His special work* on the earth. This was His report to the Father in which He enumerated the things He had accomplished with the twelve:

- I have revealed You (lit., "Your name") to those whom You gave Me (17:6);
- I gave them the words You gave Me (17:8);
- I protected them and kept them safe (17:12);
- I have given them Your word (17:14);
- As you sent Me into the world, I have sent them into the world (17:18);
- I have given them the glory that You gave Me (17:22).

In His account to the Father, Jesus also described the status of the disciples at the end of their training:

- They were Yours; You gave them to Me (17:6);
- They have obeyed Your word (17:6);
- They know that everything You have given Me comes from You (17:7);
- They believed that You sent Me (17:8);
- They accepted the words I gave them (17:8, paraphrase);
- They knew with certainty that I came from You (17:8);
- They are not of the world any more than I am of the world (17:14, 16).

In order to obtain a complete picture of the disciples, we must also look at the things Jesus asked of the Father on their behalf as He prayed for them:

- Protect them by the power of Your name (17:11);
- That they may be one as We are one (17:11);
- That they may have the full measure of My joy within them (17:13);
- My prayer is not that You take them out of the world but that You protect them from the evil one (17:15);
- Sanctify them by the truth (17:17);
- I pray also for those who will believe in Me through their message, that all of them may be one (17:20-21);
- May they also be in us: . . . I in them and You in Me (17:21, 23);
- May they be brought to complete unity to let the world know that You sent Me and have loved them even as You have loved Me (17:23);
- I want those You have given Me to be with Me where I am

(17:24);
– That the love You have for Me may be in them and that I
myself may be in them (17:26).

This prayer shows us not only how important it was for Jesus to
instruct, to mold, and to shape these men, but also how important the
Twelve were for His whole plan with humanity, as the ones who would
continue His purposes in the world. The prayer of John 17 also
portrays to what great extent they were one with Him, so much so that
He would continue His ministry through them.

The image portrayed in John 17 was not one created by John and
reflected back to Jesus. The basic ideas in this prayer can be clearly
seen in the instructions Jesus gave to His disciples in the first phase of
their training, in the tenth chapter of Matthew. There we notice the
same unity between the Father, the Son, and the disciples: "He who
receives you receives Me, and he who receives Me receives Him who
sent Me" (Matt. 10:40).

When one studies the process of the disciples' training, it is evident
that Jesus was concerned with more than just giving them the *content*
of His teaching so that they could pass it on to others. On the contrary,
Jesus also desired to help them understand their own place and
function in His plan, and He wanted them to be aware of the violent
opposition they were going to face as they would go out to fulfill their
mission; not the least of His intentions was to teach them exactly what
to do in a situation of such violence.

Let us start by analyzing the function of the disciples. We begin
with the statement of the risen Lord as He defined the function of the
disciples in these words: "You shall be My witnesses both in
Jerusalem, and in all Judea and Samaria, and even to the remotest part
of the earth" (Acts 1:8). His announcement at this moment was the
culmination of His systematic teaching on *what it means to be a
witness* and on *what the function of a witness entails*. We should keep
in mind the Greek terms employed in this discussion. The word for
witness is μάρτυς (gen. μάρτυρος). The verb for bearing witness is
μαρτυρεῖν, and the noun for the action of bearing witness is μαρτυρία.
The other words of special interest for our theme are "to confess,"
ὁμολογεῖν, and "confession," ὁμολογία.

The actual training of the disciples for their role as witnesses
started when Jesus sent them two by two to preach in the villages and
towns of Galilee, an action presented to us in Matthew the tenth
chapter. The practical instructions Jesus gave them were not only

appropriate for that immediate situation but were even more fitting for the much greater mission on which they would be sent in the future. Jesus warned them of the violent reaction their preaching would provoke in some places: "They will deliver you up to the courts, and scourge you in their synagogues; and you shall even be brought before governors and kings for My sake, as a testimony (μαρτύριον) to them and to the Gentiles" (Matt. 10:17-18). Although the action of witnessing in such environments can bring severe punishment or even death, the disciples were summoned to boldly witness and confess Christ. The things that Christ taught them in private, they must shout in the marketplaces. Both here and in a different context in Luke, this challenge is accompanied by a promise and a threat: "Every one therefore who shall confess (ὁμολογήσει) Me before men, I will also confess (ὁμολογήσω) him before My Father who is in heaven. But whoever shall deny Me before men, I will also deny him before My Father who is in heaven" (Matt. 10:32-33; Lk. 12:8-9).

The concept of witness was further developed in Jerusalem, where Jesus gave the disciples instructions regarding the future. There will be a time of calamities, of wars, and of tribulation. Notwithstanding these things, the disciples must continue their work of witnessing, because "this gospel of the kingdom shall be preached in the whole world for a witness (μαρτύριον) to all the nations" (Matt. 24:14). In the parallel text in Mark's Gospel, the statement about witness is placed after the announcement that they will be arrested and taken before the religious or civil authorities (Mk. 13:9-11; cf., Matt. 10:17-18). H. Strathmann says that the phrase εἰς μαρτύριον αὐτοῖς in these places does not mean a witness to them so that they may believe, but an incriminating witness against them at the last judgment.[3] Against Strathmann's view and in support of the view for which I shall argue further, Cranfield offers a useful explication:

> . . . it is surely better to allow for the various ideas which are involved in the witness-imagery rather than to insist on choosing between "witness to" and "evidence against." We suggest that the meaning here is threefold: first, that the disciples' profession of Christ before the tribunals of governors and kings will be a piece of evidence for the truth of the gospel; secondly, it will be a piece of evidence for the truth of the gospel offered to their prosecutors (αὐτοῖς probably including both the governors and kings, who otherwise might not have heard the gospel, and also the disciples' Jewish persecutors); and thirdly, if the evidence for the truth of the gospel which this courageous profession of Christ's name presents

is not accepted by the persecutors and judges, then at the final judgment it will be evidence against them.[4]

The Lukan version of the phrase should help us see the intent to conversion. In Luke 21:13, the arrest is said to "lead to an opportunity for your testimony" (ἀποβήσεται ὑμῖν εἰς μαρτύριον; lit., "it will turn to you for a testimony"). Then, both in Matthew 10:19-20 and in Mark 13:11, the disciples are told not to worry beforehand about how or what they will speak to the authorities, because it will be the Holy Spirit who will speak through them; the involvement of the Holy Spirit in their task of witnessing is certain and sure. Again, Luke understands this to mean: "for I will give you utterance (lit., a mouth) and wisdom which none of your opponents will be able to resist or refute" (21:15). The context of this assurance is the preaching of the gospel to all the nations of the earth. Hence, we may safely conclude that the purpose of witnessing is to convince the nations about the truth of the gospel and to bring them to believe in Jesus Christ.

This interpretation of the function of the witnesses of Christ is strongly confirmed by the Gospel of John. John conceived his entire Gospel as his own "witness" to Christ. He testified to this in the conclusion of his book: "This is the disciple who bears witness (ὁ μαρτυρῶν) of these things, and wrote these things; and we know that his witness (μαρτυρία) is true" (John 21:24). In this Gospel, the concept of witness is used more than in any other book of the Bible. Here is C. K. Barrett's summary of the use of the word in the Gospel of John:

> Witness (μαρτυρεῖν, μαρτυρία) holds an important place in the thought of the gospel. The Baptist (1.7f., 15, 32, 34; 3.26; 5.33), the Samaritan woman (4.39), the works of Jesus (5.36; 10.25), the Old Testament (5:39), the multitude (12.17), the Holy Spirit and the apostles (15.26f.), God the Father Himself (5.32, 37; 8.18), all bear witness to Jesus. Jesus Himself . . . bears witness to the truth (18.37; cf. 3.11), in conjunction with the Father (8.13-18) whose consentient testimony validates His own. Witnesses in turn testify to the truth of the gospel record (19.35; 21.24).[5]

Out of this multitude of witnesses, we are interested here mainly in the function of the apostles as witnesses. In the upper room, Jesus told His disciples that He is the vine and they are the branches, and that their function is to bear fruit (John 15:1-8). It is common knowledge that a vine produces fruit only through its branches. By this metaphor, therefore, Jesus was telling His disciples that He had made Himself dependent upon them to be fruitful in the world. He declared to them in no uncertain terms what His purpose was for them: "I chose you, and appointed you, that you should go and bear fruit" (15:16). They would bear fruit by being His witnesses, a task for which they were now qualified because they had been with Him from the beginning (15:27).

Allison A. Trites, in *The New Testament Concept of Witness*, discovered that the Gospel of John follows the pattern of Isaiah very closely. What is of interest for us here is the parallel between the identity and function of the witnesses in Isaiah and the identity and function of the witnesses in John's Gospel:

> Isaiah's "Book of Consolation" speaks of Israel both as God's witness and as his servant (Isa. 43:10, 12; cf., 41:8f.; 44:8); the same combination appears in John's Gospel. Jesus plainly assumes the role of a servant in John 13:1-17 (in fact he deliberately gives them a ὑπόδειγμα, 13:15), and great stress is laid on his task as a witness (Jn. 3:32-4; 8:13-4, 18:37). Similarly, the disciples of Jesus are called to be both servants (13:14-17; 15:20) and witnesses (15:27; cf., 1:6-8, 15, 19ff.; 19:35; 21:24).[6]

Trites defines the role of the witnesses in the Gospel of John as follows:

> The apostles, like the witnesses in the Old Testament lawsuit, have a two-fold role; they are both witnesses to the facts of the life of Jesus, for they have been with him "from the beginning" (15:27; cf., 1 John 1:1), and they are also advocates, defending him, commending him and trying to convince his opponents that he is Messiah, and Son of God.[7]

The Persecution of the Witness

Right from the beginning of His public ministry, Jesus knew exactly who He was, and He had a clear plan of action. He knew what He himself had to achieve through His own death, and He knew what His disciples' function and ministry would be after He had completed His own earthly ministry. We have already seen that Jesus followed the pattern given in Isaiah: the pattern of the Servant of the Lord as God's witness to a world that is in darkness and of the servants who are also called to be God's witnesses to that perishing world.

Jesus also knew that the world would kill Him, but He knew that He would save the world by His act of dying. He had been called "to give His life as a ransom for many" (Matt. 20:28). Additionally, Jesus was aware of the fact that His disciples were going to meet the same kind of violent resistance from the world, and that they were going to be killed like Him. This is why He consistently taught them about their future destiny, and a substantial part of that teaching was about their suffering and death. We are going to explore this teaching in the pages to follow, but my purpose is not only to point out that the disciples were forewarned about the violence they would encounter; rather, in our exploration of the Scriptures, we must also uncover the final goal of their suffering and dying for Christ. Were these events just the incidentals of a risky job, or were they similar to His own suffering and dying, possessing a deeper meaning and a farther-reaching function?

Jesus clearly saw a parallel between His ministry and destiny, on the one hand, and the ministry and destiny of His disciples, on the other. We have already heard Jesus reporting to His Father that He has sent them into the world as the Father had sent Him into the world (John 17:18). After His resurrection, Jesus repeated these words to His disciples: "As the Father has sent Me, I also send you" (John 20:21). How far does the parallelism go? John the Baptist defined Jesus' position and function in the world with these words: "Behold the Lamb of God who takes away the sin of the world" (John 1:29). When Jesus sent His disciples into the world, He defined their position with these words: "Behold, I send you out as lambs in the midst of wolves" (Lk. 10:3). The "lambs in the midst of wolves" is the most hopeless image one could ever conceive: the lambs have no hope of staying alive there for five minutes, let alone of converting the wolves! Nevertheless, it is clear from all of Jesus' teachings that His aim is exactly the conversion of the wolves into lambs! Could Jesus be intimating that by means of their deaths, the lambs would achieve the conversion of the wolves? Let us keep this question in mind as we continue to study the teachings of Jesus.

Jesus commenced the preparation of His disciples for persecution and violence in the Sermon on the Mount, when He said, "Blessed are you when men cast insults at you, and persecute you, and say all kinds of evil against you falsely, on account of Me. Rejoice, and be glad, for your reward in heaven is great, for so they persecuted the prophets who were before you" (Matt. 5:11-12). Later in the same sermon, He added: "Do not resist him who is evil; but whoever slaps you on your right cheek, turn to him the other also. . . . love your enemies, and pray for those who persecute you in order that you may be sons of your Father who is in heaven" (5:39, 44-45).

Several important features of this teaching of Jesus will be developed at length later, but we need to introduce them here. The most basic one is that this suffering is "on account of Me." It is for Christ's cause. Men and women suffer in His service, for the fulfillment of His purposes in the world. Next, Jesus directed their attention to the fate of the prophets. They had been God's messengers to past generations. When Jesus said, "the prophets who were before you," He meant that they, the disciples, were in the line of the prophets; that is, they were God's messengers to the world of their time. They had been chosen exactly for this purpose, to be sent to preach God's message given to them by Jesus. We have already shown that Jesus Himself knew that He was in the great line of prophetic succession, and that He, like the prophets before Him, would meet violence, persecution, and death (Matt. 17:12; 23:33-36; Mk. 6:4; Lk. 13:34). But following that, His disciples would take over and would continue His function and ministry as Prophet.

Another important item in this teaching is that the disciples were not only to stoically accept the evil done to them by others, but they were to also love the evil-doers; as witnesses, the disciples' role was to bring the latter to God and to salvation. The disciples were in the service of the very people that would meet them with abuse and ill-treatment. The reason why the disciples had to adopt such an attitude towards the very people who would hate them and kill them is that they were the sons of a Father who loves those who revile Him; the Father still gives them the light and warmth of the sun and the blessing of the rain (Matt. 5:45). Later on, the disciples would also come to understand that the Father has sacrificed His only begotten Son for the people who hate Him (John 3:16).

One more important item in the teaching of Jesus in the Sermon of the Mount is the promise of great rewards in heaven for accepting suffering in the service of Christ. Jesus began this particular idea in Matthew 5:12 with the words: "for your reward in heaven is great." Further on in the same sermon, Jesus emphasized the fact that there would be rewards for a service rendered properly to God: for the giving of alms in secret, for praying in secret, and for fasting in secret: "your Father who sees in secret will repay you" (Matt. 6:6). Jesus concluded this instruction with these words: "Do not lay up for yourselves treasures upon earth, . . . but lay up for yourselves treasures in heaven" (6:19-20).

For many evangelicals the thought of being paid or rewarded by God for the things they have done for Him seems too "commercial," "beneath their dignity," and even "repugnant." Is it not more dignified and morally right, they say, to serve God "out of love," without any thought of future reward? One may detect in this attitude a great quantity of human pride, but the main response we have for these people is that God does not act according to our own ideas. We had better listen to what *He* has to say about these matters.

On a more theological level, most Protestants reject the concept of rewards because it seems to contain the idea that man can merit something from God, and thus it seems to deny the New Testament teaching that we receive everything from God by grace. I shall discuss this issue later on in this dissertation. At this stage I simply plead with the reader to look open-mindedly at what Jesus and the rest of the New Testament teaches with respect to rewards. First, we must accept the Word as it is given. Only after we have done that, can we find answers to our theological questions. If Jesus said that even the one who gives a cup of cold water to one of His little ones, because he is a disciple, shall not lose his reward (Matt. 10:42), then we have to accept that it will be so, and adjust our theology accordingly.

Let us take a closer look at the instructions Jesus gave His disciples regarding suffering and self-sacrifice in the tenth chapter of Matthew's Gospel. This is indeed a long lesson, from verse 16 to verse 42. I shall not undertake a detailed exegetical study of it, but shall simply underscore the most important points: the ones that have been the guidelines for Christians under persecution over the centuries and are clearly a part of what our theology of suffering and martyrdom must be.

The stage is set with the description of the position of God's messengers in the world: "Behold, I send you out as sheep in the midst of wolves" (Matt. 10:16a). Isaiah had previously described the position of the Servant of the Lord in the midst of His persecutors using the same imagery: "He was oppressed and He was afflicted, yet He did not open His mouth; like a lamb that is led to the slaughter, and like a sheep that is silent before its shearers, so He did not open His mouth" (Isaiah 53:7).

It is obvious that now Jesus was giving His own disciples the same position which He Himself had taken. He said this in unmistakable terms in the course of the lesson: "A disciple is not above his teacher, nor a slave above his master. It is enough for the disciple that he become as his teacher, and the slave as his master. If they have called the head of the house Beelzebul, how much more the members of his household" (Matt. 10:24-25)! In the upper room, Jesus reminded His disciples of these words, repeating them after He had washed their feet (John 13:16); He further explained His earlier statement by saying: "Remember the word that I said to you, 'A slave is not greater than his master.' If they persecuted Me, they will also persecute you; if they kept My word, they will keep yours also" (John 15:20).

Immediately after Jesus described their position in the world, He gave them this warning: "Therefore be wise (φρόνιμοι) as serpents and innocent as doves" (Matt. 10:16b, NKJV). In fact, during a time of persecution, it is very easy to lose one's self-control and do foolish things. Some, due to fear, may compromise with the enemy; others, because of courage wrongly understood, may provoke the authorities, deliberately attracting persecution. Wisdom is needed to know how to stand, to know what to do and what not to do, so that if suffering comes, it will undoubtedly be for Jesus' sake, and not for the sake of a foolish action. Wisdom and innocence are absolutely necessary in the midst of persecution, so that Christ's disciple might make the right decisions and might stay on the true course in order to fulfill God's purposes.

Then, Jesus explained to them exactly what it means to be a lamb among the wolves: it means to be arrested, interrogated, and tortured. From His continuing discussion, we glean one of the most interesting and most important pieces of information. The disciples would be sent out as lambs precisely in order to witness to the very people who would beat them and interrogate them; however, Jesus reassured them with this great promise: "But when they deliver you up, do not become anxious about how or what you will speak; for it shall be given you in that hour what you are to speak. For it is not you who speak, but it is the Spirit of your Father who speaks in you" (Matt. 10:19-20).

It is very instructive to listen to Christians who have just come from an encounter with hostile authorities. They express the greatest amazement regarding the way they spoke to those authorities. They just cannot explain how the words came to them, and how they were able to speak about their Lord and about their faith with such courage and eloquence! This promise of the Lord is one of the most frequently fulfilled assurances and one of the most beautiful experiences Christians can have during times of persecution. The author of this dissertation does not speak here from books found in the library, but from the experiences of the pastors and elders who taught him as he was growing up in Romania; he also speaks from his own experience of very many and very long interrogations by the Romanian secret police and by other communist authorities. It is indeed the Holy Spirit who speaks through a frightened and normally timid Christian. This is not merely a theory; it is the actual, concrete, and substantiated experience of more than nineteen centuries of Christian witness in persecution.

In Matthew 10:22, the Lord again reminded His disciples that the hate of the world was "on account of My Name." The disciples would be hated by the world because of the fact that they faithfully follow Christ and His teaching. Now, in such situations the common "wisdom" would be to keep quiet. There are many "wise" and well-intentioned friends who argue that one can be a Christian "in his heart," or that one can be a Christian in secret. But Jesus did not leave that possibility open to His disciples when He gave them this command: "What I tell you in the darkness, speak in the light; and what you hear whispered in your ear, proclaim upon the housetops" (10:27).

Just to make sure that what He wanted to say was absolutely clear to them, Jesus explained: "Everyone therefore who shall confess Me before men, I will also confess him before My Father who is in heaven. But whoever shall deny Me before men, I will also deny him before My Father who is in heaven" (10:32-33). It is extremely hard not to fear the threats of the persecutors, while it is so much easier to cave in and say, "I am not a Christian," thereby denying Christ. However, one can also deny Christ by simply keeping silent, by staying hidden. In the midst of persecution only two options are open to a Christian: either to confess Christ or to deny Him.

In Matthew 10:32-33, the promise of rewards in heaven takes the form of Jesus' confession of His disciple before the Father in heaven. The Son will testify to His Father that this brother or sister of His has won the victory. Such a testimony of Christ in heaven will have eternal consequences, and we shall come to see them later on in our study.

The sheep and the lambs sent to the wolves must be prepared to die. They must have a clear understanding of why they go to the wolves, and they should clearly know why they must accept the possibility of being killed by the very wolves that they are trying to save. The issue of dying on the field of duty was explained by Jesus, and Matthew's account of it begins in verse 28 of the tenth chapter of his Gospel. Jesus started out with the most basic factor: "Do not fear those who kill the body" (10:28a). Now, Jesus did not say that they *might* "kill the body." He said outright that they *will* "kill the body." Jesus wanted His disciples to take it as certain that these people had the power to kill, and that they would most likely kill their physical bodies. Jesus warned them against false expectations: the ones they would face are indeed real, cold-blooded killers.

Once the disciples have accepted this basic fact, they must also be aware of the next two fundamental and crucial facts. The first is that the power of the killers is limited; they can kill *only the body*. But a person is not only a physical body; one also has a soul. When they kill the body, one's real self is not touched. We can better understand what Jesus was saying if we look at how He developed this issue later on in what is called the Olivet Discourse. I will quote from the Gospel of Luke: "But you will be delivered up even by parents and brothers and relatives and friends, and they will put *some* of you to death" (Lk. 21:16). We should notice that the word *some* was added to the text. What Jesus actually said was θανατώσουσιν ἐξ ὑμῶν, which means "they will kill of you." This can be understood to mean "some of you," but it can also mean "they will kill *part* of you." We have to consider the latter possibility because of what follows in the text: "Yet not a hair of your head will perish" (21:18). How can it be that they will kill you, but not a hair of your head will perish? The only explanation is in Jesus' teaching about the resurrection of the body. In effect, Jesus was saying to them: they will certainly kill your body, but even this physical body that is killed will not perish, not even a single hair of your head, because your Father will bring your body back to life!

The sovereignty of God is the second basic principle that is absolutely important for one to comprehend when he or she faces death for the cause of Christ. Jesus continued to explain that God is the only one "who is able to destroy both soul and body in hell" (Matt. 10:28b). He is the only one whom we should fear. Indeed, during a time of persecution it is very important to fear Him, especially because of the danger of denying Christ (10:33), the danger of loving one's family more than one loves Christ (10:37), and the danger of loving one's own life more than Christ and thus not being willing to lose it for Christ's sake (10:39; cf. Lk. 9:24). Persecution is a dangerous ground, yet much more perilous than the threat of those who kill the body is the possible failure to be what the Almighty God expects us to be. That is precisely what we ought to fear!

Because God is sovereign, He is in absolute control of even the smallest and most insignificant things in this world. When a sparrow dies, God is there. He is certainly involved in that fact; it is not "apart from your Father" (Matt. 10:29). But we are not sparrows, and we are not insignificant as the sparrows are. We are the children of the sovereign, Almighty God! He tells us Himself that we are very precious in His eyes (10:31). He is so careful with us that He has even numbered the hairs on our head. He knows about all of them, He cares about them, and He takes care of them. He goes that far in His involvement in our lives!

Now, is it not strange that this sovereign, Almighty God allows His children to be exposed to the danger of being killed by evil people, that He actually allows them to be tortured and killed by evil people? Yet this is exactly what Jesus emphatically stated in Matthew the tenth chapter: "Do not think that I came to bring peace on the earth; I did not come to bring peace, but a sword. For I came to set up a man against his father, and a daughter against her mother, and a daughter-in-law against her mother-in-law, and a man's enemies will be the members of his household" (10:34-36). Jesus called His people to lose what they have dearest in this world—their families—and to lose their own lives, as well (10:37-39). Why? What are God's purposes with actions that seem so unreasonable and so cruel to us? Did Jesus offer some explanation for why these things happen? Indeed He did, but He proceeded just like Isaiah and Daniel: He did not disclose everything at once, but gradually. He gave a series of lessons on these issues, and in each one He added further information. We have to proceed in the same way. Because these explanations will find their full development later on, I will only briefly introduce them here.

In the lesson of Matthew the tenth chapter, Jesus gave the disciples three reasons explaining why the children of God are exposed to sacrifice, to suffering, and to physical death. These were repeated by Jesus in many other lessons, and this fact shows the importance He gave to them. The first rationale was already given at the beginning of the lesson: the disciples are to be Christ's witnesses, sent out with the task of convincing the evil world to come back to God. The second rationale is repeated three times in this lesson: "He who loves father and mother more than Me *is not worthy of Me*; and he who loves son or daughter more than Me *is not worthy of Me*. And he who does not take his cross and follow after Me *is not worthy of Me*" (10:37-38, italics mine). The concept of being worthy (ἄξιος) is a very important one in the teachings of Jesus and in the rest of the New Testament. Again and again, we are told that the dangers which the witnesses encounter become a test of the disciples' worthiness.

The third reason for the suffering and death of the disciples is that in God's economy and methodology, one finds his life by losing it (10:39). We shall explore this strange method of God in more detail at a later stage in our study.

The Cross of the Christian

In the lesson Jesus gave to His disciples in the tenth chapter of Matthew on witnessing with the price of suffering, sacrifice, and death, He introduced for the first time the concept of the cross of His followers: "He who does not take his cross and follow after Me is not worthy of Me" (10:38). This saying is repeated in Matthew 16:24 in this form: "If anyone wishes to come after Me, let him deny himself, and take up his cross, and follow Me" (parallel texts in Mk. 8:34 and Lk. 9:23; in the Lukan version, it is "take up his cross daily"). We find Jesus repeating this saying one more time in Luke 14:27, in an even more categorical form: "Whoever does not carry his own cross and come after Me cannot be My disciple."

What is the cross of the believer? It seems to be so important to Jesus, but there is no clarity in our understanding of what it means. Once we establish what it is, we have to ask a further question: What does *the cross of the Christian* achieve in God's economy? We know what the cross of Christ means, and we know very well what it achieves. Shouldn't we also know the meaning of our own crosses and their purpose in God's strategy? It is quite peculiar that, as far as I can establish, these questions have never been asked by Protestant theologians before.

I have scanned over seventy commentaries on the Gospels of Matthew, Mark, and Luke to see what they say about the phrase "take up his cross." Some of my findings are worthy of particular attention. In the first place, Thomas Lindsay quotes Rutherford's deeply meaningful comment on Jesus' injunction to take up our cross: "Christ's cross is the sweetest burden that I ever bore; it is such a burden as wings are to a bird, or sails to a ship, to carry me forward to my harbor."[8] I have included this quote in order to forestall the following possible misunderstanding: Christ does not invite us to carry *His* cross. *He* carried *His* cross *for us*. Now, He invites us to take up *our own* cross and follow Him.

There are commentators, such as Brascomb,[9] Nineham,[10] and others, who consider that it was meaningless for Christ to speak of carrying a cross before His own crucifixion took place. They consider these sayings to be a creation of the church put into the mouth of Jesus.

There are other commentators, on the other hand, who show that it was indeed humanly possible for Jesus to use the metaphor of carrying the cross. Alan Menzies writes that "the figure does not involve a knowledge of the mode of Jesus' own death; everyone in Palestine was familiar with the incidents of crucifixion."[11] Taylor writes that "death by crucifixion under the Romans was a sufficiently familiar sight in Palestine to be the basis of the saying."[12] Moule takes a step further, affirming that "it is by no means improbable that Jesus had already foreseen that it would be by the Roman death of crucifixion that he himself would be executed."[13] Rawlingson also thinks that "the Lord may have adopted a figure from the Roman method of execution in order to express the ideas of severest suffering and ultimate risk,"[14] And Hooker quotes Plutarch who long before Christ wrote in his *De Sera* that "every criminal who is executed carries his own cross."[15]

Now we turn to what the commentators have to say about the meaning of the phrase "take up his cross." Unfortunately, at the popular level, the "cross" of the believer has been trivialized into meaning everything that is unpleasant. Hence, the reminder made by Geldenhuys is a timely and necessary corrective: "The 'cross' is not the ordinary human troubles and sorrows such as disappointments, disease, death, poverty and the like."[16]

From this extreme, we cross to the other, in which the phrase is completely spiritualized. For example, Morris writes that "taking up the cross meant the utmost in self-denial."[17] Wuest states a similar opinion: "The cross was the instrument of death. Here it speaks of death to self."[18] Ironside writes: "To take a cross is to acknowledge our identification with Him as the rejected one."[19] McGarvey would agree, saying, "To take up his cross is to endure reproach or dishonor in the eyes of the world."[20] Earle promotes the following elaborate spiritualization: "Denying one's self and taking up one's cross are crises in Christian experience. In conversion a person denies himself to follow Christ, who is the new center of orientation. In sanctification one must take up his cross of full submission to the will of God."[21] Ryle also talks about "the cross of doctrine and the cross of living a life which the world ridicules as too strict and righteous."[22]

I have selected these quotes in order to show how far some commentators have strayed from the actual meaning Jesus intended to convey when He spoke about the cross of the disciples. Yet there are a few commentators who are primarily concerned with showing what *Jesus Himself* meant when He used this phrase. For example, Allen writes: "The thought in Matt. 10:38 is no doubt of death in persecution. The disciples would be dragged before courts of justice (v. 17), they would be killed by their relatives (v. 21). But they were not to fear physical death."[23] Then, regarding Matthew 16:24, he says, "Here the meaning clearly is that the disciples must be ready to face death in allegiance to their Master and after His example. The cross need mean no more than violent death."[24] Tasker writes that to take up one's cross means to "be willing to suffer a martyr's death, like a condemned criminal forced to carry the cross beam to the place of execution."[25] In harmony with Tasker, Cranfield also affirms that "the meaning here is that the disciple must be ready to face martyrdom."[26]

Continuing the same idea, Maclaren says: "At that time they would only partially understand what the taking of the cross was, but they would apprehend that a martyred Master must needs have for followers men ready to be martyrs too."[27] Manson agrees: "In the original sense the demand of Jesus is equivalent to a man's putting on the hangman's rope about his neck. Thus only can the disciple follow Christ, for the path which he treads now is the path of martyrdom."[28] I conclude this list with Bowie who comments that "to the first disciples it involved physical danger, and martyrdom for some of them. In the dark periods of history all down the years there have been others who have dared to pay that ultimate price."[29]

As an example of a total misunderstanding of the times, I will include Sadler's evaluation, penned in 1895: "The earliest disciples had to bear the cross of persecution, even to death. Few, if any, have to bear such a cross in this day."[30] It is true that in the England of Sadler's time, there was no religious persecution, but there was much persecution taking place in other countries, even on the European continent, not to mention on the other continents. But of course, Sadler could not know at that time that the coming century was going to see the greatest number of martyrs in Christian history.

I have thus far tried to demonstrate that there have been commentators who have discerned that Jesus specifically prepared His disciples for martyrdom. But we may still ask: Why did this have to be a part of the disciples' training, and why did Jesus appoint them to be martyrs? For the answers to these questions, we get no help from the commentators. Therefore, let us look at the passage in Matthew 16:13-28, as well as at the parallel passages in Mark 8:27-38 and in Luke 9:18-27, in order to discover the context of the command to take up the cross; the larger context of Jesus' words should help us capture their meaning.

This passage relates what happened at Caesarea Philippi. From this place, Jesus was going to travel straight to Jerusalem to meet His death. For the past three years, He had been intensively training these disciples. Even though on the way to Jerusalem and during the last week there, Jesus would give them some of the most important lessons of their entire education, we may still consider that Caesarea Philippi marked the end of the "regular" school, if we may call it that. Accordingly, we may then interpret what took place at Caesarea Philippi as their final examination. After the disciples had passed that examination, Jesus began speaking to them as graduates, looking with them toward the future that would be theirs.

First of all, in this final examination, Jesus wanted to make sure that the disciples had a clear understanding of who He was. Therefore, when Peter confessed that Jesus was "the Christ, the Son of the Living God" (Matt. 16:16), the examination was over; they had passed the test. They had graduated. Now they were ready to look to the future, to their job out there in the real world. At this point, Jesus let the disciples in on the final goal of His ministry. Now that they knew exactly who He was, they were prepared to learn the purpose of the Messiah and the reason for the coming of the Son of the Living God into the world. Thus, Jesus declared His purpose to them with these words: "I will build My church" (16:18).

Now, some scholars consider that Matthew 16:18 is not an authentic saying of Jesus. Let us settle this issue by reviewing the total picture of Jesus' strategy. Right from the beginning of His ministry, Jesus selected a group of men with the purpose of training them to be the messengers of His gospel. As He was training them in the *content* of that gospel, He warned them repeatedly that their mission would provoke persecution and death. It is only natural, then, that Jesus would also give them the reasons why this would happen and would inform them of the goal to be achieved through their mission. But even more than that, is it not reasonable to expect that Jesus had had this specific goal in mind *all the time*? One does not train people for a mission involving danger, suffering, and death without having a very clear and a very great purpose in mind to achieve through them! Therefore, a time had to come when Jesus would clearly define and express this goal to His disciples.

On the one hand, it is true that Jesus' goal and purpose appear clearly after His resurrection, when the actual sending of the disciples occurs: "Go therefore and make disciples of all the nations, . . . teaching them to observe all that I commanded you." (Matt. 28:19-20). On the other hand, it would be rather strange to think that Jesus did not give His disciples His vision of the conquest of the world through the preaching of the gospel at any other time, previous to His resurrection.

I suggest that here in Caesarea Philippi, Jesus decided that the proper time had come for Him to explain His vision and purpose to the disciples. He had had it in mind from the very beginning, and during their entire time together, He had been training these twelve men to be the agents through whom He would accomplish His vision and purpose. This plan, as I stated above, was that He would build His church. For the disciples, the implication of this was that they had to go into all the world and to disciple all the nations.

I want to make two further comments on Matthew 16:18. In the first place, after Jesus announced His plan of building His church, He looked into the future and saw that all hell was going to begin assaulting her. He knew that it was going to be a total war, and that all the kingdom of evil would be let loose upon her. Satan would muster all his forces against the new reality of the church of Christ. Because Jesus knew that this would happen, He had been showing His disciples from the start how to meet the violence that would be unleashed against them. Now, at the end of their schooling, He reassured them by giving them the promise that "the gates of Hades shall not overpower it" (16:18b).

My second comment regards the words, "you are Peter, and upon this rock I will build My church" (16:18a). We should not be distracted by the enormous amount of debate on how the church would be built on Peter. Instead, let us discern the most important point that Jesus was making here. He was announcing the purpose of His coming in the flesh upon the earth and the goal of His entire ministry: He had come in order to build His church. Then, in the same breath, Jesus also informed Peter that he was going to play a key role in the accomplishment of His purpose and goal! Whatever else is contained in the words "upon this rock I will build . . . ," one thing is clear: at that moment, Jesus took Peter into a very close partnership with Him for the fulfillment of His great plan. But He did not choose Peter alone. The lesson that follows in the sixteenth chapter of Matthew and the rest of the instructions that Jesus would later give them make it clear that the disciples as a group were given key and vital roles in the realization of His purposes in history.

Now then, when someone announces a great plan of action, as Jesus had just done, it is reasonable to expect that person to follow it up by showing how such a great plan is going to be implemented. In my understanding of this text, all the verses including and following verse 21 embody Jesus' explanation of what will have to be done in order to achieve His purpose. Two things were necessary for Jesus to fulfill His plan. The first was that He had to go to Jerusalem, to take up His cross and die on it (16:21). After He had declared this to the disciples, however, Jesus did not go on to explain the way His dying on the cross would build His church. He explained this later on in Jerusalem, when the Greeks wanted to see Him and He took this as a sign that the time of His crucifixion was drawing near (John 12:20-23).

Hence, in John 12:24-35, we find Jesus explaining to His disciples why He had to die; in the process, He revealed to them two crucial concepts. The first is the basic principle of what fruitfulness entails and demands in God's economy: "Truly, truly, I say to you, unless a grain of wheat falls into the earth and dies, it remains by itself alone; but if it dies, it bears much fruit" (12:24). The second idea is the application of the first principle to His own death on the cross: "And I, if I be lifted up from the earth, will draw all men to myself" (12:32). John wanted to make it very clear to his readers that Jesus chose those exact words in order to "indicate the kind of death by which He was to die" (12:33). Christ's plan to "draw all men" to Himself represents the same thing as His plan to build His church, but by wording it in this way, Jesus was telling them that He could accomplish His goal only from the cross. Once again, just as He had done in Matthew 16, Jesus involved His disciples in the process. Immediately after announcing the principle of fruitfulness in God's economy, based upon which He

Himself would act, He drew the disciples into it, as well: "He who loves his life loses it; and he who hates his life in this world shall keep it to life eternal. If anyone serves Me, let him follow Me; and where I am, there shall My servant also be; if anyone serves Me, the Father will honor him" (12:25-26).

Coming back to Matthew 16, when Jesus broke the news of His imminent death in Jerusalem, the disciples were shocked, and their shared horror was expressed by Peter. Jesus rebuked Peter for this, and the essence of His rebuke was that Peter was not thinking as God thinks; *he was thinking as men do* (16:23). The implication is that when Jesus spoke about the way of the cross, *He was thinking in the same way that God thinks*. In fact, the method of the cross represents *the mind of God*.

In the following verses, Jesus went on to tell the disciples the second thing that He needed in order to be able to accomplish His plan of building His church; namely, the disciples had to come to the place where they would pick up their own crosses and would follow after Him. They would have to do what He was about to do. Jesus explicitly told them that He expected them to lose their lives for His sake (16:24-25). In other words, if we take the most complete form of the saying as it is found in Mark's Gospel, Jesus expected each disciple to lose "his life for My sake and the gospel's" (Mk. 8:35). "For the sake of the gospel" signifies the ministry of making disciples of all nations, thereby building the church of Christ. Ultimately, this ministry will demand that the disciples accept to die as their Master had died.

Today, we "spiritualize" these words, but when Jesus spoke them He meant them quite literally. He was about to send them into the world as sheep among wolves, and He had already told them that they were going to be killed in the process of carrying out their ministry. The tradition of the church tells us that all of them died as martyrs, with the exception of Judas. The last verse of the chapter makes sense if we see it in this context: "Truly I say to you, there are some of those who are standing here who shall not taste death until they see the Son of Man coming in His kingdom" (Matt. 16:28). Some of them, that is, eleven of them, were going to taste death for Him and for the gospel. But then, we are compelled to ask, what is the point of the promise that Jesus made to them? It is precisely this: Matthew 16:28 is Jesus' promise to the martyrs, that before they go to their martyrdom they will literally see Christ in His glory as King of kings. No torture is too difficult after such a vision.

We see this promise being fulfilled in the experience of Stephen, the first Christian martyr: "But being full of the Holy Spirit, he gazed intently into heaven and saw the glory of God, and Jesus standing at the right hand of God; and he said, 'Behold, I see the heavens opened up and the Son of Man standing at the right hand of God' " (Acts 7:55-56). As I see it, this promise to the disciples was also fulfilled in Matthew 28:18, when, just before ascending into heaven, Jesus solemnly declared, "All authority has been given to Me in heaven and on earth." After they saw Him in that position as King over the whole universe, all fear was gone from their hearts. Dying for *this* King was no longer a difficult thing to do.

We have established, then, that in order to build His church, Jesus needed His own cross as well as the crosses of the disciples, His death as well as their deaths. This is, in effect, what He told them in the sixteenth chapter of Matthew. And now we come to the most crucial question for our theology of suffering and martyrdom: While we know the function of the cross of Christ, *what is the function of the cross of the disciple?* Jesus explained His own death as "a ransom for many" (Matt. 20:28; Mk. 10:45). In His words over the cup, He explained this by saying, "This is My blood of the covenant, which is poured out for many for forgiveness of sins" (Matt. 26:28). After the resurrection, He further explained: "Thus it is written, that the Christ should suffer and rise again from the dead the third day; and that repentance for forgiveness of sins should be proclaimed in His name to all the nations, beginning from Jerusalem" (Lk. 24:46-47).

There is no indication whatsoever that Jesus gave the same function to the death of His disciples. Neither is there the slightest indication that the disciples understood their suffering and death as having something to do with the problem of the sins of the world. The rest of the New Testament is emphatic in its teaching that the sacrifice of Christ for the sins of the world was a one time event, never to be repeated or supplemented. Peter wrote: "For Christ also died for sins once for all, the just for the unjust, in order that He might bring us to God" (1 Peter 3:18). The author of the Epistle to the Hebrews was also categorical, saying that Jesus did not need to suffer many times: "but now once at the consummation of the ages He has been manifested to put away sin by the sacrifice of Himself"; then He added that Christ has only been "offered once" (Heb. 9:26-28).

Once we have excluded the possibility that the disciple's suffering and death might have something to add to the saving function of the cross of Christ, we still have to discover the true function of the cross of the disciple. For this we must go back to the words of Jesus: He asked His disciples to take up their own crosses and to die for His sake and for the sake of His gospel (Mk. 8:35). Jesus did not call people to a cause; He called them to *Himself*. He expected them to leave everything else for Him and to love Him more than anything else in this world: "He who loves father or mother more than Me is not worthy of Me; and he who loves son or daughter more than Me is not worthy of Me" (Matt. 10:37).

Jesus united Himself with the disciple in such a way that "he who receives you receives Me, and he who receives Me receives Him who sent Me (Matt. 10:40; cf., John 17:23, 26). Jesus had great plans with them in heaven, but until then, they had a job to do on earth. Their job was to show, to witness, and to confess Him to the whole world, and "everyone therefore who shall confess Me before men, I will also confess him before My Father who is in heaven. But whoever shall deny Me before men, I will also deny him before My Father who is in heaven" (Matt. 10:32-33). Confessing Christ and preaching the gospel are two ways of expressing the same action; either way one says it, it will be a dangerous activity, because it will bring hate, persecution, and even death to the confessor. This is the cause for which Jesus called His disciples to suffer and to sacrifice themselves. This is the meaning of the cross of the disciple.

Let us stay a few more moments with the text of Scripture before we try to formulate the meaning of the cross of the believer in theological terms. In Luke 24:46-47, the risen Lord said that it was written "that the Christ should suffer, . . . that repentance for forgiveness of sins should be proclaimed in His name to all the nations." From this we conclude that the process of the salvation of the world consists of two parts: the first is the suffering of Christ for the sins of the world, and the second is the proclamation of His salvation "to all the nations." The second part of the process is in fact the mission of the disciples: they are to go into all the world to preach, confess, and witness Christ and His salvation.

In the Epistle to the Romans, Paul writes that people have to believe in order to be saved. Then he asks the obvious questions: "How shall they believe in Him whom they have not heard? And how shall they hear without a preacher?" (Rom. 10:14). As His Master had known, the Apostle Paul also knew that preaching is a dangerous business, bringing much suffering to the one who preaches the Word.

Paul explained his own sufferings having this reality in mind: "For this reason I endure all things for the sake of those who are chosen, that they also may obtain the salvation which is in Christ Jesus and with it eternal glory" (2 Tim. 2:10). The distinction between the two aspects of the process of salvation are perfectly plain in this text: salvation is in Christ Jesus, and nowhere else; but the issue that remains to be solved is how people will obtain Christ's salvation. The Scripture is unmistakably clear that salvation cannot reach all the nations without the self-sacrifice of a messenger.

At the end of an exposition I once made in England on this theme, an old friend of mine, Rev. Leith Samuel, came to me and said: "Joseph, I saw you struggling to find the proper words for this theology, and I started to think how I could help you. Here is what I came up with. Why don't you put it this way: The cross of Christ is for propitiation, whereas our crosses are for propagation." I almost shouted for joy. Yes, indeed, this was the most succinct theological formulation of the partnership between the cross of Christ and the crosses of the believers. His cross worked vertically, reconciling us with God; our crosses work horizontally, delivering to others what Christ has procured for us all.

What, then, is the cross of the believer? It certainly does not mean having a nagging wife or a rude husband. It does not consist of the mortification of the body, and it should not be identified with self-denial, either. Self-denial means giving up the right to rule your own life and accepting that Jesus Christ should rule it. Self-denial also means that you cease to live for self, choosing to live for Christ and for serving other people. Self-denial means total surrender to Christ and to the service of other people.

To take up your own cross and bear it means to voluntarily and sacrificially involve yourself in the job of building the church of Christ. It means that the main occupation of your life will now be witnessing Christ to others, making disciples, and teaching them to do all that Christ has taught you to do. This will of course consume your time and your material resources. It will most likely provoke ridicule and derision from others. It might demand that you leave your own country for the mission field, and it might even cost you your own life. This is your cross, and this is how you become a partner with Christ in fulfilling His purposes for mankind.

Recently, another friend sent me a copy of a sermon delivered in the year 1856, containing this very idea. I will quote the relevant passage:

> As Jesus by His sacrifice purchased redemption, we by ours must make it known; and as there were difficulties which He had to remove before He could bring salvation to our race, so there are difficulties which we have to encounter in spreading it abroad. In this respect His priesthood and ours are strikingly analogous, and it is to give us the opportunity of showing that we are imbued with the same mind that was also in Him that so many obstacles have to be surmounted in the work of the world's conversion.[31]

I must also add that in 1693, Thomas Shepherd expressed this idea in song:

> Must Jesus bear the cross alone,
> And all the world go free?
> No, there's a cross for everyone,
> And there's a cross for me.

This was the teaching that Jesus gave to His disciples at Caesarea Philippi. There He revealed to them His purpose for being in the world, He informed them of the way He intended to achieve this purpose, and He also told them what their involvement would be in His great plan. This was nothing other than a candid training for martyrdom. Jesus' plan was to send these people into hostile environments, and He knew that they were going to be killed. Hence, He gave them this teaching in order to prepare them for the task of witnessing and dying for Him and for the gospel. Peter was shocked when he heard about the coming death of Jesus in Jerusalem; but he probably would have been overwhelmed if he had then heard about his own calling to follow Christ on the same road. However, it is more likely that neither he nor the others could have understood or accepted this information at that time. In support of this, Mark tells us that after Jesus' second prediction of *His own* sufferings, "they did not understand this statement, and they were afraid to ask Him" what it meant (Mk. 9:32).

Future Rewards in Heaven

Why should somebody accept to die like a criminal by means of the most cruel form of execution? What could motivate somebody to voluntarily pick up and place on his back that horrible instrument of torture and death? Jesus was of course aware of the fact that a man must be very strongly motivated before he will agree to undertake such an action. Accordingly, while they were in Caesarea Philippi, Jesus gave His disciples two different incentives for what they were about to do. The first incentive was in the assurance that "whoever loses his life for My sake shall find it" (Matt. 16:25); and the second was in the following promise: "For the Son of Man is going to come in the glory of His Father with His angels; and will then recompense every man according to his deeds" (16:27).

Do these incentives render real motivation? They certainly ought to! Yet, does this second promise represent an actual incentive for most Christians in our time? The answer to this question is resoundingly negative. But why is this so? The promises of Jesus strongly and effectively motivated the church of the first centuries, because the Christians of that time believed that there would be very real and very great future rewards for martyrdom. Unfortunately, the faith in great rewards for sacrifice and self-sacrifice has almost disappeared from modern Christianity.

There are many reasons for today's absence of interest in heaven and for our lack of a true understanding of heaven. One reason is found in the general secular mentality that dismisses anything beyond this earthly reality. Many Christians are intimidated by the jibe "pie in the sky by and by." Another reason, coming from the other extreme, is the teaching of some Protestant theologians who in their effort to ensure that salvation is "by grace alone" from beginning to end exclude any discussion about "works" and rewards for moral living. We should try to set aside both of these prejudices as we study the entire teaching of Jesus on heaven, future rewards, and their implications for life in eternity; only then can we determine whether rewards are a proper motivating factor or not.

We have already quoted the admonition that Jesus gave His disciples in Matthew 6:20-21 to lay up for themselves treasures in heaven. It came at the end of the teaching on the giving of alms, on praying and fasting in secret; these are actions which the Father promises to repay or reward. Hence, we may conclude that these "works," such as praying, fasting, and the giving of alms, are just some of the ways in which one can lay up for himself treasures in heaven. This is confirmed by a subsequent teaching of Jesus recorded by Luke: "Sell your possessions and give to charity; make yourselves purses which do not wear out, an unfailing treasure in heaven, where no thief comes near, nor moth destroys. For where your treasure is, there will your heart be also" (12:33-34).[32]

From many of Jesus' sayings, it is obvious that our hearts should be in heaven, not in the riches of this world. But how many Christians today believe that giving sacrificially to the poor actually makes them rich in heaven, and that these riches in heaven will literally matter for eternity? The test to which Jesus submitted the young rich ruler was precisely this: Jesus asked him to part with his earthly riches by giving them to the poor, so that he could thereby obtain a heavenly treasure. His failure to pass this test prompted Jesus to comment on the extreme difficulty "for a rich man to enter the kingdom of heaven" (Matt. 19:23). The young man proved that his heart was not in the things of God, but in his earthly riches. Even though he had assured Jesus that he had kept all the commandments, the rich young ruler had actually demonstrated to Jesus that he had failed to fulfill the greatest of all the commandments—the command to love God with all his heart.

The term "kingdom of heaven" in the teaching of Jesus has given rise to considerable controversy in the past and warrants our attention at this juncture. We find it only in Matthew's Gospel, where the author uses it alternatively with "the kingdom of God" (19:23-24). In the parallel texts in the other Gospels, the phrase always appears as "the kingdom of God." It is generally held that Matthew, who wrote his Gospel for the Jews, wanted to avoid repeating the name of God too frequently, and thus replaced it with the word "heaven." The other Evangelists, writing for a gentile audience, did not have this reticence; hence, they always used the phrase "kingdom of God." But how do we explain that Jesus, a Jew speaking to the Jews, deliberately used the phrase "kingdom of heaven" Himself? Moreover, what if He used it not only for its rhetorical value, but for its literal meaning, as well? Perhaps He wanted to imply that when He spoke of the kingdom of *God* (hence the alternative use of the two terms: "the kingdom of heaven" in 19:23 and "the kingdom of God" in 19:24), He was speaking of a heavenly reality, as well? Let us see if we can find some indications that this was in fact the case.

When the Pharisees asked Jesus when the kingdom of God would come, He answered and said that it will not come "with signs to be observed," nor will it be a place on this earth, so that one could say about it, " 'Look, here it is!' or 'There it is!' For behold, the kingdom of God is in your midst" (Lk. 17:20-21). The Greek phrase ἐντὸς ὑμῶν can also mean "in you"; but whichever translation we choose,

Jesus' meaning is clear: the kingdom of God is not to be understood as a geographic reality on this earth. We also have Jesus' statement to Pilate: "My kingdom is not of this world. If My kingdom were of this world, then My servants would be fighting, that I might not be delivered up to the Jews" (John 18:36). Again, it is obvious that Jesus understood the "kingdom of God" to mean a heavenly reality.

The clearest indication we have in support of a heavenly meaning for the phrase "kingdom of God" is in Jesus' dialogue with the rich young ruler, recorded in the nineteenth chapter of Matthew's Gospel. Jesus told him to sell his earthly riches so that he would have treasure in heaven. After the young man had turned down the offer, Jesus remarked about the difficulty of a rich man "to *enter* the kingdom of heaven" (Matt. 19:23; italics mine). Is it reasonable to suppose that when Jesus spoke to the rich young ruler about "treasure in heaven" and later when He commented on "the kingdom of heaven," He was actually referring to two different places? I suggest that the answer to this question is negative. After studying the above passage, as well as the other passages which discuss the kingdom of God, my conclusion is that when Jesus talked about the kingdom of God, He was referring to a kingdom primarily in heaven. On the one hand, it is true that this kingdom came down to earth in Jesus Himself, and that His kingdom is now active here; we are its agents as it extends its borders across the globe. On the other hand, we must always remember the truth articulated by Paul in Philippians 3:20, namely, that "our citizenship is in heaven."

Previously, in the tenth chapter of Matthew, Jesus had taught that the soul of a man does not die when the body dies. The enemies that kill the body cannot kill the soul. Only God "is able to destroy both soul and body the in hell" (Matt. 10:28). Jesus also spoke of a future resurrection of the dead, but at the same time He indicated that Abraham, Isaac, and Jacob were alive at that very moment (Matt. 22:23-32). By telling us the story of the rich man and Lazarus, Jesus not only made the point that when people die physically they go to different places in another world; He also stated that there was sufficient evidence for this fact in "Moses and the Prophets" (Lk. 16:19-31). For this reason, there is no need for somebody to be raised from the dead in order to prove it.

Yes, the soul goes to the other side, but what will it have there? Jesus gave us an important illustration in the story of the rich man whose land was very productive. With all that his land had produced, he planned to fully enjoy himself, eating, drinking, and being merry for many years to come. Notwithstanding, God calls him a "fool" and tells him that He will require his soul that very night (Lk. 12:20). When he had finished telling the story, Jesus declared: "So is the man who lays up treasure for himself, and is not rich toward God" (12:21).

According to Jesus, one can lay up treasure for himself down here, but then he is poor toward God. If, on the other hand, one lays up treasure for himself in heaven, then he will be rich toward God. We must now find out what Jesus taught the disciples about the content of these riches, treasures, or rewards in heaven. The most basic information that we can find about this is in Jesus' parables about the stewards who were entrusted with the administration of their Master's goods. Since Jesus used this picture quite frequently (Matt. 24:45-51; 25:14-30; Lk. 12:35-44; 16:1-13; 19:12-27), we can legitimately conclude that this portrait contains a very important message that He particularly wanted to convey.

What is of interest for us is the reward offered to the faithful steward: "Truly, I say to you, that he will put him in charge of all his possessions" (Matt. 24:47; Lk. 12:44). In order to understand the whole import of this saying, we must recognize Jesus as the "Master" in these parables. Then we must recall that the purpose of God in creating man was to put him in charge over all His creation. When Jesus spoke about the Father or about Himself putting man in charge over all of God's possessions, He was neither speaking lightly nor making flippant promises; He was speaking about the ultimate fulfillment of His purpose with mankind!

Another general statement of Jesus regarding the final destiny of God's people is the following: "Do not be afraid, little flock, for your Father has chosen gladly to give you the kingdom" (Lk. 12:32). This saying is followed by the exhortation to sell our possessions and to give them to the poor in order to have treasures in heaven; hence, it is clear that Jesus was speaking of the kingdom of heaven. Jesus' words about the little flock of God, that is, about the humble, the persecuted, and the suffering ones who will be given the kingdom, should immediately remind us of the same promise in Daniel, where "the sovereignty, the dominion, and the greatness of all the kingdoms under the whole heaven will be given to the people of the saints of the Highest One; His kingdom will be an everlasting kingdom, and all the dominions will serve and obey Him" (Dan. 7:27).

We have already seen that the Book of Daniel is concerned with the final destiny of man, and that it gives us some of the basic character traits that God looks for in the ones to whom He will entrust dominion, authority, sovereignty, and positions of great responsibility. They are all summed up in two fundamental qualities: submission to the authority of God and obedience to God's commands. We shall find these same qualities being taught by Jesus in the New Testament.

According to Jesus, there will be different functions in heaven, and there will be higher and lower degrees of authority given to God's people in heaven. Peter heard Jesus telling the rich young ruler that if he sold all his possessions and gave them to the poor he would have treasure in heaven, and after the young man had declined the offer and left, Peter asked the Master, "Behold, we have left everything [just as You have asked the young man to do] and followed You; what then will there be for us?" (Matt. 19:27). Surprisingly, Jesus did not rebuke Peter for wanting a reward for his sacrifice, as we might have been tempted to do. On the contrary, He told him exactly what the reward of the apostles would be: "Truly I say to you, that you who have followed Me, in the regeneration when the Son of Man will sit on His glorious throne, you also shall sit upon twelve thrones, judging the twelve tribes of Israel" (19:28). This promise was repeated to all of them after the Last Supper: "You are those who have stood by Me in My trials; and just as My Father granted (διέθετό, covenanted) Me a kingdom, I grant you (διατίθεμαι, I covenant to you) that you may eat and drink at My table in My kingdom, and you will sit on thrones judging the twelve tribes of Israel" (Lk. 22:28-30). It is evident, especially from the form of the promise made at the Supper, that "judging" here means "ruling over" or "governing the affairs of." These will be the functions of the apostles in the kingdom of heaven.

In Matthew the nineteenth chapter, Jesus added that not only the apostles but everyone who has sacrificed dearly for the sake of His name "shall receive many times as much, and shall inherit eternal life" (19:29). The word that is of interest to us here is "inherit." This word indicates the moment in which and the act by which the children of God will be put in charge over the possessions of their Father. I suggest that it is one thing to *enter into* the eternal life and another thing to *inherit* something in that eternal life. We shall see this plainly in a short while.

In the parable of the minas, recorded in Luke 19:12-27, Jesus gave the disciples some more clues regarding the diversity of functions and of degrees of authority in heaven. The slave who reports that his

Master's mina "has made ten minas more" receives this verdict: "Well done, good slave, because you have been faithful in a very little thing, be in authority over ten cities" (19:17). Similarly, the servant whose mina has produced five more minas receives this verdict: "And you are to be over five cities" (19:19). No matter how reluctant we may be, we must accept the information that Jesus intimated here: in the kingdom of heaven, people will live in "cities," and some will be "in authority" over those cities. However, this implies that there will be those who will not have authority, or who will have authority over smaller matters.

Certainly Jesus taught directly that in the kingdom of heaven some will be greater than others. Thus, depending on the way a person has kept God's commandments, one "shall be called least in the kingdom of heaven," and another "shall be called great in the kingdom of heaven" (Matt. 5:19); however, there will also be those who "shall not enter the kingdom of heaven" at all (5:20). Moreover, after commenting on the greatness of John the Baptist, Jesus concluded by saying that "he who is least in the kingdom of God is greater than he" (Lk. 7:28).

It should not come a surprise to us that the disciples debated the issue of who will be the greatest in heaven many times among themselves; in doing this, they were only following up on Jesus' remarks concerning the degrees of greatness in heaven. They even approached Him with the question: "Who then is greatest in the kingdom of heaven" (Matt. 18:1)? Some may be surprised to read that Jesus did not deny the fact that some will have greater positions than everyone else in heaven; instead, He gave them the prescription for reaching those high positions (18:3). In fact, Jesus gave His disciples three prescriptions for greatness in heaven, and these are very important indeed. Before we take a look at them, let us first examine what Jesus gave them as the primary principles of evaluation in the kingdom of heaven. These principles are found in the sixteenth chapter of Luke, in the interpretation of the parable of the shrewd steward.

The parable is about the administrator of a large farming estate. The owner decided to fire him, telling the manager that he could leave after giving an account of his past administration. However, this man had no place to move his family, and the whole point of the parable is the way in which he made arrangements with the farmers on the estate to "receive [him] into their homes" (Lk. 16:4). As one farmer after another came into his office, the administrator wiped out a large part of his debts to the owner; of course, each of these grateful farmers would in the future return the favor by inviting him and his family to stay for a while in his home. What the steward did was not right in relation to the owner, yet when the owner heard of it, he praised the manager for his wisdom in securing his future. Jesus then applied this parable about the wisdom of one of "the sons of this age," by saying that the "sons of light" should exercise the same kind of wisdom in arranging their own eternal future: they ought to make friends here on earth with the help of "the mammon of unrighteousness," so that these friends "may receive [them] into the eternal dwellings" (16:9).

I will not begin speculating about what "being received into the eternal dwellings" might mean. I simply want to draw our attention to the fact that here we have another instance in which Jesus taught that what a man does with what he has accumulated here will substantially affect his situation in eternity. It follows then that wise people will obey, taking appropriate action in this regard.

However, Jesus did not end His application of this parable in verse nine of Luke 16. One can see that this discussion about "mammon" is concluded in verse thirteen, with the saying that one "cannot serve God and mammon." Of the greatest import for us in this passage are verses ten through twelve. Jesus had just related the parable illustrating how we should arrange our eternal future; then, following this parable, He moved on to some general principles concerning the manner in which our eternal future is determined by the way we have discharged our duties here on earth.

The first general principle is this: "He who is faithful in a very little thing is faithful also in much; and he who is unrighteous in a very little thing is unrighteous also in much" (16:10). The application of this principle was portrayed by Jesus in the parable of the minas, where the Master tells one of his slaves: "Well done, good slave, because you have been faithful in a very little thing, be in authority over ten cities" (19:17). The truth that Jesus communicated here is that the character we have formed on this earth goes with us into eternity. The word "faithful" (πιστός) was well translated by the New International Version as "trustworthy." The Master has entrusted His business down here to His slaves so that they might properly administer it. But these slaves are also His "sons." In the job He has given them, they themselves are formed, shaped, trained, and *tested for reliability.* Whatever faithfulness His children have demonstrated down here, that is what goes with them up there. Then, based on the quality and degree of their trustworthiness, the Master-Judge will establish the position of authority for which each of them has proven capable.

The next principle is found in Luke 16:11: "If therefore you have not been faithful in the use of unrighteous mammon, who will entrust the true riches to you?" Since the phrase "unrighteous mammon" is placed opposite to "the true riches," we can legitimately call the first "the untrue riches." These "untrue riches" are the treasures that "moth and rust destroy" and that "thieves break in and steal"; they represent the things that one can possess upon the earth (Matt. 6:19). The "true riches," on the other hand, are the things that might be entrusted to us in heaven; but if we do not faithfully administer the "untrue riches" that have been entrusted to us on the earth, no one will entrust to us the "true riches" in heaven.

Finally, the most illuminating principle is the one given in verse twelve: "If you have not been faithful in the use of that which is another's, who will give you that which is your own?" By now we know that the first clause refers to the earthly reality and the second to the heavenly one. Nothing that exists on earth is our property. Here we are "slaves," entrusted with some of the Master's things in order to test our stewardship. Our administration of these earthly things is God's barometer of our faithfulness to Him. If we fail the test, no one will give us *the things which are our own* in heaven. With this we have come full circle, back to the issue of the final purpose of God with mankind, which is to put us in charge over all creation. If we speak in terms of the Fatherhood of God and of the sonship of the redeemed people of God, then we have to speak about *inheritance*. The desire of the Father is to give everything He has to His children. His final goal with them is to put them "in charge of all his possessions" (Matt. 24:47; Lk.12:44). The question, however, is this: Have His sons and daughters proven themselves worthy (ἄξιος), trustworthy (πιστός), and faithful?

At this point, we need to clarify the issue of merit. The common misperception is that when one speaks of rewards, one is necessarily implying that somehow merit was acquired by the services rendered. But the New Testament clearly teaches that with God, one cannot earn merit; everything that God ever gives to us is by grace, and by grace alone. Since that is the case, then we cannot speak of rewards from God! This kind of reasoning has led the majority of Protestant theologians to dismiss the concept of rewards altogether. As a result, they also had to ignore the categorical New Testament teaching regarding the judgment of the Christian based on the works he or she has done after conversion. Can we find a solution to this difficult problem? We certainly can if we will simply follow the logic of Jesus' words about life here on earth and about the life to come in heaven.

Before we continue this analysis, we should point out that it was Jesus Himself who taught that we cannot claim anything from God based on merit. He told us about the slave who had worked hard all day in the fields; although he has come home very tired, the slave has no right to ask the master to serve him dinner. The slave is the one who must do that, and even after the slave has served the master his dinner, the master is still under no obligation to say even as much as a "Thank you" to him. The slave has absolutely no rights, and the master has absolutely no obligations toward his slave. That is the cruel reality, and Jesus applied this parable to *us*: "So you too, when you do all the things which are commanded you, say, 'We are unworthy slaves; we have done only that which we ought to have done' " (Lk. 17:10). No one can put God under an obligation.

However, Jesus did not refer to us solely as His slaves. He was the one who taught us to call God "our Father" and to relate to Him as sons and daughters. As our Father, He has purposed to raise us and shape us, to train us and test us, in order to one day give us dominion over all His possessions, which are ours by birthright. No father ever asks his children to earn an inheritance; rather, it is the good pleasure of the Father to give His children all that He has. The all-important question He asks is this: Are My children capable of handling their inheritance? Are they trustworthy? The principle we found in Luke 16:10 says that if we were not faithful with the things entrusted to us down here, with the things that are not our own because we are merely His slaves, then He will not give us all His possessions, the inheritance, or in Jesus' words, "the things that are your own," as our birthright because we are His sons and daughters!

In practical terms, what are these things that are not our own but are entrusted to us? I have classified them in the following categories: spouse, children, talents (natural gifts), material goods (money, houses, etc.), unsaved people, and the church. None of these are our own. They all belong to God. He has entrusted them to us for care and administration. When we will appear before Him, He will take these areas of our stewardship and will examine our faithfulness in handling each one of them. The quality of our stewardship will then determine if we are sufficiently reliable for positions of authority and ruling in heaven.

If God had wanted to make robots, He would have transformed us into what we should be instantly, by *fiat*. However, He does not want robots; He desires sons and daughters, with unique personalities, with the power of decision and the ability to handle authority. On this planet and throughout earthly history, He rears His children, training them the hard way (cf., Heb. 2:5-3:6; 12:1-14). His aim is to produce in them, through this process, a character similar to His own: "Therefore you are to be perfect, as your heavenly Father is perfect" (Matt. 5:48). It is a tragedy for Christianity that many theologians interpret the goals pronounced by Jesus in the Sermon on the Mount not as something He really wanted us to achieve, but as a series of ideals so high and inaccessible that they simply crush us into humility, making us aware that we need the grace of God. The truth, however, is that the grace of God is not only a *saving* grace, but an *enabling* grace, as well, meant to empower us to achieve God's goals in our lives!

We now come to Jesus' prescriptions for greatness in heaven. The first is given in these words: "Whoever then humbles himself as this child, he is the greatest in the kingdom of heaven" (Matt. 18:4). The key to this verse is a correct understanding of what humility means. Speaking about Christ, Paul wrote, "He humbled Himself by becoming obedient to the point of death, even death on a cross" (Phil. 2:8). Then, after James quoted the biblical proverb that "God . . . gives grace to the humble," he drew this conclusion: "Submit therefore to God" (James 4:6-7). Humility, therefore, means submission or subordination to God and total obedience to His will. This was what it meant for Jesus. His most basic concern was to do the will of the Father: "For I have come down from heaven, not to do My own will, but the will of Him who sent Me" (John 6:38). His "food" was to do the will of the Father (John 4:34). In Gethsemane, when everything in Him was shrinking at the thought of being covered with the sin of mankind, Jesus still said, "yet not as I will, but as Thou wilt" (Matt. 26:39). Whoever accepts to live by the principle of doing the will of the Father is called Jesus' "brother and sister and mother" (Matt. 12:50).

Paul wrote that the reason why God lifted Jesus to the greatest position in the universe was precisely the fact that Jesus had humbled Himself in absolute obedience to the will of God (Phil. 2:5-11). Thus, when Jesus gave the disciples the first prescription for greatness in heaven, He was only telling them His own story!

Jesus revealed the second prescription for greatness in heaven in Matthew 20:25-28 and in Luke 22:24-27. In both places Jesus began with the example of the rulers or kings of the Gentiles, who "lord it over them" and "exercise authority over them"; then He added, "It is not so among you, but whoever wishes to become great among you shall be your servant, and whoever wishes to be first among you shall be your slave" (Matt. 20:25-27; Lk. 22:25-26). Jesus was saying that "greatness" or authority over other people is exercised either by being a "boss" over them or by *serving* them. In order to understand the whole thrust of the comparison, we can explicate the part about the Gentile kings in the following manner: among the Gentiles, the greatest man is the king, and his greatness is measured by the number of subjects he has. If one man is king over one million people, he is not as great as the king who rules over a hundred million people. Now we can interpret the second part of the comparison as follows: in the kingdom of heaven, God's measure for greatness is exactly the opposite; the greatest one is the one who serves the greatest number of people.

In both passages, Jesus gave Himself as the model for this type of greatness: although He was their Lord, He served them, because He "did not come to be served, but to serve" (Matt. 20:28a). The basic character trait that God wants to develop in His children is that of servanthood, the capacity to look for the needs and the hurts of others and to live for them, to feed them, to save them, to lift them up, and to fulfill them. This character trait, according to Jesus, makes for greatness in the kingdom of heaven.

Jesus gave the third prescription for greatness to the sons of Zebedee in Matthew 20:20-24, 28b and in the parallel text in Mark 10:35-40, 45b. To understand the background to their dialogue, we must look back to Matthew 19:27-28; there Jesus told Peter that the apostles would sit on twelve thrones and would judge the twelve tribes of Israel. Apparently James and John heard this (they were always with Peter in the closest proximity to Jesus) and, talking among themselves about those thrones, the two brothers decided that they would not settle for the ones too far from the big throne in the center. So they went to their mother and asked her to intervene on their behalf, and to request that Jesus give the two best thrones to them. In my opinion, their action represents the ultimate in the human desire for greatness.

It is significant, however, that Jesus did not rebuke James and John for their desire. Instead, He did what He had always done when they had previously discussed greatness; namely, He taught them the way to obtain one of those thrones, this time by asking them the question: "Are you able to drink the cup that I drink, or to be baptized with the baptism with which I am baptized?" (Mk. 10:38). He was clearly referring here to the coming crucifixion, as His words at the end of the whole discussion indicate: "For the Son of Man [came] . . . to give His life a ransom for many" (Matt. 20:28; Mk. 10:45).

James and John answered confidently that they *could* die for the cause of Christ. Then Jesus informed them that yes, indeed, they would drink His cup, and they would be baptized with His baptism; however, *which particular throne* they would receive was something to be determined exclusively by the Father. My interpretation of this teaching of Jesus is that with these words, He revealed to them that they would have to drink the cup of martyrdom in order to obtain a throne. *Martyrdom is what would qualify them for ruling with Him.*

In conclusion, we must keep in mind the two aspects of this story. On one side of the coin is the fact that the thrones were prepared by the Father specifically for a chosen number of people (Matt. 20:23). This means that the thrones are given by grace. On the other side of the coin, however, is the fact that the chosen people have to die as martyrs in order to obtain their thrones. They have to be obedient unto death, just like their Master was before them. Only in this way can they qualify for the highest positions of ruling.

The Essentials of a Theology of Martyrdom and Rewards in the Teachings of Jesus

In the upper room, Jesus told the disciples that in His Father's house, there were "many dwelling places"; He was going to prepare a place for them there, and when the appointed time comes, He will come back, to "receive you to Myself; that where I am, there you may be also" (John 14:2-3). This promise represents the final fulfillment of the destiny of mankind. Jesus came into this world in order to save men and women from their lostness (Lk. 19:10) and to put them back on track to heaven.

As we have seen, Jesus spent a great amount of time teaching His disciples about heaven, about the positions people can have there, and about the ways in which those positions can be obtained. Jesus' teaching was not primarily about saving man from hell. That was undoubtedly a vital part of it, but we should see that a much bigger part of His teaching addressed the issue of being rich in heaven. He said bluntly that the man who does not exercise wisdom in becoming rich in heaven was a "fool" (Lk. 12:20-21). Jesus had come to die in order to redeem people from hell, but He was even more concerned to help His redeemed ones achieve greatness in the kingdom of heaven! Furthermore, He taught His disciples that among the things that will equip and prepare them for greatness are humility, utter submission to God's will and total obedience to Him in everything, servanthood, and ultimately, martyrdom for Christ and His gospel.

It was in this context that Jesus trained His disciples to go into all the world and to preach the good news of salvation to all the nations, teaching them the things of heaven. Hence, when Jesus' disciples hear the call of God today and obey Him, they display the humility that is the first prescription for greatness in the kingdom of heaven. They also demonstrate love and compassion for other people, sacrificing themselves for the salvation and education of the lost; that is servanthood, the second condition for greatness in the kingdom of heaven. Of course, the disciples' acts of obedience will bring upon them hardship and persecution. If God so chooses, they might even be called to lose their lives through martyrdom. But that will not be a tragedy! It will be the greatest honor that can be bestowed upon His disciples, since it is the condition for ruling with Christ in heaven!

Christ taught them that in God's economy, fruitfulness is achieved only by dying (John 12:24). We can now understand the double function of fruitfulness. First, the disciples' dying as martyrs will bring many people into the kingdom of God; secondly, their martyrdom will qualify them for ruling with Christ in the kingdom of heaven. Whoever "loses" his life in Christ's service, "finds" his life; at the same time, he finds the utmost fulfillment of his destiny, the attainment of a position of authority over God's creation.

To this some people may reply, "I am not concerned with positions of honor in heaven; I just want to be saved and to humbly spend eternity in whatever lowly position God may grant me there." Is this true humility? No, it is in fact a disguised form of pride, and it is also disobedience to God's intentions for His children. In Jesus' words, that person is a "fool," because he forfeits the very purpose for which God created him. Ultimately, he will find that he has "lost" his life.

Jesus' Special Promise to Those Who Will Die as Martyrs

Jesus concluded the lesson on the cross of the disciple with this exceptional promise: "Truly I say to you, there are some of those who are standing here who shall not taste death until they see the Son of Man coming in His kingdom" (Matt. 16:28). Mark said it like this in his Gospel: "some . . . shall not taste death until they see the kingdom of God after it has come with power" (Mk. 9:1), and Luke put it in these words: "there are some of those standing here who shall not taste death until they see the kingdom of God" (Lk. 9:27). Interpretations of this prediction of Jesus are very diverse. Some believe that it reflects Jesus' belief that the *Parousia* would come very soon. Some interpret it as referring to the transfiguration or to the appearances after the resurrection; others say it refers to the Pentecost experience, and still others to the destruction of Jerusalem in 70 A.D.

If we accept that the whole episode is a systematic training for martyrdom, then logically, we are led to the following interpretation. Jesus was speaking to a group of people who were literally going to die for Him and for the gospel. The one clear exception in the group was Judas. The other case that is often questioned is the death of John. According to one tradition, John died as a martyr. However, another tradition maintains that he was released from the exile on Patmos and died at an old age in Ephesus; but even if this second tradition is true, John had undoubtedly tasted the cup of persecution and had been baptized with the fire of suffering on the island of Patmos. Using the terminology of the third and fourth centuries, if John was not a "martyr," then he was a "confessor." Regardless of the manner of his death, according to Jesus' evaluation, John did drink the Master's cup, and he was baptized with His baptism.

Now then, addressing a group of people who would sooner or later die as martyrs, Jesus ended their discussion that day by presenting them with an extraordinary promise that could be paraphrased like this: "Before you go to face your martyrdom, I will grant you a vision of Myself in My royal glory." Since Jesus was seen in His heavenly glory during the transfiguration, He could possibly have been referring to that. Peter certainly understood the transfiguration as a revelation of Christ's glory, since he later says: "We were eyewitnesses of His majesty. For . . . He received honor and glory from God the Father, . . . when we were with Him on the holy mountain" (2 Peter 1:16-18).

Nevertheless, the transfiguration was only witnessed by three of them: Peter, James, and John. The other disciples were also promised such a vision. Hence, in my interpretation, the promised vision was granted when the risen Lord showed Himself to all of them, declaring, "All authority has been given to Me in heaven and on earth" (Matt. 28:18). At that moment, Jesus' promise to the future martyrs was fulfilled, because it was then that they saw Him in His position as the supreme Ruler of the kingdom of God. But we will better understand the value and the importance of such a vision when we see this promise being fulfilled in the experience of Stephen. Just before he was martyred, Luke tells us that Stephen "gazed intently into heaven and saw the glory of God, and Jesus standing at the right hand of God; and he said, 'Behold I see the heavens opened up and the Son of Man standing at the right hand of God.' " (Acts 7:55-56).

Why is this vision of Christ necessary and significant? The truth is that this vision is extremely important for the one who is going to suffer torture and death simply because when one sees the glory of Christ, his spirit is already aglow with that glory, and then his body can withstand the pain. Indeed, when he sees the glory of Christ as King, the ferocity of the torturers does not frighten any more, and the instruments of torture lose their horror. The body does not feel the pain when the soul is already full of the glory of Christ.

Across the centuries, many Christians who were faced with the frightening prospect of martyrdom were given this vision of the glory of Christ. Their testimonies attest to the fact that this experience changed their whole attitude and helped them to meet their martyrdom with composure, with joy, and yes, even with passion.

The Martyrdom of Jesus

Did *Jesus* die as a martyr? In general, evangelicals have opposed any attempt to apply to Jesus the concept of martyrdom. This opposition stems from the mistaken idea that the death of a "martyr" merely signifies the death of a "hero" for a noble cause. Thus, if one states that Jesus died "only as a martyr," this is taken to mean that His death was only a heroic act, without any atoning function or value.

This interpretation of the meaning of the word "martyr" is wrong. In an earlier chapter, we saw that the death of the Maccabean martyrs was thought to have an atoning and expiatory function for the sins of the nation. A comparable notion is found in the First Book of Enoch. Moreover, as we shall discover later in our research, Origen, in the third century A.D., attributed a similar atoning value to the death of the Christian martyrs. The problem, therefore, is not that the concept of martyrdom lacks the idea of atonement. The problem for us is to prove beyond any shadow of a doubt that only the death of Jesus, or the martyrdom of Jesus, had an atoning function and value. Secondly, we will then need to establish the distinct function and value of the deaths of the other martyrs.

As I have already mentioned, the basic meaning of the word "martyr" is "a witness who seals his or her testimony with his or her own life." Jesus Himself said to Pilate that He had come "to bear witness to the truth" (John 18:37). Furthermore, in the introduction to the Book of Revelation, Jesus is presented as "Jesus Christ, the faithful witness" (Rev. 1:5). Similarly, in the letter to the church of Laodicea, Jesus introduced Himself with the title, "the faithful and true Witness" (Rev. 3:14). His self-description is found in the context of a letter to other witnesses who are already suffering martyrdom for their testimony, and this plainly suggests that the term "witness" had already acquired the meaning of "martyr" by the time Jesus used it to refer to Himself.

The Apostle Paul came very close to calling Jesus a martyr. In his first letter to Timothy, Paul wrote that Jesus "gave Himself as a ransom for all, the testimony borne at the proper time" (1 Tim. 2:6). Here the death of Christ as a ransom for all is called τὸ μαρτύριον καιροῖς ἰδίοις, "the testimony in its own time." In the same letter, Paul challenged Timothy to "fight the good fight of faith," encouraging him to persevere in it. Paul issued this solemn charge to Timothy "in the presence . . . of Christ Jesus, who testified (μαρτυρήσαντος) the good confession (ὁμολογίαν) before Pontius Pilate" (6:12-13). Even if at the time Paul wrote his letter the word "witness" had not yet become the technical term for witnessing with the price of one's life, when he described the death of Christ, Paul used words that would soon become basic and recognizable terms in the Christian vocabulary of martyrdom.

Therefore, when we say that Jesus died as a martyr we are not departing from biblical terminology. We must simply make it indisputably clear that Jesus' death was a unique martyrdom. We must emphasize that His death was the only one to have the function of saving the lost world from the condemnation due to sin. When Jesus described His own death, He called it a "ransom for many" (Matt. 20:28; Mk. 10:45). He spoke these words in the middle of the discussion with James and John in which He informed them that they had to drink His cup and be baptized with His baptism. Jesus came very close to identifying their deaths with His death. Nevertheless, He referred to their death as their "service" and even their "slavery" for their fellow men (Matt. 20:27). Jesus' own mission was to be a servant to others, but He significantly added to this that *He* was also called to give *His* life as a ransom for many. If Jesus had ever intended to call His disciples to die as a ransom or as an atonement for others, this certainly would have been the time and place to say it, but He did not say any such thing.

At no point in His teaching did Jesus suggest or imply that the purpose of the deaths of His disciples was the same as the purpose of His own death. Later on, His apostles made it absolutely clear that Jesus' death for the sins of the world was a unique sacrifice, once and for all, complete and utterly satisfactory. We shall point to this later on in the appropriate places. Our study of Jesus' teaching up to this point shows us that simply speaking about Jesus' death as a martyrdom does not entail subtracting from His death the function of atoning for the sins of the world. Indeed, we must be careful to safeguard the uniqueness and all-sufficiency of Christ's death on the cross for the salvation of the world.

The Fight with Satan in the Teachings of Jesus

Following His forty-day solitary fast in the desert, Jesus experienced an encounter with Satan during which Satan tempted Him three times. In the course of one of those temptations, Satan showed Jesus "all the kingdoms of the world in a moment of time. And the devil said to Him, 'I will give You all this domain and its glory; for it has been handed over to me, and I give it to whomever I wish' " (Lk. 4:5-6). Contrary to what we might have expected, Jesus did not contradict the devil's affirmation. In fact, Jesus called Satan "the ruler of this world" (John 12:31). God has, in His sovereign rule, permitted Satan to keep this world in his grip for a while. Yet even during this time, Satan's power is limited by the will of God. Thus, Jesus announced to Peter that "Satan has demanded permission to sift you like wheat" (Lk. 22:31). Obviously, the devil could not take this action without asking permission from God. Jesus also added that there was a further limit to what Satan could do to Peter, since Jesus prayed that Peter's "faith may not fail" (22:32).

Jesus taught us to picture this world as a field in which the wheat and the tares grow up together. According to His interpretation, the wheat stands for "the sons of the kingdom," whereas the tares represent "the sons of the evil one" (Matt. 13:38). Hence, Jesus declared to the Jewish leaders, "You are of your father the devil" (John 8:44). Jesus also disclosed to them elsewhere that the time of Satan on this earth was limited; an eternal fire has been prepared "for the devil and his angels" (Matt. 25:41).

Since this world is still under Satan's dominion, when Jesus came into this world He entered into the "strong man's house" in order to "plunder his property" and to "plunder his house" (Mk. 3:27). Jesus' work of casting out demons and freeing possessed people was the sign "that the kingdom of God has come upon you" (Lk. 11:20). However, by His own death, Jesus would finally break the authority of Satan. For this reason, when He spoke about His own death, Jesus said, "now the ruler of this world shall be cast out" (John 12:31).

Into this general picture, we must now place the role of the disciples. When Jesus sent the twelve disciples on their first missionary exercise, we are told that "He gave them authority over unclean spirits, to cast them out" (Matt. 10:1). It appears that He gave the same authority to the seventy disciples when He sent them on a similar mission, because when the seventy returned, they reported "with joy, saying, 'Lord, even the demons are subject to us in Your name' " (Lk. 10:17). It is very important for us to notice Jesus' reaction to this report. There are two aspects to His response. First, Jesus remarked, "I was watching Satan fall from heaven like lightning" (10:18). The disciples' work of preaching the gospel and of liberating people from Satan's grasp resulted in a cosmic defeat of Satan. Later, in the Book of Revelation, one of the consequences of the martyrs' deaths will be Satan's fall from heaven (Rev. 12:9-11). Secondly, Jesus put things into an eternal perspective for the rejoicing disciples: "Behold, I have given you authority to tread upon serpents and scorpions, and over all the power of the enemy, and nothing shall injure you. Nevertheless do not rejoice in this, that the spirits are subject to you, but rejoice that your names are recorded in heaven" (Lk. 10:19-20).

Jesus had been training these men to wage war against evil and to rescue other people from the power of evil. He wanted them to know that they were above the evil spirits, due to their status as sons of God; but He also wanted them to keep in mind, always and above everything else, that they had a heavenly destiny. The most important thing for His disciples to concentrate on and to invest their energies in was *their glorious destiny and future in heaven.* Heaven was the place for which they were meant to live and the goal for which they were meant to die.

Chapter 6

Suffering and Martyrdom in
the Book of Acts

The Book of the Acts of the Apostles is the story of the spreading of the gospel of Jesus Christ over a period of approximately thirty years, from the resurrection and ascension of Jesus and the descent of the Holy Spirit at Pentecost to the year 62 A.D. Luke, the doctor-historian and the author of the Gospel that bears his name, conceived the Book of Acts as the continuation of the ministry of the ascended and enthroned Lord Jesus Christ through His apostles empowered by the Holy Spirit.

It is reasonable to look for and to find in the ministry of the apostles a clear application of the teachings of Jesus regarding the function of the disciples as witnesses. Likewise, it is certain that we will see the persecutions, sufferings, and deaths of the witnesses just as the Master had predicted. In fact, the program and outline of the Book of Acts is stated in verse eight of the first chapter; just before the risen Lord ascended into heaven, He declared to them, "You shall receive power when the Holy Spirit has come upon you; and you shall be My witnesses both in Jerusalem, and in all Judea and Samaria, and even to the remotest part of the earth." Hence, the entire book is concerned with the disciples' function of bearing witness to Jesus by preaching His gospel. The importance of the concept of witness in this book is also visible from the frequent use of the word. A. A. Trites has determined that "μάρτυς and six of its derivatives appear a total of thirty-nine times in the Book of Acts (μάρτυς, thirteen times; μαρτυρεῖν, eleven times; διαμαρτύρεθαι, nine times; μαρτύρεσθαι and μαρτύριον, twice each; μαρτυρία and ἀμάρτυρος, once each)."[1]

The Apostle Peter underscored the fact that the primary function of the apostles was to "witness," when he enunciated the qualifications required of the one who would replace Judas: "one of these should become a witness with us of His resurrection" (Acts 1:22). Then, in his sermon at Pentecost, Peter solemnly declared: "This Jesus God raised up again, to which we are all witnesses" (2:32).

Once empowered by the Holy Spirit, the apostles cannot but witness. Each one of them experienced an inner urge, a compulsion, that drove his witness in spite of the opposition, regardless of the threats and dangers: "for we cannot stop speaking what we have seen and heard" (4:20).

After Saul was met by the risen Lord on the road to Damascus, Ananias informed him that he had been chosen to see and hear Jesus for the same purpose: "For you will be a witness for Him to all men of what you have seen and heard" (22:15). Consequently, we see in Paul the same imperative of declaring to the whole world what he had seen and heard: "Consequently, King Agrippa, I did not prove disobedient to the heavenly vision, but kept declaring both to those of Damascus first, and also at Jerusalem and then throughout all the region of Judea, and even to the Gentiles, that they should repent and turn to God, performing deeds appropriate to repentance" (26:19-20).

This passion to proclaim to the whole world what one has discovered in Jesus Christ would characterize Christians across the centuries. This is just the first of many apostolic traits depicted in the Book of Acts that was to become a model for Christians in the coming years.

Right from the beginning, as Jesus had predicted, the witness of the apostles was met with anger, opposition, and violence. The reasons for this hostility were varied. In Jerusalem, the apostles' proclamation that God had raised Jesus, whom the Jews had crucified and killed, was a rebuke and a condemnation to them. By this the Jews were in fact charged with killing the Messiah, the Savior, the King of the whole world. This was an indictment too hard to accept! Even more than this, at a later stage, the Apostle Paul's teaching to the Gentiles became an attack upon the Jewish religion, due to the fact that he maintained that in order for the Gentiles to obtain God's acceptance, it was not necessary for them to be circumcised and to keep the Law. Nothing touches a more sensitive nerve than a threat to this most sacred area of every nation!

The hostile reaction to the witnesses is illustrated by the following statements from various cities in Macedonia, Greece, and Asia Minor. Those in Philippi said this: "These men are throwing our city into confusion, being Jews, and are proclaiming customs which it is not lawful for us to accept or to observe, being Romans" (16:20-21). The response received in Thessalonica was similar: "These men who have upset the world have come here also; and Jason has welcomed them, and they all act contrary to the decrees of Caesar, saying that there is another king, Jesus" (17:6-7). The accusation in Corinth was that "this man persuades men to worship God contrary to the law" (18:13). Finally, in Ephesus, they argued:

> And you see and hear that not only in Ephesus, but in almost all of Asia, this Paul has persuaded and turned away a considerable number of people, saying that gods made with hands are no gods at all. And not only is there danger that this trade of ours fall into disrepute, but also that the temple of the great goddess Artemis be regarded as worthless and that she whom all of Asia and the world worship should even be dethroned from her magnificence. (19:26-27)

This would be the pattern for all the centuries to come: the witness to Jesus and His gospel would challenge the beliefs, customs, and the political and economic interests of the people, thus becoming a perceived danger for the community. The violent reaction was, therefore, the "normal" and expected outcome.

Since Jesus had known of this beforehand, He devoted much time to the preparation of the disciples for the suffering that would be the result of their acts of witnessing. The Book of Acts emphasizes the necessity of a clear understanding on the part of the messengers of the gospel of what lies in store for them; they need to know that they will almost certainly encounter extreme violence and even death if they obey Christ and witness to others about Him. For instance, the same warning that Jesus had given to the apostles during their training was given to Saul immediately after Ananias announced to him that he had been chosen to bear the name of Jesus before Gentiles, kings, and the children of Israel: "For I will show him how much he must suffer for My name's sake" (9:16).

After Paul took the firm decision to go to Jerusalem at the end of his third missionary journey, he told the elders of the church in Ephesus, "the Holy Spirit solemnly testifies to me in every city, saying that bonds and afflictions await me" (20:23). This warning was dramatically enacted by the prophet Agabus in Caesarea:

> And as we were staying there for some days, a certain prophet named Agabus came down from Judea. And coming to us, he took Paul's belt and bound his own feet and hands, and said, "This is what the Holy Spirit says: 'In this way the Jews at Jerusalem will bind the man who owns this belt and deliver him into the hands of the Gentiles.' " And when we had heard this, we as well as the local residents began begging him not to go up to Jerusalem. (21:10-12)

The warnings given to Paul were not meant to stop him from going to Jerusalem. They were meant instead to make it unmistakably plain to him and to everybody else that the ministry "received from the Lord Jesus, to testify solemnly of the gospel of the grace of God" (20:24) involved witnessing in the midst of severe danger, including death. Paul's response to the brethren who pleaded with him "not to go up to Jerusalem" became the standard attitude of all true disciples of Christ: "For I am ready not only to be bound, but even to die at Jerusalem for the name of the Lord Jesus" (21:13).

Why were the disciples so ready to suffer and to die for the name of Jesus and for His gospel? In what follows, we shall examine how Luke represented the thinking of the disciples and how he, as the author of the book, selected and presented his material in order to convey the rationale for suffering and martyrdom for the sake of Christ.

The first element that was an essential part of the mind of the disciples was their clear understanding of the sovereignty of God. This is the key to a disciple's faithfulness in times of persecution. Luke deliberately and emphatically pointed to it as he related how the disciples and the young church first encountered the threat of punishment for preaching the gospel in Jerusalem (ch. 4).

After Peter and John had reported to the church about the threats they had received from the state and religious authorities, the church responded by joining together in prayer. Their prayer reveals to us the attitude and overall mindset of the first disciples. The prayer starts in 4:24, using a name of God that is almost unique in the New Testament: Δέσποτα, from which we have the word "despot," or absolute ruler. The word was used by old Simeon in his prayer in the Temple (Lk. 2:29); it was once employed by Paul with the meaning of "owner" (2 Tim. 2:21); and it was given an impressive use by Jude, who called Jesus "our only δεσπότην Θεόν, καὶ Κύριον" (Jude 4).

The choice of this particular name of God in the church's prayer was not accidental. Throughout their prayer, the disciples emphasized the fact that God was in absolute control over the events of history. They began the prayer by quoting the second Psalm, which portrays God mocking and laughing at His enemies as they plot against His Son, the Messiah. The enemies' actions will come to nothing, because God will give His Son the nations as an inheritance, and the Son will rule over them with a rod of iron. It was with this picture in mind that the church interpreted what had just happened to Jesus: "For truly in this city there were gathered together against Thy holy servant Jesus, whom Thou didst anoint, both Herod and Pontius Pilate, along with the Gentiles and the peoples of Israel, to do whatever Thy hand and Thy purpose predestined to occur" (Acts 4:27-28).

All of God's enemies had united in a plot against God's "Servant." And what had they done? They had only fulfilled God's purposes, determined beforehand by Him. His enemies had certainly wanted to do an evil thing, but God had transformed that evil into the fulfillment of His plan for the salvation of the world! Now some of the same enemies of Christ had started plotting again, this time against Peter and John. The logical conclusion of the church regarding their enemies was based upon their firm grasp of the Scriptures and upon their understanding of the concept of the sovereignty of God. Their reasoning was that the enemies of God would again be able to do only as much as the Sovereign Ruler had determined beforehand that they could do; and whatever He had determined that the enemies could do would surely turn out to be simply a part of the fulfillment of His ultimate plan, which is the triumph of the Messiah and of His people.

Now, with such a view of God's sovereignty and of God's enemies as merely His instruments fulfilling His own purposes, this was no occasion for a fearful prayer begging God for the protection of Peter and John against the doings of their enemies; neither was it the time for an angry prayer railing against the evil men who were attacking them. Such a prayer would have stood in opposition to the workings of God!

There were only two things for which the church could rightly pray:

    – for boldness, so that Peter and John may go on preaching the gospel, and

– for signs and wonders to accompany their preaching, so that the name of Jesus may be lifted up (4:24-30).

We have already seen in the Book of Daniel that the concept of the sovereignty of God is extremely important in times of persecution. The Book of Acts is full of the same kind of adverse circumstances being experienced by the people of God. Their enemies were so powerful and so many, while the Christians were so weak and so few! The fury and hostility of the mob and of the authorities were again and again unleashed against them, and they saw no signs that the new faith would win over the world.

When their enemies are strong and progress is slow, the faith and zeal of Christians tends to shrink and they are ready to give up. It is in this kind of situation that a deep understanding of the sovereignty of God is so vitally important. God's children must know that He is in absolute command, that He works even through His enemies, and that He is consistently accomplishing His purposes even through adversities. Only such an understanding of God's doings keeps His servants going when the road is tough and painful.

The second element in the thinking of the disciples that kept them going strong through constant adversities was their view of suffering as a *privilege* and an *honor*. It was unmistakably stated by Luke after Peter and John were beaten before the Council. They had received a savage beating; their backs had been cut by the rods, and they had also suffered the indignity of being exposed and humiliated like criminals in front of the country's top leaders. This was their reaction to such horrible treatment: "So they went on their way from the presence of the Council, rejoicing that they had been considered worthy to suffer shame for His name" (5:41). "To suffer shame" is the New American Standard Bible's translation of ἀτιμασθῆναι, which literally means "to be dishonored." This was what the beating had been meant to do, and this was how the world had perceived it. But the apostles had a different view of what had happened; they received it as a very special treatment. One had to be found "worthy" of it! Suffering was not for everybody. Since it was only given to a select number of people chosen by God, being among the people especially honored by God to suffer for His Name was a reason for great rejoicing indeed! The apostles did not return to the church complaining and soliciting pity. They went to report the joyful news: they had been counted worthy by their Lord to suffer indignity for His Name; they were among the chosen ones!

This little verse in the fifth chapter of Acts has been central to the thinking of suffering Christians over the centuries. This text placed special value on suffering for Christ and for His gospel. It taught believers to rejoice when they were given this special honor. It made suffering for Christ something to be longed for and desired.

Exactly the same attitude was illustrated later on by Paul and Silas in the Philippian jail. They had been beaten with rods, with "many stripes," and their feet had been placed in the stocks. In this painful situation, we find them at midnight singing hymns to God, giving a concert to all the prisoners around them (16:22-25). One can feel the same joy in people today when they find themselves privileged to suffer for the Lord.

After they had been released, Paul and Silas did not go back to the believers to be pitied by them. On the contrary, "they [Paul and Silas themselves!] encouraged them" (16:40). We find a similar situation in Lystra. Shortly after Paul was stoned almost to death there, he returned to them, "strengthening the souls of the disciples, encouraging them to continue in the faith, and saying, 'Through many tribulations we must enter the kingdom of God' " (14:22).

Two further comments on this last verse. First, Paul made it clear that a certain amount of suffering was the lot of all Christians. Secondly, the eyes of Christians should be fixed upon the final goal of the journey: their entrance into the kingdom of God. It is the glory of that kingdom that should make it easy to travel towards it on the road of "many tribulations" (Ibid.).

The third component constituting the mind of the disciples was their perception of the glory of martyrdom. Luke offers us a very special and elaborate presentation of the first Christian martyrdom. The most important feature of Stephen's death is the way that it followed the pattern of the trial and death of Jesus. Here are the parallel elements:

– Jesus was "mighty in deed and word in the sight of God and all the people" (Lk. 24:19). Stephen, "full of grace and power, was performing great wonders and signs among the people" (Acts 6:8).

– Jesus was accused of speaking against the Temple. Likewise, Stephen was accused of speaking against the "holy place, and the Law" (Acts 6:13). In Jesus' case, the witnesses were not able to prove that the accusations were true, but Jesus's own statement was considered proof enough for condemnation (Lk. 22:67-71). Stephen's speech provoked the same type of violent reaction

(Acts 7:54).

– Jesus told the High Priest that "from now on the Son of Man will be seated at the right hand of the power of God" (Lk. 22:69). Stephen saw "the heavens opened up and the Son of Man standing at the right hand of God" (Acts 7:56).

– When they were crucifying Jesus, He prayed for them, "Father, forgive them; for they do not know what they are doing" (Lk. 23:34). Stephen also prayed for the ones who were stoning him: "Lord, do not hold this sin against them!" (Acts 7:60).

– Before He died, Jesus prayed, "Father, into Thy hands I commit My Spirit" (Lk. 23:46). Similarly, Stephen prayed, "Lord Jesus, receive my spirit!" (Acts 7:59).

As part of their training for suffering and martyrdom, Jesus had taught His disciples that "a pupil is not above his teacher; but everyone, after he has been fully trained, will be like his teacher" (Lk. 6:40). Obviously, in relating this account, Luke had had the express intention of presenting Stephen as a "fully trained" pupil.

The martyrdom of Stephen as portrayed by Luke in the Book of Acts has been a model for Christians to emulate and strive toward throughout history. Several features of this martyrdom should, therefore, be highlighted. The first is Stephen's courage in telling his audience that their faith was misplaced and in presenting to them the true object of saving faith: the Son of Man, seated at the right hand of God. Stephen knew very well what the outcome of his testimony would be, yet he was not afraid to declare to his audience, "You men who are stiff-necked and uncircumcised in heart and ears are always resisting the Holy Spirit; you are doing just as your fathers did. Which one of the prophets did your fathers not persecute? And they killed those who had previously announced the coming of the Righteous One, whose betrayers and murderers you have now become" (Acts 7:51-52). Stephen knew that his duty was to deliver the message with which he had been entrusted by God despite the fact that it would be rejected. The people's reaction would not by any means cancel his duty because they had done the same to his own Master!

The second important feature of Stephen's martyrdom is his vision of heaven. When Jesus was training His disciples, preparing them to lose their lives for His sake, He told them that whoever was ashamed of Him and of His message, "of him will the Son of Man be ashamed when He comes in His glory, and the glory of the Father and of the holy angels" (Lk. 9:26). Then Jesus gave them this promise: "But I say to you truthfully, there are some of those standing here who shall not taste death until they see the kingdom of God" (Lk. 9:27). According to Acts 14:22, the kingdom of God is the place Christians will enter at the end of a long journey "through many tribulations." And yet, Jesus promised them that before they will die for His sake (i.e., as martyrs), they will receive a vision of that glorious kingdom. The experience of Stephen illustrates how that promise was to be fulfilled. Stephen was in front of a furious crowd that was ready to kill him, and "being full of the Holy Spirit, he gazed intently into heaven and saw the glory of God, and Jesus standing at the right hand of God; and he said, 'Behold, I see the heavens opened up and the Son of Man standing at the right hand of God' " (Acts 7:55-56).

We should begin the analysis of this vision with two technical matters. The first is the fact that Jesus was seen "standing" at the right hand of God, whereas in all other instances in the New Testament, He is portrayed as "sitting." The second is the fact that Jesus was called the Son of Man. In the Gospels, Jesus alone used the name "Son of Man" to refer to Himself. The only other people to use the title "Son of Man" in the New Testament were Stephen, in this heavenly vision, and John the Apostle, in his heavenly visions recorded in Revelation 1:13 and 14:14.

Outside of the New Testament, James the brother of Jesus was the only one to employ this designation for Jesus, and he likewise did it at the time of his martyrdom. In the *Historia Ecclesiastica*, Eusebius quotes Hegesippus, who relates the martyrdom of James. The apostle was placed upon a wing of the Temple and asked to deny that Jesus is the Messiah. He answered in a loud voice, " 'Why do you ask me respecting Jesus the Son of Man? He is now sitting in the Heavens, on the right hand of great Power, and is about to come on the clouds of heaven.' "[2] When they began to stone him because of this testimony, James "knelt down saying, 'I entreat You, O Lord God and Father, forgive them, for they know not what they do.' "[3]

E. F. Harrison states that the standing of the Son of Man could be interpreted as Jesus being ready to welcome the spirit of the martyr; however, he adds that "this will not explain the extraordinary use of the title 'Son of Man.' "[4] Then Harrison quotes Barrett who writes that while the coming of the Son of Man is to happen on the last day, the *Parousia* is here individualized to express what happens at the death of a believer: " 'Only dying Stephen was in the position to see the coming of the Son of Man. It was at the "last day," in the hour of death, that the Son of Man would be seen. . . . Only Stephen qualifies, as a dying Christian, for an individual *Parousia* of the Son of Man.' "[5]

E. F. Harrison rejects this view as not being in agreement with the other New Testament texts that describe the death of a believer. Harrison says that the solution to the problem "is to see in the combination of standing and the use of the title 'Son of Man' an indication that the Lord was here taking the position of witness and vindicator on behalf of His servant."[6] In support of this, Harrison quotes C. F. D. Moule:

> "In short, this is a double trial scene, exactly as in the scene in which Jesus witnessed a good confession before Pontius Pilate (1 Tim. 6:13) or before the Son of Man will thenceforth be exalted with the clouds and vindicated, so here Stephen is condemned and put to death, but in the heavenly court, where the books have been opened, this member of the Son of Man community is already being vindicated by the head of that community—the Son of Man par excellence; and as Stephen's witness confessed Christ before men, so Christ is standing to confess him before the angels of God. It is the more significant, if so, that the martyr with his dying is vindicated."[7]

A. A. Trites gives us an even clearer explanation:

> The Son of Man is viewed here in the light of the legal terminology of the Old Testament (where the judge is described as "sitting," the witness as "standing," and the right hand as the place of the vindicating "witness"). As Stephen had confessed Christ before the unbelieving Jews who took his life, so Christ would confess him publicly in heaven; condemned by the earthly tribunal, Stephen would be vindicated by the heavenly one.[8]

There are two distinguishable purposes for a vision of heaven given to a person on the threshold of martyrdom. The first purpose is to be a testimony for the people who are standing by, watching the execution. Once again, we have the example of Jesus. In the twelfth chapter of John's Gospel, after Jesus had announced that "the hour has come for the Son of Man to be glorified," meaning "crucified," and He had confessed that His soul was troubled, He then prayed, "Father, glorify Thy name" (John 12:27). A voice from heaven was heard by both Jesus and the people who surrounded Him, "I have both glorified it, and will glorify it again" (12:28). Then Jesus explained to the multitude the purpose of this intervention from heaven: "This voice has not come for My sake, but for your sakes" (12:30).

A heavenly testimony of this kind can impact its hearers in a variety ways. Hence, Jesus went on to explain that the glorification of the Father will accomplish three things:

– the judgment of this world,
– the casting out of the ruler of this world, and
– the drawing of all people to Himself (12:31-32).

In a similar manner, Stephen's testimony—he saw "the heavens opened up and the Son of Man standing at the right hand of God,"— had the immediate effect of terrible judgment upon its hearers (Acts 7:56-57). They were the ones who had condemned Jesus to death. The fact that Jesus was seen in the glory of heaven was proof that they had been horribly wrong to kill the Messiah. They could not stand to hear such a judgment and therefore killed Stephen just as they had killed Jesus. Nevertheless, Stephen's testimony did have an impact on at least one of the people who were standing by, namely, on Saul. Much later in his life, Saul, who had become the Apostle Paul, said with a lingering echo of pain in his words, "Lord, they themselves understand that in one synagogue after another I used to imprison and beat those who believed in Thee. And when the blood of Thy witness Stephen was being shed, I also was standing by approving, and watching out for the cloaks of those who were slaying him" (Acts 22:19-20). Saul, the persecutor, met by Jesus on the road to Damascus, was afterward told by Ananias, "For you will be a witness for Him to all men of what you have seen and heard" (22:15). Thus, the persecutor became the witness-martyr.

The testimony of the vision of heaven given to Stephen before he died has inspired and encouraged Christians over the centuries, and many would-be martyrs were given such visions before they had to face their own martyrdom.

The second purpose of a vision of God's glory, of Christ, and of the beauty of heaven is for the martyr himself. It has a transforming impact upon that person. The glory is so great that the tortures are no longer worthy of being taken into consideration after one has seen it (Rom. 8:18). The body does not feel the pain when the spirit is enthralled by the glory of heaven. Joseph Parker, in his commentary upon this text, captures its meaning:

> In great dangers God shows us great sights. What did Elisha ask the Lord to do in the case of the young man who saw the gathering hosts surrounding his prophet master? Elisha's brief but comprehensive desire was "Lord, open his eyes that he may see."

> That is all we want. The enemy is near, I know it: but the friend is nearer.[9]

And then these superb words:

> When the Spirit is inspired, when the heart is sanctified, when heaven is opened, when Christ rises to receive the guest, there is no flesh, there is no pain, there is no consciousness but in the presence of God, the absorption of the heart in the infinite love. If you feel the body it is for want of the thorough sanctification of the spirit. If the flesh is an encumbrance to you it is because the spirit has not finished its education.[10]

The next feature of Stephen's martyrdom that we want to look at is his prayer for the forgiveness of his enemies and killers. The meaning of this prayer is found not in the imitation of the Master or in the greatness of a forgiving heart, although these are certainly a part of it. The primary point is the function of the witness. He is there to testify to the love of God manifested in His Son Jesus Christ. His job is not only to express it in his verbal testimony, but to demonstrate it by his own suffering and by his love that forgives the ones who inflict the pain. He is there to meet the hate with love and to conquer the evil by accepting suffering and by forgiving the ones who inflict it. I call this the aggression of love. The witness is not a passive victim, but the aggressor, the fighter. He takes the initiative to the end. Even his last prayer, by which he entrusts his soul into the hands of the Master, is part of that aggressive testimony. It is a demonstration of a victorious spirit unto the end.

Finally, the most important element in the martyrdom of Stephen is the leading and empowering role of the Holy Spirit. Luke introduces Stephen to us on the occasion of his election as a deacon; Stephen is presented as "a man full of faith and of the Holy Spirit" (Acts 6:5). Then, in the context of preaching "the word of God," we are told that "Stephen, full of grace and power, was performing great wonders and signs among the people" (6:8). At the climax of his address to the Sanhedrin, Luke writes that Stephen "being full of the Holy Spirit, . . . gazed intently into heaven and saw the glory of God, and Jesus standing at the right hand of God" (7:55).

The prominence of the Holy Spirit in the action of witnessing to Christ and His gospel is visible in the entire Book of Acts to such an extent that the book has been commonly surnamed "The Acts of the Holy Spirit."[11] In fact, Luke starts his book with the appearance of the risen Christ to His apostles during which He gave them the following promise: "You shall be baptized with the Holy Spirit not many days from now" (1:5). Just before He ascended into heaven, Jesus gave them the clearest indication of the role of the Holy Spirit in their ministry of witnessing: "but you shall receive power when the Holy Spirit has come upon you; and you shall be My witnesses both in Jerusalem, and in all Judea and Samaria, and even to the remotest part of the earth" (1:8).

The power of the Holy Spirit was manifested in the boldness of the Apostle Peter when he preached at Pentecost (ch. 2) and when he spoke in the Temple (4:8). Then, it was manifested in Stephen and in the Apostle Paul (e.g., 9:27; 19:8; 28:31). These accounts represent a series of cases that illustrate the fulfillment of Jesus' promise given to His witnesses: "But when they deliver you up, do not become anxious about how or what you will speak; for it shall be given you in that hour what you are to speak. For it is not you who speak, but it is the Spirit of your Father who speaks in you" (Matt. 10:19-20).

The second martyr in the Book of Acts is James, the brother of John. Although he was the first apostle to die as a martyr, his story was given only the short space of four verses (Acts 12:1-4). The next fifteen verses are dedicated to Herod's attempt to follow up the killing of James with the killing of Peter; these verses also recount Peter's miraculous rescue from prison by an angel. We can only speculate why James was not given more attention by the author. One reason may be the fact that the story of Stephen had already served Luke's purpose in presenting an example of martyrdom according to the pattern established by Jesus. A second reason may be the fact that James's martyrdom was followed closely by the rescue of Peter; putting the two together served Luke's purpose in showing the sovereign rule of God in the life of His messengers. God allowed James to be martyred, while at the same time, He sent His angel to rescue Peter, whose job on this earth had not yet been completed.

It is not the business of the messengers to decide what will happen to them or when it will happen. They simply have to go on witnessing with boldness in the power of the Holy Spirit as He leads them, no matter what may happen to them. God may have preordained a short testimony for them, followed by a violent encounter with a hateful world and then the opening of the heavens to receive them into glory. On the other hand, God's plan may hold in store for them a long journey through many tribulations before they can enter into the resplendent kingdom of God. While it is the sovereign Lord who decides the length of each ministry, the end of each will still be the same glorious one.

Chapter 7

The Teaching of the Apostle Paul

Of all the outstanding people of God in the New Testament, the Apostle Paul has the longest record of suffering for Christ and His gospel. A countless number of times, he faced the possibility of being killed for his preaching and for his stand for Jesus. He was also the one to write extensively concerning the meaning and purpose of suffering and death in the service of Christ, drawing upon his own experience as well as upon the experiences of other Christians. Paul's epistles are indeed of the greatest importance in the development of a theology of suffering, martyrdom, and rewards in heaven.

There is an enormous quantity of literature written about the writings of Paul: commentaries on his letters, monographs on the themes of his writings, and lengthy attempts to systematize his theology. They offer help as well as create difficulty for our present endeavor. While they help because we can find so much in the way of explanations of his writings, they also make selecting what is most important for our subject more difficult.

John S. Pobee recently presented a doctoral dissertation to the University of Cambridge, under the title of "Persecution and Martyrdom in the Theology of Paul."[1] Most of his work is concerned with the following two things: the concept of martyrdom in the Jewish literature of the intertestamental period and the way in which the author thinks that Paul used the ideas from that literature to explain the death of Jesus. Pobee devotes a mere fifteen pages to the persecution of the apostle himself [2] and only fourteen pages to the persecution of the church.[3] While Pobee's research provides us with extensive material pertaining to our subject, I do not agree with the way he interprets that material and with the way he interprets Jesus and Paul in light of intertestamental literature. His study shows that he is not at all interested in applying the ideas he has discovered in that literature to present day Christian life and thought. In contrast, this was exactly *my* main purpose in conducting this research.

It is important to draw attention to the fact that in recent decades, many theologians have believed that the interpretation of Jesus' death as a ransom, propitiation, or expiation for sins was a product of the influence of Maccabean literature. The Maccabeans, as we have seen, believed that the death of a martyr atones for the sins of a nation. Sam K. Williams' volume, *Jesus' Death As A Saving Event: The Background and Origin of a Concept*, is just one example of a book that presents this type of interpretation of the death of Jesus.[4]

It was of utmost significance for Christian theology when at the beginning of this century, liberal theologians presented the death of Jesus as the death of a martyr, and they understood this to mean the death of a hero for the sake of his own ideas. Fundamentalist theologians reacted with passion against this interpretation, and they did so obviously in order to preserve the atoning and redemptive function of the death of Christ. Today the situation has been completely reversed. There are theologians today who insist that the death of Christ was indeed a martyrdom, thereby necessarily having the same function and purpose as the deaths of the Maccabean martyrs; in this way, they think that they can prove that Christ's death was for the purposes of ἱλαστήριον and of ἀντίψυχον.

Consequently, the task of evangelical theologians at this time is twofold. First, we must determine to what extent the thinking of the Apostle Paul was influenced by Maccabean literature; and, secondly, we must strive to prove that regardless of this influence, Paul believed that Christ's death was a unique sacrifice for sin, even though he may have been employing a concept inherited from the Maccabeans. In spite of the fact that this project is not within the scope of this dissertation, I mention it here because it is useful to be aware of the way in which the concept of Christ's death as a martyrdom has completely changed its content in recent years.

In order to reach our ultimate goal, which is the formulation of a systematic theology of suffering and martyrdom for our own times, we must first take a comprehensive survey of the ideas concerning suffering and martyrdom in the Bible, as well as in the history of Israel and the history of Christianity. In accordance with this plan, we are now ready to examine each of the relevant Pauline epistles in order to select from them the ideas that are important to our subject.

1 and 2 Thessalonians

In almost every city where Paul preached the gospel of Jesus Christ, there was an adverse reaction in the form of violence either toward him or toward the new converts. The reason for this hostility can be explained by citing the fact that every community has certain elements that it holds dear and considers vital for its very existence. Among the most precious are a community's religious beliefs and practices. Whenever these elements of culture are threatened, the community reacts in self-defense, often with violence. Very rarely does a community preserve its calm, waiting patiently to analyze the facts and to search serenely for the truth or falsity of the new ideas brought to them from the outside. Even when people do begin to consider the arguments, their judgment can be easily swayed by economical or political interests or by other such external considerations.

Paul encountered this reality wherever he went. Yet he was convinced that the message which he had been given to communicate to others *was* the truth, and he believed that it was a matter of life and death for people everywhere to hear and to believe the truth of the gospel of Jesus Christ. Out of this conviction and out of his love for people arose the apostle's readiness to risk being reviled, beaten, and even killed.

Paul's involvement in the spreading of the gospel of Jesus Christ was completely voluntary, even though from the outset he had been fully aware of the suffering which this action might bring upon himself and upon those who would accept his message. Of course, it is unthinkable that he would embark on such a mission without first possessing a clear understanding of the reasons why he should submit himself to such sufferings and why the recipients of the message should risk persecution, suffering, and death at the hands of their own countrymen. In his letters, Paul explained both his own reasons for suffering and the reasons for the suffering of his converts. Let us explore his rationale as it is found in his letters to the Thessalonians.

The Christians in Thessalonica suffered a great deal of persecution at the hands of their countrymen soon after the time of their conversion (1 Thess. 2:14), so that Paul was justified in saying to them that they "received the word in much tribulation" (1:6). After he had spent some time with them, Paul was forced to leave Thessalonica, and now he was greatly concerned that they might "be disturbed by these afflictions," and that "the tempter" might provoke them to renounce or to give up their new faith (3:3).

The first thing that Paul wrote to these persecuted Christians was that in their suffering, they had become "imitators" of him and of Christ (1:6) and of the churches in Judea (2:14). This imitation refers to the basic fact that the Jews "both killed the Lord Jesus and the prophets" (2:15). We have already observed how Jesus Himself portrayed the prophets as God's messengers, martyred by the obstinate nation of Israel. Jesus was well aware that He and His disciples were going to receive the same type of treatment. However, this persecution was a reason for joy because of the great heavenly reward awaiting those who had suffered in their lifetime on earth (Matt. 5:10-12). Paul himself expressed his joy by singing praises to God in the prison of Philippi, just before traveling on to Thessalonica.

The Apostle Paul commended the Thessalonians for "having received the word in much tribulation with the joy of the Holy Spirit" (1 Thess. 1:6). But why should persecution, suffering, tribulation, and affliction be reasons for rejoicing? Normally, these things produce pain and anguish; ordinarily, they disturb people and discourage them. One must have very serious reasons for finding joy in things that usually kill all joy. In his message to the Thessalonians, Paul enumerated and explained these reasons to them, and we must listen very carefully, without allowing our prejudices to impede our comprehension of what he had to say.

Paul had already told them, repeatedly, when he was with them, that they were going to suffer afflictions because "we have been destined for this" (3:3). The entire letter is strong on predestination and on the sovereign rule of God over everything that happens. Thus, the Thessalonians have been elected by God; they were "His choice" (1:4). He repeated this fact in the clearest possible terms: "For God has not destined us for wrath, but for obtaining salvation through our Lord Jesus Christ" (5:9), and again in the second letter: "because God has chosen you from the beginning for salvation through sanctification by the Spirit and faith in the truth" (2 Thess. 2:13).

Satan was the one who had been hindering Paul's return to Thessalonica (1 Thess. 2:18), and "the man of lawlessness" was going to come with the power of Satan (2 Thess. 2:3-9). However, all the frightening activity of deception effected by the forces of evil turns out to be only a part of God's greater plan and strategy. Since people "did not receive the love of the truth so as to be saved, . . . for this reason God will send upon them a deluding influence so that they might believe what is false, in order that they all may be judged" (2:10-12). It is of the greatest importance for God's people to know that He has ordained these things, and that He is in control even over Satan and his agents. The adverse events, the afflictions, and the tribulations all ultimately serve the purposes of God.

Paul referred to these tribulations as "God's righteous judgment," intended to achieve two purposes: first, they serve to prove Christians "worthy of the kingdom of God" and of glory (1:5, 11); and secondly, they bring "retribution to those who do not know God and to those who do not obey the gospel of our Lord Jesus" (1:8), and "who afflict" His children (1:6).

Let us consider the concept of "worthiness" for the kingdom of God. This concept was first formulated in the New Testament by Jesus Himself. In the context of His teaching on the resurrection of the last day, He spoke of "those who are considered worthy to attain to that age and the resurrection from the dead" (Lk. 20:35). We have already examined what Jesus taught about "faithfulness" (translated by the NIV as "trustworthiness" in Lk. 16:11-12) in the jobs entrusted by the King to His servants, and how that faithfulness or trustworthiness determines positions of greater and smaller authority in heaven. Paul employed the same concept and the same pattern of thought in his teaching to the Thessalonians.

When he had been with them, instructing them in the basics of Christianity, Paul had exhorted, encouraged, and implored them to "walk in a manner worthy of the God who calls you into His own kingdom and glory" (1 Thess. 2:12). Now in his first letter to them, all the moral counsel that Paul offered them had in view the kind of people they were going to be "at the coming of our Lord Jesus with all His saints" (3:13). They were to walk in a way that would "please God" (4:1). In addition, Paul emphasized that the will of God for them was their sanctification (4:3). He warned them that a man must not defraud his brother, because "the Lord is the avenger in all these things" (4:6). He even went so far as to write that the one who rejects this teaching about holy living "is not rejecting man but the God who gives His Holy Spirit to you" (4:8).

Everyone agrees that the second coming of Christ is one of the main concerns of these two epistles. However, I suggest that although Paul clarified for the Thessalonians some of the things that will occur before and at the time of Christ's second coming, his greatest emphasis was not on these last events. Paul's supreme concern in these two letters was quite a different one, found in the following anxious question he posed to them: *In what state will the Thessalonian Christians be found at the coming of Christ?* Paul expressed it in this way: ". . . we night and day keep praying most earnestly that we may see your face, and may complete what is lacking in your faith" (1 Thess. 3:10). His prayer for them was that their love for one another and for all people might increase, "so that He may establish your hearts unblamable in holiness before our God and Father *at the coming of our Lord Jesus* with all His saints" (3:13, italics mine). He emphasized his concern again at the conclusion of the first letter, telling them that he prays that God Himself may sanctify them entirely and that their "spirit and soul and body [may] be preserved complete, without blame *at the coming of our Lord Jesus Christ* (5:23, italics mine).

In the second letter, Paul first expressed his joy "for your perseverance and faith in the midst of all your persecutions and afflictions which you endure" (2 Thess. 1:4). The reason he was so proud and glad for them was precisely because their suffering was "a plain indication of God's righteous judgment so that you may be considered worthy of the kingdom of God, for which indeed you are suffering" (1:5). This will happen "when He comes to be glorified in His saints on that day" (1:10). Yet perseverance in persecution was not enough. The Thessalonians also needed an inner transformation and the practical application of their faith: "To this end also we pray for you always that our God may count you worthy of your calling, and fulfill every desire for goodness and the work of faith with power; in order that the name of our Lord Jesus may be glorified in you, and you in Him" (1:11-12).

A red flag may be raised at this point that this teaching comes close to "salvation by works." Consequently, let us read what Paul wrote about salvation in these two letters. He started by advising his readers to put on "as a helmet, the hope of salvation," indicating that he spoke about a future event (1 Thess. 5:8b); then he added: "For God has not destined us for wrath, but for obtaining salvation through our Lord Jesus Christ, who died for us, that whether we are awake or asleep, we may live together with Him. Therefore encourage one another, and build up one another" (5:9-11). The second time he wrote about salvation, he said this: ". . . because God has chosen you from the beginning for salvation through sanctification by the Spirit and faith in the truth. And it was for this He called you through our gospel, that you may gain the glory of our Lord Jesus Christ. So then, brethren, stand firm and hold to the traditions which you were taught" (2 Thess. 2:13b-15). These are two very loaded texts, and we must try to understand exactly what Paul wanted to say through them.

First of all, the word translated by the New American Standard Bible as "*obtaining* salvation" (1 Thess. 5:9, italics mine) is the same word which is then translated as "*gain* the glory" (2 Thess. 2:14, italics mine). In both places, the Greek word used by Paul is περιποίησιν; it means *possession*. We find this term translated in this way in 1 Peter 2:9: "a people for God's own *possession*." The text that helps us to get at the meaning of it is Ephesians 1:14, where the Holy Spirit is said to be "the guarantee of our inheritance until we acquire possession of it" (RSV).

There is no justification in translating περιποίησιν as "obtaining" when it refers to salvation, and then changing it to "gaining" when it refers to glory, as the New American Standard Bible has done. Because both are future events, it would be best to keep the basic meaning of *possession* in each case, translating the phrases in the following way: "for acquiring *possession* of salvation" and "that you may acquire *possession* of glory."

In some of his other epistles, Paul used the term: "*inherit* the kingdom of God" (1 Cor. 6:9; Gal. 5:21; Eph. 5:5). Now, in *all* those places, *inheriting*—acquiring possession of the kingdom of God—is conditioned by moral living! Here is the crux of the interpretation. In the Thessalonian correspondence, Paul made it absolutely clear that God elects, predestines, and calls people to salvation and to the possession of His kingdom and glory. Christ died for us in order that we might "live together with Him," both here and in His future kingdom (1 Thess. 5:10). Furthermore, Paul added that the fulfillment of the goal of having the name of Christ glorified in us, and of ourselves being glorified in Him, will be "according to the grace of our God and the Lord Jesus Christ" (2 Thess. 1:12). Above all, it is God in

His faithfulness who will make all these things come to pass (1 Thess. 5:24; 2 Thess. 3:3).

However, we are also told that the tribulations are needed in order to prove us *worthy* of possessing the kingdom. We have to suffer for the kingdom and are exhorted and implored to walk *worthy* of God and His kingdom. After we are warned of the danger of rejecting the call to moral living, we are taught that our goal must be to be found without blame, holy, and complete at the coming of Jesus.

In the Pauline doctrine of salvation, we discover two levels of action: the one above is the plane of God's actions, and the one below is the plane of man's actions. On the higher level, God does the electing, the calling, the saving, the keeping, the sanctifying, and the glorifying. On the level below, the individual has to believe, to be zealous for good works, to deny himself or herself, to serve God and other people, to strive for perfection and holiness, to persevere, to endure hardship, and to aim to be found worthy of God's calling. How can we reconcile these two lines of action? Protestant theologians, in order to save the *sola fide* and *sola gratia* of salvation, have emphasized only God's line of action, while they have minimized or explained away the second one. Is it necessary to do this? Isn't there a way in which we can take both parts seriously, maintaining God's side of the equation while still doing justice to the biblical teaching about the importance of good works and moral living for our eternal state?

Let us approach this subject from another angle. Paul taught that Christians have to grow. He rebuked the Corinthians for remaining "babes in Christ" (1 Cor. 3:1). He wrote that the purpose of the ministries of the church is to help the saints reach maturity (Eph. 4:11-16). He exhorted them to run toward perfection (Phil. 3:12-15) and toward holiness (1 Thess. 4:3-8, et seq.). The questions we should ask are the following: Does our obedient accomplishment of these things have an impact upon our eternal state and eternal well-being? Will it matter in eternity if we did these things or if we didn't bother?

To formulate the problem in another way, let us suppose that there are two decent, young Christian men in America. One of them is concerned with the situation of the primitive people in the jungle of the Amazon and decides to go to them as a missionary. He finds his tribe, lives with them in primitive conditions, learns their language, translates the Bible into their language, introduces them to Christ, and lifts them up to a new life. The other man does not care about others. He accumulates riches for himself and lives a life of comfort and ease.

Yes, he goes to church and tithes his money, yet he limits himself to the minimum of what is commonly meant as being a Christian. The question then is this: When these two individuals get to heaven, will there be a difference in their eternal condition?

We can also consider another case: suppose that there are two Christian women in a country in which Christianity is viciously persecuted. One of them keeps a low profile, so that few people, if any, know that she is a Christian. The other one is a shining light and many are converted through her testimony. As a result, she is persecuted, then arrested, tortured, and killed. My question is the following: When these two ladies arrive in heaven, will there be a difference in their eternal state?

Most Protestant theologians would agree that some Christians will be welcomed into heaven with praise and that others will be received before the judgment seat of Christ with censure and disapproval; nevertheless, these theologians believe that any such negative reactions will soon be forgotten, since all the saints will enjoy the same felicity in heaven. If the ones who have worked, sacrificed, and suffered for the cause of Christ would have a different status in heaven, many say that this would imply earning something by their work, sacrifice, and suffering. They fear that in such a scenario, the role of the grace of God would be dramatically reduced, making it impossible to maintain that everything was *sola gratia*.

My thesis is that a Christian's zeal for good works and his aim to prove himself worthy of God and of his calling have a great impact upon the nature of his eternal state. The practices of self-denial, of serving God and other people, of striving for perfection and holiness, of persevering and enduring hardship for the cause of Christ all matter with respect to what a Christian's position in heaven will be. When the child of God enters into the heavenly kingdom, he will surely reap the consequences of the deeds he has performed while on earth. For precisely this reason, one of the purposes of this dissertation is to logically and organically integrate into our Protestant thinking a theology of good works on earth and of rewards in heaven *without* losing our distinctive belief in the grace of God that is at work in all things, at every stage in our lives, from start to finish.

As we continue to study the Pauline epistles, the following truth will emerge: the two planes of action, that of the saving and enabling grace and that of man's action, must be accepted as equally true and equally important. It will also become evident that we can build a theology of moral living and rewards without introducing the concept of human merit and without jeopardizing in any way our theology of grace, which insists that all the praise and glory be given only to God.

Before we continue our exploration, we need to further clarify the issues that are at stake. The question was asked whether a Christian's good works, suffering, self-sacrifice, and martyrdom will yield consequences for his eternal state. We indicated that most Protestant theologians would answer this query in the negative, and that they would then be forced to follow up their answer with the statement that everybody will be equal in heaven.

If we take the other position and give a positive answer to this question, accepting that there will be a difference in heaven due to our performance in the Christian life on earth, we will likewise be obligated to buttress our answer with some affirmations about the nature of that difference in heaven. Will it be a remunerative difference or a structural difference? A remunerative difference would mean that some may be given bigger treasures or bigger rewards (whatever those treasures or rewards may be), but we will all have the same stature or position in heaven. A structural difference, on the other hand, would mean that there will actually be differences of status or ranking in the heavenly kingdom. The Scriptures teach that as we obey God more and more in this life, as we strive toward maturity and holiness, as we display the fruit of the Spirit and pass victoriously through sufferings, temptations and trials, we become more and more like Christ, increasingly reflecting His character. Then, when we get to heaven, the structure of our inner man will be of a radically different quality as a direct result of our godly living. Therefore, because of our Christlike character, God will be able to entrust us with much higher positions or responsibilities in heaven.

Another important question should be raised here. Will not all of God's children be glorified and perfected? Yes, the Scripture says that all will be glorified (Rom. 8:29-30), and that all will be perfected (1 Peter 5:10). But what if that perfection does not entail equal status and identical capacities? What if there will be differing degrees and statures, while at the same time, everyone will be perfect, where they are, in their smaller or greater capacities?

Let us return to our discussion of the nature of salvation in the Thessalonian correspondence. We were commenting on the word περιποίησιν, translated by the New American Standard Bible in one case as *obtaining* and in another case as *gain*. I suggested that the basic meaning of the word is *possession*. Therefore, the best translation for 1 Thessalonians 5:9 would be this: we have been destined and ordained "for the possessing of salvation." The parallel translation of 2 Thessalonians 2:14 would be that God has called us "for the possessing of the glory of our Lord Jesus Christ." In the second passage, verse 13 states that God has chosen us for salvation. Verse 14 is thus an explanation of the previous verse: salvation means reaching that stage in our spiritual pilgrimage in which we possess the glory of Christ!

The Apostle Paul also said that this salvation is worked out by the sanctifying work of the Holy Spirit (God's plane of action) and by faith in the truth (obviously man's plane of action). The second level of action is strengthened by the exhortation that follows in 2 Thessalonians 2:15. Because the Thessalonians knew what a great destiny awaited them in heaven, they were told to "stand firm," following the teachings they had received both verbally when Paul was with them and in written form in the epistles.

It is very important to see how the whole discussion is concluded. The two epistles speak about the coming of Christ and about the glory and the kingdom that will be the possession of the Christian who has been faithful in sufferings and afflictions, and who has led a holy and godly life. The complete vision of what the faithful Christian's glorious destiny will be after the coming of Christ is summarized by Paul in his prayer in 2 Thessalonians 2:16-17. In this prayer, Paul declares that "our Lord Jesus Christ Himself and God our Father . . . has loved us and [has] given us eternal comfort and good hope by grace." Comfort is what suffering people need most. Jesus Christ and God the Father give the suffering ones "eternal comfort and good hope" (2:16b); in other words, the Father and the Son give them the promise of the possession of God's glorious kingdom. Paul announces this bright reality so that the Thessalonians' hearts might be both comforted and strengthened "in every good work and word" (2:17b).

There are two more things to be said. The first is that "the Lord is faithful, and He will strengthen and protect you from the evil one" (2 Thess. 3:3). This is an unquestionably vital thing to know when undergoing persecution and afflictions. The second thing to note is Paul's prayer that their hearts should look steadily "into the love of God and into the steadfastness of Christ" (3:5). However painful the afflictions are, they cannot separate us from the love of God, who is always with us in our trials. Furthermore, we are called to imitate

Christ. He went through Gethsemane and Calvary with ὑπομονή: steadfastness, patience, and endurance. He did not run away, and He did not give up. Through patience and endurance He won the victory and the glory. That should also be the way of the Christian.

One last note about "those who have fallen asleep in Him," mentioned in 1 Thess. 4:13-17 (NIV). Some commentators consider them to be the martyrs.[5] I take another position, however, in agreement with D. E. Hiebert, whom I will quote in this matter:

> Some hold the meaning to be that they have "fallen asleep through Jesus" as martyrs for the faith. But in that case we would expect the accusative with the preposition rather than the genitive (διὰ τοῦ Ἰησοῦ), "on account of" or "for the sake of" Jesus. Moreover, Lunemann asserts that "the indications in both Epistles do not afford the slightest justification of the idea of persecutions which ended in *bloody death*. To restrict the reference to martyrs would inappropriately limit this message of comfort to a very small portion of believers. Clearly the problem agitating the Thessalonians was wider than death by martyrdom; it is natural to assume that since the missionaries had left, some of the members had died a natural death."[6]

1 and 2 Corinthians

The Corinthian correspondence is an essential part of our investigation. Paul's ministry was being questioned in Corinth, and he had to defend it. In the process, his letters became very personal. In fact, no other epistles contain as much personal information and explanation as do Paul's First and Second Epistles to the Corinthians. Compared to all the other apostles, the Apostle Paul had suffered the most severe afflictions for the longest period of time, and here we find him interpreting his sufferings, telling us what he understood to be their purpose and meaning.

We shall see that most of the ideas sketched in the Thessalonian correspondence are nearly fully developed here. Some of them Paul further developed in his letter to the Romans, in the epistles from prison (Ephesians, Philippians, and Colossians), and in the Pastoral epistles (1 and 2 Timothy and Titus). For a more comprehensive view, I shall at times refer to these other letters as we discuss the ideas developed in 1 and 2 Corinthians, although separate attention will be given to each of them later on in this study.

There was a crisis of relationship between the church in Corinth and its founder, the Apostle Paul. After his departure from Corinth, new preachers and teachers came to the young church and persuaded the immature believers to adhere to a new type of theology. They were taken in by the spiritual gift of speaking in tongues, and they considered themselves to be like the angels. They saw themselves as rich, full, and already reigning with Christ (1 Cor. 4:9-13). Gordon Fee aptly calls this a "spiritualized eschatology" or "an 'over realized' eschatological view of their present existence."[7] They felt that they had already acquired a special power and a heavenly existence.

From this perspective, they looked at the Apostle and saw his weakness, his suffering, and the fact that he was always in trouble; they interpreted this as an indication that he was not a true apostle. It was this Corinthian view of themselves and of Paul that the apostle had to address. In the process, Paul gave us a theology of the cross (*teologia crucis*) and a theology of glory (*teologia gloriae*).

Paul began his first letter by confronting the Corinthians with the amazing fact that the Almighty God revealed Himself to us in His Son Jesus Christ in utter weakness; His Son suffered and even died on the cross. The way God came down to us can only be called "the foolishness of God" and "the weakness of God" (1:25). But this method of the cross, which for the Jews is a stumbling block and for the Gentiles simply foolishness, proved to be "God's wisdom" and "God's power" (1:21-25).

What Paul wanted to convey was that this way of humiliation and weakness, of suffering and self-sacrifice, is God's way of action; it is God's way of being involved with mankind, and His way of solving the problems of mankind. But it is not only God's way; it must be the way of all the people of God and especially of God's ministers and agents. This is so because God's people and His ministers are not separate from God. It is God who operates in and through them. In this manner, they form a partnership. Paul stated this right from the beginning of 1 Corinthians, writing that "you were called into fellowship with His Son, Jesus Christ our Lord" (1:9). Then he referred to the apostles as "God's fellow-workers" (3:9). In the letter to the Philippians, he made it clear that he was speaking about "the fellowship of His sufferings" (3:10).

In 2 Corinthians, Paul wrote that "the sufferings of Christ are ours in abundance" (2 Cor. 1:5), and that he was "always carrying about in the body the dying of Jesus" (4:10). In Romans, Paul stated that being co-heirs with Christ is conditioned upon suffering with Him (Rom. 8:17). The culminating statement is in Colossians 1:24, where Paul says that he completes "that which is lacking in Christ's afflictions."

We must now try to understand what Paul meant by this partnership with Christ in His sufferings. From the outset, it is important to be aware of the fact that many Protestant theologians today spiritualize this concrete reality to such an extent that they simply do away with the concept that Christians might in some way participate in the sufferings of Christ. Wilhelm Michaelis is a typical member of this category of interpreters. Commenting on the concept of sharing in the sufferings of Christ (τοῦ Χριστοῦ παθήμασι) in 1 Peter 4:13, he writes: "The sufferings of Christians are not here derived from the passion of Christ or the necessity of participating in His. What is stated is rather that Christians as πάσχοντες do in fact follow in His steps."[8] His understanding of Romans 8:17 (εἴπερ συμπάσχομεν), in conjunction with 1 Corinthians 12:26, leads Michaelis to conclude: "This undermines the possibility that συμπάσχομεν might denote a common participation of Christ and Christians in a common suffering."[9] His final verdict is that "the πάσχειν of Christians is a συμπάσχειν because Christ leads them to suffering."[10] Accordingly, Michaelis' view of Philippians 3:10 is that "there can be no idea of a fellowship of suffering in the sense of a true passion mysticism accessible to all at all times."[11] Michaelis comes to this final determination:

> The genitive τοῦ Χριστοῦ does not, then, denote a relation of the παθήματα of the apostle (or of the Corinthians or any Christian) to the παθήματα of Christ Himself, whether by analogy, or as a continuation, or as a mystical, or non-mystical imitation. The necessity of Christian suffering is not based on the fact that there has to be analogy, continuation or imitation, but on the fact that Jesus—because there are necessarily παθήματα τοῦ νῦν καιροῦ (Rom. 8:18), and hence the way to the kingdom of God is through tribulation (Acts 14:22)—holds out before His disciples the prospect of afflictions.[12]

We may wonder what could possibly be the reason for this radical denial of the plain meaning of the words of Scripture. Michaelis himself gives us the answer in these words: "It can hardly be the apostle's intention to speak of a soteriological significance of the sufferings of Christians. Christ, His name and the kingdom of God cannot be the subject of soteriological effort."[13]

This common Protestant fear is a result of the fact that the Roman Catholics have interpreted Colossians 1:24 to mean that Paul was adding his own atoning sufferings to the atoning sufferings of Christ, and that one can benefit from Paul's redemptive sufferings by buying indulgences. It also appears that Michaelis believes that the only sufferings of Christ are the ones He underwent when He died on the cross for our sins; if we speak of the Christian's participation in *those* sufferings, then the sufferings of the Christian would have atoning value, just like the sufferings of Christ. We will deal with this issue below.

Before we do this, however, I want to present another reason for which the theologians are reluctant to accept a real participation of the Christian in the sufferings of Christ. It is found in the traditional doctrine of the impassibility of God. This doctrine was formulated by Christian theologians during the period of time from the second to the fifth centuries. It presents God as "*apathes*," as not moving, not changing, and not suffering. Reflecting this doctrine, the Council of Chalcedon made this pronouncement: "The synod deposes from the priesthood those who dare to say that the Godhead of the Only-begotten is passable."[14]

Our century has witnessed a dramatic change in this field. As early as 1924, William Temple rejected this view of God. In his book *Christus Veritas*, he pointed out that "there is a highly technical sense in which God, as Christ revealed Him, is 'without passions'; for He is Creator and supreme, and is never 'passive' in the sense of having things happen to Him except with His consent; also He is constant, and free from gusts of feeling carrying Him this way and that." However, Temple went on to show that most theologians understand "impassible" to mean "incapable of suffering"; his response to this interpretation was that "in this sense its predication to God is almost wholly false."[15]

In 1926, J. K. Mozley, in his book *The Impassibility of God*, signaled the growing reaction against this conception of God. The change was substantially helped by the studies of the concept of God in the Old Testament. I mention the works of H. Wheeler Robinson, especially *Suffering: Human and Divine*,[16] that of the Jewish scholar Abraham Heschel, *The Prophets*,[17] and more recently, the work of Terrence E. Fretheim, *The Suffering of God: An Old Testament Perspective*.[18] These works and others like them give us an overwhelming amount of data that should convince us that the God of the Old Testament is not the impassible God of Greek philosophy; on the contrary, He is a passionate God deeply involved with His people, suffering with them and because of them.

In the field of New Testament studies, much work has been done by the German theologians of the school known as *Kreuzetheologie* (The Theology of the Cross). Starting with Luther's "theology of the cross" and with Barth's theology of the humility of God, these theologians have tried to understand the nature of God as it was revealed in the cross of Jesus. Their conclusion was that God's participation in the suffering of the world should be taken with the utmost seriousness. In this line of thought, the most important works to mention are those of Jürgen Moltmann, especially *The Crucified God, The Future of Creation,* and *God in Creation.*[19] Also deserving mention here is the work of Paul Fiddes of the University of Oxford, *The Creative Suffering of God,*[20] and from the other side of the world, *The Theology of the Pain of God,* written by the Japanese author Kazoh Kitanori.[21]

The evangelical theologian John R. W. Stott, in his book *The Cross of Christ,* has written a sub-chapter entitled "The Pain of God."[22] After his survey of both the theological and the biblical material, Stott concludes: "There is good biblical evidence that God not only suffered in Christ, but that God in Christ suffers with his people still."[23]

The image of a God who is completely detached from His creation, unmoved by what happens in His creation, is contrary to what we find in the Bible. It is enough to direct our attention to the images used by Jesus and by Paul. Jesus taught His disciples to think in terms of a vine and its branches. He, Jesus, is the vine; they, the apostles, are the branches (John 15:1-5). In His prayer to His Father, Jesus extended this relationship to include the Father: "I in them, and Thou in Me, that they may be perfected in unity" (John 17:23). This is a real, organic unity, and in it, there is a sharing of both joy and sorrow, both happiness and pain. Jesus Himself gave us the best illustration of this unity and sharing in His pronouncement of what will take place at the last judgment: "to the extent that you did it to one of these brothers of Mine, even the least of them, you did it to Me" (Matt. 25:40). The same identification in suffering was expressed by the risen Lord on the road to Damascus, when He stopped Saul, who was busy persecuting the church, and asked him: "Saul, Saul, why are you persecuting *Me*?" (Acts 9:4, italics mine).

In his own writings, Paul simply expanded the teaching of his Lord, using closely related images. In 1 Corinthians, the image of the head and the body is extensively developed: Christ is the Head, and Christians are the members of the body. This is the image of a living organism in which common participation and common sharing is the rule of life. Paul pointed specifically to the fact that "if one member suffers, all the members suffer with it; if one member is honored, all the members rejoice with it" (1 Cor. 12:26). Certainly, we can also interpret this text to mean that if the members of the body suffer, *the Head also suffers with them.*

Such an extension of the meaning of the body image is legitimized by the other metaphor used by Paul to describe the relationship between Christ and His people: the metaphor of the bridegroom and bride, or of the husband and wife. Hence, Christ "loved the church and gave Himself up for her" (Eph. 5:25). However, the work of Christ is not yet finished. He is still involved in giving Himself up for her in the work of sanctification, perfecting her until He can finally present her to Himself "holy and blameless" in heaven (5:27).

In this last image, we notice that the driving force is the love of Christ and of God. Love means involvement, participation, sharing, self-giving, and supremely, the yearning for union. The New Testament images of the relationship of God with His people do not leave any room for a detached or apathetic God. Contrariwise, they give us the assurance that He participates with us in our pilgrimage, in our tribulations and struggles until we reach His goal for our existence. Only when we are sure that *He* participates *with us* in our sufferings are we ready to consider the whole scope of *our* participation *with Him* in fulfilling *His* purposes in history.

We are now prepared to return to our analysis of the Corinthian correspondence. Our focus has been on the theme of the believer's participation in the sufferings of Christ. For more information on this theme, we can go directly to the Second Epistle of Paul to the Corinthians, because it is there that he developed this topic in an extended way. Let us begin with Paul's words in 1:3-7:

> Blessed be the God and Father of our Lord Jesus Christ, the Father of mercies and God of all comfort; who comforts us in all our affliction so that we may be able to comfort those who are in any affliction with the comfort with which we ourselves are comforted by God. For just as the sufferings of Christ are ours in abundance, so also our comfort is abundant through Christ. But if

we are afflicted, it is for your comfort and salvation; or if we are
comforted, it is for your comfort, which is effective in the patient
enduring of the same sufferings which we also suffer; and our
hope for you is firmly grounded, knowing that as you are sharers
of our sufferings, so also you are sharers of our comfort.

What is the meaning of the phrase "sufferings of Christ" in this
text and in general in Paul's writings? The basic fact with which we
should start is that when Paul addressed the issue of God's solution for
the sin of mankind, he always spoke about "*the death* of Christ" or
simply about Christ being "given up" or Christ "giving Himself up"
for us. Paul did not insist upon the sufferings of Christ *on the cross*. It
was *the death* of Christ, the fact that He replaced us or substituted
Himself on our behalf, that produced our salvation from the
condemnation we deserved for our sins.

When Paul talked about Christ's *sufferings*, on the other hand, he
spoke in such a way that they appear to be something contemporary
with us. For example, when Paul wrote that we are co-heirs with
Christ "if indeed we suffer with Him" (Rom. 8:17), he could not have
meant that we should somehow endeavor to enter into the sufferings
that Christ had already endured on the cross. Paul *could* say, however,
that when Christ died, we all died (2 Cor. 5:14; cf. Rom. 6:3-11),
because God included us in His death. But "suffering with Christ" is a
condition of becoming co-heirs with Christ, and if we are to suffer
"with Christ," we can do so only if His sufferings are
contemporaneous with ours. In 2 Corinthians 1:5, Paul could
meaningfully say that "the sufferings of Christ are ours in abundance,"
only if somehow the sufferings that he experienced were suffered by
Christ with him; or, more exactly, if Christ suffered those tribulations
through him, in his body, due to the fact that Christ lives in him. It is
only in this sense that we can also understand what Paul meant when
he wrote that in his own body he completes "that which is lacking in
Christ's afflictions . . . on behalf of His body (which is the church)"
(Col. 1:24).

Whatever the full meaning of this entire statement might be, here I
merely want to point out that, according to the Apostle Paul, these
afflictions of Christ are going on right now, and they must be
supplemented or completed. Hence, the "sufferings of Christ"
mentioned in 2 Corinthians 1:5 definitely cannot be identical to the act
that took place two thousand years ago on the cross at Calvary.
Christ's suffering on the cross was an act that was once and for all,

complete, with no need of something being added to it. Therefore, these sufferings or afflictions of Christ, that are contemporary with us and in which we are called to participate, must be completely dissociated from what happened at Calvary. Moreover, they must have a different purpose and meaning; this is exactly what we have to discover in our investigation of the Pauline literature.

In 2 Corinthians 1:3-7, the term "comfort" was used by Paul to mean deliverance, revival, re-making, and, in a word, salvation. Thus, when Paul wrote that "if we are afflicted, it is for your comfort and salvation," he was only using the Hebraic strategy of repetition with the purpose of emphasizing an idea; what he wanted to stress was that there was indeed a sense in which Paul's afflictions work for their salvation. The question is in what sense his afflictions work for their salvation. We know that for Paul, salvation is both an accomplished fact (Eph. 2:8-9) and a continuing process (1 Cor. 1:18); in addition, it is also an eschatological event (Rom. 5:10). Salvation is much more than the reparation of what went wrong in the fall. Salvation is the whole process by which God's final purpose with mankind is completed. It is in this process that Paul has a role to play with his entire ministry of preaching, teaching, suffering, and self-sacrifice. When he said to the Corinthians, "I will most gladly spend and be expended *for your souls*," he was referring precisely to this role that God had given him (2 Cor. 12:15, italics mine).

Let us go through 2 Corinthians to find out what things the sufferings of Paul, which are the sufferings of Christ in his body, are said to achieve. To begin with, we see that the comfort which flows from Paul's sufferings to the Corinthians "is effective in the patient enduring of the same sufferings which we also suffer" (1:6). Commentators remind us that we do not have any information about the persecution of the Christians in Corinth at that time. While it appears that there may have been no dramatic instances of persecution worth recording, we have sufficient reason to believe that in an area with so much anti-Christian sentiment, many of the Christians in Corinth did experience violent repercussions for their faith and because they were different from their society. For this reason, Paul felt justified to acknowledge that they suffer as he does. But there is something more here. The Corinthians join Paul in his sufferings and help him *through their prayers*. The favor of deliverance was repeatedly given to Paul "through the prayers of many" (1:11). Therefore, the lesson he had learned, "that we should not trust in ourselves, but in God who raises the dead," became their experience, as well, so that they all gave praises to God alone (1:9). This is one clear way in which Paul's sufferings work for their comfort and salvation.

In the second chapter, Paul shows them another way in which his sufferings work for others: "But thanks be to God, who always leads us in His triumph in Christ, and manifests through us the sweet aroma of the knowledge of Him in every place" (2:14). Adding another important piece of information, Paul said that "among those who are being saved . . . [this is] an aroma from life to life" (2:15-16).

The phrase translated "leads us in His triumph," θριαμβεύοντι ἡμᾶς, is difficult to understand and to translate. Its most obvious meaning is "to lead (as a prisoner of war) in one's triumphal procession," and hence, "to expose to shame and disgrace." Victor Furnish agrees with P. Marshall that "it is most likely that the allusion intends to call up the picture of public humiliation and shame. . . . If so, the meaning here is not unlike that in 1 Corinthians 4:9b, where, in an allusion to the theater, Paul describes the apostles' sufferings as "a spectacle (θέατρον) to the world."[24] The meaning is best given by Philip Hughes:

> The picture he conjures up is that of the splendor of a Roman triumphal procession, in which the victorious general led his captives as a public spectacle before the multitudes of onlookers. We who were God's former enemies (Rom. 5:10) have been overcome and taken captive by Him and are led and displayed by Him to the world, not just on one passing occasion, but every day and everywhere. From justification until glorification the redeemed sinner is on exhibition as a trophy of divine grace. But Paul is speaking more particularly of himself and his apostolic ministry. For him, the triumphal procession in Christ's train began at Damascus and continued without cessation through all his labors and journeying to his martyrdom at Rome."[25]

The specific purpose of this life of suffering is important for our study. It is through a life of suffering that God "manifests" the knowledge of Himself, because this kind of life best illustrates who God is, what His nature is, and especially how He loves people. And for those "who are being saved," this increased knowledge of God is "an aroma from life to life," because the greater the knowledge of God, the more abundant is His life in them.

In chapter 3, Paul continues to explain the ministry of the apostles, this time "as servants of the new covenant" (3:6), setting up a comparison with the ministry of Moses. Moses' face reflected the glory of the old covenant, but it was a fading glory (3:7, 11). In contrast with that fading glory, Paul writes that "we all, with unveiled face, are reflecting like mirrors the glory of the Lord, and are being transformed into the same image from glory to glory, just as from the Lord, the Spirit" (3:18, Jerusalem Bible). I support the view of commentators such as W. L. Knox,[26] Dupont, Allo, and W. C. van Unnik,[27] who argue that the middle participle κατοπτριζόμενοι should be translated "reflecting as a mirror does." Paul was consistent in what he said. In chapter two, he stated that through the suffering apostle, God "manifests" the knowledge of Himself to other people. Now, in chapter 3, he states that God's servants "reflect" the glory of God.

This train of thought is continued in the fourth chapter of 2 Corinthians where Paul tells us that the problem with unbelieving people is that their minds have been blinded by "the god of this world," in order that "they might not see the light of the gospel of the glory of Christ, who is the image of God" (4:4). To enable unbelievers to see His light, God "has shone in our hearts to give the light of the knowledge of the glory of God in the face of Christ" (4:6). Immediately after he made this statement, Paul embarked upon a description of the sufferings of the apostles. These sufferings consist in "always carrying about in the body the dying of Jesus" (4:10). Once again, we see that the sufferings of the apostles are the sufferings of Jesus! The culminating point of this passage is in Paul's statement of the purpose of suffering: "that the life of Jesus also may be manifested in our body" (4:10).

Unbelievers cannot understand the gospel. No logical arguments will work with them, because their minds have been blinded. We are reminded of what Mark told us in his Gospel: only when the centurion saw how Jesus died, "he said, 'Truly this man was the Son of God!' " (Mk. 15:39). His eyes were opened when he saw the way Jesus died. In the same way, when other Christians are "delivered over to death for Jesus' sake," Christ is "manifested" in their "mortal flesh" (2 Cor. 4:11).

We should also remember Jesus' words to Pilate: He had come into this world in order "to bear witness (μαρτυρήσω) to the truth" (John 18:37). It is clear from the entire context of John's Gospel that Jesus (who on the previous evening had said to Thomas, "I am . . . the truth"; 14:6) made His witness (μαρτυρία) by dying (His martyrdom).

Hence, in the witness of suffering and dying for the gospel, the truth shines in such a way that it penetrates the blinded eyes of unbelievers; they regain their ability to see and their minds regain the ability to comprehend. But Paul understood that this process must be repeated again and again by the ministers of Christ, as long as there are still unbelievers who cannot otherwise regain their sight.

Paul concludes this description of the function of martyrdom with the words, "so death works in us, but life in you" (2 Cor. 4:12). The sufferings of the servants of Christ do not *produce* "life"; rather, the life is "the light of the knowledge of the glory of God in the face of Christ" (4:6; cf. John 1:4, "In Him was life, and the life was the light of men."). The only question remaining to be answered is how that life can be *manifested* to unbelievers, but we have already learned God's solution to this problem. When one accepts to manifest the life of Jesus, then one accepts to die for Jesus' sake.

Paul's entire discussion, begun in the first chapter of Second Corinthians, about the purpose of the cross of Jesus and about the suffering and dying of the ministers of Jesus, reaches its climax in 2 Corinthians 4:15: "For all things are for your sakes, that the grace which is spreading to more and more people may cause the giving of thanks to abound to the glory of God." Most commentators agree that the phrase "all things" refers to all the sufferings of the ministers of Christ described in the previous verses and chapters. Although the syntax of the verse is difficult, one thing is clear: all these sufferings are for the purpose of spreading the grace of God. Theologians concur that in Paul's writings there are two kinds of grace: saving grace and enabling grace. Both originate in the cross of Christ, and Paul had both of them in mind here in 2 Corinthians 4:15. The grace of God in this passage is a saving grace, because it opens the eyes of unbelievers and brings them to the saving knowledge of Christ. It is also an enabling grace, because the whole church is brought into participation with the suffering ones by means of the church's prayers for them; for this reason, the victory belongs to all of them. In addition, the entire body acquires a stronger trust in God, and they consequently thank God and give Him the glory all the more (2 Cor. 1:11; 4:1-15). There is, indeed, more life in the church because of the suffering of the martyrs.

To summarize what we have learned so far from Paul's discussion about the purpose of his sufferings, which are, in fact, the sufferings of Christ since Christ lives in him, let us enumerate what the sufferings

of Paul are said to do:
- they manifest through him the sweet aroma of the knowledge of Christ in every place;
- they reflect the glory of the Lord as in a mirror;
- they enable unbelievers to see the light of the knowledge of the glory of God in the face of Christ;
- they manifest the life of Jesus in and through a mortal body or flesh;
- they spread the saving and the enabling grace of God in Christ;
- they cause the church to experience the life of Christ more abundantly.

What Christ achieved on the cross is God's work unique and complete. But what was achieved at Calvary now has to be delivered to humanity worldwide, and exactly this is done by people who accept suffering and self-sacrifice for Christ and His gospel as their way of life.

Martyrdom in the Corinthian Letters

Throughout his missionary journeys, Paul encountered death many times. Suffice it to mention the stoning that left him for dead in Lystra (Acts 14:19-20) and the situation that made him despair of life in Asia (2 Cor. 1:8-12). Due to these repeated experiences that brought him so close to death, Paul was forced to consider the issue of dying for Christ and His gospel and to offer an adequate explanation of its special significance. Let us look specifically at what Paul says in the Corinthian correspondence about dying as a martyr.

Here is what he writes in 1 Corinthians 4:9 and 13: "For, I think, God has exhibited us apostles last of all, as men condemned to death; because we have become a spectacle to the world, both to angels and to men. . . . when we are slandered, we try to conciliate; we have become as the scum of the world, the dregs of all things, even until now." Most commentators understand that being exhibited "last of all, as men condemned to death" suggests the festivals in which the last ones in the procession are either the gladiators or those who will simply be thrown to the beasts.[28] The editors of the New International Version have translated it as, "God has put us apostles on display at the end of the procession, like men condemned to die in the arena" (4:9). The image is that of a conquering general who returns to Rome in triumph, bringing with him, at the end of his armies, the captives who will die in the arena as a spectacle for the Roman public. In either case, the metaphor is intended to show the utter humiliation of the apostles. They are a θέατρον, meaning literally, "what one sees at a theater," i.e., at a play or a spectacle. Paul adds that the spectacle is for the whole cosmos, both for angels and for men.

This description reminds us of Job, whose sufferings were also watched by all the "children of God," as well as by Satan.[29] It is a classical description of martyrdom and it has been used by would-be martyrs around the globe as an inspiration, an encouragement, and a model. We should observe that for Paul, God was the one who determined that the apostles should be martyrs. Paul realized that this was their basic call and function. Martyrdom did not signify some unfortunate turn of events that might tragically come upon them. Paul, of course, knew that it was the commission given by Jesus to His apostles. Hence, the details of Paul's description of the apostolic martyrs "are clear reflections of the teaching of Jesus."[30]

Two words in this description must retain our attention. Paul writes that the apostles "have become as the scum of the world" (περικαθάρματα) and "the dregs of all things" (περίψημα). Here is how F. F. Bruce explains them:

> The περικαθάρματα are the impurities removed and thrown away when a vessel is cleaned, but the word was used in a derivative sense of the "scapegoat" type of victim on to which the guilt of a community was unloaded, and this victim might be a human being. If Paul is using the word in this sense, it would fit in well with his comparison of the apostles to the condemned criminals in the amphitheater.
>
> **the offscouring of all things:** Gk., περίψεμα that which is scraped off (περίψαω), has a similar meaning to περικαθάρματα both primarily and derivatively, "especially of those criminals, generally the vilest of their class, whose blood was shed to expiate the sins of the nation and to avert the wrath of the gods" (J. B. Lightfoot, on Ignatius, *Eph.* 8. 1, where Ignatius calls himself the περίψεμα of his Christian friends, their substitutionary sacrifice; cf. *Eph.* 18.1, where he calls himself the περίψεμα of the cross, its devoted slave).[31]

It is instructive to add to this the comments of C. K. Barrett:

> It is very difficult to assess the precise meaning, and especially the precise nuance, of the words *scapegoats* (περικαθάρματα) and

scum (περίψεμα). The former is built upon the root meaning "to cleanse," and may refer simply to the filth cast out in the process of cleansing. The word (or a simple form of it, περικαθάρμα; see parallels in Lucian given by Betz, p. 67, note 7) was also used however to denote the means by which a people or city might be morally or religiously cleansed, thus for a human sacrifice (details are given by Lietzmann); but since it became customary for the most worthless of men (cf. verse 9, *men under sentence of death*) to be used for this purpose the word in this connection also became a term of abuse; Epictetus (III. xxii. 78), for example, says that Priam "begot fifty rascals (περικαθάρματα)." Its one use in the LXX (Prov. xxi 18; Hebrew, *kopher*) suggests that is did not altogether lose its sense of sacrificial cleansing; *scapegoats* may perhaps convey the double meaning of despised persons who nevertheless perform a vicarious service for the community. This would accord with Paul's view of his mission (cf. Col. i.24).

Scum is a word with similar meaning, though the sense of sacrifice and atonement is perhaps not so easy to establish (it may occur at *Tobit* v. 19, but this is disputed); hence the rendering here. It should also be noted however that Ignatius uses the word in another sense. At *Ephesians* viii, 1, he uses it to say to his readers, "I am your meanest, most devoted servant"; at xviii, 1, "My spirit is an abject and devoted servant of the cross" (see Lightfoot's notes). Ignatius may have derived his use of the word from Paul, and it would suit the context of 1 Corinthians iv if Paul were here to describe himself in his apostolic office as the servant of all men (taking περίψεμα as masculine); on the whole, however, though with some hesitation, we may retain *scum of the earth* (taking περικαθάρματα as neuter).[32]

The comments on these two words show us how deeply involved the descriptions that Paul gives to the sufferings of the apostles truly are. A clarification is needed here regarding the idea that Paul might have attributed an expiatory function to his sacrificial living and dying for the gospel.

All the way through the Corinthian correspondence, Paul went out of his way to point out that he had nothing of his own but only what he had received from Christ, by God's mercy and grace (e.g., 2 Cor. 4:7). The work of Christ is of such a nature that no man can boast before God (1 Cor. 1:29). The apostles do not *produce* but only exhibit, manifest, and reflect to others what comes to them from God in Christ (e.g., 2 Cor. 2:14; 3:18; 4:3-6). The apostle is weak for this very purpose in order that everyone may see that the power of salvation is not from him but from God (2 Cor. 4:7; 12:9-10). There is absolutely nothing in all of Paul's writings which would indicate that his sufferings and his dying for Christ would have expiatory or atoning value, either in the Corinthian correspondence or in the other epistles.

Let us continue, then, to analyze what Paul himself said, without ambiguity, about the multiple purposes of his sufferings and martyrdom. Why did he write about these issues? "I do not write these things to shame you, but to admonish you as my beloved children" (1 Cor. 4:14). The word νουθετεῖν is a Pauline one (cf. Acts 20:31; Rom. 15:14; Col. 1:28; 3:16; 1 Thess. 5:12, 14; 2 Thess. 3:15). It has a rich and significant meaning, namely, to teach in a directive way, to rebuke, to warn, and to challenge. Paul desired to do this as would a father training his children. The climax is found in these words, "I exhort you therefore, be imitators of me" (1 Cor. 4:16). We should notice that this exhortation comes at the end of a passionate portrayal of the sufferings and martyrdom of the apostles. *This* is what Paul called the Corinthian Christians to imitate! "For this reason," in order to bring them to this type of living, Paul had sent Timothy to them, to "remind you of my ways which are in Christ" (4:17). Sacrificial living is both what Christ Himself demonstrated in His own earthly living and what "life in Christ," the true Christian way of living, really is.

Why should one accept a way of life that for most people seems so dreadful? Simply because this kind of life, lived in apparent weakness, is the only truly powerful life. Far from being a sign of His weakness, as the world interpreted it, the sacrificial death and resurrection of His Only Son was an extraordinary manifestation of God's power (1:18-25). It follows then that whoever enters into the kingdom of God has at his disposal this same power of God that raised Christ from the dead; that is, the believer is given the same power in order to carry out the same kind of activity—the giving of oneself to a life of self-sacrifice and even to death for others (4:19-20). The Corinthians had wanted to be kings. They had wanted to have the power that comes with reigning (4:8). Paul showed them that the true power, the power of the kingdom of God, manifests itself in the "weakness" of the cross of Christ and in the self-sacrifice of the imitators of Christ.

The next depiction of the martyrdom of the apostles is found in 2 Corinthians 4:8-12. We have already analyzed it and have seen that its outcome was the spread of grace—the spread of the salvation already procured by Christ on the cross.

There is a third description of the afflictions of the apostle and it is located in 2 Corinthians 6:3-10. At the conclusion of this dramatic narration, Paul indicates another outcome of his suffering: "as poor yet making many rich, as having nothing yet possessing all things" (6:10). We can capture the exhilarating feeling Paul has when he says that he is making many people rich, if we go on to chapter eight and listen to him speak about the special "grace of God" that was given to the Macedonians. They were so utterly poor and were going through such "a great ordeal of affliction" that Paul simply overlooked them, when it came to the collection for the saints in Jerusalem (8:2). But they begged Paul "with much entreaty for the grace (χάριν) of partnership (κοινωνίαν) in the service (διακονίας) of the saints" (8:4, literal translation).

Paul calls giving to the saints out of one's personal poverty a "grace." Paul sent Titus to Corinth to "bring also to completion this act of grace on [their] part" (8:6, NIV). Now he urges them again to abound or "excel in this grace of giving" (8:7, NIV). For what reason? "For you know the grace of our Lord Jesus Christ, that though He was rich, yet for your sake He became poor, that you through His poverty might become rich" (8:9, NASB). Strange grace, indeed, that someone becomes poor in order to enrich others! But that is the grace of Christ, and Christians have to learn to practice this grace by becoming poor so that they might enrich others! It is the lesson that Paul learned from Christ. In accordance with Christ's example, Paul accepted a life of afflictions and of poverty in order to make many people rich. That is why he was able to write to the Corinthians, "Be imitators of me, just as I also am of Christ" (1 Cor. 11:1).

Paul invites them to imitate the example of Christ and that of his own life after he talks about this strange attitude of unselfishness: "Let no one seek his own good, but that of his neighbor. . . . just as I also please all men in all things, not seeking my own profit, but the profit of the many, that they may be saved" (1 Cor. 10:24, 33).

How did Paul come to learn this attitude or, to use his own language, this grace? He tells us the story in 2 Corinthians 5:13-17. He begins by saying that a life like his, characterized by constant affliction and constant dying, may be considered by some to be sheer madness. But if that is the case, then he is mad for God. On the other hand, his way of life may also be one of a "sound mind," and if that is true, then "it is for you" (5:13). Then Paul explains himself. It is the love of Christ that "constrains" him to live such a life. Paul refers to the love of Christ as he saw it on the cross at Calvary. Paul meditated on the meaning of that love on the cross and came to see it as the most unselfish act that has ever taken place on this planet. He knew that when the first man fell, he placed himself in the center of the world. Man became a selfish, self-centered being. With His absolutely unselfish act of dying on behalf of the selfish creatures of mankind, Christ "died for all, that they who live should no longer live for themselves, but for Him who died and rose again on their behalf" (5:15). If we look carefully at the explanatory links between this verse and the following two verses, we can see that "the new creature" of verse 17 is the one achieved by Christ by His death described in verse 15; "the new creature" is a person who stops living for self, a person who gives up his self-centeredness. Constrained by the love of Christ on the cross, he lives for Christ and, consequently, for other people.

Because of this radical transformation under the cross, Paul was able to live a life of poverty in order to enrich many others. As a result of this transformation, he stopped seeking his own profit and began living for the profit of many. He saw in the selfless act of Jesus the most attractive model he could ever find, and that is why he decided to be an imitator of Christ.

The most extensive of all descriptions of Paul's afflictions is offered in 2 Corinthians 11:23 through 12:10. Instead of my own remarks on Paul's staggering list of unspeakable sufferings that he had endured in the long course of his ministry for Christ and the gospel, I will cite John Chrysostom:

> The martyr dies once for all: but that blessed saint, in his one body and one soul endured so many perils as were enough to disturb even a soul of adamant; and what things all the saints together have suffered in so many bodies, those all he himself endured in one. He entered into the world as if in a race-course, and stripped himself of all, and so made a noble stand; for he knew the fiends that were wrestling with him. Wherefore also he shone forth brightly at once from the beginning, from the very starting-post, and even to the end he continued the same; yea, rather, he even increased the intensity if his pursuit as he drew nearer to the prize.[33]

The conclusions that Paul drew from this last presentation of his afflictions demand special attention. He started the First Epistle to the Corinthians by describing "God's weakness" in the cross of His Son, a weakness of self-sacrifice that turned out to be God's strength and power. Now Paul tells us about his own weakness and about what

Jesus taught him: "My grace is sufficient for you, for My power is perfected in weakness" (12:9a); Paul then adds, "Most gladly, therefore, I will rather boast about my weaknesses, that the power of Christ may dwell in me " (12:9b). The Apostle Paul knew that he did not have any power of his own. Rather, he had learned that the greatest thing a man can obtain is the power of Christ dwelling in him; and Christ's power is the power of living, of suffering, and of dying for others.

There is yet another thing that must be emphasized here. Paul related his weaknesses along with the insults, the distresses, the persecutions, and the difficulties that he suffered "for Christ's sake" (12:10). Paul never purposefully sought these things. His only preoccupation was the cause of Christ, the spreading of Christ's gospel. The sufferings came to him as a consequence of his pursuit after the purposes of Christ. This fact is very important to underline, because it is too easy to miss it and to seek the sufferings deliberately, believing that there is something special in suffering for the sake of suffering itself. We shall see how this anomaly will unfortunately develop in the centuries to follow.

The impression we might get from Paul's lengthy narration of his own sufferings is that he relates them in order to defend himself and his ministry. However, in 2 Corinthians 12:19, he specifically denies this, saying that he has not been defending himself; rather, these stories were intended for their edification. Everything Paul does, suffers or writes is for the sake of Christ, for the sake of the gospel, and for the sake of building up the church of Christ.

The issue of martyrdom also surfaces in 1 Corinthians 15:29-33, in these two phrases: "baptized for the dead," and "I fought with the wild beasts at Ephesus." The discussion in this entire passage dwells on the fact that the dead will one day be resurrected. Some in Corinth denied that there will ever be such an event, and Paul here strongly argues in favor of it. In the course of his long and passionate discourse, Paul brings forward two logical arguments: First, if there will be no resurrection, why are some people "baptized for the dead"? What would they gain from this baptism if the hope of a resurrection was empty and misguided? Secondly, if there will be no resurrection, why is he, Paul, in danger every hour, why does he die daily, and why did he even fight with the wild beasts in Ephesus?

Let us begin with the baptism for the dead. Most commentators take this to mean that the Corinthian believers practiced a ritual in

which some people were baptized on behalf of their deceased friends
or relatives. This theory supposes that Paul did not approve of this
practice, but he nevertheless used it as an argument to support his
point about the resurrection. His argument was that this practice has a
rationale only if there is, in fact, a future for the dead; only if the dead
will one day be raised, can someone else's baptism on their behalf help
them to attain a resurrection to everlasting life. The problem, though,
is that no such practice is known to have existed in Corinth or
anywhere else. If it had existed, Paul would certainly have fought
against it. Moreover, if it had existed in Corinth, and Paul did not
oppose it but used it as an argument for the resurrection of the dead,
most certainly it would have continued and we would have heard more
about it.

Fortunately, there is another explanation for Paul's mention of
baptism for the dead, and it is found in martyrdom. Jesus had used the
word "baptism" to signify His death on two occasions. In Luke 12:50,
Jesus said, "I have a baptism to undergo," and in Mark 10:38, He
asked James and John, "Are you able . . . to be baptized with the
baptism with which I am baptized?" The French commentator F.
Godet argues that:

> under the influence of such sayings, there was formed in the
> primitive church a new expression such as that used here by the
> apostle, to denote the bloody death of martyrdom. The words "for
> the dead," would thus signify: to be baptized, not as the believer is
> with the baptism of water to enter into the church of the living, but
> to enter into that of the dead, the word dead being chosen in
> contrast to the church on the earth and to bring out the heroism of
> that martyr-baptism which leads to life only through communion
> with the dead. Thereby the article ὑπὲρ before νεκρῶν is fully
> explained; such baptized ones certainly form a class of Christians
> by themselves.[34]

The Greek commentator Spiros Zodhiates strongly argues for this
interpretation of the phrase, as well. With his intimate knowledge of
the Greek language, he interprets the phrase to mean either:

> "baptized over the dead," that is to say, solemnly admitted
> publicly into the visible church of Christ, as if the dead bodies of
> those who were similarly admitted into the church before them
> were lying beneath their feet. Metaphorically it means in the
> prospect of death and as a continuance of the testimony of those
> who have heroically died for the faith. Or "baptized in the

prospect of death."[35]

To these statements I want to add that in 1 Corinthians, Paul employed the term "baptism" several times with quite a variety of senses. In 1:13, he asks if anyone had been "baptized in the name of Paul." In 10:2, he writes about the people of Israel in the wilderness being "baptized into Moses in the cloud and in the sea." Then, in 12:13, he states that "by one Spirit we were all baptized into one body." So we see that for Paul, the concept of baptism was very fluid, capable of many uses. It should not surprise us, then, if he also used it in the sense in which it was used by his Master, namely, to designate martyrdom. Hence, the only linguistic problem we find is that in every other case, Paul phrased it as baptism "into" ($\epsilon\iota\varsigma$), whereas in this case, he formulated it as baptism "for" ($\dot{\upsilon}\pi\grave{\epsilon}\rho$). The reason may simply have been this: Paul could not theologically say "baptism into the dead" or "into the death." He wanted to indicate that he meant the "baptism of death"; but at the same time, he also needed to use this idea as part of his argument for the resurrection. He chose, therefore, to call it "the baptism for the dead," that is, the baptism that conveys or transfers a person into the ranks of the dead.

If we accept this explanation for the phrase "baptism for the dead," then we can see Paul's natural and logical transition to the question in the next verse: "Why are we also in danger every hour" (15:30)? Paul immediately adds that he is not only in constant jeopardy but he, in fact, dies daily. In the previous sentence, he had pointed to the martyrs and had asked why they would ever accept martyrdom if the dead will never be resurrected. Now, he directs their thoughts to his own situation and asks, "Why do I also face martyrdom constantly? My own daily martyrdom has meaning only if there is a resurrection of the dead." In this way, the whole text has both a clear meaning and a logical connection.

The other question in this text had to do with Paul's fight with the wild beasts in Ephesus. Was this an actual experience or was he speaking metaphorically? Most modern commentators consider this to be a figurative speech. However, a long line of theologians, beginning in the second century and coming down into modernity, have read it literally. They have reasoned that although Paul was a Roman citizen, he had somehow been condemned to the arena to face the wild beasts, but in a miraculous way, had been saved from death.

In an article published in 1923, C. R. Bowen convincingly brought together all the arguments for a real experience of Paul in the arena at

Ephesus.[36] I believe that Bowen has successfully proved the case. Only a real experience could provide Paul with his needed argument in this passage. In effect, Paul was asking the Corinthians, "If there will be no resurrection, why would I accept to face constant, deadly dangers, like the one I faced in Ephesus, when I was thrown to the wild beasts in the arena? What would it profit me? What would I gain?" Furthermore, based on what we have learned so far, I think it would be reasonable and justifiable to paraphrase Paul's question like this: "If there is indeed a resurrection from the dead and if I die daily, eventually suffering the death of a martyr, *what is my gain in that case?*" This last question then prompts us to ask: What was Paul's motivation for living a life of self-sacrifice and for accepting the prospect of martyrdom?

We have seen that Paul's way of life achieved very many things for the sake of Christ, for the sake of the gospel, and for the sake of the church. We have also seen that such a life is the closest imitation of Christ Himself and that the power of Christ is present only in this kind of life. These things might be considered sufficient reasons or motivations for accepting a life of suffering and self-sacrifice. But as we examined Paul's letters to the Corinthians, we became aware of the fact that, while these reasons are real and incredibly important, they are not sufficient. Paul himself said that if only for this life we have put our trust or hope in Christ, then "we are of all men most to be pitied" (1 Cor. 15:19). There must be a life beyond this one, a life in which we will harvest the rewards for our constant dying on earth, thereby making a sacrificial life worth living. This was the whole purpose of Paul's great discourse on the resurrection of the body in 1 Corinthians 15. For this reason, the chapter concludes with these words: "Therefore, my beloved brethren, be steadfast, immovable, always abounding in the work of the Lord, knowing that your toil is not in vain in the Lord" (15:58).

In the Thessalonian correspondence, we learned that we have been predestined and called to share in the glory of Christ. However, in order to be found worthy of God and worthy of His kingdom, we must fight our way to that destiny through many tribulations. We must make sure that at the coming of Christ, we will be found spotless and holy, without stain or blemish. Only in a condition of holiness and purity can we be found qualified and worthy of sharing in the glory of Christ.

The Apostle Paul's Teaching on Rewards in Heaven

I am tempted to assert that the most succinct summary of Paul's entire message is found in 1 Corinthians 2:7: "We speak God's wisdom in a mystery, the hidden wisdom, which God predestined before the ages to our glory." Before time began, God predestined us for glory. "God's wisdom" is the way in which He is going to achieve this final goal with His elect. It first of all involved the crucifixion of "the Lord of glory" (2:8). The question that concerns us here pertains to the actual content of "our glory," and I believe that the answer is given in verse 9: "our glory" will be "all that God has prepared for those who love Him." The things which have been prepared for us are so glorious, so amazing, and so wonderful that human "eye has not seen and ear has not heard" anything like them; they are things that the human mind cannot imagine or comprehend. Paul knew something about them because he had once been "caught up to the third heaven" and had "heard inexpressible words, which a man is not permitted to speak" (2 Cor. 12:2, 4). We may suppose that he did not only hear them with his ears, but he also saw them with his own eyes and beheld the indescribable beauty of heaven.

It should be noted that this vision of heaven had the same purpose and value for Paul as the vision given to Stephen had for him before he died the martyr's death. Calvin wrote that the vision took place "for the sake of Paul himself, for one who had such arduous difficulties awaiting him, enough to break a thousand hearts, required to be strengthened by special means that he might not give way, but might persevere undaunted."[37] Philip Hughes adds the pertinent comment that this vision of heaven "must have exercised an incalculable influence on Paul's whole ministry and apostleship, providing, it may be, a key to his astonishing zeal and indefatigable labors through which untold blessing flowed not only to his own generation but to every subsequent generation in the history of the church."[38]

Indeed, it was that vision of heaven that inspired Paul and gave him the ultimate motivation for a life of suffering and martyrdom. We shall see more of this as we follow his arguments. Paul unambiguously taught the Corinthians that in heaven, there would be rewards for the works done by Christians on earth. "Each will receive his own reward (μισθὸν, pay) according to his own labor" (1 Cor. 3:8). This will happen on "the day" (3:13), short for "the Day of the Lord" or "at the coming of the Lord." On that day, each man's work will be tested by fire. It will be a test of quality. The works may prove to be either of "gold, silver, [and] precious stones, [or of] wood, hay, [and] straw" (3:12). If the works prove to be worthy, the man "shall receive a reward" (3:14). If the man's works prove to be worthless, "he shall suffer loss; but he himself shall be saved, yet so as through fire" (3:15). We are reminded that Paul wrote to the Thessalonians that they must be proven "worthy of the God who calls you" (1 Thess. 2:12), and "worthy of your calling" (2 Thess. 1:11). Now we see that at least a part of that worthiness will be determined by the quality of one's works. We are not told at this point what the rewards will be, but if we follow Paul's writing carefully, we will come to understand the content of the rewards, as well.

The first indication comes at the end of the same chapter: "So then let no one boast in men. For all things belong to you, whether Paul or Apollos or Cephas or the world or life or death or things present or things to come; all things belong to you, and you belong to Christ; and Christ belongs to God" (1 Cor. 3:21-23). Paul went out of his way to help us comprehend that the whole "cosmos," the whole universe belongs to the ones who belong to Christ. This was emphasized in the second letter, where Paul stated that although down here we are poor and have nothing, we nonetheless possess "all things" (2 Cor. 6:10). We are God's children, and all that the Father has, His children also have. However, they have not yet entered into the exercise of that ownership. To unravel the concept of inheritance, we need to jump ahead to Paul's Epistle to the Romans, where he makes it plain for us: "The Spirit Himself bears witness with our spirit that we are children of God, and if children, heirs also, heirs of God and fellow heirs with Christ, if indeed we suffer with Him in order that we may also be glorified with Him" (Rom. 8:16-17).

Three important things should be noticed here. First, the status of being heirs of God and co-heirs with Christ comes by natural right. It is in the very nature of a child of God to also be an heir of God and a partner with Christ in the inheritance, "the first-born among many brethren" (Rom. 8:29). Secondly, the actual possession of the inheritance is conditioned upon partnership with Christ in suffering. And thirdly, entering into the possession of the inheritance also means being "glorified with" Christ. With these points in mind, we now turn to the sixth chapter of 1 Corinthians.

In this passage, Paul is explaining the issue of Christians taking other Christians to court. In the first place, Paul wanted to teach them that they ought to appoint judges from among themselves to solve whatever problems may arise, and secondly, that they ought to lead pure, moral lives so that no such cases would ever appear among them. To support his admonitions, Paul reminds them of what the children of God will be after the coming of Christ. He then asks the Corinthians three questions, consisting of basic things that they should already know about their future heavenly existence:

1. "Or do you not know that the saints will judge the world?" (1 Cor. 6:2);
2. "Do you not know that we shall judge angels?" (6:3);
3. "Or do you not know that the unrighteous shall not inherit the kingdom of God?" (6:9).

After this third question, Paul enumerates a series of sins, repeating his earlier warning that they should not deceive themselves into believing that those who practice such sins "shall inherit the kingdom of God" (6:9-10). These three questions have to be taken together in order to see their total impact and meaning.

The kingdom of God is the eschatological situation in which the rule of God has been established over the entire cosmos. For the children of God to inherit the kingdom of God means for them to be put in charge over all of God's possessions—over the whole universe (Matt. 24:47). The inheritance includes the fact that "the saints will judge the world" (κόσμον), and that "we shall judge angels" (1 Cor. 6:2, 3). It is true that in the Corinthian context, Paul spoke of a judgment in the courts; but when he refers to the future judgment given to the saints (Dan. 7:22, 27), we must then understand the word "judge" in its other Hebrew meaning of "ruling" or of "exercising authority." This is because we know that in the New Testament, the final judgment belongs to God and to Christ. The judgment of the world and of the angels by the saints after the Second Coming of Christ is a beautiful picture of the children of God having been put in charge over the affairs of the kingdom of God; and this is the same as saying that they have inherited the kingdom of God.

We must add here what Paul writes in Colossians 3:23-24: "Whatever you do, do your work heartily, as for the Lord rather than for men; knowing that from the Lord you will receive the reward of the inheritance." This text completes the portrait and allows us to see the total picture of what Paul started to tell us in the third chapter of 1 Corinthians. We shall receive a reward for our good works, and this reward is the inheritance of the kingdom of God. To inherit the kingdom of God means to be put in charge of the affairs of the whole cosmos, as judges and rulers both of the material world and of the spiritual beings. Yet one can be saved and not receive any reward; one can be saved and not inherit the kingdom of God. This is due to the fact that the reward of ruling with Christ is received as a result of suffering with Christ (Rom. 8:17, confirmed by 2 Tim. 3:12) and of leading a moral life as a Christian here on earth (1 Cor. 6:9-10, confirmed by Eph. 5:5).

Let us make one thing eminently clear. All this teaching about rewards—and we have not gleaned all of it yet—is found in the Pauline letters side by side with the strongest teaching one could ever find about the grace of God, against any human boasting (see 1 Cor. 1:29-31; 4:7; 10:13; 15:10; 2 Cor. 3:5; 4:7; 9:8; 12:9). Paul could not have been more lucid than in the fourth chapter of Romans, where he explains that "the promise to Abraham or to his descendants that he would be heir of the world" was to be obtained "by faith," in order to be "in accordance with grace" (Rom. 4:13, 16). This was obviously the promise of the inheritance of the kingdom of God. Men and women cannot earn anything before God (4:2). Whatever we receive is by grace, by God's good pleasure to give all that He has to His beloved children.

There is something else that comes into the picture at this juncture, namely, the question whether a child of God is actually capable of handling the inheritance. In the Thessalonian correspondence, this capacity was expressed as the condition of being "worthy of the kingdom of God." Here, in the Corinthian correspondence, Paul uses the concept of *pleasing God.* Right from the beginning of the first letter, Paul writes that "Jesus Christ . . . shall also confirm you to the end," in order that they may be found "blameless in the day of our Lord Jesus Christ" (1 Cor. 1:8). Paul develops this concept at the end of chapter nine and at the beginning of chapter ten. The discussion is about Paul's ministry of preaching the gospel. In 1 Corinthians 9:18, he asks the question, "What then is my reward?" The commentators look for the answer to follow immediately but it does not. It comes only in verse 23: "I do all things for the sake of the gospel, that I may become a fellow partaker of it." The word συγκοινωνὸς is the key to a right interpretation. Barrett helps us here:

> Paul does not mean, "a partner with the gospel" (in the work of salvation; this would require αὐτῷ, not αὐτοῦ); nor does he mean

"one who shares in the work of (preaching) the gospel." His word means participation in (the benefits of) the gospel; and his participation is not guaranteed (cf. verse 27).[39]

How could the Apostle Paul be sure that he would have a share in the benefits of the gospel? Paul's answer is this: by running the race in such a way as to win the prize (9:24). To use another metaphor, Paul could be certain of his share in those benefits if he consistently kept his own body under strict discipline "lest possibly, after I have preached to others, I myself should be disqualified" (9:27). The key word in verse 27, translated here as "disqualified," is ἀδόκιμος. It comes from the verb δοκιμάζω, to test, or from the noun δοκιμή, testing, and it indicates the failure to pass the test. We shall return to this concept after we have examined Paul's entire argument in this Scripture, since Paul did not finish his idea where chapter nine ends. He continues in chapter ten with: "For I do not want you to be unaware, . . ." and gives us the example of the failure of the Israelites in the wilderness. They had just experienced God's deliverance from the bondage of Egypt. They had been baptized into Moses, and every day they ate "spiritual food" and drank "spiritual drink" (10:3-4; a quite obvious allusion to the Corinthians' own experience of redemption, baptism, and participation in the Lord's Supper). "Nevertheless, with most of them God was not well-pleased" (10:5). Because God was not pleased with them, they were disqualified and did not enter the promised land, which was to have been their inheritance. Instead, they perished in the wilderness. Only two of them, Joshua and Caleb, were pleasing to God and were qualified to enter into their own land.

Repeating himself twice, Paul makes it doubly clear in 1 Corinthians 10:6 and then in verse 11 that these things from Israel's history should serve us as examples or "types" (τύποι), as patterns for our own pilgrimage. Paul concludes this discussion by resuming his explication of the concept of testing, this time, though, using the word "temptation" (πειρασμός). His argument works like this: just as the Israelites were tested (and were disqualified) in the wilderness, you are being tested in order to be found worthy and qualified. However, you should know that no temptation (i.e., testing) will come to you beyond that which you can bear and beyond that which is common to mankind. Even more than this, since God is faithful to you, in each of your trials He will provide you with enough assistance to enable you to pass the test successfully (10:13). Nonetheless, the responsibility for qualification still remains your own.

By now, the answer to the question about the rewards for preaching the gospel should be obvious. Paul was looking forward to obtaining the prize of the inheritance in the New Canaan, that is, in the kingdom of God. He knew that, like the Israelites of the Old Testament, he was undergoing a variety of tests. Due to this awareness, Paul always took great care and struggled hard to pass all the tests in such a way that at the end, God could say to him, "I am well-pleased with you"; with that, the Lord would be declaring that Paul was indeed qualified to share in the final and glorious promise of the gospel, the inheritance in the kingdom of God.

We should take a closer look at the concept of testing. Paul clearly implies that it is God who initiates the test and who watches its outcome. God Himself found Paul δεδοκιμάσμεθα, tested and approved, and thus considered him worthy of being entrusted with the gospel (1 Thess. 2:4). God's main means of testing is through afflictions. Paul writes about the Macedonians being ἐν πολλῇ δοκιμῇ θλίψεως, "in a severe test of affliction" (2 Cor. 8:2; KJV). Not only afflictions, but even false teachings come as a test; their role is to bring to light those among the Corinthians who are οἱ δόκιμοὶ, the tested and approved, i.e., the genuine ones. The final test, however, will take place at the coming of Christ, when each man's work ἐστι τὸ πῦρ δοκιμάσει, will be tested and revealed by fire (1 Cor. 3:13).

We should not get the impression that this process of testing is limited to a verification of the quality of the one submitted to the test. On the contrary, the Scriptures tell us that testing has a further purpose and outcome. The very process by which one is tested produces in that person something of great importance, having eternal consequences. Paul was joined by the Apostles James and Peter in this teaching, and we must assess them together in this matter, which is key to our whole investigation.

We start with what Paul says on this topic in the Epistle to the Romans. Paul states that all men "fall short of the glory of God," and that this is the utmost damage produced by sin (Rom. 3:23). Consequently, the ultimate goal of the process of salvation is the restoration of the glory of God to the children of God (8:17-18, 21, 28-30). Throughout this process, tribulations and testings play a major and indispensable part. Following Paul's argument, as it is developed in the last part of chapter three and in chapter four, we go on to read that through the sacrifice of Christ, God has procured for us His justification, and we receive it by faith. Then, in chapter five, Paul looks at what comes after this act of God by which we are justified. Now that we have been introduced "by faith into this grace in which we stand," we look forward to its final outcome: "we exult in hope of the glory of God" (5:2). Hope in the New Testament always refers to the future; hope expresses the content of what we expect from the future. The most succinct expression of this is given by Paul in Colossians 1:27, "Christ in you, the hope of glory."

Thus, at the beginning of the process of salvation, we were reconciled with God; at the end of this process, we will receive the glory of God. In the interval, the process of salvation consists of a chain of events among which are tribulations that produce perseverance and endurance (Rom. 5:3). These, in their turn, will produce δοκιμή (translated by the NASB as "proven character," and by J. B. Phillips as "mature character" in 5:4). Finally, this δοκιμή provides the basis for our hope of glory. John Murray put it this way:

> These tribulations bear the fruit of patience. Patience is not the passive quality which we often associate with this word; it is endurance and constancy (cf. Matt. 10:22; Rom. 2:7; 2 Cor. 1:6; 2 Thess. 1:4; Heb. 10:36; James 1:3; 2 Pet. 1:6). this constancy works approvedness, the triedness which is proven by testing (cf. 2 Cor. 2:9; 8:2; 13:3; Phil. 2:22). And this approvedness works hope.[40]

John Stott cogently explains this process:

> If suffering leads to glory in the end, it leads to maturity meanwhile. Suffering can be productive, if we respond to it positively, and not with anger or bitterness. *We know* this, especially from the experience of God's people in every generation. *Suffering produces perseverance* (3, *hypomone*, endurance). We could not learn endurance without suffering, because without suffering there would be nothing to endure. Next, *perseverance* produces *character*. *Dokime* is the quality of a person who has been tested and has passed the test. It is "a mature character" (JBP), "the temper of the veteran as opposed to that of the raw recruit." Then the last link in the chain is that *character* produces *hope* (4), perhaps because the God who is developing our character in the present can be relied on for the future too.[41]

Peter speaks in the same fashion. He says that it is necessary to be "distressed by various trials (πειρασμοῖς)," in order that the proving (δοκίμιον) of our faith, which must be "tested (δοκιμαζομένου) by fire" just as gold is tested by fire, might have as its final result "praise and glory and honor at the revelation of Jesus Christ" (1 Peter 1:6-7).

James is more specific, giving us more details regarding this process. He starts by exhorting us to "consider it all joy" whenever we encounter various trials (πειρασμοῖς; James 1:2). He also gives us the reason for such a response, namely, because we know, or we ought to know, that these πειρασμοῖς represent "the testing" or proving (δοκίμιον) of our faith, which in turn "produces endurance" (κατεργάζεται ὑπομονήν; 1:3). The next sentence categorically states that the change produced in us is unquestionably a structural change: "And let endurance have its perfect result, that you may be perfect (τέλειον) and complete (ὁλόκληροι), lacking in nothing" (1:4). James develops this theme further in verse 12: "Blessed is a man who perseveres under trial (ὑπομένει πειρασμόν); for once he has been approved (δόκιμος γενόμενος), he will receive the crown of life, which the Lord has promised to those who love Him."

The final goal of this entire sequence is God's verdict given in one word: δόκιμος, approved. Paul exhorted Timothy, saying that this is the end result to which he must aim: "Be diligent to present yourself approved (δόκιμον) to God as a workman who does not need to be ashamed, handling accurately the word of truth" (2 Tim. 2:15). The opposite of the δόκιμος, the ἀδόκιμος, is the one who has been tested and rejected, the one who has failed the proving of his faith. This is exactly the condition that Paul feared; consequently, he declared to the Corinthian believers, "I buffet my body and make it my slave, lest possibly, after I have preached to others, I myself should be disqualified (ἀδόκιμος, 1 Cor. 9:27).

Through all the trials of life, and especially through the tribulations that come to us for the sake of Christ and His gospel, God's chief aim is to produce in us a special character. We still need to explore the nature of that character, and we shall do so in our study of Ephesians, Philippians, and Colossians. Up to this point, we have learned that the character formed in us by the testing of our faith must be well-pleasing to God; it must meet with His pleasure (1 Cor. 10:5; 1 Thess. 2:4). In other words, God has to be pleased with our character when we go up to meet Him and stand before the judgment seat of Christ. Hence, the following words of Paul provide a fitting conclusion to our discussion: "Therefore also we have as our ambition, whether at home or absent, to be pleasing to Him. For we must all appear before the judgment seat of Christ, that each one may be recompensed for his deeds in the body, according to what he has done, whether good or bad" (2 Cor. 5:9-10). But Paul's thought is not yet finished, so we need to read verse 11, as well: "Since, then, we know what it is to fear the Lord, we try to persuade men. What we are is plain to God, and I hope it is also plain to your conscience" (5:11, NIV). With this last remark, Paul intimates that his diligence in the ministry is motivated by his terror of that last judgment and of the possibility of being found ἀδόκιμος.

We have now arrived at the heart of Paul's motivation for his life of discipline, suffering, self-sacrifice, and eventual martyrdom. In order to capture the full force of his teaching about the judgment seat of Christ, we must return to the fourth chapter of 2 Corinthians, where Paul gave us the most comprehensive description of his ministry. His mission is concerned with "the light of the gospel of the glory of Christ, who is the image of God" (2 Cor. 4:4), and with " the light of the knowledge of the glory of God in the face of Christ" (4:6). *This* is the "treasure" that Paul carries in a weak and humble "earthen vessel" (4:7). His tribulations, sufferings, and constant dying are all "for Jesus' sake," in order to spread the grace of God and to enrich the church of God with abundant life (4:11-12).

Next, Paul explains what is happening to his own person even as he endures these tribulations and sufferings. While his "outer man is decaying," his "inner man is being renewed day by day" (4:16). Now, the "inner man" is what will leave the body at death "to be at home with the Lord" (5:8). The "inner man" is the one who will be assessed at the judgment seat of Christ and must be found "pleasing to Him" (5:9-10). We see that not only *what we have done* will be brought to judgment, but also *what we have become* in the process of daily renewal through our afflictions will be judged! Both James and the Apostle Paul wrote that the temptations and the afflictions work (κατεργάζεται, James 1:3; Rom. 5:3) or produce endurance. Certainly, the endurance is produced in the inner man and results in a "mature character" (Rom. 5:4), so that the inner man may become "perfect and complete, lacking in nothing" (James 1:4).

In addition to the endurance that the afflictions produce in the inner man, Paul adds another product: "For momentary, light affliction is producing for us (κατεργάζεται again!) an eternal weight of glory far beyond all comparison" (2 Cor. 4:17). We must let the full force of these words sink in: the afflictions *produce* "for us" a great amount of glory. Jesus Himself was glorified when Judas betrayed Him

(John 13:31) and when He was "lifted up" on the cross (John 12:32-33). It was because of His obedience "to the point of death, even death on a cross" that God "highly exalted" and glorified Him (Phil. 2:8-9). In the same way, it is through our obedience in the service of Christ through many trials and afflictions that the work of glorification is done in us, in our inner man. The same trials and sufferings work for us the glory that will be given to us beyond the judgment seat of Christ.

We are now ready to consider the following Pauline statements taken together:

1. The "light affliction is producing for us an eternal weight of glory"
(2 Cor. 4:17);

2. "If indeed we suffer with Him in order that we may also be glorified with Him" (Rom. 8:17);

3. "If we endure (ὑπομένομεν), we shall also reign (συμβασιλεύσομεν) with Him" (2 Tim. 2:12).

Let us enumerate all the conclusions we can draw from the above juxtaposition. We begin with the fact that we have been called to imitate Jesus. Jesus was exalted to the highest position of glory only after He had gone the way of suffering. We must also travel on the same road of suffering in order to reach the same position of glory. We have been specifically called to "suffer with Him" (Rom. 8:17). God has called us "into fellowship (κοινωνίαν, partnership) with His Son, Jesus Christ our Lord" (1 Cor. 1:9). On the other side of the judgment seat of Christ is another call for us, to another partnership with Him, a partnership in which we will share His glory (Rom. 8:17; 2 Thess. 2:14). This means, in other words, that we will be partners in ruling with Him. However, we cannot have this second partnership of glory and ruling without the first partnership of suffering for the sake of His ministry on the earth. Our partnership with Him in this life qualifies us and makes us worthy of partnership with Him in eternity.

Being glorified with Christ and ruling with Christ are aspects of the same heavenly reality. Inheriting the kingdom of God means being put in charge over God's possessions, and that means ruling over them. Just as Christ was obedient in the things that He suffered and thus was lifted up by God and was put in charge over the whole universe ("All authority was given to Me in heaven and on earth," Matt. 28:18), so we have been called to be obedient to Him, to work with Him in His work on the earth in the same sacrificial way.

Amazingly, God has promised us the same inheritance, which we will share with Christ, of ruling over the entire cosmos. The inheritance is already ours "by birthright," yet it is through obedience in God's service that we become well-pleasing to Him, qualified and worthy of our inheritance.

Let us focus in on Paul's description of what will happen at the judgment seat of Christ. "We must all appear" (φανερωθῆναι), literally, "we must all be made manifest" before the tribunal of Christ (2 Cor. 5:10). Philip Hughes explains, "To be made manifest means not just to appear, but to be laid bare, stripped of every outward façade of respectability, and openly revealed in the full reality of one's character."[42] It is crucial for us to be aware of the things that will come under scrutiny at that judgment. It will be a judgment of every man, "according to what he has done, whether good or bad" (πρὸς ἃ ἔπραξεν, 5:10). A remark in Hughes' commentary about these words is worth being quoted in full:

> The aorist is interesting: looking back from Christ's tribunal, the whole life of the individual Christian is seen as a unity. This concept is strengthened by the rather unexpected addition in the neuter singular (following the neuter plural) of εἴτε ἀγαθόν εἴτε φαῦλον, "whether it be good or whether it be worthless." "The change to the neuter singular is significant," says Plummer. "It seems to imply that, although persons will be judged one by one and not in groups, yet conduct in each case will be judged as a whole. In other words, it is character rather than separate acts that will be rewarded or punished. It is a mistake to suppose that any act, however heroic, can secure eternal life. We must ask, not τί ποιήσας κληρονομήσω; (Lk. x. 25), but τί με δεῖ ποιεῖν (Acts xvi. 30). It is habitual action that will be judged. And this explains the aorist; it is what he did during his lifetime that is summed up and estimated as a total.[43]

Barrett poses the question whether the teaching given here by Paul is consistent with his doctrine of justification by faith. His answer is also worth quoting:

> Paul saw no inconsistency, for his references to judgment are much too frequent, and are too closely connected with Christ, to be dismissed as an unthinking recollection of his now abandoned Jewish past. He never ceased to think that obedience to the command of God was required of all men, not least of Christians; such obedience is not abrogated but made possible by justification. This is the foundation; on it men may build, and what they build is

exposed to judgment (1 Cor. iii. 10-15). Worthless building is destroyed, but the builder is not destroyed with it.[44]

The suspicion of an apparent conflict between Paul's teaching on justification by faith and his teaching on rewards has been plaguing Protestant theologians ever since Luther sparked the Reformation with his understanding of justification by faith alone and grace alone. Protestant theologians have been suspicious of an inconsistency in Paul's theology in this regard precisely because they have not had a clear understanding of the content of heavenly rewards. When the rewards are seen for what they are, that is, when they are seen as the receiving of our inheritance, which entails being put in charge over God's possessions and being given higher or lower positions of ruling and authority in the kingdom of heaven, then it becomes obvious that God does not expect His children to *earn* these rewards.

The rewards God has in store for His children are designated to them *by His grace*. The issue is not to acquire merit in order to obligate God to give us something in exchange. Before time began, God had already decided to give this inheritance to His children. He predestined men and women to be rulers over His creation even before He created them. The issue is that God decided to build in men and women a character like His own, to fashion them in His own image; furthermore, He decided to form that character in them in the crucible of the difficulties of earthly existence. At the end of the process, God wants to see in each of His children a blameless, unselfish, self-giving, enduring, faithful, and obedient character. This is what is well-pleasing to Him, and this is His conception of a mature person who is worthy of being entrusted with great and glorious positions of ruling and authority in His eternal kingdom.

The Epistle to the Romans

We have already highlighted two key teachings in Paul's Epistle to the Romans. We have talked about the tribulations that produce the character which qualifies us for glory (Rom. 5:3-4) and about our participation with Christ in suffering as a condition for participation with Him in glory (8:16-18). Our treatment of these ideas in previous chapters should not prevent us from seeing them as integral parts of the complete picture offered to us in this letter.

In order to capture the whole message of Romans, a necessary component of my thesis, we will begin with the teaching about Adam and Christ found in the second part of the fifth chapter. Paul presents them as the two originators of humanity. Adam, as the originator of the first humanity, initiated mankind into sin, condemnation, and death. Christ came to originate a new humanity, into which He introduced His own righteousness, sanctification, and eternal life. All mankind is by birth "in Adam"; but each person is offered the possibility of being transferred from Adam and of being implanted "in Christ." Of course, Paul has already given us part of his thinking on these two heads of humanity in 1 Corinthians 15, where he told us that there were in fact two Adams: "The first Man is from the earth, earthy; the second Man is from heaven, . . . heavenly" (15:47-48).

My first aim is to point out the kind of unity that God offers us with the Heavenly Adam, with our Lord Jesus Christ. We can best understand it if we look closely at how the unity is described by Paul in Romans, the sixth and eighth chapters. In these verses, he uses the preposition σὺν (with) nine times in order to indicate the areas of our union with Christ. Here they are:

 1. "We have become united (σύμφυτοι) with Him in the likeness of His death" (Rom. 6:5);
 2. "Our old self was crucified with Him" (συνεσταυρώθη) (6:6);
 3. "We have died with Christ" (ἀπεθάνομεν σὺν Χριστῷ) (6:8);
 4. "We have been buried with Him (συνετάφημεν οὖν αὐτῷ) through baptism" (6:4);
 5. "We shall also live with Him" (συζήσομεν) (6:8);
 6. We are "fellow heirs with Christ" (συγκληρονόμοι) (8:17);
 7. "If indeed we suffer with Him" (συμπάσχομεν) (8:17);
 8. "That we may also be glorified with Him" (συνδοξασθῶμεν) (8:17);
 9. "To become conformed to the image of His Son" (συμμόρφους) (8:29).

This last one is emphasized at the conclusion of the discussion about the two Adams in 1 Corinthians 15: "And just as we have borne the image of the earthy, we shall also bear the image of the heavenly" (15:49).

While this union with Him is God's operation, we have a role to play in it, too. Therefore, my second aim is to point out the principle of cooperation (Θεοῦ γάρ ἐσμεν συνεργοί, 1 Cor. 3:9) with God in Christ, which is the principle of obedience. The starting point is in Romans 5:19, where we read that by the disobedience of Adam, the whole human race was poisoned with sin; but through the obedience of Christ, "the many will be made righteous."

Obedience is a key concept in the thinking of Paul and throughout his letter to the Romans. He saw obedience as the determining factor in our relationship with God. It emerges strongly in chapter six, where he discusses the Christian's attitude to sin. The Christian died to sin when he became united with Christ; he is "dead to sin, but alive to God in Christ Jesus" (6:11). However, this condition or status demands the active surrender of the Christian's entire being to the service of God (6:12-13), and that translates into a life of total obedience to God. For Paul, obedience was such a radical concept that he actually identified it with slavery. He talked of individuals presenting themselves to someone "as slaves for obedience," because he believed that "you are slaves of the one you obey" (6:16). Based on this view, Paul bluntly told the Christians: "You have been set free from sin and have become slaves to God" (6:22, NIV).

The Christian's slavery is a double slavery; it is both to God as a Person and to the teaching of God. Paul writes, "But thanks be to God that though you were slaves to sin, you became obedient from the heart to that form of teaching to which you were committed" (6:17, NASB). Stott remarks that what Paul was referring to in this verse "must have been a pattern of sound teaching, or structure of apostolic instruction, which probably included both elementary gospel doctrine and elementary personal ethics."[45] Barrett succinctly explains that Christians "are themselves created by the word of God, and remain in subjection to it."[46]

Our slavery to God and to His righteousness results in our sanctification (6:19). Sanctification (ἁγιασμός) has to be understood as the process "of being changed into the likeness of Christ."[47] Paul concludes this vitally important teaching by drawing our attention to the fact that from this slavery to God, "you derive your benefit, resulting in sanctification, and the outcome, eternal life. For the wages of sin is death, but the free gift of God is eternal life in Christ Jesus our Lord" (6:22-23). We have to understand the words "eternal life" as "surely here meaning fellowship with God in heaven."[48]

Whereas sin produces death, obedience to God produces a holiness that qualifies one for fellowship with God in heaven; this comes by grace as a "gift of God." Once again we are told that we cannot earn anything from God. Whatever we receive from Him comes to us as a free gift. At the same time, however, our slavery of obedience to Him and to His teaching qualifies us for His generous gift.

At the beginning of his letter to the Romans, Paul captured in one short phrase the entire purpose of his "apostleship": "to bring about *the obedience of faith* among all the Gentiles" (1:5, italics mine). It is significant that he also concluded the letter with the same phrase, stating that the mystery of God, which is Christ and His gospel, has now been manifested and has been made known to the nations, leading to the "obedience of faith" (16:25-26). A great multitude of Protestant theologians and commentators, afraid that an emphasis on obedience might jeopardize the concept of *sola fide*, interpret this phrase as "obedience of belief"; to put it in a different way, they maintain that "obedience" merely refers to people obeying the command of God to *believe* in Christ. But Paul was much too interested in bringing us to a slavery of obedience to God to limit himself here to saying that he only wanted the Gentiles to obey the command to believe.

Therefore I stand with John Stott, as well as with many others, in interpreting the phrase "obedience of faith" to mean "the obedience that *comes from* faith." Stott points out that "a true and living faith in Jesus Christ . . . includes within itself an element of submission."[49] This connotation was implied by Paul in Romans 10:3, where he writes that the Jews "did not subject themselves to the righteousness of God." A true faith "leads inevitably into a lifetime of obedience."[50] But this issue is settled by Paul himself in Romans 15:18, when he states that what Christ has accomplished through him has resulted "in the obedience of the Gentiles." Here the word "faith" is dropped and things become simple: the purpose of preaching the gospel of Jesus Christ is to bring people into His sphere of authority, utterly obedient to His rule. Paul makes this even clearer in 2 Corinthians 10:3-5, when he speaks about his ministry as a war in which the objective is to take "every thought captive to the obedience of Christ."

We have been brought into union with Christ and into partnership with Him, having the final goal of ruling with Christ in heaven. While the union with Him is accomplished and unbreakable (Rom. 8:32-39), at the same time, we have been introduced by God into a process of transformation (μεταμορφόσις). Thus, we are commanded to present our bodies as "a living and holy sacrifice" to God and to renew our minds in such a way that we can know the "good and acceptable and perfect . . . will of God" (Rom. 12:1-2). Clearly, this is a call to submission and obedience. But it is also a call to sacrificial living. Most importantly, this process of obedience and of living sacrificially in the service of God is the method by which the transformation of a person, of a character, takes place.

With this general context in mind, we are now able to understand what Paul writes in Romans 5:1-5 and in 8:16-18. Now that we have been reconciled with God and are united with Christ, we are thrown by our loving Father into various afflictions, because sufferings and tribulations produce in us the character that is required for life in glory. We have been called to be fellow-sufferers with Christ, which means that we have to make His goals our goals, His purposes our purposes, and His method of the cross our method. We must manifest Him and His life in us, spreading the grace of His salvation with the price of our comfort and even with the price of our own lives. We will be qualified for being glorified with Him only if we accept to participate with Him in suffering.

There is only one emphasis left to be made. Whatever sacrifices we voluntarily make for Christ and His gospel, and whatever sufferings we accept for Him and for taking His salvation to a perishing world, they "are not worthy to be compared with the glory that is to be revealed to us" (8:18). We cannot excel God. His generosity toward His children is so amazingly grandiose in the life to come, that nothing should be too much for us to do for Him and with Him in this life.

We have now established the most fitting context in which to read the beautiful description of martyrdom in Romans 8:35-39:

> Who shall separate us from the love of Christ? Shall tribulation, or distress, or persecution, or famine, or nakedness, or peril, or sword? Just as it is written, "For Thy sake we are being put to death all day long; we were considered as sheep to be slaughtered." But in all these things we overwhelmingly conquer through Him who loved us. For I am convinced that neither death, nor life, nor angels, nor principalities, nor things present, nor things to come, nor powers, nor height, nor depth, nor any other created thing, shall be able to separate us from the love of God, which is in Christ Jesus our Lord.

Once we realize that our union with Christ is absolutely secure and once we have had a glimpse of the glory that is in store for us, we can advance more than victoriously through all the afflictions, all the tests, and all the temptations of this life. *They* produce the glory; let them come!

Ephesians, Philippians, and Colossians

We now turn our attention to a group of letters with a similar structure, content, and length. They were written from prison by a man who was aware that he might have to face death very soon. This was not the first time that the Apostle Paul was confronted with possibility of dying as a martyr. He had encountered it so many times throughout his entire career as a missionary that he succinctly declared, "I die daily" (1 Cor. 15:31). In addition to this, he was constantly pondering the meaning of his suffering and dying for Christ and the gospel. We have noticed this in each of the epistles that we have studied so far. In the prison epistles, however, Paul seems to go deeper into every area and into each aspect of this rich and vast subject. Most of the ideas that we discovered in the previous epistles are also present here; yet in Ephesians, Philippians, and Colossians, these ideas become more refined, and they are better defined and better framed. We will start with the more general ideas that will enable us to understand Paul's motivations for what he did. If we can grasp Paul's total mindset and frame of reference, then we will be able to capture his thinking on the purposes of suffering and martyrdom.

In each of these three epistles, we once again find the call to "worthiness" that was so prevalent in the Thessalonian correspondence. Paul entreats the Ephesians "to walk in a manner worthy of the calling with which you have been called" (Eph. 4:1). To the Philippians he writes: "conduct yourselves in a manner worthy of the gospel of Christ" (Phil. 1:27); and he prays for the Christians in Colosse that they "may be filled with the knowledge of [God's] will" and with "all spiritual wisdom and understanding, so that [they] may walk in a manner worthy of the Lord, to please Him in all respects" (Col. 1:9-10).

We saw in the letters to the Thessalonians that "worthiness" was not an abstract or a sentimental term, but a technical one: a person has to be found worthy of being entrusted with responsibilities in the kingdom of God. Once again, when Paul speaks of being "worthy of your calling," we should remember to what we have been called: "He called you through our gospel, that you may gain the glory of our Lord Jesus Christ" (2 Thess. 2:14). The same call to future glory is emphasized by Paul at the beginning of each of these three letters.

The condition of worthiness entails our being in a state that will "please Him in all respects" when we go to meet Him on that last day

(Col. 1:10). We have been commanded to "walk as children of light," and that means that we have "to learn what is pleasing to the Lord" (Eph. 5:8, 10). Of course, what will please God in the end is our holy, mature, complete, and perfect character, conformed to His own image. In other words, He wants us to be "blameless," without reproach, and without defect. In Ephesians 1:4, we read that "before the foundation of the world," God chose us "that we should be holy and blameless before Him." Paul prayed for the Philippians that their love may grow "in real knowledge and all discernment," so that they might pursue only "the things that are excellent, in order to be sincere and blameless until the day of Christ" (Phil. 1:9-10).

Christ came into this world for a specific purpose. He reconciled us "in His fleshly body through death," with this goal in mind: "in order to present you before Him holy and blameless and beyond reproach" (Col. 1:22). Paul portrayed this ministry of Christ superbly to the Ephesians in his memorable words to husbands: "Husbands, love your wives, just as Christ also loved the church and gave Himself up for her; that He might sanctify her, . . . that He might present to Himself the church in all her glory, having no spot or wrinkle or any such thing; but that she should be holy and blameless" (Eph. 5:25-27). However, this work of Christ was not completed at Calvary. Christ is still involved in the life of His church. He "nourishes and cherishes" her in order to make her what He wants her to be in the end (5:29).

To better comprehend Christ's work as an unfinished task, we must observe two other important things in this matter. First of all, Paul considered the unfinished work of Christ to be the essence of his own ministry: "admonishing every man and teaching every man with all wisdom, that we may present every man complete (τέλειον) in Christ" (Col. 1:28). Since the job is not an easy one, Paul emphatically adds, "for this purpose also I labor, striving according to His power, which mightily works within me" (1:29). Secondly, we have been called to work hard in order to accomplish the purposes of God within us. Immediately after the hymn with which he presents Christ as the supreme model, who through humility, submission, and obedience unto death was highly exalted by God, Paul writes to the Philippians that they should persevere in this Christlike obedience; in practical terms, that means to "work out your salvation with fear and trembling" (Phil. 2:12). The final purpose, as in the case of Christ, is to be glorified by God: "that you may prove yourselves to be blameless and innocent, children of God above reproach, . . . so that in the day of

Christ I may have cause to glory because I did not run in vain nor toil in vain (2:15-16). Then Paul makes it clear to the Philippians that a life of faith modeled after Christ entails "sacrifice and service" (2:17). Paul himself was ready to be sacrificed for this purpose, and he anticipated the prospect of martyrdom as a reason for great rejoicing.

Paul did not want to risk giving a wrong impression, letting us think that we must do this work of completing our salvation alone; therefore, he assured his readers that "it is God who works in you, both to will and to work for His good pleasure" (2:13). Again we are reminded of the two levels of action: God is the One who predestines, saves, and abundantly provides all the necessary supplies, accomplishing His own purposes in His children; then, God's children are the ones who have to believe, to sacrifice themselves, to work hard, and to persevere, proving themselves worthy. These are not contradictory or conflicting lines of action; rather, they complement each other perfectly.

The actions that Christians are called to take in order to become pleasing to God are further developed in these letters in two ways. Primarily, the children of God are exhorted to grow toward perfection or maturity. All the ministers of the church are given for the purpose of "equipping . . . the saints for the work of service, to the building up of the body of Christ," until they all attain "to a perfect (τέλειον) man, to the measure of the stature which belongs to the fulness of Christ" (Eph. 4:12, 13). Paul goes on to insist that "we are to grow up in all aspects," and this is "into Christ," the Head of the body (4:15). The growth is said to be "into Christ" both because everything that happens to the Christian happens "in Christ," and because our goal is to grow into the image of Christ.

This brings us to the second way in which our transformation is taught in these epistles, and that is by means of the concept of the "new man." At our conversion, we laid aside "the old man," and "put on the new man," but this new man has to be renewed "according to the image of the One who created him" (Eph. 4:22-24, NKJV). This is done by the renewal of the mind and by acquiring the "true knowledge" (Col. 3:5-10, NASB). Both in Ephesians and in Colossians, this teaching is given in the context of instructions about moral behavior. The renewal of "the inner man" (Eph. 3:16) happens as we learn to apply the love of Christ in our own relationships, as we learn to give up worldly practices, and as we learn to live according to God's commandments. This actually means that we should "be

imitators of God, as beloved children" (5:1). As we imitate our Father
in our attitudes and behavior, our inner structure is increasingly being
conformed to His image. Why should we bother with these matters?
Paul resolutely tells us why: "For this you know with certainty, that no
immoral or impure person or covetous man, who is an idolater, has an
inheritance in the kingdom of Christ and God" (5:5).

We have reached exactly the same conclusion as in the previous
epistles: the result of our obedience to Christ on this earth will not be a
mere pat on the back at the judgment seat of Christ; conversely, our
disobedience will not bring us a simple rebuke that shall be quickly
forgotten amidst the bliss of heaven, as most preachers in the West
tend to say. On the contrary, the outcome of either our obedience or
our disobedience will be much more serious than that. Either our
obedience will have produced in us a structured and perfected
character, a "self" made in the image of God, or our disobedience will
have produced a character that is not well-pleasing to God, that is
unworthy and incapable of being entrusted with the inheritance. I
should point out that in Ephesians, Paul refers to people without Christ
as "the sons of disobedience," showing us again how central the
concept of obedience was to his thinking (2:2; 5:6).

It is time to turn our attention to a key feature of the prison
epistles, namely, their emphasis on heaven. In Ephesians, all our
spiritual blessings are located "in the heavenly places" (1:3, ἐν τοῖς
ἐπουρανίοις, lit., "in the heavenlies"). Christ is seated there at the
right hand of God (1:20) and He has "seated us with Him in the
heavenly places" (2:6). Paul can assert this fact for two reasons. First,
believers are already with Christ "in the heavenlies," because they are
"in Christ." Secondly, Paul can assert this because he speaks from the
perspective of the sovereign predestination of God, from which point
of view he may say that God's children have already been glorified
(Rom. 8:30).

Similar to Ephesians, the letter to the Colossians mentions heaven
right from the start, as Paul commends the Christians in Colosse for
their faith in Christ and for their love for all the saints. He writes that
this faith and this love exist "because of the hope laid up for you in
heaven, of which you previously heard in the word of truth, the
gospel" (Col. 1:5). As we have already indicated, in the New
Testament hope refers to the future. Often it expresses *the content of
what we expect from the future*. Hence, we can take this to mean that
the Colossians' faith and love are motivated by the great riches that

are stored up for them in heaven. A few verses later, Paul refers to these riches as "the inheritance of the saints in light" (1:12), and still further down, he writes that "the riches of the glory of this mystery" can be summed up in these words: "Christ in you, the hope of glory" (1:27).

Paul was convinced of the vital necessity that Christians know about these riches, that they know exactly how great and how glorious they are. For this reason, he prayed "that the eyes of your heart may be enlightened, so that you may know what is the hope of His calling, what are the riches of the glory of His inheritance" (Eph. 1:18). The saints must also be aware of the fact that the Holy Spirit was given to them "as a pledge" that they will receive the inheritance (1:14). Paul could not overemphasize the importance of deeply knowing these things and letting oneself be influenced by them, being determined, conditioned, and motivated by them. Thus, Paul commanded us to keep these truths constantly in our minds, pursuing them and meditating on them:

> If then you have been raised up with Christ, keep seeking the things above, where Christ is, seated at the right hand of God. Set your mind on the things above, not on the things that are on earth. For you have died and your life is hidden with Christ in God. When Christ, who is our life, is revealed, then you also will be revealed with Him in glory. (Col. 3:1-4)

In Philippians, Paul went even further, affirming that the "enemies of the cross of Christ" are characterized by a corrupt frame of mind that determines them to "set their minds on earthly things" (Phil. 3:18-19). In opposition to them, Paul gave himself and his own attitude as a positive example, saying that "as many as are perfect, have this attitude" (3:15). He declared to them, "I press on toward the goal for the prize of the upward call of God in Christ Jesus" (3:14-15). Yet what was the reason for Paul's concentration and insistence upon the subject of heaven? The answer is plainly given in the following verses:

> For our citizenship is in heaven, from which also we eagerly wait for a Savior, the Lord Jesus Christ: who will transform the body of our humble state into conformity with the body of His glory, by the exertion of the power that He has even to subject all things to Himself. (Phil. 3:20-21)

Having situated ourselves in this general context, we can now examine what Paul had to say in these three letters about suffering and martyrdom. It is important to know that it was this vision of heaven that motivated Paul to advance with Christ into the ministry of suffering and sacrifice. His vision of the life awaiting us in heaven came from the teaching of Jesus Himself, and this teaching exists strongly and ubiquitously in Paul's writings.

In Philippians and Colossians, we repeatedly encounter the concept of participation with Christ in His sufferings. The letter to the Philippians is concerned with suffering to such an extent that E. Lohmeyer calls it "a tractate on martyrdom."[51] Unfortunately, most English-speaking commentators reject this view. One exception, however, is J. L. Blevins.[52]

The culmination of Paul's discussion on suffering in the epistle to the Philippians comes in the third chapter, verses 10 and 11. In this passage, suffering is presented as the Apostle's supreme goal: "that I may know Him, and the power of His resurrection and the fellowship of His sufferings, being conformed to His death; in order that I may attain to the resurrection from the dead." Regarding the importance of this text, Gordon Fee writes that "the language 'participation in *his* sufferings' gives the clue to everything."[53] Fee also believes that "here is quintessential Paul, and a quintessential expression of the New Testament view of Christian life."[54]

The first issue that we need to settle, an issue that we have already partially addressed in our discussion of the Corinthian correspondence, is the following question: Which sufferings of Christ was Paul speaking about here? Was he referring to Christ's historic sufferings at Calvary, of His being tortured and crucified, or to His sufferings that are going on now, sufferings that were contemporaneous with Paul and have been coexistent with all the sufferings of Christians up to the present time and will be until His second coming? Many Protestant theologians say that in Philippians 3:10, Paul was referring to the historic sufferings of Christ. The believer's participation in Christ's sufferings is commonly interpreted as "mystical, in the sense of a real connection between believer and divinity in which there may be an actual sharing of experience, but not necessarily a merging of personalities."[55]

Albert Schweitzer gives us the most literal interpretation of this mystical union, calling it a "physical solidarity."[56] The proponents of this view hold that the mystical union has been achieved through baptism. Merrill Proudfoot, asking how Paul could say that he and the

Corinthians experience the sufferings of Christ, answers in this way: "It is because they have entered by baptism into a realistic bond with Christ that enables them through the medium of the Spirit to experience Christ's experiences—that is, of course, soteriological experiences of death and resurrection."[57] Proudfoot develops the theory that due to the unity of the body of Christ, a man like Paul can become a sort of electrical conductor through which comfort and salvation are transmitted from Christ to the other members of the body of Christ.[58]

There is nothing in Paul's writings to suggest such a transmission. We have already seen that Paul spoke in terms of "manifesting," of "reflecting," and of "spreading" the gospel of Christ through his own sufferings.

On the opposite end of the spectrum are those evangelical interpreters who consider that "participation" in the sufferings of Christ actually means "imitation" of the sufferings of Christ. This is the view of Gordon Fee:

> The "participation" inherent in κοινωνία means that Paul participates in the same reality as exemplified in Christ's sufferings; the "connection" between the two is that Paul's sufferings reflect Christ's inasmuch as they have the same goal. Christ's sufferings, which culminated in his death, were "for our sakes"; Paul's—and by implication the Philippians' as well—are for "the sake of the gospel," both in the sense of "because of" and "in behalf of."[59]

H. J. Michael explains the participation as an "inward experience" of the believer. He starts by saying that "by knowing Christ in the fellowship of His sufferings Paul does not mean enduring outward sufferings similar to those which He endured in the days of His flesh"; then Michael writes that "to know Him in the fellowship of His sufferings is to pass through an experience possessing some analogy with His passion."[60] Another example of this type of "spiritualization" of the text can be seen in Moises Silva's *Philippians*.[61]

What these two categories of commentators have in common is their fear or reluctance to accept the notion that, in one way or another, Christ is still suffering. They are reluctant to admit this reality because in their view, the possibility that Christ might still be suffering would necessarily mean that His work of redemption was not completed at Calvary. We have already asserted that this conclusion is not at all a necessary one. Paul never spoke about Christ's atoning or redemptive action on our behalf in terms of sufferings or afflictions. He always spoke of the atonement in terms of "the cross," "the blood," or "the death" of Christ, and of His being "given up" or of His "giving Himself up" for us.[62] The only places in the New Testament where the sufferings of Christ are referred to in connection with His death are in 1 Peter 2:21-24 and in 3:17-18. However, Peter also talked about a kind of suffering in which Christians "participate in the sufferings of Christ" (1 Peter 4:13, NIV).

As we indicated above, whenever Paul referred to the sufferings of Christ, he always did so in the context of an explication of his own sufferings for Christ. Furthermore, he always implied that the sufferings of Christ are something contemporaneous with himself, so that he can share in them; they are also concurrent with us, so that we can "suffer with Him" (συμπάσχομεν, Rom. 8:17). Let us now examine *how* we can participate in the sufferings of Christ that are contemporary with us.

Paul writes that through the agency of the Holy Spirit, we were baptized into the body of Christ (1 Cor. 12:13), we were planted in Christ and were united with Christ (σύμφυτοι, Rom. 6:5). Due to our being "in Christ," when Christ was crucified and died on the cross, we were crucified with Him, and we died with Him (6:6-8). In Colossians 3:1, Paul also tells us that we "have been raised up with Christ." Our inclusion into Christ and our participation with Christ in His historic death and resurrection is a divine act that has been *done to us*. We are not asked to do it ourselves. We are simply called to let this miraculous reality sink into our minds by considering ourselves "to be dead to sin, but alive to God in Christ Jesus" (Rom. 6:11). All of God's blessings and riches are ours by virtue of the fact that we are "in Christ."

But there is a reverse side to this spiritual reality and that is the fact that Christ *lives in us*. The concept of "Christ in us" was introduced by Jesus, who twice used the phrase "I in them" in John 17:23 and 26. Paul expressed the same reality in the memorable words to the Galatians: "I have been crucified with Christ; and it is no longer I who live, but Christ lives in me" (Gal. 2:20).

Now, if Christ lives in Paul, it means that Christ performs His purposes through him, and Paul is careful to say so. He puts it this way in Romans: "For I will not presume to speak of anything except what Christ has accomplished through me, resulting in the obedience of the Gentiles by word and deed" (Rom. 15:18). Luke captured the same attitude when he reported that the Apostle Paul, after he had arrived in Jerusalem, "began to relate one by one the things which God had done among the Gentiles through his ministry" (Acts 21:19). Even when Paul says in the first chapter of Colossians that *he* does the job of admonishing and teaching in order "that we may present every man complete in Christ," he is careful to add that he is "striving according to His power, which mightily works within me" (Col. 1:28-29). The obvious conclusion is that *all of Paul's ministry* is in fact *Christ's ministry*, in the sense that Christ Himself lives in Paul and works His purposes through him. If this general statement is true, then the subordinate statement is also true, that whenever Paul suffers as the agent of Christ, it is in fact Christ who suffers through him. Paul's sufferings are the sufferings of Christ through him.

With all these facts in mind, we now direct our attention to Colossians 1:24, the most controversial of Paul's statements about our partnership with Christ in His afflictions. What follows is a personal translation, conforming exactly to the wording of Paul: "Now I rejoice in my sufferings for you and I complete what is lacking in Christ's afflictions in my body for His body, which is the church."

Let us first repeat the question we had asked earlier: Which afflictions of Christ was Paul speaking about? Hendriksen answers that Paul was referring to "the afflictions that Jesus suffered while on earth," and quotes Percy, who calls this " 'the only possible interpretation' "; he also quotes Ridderbos: " 'Our conclusion can be no other than this, that the expression *the afflictions of Christ* points to the historical suffering of Christ.' "[63]

I cited Hendriksen because he is the most typical of the evangelical commentators at this time. As we shall see, he reacts here to the Roman Catholic, as well as to some Protestant, commentators who perceive in Paul's statement a call to some Christians to take upon themselves a suffering that has atoning value. To illustrate the latter position, I refer to W. L. Knox, who writes that "Christ . . . through His servants must continue to suffer until the whole quantity of suffering needed for the redemption of the world was completed."[64] How does Hendriksen counter such a theory? First, he remarks:

> Of course, this does not mean that there was anything lacking in the atoning value of Christ's sacrifice. It does not mean that good works, the suffering in purgatory, faithful attendance at mass, the purchase of indulgences, or any other so-called merits can be or need be added to the merits of our Lord. Among the many

passages that would refute such a theory are Col.1:14; John 19:30; Heb. 10:11-14; and 1 John 1:9.[65]

Then, Hendriksen adds:

> But we have no right, in the interest of Protestantism in its struggle with Roman Catholicism, to change the clear grammatical and contextual meaning of a passage. We should bear in mind that although Christ by means of the afflictions which he endured rendered *complete* satisfaction to God, so that Paul is able to glory in nothing but the cross (Gal. 6:14), *the enemies of Christ were not satisfied!* They hated Jesus with insatiable hatred, and wanted to add to his afflictions. But since *he* is no longer physically present on earth, their arrows, which are meant especially for *him*, strike his followers. It is in that sense that all true believers are in his stead supplying what, as the enemies see it, is lacking in the afflictions which Jesus endured.[66]

On the contrary, there is no basis in the text for attributing this statement to the enemies of Christ. It was *Paul* who said it! The action of completing the afflictions of Christ is *his* action, not that of Christ's enemies. Therefore, let us see if we can give this text a reasonable explanation, resting on our basic presupposition that Paul was talking about the afflictions or sufferings of Christ that were contemporary with his own sufferings. We have to start by making it absolutely clear that for Paul the problem of the sin of mankind was completely and absolutely solved by God in Christ (cf. Rom. 3:21-25; Eph. 2:12-18; Eph. 5:25-29; etc.). The salvation of men and women is from beginning to end the work of God in Christ (Rom. 5:1-11).

In addition, we must take what Paul says in Colossians 1:24 as literally and as strongly as we can: the afflictions of Christ are "on behalf of His body (which is the church)." These are not sufferings for sin. They are sufferings for some other purpose, related to Christ's own body. In the last century, J. B. Lightfoot made the distinction between the sufferings of Christ that were satisfactory, having sacrificial efficacy, and *aedificatoriae*, being useful for edification.[67] In 1956, C. F. D. Moule, in his book *The Sacrifice of Christ*, wrote about the "strange paradox" at the heart of Christianity, arising from "the finality and yet constantly repetitive nature of salvation—the finished work of God in Christ, over against his continued work in the body of Christ which is the church."[68]

More recently, in a study entitled "Interchange and Suffering," Morna Hooker wrote: "The interpretation of Christ's death as a once-for-all event is one model used by the New Testament writers, but it is not the only one. When Paul speaks of Christ's death in relation to sin, then he describes it in once-for-all terms. But the theme of dying-to-live is an ongoing process, in which the Christians share."[69] M. Hooker discusses the relationship between the sufferings of Christ and those of Christians as an "interchange," or a participation of one into the other. In some way, Christ participates in our condition and we participate in His status. E. P. Sanders, in *Paul and Palestinian Judaism*, considers the participation of the believer in Christ to be the key concept of the theology of Paul, emphasizing that "the participatory union is not a figure of speech for something else: it is, as many scholars have insisted, real."[70] I would just add that it is not only the participation of the believer in Christ but also the participation of Christ in the believer that is *real*.

Returning to the words of Paul in Colossians 1:24, let us focus in on this particular portion of the verse: "I complete what is lacking in Christ's afflictions in my flesh." Paul does not speak here about the afflictions of Christ in general as a fixed amount that must be completed. He speaks about the specific afflictions of Christ *in his own body. They* are not yet complete and must be completed. Let us see if we can corroborate this assertion with other sayings of Paul. Paul believed that we were "created in Christ Jesus for good works"; we were planted in Him with a purpose, having certain jobs that God wants to achieve through us (Eph. 2:10). These good works were "prepared beforehand" by God "that we should walk in them" (Ibid.). We ourselves do not choose the good works that we desire to do for God. On the contrary, we must discover the good works that God has already chosen for us to fulfill. I suggest that a part of these "good works," prepared by God for Paul to walk in, were the sufferings and afflictions that Jesus showed him beforehand that "he must suffer" for His name's sake; Paul knew very well that there was a certain quantity of "how much he must suffer" that had been prepared by God for him (Acts 9:16). Since he was cognizant of this reality, Paul was entirely willing to complete those sufferings in his own body, well aware of the fact that Christ Himself was suffering in him at the same time.

The next important aspect of the afflictions of Christ, suffered by Paul in his own body, is that they were "for the body of Christ, which is the church" (Col. 1:24, personal translation). The biggest mistake made by most commentators with respect to this verse is that they take it out of context and discuss it as a completely independent unit. When

I look at it in its context, I see a striking similarity between this verse in Colossians and Ephesians 5:25-32. To understand this better, let us analyze the whole Colossians passage from verse 21 to verse 29.

In Colossians 1:21-22, Paul gives them his entire message in a nutshell: "And although you were formerly alienated and hostile in mind, engaged in evil deeds, yet He has now reconciled you in His fleshly body through death, in order to present you before Him holy and blameless and beyond reproach." Then, he tells them that this is "the hope of the gospel," and that this hope has been proclaimed worldwide; of this gospel, he, Paul, "was made a minister" (1:23). In verse 24, Paul relates the sufferings that he has had to bear for the church. The remaining verses in this chapter are simply an elaboration of verse 24, explaining the actual content of the suffering ministry of Paul for the church. In essence, the final goal, as well as the mystery, of the gospel that he preaches is "Christ in you, the hope of glory" (1:27). Paul's ministry is to "proclaim Him, admonishing every man and teaching every man with all wisdom, that we may present every man complete (perfect) in Christ. And for this purpose also I labor, striving according to His power, which mightily works within me" (1:28-29).

The key to the interpretation of Colossians 1:24 is to see the parallels between Colossians 1:21-29 and Ephesians 5:25-32. In Colossians 1:21-22, Paul tells the believers in Colosse that Christ died for them in order to present them before Himself "holy and blameless and beyond reproach." In the parallel passage in Ephesians, Paul writes that Christ "gave Himself up for" the church so that "He might present to Himself the church in all her glory, having no spot or wrinkle or any such thing; but that she should be holy and blameless" (5:25, 27). In Ephesians, it is Christ Himself who works toward this goal, as He "nourishes and cherishes" her (5:29). However, in Colossians 1:28-29, Paul writes that his own preaching and teaching have this purpose of presenting "every man complete (perfect) in Christ," and that "for this purpose also I labor, striving according to His power, which mightily works within me." What is clear from the comparison of these two passages is that Paul had no difficulty in saying that the work of Christ is his work and that his work is the work of Christ.

The goal of Christ is to sanctify and to perfect His church, in order to present her to Himself "holy and blameless and beyond reproach" (Col. 1:22). But He does not carry out this task alone. He works through the ones who voluntarily take His goal and make it their own supreme goal. Furthermore, Christ's objective cannot be achieved easily. It demands *labor* and *agony*—these are the two words Paul uses in Colossians 1:29 to describe what he has experienced as he has worked toward this end. We can feel his agony in the following words: "Apart from such external things, there is the daily pressure upon me of concern for all the churches. Who is weak without my being weak? Who is led into sin without my intense concern?" (2 Cor. 11:28-29); and in these words, as well: "My children, with whom I am again in labor until Christ is formed in you" (Gal. 4:19). These are voluntary sufferings. Paul purposefully and deliberately chose to make Christ's concerns his own concerns. Most significantly, he invites us to join him in this agony. If we accept his invitation, it means that we will simply be completing *in our bodies* what is lacking in the sufferings of Christ for the fulfillment of His plan.

The words of J. B. Lightfoot concerning the edificatory sufferings of Christ serve as a good conclusion to our discussion thus far:

> It is a simple matter of fact that the afflictions of every saint and martyr do supplement the affliction of Christ. The church is built up by the repeated acts of self-denial in successive generations. They continue the work which Christ began. They bear their part in the sufferings of Christ.[71]

The last, but not the least, element that I want to discuss in Colossians 1:24 is the phrase with which Paul begins the entire statement: "I rejoice in my sufferings for your sake." For Western Christians, for so long under the lamentable influence of preachers and theologians who have played down or glossed over the reality of suffering with Christ, it is very surprising to hear that someone can rejoice in sufferings; but for Paul, the joy of suffering with Christ was a vivid reality. The most striking example of this phenomenon is Paul's entire letter to the Philippians. I pointed out earlier that this letter contains so much material about suffering that some commentators have felt compelled to consider martyrdom as its main theme and concern. In spite of this or, may I say, because of this, Philippians is also called the letter of joy. No other letter of Paul is as full of joy as this one (joy is mentioned ten times in four chapters!).

Why, then, did Paul find so much joy in suffering? In order to answer this question, we must first define suffering in the fullest sense of the word. We will start with a very significant statement made by the Apostle at the beginning of the letter. In 1:7, he tells the

Philippians that he has them in his heart in a special way because "both in my imprisonment and in the defense and confirmation of the gospel, you all are partakers of grace with me." What is of interest for us in this verse is the way in which Paul spoke of grace. Of course, there are those who will downplay the concept of suffering by saying that Paul was either alluding to saving grace (e.g., Martin, Motyer, O'Brian) or to his own apostolic ministry (e.g., Collange, Bruce, Hawthorne, Silva, Melick). Fee, however, says that "in the light of v. 29 where the verb of this now occurs in conjunction with their mutual suffering for Christ (ὑμῖν ἐχαρίσθη, 'you have been "graced" '), Paul very likely is referring to the 'grace' of being 'partners together in the defense and vindication of the gospel' even in the midst of present 'chains.' "[72]

In Philippians 3:10, Paul expresses his goal of being a "partner with Christ in His sufferings" (κοινωνίαν τῶν παθημάτων αὐτοῦ, literal translation). He, therefore, experiences a special joy because the Philippians have also been partners with him both in his sufferings (τοῖ δεσμοῖς μου, "in my chains") and in the cause of the gospel (1:7a). Paul calls their partnership a "partnership in the grace" (συγκοινωνούς μου τῆς χάριτος, 1:7b). As Fee points out, we must bring in verse 29 in order to get the complete picture: "For to you it has been granted for Christ's sake, not only to believe in Him, but also to suffer for His sake." The word translated in English as "granted" is ἐχαρίσθη, which is the cognate verb of the noun χάρις, grace; ἐχαρίσθη literally translated is "you were graced," or "you were given the grace." In three other places where the word appears in Paul's letters, it is usually translated as "the free gift" or "the gift freely given" (Rom. 8:32; 1 Cor. 2:12; Gal. 3:18). This method of translation has led to the impoverishment of God's Word and to the loss of the concept of grace in these places, especially in Philippians 1:29.

What Paul wanted to communicate to the Philippians was that they had initially been given the grace to believe in Christ (the grace of salvation); but then, they were also given this new grace, the grace of suffering for Christ, through their involvement in persecution and their participation in the battle for the spreading of the gospel.

Let us remember that in the eighth chapter of 2 Corinthians, Paul wrote about the Macedonians (that is, the Philippians and the Thessalonians!) that they had the special grace of giving to the needs of the Jerusalem saints out of their own poverty. The church's grace of giving is illustrative of "the grace of our Lord Jesus Christ, that though

He was rich, yet for your sake He became poor, that you through His poverty might become rich" (2 Cor. 8:9). The "grace" in this passage is one of sacrificial giving, a grace that is very costly for the giver. Now in Philippians, Paul introduces a new dimension of grace, or a new kind of grace, the grace of suffering for the cause of Christ.

Our problem in the West is that we have always been taught that grace is the free gift of God given *to us*. We were never taught that grace is something meant to transform us into *sacrificial givers to others*, leading us into a sacrificial involvement in the cause of Christ and His gospel.

In addition, it is especially important to grasp the joy that this "grace" brings. One of the very first things that Paul tells the Philippians is that in every prayer for them he rejoices because of their "participation (κοινωνία, partnership again) in the gospel from the first day until now" (Phil. 1:4-5). This partnership in the gospel means "striving together for the faith of the gospel" (1:27) in the midst of violent opposition (1:28). It was this active spreading of the gospel that involved them in the additional, special grace of suffering for the cause of Christ (1:29).

The joy that Paul has in this grace of suffering harmonizes perfectly with the joy that Peter and John experienced when they were "considered worthy to suffer shame for His name" before the Council in Jerusalem (Acts 5:41). This joy comes, first of all, from the sheer beauty of being partners with Christ in His divine ministry carried out in humility and through self-sacrifice. When we capture the wonder and the splendor of His divine humility and His total self-sacrifice for others, then we will be truly inundated with the joy of the privilege (grace) of being partners with Him in His ministry on earth.

There are other benefits from a partnership with Christ and with like-minded Christians in suffering. Paul described to his Philippian partners the benefits that had come to him as a result of his imprisonment and suffering for Christ. The first one was the impact his imprisonment had on the non-believers in Rome. Since Paul was in chains *for Christ*, people were naturally curious about who Christ was and about what He had done for Paul and for them. Such interest in Christ in the high society of Rome could not have been provoked by any other means. Hence, Paul rejoiced in his sufferings precisely because his "circumstances have turned out for the greater progress of the gospel" (Phil. 1:12). The second reason for his joy was the impact on the Christians in Rome. Because of the great apostle's imprisonment, they learned to trust in the Lord in a new way; they learned to trust in Him not only when everything was going well but also when they faced hardships and calamities. This new trust in the Lord gave them "far more courage to speak the word of God without fear" (1:14). The simple, timid Christians of Rome were thus transformed into courageous personal evangelists, and that was surely a great reason for rejoicing.

Then, there was a third impact of Paul's sufferings, but here we must step cautiously, because we are treading on holy ground. At this point, Paul begins to discuss his possible martyrdom. He had faced death so many times before, that this was not a new situation for him. It was just another instance when he had to be ready. Furthermore, he made it perfectly clear that for him personally, to die would be a gain (1:21), since death simply means "to depart and be with Christ, for that is very much better" (1:23). However, for the sake of the Christians it might be necessary for him "to remain on in the flesh" (1:24). Nevertheless, this was not his own decision to make. His Lord and Master was the One who would determine his future.

At the same time, Paul was completely certain of what his own responsibility was in this situation: "that I shall not be put to shame in anything, but that with all boldness, Christ shall even now, as always, be exalted in my body, whether by life or by death" (1:20). Paul placed a great emphasis on his desire that "Christ shall . . . be exalted (μεγαλυνθήσεται, shall be magnified) in my body." We already know that Paul considered his ministry to consist of "manifesting" and "reflecting" Christ to others, enabling the blind men and women of this world to see "the glory of God in the face of Christ" (2 Cor. 4:6). We also know that Paul believed that this purpose could be achieved only if his body was broken by sufferings, by beatings, and eventually by death. Once again, we catch a glimpse of Paul's unique, overarching concern to have Christ magnified; to stand in his chains and in his martyrdom in such a way that unbelievers might clearly see the beauty and greatness of Christ, His goodness and grace, and ultimately, the divinity of Christ! Paul did not simply want to die because it would be "very much better" for him personally (Phil. 1:23); rather, he wanted his martyrdom to have maximum effectiveness for the cause of Christ.

We need to remember at this point that John the Evangelist had an identical view with respect to martyrdom. In his Gospel, John relates how Jesus told Peter that one day, when he was old, someone would bind him and take him to a place where he did not wish to go. Then, John explains: "Now this He said, signifying by what kind of death he would glorify God" (John 21:19). *The ultimate goal of the martyr's death is to glorify God.* Knowing that, Paul aimed at nothing else, rejoicing because he had been given the privilege, that is, the grace, to glorify God in this way. It is truly significant and right that the inscription on the Martyrs' Monument in Oxford, England, where Bishops Cranmer, Latimer, and Ridley were burnt at the stake, is a direct quote from Philippians 1:29. Indeed, martyrdom *is* the supreme grace of suffering for Christ and for the gospel.

Let us continue to explore the meaning of the grace of suffering for Christ. In 1:7, this grace, in which the Philippians were partners with Paul, was for the "defense and confirmation of the gospel." Then, in verse 27 of the same chapter, Paul exhorts the Philippians to conduct themselves "in a manner worthy of the gospel"; he wants to be sure that they "are standing firm in one spirit, with one mind striving together for the faith of the gospel." This should be so precisely because they have been "given the grace to suffer for Christ" (1:29, personal translation).

Here we find a clear combination of the two actions: working for the gospel and suffering for Christ. In fact, this combination was conceived by Christ Himself. He said to His disciples: "For whoever wishes to save his life shall lose it; but whoever loses his life for My sake and the gospel's shall save it" (Mk. 8:35). The cause of Christ *is* the cause of the gospel, and the cause of the gospel *is* the cause of Christ. When one lives for Christ, he automatically lives for the gospel, as well. This is true because the gospel contains the message *of* Christ and *about* Christ. Living and striving for the gospel means doing everything, however costly, even if it costs you your own life, to take the message of Christ and about Christ to other people. Therefore, living for Christ means actually living for other people, doing everything so that they can obtain Christ, and teaching them to live with and for Christ. In conclusion, the grace of suffering for Christ in Philippians 1:29 is the same grace that is mentioned in 2 Corinthians 4:1-15, where we read that Paul was called to spread the knowledge of Christ to the blind people of the world. He demonstrated obedience to his calling by accepting to be constantly delivered unto death for Jesus' sake, so that the life of Jesus could be manifested in his mortal body. *Everything* Paul did was for this purpose, namely, for the purpose of spreading the grace of God to more and more people.

Now, why should one accept such a life and such a ministry? Let us recall Paul's explanation and reasoning in 2 Corinthians 5:13-17. Paul had conceded that, humanly speaking, his way of life was sheer madness. But when he had contemplated the cross and the death of Christ for all men, he had seen there the most unselfish love that one could ever have demonstrated for another. He had seen the Son of God hanging on that cross wholly for others. Paul realized that the problem of mankind was self-centeredness; all human hearts were full of selfishness. But he also knew that the purpose of Christ's death was to change those who lived for themselves into people who live for Christ and for others. To change self-centered people into people who live for Christ and for others means to effectuate a new creation. Unselfish men and women are new creatures, indeed.

My argument at this point is that in the first two chapters of Philippians, Paul follows exactly the same line of reasoning as in 2 Corinthians chapters four and five. We should take another look at the text in Philippians, keeping in mind what Paul had written to the Corinthians.

In the first chapter of Philippians, Paul spoke about his own chains, about the possibility of dying in the service of Christ, and about his desire that Christ should be magnified in his own body. He expressed his joy because the Philippians had become partners with him in the grace of suffering for Christ and for the gospel. With all this in mind, he went on to write chapter two, which for him, of course, was not a new chapter. He was simply continuing his argument, and that is why chapter two begins with the word "therefore." Gordon Fee writes: "The conjunction is inferential ('in consequence of what I said') and is probably intended to pick upon the whole of vv. 27-30."[73] Fee is of the opinion that "therefore" links the second chapter with the exhortation of 1:27. In verse 27, Paul had called the Philippians to "live as 'citizens' worthy of the gospel by standing firm in one spirit against the opposition"; in a footnote, Fee adds that in this case, "the theme of suffering, as with its counterpoint, serves as a kind of 'leitmotif' in the letter, not as its primary theme"[74] The suspicion Fee and others have is that if "therefore" links the second chapter with what Paul had written in 1:29-30, then logically, we would have to consider chapter two as Paul's "theological explanation of suffering."[75]

I have already pointed out that the entire first chapter has as its main theme Paul's chains and his possible martyrdom; the other main idea is his joy in being partners with the Philippian Christians in the grace of suffering. The conjunction "therefore" links the second chapter with this theme, which Paul is about to explain. Yes, what follows is, indeed, his "theological explanation of suffering." Paul begins with these words: "If therefore there is any comfort in Christ" (2:1, the NASB uses "encouragement" instead of "comfort"). Remember that in 2 Corinthians 1:3-7, Paul amplified the theme of comfort, asserting that as he shared in the sufferings of Christ, he received Christ's comfort and was thus able to comfort the Corinthians. Now, in Philippians 2:2, Paul is pleading with the believers in Philippi to make his joy complete by being a certain kind of people (2:2). The essence of the kind of character that they should have is this: "Do nothing from selfishness or empty conceit, but with humility of mind let each of you regard one another as more important than himself; do not merely look out for your own personal interests, but also for the interests of others" (2:3-4).

One can immediately see that this is an attack on self-centered living, exactly as in 2 Corinthians 5:15! There, Paul had written that it was in contemplating the death of Christ that he had understood the purpose of His death, namely, that people should no longer live for themselves. Now, Paul is once again directing our attention to the example of Christ in His humiliation, His obedience to the Father, and His self-sacrifice for others. In the process, he gives us one of the most magnificent descriptions of Christ ever written.

Before we take a closer look at Philippians 2:5-11, we have to realize that in the previous verses, Paul is primarily concerned with the way the Philippians think—the way they approach life and their basic attitude of mind. We see this for the first time in the second verse of chapter two. M. Silva's translation captures the full force of Paul's idea: "adopt the same frame of mind, sharing the same love—[yes] you must adopt the only frame of mind [that is proper for those who are] united in their soul."[76] In the third verse, Paul shows us that there are only two basic ways of thinking when it comes to assessing other people and to determining one's attitude toward them. One way of thinking is characterized by "selfishness or empty conceit." Paul refers to the other way of thinking as "humility of mind" (ταπεινοφροσύνη); he further defines it as "considering (ἡγούμενοι, deeming, thinking, counting) others better than yourselves." The climax of this exhortation is in his appeal to the Philippians that they should *think* in the same way Jesus Christ thinks. After he pleads with them to capture the mind of Christ, Paul plunges into his description of Christ's way of thinking.

The text of Philippians 2:5-11 is one of the most important Christological passages in the New Testament. To a large extent, our understanding of Christ, of His divinity, and of His incarnation depends on the interpretation we give to several key words in this passage. Although most of them are beyond the scope of this dissertation, the one key word that does interest us in particular is ἁρπαγμον, since it is essential for an accurate understanding of the mind of Christ. It appears in verse 6, in Paul's first statement about Christ's way of thinking: "who, although He existed in the form of God, did not regard (ἡγήσατο, did not deem, consider, or think; the same word as in 2:3) equality with God ἁρπαγμὸν" (translated by the NASB as "a thing to be grasped"). This sentence is meant to show us what the mind of Christ is not; in the following sentences, Paul tells us positively what the mind of Christ is like. There are difficult words in those sentences, as well, but they are all easier to understand when we find an adequate translation for ἁρπαγμὸν.

Traditionally, the word ἁρπαγμὸν was taken to mean either something to be held fast, something to cling to tightly, or a thing to be snatched or violently seized. These translations or interpretations have led to many varying theological speculations, leaving many people skeptical that these words really do accurately express the mind of Christ. Two recent linguistic studies have shed new light on the meaning of ἁρπαγμὸν, and they have shone a new and satisfying light on the essence of our Lord's way of thinking. R. W. Hoover, after a detailed study of the use of this word in the Hellenistic world, came to the conclusion that its meaning must be "accordant to the phrase ἁρπάζειν τὸν καιρόν (catch the moment, seize the moment), and it should be translated 'something to take advantage of.' "[77] Based upon this linguistic research, Hoover offers this translation of the ἁρπαγμός sentence: "he did not regard being equal with God as something to take advantage of," or, more idiomatically, "as something to use for his own advantage."[78]

Again after a lengthy consideration, C. F. D. Moule came to the conclusion that ἁρπαγμός does not mean "something not yet possessed but desirable (to be snatched at, *res rapienda*), nor something already possessed (*res rapta*) and to be clung to (*retienda*), but rather it denotes the act of snatching (*raptus*)."[79] In this case, "snatching" has no object. If one asks "snatching what?" then one has missed the point. It would be analogous to arguing that the saying, "It is more blessed to give than to receive," has no meaning because we are not told what to give and what to receive! Moule goes on to say that ἁρπαγμός means simply "taking" or "snatching," as opposed to "giving away"; it is a symptom of πλεονεξία, or acquisitiveness. The point of the passage, according to this understanding of the term, is that, instead of imagining that equality with God meant *getting*, Jesus, on the contrary, *gave*—He gave until he was "empty."

Further on, Moule states that Jesus "thought of equality with God not as πλήρωσις but as κένωσις, not as ἁρπαγμός but as open-handed spending—even to death."[80] And still further, he explains, "Essentially, it is all at one time and on one level; there is no ultimate question of descent or ascent, of loss or compensation, because what is *styled* κένωσις is, itself, the height of πλήρωσις: the most divine thing is to give rather than to get."[81]

Gordon Fee draws the following conclusions from this interpretation of ἁρπαγμόν:

> God-likeness did *not* mean for Christ to be a "grasping, seizing" being, as it would for the "gods" and "lords" whom the Philippians had previously known; it was not "something to be seized upon to his own advantage," which would be the normal expectation of lordly power—and the nadir of selfishness. Rather, His "equality with God" found its truest expression when "He emptied himself."[82]

Below this, Fee adds: "The concern is with divine selflessness: God is not an acquisitive being, grasping and seizing, but self-giving for the sake of others."[83] M. Silva succinctly summarizes the whole debate about the meaning of this verse: "Christ refused to act selfishly."[84]

After this exposition of what the mind of Christ is not, Paul puts it in positive terms: He "emptied Himself, taking the form of a slave . . . He humbled Himself by becoming obedient to the point of death, even death on a cross" (2:7-8). This is yet another place in which Paul describes how Christ, by His death, procured our salvation. However, this is not the central point he wants to make here. He is describing Christ's way of thinking, and Christ's way was to give Himself totally to the service of others, acting with the mentality of a slave, of one who is completely humble and utterly obedient to his owner. This slave-mentality was an attitude that Jesus Himself had taught during His earthly ministry. He had explained to His disciples that a slave who has worked all day in the fields cannot expect his master to serve him dinner. And even after the slave has prepared and served the dinner to his master, he cannot claim even a single word of gratitude from his master. Jesus then applied this parable to His disciples, relating it to their service to God: "So you too, when you do all the things which are commanded you, say, 'We are unworthy slaves; we have done only that which we ought to have done' " (Lk. 17:10).

The Epistle of James best illustrates the fact that humility entails this slave-mentality which results in absolute obedience to God. James quotes Proverbs 3:34, stating that "God is opposed to the proud, but gives grace to the humble." Afterward, he draws this conclusion: "Submit therefore to God" (James 4:6-7). To be humble means to submit, to put yourself under someone else's authority and to be totally obedient to that authority. Peter quotes the same saying from Proverbs, reaching a similar conclusion: "Humble yourselves, therefore, under the mighty hand of God, that He may exalt you at the proper time" (1 Peter 5:6).

Regarding the general meaning of this text, Gordon Fee explains:

> But quite apart from its function in the argument, this narrative has significance all on its own. Here is the closest thing to Christology that one finds in Paul; and here we see again why the "scandal of the cross" was so central to his understanding of everything Christian. For in "pouring himself out" and "humbling himself to death on the cross," Christ Jesus has revealed the character of God himself. Here is the epitome of God-likeness; the preexistent Christ was not a "grasping, selfish" being, but one whose love for others found its consummate expression in "pouring himself out," in taking on the role of a slave, in humbling himself to the point of death on behalf of those so loved.[85]

We come now to the exaltation of Christ:

> Therefore also God highly exalted Him, and bestowed on Him the name which is above every name, that at the name of Jesus every knee should bow, of those who are in heaven, and on earth, and under the earth, and that every tongue should confess that Jesus Christ is Lord, to the glory of God the Father. (Phil. 2:9-11)

After describing the self-humiliation of Christ, Paul presents the act by which God exalted Christ to "the place of supreme authority;"[86] in other words, Christ was exalted to the highest position "as God's vice-regent in the government of the universe."[87] The theological debate over the exaltation of Christ, as it was depicted by the Apostle

Paul, is significant for us because it directly relates to the key issue of this dissertation.

Hawthorne points out correctly that this part of the story "opens with a strong inferential conjunction (διὸ) followed immediately by a second conjunction (καὶ) denoting that the inference is obvious. Together they may be translated, 'As a consequence, therefore.' "[88] What is the inference that these conjunctions make? Some commentators say that the exaltation is the reward given by the Father for His Son's self-abnegation (Michaelis, Moule). On the other side of the table, there are those commentators who, as Hawthorne puts it, consider the exaltation to be "a gracious gift that excludes any idea of merit on Christ's part" (Collange, Gnilka, Martin).[89] In order to avoid these two extremes, Hawthorne says that the Son's exaltation was:

> the natural or logical outcome of His humility. . . . In other words, these conjunctions affirm what Jesus taught, namely that in the divine order of things, self-humbling leads inevitably to exaltation. This is an inflexible law of God's kingdom that operates without variance, equally applicable for Christians at Philippi as for Christ Himself.[90]

Hawthorne's interpretation is a painful reminder to me of the Marxist philosophy that we, under communist rule, were forced to swallow; this philosophy promotes the idea that there are laws inherent in the nature of matter, such as the law of evolution or the law of history, which says that capitalism is always inexorably followed by communism. It seems to me that Hawthorne even places God under the authority of such "laws," since he makes them applicable to Christ. Why do we witness this effort to find some other explanation than the one clearly given by Paul, that *God Himself* exalted Jesus? The answer is located in the fear of so many Protestant theologians of admitting any idea of rewards into their theological system. Hence, in most Protestant interpretations of these verses, "the notion of reward . . . [is] quickly dismissed . . . as reflecting a medieval aberration."[91]

In his monograph study of Philippians 2:5-11, R. P. Martin offers an extended discussion of this issue. He starts out by quoting Michaelis, who introduces the notion of recompense: " 'As the humiliation signifies the obedience of Christ as self-humiliation, so the Exaltation is shown as Exaltation by God as He recompenses this obedience.' "[92] Martin continues:

> Many commentators take this view, especially those who write
> from a Roman Catholic standpoint. Thus, D. M. Stanley insists
> that the conception of Christ's exaltation as a personal reward for
> his obedience in undergoing death is characteristic of the theology
> of the whole passage. This is the one place in the whole corpus
> Paulinum where Christ's glorification appears in the context of his
> merit.[93]

Martin then explains that "this line of reasoning has been opposed
since the time of the Reformation," and quotes Vincent in support of
this: " 'The idea of Christ's receiving his exaltation as a reward was
repugnant to the Reformed theologians.' "[94] Martin points to Calvin's
translation of διὸ καὶ as *quo facto*, "which done," adding that these
conjunctions show here "a consequence of the action not the cause or
reason."[95] Martin maintains that "it is extremely doubtful whether this
rendering of διὸ καὶ by 'consequently' can be sustained. But equally
there is no place for the notion of merit."[96] Martin believes that the
solution to this problem was expressed by Bultmann when he wrote
that when Jesus spoke of rewards, He promised them "to those who are
obedient without thought of reward."[97] Here is Martin's conclusion:

> And in the context of the hymn, this is exactly the sense. It is not
> so much the thought that because He rendered this obedience that
> He was glorified as, having accomplished the mission He came
> into the world to fulfill, God interposed and reversed the seeming
> finality of death in raising Him to the place of dignity. The
> obedience of Christ did not force the hand of God, as a doctrine of
> merit implies. The action of God is but the other side of that
> obedience, and a vindication of all that the obedience involved.[98]

I cannot agree that Bultmann solved the problem of rewards. First
of all, nowhere did Jesus say that rewards will be given only to those
who do not think of them or work for them. By the very fact that He
again and again told His disciples about rewards in heaven, He
conditioned them to think about rewards and to be motivated by them.
But even conceding the point that one ought not to be obedient merely
for the sake of a reward, as Bultmann insists, the issue of rewards still
remains intact. Jesus did promise rewards "to those who are obedient
without thought of reward."[99]

The real question we need to ask is this: Is there a way in which we
can speak about rewards without implying "merit," and without
implying that God is somehow under obligation to those who have
done something in His service? Indeed, the concept of merit was

excluded by what Jesus taught in Luke 17:7-10, namely, that a slave cannot expect even a word of thanks from his owner. This notion was also excluded by Paul in Romans 4:1-18 and in Galatians 3:18, when he said that Abraham's inheritance was granted to him "by means of a promise," meaning "by grace." We have already established the fact that if our rewards in heaven will in fact be our "inheritance," then we are not called to earn the rewards or to purchase them, so to speak, by our work for God (*that* would imply merit). We are called, instead, to obedience in God's school, as He prepares us for ruling with Him. Through obedience, we become qualified to be placed in charge of God's possessions, that is, we become qualified to obtain our inheritance.

If my thesis is correct, it should be applicable to the description of Jesus in Philippians 2:5-11, as well. We have already seen that Christ considered His equality with God, or His divine essence, to *be* self-giving (not ἁρπαγμὸν, not grasping or being acquisitive); He expressed His divine essence by emptying Himself, by becoming a slave, and by being totally obedient to His Father and totally given to the salvation of others, even to the point of death on a cross.

In the Epistle to the Hebrews, Jesus is said to have been "faithful" to His Father "as a Son" (3:6); therefore, "He has been counted worthy of more glory than Moses" (3:3), who had been faithful "as a slave" (3:5). In the previous chapter, it is written that "Jesus, because of the suffering of death," was "crowned with glory and honor" (2:9). In view of these texts, we are justified in affirming that for Christ to have been "faithful as a Son" means to have been faithful to His divinity. Christ was consistent with His divine nature when He gave Himself up for us and when He sacrificed Himself for us. By this action, He demonstrated the true character of God as a self-giving Being. Self-sacrifice belongs to the very nature of God. Hence, God was being consistent with His nature when He chose to make suffering His way of achieving His purposes in human history.

Let us take a deeper look into the nature of God. In a small book entitled *Suffering: A Test of Theological Method*, Arthur C. McGill has an amazing chapter called "Self-giving as the Inner Life of God." In it, McGill makes a comparative study of the opposing ways in which Arius and Athanasius conceived of the nature of God. McGill points out that according to Athanasius, a beautiful portrayal of the essence of divinity is found in the passages from John's Gospel that describe the relations between the Father and the Son. Here are the texts that describe the Father:

    – "All things that the Father has are Mine," says the Son (John 16:15).

    – "Just as the Father has life in Himself, even so He gave to the Son also to have life in Himself" (5:26).

    – "Whatever the Father does, these things the Son also does in like manner. For the Father loves the Son, and shows Him all things that He Himself is doing" (5:19-20).

    – "The Father loves the Son, and has given all things into His hand" (3:35), "in order that all may honor the Son, even as they honor the Father" (5:23).

On the basis of these texts, what is the decisive mark of the Father? It is the love by which He "gives" all things to the Son, including the honor and reverence due to Him as God. Here are the texts in which the Son describes Himself:

    – "I do not seek My own will, but the will of Him who sent Me" (5:30).

    – "I do nothing on My own initiative, but I speak these things as the Father taught Me" (8:28).

    – "And whatever you ask in My name, that will I do, that the Father may be glorified in the Son" (14:13).

    "He who believes in Me does not believe in Me, but in Him who sent Me" (12:44).

According to these verses, what is the decisive mark of the Son? It is the love by which He yields all the glory back to the Father. McGill continues to summarize Athanasius' view of God:

> What constitutes the essential mark of God's divinity, therefore, is love, the bestowing love of the Father for the Son and the adoring love of the Son for the Father. Let us put the matter another way. Between the Father and the Son there exists a relationship of *total and mutual self-giving.* The Father and the Son are not just entities who contain within themselves a divine level of reality, and who tenaciously hold onto what they have, in the fashion of Arius' God. The Father and the Son have divine reality in a state of action, in the action of total self-communication. In fact, Athanasius' point is that this state of action, this act of self-giving is the *essential mark of God's divinity.* The Father and the Son do not have their identity in terms of the reality that they possess and hold onto within themselves, but in terms of their giving this reality to the other. If God's reality in Himself is the relation between Father and Son, then God is this staggering dynamism of

mutual self-communication. Because the Father holds nothing back but gives all His glory to the Son, and because the Son holds nothing back but offers all that He has to glorify the Father, God within Himself is supreme in the order of love.[100]

In a later passage, McGill quotes from the *Epistle to Diognetus*, an early Christian writing in which the following question is asked: Why did God send His Son? McGill paraphrases the author's answer: "To rule as a tyrant, to inspire terror and astonishment? No, He did not. No, He sent Him in gentleness and mildness. To be sure, as a king sending his royal son, He sent Him as God. But He sent Him as to men, as saving and persuading them, and not as exercising force. For force is no attribute of God."[101] McGill then draws this conclusion about the nature of God:

> "Force is no attribute of God," that is the basic principle for the Trinitarian theologians. God's divinity does not consist in His ability to push things around, to make and break, to impose His will from the severity of some heavenly remoteness, and to sit in grandeur while all the world does His bidding. Far from staying above the world, He sends His own glory into it. Far from imposing, He invites and persuades. Far from demanding service from men in order to enhance Himself, He gives His life in service to men for their enhancement. But God acts toward the world in this way because within Himself He is a life of self-giving.[102]

With all this we come back to Philippians 2:5-11. Gordon Fee summarizes its importance in these words:

> Here is the very heart of Pauline theology, both of his understanding of what God has done and is doing in our fallen world. Here is where the one who as "equal with God" has most fully revealed the truth about God; that God is love and that His love expresses itself in self-sacrifice—cruel, humiliating death on a cross—for the sake of those He loves.[103]

But what about the exaltation of Christ? First of all, Christ proved to be faithful to the essence of deity and was thereby considered worthy of the highest glory (Heb. 3:2, 6). Consequently, Christ was put in charge over the whole universe. However,—and this is a crucial point to comprehend—the Son did not have to earn it because it had already belonged to Him as the Son of God. It was the good pleasure of His Father that the Son should be the heir of God. Thus, in Philippians 2:9, Paul did not say that Christ was *rewarded* the highest position in the universe; Paul wrote instead that God "bestowed it on Him" or "granted to Him" this position. The word used by Paul is ἐχαρίσατο, meaning "graced" or "given by grace" (the same word which was used in 1:29 about the Philippians being "graced" or being "given the grace" to believe and suffer for their Lord). Of course, Christ was rewarded for His faithfulness expressed in self-sacrifice and obedience unto death. Nevertheless, God's rewards are always "by grace." On the other hand, they are only given as a consequence of obedience in suffering and in self-sacrifice for others.

There is still more to this concept of rewards. The entire account of Christ was included in this letter for the purpose of showing us the mind of Christ, His way of thinking and being. Philippians 2:5-11 has the further purpose of helping us learn from Him and of showing us how to become like Him. We are promised that Christ Himself will come with us and will live in us, if we accept a life of obedience, of humility, of suffering, and of self-sacrifice for others. He then promises that His own image will be built in us, as He lives this kind of life through us. Increasingly, we will be transformed into His likeness. *Therefore, the real reward is our becoming like Christ!* When we shall come to look at the Epistle to the Hebrews, we shall see that this principle was true of Christ Himself: He was "perfected" through His suffering (Heb. 2:10; 5:8). What Hebrews teaches serves to strengthen my point about Christ's example and about Paul's call to the Philippians and to us, to "think" like Him and to become like Him.

At this time, I must mention the fact that I do not agree with those scholars who follow Kassemann in saying that the content of Philippians 2:5-11 was not presented by Paul as something that we should imitate. Kassemann starts from the premise that the "Jesus of history" did not interest Paul very much; he goes on to say that Paul was primarily concerned with the "Christ of Faith," and therefore, Kassemann concludes, Paul simply admonished the Philippians "to conduct themselves toward one another as is fitting within the realm of Christ."[104] For an evaluation and rejection of this theory I refer the reader to Peter O'Brian, who closes his appendix on this issue with this statement: "We conclude that the Christ-hymn presents Jesus as the supreme example of the humble, self-sacrificing, self-giving service that Paul has just been urging the Philippians to practice in their relations one toward another (vv. 1-4)."[105]

There is yet another attitude to this passage that we should analyze. It is the attitude of R. M. Hawkins, who considers Philippians 2:5-11 to be a post-Pauline interpolation into the text of the letter. He rejects the passage because he believes it is not worthy of Paul. In his opinion, the effect of this passage as a whole on the readers must have been:

> to make each proud self-glorifying Christian think, "I will be like Christ; I will ever be conscious of my true dignity; I will stoop to a temporary subjection of myself to my fellow in the hope that God will see the merit of my self-abnegation, and exalt me far above this fellow to whom I temporarily submit myself." It could but accentuate the divisions and the rivalries, although it suggested the method of humility as the goal to the realization of the superiority each one thought himself to possess. Such an assumption of humility as a means to self-exaltation is utterly contemptible.[106]

I include this quote not only as an oddity, but also as an example of a total misunderstanding of the character of Christ and a complete misunderstanding of the real effect that Paul intended this passage to have on his readers. I believe that what I have already said above regarding the nature of God as self-giving, self-sacrificing love, and what I have said regarding our becoming like God by developing the same mentality and character shows beyond a shadow of a doubt that there is nothing "contemptible" here.

What we must keep in mind at all times is that "God is in the process of recreating us in His image," and in this process, "we are not called simply to 'imitate God' by what we do, but to have this very mind, the mind of Christ, developed in us, so that we too bear God's image in our attitudes and relationships within the Christian community—and beyond."[107]

The fear of some Protestant theologians is that our theology will inevitably enter into conflict with the gospel of grace preached by Paul, if our emphasis upon the imitation of Christ, for the purpose of growing and being conformed to His image, leads us to emphasize obedience and hard work. I will let Gordon Fee speak once more on our behalf:

> That Christ serves for us as a paradigm for Christian life is not as some fear, a betrayal of Paul's gospel. On the contrary, it reinforces a significant aspect of his gospel, namely that there is no genuine *life in Christ* that is not at the same time, by the power of the Holy Spirit, being regularly transformed into the *likeness of Christ*. A gospel of grace, which omits obedience, is not Pauline in any sense; obedience, after all, is precisely the point made in the application that follows (v. 12).[108]

Finally, as a last remark on Philippians 2:5-11, I want to point out just how essential this passage is for the development of a theology of suffering, martyrdom, and rewards in heaven. With the risk of over-exploiting Gordon Fee, I will cite him once more:

> Moreover, there is also an emphasis in this letter on *imitatio* with regard to suffering (1:29-30; 3:10, 21). Those who are privileged to believe in Christ are also privileged to suffer for him; indeed to share in those sufferings is part of knowing him. Hence, this passage, with Christ's humbling himself to the point of death on the cross, will also serve as the theological ground for that concern. That, indeed, seems to make the best sense of the otherwise unusual emphasis in 3:10 that knowing Christ includes the "participation in his sufferings, being conformed to his death." Thus Christ's death once again serves as paradigm.[109]

We now turn our attention to the way Paul applied the example of Christ to the Philippian Christians. The following excerpts are Paul's key applications of the teaching in Philippians 2:5-11:

> So then, my beloved, just as you have always obeyed, . . . work out your salvation with fear and trembling; . . . that you may prove yourselves to be blameless and innocent, children of God above reproach . . . so that in the day of Christ I may have cause to glory because I did not run in vain nor toil in vain. But even if I am being poured out as a drink offering upon the sacrifice and service of your faith, I rejoice and share my joy with you all. And you too, I urge you, rejoice in the same way and share your joy with me. (2:12, 15a, 16b, 17, 18)

For a general setting of this passage, I want to draw our the attention to Paul's allusion to the song Moses delivered just before his death, in which Moses predicted the failure of Israel to serve the Lord (Deut. 32:5, used in Phil. 2:15). Paul was also at the end of his life as he was writing this letter; hence, the repeated references to the possibility of his own death (1:20-24; 2:16-17; 3:10). We also have to remember that in 1 Corinthians 10:1-13, Paul cited the failures of Israel in the wilderness as examples of actions that the Corinthians ought to avoid, warning them about being in a situation in which they will not be worthy of obtaining what God has in store for them. Additionally, Paul used Israel's disqualification to illustrate his own fear of being "disqualified" and of being unworthy of obtaining the benefits of the gospel after he had preached it to others (1 Cor. 9:23-27). The Apostle Paul himself was fearful of the judgment seat of

Christ! His greatest ambition was, therefore, to be pleasing to God (2 Cor. 5:9-11). In fact, in Philippians 2:16, Paul expresses exactly the same goal as in 2 Corinthians 5:9; his highest aim was "that at the day of Christ I may have cause to glory" (Phil. 2:16).

With this general picture in mind, we can now focus on our main points of interest in this passage on ethical living. Paul began with the issue of obedience, because he had just given them the example of Christ's obedience, even unto death on a cross. According to Paul, obedience has two aspects. Its primary aspect is the total submission to a higher authority. It is described in Romans 12:1 as the presentation of one's body as "a living and holy sacrifice, acceptable to God." It is the total surrender of self-rule, and it entails ceasing to live for oneself, thereafter living solely for the Master. The obedient fulfillment of specific rules or commands is merely the secondary aspect of obedience. One's obedience to rules has no value if the self has not been first surrendered, if one's total mentality is not that of a slave whose essence is to obey.

In Philippians 2:12, after the general mention of obedience ("you have always obeyed"), Paul gives them the specific command that they should continue to obey, working "out [their] salvation with fear and trembling." By "salvation," Paul means the total process that commences in justification and reconciliation with God, continuing through the Holy Spirit's work of sanctification to the final moment of glorification. Calvin wrote that here "salvation is taken to mean the entire course of our calling, and that this term includes all things by which God accomplishes that perfection, to which He has determined us by His free election."[110] F. W. Beare points out the fact that Paul always spoke of salvation as "the eschatological fulfillment of the hope of the gospel, the winning through to the goal, the attainment of the final blessedness."[111] To be more specific, Paul was concerned with the process by which the Philippians would have their character developed until the day of Christ, when they will be presented before Him "blameless and innocent, . . . above reproach (2:15: cf. 1:10). When Paul contemplated the judgment seat of Christ, he experienced exactly this attitude of fear and trembling to which he now called them (2 Cor. 5:10-11). Moreover, the issue for the Philippians was the same as for the Corinthians, namely, how to obtain God's εὐδοκία, or good pleasure (2 Cor. 5:9; Phil. 2:13).

Paul, however, was quick to add that "it is God who is at work in you, both to will and to work" toward the goal of being well-pleasing to Him (2:13). As a matter of fact, Paul was simply repeating what he had written at the beginning of the letter, when he commended the Philippians for their "participation in the gospel from the first day until now" (1:5). So that they will not think that they have achieved merit from their participation, Paul adds, "For I am confident of this very thing, that He who began a good work in you will perfect it until the day of Christ Jesus" (1:6).

What we have here is yet another perfect example of the two planes of action that are always parallel to each other in the thinking of Paul: the divine plane on which God does everything from beginning to end, and the human plane on which man is called to do all that God is doing in him. Many theologians point out that in Paul we find both the indicative mood, in which we are told what we are and what we have in Christ, and the imperative mood, in which we are commanded to become what we are in Him and to obtain what we have in Him. The accepted phrase is that we are commanded to be what we are. For example, each of the nine things listed by Paul in Galatians 5:22-23 as "the fruit of the Spirit," are in other places commanded *of us* to actualize in our lives; we are expected to actively pursue, develop, and achieve these fruits in ourselves.[112]

For "the finest interpretative summary of Philippians 2:12-13," I refer the reader to John Murray's *Redemption: Accomplished and Applied*.[113] But what does it mean to "work out your salvation" in practical terms, and why are we commanded thus? Paul explained it in these words: "that you may become (γένησθε) blameless and pure, children of God without fault" (2:15, NIV). The key to the interpretation of this text is in the word γένησθε, translated by the New American Standard Bible as "may prove yourselves to be." O'Brian rejects this translation for two reasons. The first one is linguistic. The sentence begins with: "Do everything (πάντα ποιεῖτε) in order to (ἵνα) . . ."; the preposition ἵνα introduces a clause of purpose, in order to say, in other words, that you must do everything for the purpose of becoming blameless.

The second reason for O'Brian's rejection of this translation is logical. If we translate the word as "prove yourselves to be," then it would mean that "the Philippians were already 'blameless and flawless' in God's sight and were now to demonstrate it in their behavior."[114] Strangely enough, although O'Brian strongly advocates the idea of becoming, he denies that the phrase "becoming blameless and flawless" is "in a future eschatological sense with the apostle looking to the Philippians' ultimate perfection at the Parousia. Rather, [Paul] desires that they be blameless and faultless now in the midst of a corrupt and sinful world."[115] Yet how can this statement refer to the present when the key word in it is "becoming," a word that indicates future fulfillment? O'Brian's explication provides further proof of the fact that one's theological interest colors one's interpretation. Beare admits that γένησθε might be translated "show yourselves to be," yet he adds that "the stronger sense, conveying the thought of character changed by divine grace, is probably justified in the context of the epistle as a whole."[116] Hawthorne makes this point clearer:

> All the injunctions Paul lays upon the Philippians (2:3, 4, 12-14) are for a purpose: that (ἵνα) they might become (γένησθε) better people than they are. Characterized by assertiveness (ἐρίθειαν), conceit (κενοδοξίαν), grumbling (γογγυσμῶν), argumentativeness (διαλογισμῶν), the Philippians are promised that improvement is possible. They can become blameless (ἄμεμπτοι), flawless (ἀκέραιοι), faultless (ἀμώμητα) children of God. But for Paul this radical transformation is possible only when there is a humble positive response of the human will to the demands of God (note the preponderance of the imperative mood here) linked together with the creative force of divine grace.[117]

The fact that Paul had in view "the day of Christ" is shown by two immediate indicators. First, by the fact that twice previously, in verses 1:6 and 10, he had linked their character with "the day of Christ." Secondly, he mentioned "the Day of the Lord" again in 2:16, immediately after this exhortation. We shall also see that Paul's own striving has in view the future day when he hopes to gain "the prize" (3:8-14).

We notice in this epistle exactly what we observed in the Thessalonian and in the Corinthian correspondence: Paul's concern is with the state or condition in which these Christians will be found at the judgment seat of Christ. Will God be pleased with what He sees in their character? Of course, God loves all of His children, but will He *like* them?

But here we find that Paul was preoccupied with yet another aspect of this issue. He wanted the Philippians to be men of character and to pass the scrutiny of the judgment seat of Christ, because he had in mind his own situation there: "so that in the day of Christ I may have cause to glory because I did not run in vain nor toil in vain" (2:16). Many commentators are rather embarrassed that Paul expressed a desire to glory in his ministry in this life (lit., εἰς καύχημα ἐμοὶ, "for a boast to me"). Instead of being embarrassed, we should remember the words of Paul to the Corinthians about each man's work being tested by fire at "the day" (1 Cor. 3:12-15). The Philippians are Paul's "work," and if they do not pass the quality control, he will suffer loss! He will have no reward and will have toiled in vain! But he is confident that the actual outcome will be different. That is why he calls them "my joy and crown" (Phil. 4:1). Paul expands this idea in his first letter to the Thessalonians, when he tells them of his confidence that "in the presence of our Lord Jesus at His coming," they will be his "hope or joy or crown of exultation," and his "glory and joy" (1 Thess. 2:19-20). Paul took his belief in the rewards that will be his beyond the judgment seat of Christ extremely seriously, and this is evident from the way he invested his whole life in these people!

At the end of this passage in Philippians chapter two, Paul resumes his discussion of the possibility of his own martyrdom: "But even if I am being poured out as a drink offering upon the sacrifice and service of your faith, I rejoice and share my joy with you all. And you too, I urge you, rejoice in the same way and share your joy with me" (Phil. 2:17-18). I will allow F. F. Bruce to have the first word on this subject:

> Paul comes back to the present situation. He hopes for a favorable verdict in the imperial court, but he cannot be sure; the case might go the other way, and he might be sentenced to death. If so, the sentence would probably be carried out by decapitation. How would Paul view that prospect?
>
> The life and service of Christians could be described as a sacrifice. When a sacrifice, such as a burnt offering with its accompanying cereal offering, was presented in the temple at Jerusalem, a drink-offering or libation of wine or olive oil might be poured over it or beside it. This was added last, and completed the sacrifice. **If I am being poured out like a drink offering**, says Paul, let me be poured out as a libation **on the sacrifice and service coming from your faith.** When Paul says if I am being poured out like a drink offering (Gk., εἰ καὶ σπένδομαι), he is not thinking of a literal libation of blood such as was poured out in some pagan cults (cf. Ps. 16:4: "their libations of blood"); he is thinking of the willing yielding up of his life to God.[118]

As usual, however, there are people who do not like the idea of martyrdom, and who accordingly deny that Paul was referring here to his own imminent execution. Hawthorne is one interpreter who takes this view. His main reason for rejecting the allusion to martyrdom is that "the note of joy—χαίρω καὶ συγχαίρω πᾶσιν ὑμῖν—would then strangely be sounded for martyrdom: 'I am glad and glad with all of you that I am to be put to death.' Ignatius may have said this, but hardly Paul."[119]

Moises Silva responds to the above statement very well:

> This is a startling objection. Is there anything more characteristic of Philippians than Paul's juxtaposing of joy and adversity? Paul's words in 1:18-20 are particularly relevant here, for that passage too contains a repetition of χαίρω (v.18), and the joy in view is not affected by the possibility of death (εἴτε διὰ ζωῆς εἴτε διὰ θανάτου, v.20).[120]

For the significance and beauty of Paul's image of martyrdom in this place, we should go back to F. F. Bruce's commentary:

> Charles Wesley, in memorable lines, prays that his life may be a perpetual sacrifice, kindled "on the mean altar of my heart" by the flame of the Spirit:
>
> > Ready for all thy perfect will,
> > My acts of faith and love repeat,
> > Till death thy endless mercies seal,
> > And make the sacrifice complete.
>
> Paul's imagery is similar, with one material difference; *his* death should make *their* sacrifice complete. A martyr's death would be the crown of his own life of apostolic service, but he is willing that it should be reckoned not to his credit but to theirs. If so, "nothing is here for tears"; such a prospect causes him to **rejoice**, as it should them.[121]

A similar perspective is found in Ephesians 3:13, where the same apostle in chains writes to his beloved church: "Therefore I ask you not to lose heart at my tribulations on your behalf, for they are your glory." A. T. Lincoln comments on this verse, saying:

> In Paul's thought one of the relationships between suffering and glory is that the former is a precondition of the latter (cf. 2 Cor. 4:17; Rom. 8:17, 18). But the one who suffers is the one who is later glorified, while here in Eph. 3:13 the one who suffers is Paul but those who are glorified are believers. Such a relationship, whereby apostolic suffering mediates salvation to others, is present in Paul's thought but expressed in different terms in 2 Cor. 1:6 ("if we are afflicted, it is for your comfort and salvation") and 2 Cor. 4:12 ("so death works in us, but life in you"). It is this

concept of Paul's afflictions mediating the salvific benefits of Christ's sufferings to believers that is expressed here in Ephesians in terms of his sufferings and their glory. Suffering still must come before glory for the readers, but it is Paul who has fulfilled the condition of suffering for them, ὑπὲρ ὑμῶν.[122]

Paul challenged his friends in Philippi to "do nothing from selfishness," but to "regard one another as more important than himself; [to] not merely look out for [their] own personal interests, but also for the interests of others" (2:3-4), since Christ did the same when He died for us. Paul illustrated this principle by his own attitude and way of life. He was even willing to let his own sacrifice bring glory to others, even though it was meant to bring heavenly glory to him. That is Christlikeness in deed!

We have now arrived in our journey through Philippians at the passage in which Paul's own view of his impending martyrdom is revealed. The third chapter of this letter contains one of the most personal and most intimate self-descriptions written by the great apostle. Paul begins by telling us who he was before he met Christ and what he has lost in order to "gain Christ." He speaks about "the surpassing value of knowing Christ Jesus [his] Lord" (3:8). Then he turns to his life at present and to his goals for the future. These are well-known verses, much memorized and often the subject of sermons in our evangelical churches:

> that I may know Him, and the power of His resurrection and the fellowship of His sufferings, being conformed to His death; in order that I may attain to the resurrection from the dead. Not that I have already obtained it, or have already become perfect, but I press on in order that I may lay hold of that for which also I was laid hold of by Christ Jesus. . . . I press on toward the goal for the prize of the upward call of God in Christ Jesus. (Phil. 3:10-12, 14)

We have already discussed the concept of participation with Christ in His sufferings. Here we are mainly interested in Paul's view of martyrdom and in his view of receiving the prize at the day of Christ. The issue of partnership with Christ in suffering will now be treated only in that context.

Let us begin with verse nine, with the phrase, "and may be found in Him . . .". It seems so strange that most commentators put a period after this phrase, assuming that Paul's goal was to be "found in Christ." If this is a right interpretation, then it seems that the only issue is *when* this should happen. Hendriksen apparently understands the phrase to refer to the present time: "It is Paul's great aim that in the observation of all his fellow-believers he may be *found* to be completely *in Him*, that is, in union with Christ.[123] On the other hand, James Moffat says that Paul means "to be found at death in Him."[124]

O'Brian also includes the qualifier written by Paul in the rest of verse nine and writes: "We prefer to understand the clause as modal, indicating the manner in which he will be found perfectly in Christ, that is, as one who does not have a righteousness of his own." As to the *when* of being "found in Christ," O'Brian suggests that "the whole clause" could be taken to indicate what Paul will possess "as he stands before God's tribunal, that is, when he is fully united with Christ"; nevertheless, he still considers it best to interpret it as the righteousness which Paul "has as a Christian, . . . in the here and now as well as on the final day."[125]

In my view, Paul considered the condition of being "in Christ" as the most basic fact of a Christian's existence. Furthermore, being "in Christ" does not suffer any modifier; one cannot be *more* "in Christ" or *completely* "in Christ" or *perfectly* "in Christ." One is either "in Christ" or "without Christ." In Philippians 3:9, Paul knows that he *is* "in Christ," so there is no need for him to desire to be found where he already is. There is no indication that at any time, Paul was afraid that he could "get out of" Christ by a mistake or failure. He was absolutely confident that nothing could ever separate him from the love of God which is his "in Christ" (Rom. 8:32-39).

Instead, what Paul is saying in this verse is that he is concerned to be found in a certain way, or to be found as a certain kind of person, "in Christ." The first thing he says regarding this matter is that he wants to be found having not his own righteousness, but the righteousness that God gave him in Christ. Paul does not stop there, however. He also desires the things that come to him from knowing Christ and the power of His resurrection, from a partnership with Him in His sufferings and from dying a death like His; in addition, Paul desires the things that will make him perfect and will qualify him to win the prize (Phil. 3:10-14).

We know how passionate Paul was to be found blameless, holy, perfect, and well-pleasing to God at the judgment seat of Christ. Hence, I believe that we ought to interpret the phrase, "and may be found in Him . . ." (3:9), in the following way: Paul is expressing his determination to be found qualified for "the prize of the upward call of God in Christ Jesus," when he stands before the judgment seat of

Christ (3:14). With this in mind, in verses nine through fourteen, he offers a description of how he wants to be found and of how he believes he will become qualified for the prize.

In order to understand Philippians 3:10-11, we must look at its context, and we must grasp the total frame of mind exhibited in this entire chapter. The first thing we have to notice, identical to what we saw in Philippians 2:5-11, is the fundamental importance Paul gave to the way people think. The primary aim of his ministry was *to take "every thought captive to the obedience of Christ"* (2 Cor. 10:5, italics mine). This particular aim was a product of his belief that people are changed into what God wants them to be only as they *renew their minds* (Rom. 12:2). When people hear the "truth . . . in Jesus" and are "taught in Him," they are commanded, with reference to their old way of life, to "lay aside the old self" and to "put on the new self"; this can only be accomplished by being "renewed in the spirit of your mind," because "the new self . . . in the likeness of God has been created in righteousness and holiness of *the truth*" (Eph. 4:21-24, italics mine). In other words, this "new self . . . is being renewed *to a true knowledge* according to the image of the One who created him" (Col. 3:10, italics mine).

According to Paul, there are two kinds of minds: the mind according to the flesh (φρόνημα τῆς σαρκὸς) and the mind according to the Spirit (φρόνημα τοῦ πνεύματος), the one spelling death and the other one life (Rom. 8:6). At the close of his discussion about *the wisdom of God*, Paul declared that "we have the mind (νοῦν) of Christ" (1 Cor. 2:16). In the same spirit, in the second chapter of Philippians, the key exhortation of Paul to the Philippians is to have "the same mind . . . [and] attitude" as Christ (Phil. 2:2, 5); they ought "to think" (φρονείσθω) like Him (2:5, literal translation). Lastly, we saw that the essence of the mind of Christ was the total giving of Himself in humility and self-sacrifice for the salvation of others even with the price of death on a cross.

Now, in the third chapter of Philippians, Paul tells us how he himself thinks; he opens *his own mind* to us. He uses the words "I counted" (ἥγημαι) and "I count" (ἡγοῦμαι, consider, think) three times in verses seven and eight to indicate how he has changed his perspective with respect to the things of the flesh. At one time in the past, these had been his supreme values, whereas now he thinks of them as being rubbish. He has a new mental outlook, and what is of "surpassing value" for him now is "knowing Christ Jesus my Lord"

(3:8). Paul's present goal is to know Him in the most intimate fellowship possible (3:10). He, of course, does not consider (λογίζομαι, reckon or think) himself as having "arrived" at the goal, or as having been perfected already. Instead, Paul sees himself as running, with his whole being engaged in this race "toward the goal for the prize of the upward call of God in Christ Jesus" (3:14).

In conclusion to his comprehensive description of the way he thinks about life, the Apostle Paul calls the Philippians to join him: "Let us think this way" (τοῦτο φρονῶμεν, 3:15, personal translation). Next, he turns and violently condemns the "enemies of the cross of Christ" (they are people in the church!), because they have "set their minds on earthly things" (3:19). In contrast to these people, our inner eyes should eagerly and perpetually search the horizon for the coming of our Savior, the Lord Jesus Christ, because "our citizenship is in heaven"; we, at present, are confidently expecting the transformation of our earthly bodies "into conformity with the body of His glory" (3:20-21). In the parallel Epistle to the Colossians, Paul says directly that we should concentrate our minds on things above (τὰ ἄνω φρονεῖτε) as we anticipate the moment when we shall be "revealed . . . with Him in glory" (Col. 3:2-4).

We have surveyed the way that Paul thought and the way he exhorted other Christians to think, because it is only after we have captured his total mindset that we can really grasp what he wanted to communicate in Philippians 3:10 through verse 14. Above all else, Paul wanted to know Christ. We know that in order to come to know Christ, one has to first attain the mind of Christ; one must think the way Christ thinks. Paul explained this truth in Philippians 2:5-8. The mind or attitude of Christ led Him to a voluntary incarnation into a life of humility and total obedience to the Father, into servanthood and self-sacrifice for the salvation of others. Christ knew that His equality with God, His divine essence, was not expressed by grabbing, snatching, or accumulating for Himself; rather, His essence was to empty Himself by utterly giving Himself to the service of others. His thinking was that "it is more blessed to give than to receive" (Acts 20:35). Christ expressed that kind of thinking by a life of suffering and by dying on the cross for others.

Paul called the Philippians to develop this same kind of thinking, but he also showed them how he applied it in his own life. How did he propose to know Christ in the most intimate way of knowing? Paul's answer is in the word κοινωνία: fellowship, partnership, and participation together with Christ in the affairs of Christ. In fact, there are three distinct elements in this κοινωνία: the power that is needed for it, which is the power of *His* resurrection, the sufferings of Christ, and the death of Christ.

Let us see how these three work together. Some commentators wonder why Paul started with the power of the resurrection. They feel that the logical sequence would be suffering, death, and resurrection. The answer is found in Ephesians 1:18-25, a parallel passage to Philippians 2:5-11 and 3:9-14. Initially, we read Paul's intense prayer that the eyes of our hearts might be enlightened so that we may know the extraordinary and glorious riches that will be our inheritance in heaven; in his conclusion, we read that Christ is seated at the right hand of God "in the heavenly places" as the supreme ruler over the universe. He was lifted up to that position by the power of the resurrection. But the main point in the prayer is this: the power that raised, transformed, and installed Jesus as "head over all things," now works "toward us who believe" (Eph. 1:19, 22). That power of "surpassing greatness" is now directed by God toward His other children who have the same destiny of obtaining the inheritance, that is, of being assigned places of authority or dominion over His creation, just as Jesus was placed "over all things"!

But how can we reach that glory? Romans 8:17 gives us the answer: by becoming partners with Christ in His sufferings! The point Paul makes in Philippians 3:10 is that in order to be able to go with Christ into that partnership of suffering, we have to know in ourselves, in our own experience, the power of His resurrection. We have already seen that to participate with Christ in His sufferings means to make His affairs our affairs; this idea is expressed in Philippians as "participation in the gospel" (1:5), as "striving together for the faith of the gospel" (1:27), and "experiencing the same conflict" as Paul was experiencing with a hostile world (1:30). Of course, this is the grace of suffering for the sake of Christ (1:29). In the letter to the Colossians, the grace of suffering for Christ's sake is expressed as suffering on behalf of the church (1:24), which means getting involved sacrificially to admonish and teach each man and woman until we are able to present everyone "complete in Christ" (1:28-29).

This is not something that we simply wait for, hoping that perhaps someday, somehow, some suffering for Christ might come to us. Certainly, the Scriptures do not teach us to pursue suffering for its own sake. Rather, suffering for Christ means, first of all, being aware that

Christ is still in pain for a dying world and is still at work perfecting His body, the church; it involves becoming concerned with His concerns and agreeing with Him that it is happier to give than to receive. Then, as a result of this, it means pouring ourselves into the service of others until we empty ourselves in order to fill others, until we become poor in order that they may become rich, and until we sacrifice ourselves in order that they may be blameless at the judgment seat of Christ.

And as we take the gospel of life and light and glory to the blind people of the world, we will undoubtedly disturb their earthly pursuits and they might even react by killing us. It happened to our Forerunner, and He Himself said that it most certainly will happen to us if we follow in His footsteps. But in His kingdom's economy, one wins by losing, and one lives by dying. Ultimately, conforming our own story to the story of the Master, and enduring a death like His for the sake of others, is the supreme beauty, the supreme grace, the supreme privilege, the supreme honor, and the supreme glory! This is exactly what Paul tried to convey when he expressed his goal of "being conformed to His death" (Phil. 3:10).

Earlier, he had exhorted the Philippians to think like Christ by accepting to live wholly for others and by even being willing to die for others; now, in 3:10, he is simply saying that he himself wants to walk on the same road! There are linguistic and logical similarities between what he said about Christ in 2:5-8 and what he says about himself here. Jesus took the form (μορφήν) of a slave whose essence is absolute obedience. He humbled Himself to that position and became obedient unto death, even death on a cross. In the same spirit, Paul wants to conform (συμμορφούμενος) to Christ's lowly, humble position and to die a death like "His death" (3:10).

Protestant theologians in the West typically spiritualize this text to death, because they are so afraid of anything that would bring us closer to a Roman Catholic interpretation of suffering and martyrdom, and *especially*, because they want to run away from any idea of an obligatory call to a literal suffering and sacrifice for Christ and for His gospel. It will suffice to give just one example of this kind of interpretation:

> Union with Christ implies that all of Christ's redemptive experiences are duplicated unredemptively in the believer. The Christian, accordingly, suffered with Christ (Rom. 8:17), was crucified with him (Rom. 6:6), died with him (Rom. 6:8; 2 Tim.

2:11), was buried with him (Rom. 6:4; Col. 2:12), made alive with him (Col. 2:13), raised with him (Col. 2:12; 3:1), made joint-heirs with him (Rom. 8:17), is glorified with him (Rom. 8:17), enthroned with him (Col. 3:1; Rev. 20:4), and reigns with him (2 Tim. 2:12; Rev. 20:4).[126]

In addition, it is baffling to observe the way in which the Bible's conditional statements, such as the promises conditioned upon our suffering with Christ (i.e., if we suffer, we will be joint-heirs with Him and will be glorified with Him, Rom. 8:17; we will reign with Him, 2 Tim. 2:12 and Rev. 20:4) are said to be somehow "duplicated . . . in the believer," with no obligation on the part of the believer at all.[127] This *is* a very attractive and easy religion, indeed!

We have arrived at the most difficult Pauline statement for our Protestant colleagues: "in order that I may attain to the resurrection from the dead" (Phil. 3:11). There are two specific difficulties in this text. The first one is Paul's obvious uncertainty regarding the resurrection. Our difficulty is created by the fact that the resurrection from the dead will happen to everybody, saved or unsaved, whatever sequence of events is construed from the New Testament information on this subject. Moreover, in many of his letters, including the one to the Philippians, Paul made his certainty very clear that if he died before "that Day," he would go to be with the Lord, and that he would be among the resurrected ones "in Christ" when the Lord will come for the last judgment (1 Cor. 15:23; 2 Cor. 5:1-8; Phil. 1:21-23; 2 Tim. 4:6-8). On the other hand, Paul was also absolutely sure that if he did not die before the Day of the Lord, then he would be among those who will be taken up to meet the Lord in the air (1 Thess. 4:16-17). In view of this hope and certitude, why did Paul speak in such uncertain terms in Philippians 3:11?

The second difficulty lies in the word translated into English as the "resurrection." That was not the word used by Paul. Philippians 3:11 is the only place in which Paul used the term "ex-resurrection" (ἐξανάστασιν). For what reason did he employ this particular term and what did he mean by it? Our problem no longer exists if we simply take it exactly as it is written: Paul wanted to attain to the extra-resurrection! There are two other passages in the New Testament that can help us understand Paul's desire. The first is in the eleventh chapter of Hebrews, referring to the martyrs. After they had been tortured, they were offered release if they would only choose to give up their testimony; however, they refused and gave up their lives instead.

The author of Hebrews explains that the martyrs took this action "in order that they might obtain a better resurrection" (Heb. 11:35). What we have here is the scriptural teaching that there will be a special resurrection given only to the martyrs. This assertion is also found in Revelation 20:4-5, where we read that *only the martyrs* will be resurrected to reign with Christ for a thousand years. John wanted to make sure that he was correctly understood, because he emphatically added that "the rest of the dead did not come to life until the thousand years were completed. This is the first resurrection" (Rev. 20:5).

Now, I am aware that this view is vehemently opposed by most Protestant theologians. Notwithstanding, this is how Christians in the first centuries of the church's history understood these texts. It was this special promise made to the martyrs, among many other special promises, that transformed the horrible tragedy of martyrdom into the most desirable event that a child of God could ever experience. The strength of Christianity in times of great persecution was constituted and informed precisely by this belief in a special resurrection for those who had suffered martyrdom. This conviction is what made Christianity victorious throughout the ages. Here I stand, so help me God!

Paul wanted to become a martyr because, among other things, he wanted to participate in this extra-resurrection from the dead. That is why he included the words "if somehow" or "if possible" (NRSV). If we take Paul literally in what he said about wanting to die as his Lord had died, in the service of God's purposes for mankind, then we should also take him literally when he says that he desires the "extra-resurrection," or as Hebrews has it, "the better resurrection," which according to Revelation, means reigning with Christ for a thousand years.

We should not forget, however, that Philippians 3:10-11 represents only a small part of the larger picture. First of all, Paul's purpose was to convey the manner in which he would achieve his aim of knowing Christ. He would reach this goal by imitating Christ in His essence of self-giving, by living a life of self-sacrifice like Him, and by dying for God's purposes as Christ had died. It was a knowledge of the Other acquired by identification with the Other. But we should also keep in mind Paul's conviction that Christ lived all these actions in him and through him. Paul only participated voluntarily, wholeheartedly, and joyfully in the ministries of Christ. This is how Paul came to know Him better; his was a knowledge acquired by symbiosis and synergesis, by living together and working together with Christ in the most intimate way.

Yet even this aim of knowing Christ is part of a still larger picture. All this time, Paul has had in mind "the upward call of God in Christ Jesus" (Phil. 3:14). We already know what Paul meant by that call; we have seen it expressed in varying terms such as gaining "the glory of our Lord Jesus Christ" (2 Thess. 2:14) or receiving "an inheritance in the kingdom of Christ and God" (Eph. 5:5). However, Paul must first present himself before the judgment seat of Christ, where all his work will be tested by fire; he himself must be found blameless and well-pleasing to God, before he can be declared worthy of the kingdom of God.

Therefore, Paul continued his description of his own outlook on life, his own way of thinking about this earthly existence, by telling the Philippians that he has not yet been made perfect and has not yet reached the goal. He is still in the midst of the struggle through which he strives to become what God wants him to be in the end, step by step acquiring and developing the kind of character God Himself is working in him. Yes, Paul wants to win the prize; he wants to pass the final exam of God and to hear His final verdict: δόκιμος, tested and approved for ruling with Christ. This is the whole picture of Paul's way of thinking, the essence of his world-view. Hence, Paul's single piece of advice to his readers is: "Think like me" (τοῦτο φρονῶμεν, Phil. 3:15, personal translation). Paul must have felt that he needed to explain this further, because he added, "Brethren, join in following my example, and observe those who walk according to the pattern you have in us" (3:17).

There are a few other items in Paul's prison epistles that call for our attention. One is the overall destiny of mankind. God made men and women in His own image, with the purpose of giving them dominion over His entire creation, according to Genesis 1:26-28 and Psalm 8. However, they failed the test of obedience. We have just seen that both in Romans and in the letters from prison, obedience is the key element in man's relationship with God. In addition, we are here presented with the Son of God as the Second Man, who gave God His total obedience, and as a direct consequence, was lifted up by God and installed as Lord over all creation. Both descriptions of the exaltation of Jesus, in Ephesians 1:19-23 and in Philippians 2:9-11, contain words that were taken directly from Psalm 8. Jesus is presented in these verses as the one Man who achieved the destiny of all men. He is given to us as the pattern, because God predestined us "to become conformed (συμμόρφους) to the image of His Son" (Rom. 8:29). Now we know that we become conformed to Christ's image by claiming the power of His resurrection in our own self-sacrificial living and, if God so chooses, in our dying in His service for the salvation and spiritual growth of other people.

God's whole strategy for transforming us into the kind of people He ultimately wants us to be has become perfectly clear. And what a glorious picture it is! When one really sees it, one gasps in awe and wonder. This is reason for joy, indeed! It is not a different joy than the one produced by suffering for Christ and by martyrdom for His sake. It is the joy that arises in our hearts when we stand in awe before the beauty and majesty of our heavenly destiny. Suffering and martyrdom are part of the race and the journey. They are the tools God uses in preparing us for that glorious destiny. We can rejoice in them because we know what they produce (2 Cor. 4:16-17). In 1973, when I was risking my life in the battle for more rights for our churches under the communist tyranny of Romania, my wife Elisabeth shared with one of my students at the Baptist Seminary in Bucharest that we might go through great troubles and sufferings. In response, the student replied with a shining face, "But, sister, if we go through sufferings, it simply means that we are on The Way!" My wife understood what he meant perfectly. He was, of course, using the language of the Book of Acts (Acts 22:4; 24:14, 22), encouraging her by saying that our suffering was the blessed proof that we were on the right track. We were making it! Consequently, we rejoiced in our suffering because it gave us the assurance that we were indeed on the way to the fulfillment of our heavenly calling. After all, when the mind is caught up in heaven, the pains of this earth are turned to naught. The body does not feel the pain if the spirit is in heaven!

The letter to the Philippian saints is indeed a manual for martyrdom. Precisely because its nature is such, it is also a book of joy. Sixteen times in four short chapters Paul speaks about joy and rejoicing. He was in prison, in chains, writing about his imminent martyrdom to friends who were themselves going through a bitter persecution. He congratulates them for being partners with him and for sharing with him in the grace of suffering for Christ and for His gospel. Therefore, "rejoice in the Lord always; again I will say, rejoice!" (Phil. 4:4).

There is one other martyrological motif that I want to highlight in these letters from prison. It is the battle with the cosmic principalities and powers. Paul had earlier described the apostles' suffering and martyrdom as a spectacle for these cosmic powers (1 Cor. 4:9). Here, in Colossians 2:15, he writes that when Christ died on the cross, He "disarmed the rulers and authorities, [and] He made a public display of them, having triumphed over them." Even so, Paul tells the Christians in Ephesus that we must wage war "against the rulers, against the powers, against the world forces of this darkness, and against the spiritual forces of wickedness in the heavenly places" (Eph. 6:12). How can we do battle with and defeat forces that we cannot even see and of whose existence we might not even be aware?

In order to answer this question, we need to remember the experience of Job. He was certainly not aware of the dramatic events that were taking place in heaven. He simply discovered one day that all he had built during a lifetime was suddenly lost and ruined; furthermore, without any prior warning, he found himself in the most miserable state of suffering. Nevertheless, Job kept his faith in God, and his faithfulness to God remained undaunted and firm. Job had no way of knowing that God was at that moment demonstrating something special to the cosmic beings; he could not have fathomed that, by means of his faithfulness to God, he was dealing a heavy blow to Satan.

Now, when we read Ephesians 3:10—"in order that the manifold wisdom of God might now be made known through the church to the rulers and the authorities in the heavenly places" (ἐπουρανίοις)—can we give it a similar interpretation? How does God demonstrate His wisdom to "the rulers and the authorities" through His church? The answer is clear: by nothing other than the way of Job! God demonstrates His wisdom through the faithfulness of His children; through their refusal to remain on the easy road of self-satisfaction and self-centeredness, and through their willingness to take the way of the cross, the way of self-sacrifice and of living and dying for others. When the early Christians were led into the arena to be thrown before the wild beasts, they understood that they were actually engaging in a supreme battle with Satan and his forces. They were absolutely aware of the fact that they were a spectacle to the entire universe, and they knew with utmost certainty that God was going to achieve a great victory through their faithfulness unto death.

1 and 2 Timothy

The letters to Timothy are the last messages we have from the Apostle Paul. When these letters were written, Paul was sure that he would soon be sentenced to death as a martyr. These messages were addressed to his closest disciple and co-worker, the man to whom Paul would entrust the continuation of his ministry. It is only natural to expect, therefore, that among other important last instructions, Paul would give Timothy a solid teaching regarding suffering and martyrdom for Christ and His gospel, as well as regarding rewards in heaven. Our expectations are not disappointed when we read 1 and 2 Timothy. In both letters, and particularly in the second one, we find a teaching that has been guiding, inspiring, and encouraging Christians facing persecution and martyrdom ever since these words were penned.

In the first letter, we find only one exhortation to Timothy that relates directly to our subject of research. We also find a piece of instruction given to rich Christians that includes important ideas about rewards in heaven. We shall reserve this last issue for the end of this chapter and concentrate now on the instructions given to Timothy.

Here is the essence of Paul's exhortation: "Fight the good fight of faith; take hold of the eternal life to which you were called, . . . I charge you in the presence of God, . . . that you keep the commandment without stain or reproach until the appearing of our Lord Jesus Christ" (1 Timothy 6:12-14). In the face of so much opposition to faith in the gospel of Christ, the ministries of Paul and of Timothy were constant battles. Although the two terms, ἀγωνίζου and ἀγῶνα are athletic, here the idea of a sports competition does not fit, because Paul was referring to his own personal warfare with evil.[128] Jesus said that He had come into this world as one who enters a strong man's domain and binds him, in order to take away his goods (Matt. 12:29). Following in His Master's footsteps, Paul saw himself and his co-warrior in the same battle; he was in a war for the minds of men and women, employing "weapons of warfare" that are "divinely powerful for the destruction of fortresses" (2 Cor. 10:4). When one is in the midst of a war, one has to be ready for suffering and for dying in the field of battle. This idea will emerge more clearly in the second letter, but it is still intimated here, as we shall see in a moment. But first, I want to indicate that, as usual, all of Paul's instructions to Timothy are mainly concerned with the young leader's condition on the final day, at "the appearing of our Lord Jesus Christ" (1 Tim. 6:14). Timothy is commanded to live in such a way as to be "unspotted" (ἄσπιλον) and "without reproach" (ἀνεπίλημπτον) on that day (ibid.).

Of special interest to us in these verses is Paul's reference to the "confession" made by Timothy (6:12) and to the "confession" made by Jesus (6:13). In verse 12, Paul exhorts him to "take hold of the eternal life to which you were called, and did confess (ὡμολόγησας) the good confession (ὁμολογίαν) in the presence of many witnesses" (literal translation). Then, in verse 13, Paul says to Timothy, "I charge you in the presence of God, who gives life to all things, and of Christ Jesus, who testified (μαρτυρήσαντος, witnessed) the good confession (ὁμολογίαν) before Pontius Pilate" (NASB). These words have generated many heated debates among modern commentators, but in the second through the fourth centuries, they were commonly used when speaking about martyrdom.

The first piece of information we want to know is *when* Timothy made his confession; then, we are interested in *what* the content of that confession was; lastly, we want to know *how* Timothy's confession was linked with the witness of Jesus. Likewise, we can ask similar questions with regard to the witness of Jesus. Most modern commentators say that Timothy's confession was made either at his baptism or at his ordination. The problem with both of these suggestions is that Timothy was baptized and called to work with Paul very early in the life of the Christian church, and it is doubtful whether at that stage the church had a set formula for baptism or for ordination.

Much more probable is the suggestion that Timothy made his confession of faith "when on a trial before a heathen judge."[129] Only in this case would his witness be similar to the witness made by Jesus before Pilate. Another linguistic indication that has to be taken into consideration is that in the later martyrological terminology, a Christian who withstood the test of the trial and the torture following the sentencing was called a "confessor." Only after the actual execution had taken place would his witness be called a μαρτυρία, martyrdom. In keeping with this specific use of the term "confessor," Paul refers to Timothy's action as ὡμολόγησας, "you did confess," and to the action of Jesus as τοῦ μαρτυρήσαντος, "who witnessed." One could argue here that it is at best doubtful that such advanced, technical terms for martyrdom would already be in use when Paul was writing this letter. However, one thing is sure: in Paul's defense before the people in Jerusalem, he spoke of the stoning of Stephen in clearly defined martyrological jargon: "when the blood of Thy witness (μάρτυρός) Stephen was being shed" (Acts 22:20).

Three other instances where the term "witness" was used in the New Testament serve to elucidate the issue and to support our claim. In 1 Timothy 2:6, after stating that Jesus "gave Himself as a ransom for all," Paul adds these strange words: "the witness borne at the proper time" (τὸ μαρτύριον καιροῖς ἰδίοις; the NASB has translated it as "testimony"). Spicq comments that this phrase is "so elliptical as to be almost unintelligible."[130] Secondly, in 2 Timothy 1:8, Paul advises Timothy not to be ashamed of "the witness of our Lord" (τὸ μαρτύτιον τοῦ Κυρίου ἡμῶν; again, the NASB uses the word "testimony"). If we add the fact that Jesus Himself told Pilate that He had come into this world "to bear witness (μαρτυρήσω) to the truth" (John 18:37), it becomes clear that we are already in a milieu in which bearing witness is accompanied by death. Hence, sometime during the first century A.D., the term "witness" acquired the new meaning of "martyr." Of course, in the Greek language, the same word is used to signify both witness and martyr; the only issue, then, is to discover when the word "witness" came to possess this new meaning. My opinion is that we have sufficient evidence to be able to argue that the new meaning was already popularly used and recognized by the time Paul gave his speech in Jerusalem, recorded in Acts 22, and undoubtedly by the time he wrote his letters to Timothy.

Therefore, we can legitimately affirm that in 1 Timothy 2:6, Paul was clearly representing the death of Jesus as a martyrdom (μαρτύριον). Hanson writes about Jesus' "witness" before Pilate, mentioned by Paul in 1 Timothy 6:13, that "if we are to be influenced by 2:6, . . . the witnessing was simply Christ's self-giving in death."[131]

Paul appreciated the fact that Timothy had already withstood the test of being a confessor. Then, he immediately directed Timothy's attention to the witness to death made by Jesus. We should notice that he linked these two by pointing to God "who gives life to all things" (1 Tim. 6:13). Earlier, when Paul wrote to the Corinthians about his near-death experience in Asia, he told them that this had happened to him "in order that we should not trust in ourselves, but in God who raises the dead" (2 Cor. 1:9). When you know that God gives life to everything and even raises the dead, then you are able to confidently go into a ministry that you know might cost you your own life. Paul expressed this idea in his second letter to Timothy: "For this reason I also suffer these things, but I am not ashamed; for I know whom I have believed and I am convinced that He is able to guard what I have entrusted to Him until that day" (2 Tim. 1:12).

It is to this second letter that we now turn our attention. The Second Epistle to Timothy is the message of a man who has become aware that he would certainly be martyred for Christ and His gospel. He pens his last words to his "beloved son" (1:2), to whom he gives his last commission, and with whom he shares his most intimate thoughts about his life, his faith, and his expectations for the future. In the process, we gain one of the deepest meditations on suffering and martyrdom, and yes, indeed, on rewards in heaven.

First of all, Paul sends Timothy an invitation to suffering: "Therefore do not be ashamed of the testimony of our Lord, or of me His prisoner; but join with me in suffering for the gospel according to the power of God" (1:8). The text is directly inspired by the words of Jesus in Matthew 10:32-33: "Everyone therefore who shall confess Me before men, I will also confess him before My Father who is in heaven. But whoever shall deny Me before men, I will also deny him before My Father who is in heaven." However, when Paul wrote about the "witness of our Lord," he was not referring to this witness of Christ in heaven. Timothy was in no danger of being ashamed of that. Instead, Paul was referring, as we have already indicated, to the witness Jesus made by His death. God has so ordained that whatever He achieves, He accomplishes through His children's voluntary suffering. For this reason, the gospel, which is God's plan in action, requires voluntary sufferers; hence the invitation to "join with me in suffering for the gospel" (2 Tim. 1:8). The actual words Paul used here are much more condensed than their English translation: συγκακοπάθησον τῷ εὐαγγελίῳ; the literal translation is to "suffer bad [treatment or hardship] with the gospel" (τῷ εὐαγγελιῳ is a dative instrument).

The cause of the gospel, the cause of reaching a dying world with God's salvation, demands sufferers. Paul will explain why this is so in the second chapter. For the moment, he simply wants to assure Timothy that if he accepts this ministry of suffering, he will not do it in his own power, but in the "power of God." Paul himself was given this "holy calling" (1:9) and was appointed preacher, apostle, and teacher of the gospel. It is for this reason that he also suffers these things. Yet Paul was confident because he knew that God "is able" to carry him through "until that day" (1:12). Again we see Paul with an eye toward "that day," the day when he will stand before the Lord. We shall see what he has to say to Timothy about "that day" in a short while.

It is in the second chapter that Paul fully develops his teaching about suffering for the gospel. He starts by repeating his invitation to suffering: "Suffer hardship with me, as a good soldier of Christ Jesus" (2:3). Again Paul employs the combined word of 1:8, συγκακοπάθησον, this time without any qualifier. In addition, Paul introduces a new reason for his suffering: he suffers because he has accepted to be a good soldier of Jesus Christ. We find ourselves once more in the war situation depicted in 1 Timothy 6:12. Here, in the second chapter of 2 Timothy, Paul multiplies the metaphors, selecting three types of people who have jobs involving them in hardship: the soldier, the athlete, and the farmer. The soldier has to give up his entanglements "in the affairs of everyday life" (2 Tim. 2:4); the athlete has to submit to the rules of his sport; and the farmer has to be dedicated and hard-working in order to bring in his crops. Paul's emphasis, however, is not on the difficulties, but rather on the final result of the effort expended by each of these individuals. The soldier pleases the one who enlisted him, the athlete wins the prize, and the farmer receives his share of the crops. Barrett formulates the purpose of this passage in this way:

> The main point of this small paragraph (vv. 3-7) as a whole is to exhort Timothy to take his share of hardship; and the metaphors, when duly pondered, suggest that beyond warfare is victory, beyond athletic effort a prize, and beyond agricultural labor a crop. In the same way, Timothy's share of hardship will be followed by reward.[132]

In order to make his point, Paul directs Timothy's attention to the example of Christ: "Remember Jesus Christ, risen from the dead, descendant of David, . . ." (2:8). The term "remember" here stands for "think of" or "consider." Paul wants Timothy to consider the fact that Christ accepted to die, but now He is risen and exalted; He accepted to become a man, a descendant of David, but now He is the ruler of the universe. What happened to Christ will happen to him (2:12), which means, of course, that Timothy will be given the reward!

Before he reaches the issue of rewards, Paul offers his own situation as an example for Timothy to follow. He speaks of "my gospel, for which I suffer hardship even to imprisonment as a criminal; but the word of God is not imprisoned" (2:8-9). In this whole passage, Paul is extremely concise in his statements; again and again we need to fill out his thoughts, as we did with Paul's example of the three kinds of people involved in hardship and with the example of Christ. In these verses, Paul's thought must be continued in this way: the word of God is not imprisoned; on the contrary, says Paul, due to my imprisonment, it spreads to areas it would never have otherwise reached (cf. Phil. 1:12-14). Paul himself confirms our explication, since he goes on to state the specific purpose of his own sufferings in the clearest possible terms: "For this reason I endure all things for the sake of those who are chosen, that they also may obtain the salvation which is in Christ Jesus and with it eternal glory" (2 Tim. 2:10).

The prepositional phrase at the beginning of the sentence, "for this reason," makes it absolutely clear that what follows is Paul's explanation of the purpose or goal of his sufferings. But first, there are two very important divine actions that must be recognized. One is that God *elects*, and the other is that *salvation is in Christ Jesus alone*, only in Him and nowhere else. Having established the fact that salvation was worked out by Jesus Christ and the fact that God elects people for salvation, there is still one link missing: how will people obtain the salvation available in Christ and for which they have been elected? They have to believe the gospel of Jesus Christ, but before that can happen, they have to hear it. In his letter to the Romans, Paul had asked, "How shall they believe in Him whom they have not heard? And how shall they hear without a preacher?" (Rom. 10:14). Here we come to the crux of the matter. When a Christian goes to tell others about Christ, the non-believers are disturbed and react violently against that person. But in most cases, as the messenger of the gospel accepts the violence and meets it with love, the eyes of the spiritually blind are opened, and they see "the glory of God in the face of Christ" (2 Cor. 4:6). That is how they obtain the salvation that is in Christ!

Since God's salvation is available to all men and women, the only question is who will deliver it to them. Moreover, this process of salvation-delivery is very costly for the carrier; some type of suffering will always be involved for the one who takes the Good News to others. It is crucial to notice here that Paul was never ambiguous about his sufferings possibly adding something to salvation itself, in the sense that his sufferings could have some atoning or redemptive value in themselves. There is no such thought anywhere in his writings. Salvation is totally and completely the work of Christ and the gift of God. It is all by grace. The only purpose for Paul's own sufferings is to carry that gift to people everywhere. Suffering has no value in itself, and one should not seek suffering for its own sake. Suffering has value only if it comes as a consequence of the fact that one has embraced the cause of Christ and has invested all that one has and all that one is in the service of the delivery of the gospel. These are the sufferings of Christ, and it is only in the cause of the gospel that one becomes a partner with Christ in His sufferings.

At this juncture we are ready to receive one more detail that Paul offers regarding rewards in heaven:

> It is a trustworthy statement:
> For if we died with Him, we shall also live with Him;
> If we endure, we shall also reign with Him;
> If we deny Him, He also will deny us;
> If we are faithless, He remains faithful; for He cannot deny Himself.
> Be diligent to present yourself approved to God as a workman who does not need to be ashamed, handling accurately the word of truth. (2 Tim. 2:11-13, 15)

This is yet another text that Protestant interpreters tend to spiritualize until it loses all of its intended meaning. In essence, the repeated ifs of these clauses are not taken seriously as literal conditionals. For example, one American theologian told me that all saved people will reign or rule with Christ. When I quoted 2 Timothy 2:12 to him and asked how he would interpret it, he candidly said: "All Christians will rule with Christ. But now, down here, for the people who go through persecution, it is encouraging to be told that one day they will rule with Christ." My reaction was to say that if such were the case, it would amount to dishonesty and deception on the part of God!

Barrett is one of the few commentators who believe that this passage refers to martyrdom. Nevertheless, he still spiritualizes the part about rewards until *it* amounts to nothing.[133] John Stott is closer to giving us the real meaning of the text, but he does not mention martyrdom. Here is how he puts it:

> The death with Christ which is here mentioned must refer, according to the context, not to our death to sin through union with Christ in his death, but rather to our death to self and to safety, as we take up the cross and follow Christ. So the Christian life is depicted as a life of dying, a life of enduring. Only if we share Christ's death on earth, shall we share his life in heaven. Only if

we share his sufferings and endure, shall we share his reign in the hereafter. For the road to life is death, and the road to glory suffering. (cf. Rom. 8:17; 2 Cor. 4:17)[134]

Before I make my own comments on this important text, I must point out that 2 Timothy 2:11 is one of the five places in the Pastoral epistles where Paul begins a statement with the words, "It is a faithful saying" (the NASB has translated it as "It is a trustworthy statement"). Most scholars believe that Paul used this phrase to introduce a popular saying which was already familiar to the readers of his time. The problem with this theory is that the first part of the quote is very similar to what Paul wrote in Romans 6; only the second part seems to be a maxim that was in circulation at that time. J. H. Bernard gives us a plausible scenario:

> It thus appears that clauses 1, 2, 4 of this remarkable hymn are little more than reproductions of phrases from St. Paul's Epistle to the Romans, clause 3 being based on words of Christ. It does not seem an improbable conjecture that the hymn was actually composed at Rome in reference to the earlier persecutions of Christians under Nero, and that it thus became known to St. Paul during his second imprisonment in the imperial city. If this be so, he is here, as it were, quoting a popular version of words from his own great Epistle, which had become stereotyped by liturgical use.[135]

Whichever way this text was created, as we have it in chapter two, it is part of a lengthy meditation on the purpose of suffering for Christ and His gospel and on the rewards for such suffering. It clearly has in view the judgment at the seat of Christ: "Be diligent to present yourself approved to God as a workman who does not need to be ashamed, handling accurately the word of truth" (2 Tim. 2:15).

We are, by now, well acquainted with Paul's concern for the way in which we shall be found at the judgment seat of Christ. Paul has already shown us that the suffering and work of Christ at Calvary has had only one purpose ever since that event took place, namely, to present (παραστήσῃ, Eph. 5:27) His church blameless, holy, and perfect to Himself in heaven. We also remember Paul having said that his own toils and struggles have been for the purpose of presenting (παραστήσωμεν) "every man complete (perfect) in Christ" (Col. 1:28). Now, we see Paul pleading with Timothy to struggle and toil diligently in order to present (παραστῆσαι) *himself* in the same way for the final examination of Christ and of God (2 Tim. 2:15).

In addition to this, we should remember that one of the key purposes of the afflictions that come our way is to test (δοκιμάζω) us; furthermore, the tests have the goal of producing a godly character (δοκιμή) in us (Rom. 5:4). The final determination and verdict at the end of the production line will then be either tested and approved (δόκιμος), or tested and disqualified (ἀδόκιμος). Paul wrote to the Corinthians that he has worked for the gospel so that he might have a share in it, and that he has worked hard and has kept himself under strict discipline so that, after he has preached the gospel of glory to others, he himself might not be disqualified (ἀδόκιμος, 1 Cor. 9:23-27). In 2 Timothy 2:6, Paul also tells Timothy to toil diligently, following the example of the hard-working farmer, in order to have the first share in the crop and to be found "approved" (δόκιμος) by God at the final judgment. The dreadful alternative to this verdict would be to hear God declare him ἀδόκιμος, and what a frightening shame that would be!

Looking back upon the ground we have covered, we can now observe how consistent this great apostle has been throughout all of his writings. But we have not yet asked the most burning question: What will take place *after* the judgment seat of Christ? What will happen to the one who will be "ashamed" because of being "disqualified"? We know one thing for sure: that man will have no reward in heaven, and even worse, "he shall suffer loss," although "he himself shall be saved, yet so as through fire" (1 Cor. 3:15). Ought we also to apply to him the many warnings Jesus gave to "the evil slave" or to "the unworthy slave" who did not fulfill the jobs given to him by his Master (e.g., Matt. 24:48-51; Matt. 25:24-30; Luke 12:45-48; Luke 19:20-26)? Should we take seriously His warnings about the slave (*His* slave) who will be found "unworthy" and will be severely flogged or thrown into the outer darkness? I do not wish to speculate, but only to look carefully at what the Son of God said and at what the Word of God actually says; most of all, I want to echo Paul's words when he spoke of the judgment seat of Christ: "Therefore knowing the fear of the Lord, [I] persuade men," not to play with fire (2 Cor. 5:11)!

On the other hand, what will eternity be like for the one who did suffer with Christ, who endured hardship with Christ, and who died with Him and for Him? Thankfully, there is more information available to us regarding this last question. Paul introduces it as "a faithful saying," or, as the NASB has translated it, "a trustworthy statement": "For if we died with Him, we shall also live with Him. If we endure, we shall also reign with Him" (2 Tim. 2:11-12).

We know that Christ came down to us as a slave, and that He toiled, agonized, and died for the sake of others. "Therefore also God highly exalted Him," and made Him the ruler of the cosmos; now He reigns over the entire universe (Phil. 2:9-11). Christ has been presented to us as the paradigm, and we have been called to the same destiny. Furthermore, we know that being given authority as a son over the Father's possessions means obtaining the inheritance. Therefore, reigning with Christ means being co-heirs with Christ. In view of this, it makes complete sense to refer here to what Paul writes in Colossians 3:23-25 to the slaves in that church: "Whatever you do, do your work heartily, as for the Lord rather than for men; knowing that from the Lord you will receive the reward of the inheritance. It is the Lord Christ whom you serve. For he who does wrong will receive the consequences of the wrong which he has done, and that without partiality." For we "know with certainty, that no immoral or impure person or covetous man, who is an idolater, has an inheritance in the kingdom of Christ and God" (Eph. 5:5; cf. 1 Cor. 6:9-10; Gal. 5:19-21).

Let me emphasize again that the issue here is not about merit. No father demands that his child "earn" the inheritance. It is the good pleasure of the Father to give His child all that He has. It is in the nature of fatherhood to desire to see a child become a mature, responsible, capable person to whom a father can entrust his possessions. Without any doubt, whatever position God gave to Christ, it was by grace (ἐχαρίσατο αὐτῷ, Phil. 2:9). Paul made it eminently clear that the inheritance is not "based on law," but is "based on a promise" (Gal. 3:18), and that means that it is given "by grace" (cf. Rom. 4:1-18).

We have so far learned that the main content of rewards in heaven is ruling with Christ, and that this ruling with Christ is the same as obtaining the inheritance. I strongly believe that by understanding and establishing these two premises, we have achieved a solid base for a theology of rewards. At the same time, we have also securely founded a theology of works and a theology of suffering and dying with and for Christ, from which the notion of merit, of earning something from God, has been completely excluded.

God is not waiting up in heaven until we earn and therefore merit from Him some privileges, treasures, and positions in His kingdom. God is in the business of training His children as they do their jobs down here for unspeakably great responsibilities up there. As this process unfolds, He purposes to produce in us a character like His own and to conform us to His own image. God will not produce these things automatically. Instead, He chose to place us in the midst of an evil society full of hardship and difficulty, commanding us to tackle it according to His rules of engagement and in His own way. In the meantime, He provides us with all the power we need to accomplish His will (2 Cor. 9:8). He promises that no test will be beyond our ability to stand because He will always provide the way to victory (1 Cor. 10:13). It is God Himself who, in the last analysis, "is at work in you, both to will and to work for His good pleasure" (Phil 2:13), in such a way that we shall never be able to boast that *we* achieved something. As Paul declared about himself, we will only be able to tell of what *Christ* did through us (Rom. 15:18). Through this entire process we become *qualified*, and we become *worthy*, that is, *capable* of handling authority for ruling, for governing responsibly with Christ over the affairs of His whole creation, in accordance with the initial purpose of God in creating man (Gen. 1:26-28, Psalm 8).

One more thing must be said regarding the first "if" on Paul's list of conditions sent to Timothy: "If we died with Him, we shall also live with Him" (2 Tim. 2:11). John Stott gives us a starting point into its interpretation, by stating that this is "our death to *self* and to *safety*, as we take up the cross and follow Christ."[136] I have defined taking up our own cross and following Jesus as our voluntary and self-sacrificial involvement with Christ in spreading the gospel and in fulfilling all the other purposes of Christ in and through our own lives. This definition is in complete accord with what we found to be Paul's understanding. In order to adequately comprehend this "death to *self* and to *safety*," we must return to one of the most essential texts in Paul's writings: "For the love of Christ constrains us, having concluded (κρίναντας, judged, pondered deeply and arrived at the deepest understanding of) this, that one died for all, therefore all died; and He died for all, that they who live should no longer live for themselves, but for Him who died and rose again on their behalf" (2 Cor. 5:14-15; the NASB has "controls" instead of "constrains").

We have seen that the essence of the divine nature is not to grab for Himself, but to give until He is empty. His nature is characterized by a selfless, altruistic attitude of self-giving, suffering, and dying for the utmost benefit of unworthy humans, whom Christ wants to make His own brothers and sisters, bearing His own image (Phil. 2:5-8;

Rom. 8:29-30). We have also seen that in the fall, God's image in human beings was damaged; they became selfish and self-centered creatures. Man set himself up as the center of the world; and when there is an entire world consisting of billions of people who all consider themselves to be the center of the world and who want to grab everything for themselves, therein exist all the conditions for misery and self-destruction. Beyond the purpose of atoning for our sins and of reconciling us to God, the key purpose of Christ's death for us, said Paul, was to recreate us and to remake us according to His own image. He died so that we would stop living for ourselves and would begin living for Christ and, by implication, would begin living for others. *This* is the content of the "new creature . . . in Christ" spoken about in 2 Corinthians 5:17!

When we truly understand the love of Christ on the cross, when we deeply ponder its meaning as Paul had done, we come to see the beauty of a life completely spent for others, and we are conquered by this beauty; hence, we come to desire to live likewise. As we begin living that kind of life, we die "to self and to safety," becoming men and women of a new kind on this planet; living with Christ and for Christ, we begin looking not for our own interests but for the interests of others, in order that they may be saved and may be presented blameless and complete at the judgment seat of Christ. In the meantime, we undergo different struggles and hardships, much suffering, and perhaps even martyrdom. However, if we endure these things, we will reign with Christ, because we will have become *what He is* in the course of our partnership with Him in His purposes on earth. As we are transformed into self-giving and self-sacrificing people, we acquire more and more of the character of Christ, and we become increasingly conformed to His image. This is the qualification required for being given dominion, for being put in charge over all of God's possessions, for being co-heirs with Christ, and for ruling and reigning with Christ.

With all this in mind, we are ready to look at the final, extremely personal testimony of the Apostle Paul:

> For I am already being poured out as a drink offering, and the time of my departure has come. I have fought the good fight, I have finished the course, I have kept the faith; in the future there is laid up for me the crown of righteousness, which the Lord, the righteous Judge, will award to me on that day; and not only to me, but also to all who have loved His appearing. (2 Tim. 4:6-8)

We should definitely add to this verses 17 and 18:

> But the Lord stood with me, and strengthened me, in order that through me the proclamation might be fully accomplished, and that all the Gentiles might hear; and I was delivered out of the lion's mouth. The Lord will deliver me from every evil deed, and will bring me safely to His heavenly kingdom; to Him be the glory forever and ever. Amen.

Our response to these words should be to bow down with Paul, acknowledging that whatever we have accomplished, it was done by Him, and He is indeed the only One worthy of our praise. To Him alone do we give all the glory forever.

This is the profoundly moving testimony of a man of God who gave himself totally to the service of Christ and of His gospel. For the purposes of this investigation, there is one specific item we must consider in particular in Paul's testimony. In all his previous letters and in all his exhortations, including this one addressed to Timothy, Paul had warned about the judgment seat of Christ, the fearful moment when the slave must hear the verdict of his Lord, a verdict that will decide his position in the eternal kingdom of God. But now, when he is on the point of going there, Paul does not exhibit any anxiety about that judgment. He simply expresses his certainty that he will surely receive "the crown of righteousness, which the Lord, the righteous Judge, will award to me on that day; and not only to me, but also to all who have loved His appearing" (4:8). Why all of a sudden this absolute certainty?

Let us try to understand Paul's mind. In Philippians 3:9, he told us that his aim was to "be found in Him, not having a righteousness of [his] own," but having "the righteousness which comes from God on the basis of faith," because he believes in Christ and relies only on the work of Christ on his behalf. Here in 2 Timothy 4:7, Paul has arrived at the end of his journey of faith, and he has "kept the faith"; that is, he has remained in that position of total dependence on Christ alone for his acceptance into God's eternal kingdom. At this moment, Paul is completely confident of the reception with which he will be welcomed in heaven. But what did he mean by "the crown of righteousness"? Paul certainly did not work for that righteousness; it was all the work of Christ for him. Then why will Paul be given a crown for something that has been entirely the work of someone else? In fact, that is the whole point of the matter: Paul will receive the crown because of his total reliance on the finished work of Christ on the cross for him. Precisely this crown shows that he has no merit for being there. It seems that on Paul's crown, these words are written: *I am here because of Jesus; therefore, let all the glory be given to Him!*

Yes, Paul will be judged before the judgment seat of Christ, but Paul himself has said that we should not "go on passing judgment before the time, but wait until the Lord comes who will both bring to light the things hidden in the darkness and disclose the motives of men's hearts; and then each man's praise will come to him from God."(1 Cor. 4:5). Paul lived according to his own preaching to others. He was assured and content that the whole matter was in good hands: "the one who examines me is the Lord" (1 Cor. 4:4). He did not know what that verdict would be that will determine his rewards, his share in the inheritance, and his ruling position. Nevertheless, he knew and rejoiced in the fact that he would be present before God's throne of judgment, entirely due to and based on the righteousness of Christ alone.

We still need to translate into modern idiom the following statement of Paul, which he wrote using the common language of martyrdom of his own day: Paul knew that he was "being poured out as a drink offering" (2 Tim. 4:6); that is, he knew that he would soon be martyred. Yet he still declares that "the Lord will deliver me from every evil deed, and He will save me into (εἰς, into or toward) His heavenly kingdom" (4:18, literal translation). Let us try to understand exactly what Paul meant by this. Jesus had taught him, saying, "Do not fear those who kill the body, but are unable to kill the soul" (Matt. 10:28). Going even further than this, Jesus said, "They will put . . . you to death, . . . yet not a hair of your head will perish" (Luke 21:16b, 18). How can this be? The answer is simple: although we will be put to death, God will raise us up again "imperishable" (1 Cor. 15:42). This awareness caused Paul to write that even though they will kill his body, the Lord will "save," keep, and preserve him in His heavenly kingdom. When they will kill his mortal body, he will finally go to be with his Lord, and it is "very much better" there with Him (Phil. 1:23).

In conclusion to our study of Paul's teaching on suffering, martyrdom, and rewards in heaven, a teaching that also led us to explore the interrelated issues of our works and of the judgment of Christ based on our works, we may ask ourselves how this teaching can apply in an area of the world in which there is no persecution and no possibility of martyrdom. Will Christians in such a situation miss something? With this question in mind, we now turn to Paul's specific instructions addressed to affluent people. Paul says to Timothy:

> Instruct those who are rich in this present world not to be
> conceited or to fix their hope on the uncertainty of riches, but on
> God, who richly supplies us with all things to enjoy. Instruct them
> to do good, to be rich in good works, to be generous and ready to
> share, storing up for themselves the treasure of a good foundation
> for the future, so that they may take hold of that which is life
> indeed. (1 Tim. 6:17-19)

On the most superficial level, this text is used as a pious call to the
rich to be generous in their giving. In its most vicious interpretation, it
is used as a justification for indulgence, because, after all, *God* gives
us all these riches in order for *us* "to enjoy" them (6:17). Let us make
an effort to unravel the extraordinarily important issues raised by Paul
in this direction. All these issues are basic and essential for our nature,
for our character, and for our eternal future.

Paul began with one of his favorite topics: the manner in which
people think of or perceive their total existence. "Charge them not to
be high-minded," Paul says in 6:17 (ὑψηλοφρονεῖν, think about
themselves in the highest degree; literal translation). The people to
whom Paul was referring saw themselves as special to God because
they had been given great wealth; they thought that God wanted them
to simply enjoy what he had lavishly bestowed upon them. Is not such
a theology being disseminated right now throughout one sector of
Western Christianity? But what was Paul suggesting? Paul knew the
teaching of Jesus on this subject very well, and we must go back to that
now. Let us see the total picture depicted by Christ:

> And the Lord said, "Who then is the faithful and sensible steward,
> whom his master will put in charge of his servants, to give them
> their rations at the proper time? Blessed is that slave whom his
> master finds so doing when he comes. Truly I say to you, that he
> will put him in charge of all his possessions. But if that slave says
> in his heart, 'My master will be a long time in coming,' and
> begins to beat the slaves, both men and women, and to eat and
> drink and get drunk; the master of that slave will come on a day
> when he does not expect him, and at an hour he does not know,
> and will cut him in pieces, and assign him a place with the
> unbelievers. And that slave who knew his master's will and did
> not get ready or act in accord with his will, shall receive many
> lashes, but the one who did not know it, and committed deeds
> worthy of a flogging, will receive but few. And from everyone who
> has been given much shall much be required; and to whom they

entrusted much, of him they will ask all the more." (Lk 12:42-48)

When God entrusts earthly riches to someone, that individual becomes a steward. In God's view, he is rich for others; the whole purpose of his being wealthy is so that he can feed others. Of course, Jesus was speaking metaphorically in this passage; consequently, we need to "translate" Jesus' words in this parable on the basis of the whole corpus of His literal teaching.

Jesus' main concern was with the great multitude of peoples that were without a shepherd. He was grieved that while the harvest was ripe and plentiful, the laborers were so few (Matt. 9:36-38). He then called His own disciples to feed these multitudes (Mark 6:37). However, this command was not only addressed to His disciples there and then; rather, it was a charge that is valid for all those who claim to belong to Him. We are all stewards who have been called to feed the starving people of the world with the gospel. Everything we have has been given to us in order for us to feed them.

One of the slaves in Jesus' parable could not believe that the owner would ever come back to judge him for what he had done with what was entrusted to him. This is the basic problem with evangelical Christians today. We simply cannot believe this teaching of Jesus, so we do not take it seriously! We are not afraid of the judgment seat of Christ. Just like that slave, we start eating and drinking (not necessarily alcoholic drinks), and the things we received in order to help others, we enjoy by ourselves! We do not realize that we are robbing God by our actions, exactly as the children of Israel were doing in the time of the prophet Malachi (Mal. 3:8-10). Furthermore, at that time, the Israelites were only asked to give ten percent of their income; with us, Christ is much more demanding.

The real issue at stake here is the inner nature of the steward: is he self-centered and arrogant, thinking that he is the one who deserves everything, wanting to accumulate all that he can in order to appear rich and great? This is the spirit of greed, of acquisitiveness, and of snatching for oneself that is perverting human nature. When Christ came into our world, He demonstrated exactly the opposite kind of spirit. His spirit is one of giving and of giving to the point of utter emptiness. Jesus demonstrated a spirit of servanthood and concern for others. He was primarily interested in feeding others, in healing them, rescuing them, and remaking them even with the cost of His own life. Today, Jesus says to all of us: "Learn from Me, for I am gentle and humble in heart" (Matt. 11:29). He calls us to humble ourselves, to spend ourselves and our riches for others just as He did: "For I gave you an example that you also should do as I did to you. Truly , truly, I say to you, a slave is not greater than his master; . . . If you know these things, you are blessed if you do them" (John 13:15-17).

Therefore, the instructions Paul gave to the wealthy are not at all a superficial matter. These actions of humility and generosity are a working out of one's nature. Hence, riches become a test for us; how we handle them will show others whether we are selfish, greedy, and acquisitive or we are like Christ, altruistic, self-giving, and self-sacrificing. These riches will serve to show if we should be declared δόκιμος, tested and approved, or ἀδόκιμος, tested and disqualified. This is exactly what Jesus taught us in the following passage:

> He who is faithful in a very little thing is faithful also in much; and he who is unrighteous in a very little thing is unrighteous also in much. If therefore you have not been faithful in the use of unrighteous mammon, who will entrust the true riches to you? And if you have not been faithful in the use of that which is another's, who will give you that which is your own? (Lk. 16:10-12)

In these verses, our Lord laid down three basic principles. The first principle is this: The faithfulness or unfaithfulness you demonstrate in the things entrusted to you for administration on this earth reveals your character as either reliable or unreliable (16:10). Jesus showed us the application of this principle in the parable of the minas. The slave who had been faithful down here was given authority over ten cities or over five cities (depending on the degree of faithfulness) when the king came back with His kingdom (Lk. 19:11-26).

The second principle contrasts "the true riches" with all the riches that are entrusted to us on earth, referred to as "unrighteous mammon" (16:11); this means that the material goods we have (i.e., house, fields, money, shares, etc.) are not the real or true riches. Our material possessions are eaten by moths and are subject to rust; in other words, in one way or another, they will all perish, decompose, and cease to exist. The true riches are in heaven (Matt. 6:19-21). For this reason, Paul did not look at "the things which are seen," but cared only for "the things which are not seen; for the things which are seen are temporal, but the things which are not seen are eternal" (2 Cor. 4:18). Hence, the second principle states that if you have not been faithful in the administration of these untrue riches, that is, if you have not used them for the purposes of the King, but only for your own enjoyment, you will not be entrusted with the true riches. You will have proven unreliable in the administration of God's possessions. You will have failed the test. As a result, God's verdict for you will be ἀδόκιμος.

The third principle says that all you have on this earth is not your own. Your wife is not your own; she belongs to God, who entrusted her into your care. Your children are not your own; they likewise belong to God, who entrusted them into your care so that you would shape a holy and godly character in each of them. Your talents are not your own either. In fact, you have nothing in yourself about which you could say, "This is mine; I can boast with this" (1 Cor. 4:7). Neither are any of your material goods your own; they also belong to God. They have been entrusted to you only for administration, as shown by the second principle. However, Jesus did mention some things that are your own (Lk. 16:12). What are these things? They are precisely everything that God has, the whole universe, for "all things belong to you" (1 Cor. 3:21-22). They are your birthright and your inheritance. Here, then, is the essence of the third principle: If you have not been faithful in the administration of the things which were not your own, you will not be entrusted with the things that are your own. You will not be given your own inheritance because when you were tested for reliability, you were found unworthy and unqualified, incapable of exercising authority over God's possessions. You were thus declared incapable of ruling and reigning with Christ.

Again we see how all things in the teaching of Jesus and in the teaching of Paul fit coherently together. As we go back to Paul's instructions to rich Christians, let us visualize these two different ways of living in contrast to each other. Paul commanded:

1. "Do not set your hope on the riches of uncertainty, but . . .
2. accumulate your treasures as a foundation for the future, for the real life in eternity" (1 Tim. 4:17, 19; free translation).

We live the first type of life by having a mentality that says: I am great; I deserve it. I will, therefore, accumulate for myself; I will keep it all and enjoy myself (4:17a). We follow the second model by doing good, by being rich in good works, by being generous, and by sharing with others (4:18). Some people believe that all of God's blessings have to be enjoyed here on earth. These individuals are the ones who set their hope on the riches that are not the "true riches." According to Paul, they are Christians who behave like "enemies of the cross of Christ"; he described them in this manner because they "set their minds on earthly things" (Phil. 3:18-19). These Christians are actually "enemies of the cross of Christ" because "the cross of Christ" necessarily entails a humble mind, a servant spirit, and a constant activity of sacrificial giving to others; all of these are, of course, lived out with our eyes fixed on the glory of heaven.

Jesus taught us to accumulate treasures in heaven by using our earthly possessions to serve the peoples of the world who are in need of the gospel. The Lord plainly and forthrightly commanded us: "Sell your possessions and give to charity; make yourselves purses which do not wear out, an unfailing treasure in heaven" (Lk. 12:33). Paul added to this that if we do accumulate our treasures in heaven by using our possessions in the service of Christ and His gospel, we thereby lay *a foundation* for our eternal life. The question, then, is whether we will build here or we will build there. Why should we build here, seeing as we will not stay long on this earth? Why not build in eternity?

The foundation for our life in heaven is clearly being laid by us in this life on earth. This "foundation" is in fact our own character. By giving to others the things we have on earth, we become more and more like our Lord who became poor in order to make many people rich. That is the grace of Christ, the grace of giving.

We have come full circle again, and the only question left to ask is this: Do we believe what the Word of God says? Do we have the mind of Christ? If we develop the world-view outlined by Jesus and by Paul, and if we apply it to our own way of life, we *will become* like Christ. The real reward turns out to be this becoming; after all, is it not the most extraordinary thing in the universe to have a character that is conformed to the image of our Father and of our Lord Jesus Christ?

Judgment Based on Works for Rewards

Protestant theologians have always been uneasy about the fact that while salvation is said to be by grace alone and by faith alone, God's judgment, even of believers, is always presented in the New Testament as being a judgment of our works. Moreover, it is written that after the judgment, there will be rewards for the works that were good, and punishments for those that were bad. In a small book entitled *The Biblical Doctrine of Judgment*, Leon Morris deals with this issue. Here is how he presents the total picture:

> It is the consistent teaching of the New Testament that judgment will be according to works (Mt. xvi. 27; Rom. ii. 6; 1 Cor. iii. 8; Rev. xxii. 12; etc.). The principle is worked out in Matthew xxv.

31-46. The Son of Man says to those who are to inherit the kingdom, "I was hungered, and ye gave me meat: I was thirsty, and ye gave me drink: I was a stranger, and ye took me in; naked, and ye clothed me: I was sick, and ye visited me: I was in prison, and ye came unto me." All this is explained in the words, "Inasmuch as ye did it unto one of these my brethren, even these least, ye did it unto me." A similar explanation is given of the fate of those who go away "into eternal punishment." In similar fashion, though without the concrete examples, Paul shows how judgment will work in Romans ii. 5-16. In this respect it is worth pointing out that from 1 Corinthians iii. 8 we learn that every man "shall receive his own reward according to his own labor."[137]

Morris goes on to write about the difficulty of reconciling salvation by grace and the judgment of works:

There is a difficulty in that salvation is always regarded as due to the good gift of Christ, whereas judgment is invariably on the basis of works. Such a passage as 1 Corinthians iii. 10-15 seems to give the reconciliation. "Other foundation can no man lay than that which is laid, which is Jesus Christ." That is to say, salvation comes only from what Christ has done. But men must live out their Christian lives and this is likened to a process of building: "But if any man buildeth on the foundation gold, silver, costly stones, wood, hay, stubble . . ." That is to say, some men build carelessly. Their service to Christ is shoddy and half-hearted. Others build with care, putting their very best into all of life, regarded now as the living out of the faith. And, says Paul, "the day shall declare it, because it is revealed in fire; and the fire itself shall prove each man's work of what sort it is. If any man's work shall abide which he build thereon, he shall receive a reward. If any man's work shall be burned, he shall suffer loss: but he himself shall be saved; yet so as through fire."[138]

This is not an actual "reconciliation" of grace and works. The main reason Protestant theologians cannot find the much desired harmonization of grace and works is because they do not possess a clear understanding of the rewards given in heaven. Morris has only this to say about rewards:

But that does not mean that God is to put all men on a flat level in the hereafter. Here and now the man who gives himself wholeheartedly to the service of Christ knows more of the joy of the Lord than the half-hearted. We have no warrant from the New Testament for thinking that it will be otherwise in heaven.[139]

What is most significant is the Protestant reluctance to accept the notion of rewards and the consequent refusal to see them as a motivation for working for Christ and His gospel, as the whole New Testament teaches us to do. Morris displays this very refusal in the following words:

> There are some who object to the whole idea of eternal rewards, affirming that it is not true Christian service if we serve simply for reward. This affirmation may unhesitatingly be endorsed. Selfishness is not less selfishness because it is directed toward spiritual rather than material ends. If we serve for reward then that in itself indicates that we have not begun to understand the Christian way, and that there awaits us only condemnation.[140]

The reluctance seen here is due to a tragic lack of understanding of the true nature of rewards. Contrary to what theologians such as Morris may think, heavenly rewards are not just some decorative medallions in which we can take pride. The deepest reward *is* in the very fact that we will become what our Creator intends us to become. It is the reward of being made into the likeness of Christ. When we will be like Him, we will be qualified to share with Him in the inheritance, and to work with Him in important positions of high responsibility over the whole universe. If we understand rewards according to their true nature and essence, then we will no longer be ashamed to work for them, because in working for the rewards, we will actually be working toward the final goal for which our Father made us and for which He is busy training us.

Chapter 8

Hebrews: The Final Destiny of Man

The Epistle to the Hebrews was written to a group of Christian Jews who in their "former days" had endured severe persecution for their faith (Heb. 10:32). Their property had been plundered, and they had been exposed to public shame and to the insults and ridicule of their society. When some of them were imprisoned, the ones who still retained their freedom were not ashamed to show their solidarity with their brethren in chains (10:33-34). It appears, however, that none of them had been executed (12:4). It also appears that these Christians were now facing a new challenge, and as a result, some of them were drifting away from the Christian church (10:23). Perhaps, this challenge came from the Jews who realized that keeping this new faith called Christianity involved a complete break with their Mosaic religion. This break not only implied a total separation with something that belonged to their very nationhood, but it also meant losing the protection that adherents to the Jewish religion enjoyed from the Roman imperial government. Whatever their specific situation may have been, the danger of renouncing the Christian faith was now present, and the author wrote to them with the purpose of convincing them of the superiority of the Christian faith and of the great worth of suffering and dying for this faith.

Although in the fourth century A.D., the letter was attributed to the Apostle Paul, the most likely candidates for its authorship are

Barnabas, Apollos, and Luke. While the language, images, and symbols all indicate that this epistle was not penned by Paul, the theology of Hebrews is very much like Paul's theology, and we shall soon discover that this letter completes and strengthens what we found in Paul's writings pertaining to our study.

The author begins by accentuating the full divinity of Jesus Christ, the Son of God. He also shows that Christ is above the angels in rank, that He is superior to Moses in His function on the earth, and that Christ has introduced a better covenant than the one given through Moses. The author also points out that Christ is the High Priest who, by His own blood, made the sacrifice of cleansing for the sins of mankind; through His death on the cross, Christ re-opened man's free access to God. The climax of the passage is in the statement that Christ is now seated at the right hand of God as the heir of all things, having the name that is above all other names in the universe.

Parallel to all these ideas, the author develops another theme that runs throughout the whole letter: the destiny of man and how God is achieving that destiny in this present world. He commences this theme by quoting the eighth Psalm, which we know is based upon Genesis 1:26; with this Scripture, the author shows that in God's overall plan, man is destined to have "all things in subjection under his feet" (2:8a). The author qualifies this by saying, "But now we do not yet see all things subjected to him" (2:8b). He also makes the interesting opening remark that it is not the present world that God plans to submit to man but "the world to come, concerning which," the author says, "we are speaking" (2:5).

The main idea that the author conveys in this beginning passage is that the Son of God, after becoming the Man Jesus, was the first man to fulfill the destiny of mankind. He demonstrated absolute obedience and faithfulness to God by suffering death for all and because of this, God crowned Him with glory and honor, making Him heir of all things (1:2; 2:9). Yet Christ accomplished this only after He united himself with mankind, sharing with them a human body. Therefore, in being the first to fulfill man's destiny, He became the Pathfinder, the Pioneer (ἀρχηγὸν, 2:10), the Forerunner (πρόδρομος, 6:20), and the Example that other men must look to and learn from if they want to share in the same destiny (12:2), since God's intention is to bring "many sons to glory" (2:10).

The most amazing thing in this divine plan is that God chose "to perfect the Pioneer through sufferings" (2:10; the NASB translates ἀρχηγὸν as "the author of their salvation"). This fact is so incredible that the author of Hebrews felt obligated to preface this statement with the words, "*it was fitting* for Him, for whom are all things, and through whom are all things"; this is the only place in the entire Bible where it is stated that a certain action befits God![1] This verse is especially astonishing because the epistle started out with a description of Christ as "the effulgence of God's glory and the very image of His being" (1:3).[2] If Christ has the nature and the essence of God, how is it possible that He needed perfecting? Was not Christ perfect in every way already? Typically, most Protestant theologians answer these questions by stripping Hebrews 2:10 of all its radical and significant meaning. Here is how F. F. Bruce does it:

> The perfect Son of God has become his people's perfect Savior, opening up their way to God; and in order to become that, he must endure suffering and death. The pathway of perfection which his people must tread must first be trodden by the Pathfinder, only so could he be their adequate representative and high priest in the presence of God. There is much in this epistle about the attainment of perfection in the sense of unimpeded access to God and unbroken communion with him, but in this as in other things it is Christ who leads the way.[3]

The essence of Bruce's explanation is this: the perfecting through suffering was not something that touched and effected Jesus' inner structure. It was only a question of status; through the suffering, He obtained the function of "adequate representative and high priest in the presence of God."[4]

Why is this issue so important for us? It is vitally important because Christ is presented as our Forerunner and Model; all that happened to Him has to happen to us. Particularly, if He was perfected through sufferings, we must be perfected by the same method. That is exactly the purpose of suffering that is presented throughout the whole letter to the Hebrews, especially in 12:5-11. Now, the problem we encounter if we "explain away" what the Bible says is this: if suffering only changes one's status, and if, as Bruce writes, "the attainment of perfection" is used in this epistle only "in the sense of unimpeded access to God and unbroken communion with him," then logically, we have to conclude that believers are called to suffer in order to obtain "unimpeded access to God and unbroken communion with Him."[5] Yet this conclusion clearly contradicts what the author of Hebrews himself says, namely, that unimpeded access to God was procured for us by the sacrifice of Christ on the cross (10:19-21).

No, we cannot limit the result of Christ's suffering to the mere changing of His status and our status. It is clear from what the author says about the effects of Jesus' suffering, as well as about the effects of His brothers' suffering, that suffering decidedly impacts and affects the inner being of the one who successfully passes through that experience.

Hence, we must approach the issue of Jesus' perfection through suffering from another angle, not the angle of His divinity; we have to take His humanity seriously and solve the problem from that perspective. We should start with what Luke writes about the child Jesus: "And He went down with them, and came to Nazareth; and He continued in subjection to them; and His mother treasured all these things in her heart. And Jesus kept increasing in wisdom and stature, and in favor with God and men" (Lk. 2:51-52).

However difficult it might be for us to reconcile the coexistence of the divine nature with the human nature in the Person of Christ, we have to accept the fact that the boy Jesus grew just as all human beings grow, not only physically but also intellectually. It follows, then, that He went through the same process of learning, and through that process of learning and growing, He increased in wisdom.

In the same way, we must also accept the information given in the letter to the Hebrews. The author emphasizes that it was necessary for Him "to be made like His brethren *in all things*" (Heb. 2:17, italics mine). In the same context we are told that "He Himself was tempted in that which He has suffered" (πέπονθεν αὐτὸς πειρασθείς), and *that is why* "He is able to come to the aid of those who are tempted" (2:18). Jesus did not merely obtain a new status; on the contrary, in His suffering, Jesus acquired a kind of knowledge that could have been His only if He accepted to become a man, to feel what humans feel when they suffer and when they are tempted. In addition to this, Jesus needed this kind of knowledge in order to be able to help others in similar situations. This idea is explicitly stated in Hebrews 4:15: "For we do not have a high priest who cannot sympathize with our weaknesses, but one who has been tempted in all things *as we are, yet* without sin" (italics mine).

The author continues to pursue this concept, telling us that Jesus "learned obedience from the things which He suffered," and it was through this process that He was perfected; this process happened "although He was a Son" (5:8-9). We will be able to recognize the increased emphasis of the author if we take note of the well-established Greek saying inserted here about the method of learning by suffering: ἔμαθεν ἀφ ὧν ἔπαθε. It is a poetic phrase taken from Greek literature, and it conveys the idea that we learn through our suffering.[6]

What did the author mean when he said that Christ "learned obedience"? Of course, Christ had been obedient to His Father when He had agreed to become a man and to save the world by His suffering and death. We can be sure that Christ had known exactly what obedience would entail for Him as the Incarnate Son of God. But what did obedience mean for Him as a human being? To find the answer to this we must first respond to the more general question of what obedience means for *all* human beings. Why it is so difficult for man to obey God? What is the nature of the temptation to disobey?

I would describe the human condition upon the earth as a delicate balance between being in possession of authority and being in submission to authority. On the one hand, man was created with the capacity to rule and to exercise authority. On the other hand, man was intended to live under the authority of God, to submit to Him, and to obey Him. In other words, man has to exercise his authority under the authority of God. In the end, the test of his capacity to rule is his capacity to obey. However, it is difficult to feel empowered with authority and still gladly submit to the authority of another. Man's temptation is to exercise his authority independently, without recognizing God's absolute authority.

When Christ entered the human condition, He came face to face with this human difficulty of keeping the balance between having authority and still being totally dependent upon the Father and totally obedient to the Father. It is not enough, however, to simply say that Jesus passed this difficult test. It is likewise not enough to say that as a Man, He merely learned "what obedience to God involved in practice in the condition of human life on earth."[7] Hebrews 2:10 tells us that *He was perfected* through what He suffered. Let us approach this issue by asking the following question: As a human being, didn't His acquisition of new knowledge and of the capacity to understand humans and to sympathize with them have the effect of developing a new dimension in His Person? When He became a man, putting on the new dimension of humanity, did this not entail a completion of His Person? If Paul was able to say that the church as His body is His "fulness" (Eph. 1:23), could we not say the same regarding His physical body? I believe that in our Christology, we should make more room for a process by which Christ increased in knowledge not only as a young boy (Lk. 2:52), but all the way through His life on the earth. Only when we allow for this process of growth in the manhood of Christ, are we able to truly see Him as both our Forerunner and as our Example.

I believe that the author of this epistle wrote the words of Hebrews 12:5-11 with this very idea in mind. After instructing his readers to fix their eyes on Jesus, who had "endured such hostility by sinners against Himself" (12:3) and who had "endured the cross, despising the shame" (12:2), the author begins to expand on the way God trains *all* His children by means of παιδείας (12:5, translated as "chastening" in the King James Version and as "discipline" in modern versions). In order to support this teaching with Scripture, the author quotes Proverbs 3:12, "For those whom the Lord loves He disciplines, and He scourges every son whom He receives." Then he goes on to say that "all" the sons of God "have become partakers" of God's discipline, and this is in fact a sign to each one that he is a genuine son and not an illegitimate child (Heb. 12:8).

In the following verses, the author tells us the purpose of this discipline: "He disciplines us for our good, that we may share His holiness" (12:10); because "to those who have been trained by it (γεγυμνασμένοις, trained as in a gymnasium), afterwards it yields the peaceful fruit of righteousness" (12:11). The author is obviously not referring here to the juridical righteousness that is given to us by faith in Christ. The righteousness in 12:11 is an inner quality of "rightness," or of uprightness of character. It defines the holiness that God aims to produce in us through the suffering inflicted in the discipline. Making the much needed distinction between justification and sanctification, M. Erickson writes: "Justification is a forensic or declarative matter . . . while sanctification is an actual transformation of character and condition of the person. Justification is an objective work affecting our standing before God, our relationship with Him, while sanctification is a subjective work affecting our inner person."[8]

We should keep in mind that the author deliberately presents this teaching immediately following his survey of the history of the sufferings of God's people in ages past, in which he places great emphasis upon the history of the persecutions and martyrdoms of the Maccabean heroes (ch. 11). Why did all these dreadful things occur? Why does God allow such things to happen? Remember the words with which our author began his discussion of the sufferings of the Pioneer: God considered it "fitting" (2:10). The Father considered suffering to be the appropriate method by which He would perfect first His only begotten Son and then all those other sons and daughters for whom His Son would become the Example! For this reason, suffering, persecution, and martyrdom are not the fated tragedies of a miserable earthly existence; they are clear indications that one is in God's "gymnasium," in the place where God is forming His child into His own image of holiness and righteousness.

We should not be surprised at this teaching. It was given by Jesus Himself when He taught His disciples to be perfect just as their Father in heaven is perfect (Matt. 5:48). Significantly, Jesus gave this command in the context of His instructions to those who suffer persecution: "Love your enemies, and pray for those who persecute you in order that you may be sons of your Father who is in heaven; for He causes His sun to rise on the evil and the good, and sends rain on the righteous and the unrighteous" (Matt. 5:44-45). It seems that only in such an environment of suffering can a godly character be developed.

However, Jesus' words should not cause us to be discouraged and down-hearted. Instead, they ought to be a reason for rejoicing. When we fix our eyes on Jesus, we should see that it was "for the joy set before Him" that He endured suffering, shame, and death on the cross (Heb. 12:2). What kind of joy was the author referring to here? The author of Hebrews obviously used the Book of Isaiah and especially the fifty-third chapter as sources for his description of Jesus; therefore, it is not difficult to see that in 12:2, he was referring to Isaiah 53:11, "As a result of the anguish of His soul, He will see it and be satisfied; by His knowledge the Righteous One, My Servant will justify the many." When Jesus faced the prospect of torture, agony, and crucifixion, He looked beyond it, at its result; He fixed His eyes on the salvation and the heavenly destiny of His many brethren. He focused on the great satisfaction and joy which that harvest would give Him. For this reason, Jesus was able, a few hours before Gethsemane and Calvary, to tell His disciples: "These things I have spoken to you, that My joy may be in you, and that your joy may be made full" (John 15:11).

The same principle that applied to Jesus applies to us, as well. When we understand that these sufferings are a great honor, when we understand the extraordinary purposes that they achieve both in us and in many others through us, and when we see their ultimate result in glory, then we can rejoice even if we must endure pain, agony, and even martyrdom.

Although the author of Hebrews concentrated mainly on the perfecting work of suffering upon the one who has accepted it for the sake of Christ, he also touched upon other issues that are of special interest for us. We shall focus on them in what follows.

Rewards, Inheritance, and Heaven

In order to encourage his Jewish Christian flock to persevere and endure unto the end, the author shows them the final destiny of man and explains how that great destiny may be attained. God's ultimate goal with mankind is formulated in several different ways. In the first place, the great plan of the Creator and Sustainer of the whole universe is to bring "many sons to glory" (2:10). Secondly, God wants to submit to His children the world to come (2:5-8). Thirdly, God's desire is to give them His eternal inheritance (9:15). The fourth way in which the author depicts man's ultimate destiny is that God's children will "receive a kingdom which cannot be shaken" (12:28). The fifth and final way is the culmination of all that has gone before: God intends men and women to share in His holiness and in His perfection, and that entails that they share in His character, as well (12:5-14).

In order for all these extraordinary things to happen, God sent His Son into our world to become a man, to become a partner with humanity in flesh and blood, to undergo the same trials and temptations, and to open the way to heaven and to that eternal destiny by suffering death in humanity's stead. But now it is our turn. We have become partners with Christ in that heavenly calling (3:1), but first we must go through the same process of testing. Before He can fulfill His final plan with us, God needs to test our worthiness (3:3) and our faithfulness to Him (3:2); for this reason, we must persevere to the end (3:6, 12).

The word the author used for "partners" is μέτοχοι, a term that was used in the secular Greek of that time for "business partners."[9] Luke also employed it when he said that the sons of Zebedee were "partners" in fishing with Simon Peter and his brother (Lk. 5:7; Luke alternated it with κοινωνοί in 5:10). The term μέτοχοι denotes a true partnership in a great enterprise, ending in the ownership and administration of the whole universe. This is the "great reward" for which Christians are called to endure hardship in their partnership with Jesus (Heb. 10:35).

This partnership with Christ in suffering is best illustrated by the story of Moses recounted in Hebrews 11:24-29. Moses was faced with a difficult choice. He could either remain in the royal palace as the adopted son of Pharaoh's daughter, a situation referred to by the author as "the passing pleasures of sin," or he could relinquish the palace, "choosing rather to endure ill-treatment with the people of God" (11:25). As we know from the history recorded in the Old Testament Book of Exodus, Moses chose the second alternative. He dedicated his life to the liberation of God's people from the bondage of Egypt and to giving them the commandments of God, educating them to become a special people among the nations of the world. His choice and his subsequent actions involved Moses in hardship, toil, agony, and tears for most of his lifetime.

The key to this passage in Hebrews is the way in which the author refers to the activity of Moses on behalf of God's people as "the reproach (ὀνειδισμὸν, insult, shame) of Christ" (11:26). The author of Hebrews agreed with the teaching of the Apostle Paul that Christ was active in the deliverance of Israel from Egypt and in their sojourn through the wilderness into Canaan (1 Cor. 10:4). By choosing to spend his life for the Hebrew slaves of Pharaoh, Moses in fact chose to become a partner with Christ. All the agony of working with the stubborn children of Israel for forty years in the wilderness was in fact a sharing in the agony of Christ. This is important to understand, because in Hebrews 13:13 the author invites us to "go out to Him [Christ] outside the camp, bearing His reproach" (ὀνειδισμὸν, the same word used in the case of Moses in 11:26). Christ Himself has "suffered outside the gate, . . . that He might sanctify the people through His own blood" (13:12).

The author has made it very clear that Christ's sacrifice for the sins of the world was a "once for all" action (7:26-27; 9:24-28). Therefore, we have nothing to add to that action. But just like Moses, we still need to work for the rescue of men and women from their Egypt of sin; there is still room for agony in building up the people of God today. Whoever sees this need and dedicates himself to this task chooses to become a partner with Christ in His suffering. And the partnership still brings upon us the world's insults, ridicule, hostile persecution, and in some cases, even martyrdom.

What was the motivation that helped Moses to forgo "the treasures of Egypt" and to choose instead a life of self-sacrifice? It was very simple: "he was looking to the reward" (11:26). The author had already written so much about that heavenly destiny that he did not feel it necessary to repeat here what sort of reward he was talking about. We need to see the whole picture of the author's teaching about "the reward" in order to understand what Moses was looking for when he chose to dedicate himself to the deliverance of the people of God.

Let us look for a moment at this reward in terms of inheritance. The author struck this note right at the beginning of his letter by telling his readers that God appointed His Son to be the "heir of all things" (1:2). "All things" means, of course, the whole created universe. The author goes on to tell us that "Jesus, because of the suffering of death" was "crowned with glory and honor" (2:9), and that meant that "all things" were "subjected to Him" (2:8). Christ now "upholds all things by the word of His power" (1:3). The author uses the word "inherit" in the sense of obtaining what God has to offer. Hence, Christ "has inherited a more excellent name than" the angels (1:4). This is also the meaning of the word in the phrase "those who will inherit salvation" in 1:14; it refers to the people who will *obtain* the whole content of what God has in store for them.

Just as Christ received the inheritance or, in other words, just as He was put in charge over the whole cosmos, so His brethren are partakers with Him in the same "heavenly calling" (3:1). This is the *content* of the new covenant which He instituted in His own blood: "For this reason He is the mediator of a new covenant, in order that . . . those who have been called may receive the promise of the eternal inheritance" (9:15). These words should be linked with what Jesus told His disciples after the Supper: "You are those who have stood by Me in My trials (πειρασμοῖς); and just as My Father has covenanted (διέθετό) to Me a kingdom, I covenant (διατίθεμαι) to you that you may eat and drink at My table in My kingdom, and you will sit on thrones judging the twelve tribes of Israel" (Lk. 22:28-30; the New American Standard Bible translates διέθετο as "granted" and διατίθεμαι as "grant"). It was because of their faithful partnership in His trials that Christ covenanted to His disciples partnership with Him in the kingdom; that meant, in other words, that Christ covenanted to them partnership in ruling over all creation with Him. Therefore, "the inheritance" in the letter to the Hebrews means receiving an unshakable kingdom, as a result of the faithful endurance in suffering for the cause of Christ to the end.

Now let us examine the conditions for obtaining this reward of the inheritance, this position of ruling with Christ. Indeed, the Scriptures state several conditions that must be fulfilled by the one who desires to qualify for the inheritance. Even Christ, as the Pioneer, had to meet these conditions; He had to become fully human and He had to be tested in everything just as we are (2:17-18; 4:15). Because Christ passed all the tests successfully or, in the author's words, because "He was *faithful* to Him who appointed Him, . . . He has been counted *worthy* of more glory than Moses" (3:2-3, italics mine). However shocking it may seem to us to hear that the Son of God had to be tested and had to demonstrate His worthiness for ruling over the universe, this *is* the truth that the author of the epistle wanted to convey to us. And, very importantly, only if these things are true of Him, can He be our Example, the One whom we follow, and the One with whom we have become partners in the heavenly calling.

The example of Israel in the wilderness is given in the context of the discussion about Jesus being found faithful. The author uses this example to show that the Israelites did not obtain the promise because of their unbelief or lack of faith (ἀπιστίαν, 3:19); a few verses later the author repeats that it was "because of disobedience" (4:6). For the author of Hebrews, just like for the Apostle Paul, faith translates into obedience: "By faith Abraham . . . obeyed" (11:8). The author goes so far as to say that Christ "became to all those who obey Him the source of eternal salvation" (5:9). This is the case simply because "believing in Christ" means submitting to His royal authority and obeying Him. It is only "through faith and patience," that "the heirs of the promise" come to "inherit the promise" (6:12, 17).

Thus far we have uncovered three conditions for receiving the inheritance: faith, obedience, and patience; we now turn to the eleventh chapter for the others. The first condition we find in chapter eleven is similar to the teaching of Paul in that it pertains to the world-view and general attitudes governing one's way of life. The people who qualify to receive the inheritance are the men and women who consider themselves "strangers and exiles on the earth" (11:13), and who eagerly seek after "a the better country, that is a heavenly one" (11:16). Speaking about this type of people, the author writes that "God is not ashamed to be called their God; for He has prepared a city for them" (11:16).

The other condition that we find in this chapter is the endurance of sufferings. In chapter ten, the author talked about the persecutions that they had suffered in their "former days" and encouraged them not to throw away their "confidence, which has a great reward" (10:32a, 35b). Then he continues to explain what they need to do in order to obtain that reward: "You have need of endurance, so that when you have done the will of God, you may receive what was promised" (10:36). To illustrate his teaching, the author presents the memorable record of the heroes of the faith, ending with the Maccabean heroes who "were tortured, . . . [who] experienced mockings and scourgings, yes, also chains and imprisonment. They were stoned, they were sawn in two, they were tempted, they were put to death with the sword; they went about in sheepskins, in goatskins, being destitute, afflicted, ill-treated, . . . wandering in deserts and mountains and caves and holes in the ground" (11:35-38). The heroes described in the first part of the eleventh chapter were great achievers, whereas the ones described in this list did not achieve anything "great" on this earth. Nevertheless, the heroes listed at the end of chapter eleven were the ones to receive the greatest praise ever bestowed upon men and women in the Bible: they were people "of whom the world was not worthy" (11:38a)! We can be most certain that these men and women were found worthy of heaven!

As we read through the author's description of the sufferers and martyrs of the faith, we stumble across are two particularly cryptic statements. The first says that some "women received back their dead by resurrection" (ἐξ ἀναστάσεως) and the second, found in the latter part of the same verse, states that "others were tortured, not accepting their release, in order that they might obtain a better resurrection" (11:35). Most commentators say that the first statement refers to two of the women mentioned in the Old Testament, to the widow of Zarephath and the woman of Shunem; each one had had her son resurrected, the first by Elijah (1 Kings 17:17-24) and the second by Elisha (2 Kings 4:17-37).[10] This kind of resurrection, the commentators say, was not the most desirable one, because those boys eventually died again; the Maccabean heroes desired instead "a better resurrection" (Heb. 11:35). They wanted the resurrection to eternal life.

This interpretation of 11:35 is a possibility, and it is true that the Maccabean heroes did declare to their torturers that one day they would be raised from the dead.[11] However, it would have been rather peculiar for the author to have inserted in such a highly condensed space a comparison of the Maccabeans' hoped-for resurrection with the resurrection of the two children in the Old Testament.

Unfortunately, we cannot enter into the mind of the author in order to find out exactly to what resurrection he referred. Consequently, we cannot be sure that the "better resurrection" is said to be "better" in comparison with the resurrections mentioned in 1 and 2 Kings. It is much simpler, therefore, to assume that the Maccabean heroes believed in a special resurrection that would be theirs because they had accepted to die for their God and their faith.

We have seen how Paul linked the two words "ἐξ ἀναστάσεως," forming a special word to indicate the "extra-resurrection" that he was hoping to attain by dying as a martyr in conformity with the death of Christ (ἐξανάστασιν, Phil. 3:10-11). Without a doubt, Paul believed that the martyrs who have died for Christ's sake will be rewarded with a resurrection that will be so special that it was worth dying for; otherwise, if the "better resurrection" simply referred to the resurrection that all believers will experience at the Second Coming of Christ, it would be a meaningless goal for the martyrs. William Fuller's astute comment regarding the promises to the overcomers in the Book of Revelation fits here, as well: "A command that everyone keeps is superfluous, and a reward that everyone receives for a virtue that everyone has is nonsense."[12]

Going back to our analysis of the heroes of the faith in chapter eleven, the most important aspect of each of their stories is that they all suffered and died for "the confession of our hope" (Heb. 10:23). This is another way of saying that their sufferings and deaths necessarily had to have been for the sake of the gospel in order for them to have been genuine and accepted. These heroes did not suffer for the sake of suffering itself, but because they voluntarily joined with Christ in His sufferings for His own people, just as Moses had done hundreds of years before (11:24-26; 13:11-13). Their stories serve to reinforce the biblical teaching that we should not seek after suffering and martyrdom as such; rather, we should seek after partnership with Christ in His business here on earth. Suffering and martyrdom are the likely consequences of our partnership with Him, and if they do come, we should rejoice because we have been found worthy of being included among those given the greatest honor ever bestowed upon humans in heaven or on earth.

At the end of the extraordinary record of the Old Testament and Maccabean heroes of the faith, the author concludes by referring to them as "so great a cloud of witnesses" (μαρτυρων, 12:1). In what sense were they witnesses? Bruce answers this question negatively first, saying that they were witnesses, "not, probably, in the sense of spectators watching their successors as they in their turn run the race; . . . rather, [they were witnesses] in the sense that they by their loyalty and endurance have borne witness to the possibilities of the life of faith, . . . [and] they have borne witness to the faithfulness of God."[13]

Bruce is correct in affirming that the martyrs' witness to us includes these things; however, in their own day, the content and purpose of their witness was something else. At the beginning of the second century A.D., Ignatius wrote this about the witnesses in the Book of Hebrews: "The holiest prophets lived according to Jesus Christ, and for this reason they were persecuted; they were inspired by His grace so that the unbelievers might be fully assured that there is one God, who has manifested Himself in Jesus Christ His Son."[14] These people were *God's witnesses,* speaking on God's behalf to their own generation, ready to pay the price of persecution and even of martyrdom for their witness. And so we have come to the place where the word "witness" (μάρτυς) becomes synonymous with the term "martyr." Bruce indicates that in Hebrews 12:1 we have "one of the early examples of the beginning of the semantic change by which the ordinary Greek word 'witness' acquired its distinctive Christian sense of 'martyr.' "[15]

We have already suggested that the beginning of this semantic change could have occurred in Acts 22:20, where Paul speaks about "the blood of Thy witness Stephen." But here in the letter to the Hebrews, a theology of martyrdom is starting to take a distinct shape. We will later be able to recognize the concepts formulated in Hebrews, in the thinking of the Christian martyrs of the second and third centuries.

At this time, I want to highlight only one other extremely important idea in this letter, and that is the work of grace and the work of God in the sufferers and martyrs. Christians are not left alone to fight this terribly difficult battle on their own. To begin with, they are assisted by the angels, who are described as "ministering spirits, sent out to render service for the sake of those who will inherit salvation" (Heb. 1:14). Secondly, Christ Himself comes to their aid, because He has gone victoriously through everything that they now encounter; for this reason, He is seated on the throne of grace and is able to "sympathize with our weaknesses" (4:15). We should therefore approach His throne with confidence in order to "find grace to help in time of need" (4:16).

At the climax of his explication of suffering as the discipline that causes us to share in the holiness of God, the author writes: "See to it that no one comes short of the grace of God" (12:15a). This warning clearly indicates that the grace of God is available to each Christian as he goes through the process of being disciplined. The only problem is that the believer might not make use of it. Then, if he fails, it is only because of the fact that he did not take advantage of all the assistance that God continually made immediately available to him in order to give him a complete victory!

We reach the apex of the teaching of Hebrews in the author's benediction at the end of chapter thirteen. The God who has raised Jesus from the dead is ready to "equip you in every good thing to do His will" (13:21a); in fact, *it is He* who is "working in us that which is pleasing in His sight, through Jesus Christ," and for this reason, all the glory should go to Him alone (13:21b).

The Epistle to the Hebrews tells us that we have been called to work hard and to sacrifice our lives as we live for Christ and for others; indeed, we have been called to suffer and maybe even to die as martyrs. Then, on that final day, the glorious reward of the inheritance, of ruling with Christ over all the created universe, will be ours. In the end, however, there can be no "meriting" and no "boasting" on our part, because from the beginning, we were destined for the inheritance purely by the grace of God, and it was solely the grace of God that enabled us to qualify for it. Yes, it is *all* by grace, and we shall give all the glory to God for ever and ever.

Chapter 9

---

1 Peter: The True Grace of God

The First Epistle of Peter was written to the Christians in Asia Minor who were suffering persecution for their faith. It appears that theirs was not the type of persecution that was carried out by the state, the type that usually resulted in martyrdom, but a common suffering inflicted on those who dared to be different and who refused to take part in their society's immoral activities.[1]

The whole letter is devoted to the issue of suffering for one's faith in Christ. We shall follow Peter's presentation of this subject point by point because it provides us with very important elements in our understanding of the Biblical teaching on suffering for Christ and its consequences in heaven. Before we plunge into this detailed survey of Peter's first letter, we have to understand a very important point that Peter himself makes at the very end concerning his purpose in writing this letter about suffering: "I have written to you briefly, exhorting and testifying that this is the true grace of God. Stand firm in it!" (1 Pet. 5:12b). In this statement, we find the precise reason why the author wrote this letter, and our understanding of his stated purpose is crucial for our understanding of the entire letter. To what does Peter refer when he says that "*this* is the true grace of God"? Moreover, what does he mean by "*the grace of God*"? P. H. Davids relates the three attempts that have been made in the past to explain this statement:

First, Peter has spoken of God's grace three times (1:13; 5:5,

10), and these statements include both the future reward at the coming of Christ (1:13; 3:7; 5:10) and God's present relationship to them (5:5; cf., 1:10; 4:10, 14), which is a foretaste of the future (1:6; 2:10). Thus while their present situation may not feel like grace from God, when looked at from the proper perspective they are indeed receiving that grace.

Second, others believe that "this" refers to the suffering itself, both actual and potential, which the Christians are experiencing. Thus the very thing that the believers look on as evil is actually part of God's manifold grace (4:10).

Third, "this" may refer to the letter as a whole. In other words, Peter is saying, "I've written to you a short letter to encourage you and to testify to you that this teaching is really [i.e., 'true'] a gift ['grace'] from God."[2]

Davids says in a note that the second suggestion was made by N. Brox in *Der erste Petrusbrief*, but immediately Davids refutes it with these words:

He cites the phrase τοῦτο χάρις παρὰ Θεῷ in 2:19-20 in support. Unfortunately that differs from the χάρις τοῦ Θεοῦ here in that in the earlier passage it refers to human actions that God looks on positively and this verse refers to the grace that God grants. That ταύτην is feminine does not mean that it must refer to the feminine χάρις found earlier, for the feminine pronoun may agree with the predicate noun rather than its antecedent.[3]

Davids himself explains 5:12 in this way: "But since the phrase appears immediately after the commendation of Silvanus, most likely it refers to the letter as a whole, not to specific references to grace within it. Either way, the clause points to the encouraging fact that God is not absent from their suffering, but values it and rewards it."[4] It should sound strange to us that a statement about the grace of God is turned into a promise of God's reward. We shall understand this singular interpretation in a moment.

The crux of the interpretation of the whole matter of grace in this epistle is in 2:19-20. The New American Standard Bible offers us the following translation of it:

For this finds favor, if for the sake of conscience toward God a man bears up under sorrows when suffering unjustly. For what credit is there if, when you sin and are harshly treated, you endure it with patience? But if when you do what is right and suffer for it you patiently endure it, this finds favor with God.

Now let us have a more literal translation before us:

> This therefore is grace: if for the sake of conscience toward God a man bears up under sorrows when suffering unjustly. For what glory (κλέος) is there if, when you sin and are harshly treated, you endure it with patience. But if, when you do what is right and suffer, you patiently endure it, this is grace before God.

One can immediately see that grace is the focus of the whole passage. Peter defines grace, in essence, as suffering due to one's faithfulness to God. This is not a new and unfamiliar teaching for us; in a similar way, Paul wrote to the Philippians that besides the grace of believing in Christ, they had also received the grace of suffering for Him (Phil. 1:29). Paul also wrote to the Corinthians about the grace of becoming poor in order to enrich others, which is in fact the grace of Christ (2 Cor. 8:1-9).

It is astonishing to see the kinds of extremes that Protestant commentators will go to in order to get rid of the kind of grace we find here in First Peter. Kelly explains it away with this comment on verse nineteen of the second chapter of First Peter: "The opening clause literally reads 'this is a grace,' i.e., an act which is intrinsically attractive and thus wins God's approval (cf., the same phrase expanded in 20 below). For this sense of 'grace' (χάρις), so unlike the distinctively Pauline one, cf., Lk. 6:32-34 (sayings of Christ which, in the view of many, the present passage echoes)."[5]

Then, Kelly has this to say about verse 20: "It is no accident that, instead of using **credit** (κλέος: 'glory,' 'prestige') as in the first half of the verse, he reverts to **a fine thing** (χάρις: see on 19) in the second."[6]

Now let us examine the explanation given by Davids for verse 19:

> What "wins God's favor" (an unusual idiomatic use of the Greek word χάρις, often translated "grace"—the same expression appears in Luke 6:32-34, which could be the source of this teaching) is enduring or "bearing up under" injustice, which here refers to the insults, blows, and beatings a slave might receive if the master was in a bad mood or made impossible demands. . . . What he means, then, is that God is pleased with Christian slaves who bear up under unjust suffering, not because there is no other option or because of their optimistic character, but because they know this pleases God and conforms to the teaching of Jesus.[7]

The big question that should immediately occur to us is this: For what reason would God be pleased to see unjust suffering? We are

given no rationale for this, and so we are left with the horrifying idea
that it "pleases God" to see such injustice. But that is not all!
Regarding verse 20, Davids has this to say about the fact that a master
punishes a Christian slave for "doing good":

> This does impress God. The construction "receives credit" is
> literally "this is grace (τοῦτο χάρις) before God." There is no
> question of fame or boasting before God (and thus the change in
> vocabulary from κλέος of the first part of this verse or ἔπαινον of
> 2:14), but neither is this simply "grace" only because God's grace
> produced it. This endurance is an act that finds favor with God, on
> which he smiles with approval. It is a deed of covenant
> faithfulness to the God who has extended grace to them (1 Pet.
> 1:10,13; 3:7; 4:10; 5:5,10,12) and as such leads to the paradoxical
> joy already mentioned in 1:6-7.[8]

The unjust suffering "impresses God" and even "finds favor with"
Him, so that He actually "smiles with approval" while gazing at it!
Even more astonishing is the fact that the word "grace" is translated as
"receives credit," and later in 5:12, Davids says that God "rewards it."
Now, in the basic New Testament understanding of the term, grace
means the free gift of God; but here "grace" is made to mean exactly
the opposite: it is something that "receives credit" from God. If words
can be made to stand on their head like this, to say exactly the opposite
of what they normally say, then everything can be read in the
Scriptures!

The key to the correct understanding of this passage is in the
phrase "this is grace before God," τοῦτο χάρις παρὰ Θεῷ. The
preposition παρὰ preceding Θεῷ in the dative in the New Testament
"is used when the probing judgment of God decides the real truth:
δίκαιοι παρὰ τῷ Θεῷ before God, R. 2:13; Gl. 3:11."[9] Reisenfeld
adds that in such constructions "it is presupposed that human
judgment is misleading."[10] The best example of this is in 1
Corinthians 3:19: ἡ γὰρ σοφία τοῦ κόσμου τούτου μωρία παρὰ τῷ
Θεῷ ἐστι, "the wisdom of this world is foolishness before God."[11] The
same Greek construction can also be seen in 2 Thessalonians 1:6:
δίκαιον παρὰ Θεῷ ἀνταποδοῦναι τοῖς θλίβουσιν ὑμᾶς θλίψιν, "For
after all it is only just for God to repay with affliction those who afflict
you."

Paul's use of this phrase helps us to get at its meaning. What is of
the greatest help, though, is the fact that Peter uses it exactly in the
same way. In 1 Peter 2:4, he mentions that Christ, the "living stone,"

was "rejected by men, but choice and precious in the sight of God," παρὰ δὲ Θεῷ ἐκλεκτόν ἔντιμον. People rejected the "living stone," but God's estimation of it was different: He considered it chosen and precious. Then, fifteen verses later, we find Peter using exactly the same construction. Should we not read it in the same way? Let us then translate verse 19 following the pattern of verse 4: "From the point of view of this world, suffering unjustly is considered a tragedy, but in God's evaluation, it is grace (or, God considers that it is grace)." This rendering of 2:19 is linguistically consistent with Peter's previous sentence, and with the Pauline use of that construction. We will later find that this interpretation is also consistent with all that Peter writes in this letter about suffering for Christ, and, we will be able to understand the sense in which Peter can say at the end of his first letter that *this* suffering "is the true grace of God" (5:12).

Let us begin precisely where Peter begins. He tells his readers that through the resurrection of Christ, they were "born again to a living hope" (1:3), in order "to obtain an inheritance which is imperishable and undefiled and will not fade away, reserved in heaven for you" (1:4). We again find ourselves on familiar territory: the purpose of our salvation, its ultimate goal, is the inheritance in heaven. Furthermore, Peter declares: "You were called for the very purpose that you might inherit a blessing" (3:9). Peter does not specify what the inheritance is or what the blessing contains, but all the way through the letter, he tells us that we have been called to follow in the footsteps of Christ in suffering (2:21), and that Christ is now "at the right hand of God, having gone into heaven, after angels and authorities and powers had been subjected to Him" (3:22). Then we as believers are told that if we are partakers with Christ in His sufferings (4:13), like Peter himself was, then we will be partakers "also of the glory that is to be revealed" (5:1). Again we find that the destiny of man was illustrated and fulfilled by Christ, just as in the Epistle to the Hebrews and in the epistles of Paul.

However, this celestial destiny will be ours entirely by grace: "Fix your hope completely on the grace to be brought to you at the revelation of Jesus Christ" (1:13). Peter goes so far as to call the inheritance, "the grace of life," in the context of saying that women are "fellow heirs" with their husbands (3:7). The work of equipping the chosen ones for glory is being done by "the God of all grace, who called you to His eternal glory in Christ" (5:10). Furthermore, in the fourth chapter, Peter presents yet another interesting view of this grace of God; he writes that it is "manifold" or "varied," and that God's children have been made "stewards" of the "manifold grace of God" (4:10).

Whenever we find Peter writing about suffering, about its purpose and its achievements, we have to keep in mind that it is all a work of grace, and that God is at work through it. Consequently, there is no merit for the one who endures hardship and suffering, and there can be no boasting of its achievements.

Let us now analyze what Peter has to say about sufferings. His first comment on this subject is found right at the beginning of the letter, where he says that we have been "born again to a living hope," and this "hope" is our inheritance in heaven, in which we "greatly rejoice" (1:3-4, 6). But, before we can reach that inheritance, Peter tells us that we must go through a process of testing, a process that will purify us just as gold is purified by fire. That process, if we will have passed successfully through it, will result in "praise and glory and honor at the revelation of Jesus Christ" (1:7). The pattern is exactly the same as in Romans 5:1-10; even the key words are the same: "tested by fire" is δοκιμαζομένου and the result of the process is the "δοκίμιον of your faith." In Paul's writings, the result is δοκιμή, translated as "proven character" in modern versions of the Bible (Rom. 5:4), and the verdict at the coming of Jesus is δόκιμον (2 Tim. 2:15) or αδόκιμος (1 Cor. 9:27). Peter chose to use the form δοκίμιον, having the same meaning as δόκιμον, that is, "tested and approved," or one who has successfully passed the tests of faithfulness and reliability. We are then told that the consequence of this positive verdict will be "praise and glory and honor" (1 Peter 1:7). The "praise" will be God saying to His faithful child, "Well done, good slave," as he stands before the judgment seat of Christ. The "glory" will be sharing in the glory of Christ that was given to Him as a result of *His* sufferings (3:22; 4:13-14). *This* is certainly what "obtaining the inheritance" means, and what an extraordinary "honor" it will be to be given dominion with Christ over all of God's possessions!

When we, at present, "see" with the eyes of faith the glory of Christ that will also be ours, we "greatly rejoice with joy inexpressible and full of glory" (1:8), even though we are presently "distressed by various trials" (πειρασμοῖς, 1:6). When the mind is set on the things of heaven, the present momentary ("for a little while") sufferings, although painful, cannot overcome the unspeakable joy that overwhelms our entire being.

On the fourth of October 1974, the Romanian secret police ordered a house search of our home in Ploiesti. Seven policemen invaded our house, and in the course of seven hours, they turned every room upside down, confiscating my entire library, as well as all of my personal papers and notes. I was forced to sign each book before it was taken away, and as I was doing this, my eyes fell on a book with this title: *Joy Unspeakable and Full of Glory*, followed by the subtitle: *Is it Yours Right Now?* I stopped, staring at that book cover, and began to pray, "Lord, if this joy is not mine *now*, it will never be! Please, Lord, make it mine now!" At that very moment, my whole being felt as though it had been inundated with light. From that time on, I was no longer the victim of a house search, but the host of seven men to whom I witnessed about my faith and my Lord! The joy of the Lord had become my strength (Neh. 8:10), and all through those subsequent years of persecution, that joy was constantly with me. As a result, I often preached about "joy unspeakable and full of glory," encouraging many others with it. Amazingly, the fact that I was able to preach about joy, in *those* situations during *those* times, determined many others to stand up for the Lord in the same way.

Let us now turn our attention to the passage in which Peter speaks to the Christian slaves, telling them that their suffering for their faithfulness to God is His grace to them (2:19, et seq.). Why is it grace? Peter answers this question in verse 21: "For you have been called for this purpose, since Christ also suffered for you, leaving you an example for you to follow in His steps." Before we stop to analyze the meaning of this statement, we must understand what Peter meant by the "purpose" to which we have been called. Although this sentence shows Christ as our pattern, it does not spell out the purpose for our calling.

Peter does not end his discussion of Christ's example with these verses in chapter two. He develops it in the rest of the chapter and all the way through chapter three. In 3:8, he comes back to the issue with the words "to sum up"; in verses eight and nine, Peter summarizes what he has said thus far about suffering like Christ. His précis shows the kind of attitude a Christian should have in the midst of hardships and trouble: "Let all be harmonious, sympathetic, brotherly, kindhearted, and humble in spirit; not returning evil for evil, or insult for insult, but giving a blessing instead" (just like Christ!). Why should we be like this? Peter gives us the reason in the rest of verse nine: "For you were called for the very purpose that you might inherit a blessing."

Coming back to the issue of the inheritance, Peter affirms that it will be given to the one who demonstrates the character of Christ and that it will come as "a blessing." What form will this "blessing" take and what content will it have? Peter answers these questions by continuing to tell us more about the sufferings of Christ as the pattern we should follow. The discussion reaches its climax when Peter shows that in Jesus' case, the inheritance or the "blessing" was His exaltation to "the right hand of God," after all the beings that populate the heavens "had been subjected to Him" (3:22).

We now have before us the complete panorama of the pattern that Christ offers us! The content of the "blessing" is equivalent to the content of our calling, as Peter concludes in 5:10: "the God of all grace, who called you to His eternal glory in Christ." With this entire picture in mind, we can better understand what Peter wants to say in 2:21. When Christ suffered, He suffered for us, for our sins "once for all, the just for the unjust, in order that He might bring us to God" (3:18). "With [the] precious blood" of Christ, we were redeemed from the futile way of life that we inherited from our forefathers (1:18-19). However, in addition to the redemptive purpose of the sufferings and death of Christ, His suffering and death also had the purpose of making Him our model, example, and pattern. The word ὑπογραμμόν used by Peter for "example" is very significant (2:21). Its basic meaning can be illustrated in the following way. In the schools of Peter's time, children wrote on a slate, as we still did fifty years ago in my Romanian elementary school. The slates we used each had the entire alphabet printed in beautiful calligraphy on the top. In Peter's time, however, that was not the case; the practice then was that the teacher would come into the classroom and would write a sentence on top of each slate. After that the students would try to imitate the beautiful writing of the teacher by writing that sentence again and again until each had filled his or her own slate. Well, the sentence on the top of the slate, written by the teacher himself, was called ὑπογραμμός!

We can now appreciate the beautiful and expressive illustration that Peter gave us in 2:21. With His own life on the earth, Christ wrote a complete account of man's glorious destiny. As we see His example, we must copy it with our own lives here on earth. Then, if we strictly follow Christ's example or, switching metaphors, if we closely "follow in His steps," by taking the same road and by walking in the same way, doing exactly as He did, we will have the same heavenly positions with Him in eternity!

In chapter four, Peter continues to explain how we are to follow the example or the pattern set by Christ. First of all, we must develop the same mind, the same way of thinking that we see in Christ (4:1-2). Peter says to literally "arm yourselves also with the same mind" (τὴν αὐτὴν ἔννοιαν ὁπλίσασθε, 4:1; the NASB uses "purpose" instead of "mind"). Peter places a great emphasis on the way his readers think and on the necessity of developing a true world-view, a right way of looking at the world and at life. In 1:13, he calls them to "gird up the loins of your mind" (διανοίας, literal translation). Both the farmer who has to do very heavy work and the man who has to lift heavy things must gird up their loins. Peter uses this phrase metaphorically to show that the development of a Christian mind is heavy work! In 3:8, he writes, "Τὸ δὲ τέλος πάντες ὁμόφρονες," which can be translated as "think in the same way with regard to the end"; that end or goal is the inheritance. In the same verse and again in 5:5, Peter calls them to ταπεινοφροσύνη or humility of mind. But it is in chapter four that Peter says more about this Christian mind, which is the mind of Christ.

First of all, a person who thinks like Christ does not live according to the dictates of the flesh but lives according to the will of God. This is the basic meaning of the rather difficult text of 4:1-2. What follows from verse 3 to verse 10 explains the difference between a worldly mentality and a Christlike mentality. The essence of what Peter says is that the people of this world live for their own pleasure; they live selfish lives. But the one who becomes wise by prayer (σωφρονήσατε . . . εἰς τὰς προσευχάς, 4:7) has an unfailing and fervent love toward others, employing all the gifts given to him by God in the service of others (4:8-10). Peter portrays the same image of Christ as the one we saw in Philippians 2:1-8, where the mind of Christ means serving others and sacrificing everything one has for others!

Peter concludes that if we live like this, we will then prove to be "good stewards of the manifold grace of God" (1 Pet. 4:10). Our conclusion, therefore, is that the essence of the grace of God is in living sacrificially for others; this truth is exactly what we found earlier in the other authors we studied.

Moving on, we discover yet another aspect of suffering in the teaching of Peter. It is found in 4:12-13: "Beloved, do not be surprised at the fiery ordeal among you, which comes upon you for your testing, as though some strange thing were happening to you; but to the degree that you share the sufferings of Christ, keep on rejoicing; so that also at the revelation of His glory, you may rejoice with exultation."

In this passage, Peter includes the same elements that he had mentioned in 1:6-8. In the first place, sufferings and persecution for Christ are a "fiery ordeal" (πυρώσει, one word in Greek; 4:12a); and secondly, they have the purpose of testing the saints (πειρασμὸν, as in 1:6-7). But now, Peter introduces a new and indispensable aspect of suffering: when Christians suffer for the right cause, which is the cause of Christ, they "share the sufferings of Christ" (κοινωνεῖτε τοῖς τοῦ Χριστοῦ παθήμασι, 4:13a). In this letter, we are not told in what sense we share in His sufferings. It is true that whenever Peter speaks about the sufferings of Christ, he always refers to Christ's historic sufferings; but in this place, he does not specify to which sufferings he refers, the historic ones or the present ones. Moreover, due to the fact that Peter is so close in his theology both to the teaching of Jesus and to that of Paul, we can safely assume that Peter also shares the belief that when believers suffer, Christ is present in them through the Holy Spirit, and that Christ suffers in them in such a way that *their* sufferings are a sharing in *His* sufferings.

In order to be able to visualize the whole Petrine teaching on the concept of partnership with Christ, we must add here what Peter writes about himself in the first verse of chapter five: "Therefore, I exhort the elders among you, as your fellow elder and witness of the sufferings of Christ, and a partaker (κοινωνός) also of the glory that is to be revealed." The first thing we need to analyze here is the meaning Peter gives to the word "witness" in this sentence. The simplest way to read it is to say that Peter is describing himself as a witness of the historic sufferings of Christ. The problem with this interpretation is that while Peter was a witness of Jesus' sufferings at the trial, it is apparent from the Gospels that he was not present at the crucifixion. Hence, it is improbable that Peter used the word "witness" in the sense of an "eyewitness" to a certain event.

The whole paragraph suddenly becomes more meaningful if we interpret "witness" to mean "one who bears witness." Peter tells the elders that he is a co-elder and, by extension, a co-witness with them to the sufferings of Christ. As Peter bears witness to Christ's sufferings, death, resurrection, and exaltation, he suffers with them and with Christ because of the hostility of the world. Due to this partnership with Christ in His sufferings, Peter can then say that he is also a partner with them and with Christ in the glory of Christ that will soon be revealed.

Peter has already informed his readers that to Christ "belongs the glory and dominion forever and ever" (4:11). The good news he now gives them is that if they are partners with Him in His sufferings, they will be partners with Him in the glory and dominion, as well. We have seen that in God's plan, mankind is destined to have dominion over all creation. Christ fulfilled that destiny through His suffering and death and became the pattern for all who are called by God to the same glorious, eternal position. But the chosen ones must understand that they have to become like Christ in their character first, for only then will they be able to handle sharing His position of ruling; for this reason, their character has to be severely tested by sufferings and self-sacrifice. They have to demonstrate the same mental attitude that Christ displayed toward God and toward other people.

To that Christlike mental attitude we must now pay special attention. Here is what Peter writes: "All of you, clothe yourselves with humility toward one another, for God is opposed to the proud, but gives grace to the humble. Humble yourselves, therefore, under the mighty hand of God, that He may exalt you at the proper time, casting all your anxiety upon Him, because He cares for you" (5:5b-7).

Peter has already spoken about our need of ταπεινοφροσύνη (3:8), of humility of mind or the habit of thinking humbly. In chapter five, Peter develops this concept further. In essence, to be proud is to desire independence from God, to want to be self-sufficient and to demand to govern one's own life according to one's own self-interest. The essence of humility, on the other hand, is total submission under the authority of God and absolute obedience to God's commands. Paul refers to this second mindset as the essence of Christ and of Christlikeness in Philippians 2:5-8. Pride, the declaration of independence from God, entails a declaration of war against God. God stands against pride and will ultimately destroy it for all eternity. But to the one who accepts to live under His authority, He "gives grace" (1 Pet. 5:5), that is, *He* works His purposes of glory and dominion in that person. Only to the person who knows how to live under authority will He entrust authority over the universe. However, the "God of all grace" is the One who forms that character in us through our sufferings; by means of these trials, He will "Himself perfect (καταρτίσαι), confirm (στηρίξαι), strengthen (σθενώσαι) and establish (θεμελιώσαι) you" (5:10). Davids indicates rightly that in this verse "the focus is on character. Through their suffering God will produce a fully restored or confirmed character in them."[12]

Concerning the last item on this list of actions taken by God in order to form us, it is very puzzling that some manuscripts have actually dropped the word "establish" from the list. It literally means "to make a foundation." Commentators point to what Jesus said in His Sermon on the Mount about the one who hears the words of Christ and "acts upon them"; this person "may be compared to a wise man, who built his house upon [a foundation of] rock" (Matt. 7:24).[13] I propose that we also look at what Paul says to rich Christians; namely, if they accumulate their riches in heaven during their life on earth, then they will have built a foundation (θεμέλιον) for their future existence in eternity (1 Tim. 6:19). Peter gives us a similar idea: the character that God is building in us through suffering becomes the "foundation" for our heavenly existence.

It is important to emphasize at this juncture that God is not the author of our sufferings. Their instigator is the devil, and Christians must be aware of the fact that they are involved in a spiritual war. If they consistently resist Satan's attacks, standing firm in their faith, they will defeat him (1 Peter 5:9). The devil will then be forced to "flee from" them (James 4:7). We will see this crucial teaching become basic for the Christian theology of martyrdom in the succeeding centuries.

In spite of the fact that the devil "prowls about like a roaring lion, seeking someone to devour" (1 Peter 5:8), and in spite of the persecutions and sufferings that are painful and difficult to endure, Christians are encouraged right from the beginning of this letter with the assurance that they are "protected by the power of God" (1:5) so that they *will* be able to obtain their heavenly inheritance (1:4). It is the "God of all grace" who works His glorious purposes in their lives (5:10). Once more, we must stress the fact that although Christians are called to work hard, to fight valiantly, to endure sufferings, to give up all self-interest, and to spend themselves in living totally for others, there is no hint or suggestion that through these things they could earn something or merit something. Instead, it is through these various trials and tribulations that they become like Christ, and as a consequence, they become qualified to share with Him in His glory and dominion. This is indeed "the true grace of God" in which we are exhorted to "stand firm" unto the end!

Chapter 10

Revelation: The Contours of
a Theology of Martyrdom

Of all the books in the Bible, the Book of Revelation is the most controversial. The author of the book, the date of its writing, and especially the mode of its interpretation are all matters of great debate.

I base my own study of the book on the premise that it was written by the Apostle John, sometime around A.D. 95. Some thirty years before, the churches experienced the great persecution under Nero, when thousands of Christians died as martyrs, including the Apostles Peter and Paul. Now, a new persecution had been initiated by the Emperor Domitian. Some of the churches in Asia Minor, where John had been a shepherd of souls for many years, were already caught in this new adversity and had given the first martyrs. John himself had been deported to the island of Patmos because of his faith and testimony for Jesus Christ.

This persecution had raised many questions that were now crying out for answers. Why does God allow persecution? If Christ has conquered Satan, then where is His victory? If Christ is the King of kings, then why doesn't He intervene to stop the persecution? What is the nature of the sufferings of the Christians, and what is the purpose of these sufferings and martyrdoms in the general plan of God? What is the purpose of martyrdom? Where is the history of mankind heading? When and how will history end? How long will the suffering last? What attitude should Christians have in times of persecution? From where or from whom can they obtain the courage and the strength they need to endure torture and martyrdom for the faith? These are just a few of the questions that were asked in John's time and that are asked again and again each time a new persecution comes storming over the Christian church. John, as apostle and shepherd, had to give answers to these and other similar questions in order to maintain the spiritual health and strength of the churches. The book he wrote was meant to provide the churches with the answers they so desperately needed.

The problem we have with the Book of Revelation is that it was written in a highly symbolic language. Most of the symbols, metaphors, and images were taken directly from the Old Testament and were then applied to the new situation of the persecuted people of God. The difficulty lies in our lack of knowledge about the way in which we should "translate" this symbolic language into literal, concrete terms and into theological terms.

Because of the great amount of space it would take to offer a recital of the variety of interpretations proposed for the Book of Revelation, I shall simply describe my own approach to it. I believe the book was written to address the particular situation of the churches in Asia Minor, as described above, and it was meant to answer the above-mentioned questions as well as others related to their situation of persecution. By answering these questions, the author helps us understand God's purposes in human history and God's methods for achieving His purposes in history. Milligan was right when he wrote the following about a hundred years ago: "We are not to look in the Apocalypse for special events, but for an exhibition of the principles which govern the history both of the world and the church."[1]

Interpreters who try to understand this book by "translating" its symbols are called idealist. The problem I have with this school of thought is that most of its proponents deny that the prophecies of Revelation will ever have any specific historic fulfillment: "From the idealist's point of view the symbols portray an ever present conflict: there is no necessary consummation of the historical process."[2] I do not find this to be the necessary conclusion of the hermeneutical endeavor that is preoccupied with deciphering the book's symbolic language.

It is true that the Book of Revelation shows us the historical conflict between Christ and His followers on the one side and Satan and his people on the other. It is also true that the book gives us the principles of interpretation that we need in order to understand this conflict, precisely by giving us an understanding of the methods used by each of the chief combatants. The book also shows us that this conflict is not unending; there will be a definite end to history in the general resurrection, in the last judgment, and in the creation of a new heaven and a new earth. The symbols express objective realities, and although the last chapters of Revelation are symbolic just like the rest of the book, these symbols represent real events that will occur at the end of earthly history and at the beginning of the eternal kingdom of God.

For the interpretation of the symbols of Revelation, I am greatly indebted to G. B. Caird, one of my professors at the University of Oxford. His commentary on Revelation helped me to understand that the work of the Lamb and of His lambs represents God's method of tackling the problems posed by the evil in this world. The followers of Jesus, by accepting His invitation to pick up their crosses and do exactly what He did, continue and complete God's work of bringing the world to Himself. Because I had this basic understanding in the forefront of my mind, I was able to face the possibility of martyrdom in communist Romania under Ceausescu's dictatorship.

Although I do not agree with my professor's views on some points of doctrine and I argue with his interpretations of some passages in Revelation, particularly of the last chapters, I may state truthfully that I acquired my understanding of the symbolic language of Revelation from G. B. Caird. Nonetheless, I have also reviewed many other books on Revelation, as I shall indicate below.

My aim is not to offer a complete interpretation of the whole book. My aim is to bring to light the main ideas that relate to our theme of suffering, martyrdom, and rewards in heaven. The first main concept I want to discuss is found at the beginning of the book in the specific way John presents Jesus Christ, God the Father, and himself to his readers.

Jesus Christ is introduced first of all as "the faithful witness" (Rev. 1:5). By the time of the writing of this book, the word "witness" had already been loaded with the new meaning of one who witnesses to the truth of God and who pays for that act with his own life. Thus, the introduction of Jesus as the faithful witness (martyr) sets the stage for the entire book. With this, John is presenting Jesus as the Forerunner and Pioneer of the ones who are facing the threat of torture and execution for their faith. Yet He is not only their Forerunner *into* death; He is also their Forerunner *out of* that death by the fact of His resurrection. Hence, Christ is "the first fruits of those who are asleep" (1 Cor. 15:20). As the New Adam, the originator of a new humanity, Christ was the first to come into this new life through death and resurrection. For the people who are facing martyrdom, this fact is a great encouragement; for this reason, John tells them to look to Jesus, since He has gone before them. They now follow Him in His witness and death, but there will come a day when they will also follow Him in His resurrection. He was the first, and they are simply following in line behind Him!

Secondly, Jesus is introduced as "the ruler (ἄρχων) of the kings of the earth" (Rev. 1:5). The kings of the earth are the ones who are persecuting the Christians; however, Christ is their ruler! This is a very strange situation, indeed. Before we look into the way Christ rules over these enemy kings, we must see the whole picture of Christ given to us by John in this book.

Christ is the one who has redeemed people from all tribes and nations and tongues for God's kingdom, and He has done this by the shedding of His own blood (1:5-6; 5:9-10). Presently, He is enthroned with "His God and Father" (1:6), and He shares with God the glory and the power. God is "the Alpha and the Omega" (1:8; 21:6), but Christ is also "the Alpha and the Omega, the first and the last, the beginning and the end" (22:13). He sits on the throne with His Father (3:21), on "the throne of God and of the Lamb" (22:1, 3). When the end will come, "loud voices in heaven" will announce it, "saying, 'The kingdom of the world has become the kingdom of our Lord, and of His Christ; and He will reign forever and ever' " (11:15).

God is described as "the Almighty" (ὁ παντοκράτωρ, 1:8). This word, showing the supremacy and the sovereignty of God over all things, is used ten times in the New Testament, with nine of these instances located here in Revelation (2 Cor. 6:18; Rev. 1:8; 4:8; 11:17; 15:3; 16:7, 14; 19:6, 15; 21:22). Jesus Christ shares in this supremacy, being of the same essence as the Father ("τὸ Α καὶ τὸ Ω," 1:8; 22:13), having "the keys of death and of Hades" (1:18), and ruling over the kings of the earth (1:5). The Son is, therefore, "worthy . . . to receive power and riches and wisdom and might and honor and glory and blessing" (5:12).

John informs the Christians in the midst of persecution that Christ holds in His hand the "seven stars," which are "the angels of the seven churches" (1:20), and that He Himself stands "in the middle of the lampstands" (1:13), which represent the churches (1:20); this special information is of vital importance for these suffering believers. Christ is not only reigning on His throne in heaven; He is also present with His own people in their struggle and in their suffering. Here is yet another very encouraging piece of news: Christ knows the situation of all the churches. Each letter to the seven churches starts with these significant words: "*I know* your . . ." (2:2, 9, 13, 19; 3:1, 8, 15, italics mine).

The conclusion to be drawn from all of these statements in John's introduction is that God and His Son Jesus Christ are in control of all that happens in human history. We have already seen in the other biblical texts and in the intertestamental literature we have studied that it is incredibly important for God's people to understand the sovereignty of their God, to know that He is in command and that His purposes are being fulfilled even by His own enemies. The Book of Revelation makes this truth shine with dazzling light.

The next thing we have to observe in the introduction to this book is the way the author introduces himself: "The revelation of Jesus Christ, . . . to His slave John, who bore witness (ὃς ἐμαρτύρησε) to the word of God and to the testimony of Jesus Christ" (1:1-2). As a consequence of his witness, John was now exiled on the island of Patmos. Therefore, he could write to the persecuted Christians of the seven churches that he is a co-sharer (συγκοινωνὸς) with them "in the tribulation (θλίψει) and kingdom (βασιλείᾳ) and perseverance (ὑπομονῇ) which are in Jesus" (1:9). Again we notice the terminology of martyrdom: the witness, the suffering (or tribulation, affliction), the endurance (or perseverance, patience). Later on in the story, we shall see many dying for this testimony. It is very important to notice that right in the midst of them all is "the kingdom." The persecuted Christians have to be aware that the kingdom is theirs not only in the future tense, at the end of their struggle; they already *are* the kingdom (1:6; 5:10). Since they are "in Jesus," they *now* participate with Jesus not only in suffering with Him but also in ruling with Him. Therefore, even in their tribulations, they should act not as the victims but as the conquerors!

With this, we have arrived at the essence of this book. The basic symbol and predominant image of the Book of Revelation is that of a war. In each war, the fundamental question is this: How can we obtain the victory? By what means and methods will we defeat the enemy and conquer him? We should not be surprised to find that these are the key questions of the book and that its key words are "to conquer" and "to overcome" (and their cognates).

The pagan forces, namely, the Emperor of Rome and all the military administrative apparatus of the Roman Empire, have just launched a new assault against Christianity. All physical power is in the hands of this apparatus. How can Christians fight empty-handed against such a colossal force? The answer to this question provides the key to this book. We must, therefore, investigate this theme throughout the whole book in order to unlock the meaning of Revelation.

In the first part of Revelation, Jesus sends a message to each of the seven churches shepherded by the Apostle John. Each message ends with a promise to the one who conquers or overcomes. While each church has its different problems, all of them are caught in the major conflict with the pagan empire, and the principal concern of each one is the final victory: who will overcome and by what means?

Most commentators say that in the seven letters, we are not told who the conquerors are; however, I suggest that the author does tell us who they are in the following words addressed to the second church, the church of Smyrna: "Do not fear what you are about to suffer. Behold, the devil is about to cast some of you into prison, that you may be tested, and you will have tribulation ten days. Be faithful until death, and I will give you the crown of life. He who has an ear, let him hear what the Spirit says to the churches. He who overcomes shall not be hurt by the second death" (2:10-11).

I will approach the interpretation of this text from a personal perspective. I grew up in a persecuted church in Romania. In our home, we had a beautifully written verse centrally positioned on a wall in our living room; this is what it said: "Be faithful until death, and I will give you the crown of life." As a child, I would look in the Bible and read the preceding words about being thrown in prison for ten days; puzzled by this information, I always wondered why Jesus would give them the command to "be faithful until death," if they would be kept in prison for only ten days and then would be set free. It just did not make sense to me. In fact, this is exactly the problem we face in the twentieth century, because we do not know the difference between the purpose of imprisonment in the first century A.D. and its purpose in our time.

For us, prison is a place of punishment. One is sent there after the trial is over and the sentence has been pronounced. In ancient times, however, prison was a place of detention *before* one's trial took place. After the trial, the prisoners were either sent into exile or to a labor camp or they were sentenced to death and executed. In the case of the Christians in John's lifetime, the procedure was as follows. The Christian who had been betrayed to the authorities was asked to come before the magistrate. As he stood there alone, he was asked whether he was a Christian or not. If he answered that he was not a Christian, he would be told to prove it in this way: he had to pick up some incense from a bowl, to spread it over the flame on the altar of the emperor-god, and to declare that "Caesar is Lord." Sometimes, instead of burning incense, he had to make a libation, which meant that he had to pour some wine on the same altar and worship the emperor, acknowledging that he was "Lord." If the arrested individual performed all these things satisfactorily, he would then be given a certificate stating that he had worshipped Caesar; the certificate would enable him to leave the prison as a free man.

Of course, a Christian could not comply with such orders. He would say "Christ is Lord," not Caesar. But if he refused to worship Caesar, he would immediately be given into the hands of the torturers. The Christian would be savagely tortured for a whole day in order to force him to deny his Lord and to worship Caesar. If he endured the torture all day, at one point the torturers would cease, realizing that they could not break him. This being the case, the magistrate would simply pronounce the sentence of death: usually a public execution in the arena, most often by beheading and sometimes by crucifixion or by being thrown to the wild beasts. But there was another procedure of which we are not aware. Because the authorities did not want to let the public see the open wounds of the Christians, they would keep the Christians in prison for a short while, until the wounds inflicted by the torturers would at least superficially heal; this could mean a period of ten days or a little longer. Finally, after this short time in prison, they would be taken into the arena for the public execution.

Therefore, when the Christians in Asia Minor were told that they would be "tested" and then would have a tribulation of ten days, they clearly understood by this that what was before them was torture and martyrdom. For this reason, the following admonition was very meaningful to them: "Be faithful until death!" And the promise after that carried an even greater import: "He who overcomes shall not be hurt by the second death" (2:11).

From this view of the situation, it becomes obvious that here John was giving the saints in Smyrna the message that they would soon be tortured and killed. However, this was in fact their call to witness, just as Jesus had done, with the cost of life itself. Moreover, they were also assured that they would defeat Satan by their martyrdom, again just as Jesus had done. Their victory would come through death. Therefore, the victorious ones will not be those who avoid persecution and who escape with their lives, but those who openly witness Christ and lose their lives in the process. With Christ, one wins by losing!

In the next letter, the saints in Pergamum are praised in terms that display their endurance and faithfulness unto martyrdom: "You held fast My name, and did not deny My faith, even in the days of Antipas, My witness, My faithful one, who was killed among you, where Satan dwells" (2:13). The remarkable thing is that Antipas is called "a faithful witness," in the same way that Christ was called "the faithful witness" at the beginning of the letter. We shall soon observe how this close association between Christ and His witness-martyrs grows into an even deeper intimacy.

In the conclusion to the seventh letter, we read: "He who overcomes, I will grant to him to sit down with Me on My throne, as I also overcame and sat down with My Father on His throne" (3:21). The Lord is clearly saying here that because He overcame, His Father granted Him to sit with Him on His throne. And now, the Lord promises the churches exactly the same thing: to the one who overcomes, just as He overcame (the parallelism of the sentence obligates us to add that), He will give the same honor His Father gave Him, the honor of sitting on His throne, that is, of sharing with Him in ruling or reigning.

How did Jesus overcome? In chapter five, we are told exactly how He overcame. In verses five and six, we discover that the Lamb who had been slain (ἐσφαγμένον) "has overcome so as to open the book." In verse nine, we are told how He overcame and what He accomplished by this victory: "Worthy art Thou to take the book, and to break its seals; for Thou wast slain (ἐσφάγης) and didst purchase for God with Thy blood men from every tribe and tongue and people and nation." Christ overcame by dying on the cross. We can now read 3:21 in this way: the Lord Jesus Christ says, "To the one who overcomes by dying, as I overcame by dying, I will grant to him to sit down with Me on My throne, as My Father granted Me to sit down with Him on His throne."

The similarity between the martyrs and their Lord is further developed in chapter six. John has a new vision of heaven in which he sees "underneath the altar the souls of those who had been slain (ἐσφαγμένων) because of the word of God, and because of the testimony which they had maintained" (6:9). The fact that John uses the same word to designate how Christ was slain and how the martyrs were slain (literally, "stabbed") is intentional. It is meant to show that the method of conquest was the same in both cases.

Furthermore, in chapter six, the martyrs in heaven "were told that they should rest for a little while longer, until *the number of* their fellow servants and their brethren who were to be killed even as they had been, should be completed also" (6:11). This is an extraordinarily important piece of information for us; it tells us that God has preordained a fixed number of His children to die as martyrs!

Our next valuable clue about the war in which the martyrs are engaged is found in the twelfth chapter. In verse nine, we observe Satan being thrown out of heaven, and we learn that this defeat of Satan was accomplished by those who had accepted to die for Christ: "And they overcame him because of the blood of the Lamb and because of the word of their testimony, and they did not love their life even to death" (12:11).

We know that Christ defeated Satan by His death on the cross (John 12:31-32; Col. 2:15; Heb. 2:14; 1 John 3:8). By His own blood, He delivered us from Satan's clutches. But in Revelation 12:11, we discover that this conquest of Satan is repeated by the martyrs. Later in the text, we will learn more about the way in which the martyrs conquer Satan by their own death.

At the end of chapter twelve, we are told that "the dragon was enraged with the woman, and went off to make war with the rest of her offspring, who keep the commandments of God and hold to the testimony of Jesus" (12:17). It is obvious that what is described here is the same attack against the church, through persecution. In the next chapter, we see "a beast coming up out of the sea" (13:1), and we read that "it was given to him to make war with the saints and to overcome them" (13:7). The subsequent statement in verse ten cautions us that throughout the whole story of the beast, we need to see and discern "the perseverance and the faith of the saints." In chapter fourteen, the war with the beast continues, and in the midst of it, we are given the same clue one more time: "Here is the perseverance of the saints who keep the commandments of God and their faith in Jesus. . . . 'Blessed are the dead who die in the Lord from now on!' " (14:12-13).

The climax of this war is reached in chapter seventeen. A confederation led by the beast gathers to "wage war against the Lamb, and the Lamb will overcome them, because He is Lord of lords and King of kings, and those who are with Him . . . the called and chosen and faithful [will also overcome them]" (17:14). The structure of this passage in Greek compels us to add the phrase "will also overcome them"; the structure in Greek is the following:

καὶ τὸ ἀρνίον νικήσει αὐτούς
καὶ οἱ μετ' αὐτοῦ

and the Lamb will conquer them
and those with Him [will conquer them].

Now, having seen this, the parallel structure of the two qualifiers becomes apparent, as well:

ὅτι Κύριος κυρίων ἐστὶ καὶ Βασιλεὺς βασιλέων
κλητοὶ καὶ ἐκλεκτοὶ καὶ πιστοί

because He is Lord of lords and King of kings
[because they are] called and chosen and faithful.

The passage cannot be translated to make sense without some addition of this kind. Now, the New American Standard Bible simply adds the verb: "and those who are with Him *are* the called and chosen and faithful." I argue that the addition of this verb renders the second part of the statement, referring to the ones who are with Him, meaningless. All that John has written up to this point about those with the Lamb indicates that they are partakers with Him in the war and that they conquer with Him; in other words, it is clear that Christ continues the war through them and wins the war through them. There are four versions in English which render this passage with an added phrase similar to the one I have placed in brackets (i.e., "will also overcome them"): the J. B. Philips version, the Jerusalem Bible, the New English Bible, and Today's English Version.

Robert H. Mounce would also support my addition because he believes that "the concept of the righteous taking part in the destruction of the wicked is a standard apocalyptic theme. (e.g., 1 Enoch 98:12; 4 Enoch 38:5; 91:12; 96:1)."[3]

From all these texts about the conquerors, we see the following general picture emerging: the initial victory that was won by Jesus at Calvary must be repeated by those who follow Him; only in this manner will the forces of evil be finally overcome. Nevertheless, the question that comes to our minds when we read these things is this: Why does God specifically choose this method to conquer the evil that is in the world? We will discover God's own answer to this key question as we analyze the mission of the martyrs depicted through the symbols of the 144,000 warriors and the two witnesses.

The 144,000 appear for the first time in 7:3-4: "Do not harm the earth or the sea or the trees, until we have sealed the slaves of our God on their foreheads. And I heard the number of those who were sealed, one hundred and forty-four thousand sealed from every tribe of the sons of Israel."

In order to identify the 144,000 we need to look for clues in all the places where they appear in the book, so that in the end, we can add up all the bits of information given in each place into a complete, coherent whole. The first clue is in the fact that they are called "slaves (δούλους) of God" (7:3; the NASB has incorrectly translated δούλους as "bond-servants," while the correct term is "slaves"; hence, I have rendered the word δούλους in its proper translation throughout this dissertation). What else does John tell us about these slaves? In 10:7, we read that the mystery of God will be finished "as He preached to His slaves (δούλοις) the prophets." In 11:3, God says: "I will give to My two witnesses (μάρτυσί) to prophesy" (literal translation), and in verse 10, they are called directly the "two prophets." What we learn from these passages is that the job of the witness-martyrs, of those who bear witness to Christ, is to prophesy. In 19:10, we are further told that "the testimony (μαρτυρίαν) of Jesus is the spirit of prophecy," which can be taken to mean that the essence of prophesying is bearing witness to Christ.

In 11:18, we find another helpful clue: "And the nations were enraged, and Thy wrath came, and the time came for the dead to be judged, and the time to give their reward to Thy slaves the prophets and to *the saints* and to those who fear Thy name, the small and the great, and to destroy those who destroy the earth" (italics mine). Finally, in 19:2, we read that God "has judged the great harlot who was corrupting the earth with her immorality, and He has avenged the blood of His slaves on her."

From all these texts we understand that the slaves (also called the 144,000), the witnesses, and the prophets in Revelation are one and the same group: they are the martyrs. We should remember at this point that John had been in Jesus' school, where he had been taught that the prophets were always persecuted and in many cases were killed because of their testimony. Additionally, John had learned that there is no greater honor than to be in their company and to share in the destiny of the persecuted messengers of God (cf. Matt. 5:10-12; 23:34, 37).

Let us take a closer look at the sealing of the 144,000 in chapter seven. First of all, we need to keep in mind the fact that in the Old Testament, a census of the people was usually taken in preparation for war. Secondly, in order to understand the way John uses his symbols here, we have to notice the shift in symbols: John uses one symbol when he first *hears* a message, and then changes it to another symbol when he later *sees* that message enacted. The most obvious example of this is in chapter five, when John *hears* a voice saying, "Behold, the Lion that is from the tribe of Judah, the Root of David, has overcome so as to open the book and its seven seals" (Rev. 5:5). The symbol of the Lion indicates a warrior. Indeed, He is a warrior, because He "has overcome." However, when John turns around to *see* the Lion, lo and behold, He is a Lamb, and a Lamb that has been stabbed! Why? It is because He did not fight by means of brutal force but by means of His death on a cross! Then, in chapter seven, John *hears* the voice telling him of the 144,000 warriors. In similar fashion, the symbol changes when he *sees* them in action later on, discovering that they are the lambs who have been stabbed and who have won the war by dying as martyrs.

Let us now examine what John tells us about the war itself. In 12:17, we read: "And the dragon was enraged with the woman, and went off to make war with the rest of her offspring, who keep the commandments of God and hold to the testimony of Jesus." Then in 13:7, we are told that the beast "was given . . . to make war with the saints and to overcome them." Clearly, the beast overcomes the saints by putting them to death; this is immediately evident from the following verse, in which we are told that the Commander-in-Chief of these saints was Himself "slain." At the end of this vision, John lets us understand that what is at stake here is "the perseverance (ὑπομονὴ, endurance, patience) and the faith of the saints" (13:10).

A bit further, when the war against the saints is fully in progress, we see Jesus present on the earth in the midst of the 144,000:

> And I looked, and behold, the Lamb was standing on Mount Zion, and with Him one hundred and forty-four thousand, having His name and the name of His Father written on their foreheads. And I

heard a voice from heaven, like the sound of many waters and like the sound of loud thunder, and the voice which I heard was like the sound of harpists playing on their harps. And they sang a new song before the throne and before the four living creatures and the elders; and no one could learn the song except the one hundred and forty-four thousand who had been purchased from the earth. These are the ones who have not been defiled with women, for they have kept themselves chaste. These are the ones who follow the Lamb wherever He goes. These have been purchased from among men as first fruits to God and to the Lamb. And no lie was found in their mouth; they are blameless. (14:1-5)

All the way through this chapter, the war continues to rage. We can infer this from the fact that in 14:9-10, the ones who worship the beast receive a dreadful warning, and afterward, the saints are called to suffer and to endure unto death:

Here is the perseverance of the saints who keep the commandments of God and their faith in Jesus. And I heard a voice from heaven, saying, "Write, 'Blessed are the dead who die in the Lord from now on!' " "Yes," says the Spirit, "that they may rest from their labors, for their deeds follow with them." (14:12-13)

What follows in the rest of this chapter is a symbolic representation of the way the martyrs win the victory by accepting to be slaughtered. It is significant that verse 20 reveals the fact that this event takes place "outside the city." We know that Jesus suffered unto death outside the city, and we have heard the invitation to "go out to Him outside the camp, bearing His reproach" (Heb. 13:13).

Immediately following the description of the slaughter of the martyrs, its results are revealed:

And I saw another sign in heaven, great and marvelous, seven angels who had seven plagues, which are the last, because in them the wrath of God is finished.

And I saw, as it were, a sea of glass mixed with fire, and those who had come off victorious from the beast and from his image and from the number of his name, standing on the sea of glass, holding harps of God. And they sang the song of Moses the slave of God and the song of the Lamb, saying,

"Great and marvelous are Thy works,
O Lord God, the Almighty;
Righteous and true are Thy ways,
Thou King of the nations.

> Who will not fear, O Lord, and glorify Thy name?
> For Thou alone art holy;
> For all the nations will come and worship before Thee,
> For Thy righteous acts have been revealed." (Rev. 15:2-4)

Who are the victors? There is a clue in this text that helps us to identify them: they are the ones "holding harps of God." If we refer back to 14:2, we notice that the 144,000 are singing and "playing on their harps." Therefore, the 144,000 are first of all the warriors of chapter seven; they are also the saints who are called to "fight" by suffering and dying (ch. 13, 14); and they are the victorious conquerors with the Lamb by means of their martyrdom (ch. 15).

The theme of the war is repeated in 16:14-16, and again in 17:14, where we are told that the beast and the kings of the earth "will wage war against the Lamb." We have already seen that these will be overcome both by the Lamb *and* by those with Him, the ones who are "called and chosen and faithful" (17:14b).

Finally, the war is depicted one last time in 19:19 and the verses to follow; once more we see that "the beast was seized, and with him the false prophet who performed the signs in his presence, by which he deceived those who had received the mark of the beast and those who worshipped his image; these two were thrown alive into the lake of fire which burns with brimstone" (19:20). Satan himself is bound and thrown into the abyss for a thousand years (20:1-3).

The principal question we want to pose is whether all the wars mentioned in 11:7, 12:17, 13:7, 16:14-16, 17:14, and 19:19-20 are different events, occurring at different times or whether they are one and the same war, described in various ways from different angles, with new details provided with each new perspective?

The following two things prove to us that each of those passages describes one and the same war. First, the instigators of the war are always the same: the dragon, the beast, and the false prophet. Each time the war is mentioned, one of the three, or two of them, or all three are mentioned. The second confirmation is in the fact that the war is always waged against the same group of people: the "two witnesses" (11:3, 7), "the rest of [the woman's] offspring" (12:17), "the saints" (13:7), "the Lamb . . . and those who are with Him" (17:14), and "against Him who sat upon the horse, and against His army" (19:19). It has already been made amply clear that in the Book of Revelation, these are all different designations referring to the same group of people. In 16:14, we are only told about "the war of the great day of God, the Almighty," but the warning that follows shows that the war is directed against God's people.

This war is described in successive scenes from chapter seven to chapter nineteen. The scene located midway in this sequence portrays a rather peculiar battle: the beast comes up out of the abyss and makes war against the two witnesses, killing them both (11:7). We have established that this scene represents the same war that is described in all the other places. Therefore, the 144,000, or those who are with the Lamb, are here reduced to two martyrs, giving us a close-up view of the same large-scale struggle.

Let us look more closely at these two witnesses. In verse four of chapter eleven, we are told that "these are the two olive trees and the two lampstands that stand before the Lord of the earth." To find out the significance of the fact that they are called "olive trees," we must go back to Zechariah 4:3-14; in this Old Testament prophecy, the two olive trees are Joshua the high priest and the ruling prince Zerubbabel. In Revelation 1:6 and 5:10, we read that the ones redeemed by Christ are made priests and kings. While these verses refer to the totality of the redeemed, the two witnesses represent only a small segment of that totality. Revelation 20:6 helps us here, by informing us that the martyred witnesses are the ones who will have a part "in the first resurrection" and that "they will be priests of God and of Christ and will reign with Him for a thousand years." Since we observed in chapter eleven that the two witnesses are martyred and then they are resurrected, we conclude that they can be identified with the martyred witnesses of 20:4-6.

In 11:4, a second metaphor, namely, "the two lampstands," is used to represent the two witnesses. Back in 1:20, we were told that the seven lampstands were the seven churches. However, this cannot mean that merely two of the seven churches are represented by the symbol of the two witnesses, because each of the seven churches had given martyrs. The only reasonable solution is to understand that the two witnesses represent only the martyred members of all the churches; in other words, the two witnesses signify the totality of Christian martyrs throughout history. This supports the above statement that the two witnesses are a close-up view of the 144,000, who also symbolize the totality of Christian martyrs.

With respect to the time frame in which the war takes place, it was revealed to John that the nations "will tread under foot the holy city for forty-two months" (11:2). The two witnesses "will prophesy for twelve hundred and sixty days" (11:3), which is the equivalent of forty-two months (42 x 30 = 1260). Then, in chapter twelve, John sees a symbolic representation of Christian history, starting with the birth of Christ; he is informed that the woman, who represents the church, will spend "one thousand two hundred and sixty days" in the wilderness (12:6). During this period of time, the dragon will "make war with the rest of her offspring, who keep the commandments of God and hold to the testimony of Jesus" (12:17). In chapter thirteen, John observes the beast coming out of the sea. The beast is the one to whom "it was given . . . to make war with the saints and to overcome them" (13:7). Again in 13:5, we read that authority "was given to him . . . to act for forty-two months," for the same period of time as in chapters eleven and twelve. It should be clear from these verses that John is speaking of the entire history of the Christian church, from the time of Christ on the earth to the time of the final victory of Christ and His church.

The First Purpose of the War: Bringing the Nations to God

Reading the Book of Revelation, particularly from chapter six to chapter nineteen, is a rather frightening experience. We are given vivid descriptions of wars, natural disasters, plagues, and other such calamities that bring suffering and death to huge numbers of people. These detailed accounts are in fact an elaboration of what Jesus had said to His disciples: "And you will be hearing of wars and rumors of wars; see that you are not frightened, for those things must take place, but that is not yet the end. For nation will rise against nation, and kingdom against kingdom, and in various places there will be famines and earthquakes. But all these things are merely the beginning of birth pangs" (Matt. 24:6-8).

What is the purpose of these calamities and disasters? They are, of course, the consequences of man's rebellion, when he turned his back toward God and began living without God and against His commandments. However, disasters and plagues are not God's chosen formula for bringing mankind back to Himself. Indeed, in the conclusion to John's description of these dreadful events, we see that the plagues did not convince people to come back to God:

And the rest of mankind, who were not killed by these plagues, did not repent of the works of their hands, so as not to worship demons, and the idols of gold and of silver and of brass and of stone and of wood, which can neither see nor hear nor walk; and they did not repent of their murders nor of their sorceries nor of their immorality nor of their thefts. (Rev. 9:20-21)

Later on, at the end of another description of similar disasters, John tells us that as a result of the calamities, those left alive became angry with God and refused to turn to Him: "And men were scorched with fierce heat; and they blasphemed the name of God who has the power over these plagues; and they did not repent, so as to give Him glory" (16:9).

Plainly, natural disasters do not produce the conversion of the nations. In view of this, we are led to ask: What method or what agency does God use in order to determine the nations of the earth to turn back to Him? The answer to this all-important question begins to emerge in chapter ten. An angel tells John that when the seventh angel will sound his trumpet, "then the mystery of God is finished, as He evangelized (εὐηγγέλισε, announced the good news; the NASB has translated it as "preached") to His slaves (δούλοις) the prophets" (10:7). Some time later, the angel commands John to "prophesy again concerning many peoples and nations and tongues and kings" (10:11). This is then followed by the martyrdom of the two witnesses and their vindication by resurrection and ascension to heaven. As the seventh angel sounds his trumpet, we hear the voice from heaven explaining how the mystery of God was finished: "The kingdom of the world has become the kingdom of our Lord, and of His Christ; and He will reign forever and ever" (11:15b).

The mystery of God, mentioned in 10:7, is the process by which He establishes His rule over the world in such a way that "all the nations will come and worship before" Him (15:4). The first clue for understanding this mystery is embedded in the story of the two witnesses in chapter eleven. William Barclay is right in affirming that this chapter contains a summary of all that John is about to relate in detail in the remaining chapters; it is an outline of the entire plan of God to establish His authority upon the earth.[4]

The story of the two witnesses begins with the measuring of the temple. John is told to "measure the temple of God, and the altar, and those who worship in it. And leave out the court which is outside the temple, and do not measure it, for it has been given to the nations; and they will tread under foot the holy city for forty-two months" (11:1-2).

Since John wrote this book using symbols and metaphors, we should always make an effort to understand the realities represented by those symbols and the ideas they were meant to convey. In my interpretation, the temple is a symbol for the church. The action of measuring its inside part signifies an inner security, a quarantine for the protection of its spiritual life. But the outside court is not measured, because God does not shield the church against external attacks and does not offer her protection against suffering and physical death. The church is somehow in the situation in which Peter had been when Jesus said to him: "Simon, Simon, behold, Satan has demanded permission to sift you like wheat; but I have prayed for you, that your faith may not fail; and you, when once you have turned again, strengthen your brothers" (Lk. 22:31-32).

Evidently, God allowed Satan to sift Peter, but his inner spiritual life, his faith, was protected. In the Book of Revelation, we see God's design even more clearly. His "called and chosen and faithful" ones (Rev. 17:14) should be vulnerable only on the outside; meanwhile, they have full assurance that through all the trials, their faithfulness to the Lord is secured and protected by God Himself.

The main goal toward which we see God working in this chapter is the return of the nations to Him. When the two witnesses are martyred, here is what happens:

> And their dead bodies will lie in the street of the great city which mystically is called Sodom and Egypt, where also their Lord was crucified. And those from the peoples and tribes and tongues and nations will look at their dead bodies for three and a half days, and will not permit their dead bodies to be laid in a tomb. And those who dwell on the earth will rejoice over them and make merry; and they will send gifts to one another, because these two prophets tormented those who dwell on the earth. (11:8-10)

It is necessary for our understanding of this passage to identify the place where these events occur. John himself draws our attention to the fact that the names he gives to this place must be interpreted "spiritually" (πνευματικῶς); we would say that he is speaking "allegorically." Hence, the name "Sodom" is used to indicate the depth of the moral degeneration of the unsaved world (Gen. 19:4-11).

In other parts of Revelation, the "great city" is called "Babylon" (18:10), "the great harlot" (17:1), or "the woman" whose "mystery" turns out to be the mystery of God (17:3-7). The purpose of the entire book, and especially of chapters eleven through twenty-two, is to reveal this mystery. The "great city" is populated by all the nations of the earth. This is visible from the fact that when the two witnesses are killed, people from all nations gaze upon their dead bodies, and all those who dwell on earth rejoice (11:9-10). This means that God's people do not suffer martyrdom in one particular city alone. John is talking about a worldwide event, occurring everywhere upon this earth, because the "great city" represents the world in revolt against God, led by forces hostile to God and symbolized by the dragon, the beast, and the false prophet.

An even more important clue given to us by John is the revelation that the witness-martyrs must die "where also their Lord was crucified" (11:8). In 14:20, we are told that "the wine press" in which the blood of the martyrs is shed is located "outside the city." In Hebrews 13:12-13, we are told that Jesus "suffered outside the gate"; subsequently, we are called to do likewise and "go out to Him outside the camp" to suffer for His cause. In Revelation 14:4, John tells us that the martyrs are "the ones who follow the Lamb wherever He goes," which plainly means that they follow Him to crucifixion and death. The witnesses, by means of their martyrdom, participate in the sufferings and reproach, as well as in the sacrifice and death of their Lord; in this manner, they complete its impact on the unsaved world, as we shall immediately see.

The two witness-martyrs are also called "the two prophets" (11:10). Their ministry is to prophesy for forty-two months (11:3). We have already noted that in Revelation the words "witness," "slave," and "prophet" designate the same group of people: the soldiers of the Lamb, the ones who conquer by their costly witness, and the ones who overcome by dying.

In the Old Testament, a prophet was someone who received the Word of God and was commissioned to communicate this Word to other people. However, in the New Testament, "the Word became flesh" (John 1:14). From that time on, the prophet became someone who unites himself with Jesus, the Word; the prophet is the one through whom Jesus, the Word, expresses Himself. Furthermore, the prophet participates with Jesus in the costly witness that ultimately ends in crucifixion and death; the prophet, therefore, continues what Jesus has inaugurated and brings it to completion. John encapsulates all these truths in his description of the brethren "who hold the testimony of Jesus," explaining that "the testimony of Jesus is the spirit of prophesy" (Rev. 19:10).

As it was indicated above, throughout the Book of Revelation, "witnessing" leads to martyrdom. Jesus Himself was crucified because of His witness and that is why He is called "the faithful and true Witness" (3:14). Hence, we can understand 19:10 to mean that the testimony of Jesus inspires the prophet-martyrs. Furthermore, we can also interpret it to mean that the essence of being a Christian prophet is expressing Christ by one's words, lifestyle, endurance, and ultimately, martyrdom.

Continuing our analysis of chapter eleven with respect to the two witnesses, we discover that "fire proceeds out of their mouth and devours their enemies" (11:5); the two witnesses "tormented those who dwell on the earth" (11:10). We will be able to "translate" these symbolic statements when we remember John's previous observation concerning the Leader of the two witnesses, that "from His mouth comes a sharp sword, so that with it He may smite the nations" (19:15a). Since we know that the "sword" is the Word of God and that the Lamb smites only with that Word, we can logically deduce that the fire proceeding from the mouth of the witnesses is nothing other than the power of their testimony.

This testimony of the witnesses is extremely powerful, producing pain and tormenting the dwellers of the earth. Their testimony has this effect upon the lost world because the world is covered by thick darkness. 2 Corinthians 4:4 declares that the very minds of men were darkened by "the god of this world." Naturally, the piercingly bright light of the fire of the martyrs' testimony is very painful to eyes that have been accustomed to this darkness. Moreover, men hate the light because it exposes their evil deeds (John 3:19-20). As a result, when the witnesses shine the light of truth upon the world enshrouded by the tyranny of the lie, this truth hurts, disturbs, and infuriates those who have enjoyed living in the darkness of the lie. The truth produces pain as it strikes minds that have been dominated by the lie, particularly as the truth penetrates to consciences that have been choked by living for so long in darkness.

For these reasons, the world hates the witnesses; it stands in opposition to them and eventually puts them to death. Furthermore, this is why the nations rejoice when they see the witnesses killed. Notwithstanding their hateful glee, God intervenes and after three and a half days (another symbolic time!), He raises them from the dead and takes them up to heaven, as the world watches this miracle in amazement (Rev. 11:11-12). Passing over the symbolism of the earthquake that kills the seven thousand, we come to an especially crucial point in our study: the impact of the death and resurrection of the martyrs on the nations. In 11:13, we are informed that "the rest were terrified and gave glory to the God of heaven." This is one of the most important clues for our understanding of the whole message of Revelation: the nations were "terrified" (ἔμφοβοι). The statement that they were filled with terror in fact indicates that the nations were filled with "the fear of the Lord." How should we interpret this information?

One of my professors in Oxford, Dr. Henton Davies, explained to us in one of his lectures that the Hebrew language lacks the word "religion"; the phrase used instead is "the fear of the Lord." To "fear" a certain God means to make Him your own God and to practice His "religion." Dr. Davies referred us to the story recorded in 2 Kings 17:24-41, about the pagan people brought to repopulate the region of Samaria after the Jews had been exiled to Assyria: "And it came about at the beginning of their living there, that they did not fear the Lord; therefore the Lord sent lions among them which killed some of them" (17:25). A messenger was sent to the king of Assyria informing him that the lions had been "sent" because the colonists "in the cities of Samaria do not know the custom of the god of the land" (17:26b). So the king decided to send back to them a true Samaritan priest from among the exiles in order to teach the new population "the custom of the god of the land" (17:27b). At the king's command, the priest went back to Samaria and taught them "how they should fear the Lord" (17:28b). From the remainder of this account, we are led to conclude that to "fear the Lord" means to follow His statutes, ordinances, and commandments; to "fear Him" means to serve Him only and to bring sacrifices to Him alone (17:33-41). This text clearly indicates that "the fear of the Lord" is in fact the whole "religion" of Yahweh. It involves living under His authority, serving Him, and sacrificing to Him.

The Book of Proverbs, a textbook for the education of Israelite children, rests on the premise that "the fear of the Lord is the beginning of knowledge" (Prov. 1:7). Based on the conclusion we have drawn from 2 Kings 17:24-41, we can paraphrase this statement in the following way: "The religion of Yahweh is the basis for all science and the foundation of all systems of education." To fear the Lord means to accept that Yahweh is the true God, to submit to Him, and to live in conformity to His commandments.

Therefore, it is in this sense that John used the phrase "and the rest were terrified" in Revelation 11:13b. According to the Apostle John, the main goal of the gospel is to bring all the nations to the fear of God. He writes this in chapter fourteen, in the midst of images of the slaughter of the martyrs: "And I saw another angel flying in midheaven, having an eternal gospel to preach to those who live on the earth, and to every nation and tribe and tongue and people" (14:6). Clearly, the purpose of proclaiming the gospel is to reach *all* the nations of the world! But what is the content of this gospel? John defines it in the following statement: "And he said with a loud voice, 'Fear God, and give Him glory, because the hour of His judgment has come; and worship Him who made the heaven and the earth and sea and springs of waters' " (14:7).

When we think of the content of the gospel, we normally think of the work of Christ for our salvation. John was certainly aware of this aspect of the gospel (5:9-12), but he was more concerned now with the *goal* of the gospel. This goal is to bring the nations to the fear of God, that is, to bring them to full submission and obedience to Him as the Sovereign, giving Him all the glory and worshipping Him alone. The Apostle Paul perceived the purpose of his ministry in identical terms: to bring the nations to the "obedience of faith" (Rom. 1:5; 15:18; 16:25-26).

The song of the martyrs in heaven, recorded by John in Revelation 15:3-4, is a song that celebrates the result of their proclamation of the gospel and of their endurance until death:

> And they sang the song of Moses the slave of God and the song of the Lamb, saying,
>> "Great and marvelous are Thy works,
>> O Lord God, the Almighty;
>> Righteous and true are Thy ways,
>> Thou King of the nations.
>> Who will not fear, O Lord, and glorify Thy name?
>> For Thou alone art holy;
>> For all the nations will come and worship before Thee,
>> For Thy righteous acts have been revealed."

In conclusion, the key message of the Book of Revelation is that the only method God uses to bring the nations to Himself is through the testimony of Jesus Christ, propagated by His faithful witnesses, sealed with their blood in martyrdom, and vindicated by God through their resurrection. In God's strategy, the use of force is counterproductive. It is true that one can bend and break people by force, but the result will only be more hatred and further revolt.

Instead, God has determined to save the world by the foolishness of the cross of Christ and by the foolishness of the crosses of His children whom He has chosen and called for this very purpose. He will be consistent in using this unique method until He achieves His final goal. God will thus bring the nations to Himself by the sacrifice of His Son followed by the sacrifices of His other sons.

It serves our purpose to return to the teaching of Jesus for a moment. In the twenty-fourth chapter of Matthew, Jesus spoke about a long future of wars and natural disasters. He then enlarged the picture to include the deaths of the martyrs resulting from their faithful preaching of the gospel. Jesus made it very clear that the end of history would only come after God had completed His purposes with these witnesses. He explained this future reality to His disciples in the following words:

> Then they will deliver you up to tribulation, and will kill you, and you will be hated by all nations on account of My name. And at that time many will fall away and will deliver up one another and hate one another. And many false prophets will arise, and will mislead many. And because lawlessness is increased, most people's love will grow cold. But the one who endures to the end, he shall be saved. And this gospel of the kingdom shall be preached in the whole world for a witness to all the nations, and *then* the end shall come. (Matt. 24:9-14, italics mine)

Now, with this image before us, we should look at the general picture offered by the Book of Revelation. In chapters six through ten, John showed us the plagues and the natural disasters which have no effect in bringing the nations to God. Then in chapter eleven, he introduced the two witness-martyrs, who deliver their message faithfully, paying for it with their own lives. The result is that the nations come to fear God and to give Him glory; *then* we see the end: "The kingdom of the world has become the kingdom of our Lord, and of His Christ" (11:15). And after another panoramic view of the history of martyrdom, John shows us the end once more: "Great and marvelous are Thy works, O Lord God, the Almighty . . . for all the nations will come and worship before Thee" (15:3-4). The message rings out loud and clear: God will establish His rule over the nations by means of the faithful witness unto death of His chosen children who follow in the footsteps of His chosen Son. In God's economy, one conquers by dying.

The Second Purpose of the War:
the Martyrs Defeat Satan

On the surface of things, the war seems to have been started by the evil forces that dominate the nations of the earth. However, the Scriptures say that they were *given* to make war with the saints and to overcome them (13:7). In fact, it was Christ who began the war and who now leads it by His direct involvement with His own army, all the way to the final victory.

Chapter twelve gives us some important clues about the way the final victory will be won. The chapter begins with the image of a pregnant woman giving birth to a male child. About this child we are told that He "is to rule all the nations with a rod of iron," and that He "was caught up to God and to His throne" (12:5). It is not difficult to identify Him because the One who will lead the nations with a rod of iron is further described in 19:11-16; the fact that He was lifted up to the throne of God was already visible in chapter five, where we saw Him standing next to the throne.

Another item of special interest in chapter twelve is found in verse 17: the followers of Jesus are called "the rest of the offspring" (σπέρματος, seed), referring to the woman that gave birth to Christ. We know that the first prophecy about the birth of Christ was given by the Lord God Himself, and it was He who first used the words "her seed" (referring to Eve) when He told the Serpent: "And I will put enmity between you and the woman, and between your seed and her seed; He [her seed] shall bruise you on the head and you [your seed] shall bruise Him on the heel" (Gen. 3:15). It is very significant to read in Revelation that Jesus and His faithful witnesses are one and the same "seed." Again, we have to be consistent in our interpretation of the symbols John used. In his Gospel, John wrote these words of Jesus addressed to His disciples: "I am the vine, you are the branches; he who abides in Me, and I in him, he bears much fruit; for apart from Me you can do nothing" (John 15:5). The unity between Christ and His disciples is so strong and so organic that Jesus spoke of it parallel to and on the same level with the unity between Himself and His Father, when He said to His Father: "I in them, and Thou in Me" (John 17:23).

If we do not lose sight of this tight unity between Jesus and His witnesses, then we will not be surprised to discover that the witnesses are called to imitate His self-sacrifice, and that the results of their self-sacrifice are similar to those of His self-sacrifice. Because they are one, it is He who fights in them, and it is He who suffers in them. All that their sacrifices achieve, He achieves. John conveys this very principle when he describes the defeat of Satan in the twelfth chapter. On the surface of things, we see Michael and his angels waging war with Satan (Rev. 12:7-9). However, Satan's defeat is not attributed to them. On the contrary, the "loud voice in heaven" is heard declaring, "And they overcame him because of the blood of the Lamb and because of the word of their testimony, and they did not love their life even to death" (12:11). We have already seen that the witnesses of Jesus Christ in Revelation die as martyrs; but here in 12:11, John wanted to leave absolutely no room for doubt that he was talking about those particular witnesses who have sealed their testimony with their blood. For this reason, he concludes with this statement: "they did not love their life even to death."

How do the witness-martyrs defeat Satan through their martyrdom? John gives us the following three answers to this question. The first one has already been mentioned in chapter eleven and will be further developed in chapters thirteen through nineteen. The second and third answers are found in 12:11.

1. The deaths of the witness-martyrs have a great impact upon the darkened minds of unbelievers; their martyrdom makes the truth of God shine for the unsaved world, and as a result, people are liberated from Satan's deception.

2. The witnesses defeat Satan by the blood of the Lamb;

3. and they defeat Satan by not being afraid of dying.

Let us begin our discussion with the two points indicated in 12:11. The witnesses' first weapon is "the blood of the Lamb." This information directs our thoughts to the cross of Christ and to the way He defeated Satan on that cross. In Colossians 2:14-15, the Apostle Paul writes that Christ conquered the evil forces by His work at Calvary. As He hung there on the cross, He took upon Himself our load of sin, which was Satan's certificate of ownership over us. When He washed away those sins with His own blood, He canceled the claims of Satan over us. Therefore, when someone appropriates the blood of the Lamb, he defeats Satan, since Jesus' blood cancels Satan's right of ownership over him. Then each time Satan returns to him with the lie that he is still his owner and master, the Christian must point to the blood of Christ in order to defend his freedom. This is the first way of defeating Satan.

As we look at the Christian's second weapon against Satan, we should recall that John was the one who recorded the words of Jesus referring to His crucifixion: "Now the ruler of this world shall be cast out" (John 12:31). Moreover, Jesus taught that Satan would be cast out not only by means of His own crucifixion but also by means of the work of evangelism done by His disciples. When the seventy disciples returned from their mission and enthusiastically reported to Jesus all that they had done, He remarked, "I was watching Satan fall from heaven like lightning " (Lk 10:18). Therefore, in the twelfth chapter of Revelation, John is simply developing Jesus' teaching that the work of His faithful witnesses would cast Satan out of heaven. But how should we understand the actual "mechanism" of Satan's defeat by the disciples' witness unto death?

Here is how I understand it. We have seen that sin is Satan's title deed over a person. However, when one takes upon himself the blood of Christ and hides behind it as his shield, Satan falls defeated. Nevertheless, the Word of God tells us that there is yet another way in which Satan enslaves people, namely, by their fear of dying. In Hebrews 2:14-15, we read that Christ identified Himself with His brethren "that through death He might render powerless him who had the power of death, that is, the devil; and might deliver those who through fear of death were subject to slavery all their lives."

The devil knows about our fear of dying and seeks to intimidate us into serving him; he does this precisely by threatening to kill us if we refuse. The threat of death was a very real and concrete experience for Christians in John's time, since many were actually summoned before the local magistrate, where each was asked if he was truly a Christian. Each Christian could then see, with his spiritual eyes, the threatening figure of Satan standing behind the magistrate and saying to him: "Now I have you in my clutches; if you do not renounce your faith in Christ, I will surely torture you, and then I will kill you!" If the Christian loved this life more than anything else and wanted to save it, he would deny Christ and worship Caesar. However, by this act, he would also be accepting Satan's dominion over him, compelled by his fear of dying.

On the other hand, if the Christian loved the Lord more than his own life, and if he really believed Jesus' promise that he will never die (John 11:25-26), so that he would no longer be afraid of dying, he would then tell Satan: "You are a liar! You have no right over me because I stand under the blood of Christ. You can kill my body, but by that you are only sending me up to glory with Jesus Christ my Lord. I am not afraid of you. Therefore, I bear witness that Jesus Christ is my Lord!" If this was his response, then Satan would lose his ultimate weapon, that man's fear of dying, and he would fall flat on his face completely disarmed, just as he fell initially when Christ was sacrificed on the cross.

Why must the sacrifice of Christ and the sacrifice of His fellow soldiers take place? The simple answer is that God does not fight to win people back to Himself; He will not use force. From the beginning, Satan has used deception to win people to himself, and throughout history, he has relied on lies, hatred, brute force, torture, and death to keep people in bondage and slavery. But God cannot use the same methods. He must use methods *consistent with His own nature*. He could conceivably force His way to the nations of the world, but that would be against His own nature and character.

In addition, God has to demonstrate to the whole cosmos that *His* methods are better and more efficacious than the ones used by Satan. God has to prove that He is more credible, more convincing, and more desirable than Satan. He has to demonstrate that He can attract the nations to Himself by means of His own methods of love and self-sacrifice more effectively than Satan can keep them in slavery by his demonic methods. Finally, God has decided that in this manner, His manifold wisdom should "be made known through the church to the rulers and the authorities in the heavenly places" (Eph. 3:10).

In the First Epistle to the Corinthians, Paul tells us that the wisdom of God, which seems foolishness to the world, is in the fact that He uses the cross of Christ to win the world back to Himself (1 Cor. 1:18-2:9). And now, we know that in addition to Christ's cross, God's wisdom also brings the nations back to Himself by means of the crosses of His chosen fellow witnesses.

In this way God has made His honor depend on our faithfulness to Him. Remember the story of Job: God's honor depended on the faithfulness of this one man, and Job's endurance of suffering and his steadfast allegiance to God resulted in the shame and defeat of Satan. In His unfathomable wisdom, God has determined that His victory should always be man's victory; in other words, He has decided that His victory should always be won by His human agents. In the Book of Revelation, this fact is expressed in figurative language by the symbol of the scroll upon which the history of the nations' return to God is recorded. The scroll represents the method by which God will establish

His rule over the nations; it could not be opened except by the One who had come down to earth, accepting to be stabbed and sacrificed, thereby redeeming people for God from all the nations (Rev. 5:9-10). But the story does not end here because the Book of Revelation is meant to show us that the Lamb is not alone in this work of God. The Lamb initiated it and modeled it for us; now it is our turn to follow in His footsteps. Only when a sufficient number of people (this number has been predetermined by God, 6:11) have been found willing to witness to the power of the cross with the same faithfulness and self-sacrifice, shall the power of Satan be broken; only after that happens will the nations come back under the authority of God and only then will the wisdom of God be vindicated.

One fact must be emphatically underscored in this context: God is absolutely sovereign, and His authority extends over the forces of evil, as well. His sovereignty is manifested by the fact that even the beast and the ten horns can do only what "God has put . . . in their hearts to execute" (17:17). He has programmed them to fulfill "His [own] purpose" even through their adverse and evil actions "until the words of God should be fulfilled" (Ibid.).

Now then, the peoples of the earth have had their minds darkened by the devil. They have been enslaved by the lie of the one who is "the father of lies" (John 8:44). Their eyes will be opened only when they see the One who is the Truth sacrificing Himself; this is what Christ meant when He said: "And I, if I be lifted up from the earth, will draw all men to Myself" (John 12:32). John added the editorial note in verse 33 to make sure that no one misunderstands that Jesus had been referring to His crucifixion. However, this self-sacrifice of the Truth must be repeated again and again by His witnesses; in their case, as in Jesus' case, their testimonies sealed by their blood will attract all the nations to God.

With this last statement, we have returned to the first way in which the witness-martyrs conquer Satan by their own death: *they give credibility to the truth of God.* The experience of the centurion who led Jesus' execution was a perfect example of this principle and the pattern that we should follow. As the soldiers were nailing Him to the cross, the centurion heard Jesus praying for their forgiveness, rather than cursing them for what they were doing to Him. He heard all the other words Jesus uttered from the cross, including the confident prayer with which He entrusted His spirit into the hands of His Father before He died. Then we read what happened next: "And when the centurion, who was standing right in front of Him, *saw the way He breathed His last*, he said: 'Truly this man was the Son of God!' " (Mk. 15:39, italics mine). This is exactly what John tells us by means of his symbols in the Book of Revelation: when the nations watch the way in which the martyrs die, their eyes are opened so they can see, their mind is enlightened so they can believe, and their heart is moved so they can accept the sovereignty of God, giving Him all the glory and worshipping Him. For this reason, the statement that follows the account of the finished work of the two witness-martyrs is a fitting conclusion: "The kingdom of the world has become the kingdom of our Lord, and of His Christ" (Rev. 11:15). In chapter twelve, also as a result of the martyrs' defeat of Satan, the following announcement is made: "Now the salvation, and the power, and the kingdom of our God and the authority of His Christ have come, for the accuser of our brethren has been thrown down" (Rev. 12:10).

Let us recall that just prior to His crucifixion, Jesus gave His disciples their last lessons in martyrdom (John 13-16). He closed with these words: "In the world you have tribulation, but take courage; I have overcome the world" (John 16:33b). His Father had sent Him to conquer by the cross, and after He had won the victory and the Father had raised Him from the dead, Jesus said to His disciples: "As the Father has sent Me, I also send you" (John 20:21b). Jesus sent them into the world with the same strategy and with the same goal with which He had been sent by the Father into the world. He had overcome the world by His suffering and death and now they must overcome it by their own suffering and death. Using God's own method and His plan of action, they must bring the nations to God.

When we speak about the similarity between the sacrifice of Christ and the sacrifices of the martyrs, we should always add the following qualification with strong conviction: the sacrifices of the martyrs have no atoning function whatsoever. John makes it absolutely clear that the blood of Christ, and not the blood of the other martyrs, has redeemed people for God and the eternal kingdom. There is not the slightest indication that in one way or another the blood of the martyrs might add something to the redemptive sacrifice of Christ. The martyrs themselves were redeemed by the blood of the Lamb and have the blood of the Lamb upon them as their protective weapon. Instead, the martyrs' blood is shed to defeat Satan, to break his power of deception over the nations, and to bring these nations to the knowledge of the truth of God, so that they might submit themselves to the rule of God.

There is one other passage related to our subject that we need to try to understand. After John saw the beast coming out of the sea, he learned that "it was given to him to make war with the saints and to overcome them" (Rev. 13:7). *By whom* was he *given* to do this? The answer is that this action "was given to him" by the One who is Almighty (παντοκράτωρ). This fact is confirmed by John in 17:17, where he says that "God has put it in their hearts (of the beast and the ten kings) to execute His purpose." What is of greatest interest for us is what follows in 13:10; after having been informed about the start of the war against the saints; we hear this solemn warning: "If anyone is destined for captivity, to captivity he goes; if anyone kills with the sword, with the sword he must be killed. Here is the perseverance and the faith of the saints." The first clause tells us that some saints have been destined for imprisonment, and we know from 2:10 that in John's time, imprisonment meant preparation for martyrdom in the arena. Regarding the second clause of 13:10, a fifth century manuscript entitled *Alexandrinus* contains a statement almost identical to it: "If any man is to be killed with a sword, he is to be killed with a sword." This passage is in fact a quote from the Book of Jeremiah: "Thus says the Lord: 'Those destined for death, to death; and those destined for the sword, to the sword; and those destined for famine, to famine; and those destined for captivity, to captivity' " (Jer. 15:2).

In the prophecy of Jeremiah, these words are a judgment on the people of Israel; but in the Book of Revelation, they become God's marching orders given to the martyrs. They are His solemn command to them to advance into battle and to win by dying. I want to emphasize here that God is the One who chooses those who should die as martyrs. He *predestines* them for this function. It is not the Christian who is called to choose martyrdom. On the contrary, the Christian is called to be a witness to Jesus; he is called to spend himself and whatever he owns for the gospel and for the church. If God chooses to seal his ministry with martyrdom, the child of God has to accept it gladly. However, the Scriptures do not teach anywhere that the individual should pursue martyrdom or even suffering, as such, for its own sake.

The Book of Revelation has much more to say about the way God deals with the nations until they return to Him in repentance and obedience. We shall not take up space to go into all those details, although they are linked with the ministry of the martyrs. For our purposes, it was sufficient to have seen the essential teaching of

Revelation about the place of the martyrs in God's strategy in human history. There is only one other important issue that we must discuss here, and that is the reward of the martyrs.

The Reward of the Martyrs

The Book of Revelation has much to say about rewards. To begin with, its teaching is consistent with the rest of the Bible in affirming that the last judgment will be based on works:

> And I saw the dead, the great and the small, standing before the throne, and books were opened; and another book was opened, which is the book of life; and the dead were judged from the things which were written in the books, according to their deeds. And the sea gave up the dead which were in it, and death and Hades gave up the dead which were in them; and they were judged, every one of them according to their deeds. (20:12-13)

From this passage we learn that the judgment will be based upon the evidence contained in the book of life, as well as in the books where the works or actions of every individual were recorded. This seems to suggest a general judgment rather than one restricted to the unsaved. The information here may also appear to be in conflict with Paul's teaching that the Christian will be judged as he departs from this life to be with the Lord, at the judgment seat of Christ (2 Cor. 5:10).

Whether we speak of the death of a Christian or we refer to the general resurrection of the dead, in both cases we are dealing with an intersection of existence in time and existence in eternity. It may be that our extremely limited understanding of eternity makes us unable to *synchronize* the events that are beyond our own *cronos*. (Is eternity completely outside of time, without any sort of notion of time, or is it simply in a different "kind" of time?) The reality of our limited understanding may also apply to the difficult issue concerning the "time" of the resurrection of the martyrs. Dogmatizing in these areas is risky. We had better listen carefully to what the texts have to say and then draw from them the pertinent conclusions for our *present* existence. At least two important conclusions can be legitimately drawn, namely, that God keeps records of all our thoughts, words, and actions, and that we will all be judged according to them.

The teaching of Jesus and of the rest of the New Testament reveals that there will be both punishments and rewards for God's "slaves." Some will "receive many lashes" and some "will receive but few," while others will be cast into "the outer darkness" (Matt. 22:13; Lk. 12:47-48). What did Jesus mean by these frightening words? I must candidly say that we do not know; at the same time, we must believe Jesus! In his second epistle, John exhorted his friends to live in such a way that they "may receive a full reward" (2 John 8). This seems to indicate that our acts of disobedience done throughout our Christian life may have as their consequence the loss of the rewards that had been laid up in heaven for us as a result of our earlier acts of obedience. I believe that this is a legitimate inference from what the text says. Paul himself was clearly afraid that if he did not consistently keep his body in submission, he might be disqualified from receiving "the prize" (1 Cor. 9:23-27).

As I have indicated many times, Protestant theologians tend to dismiss the teaching of a judgment of believers according to their deeds on earth; sadly, they tend to do the same with the biblical concept of rewards in heaven. Some Protestants also trivialize the promises of punishment and the promises of rewards by interpreting them to mean merely verbal rebukes, such as a simple "Shame on you," or merely verbal praises, such as a nice pat on the back with a cheerful "Well done, good slave." No matter what the assessment will be, they maintain that both the praised and the chided children of God will be equally perfectly happy for all eternity. Nevertheless, I want to insist that the warnings of the Scriptures are much too serious to be dismissed in this fashion. What we have here is an extremely important issue affecting the destiny of every human being. These are the basic principles of God's way of dealing with mankind, and precisely our eternal future is at stake! Hence, we must pay very careful attention to what God has to say to us.

It is no mere coincidence that in Jesus' first recorded sermon, He spoke of rewards in heaven (Matt. 5:12), instructing us to accumulate "treasures" in heaven (Matt. 6:19-21), and that in His penultimate speech recorded on the last page of the Bible, His words are: "Behold, I am coming quickly, and My reward is with Me, to render to every man according to what he has done" (Rev. 22:12).

We shall now turn our attention to the rewards promised to the conquerors in the Book of Revelation, starting with the seven letters to the seven churches. Each letter ends with the promise of a reward that will be given to the one who conquers. From the beginning of our study, we have clearly seen that throughout Revelation, the ones referred to as the "conquerors" are in fact the martyrs. Of course, commentators who do not believe in any differentiation between the saved in heaven must dismiss all notions of actual rewards in heaven. Consequently, they have to say that all Christians are conquerors, and therefore, that each promise in the seven letters was addressed to and is applicable to every Christian. In response to such an interpretation, Fuller cogently replies: "A command that everyone keeps is superfluous, and a reward everyone receives for a virtue that everyone has is nonsense."[5]

Before I make any comments on the content of the rewards promised to the conquerors, I must point out that all of these promises are either introduced or followed by this warning: "He who has an ear, let him hear what the Spirit says to the churches" (2:7, 11, 17, 29; 3:6, 13, 22). In chapter thirteen, after the beast comes to make war against the saints and to kill them, a similar caution is given: "If anyone has an ear, let him hear" (13:9). What should he hear? He must hear precisely that those who have been destined for martyrdom should boldly face it and endure it, because this is "the perseverance and the faith of the saints" (13:9-10). Once again, in chapter fourteen, in the midst of the same slaughter of the martyrs, we hear the Spirit saying: " 'Blessed are the dead who die in the Lord from now on' " (14:13). The Holy Spirit is the One who accompanies the martyrs and strengthens them in their battle. It is only natural then to find that the Holy Spirit, addressing the churches, is also the One who announces the martyrs' rewards.

Regarding the content of the rewards promised to the martyrs, I have to say that some of the symbols used by John are very difficult for us to "translate"; for this reason, I will simply list them here: the privilege of eating of the tree of life (2:7); not being hurt by the second death (2:11); the hidden manna, (2:17); the morning star (2:28); and being made a pillar in the temple of God (3:12). However, there are other promises and symbols which *can* be understood (we have already explicated 3:21, and we will discuss 3:5 below), and these can become a window for us through which we can gaze into the eternal future of Jesus' faithful witnesses. Lilje writes that "all the promises about 'victory' point beyond this world to another,"[6] and Mounce rightly says that the entire Apocalypse is an exposition of this concept."[7]

Let us analyze the promise made to the conqueror in the letter to Thyatira: "And he who overcomes, and he who keeps My deeds until the end, *to him I will give authority over the nations*; and he shall rule them with a rod of iron, as the vessels of the potter are broken to pieces, *as I also have received authority from My Father*" (2:26-27, italics mine). The conqueror is promised authority to rule the nations. We should start our analysis of this promise by directing our attention to the last, qualifying clause: "as I also have received authority from My Father" (2:27b). Christ gives this authority to the conqueror just as His Father has given it to Him. All the way through the Book of Revelation we have seen the parallels drawn between Jesus and His followers: He is the faithful witness, and they also conquer by dying (2:14; 12:9-11). It is to be expected, then, that their eternal position and function will be similar to His.

The promise in Revelation 2:26-27 is a free quotation of the Messianic Second Psalm, verses eight and nine. It is significant that in the Septuagint translation, the promise is of an inheritance, "κληρονομίας," over the nations. John translates it as authority, "ἐξουσίαν," over the nations. Here we have an important confirmation of one of the key tenets of this dissertation, namely, that "the inheritance," in concrete terms, is the authority to rule.

A difficulty appears in the translation of the phrase "rule them with a rod of iron" (Rev. 2:27a). The difficulty is in the meaning of the word "ποιμανεῖ." While the Massoretic text of Psalm 2:9 translates it as "to break," the Septuagint renders it as "to tend," "to pasture," "to shepherd," and hence, "to rule." The Psalmist's allusion to the image of the potter smashing the rejected vessel (Ps. 2:9b), developed fully in Jeremiah 18:1-11, should help us find the specific meaning of the text. The image is that of a vessel which did not take the precise form desired by the potter and which has to be broken *in order to be remade*. Now, in two passages in Revelation, Jesus Himself is said to rule (to smash and break or to tend and shepherd) the nations with a rod of iron (Rev. 12:5; 19:15). However, the nations are never destroyed. They reappear time after time, until we see all of them marching into the New Jerusalem: "And the nations shall walk by its light, and the kings of the earth shall bring their glory into it. . . . And they shall bring the glory and the honor of the nations into it" (21:24, 26).

The question we must now answer is this: When and how will the martyrs rule over the nations? The nations will kill *them* just as they have killed Jesus (Acts 4:25-28). Caird gives us a good interpretation of how the nations will be smashed in order to be remade:

The psalmist had looked forward to the day when God's Messiah would **smash** all resistance to God's kingly rule and assume **authority over the nations**. John sees this ancient hope transfigured in the light of the Cross. Pagan resistance will indeed be smashed, but God will use no other **iron bar** than the death of his Son and the martyrdom of his saints.[8]

Caird limits the fulfillment of this promise to the conversion of the nations. It is my view that in light of the promises of 3:21 and 20:4-5, this limitation is unwarranted. Jesus Himself was lifted up and was given all authority in heaven and on earth. He rules the nations and guides their destiny. The promise to the conquering martyr must be taken at face value: he is promised a participation with Christ in the ruling or shepherding of the nations. How and when this will happen is a matter for speculation. But there are, as we have already seen, plenty of texts that give us the freedom and the right to use our imaginations.

In Revelation 20:4-5, the martyrs are shown to be reigning with Christ for a thousand years. We are not told *where* Christ and the ruling martyrs will be at that time. Then, we see that in the New Creation, the nations will come with their kings and will bring their treasures into the New Jerusalem (21:24, 26). How many people will rule these nations and how will they do so? What does it mean to rule over them? Perhaps we could apply here what Jesus said to the faithful slave: "Be in authority over ten cities" (Lk. 19:17). I think that indeed we can do this and we certainly should. We have sufficient data to warrant our formulation of a belief in a literal fulfillment of this promise given to the martyrs.

There are two letters in which the reward has something to do with one's "name." In the letter to Pergamum, Christ promises the overcomer a white stone with "a new name written on the stone which no one knows but he who receives it" (Rev. 2:17). To the conqueror in Sardis, Christ makes this promise, among others: "I will not erase his name from the book of life, and I will confess his name before My Father, and before His angels" (3:5b). Due to the fact that some of the things that I will say here about the meaning of the "name" in 2:17 are relevant to the promise made to the conqueror in Sardis, as well, I will explain the two passages together.

In the Bible, a name is in fact a very serious matter. It defines one's character and destiny. A new name symbolizes a changed character and a new position or situation. Abram is a good example of this concept. After a long period of testing and of unwavering faithfulness in the midst of that testing, Abram's name was changed to *Abraham*, "the father of a multitude" (Gen. 17:5). God confirmed His covenant with Abraham, giving him a new name as the sign of their new relationship and of the new position that Abraham had been granted in God's economy (17:1-8).

Of even more significance is the changing of Jacob's name. Through many events and many struggles, God shaped a new character in this man, and when this work was completed, he received a new name: Israel. Immediately thereafter, God explained to Jacob the reason for his new name: "for you have striven with God and with men and have prevailed" (Gen. 32:28).

The prophet Isaiah also said that when Jerusalem's salvation will be seen by all the nations, God will give the city a new name, obviously designating its new situation and position in God's glory (Isa. 62:2).

R. H. Charles has detected a difficulty in the fact that the conqueror is promised a new character, because the conqueror has shown by his faithfulness that he already possesses it.[9] I mention Charles' objection because it helps me to make a very important point: the new name does not mean that a new character is *given*. The new name only defines the new reality; the character formed, tested, and proven worthy in and through the tribulations is signified by this new name!

This new name, which is to be kept secret by the person who receives it, shows that there will be distinctiveness and individuality in heaven. Kiddle's comment points us in this direction:

> If this is held to be the new name of the individual Christian, granted on his inheritance of his heavenly reward where all things are made new (21:5), John is here giving full expression to an idea rare in Revelation, that the Christian will take his place among the heavenly hosts as a separate individual, not merely a nameless sharer in a general felicity.[10]

Hemer also emphasizes the fact that "this name is the peculiar possession of each individual"; after he thoroughly investigates all the biblical information available about the "white stone" on which the new name is written, Hemer draws the conclusion that "the more promising analogies of the 'white stone' seem on balance to be those which stress the individual nature of its blessing. The new name symbolizes the individual's entry into a new life, status or personality."[11] Hemer's final suggestion is that the new name indicates "a perfecting of a new and transforming relationship with Christ" as indicated by Paul in 1 Corinthians 13:9-12.[12]

But why is the new name to be kept secret? Why should no one else know it? Perhaps we can arrive at an answer if we take as our starting point this statement made by Becker: "When God gives someone a new name, this person is no longer what he was before. There will be a new type of existence for his people."[13] Kiddle pointed out that this new existence will start when one obtains his inheritance as his heavenly reward. Hemer showed us that the emphasis is placed on the individual nature of that new status. From all these starting points, I go on to say that the new name defines the new position of authority and of ruling that the conqueror receives from his Lord. However, in heaven there will be no attitude of boasting and no tendency to parade one's greater position in front of those with lesser positions. The believer's attitude is of such a nature that he will always give all the glory to God and to the Lamb, keeping the special name that defines his new status in the heavenly kingdom to himself.

As we come to the church in Sardis, we have an apparent deviation from the rule that the promise of rewards is always made to the conquerors. Here the promise starts with these words: "But you have a few people in Sardis who have not soiled their garments; and they will walk with me in white; for they are worthy" (Rev. 3:4); only after this is the conqueror introduced: "He who overcomes shall thus be clothed in white garments" (3:5). There are strong indications that the people mentioned in verse four are not a different group from the conquerors. The other place where we find that a group of people did not defile themselves (ἐμολύνθησαν), just as the people in Sardis did not soil (ἐμόλυναν) their garments, is in 14:4, where John describes the army of the 144,000 martyrs. The promise given in 3:4 is that "they will walk with Me in white." The martyrs in 14:4 are also identified as "the ones who follow the Lamb wherever He goes." In 3:4, the ones who remain pure are promised that they will walk with Christ "in white," and this promise is obviously further developed in the verse to follow: ὁ νικῶν οὗτος περιβαλεῖται ἐν ἱματίοις λευκοῖς, "he who overcomes shall thus be clothed in white garments" (3:5). Plainly, the adverb "thus" links and identifies the group mentioned in verse four with the overcomers in verse five.

The promise of white garments is repeated time after time in Revelation. The martyrs awaiting their vindication are given white robes (6:11). Standing before the Lamb, the great multitude of martyrs who have come from the great tribulation are clothed in white robes that have been washed in the blood of the Lamb (7:9, 13-14). Lastly, the armies of heaven (the martyrs) appear with Christ "clothed in fine linen, white and clean" (19:14).

A great variety of interpretations have been offered for the "white garments." Hemer puts them together in a systematic way, and for this reason, I will quote his account *in extenso*:

> W. Michaelis, on πασχω, (*TDNT* IV, 241-50), emphasizes that heavenly clothing was seen as a divine gift and signifies the heavenly glory of those adjudged righteous. So Swete finds that in Scripture white apparel denotes festivity (Eccl. 9.8), victory (2 Macc. 11.8), purity (Rev. 7.9-10) and the heavenly state (Dan 7.9), and sees these associations as meeting in the present phrase (p. 51).
>
> (3) Some older writers compare the parable of the wedding-garment (Mt. 22.11-13) and see here some specific reference to imputed righteousness or to baptismal robes (Trench, p. 167; Tait, p. 314), or to the spiritual body of the faithful in the resurrection (cf. 2 Cor. 5.1-4; so Kepler, p.67; cf. Swete). No allusion of this kind however seems necessary or likely.
>
> (4) Ramsay argued that the Roman triumph was present here in the writer's mind. Roman citizens wore a pure white toga at holidays and religious ceremonies, but especially at a triumph (SC, p. 386; cf. Juv. Sat. 10.45). Paul certainly uses the metaphor of the Roman triumph in Col. 2.15 and develops it in 2 Cor. 2.14-16. On this view the aspect of victory would be especially prominent: Sardis was notoriously a city of defeat and unfulfilled promise, from which the royal pomp of former times had departed, but where the few should walk with Christ in the triumphal procession of his final victory. It is remarkable that Tertullian understands Rev. 7.14 in this way.[14]

In spite of Hemer's remark that it does not seem "necessary or likely" that the "white garments" are to be interpreted as "the spiritual body of the faithful in the resurrection," I think that we should pursue this idea further. In fact, Caird argues for this interpretation in the following manner:

> White robes or robes of glory are mentioned several times in Jewish apocalyptic writings as tokens of heavenly existence (e.g. *1 Enoch* lxii. 16; *2 Enoch* xxii, 8). In three works, all probably written in the second half of the second century A.D., the white

robes are explicitly identified with the body of glory which, according to Paul, is to be the outward form of the resurrection life (1 Cor. xv. 35 ff.; 2 Cor. v. 1 ff.; Phil. iii. 21). Ezra sees the saints in white robes and is told by an angel, "these are they who have put off their mortal garment and have put on an immortal one" (2 Esdras ii. 39-44). Another seer has a vision of the saints in heaven "stripped of their fleshly garments" and clothed in "garments of the world above" (*Acs. Isa.* ix. 9). In the Hymn of the Soul found in the Syriac *Acts of Thomas* the soul is made to leave behind its bright robe, when it descends to Egypt to charm the serpent and bring back the pearl which it guards. On its return the robe is brought out to it. "On a sudden, as I faced it, the garment seemed to me like a mirror of myself. I saw it all in my whole self; moreover I faced my whole self in facing it. For we were two in distinction, and yet again one in likeness." The last two of these works are certainly both Gnostic in origin, yet it is likely that they enshrine a genuine tradition of the meaning of this symbol in Jewish apocalyptic writing, and that John, following the same tradition, meant his readers to understand by the **white robe** a spiritual body which would replace the body of flesh. But it must be added that he shows singularly little trace of being interested in detailed speculations about the nature of life in the world to come and its relation to bodily existence.[15]

A number of modern interpreters believe that the teaching of Paul in 2 Corinthians 5:1-8 affirms that the Christian receives a spiritual body when he moves from this earthly existence into the heavenly one. There is also a strong belief, originating in the second century A.D., that the martyrs will receive heavenly bodies and begin ruling with Christ as soon as they pass into eternity.

Returning to chapter three, let us look at the rest of the promise of future rewards made to the conqueror of Sardis: ". . . and I will not erase his name from the book of life, and I will confess his name before My Father, and before His angels" (Rev. 3:5b).

Of all the writers of the Scriptures, John was one of the strongest believers in the sovereignty of God. He writes that the names of the elect have been written in the book of life even "from the foundation of the world" (13:8). When he quotes Jesus saying that He will not erase their names from the book of life, John uses the Greek figure of speech (littotes) by which one employs a negative in order to make a stronger positive. He utilized this figure of speech in order to stress the absolute security of the one who will have his body put to death by his persecutors. When Jesus said that no one would be able to snatch His sheep out of His hand (John 10:28), He conveyed exactly the same message of security without any implication of the possibility of the opposite situation.

The important thing in this text is the subsequent positive formulation of the same promise: "I will confess his name before My Father, and before His angels" (Rev. 3:5b). Of course, these words are identical to the words of Jesus spoken to His disciples in the course of their training for martyrdom (Matt. 10:32; Mk. 8:38; Lk. 9:26; 12:8). Fuller has done a detailed study of the "name" as one's "reputation" or position in heaven, and here is his conclusion:

> There is generally a very strong bond between one's earthly works and his heavenly identity. The thought sequence seems to be the following: One's good works (including faithfulness; cf. 2:2-3, 19) produce a good reputation in heaven (cf. the recurring phrase "I know your deeds" in Rev. 2:2, 19; 3:1, 8, 15; cf. also 2:9, 13). The good reputation in turn results in receiving an honorable eternal identity (a "new name," 2:17; 3:12), which in Revelation is closely associated with rewards.
>
> Further relationship between one's works and heavenly identity is found in the treatment of martyrs. In Rev. 6:9-11 they are given white robes and in 20:4 they are given ruling positions. Hence their good works and their heavenly identities are closely associated. It is the above privileges and positions that those who deny or compromise their faith rather than their lives will lose, as implied in Rev. 3:5.[16]

Fuller adds that the Christian's "quality of eternal life (not whether there will be eternal life) is essentially determined during that Christian's earthly life. Hence the same Christian who overcomes also eats of the hidden manna (2:17), rules with Christ (2:26-28). It is this notion that makes the promise of Rev. 3:5 truly wonderful and the implied threat of the verse truly awful."[17]

Kiddle also gives us a beautiful explanation of this promise of rewards: "Lastly, the greatest reward of all, embracing all other rewards, is placed before the faithful. As conquerors, they will be acknowledged openly before the Father Himself, amidst the glory of the heavenly beings surrounding the throne, as faithful followers of the Messiah and therefore as sharers of His power and authority."[18] Yet the most succinct and superb comment belongs to Caird: "At the Great Assize Christ the Advocate will acknowledge as his colleagues in sovereignty those who have been his colleagues in suffering."[19]

At this point we have to remember the words of Christ describing the conquerors who will walk with Him or share with Him in heavenly authority; He gave the following justification for their position: "for they are worthy" (3:4). This is an awesome statement because in the Book of Revelation, this qualification, in its positive form, is predicated only to God (4:11) and to Christ (5:9, 12). Commentators are often made uneasy by this statement because they fear that somehow the "worthiness" that is attributed to humans implies "merit" or something that they have "earned" for themselves.

Once again we must understand the way in which the Word of God harmoniously blends God's sovereignty together with man's responsibility. On the one hand, it is God who has elected these people from the foundation of the world, and it is Christ who has loved them and redeemed them, making them a kingdom and priests, keeping them secure until the end. Christ accompanies them in the battle and the Holy Spirit is also present with them in their ordeal. Everything that the martyrs achieve, Christ achieves in them through the Holy Spirit. On the other hand, Christians are called to repentance, to dedication, to a rekindled passion for their Lord, to endurance, and to faithfulness unto death, even under the duress of torture. This faithfulness unto death qualifies them, that is, makes them worthy, of sharing with Christ in ruling the universe. Nevertheless, no merit and no reason for boasting exists, because it was God who predestined them for this from the start, and it was Christ through the Holy Spirit who has achieved it in them.

We should never try to separate the two lines of action so perfectly blended in Scripture. We should let the Scriptures present both sides, without ever trying to favor or magnify one side by excluding or ignoring the other. As Mounce puts it, it is "better to allow the text, even when difficult, to present its own picture."[20]

We have arrived at the last and most glorious and comprehensive promise to the conquerors, written to the overcomers of the church of Laodicea: "He who overcomes, I will grant to him to sit down with Me on My throne, as I also overcame and sat down with My Father on His throne" (Rev. 3:21). In his first letter, John told us that "the Son of God appeared for this purpose, that He might destroy the works of the devil" (1 John 3:8). Jesus defeated Satan in the first place by not giving in to any of Satan's temptations (Matt. 4:1-10; cf. Heb. 4:15). He also defeated Satan by witnessing to the truth (John 18:37; Rev. 1:5). In John's Gospel, we saw that the devil was defeated by the crucifixion of Jesus (John 12:30-32; cf. Col. 2:14-15; Heb. 2:14-15).

Because of His conquest through His death, Jesus was lifted up and enthroned as Lord of the whole cosmos (Acts 2:36; Phil. 2:5-11; Heb. 2:9). Similarly, when Jesus called His disciples to pick up their own crosses for Him and His gospel, He promised them that they would sit on twelve thrones (Matt. 19:28) and He covenanted to them the kingdom (Lk. 22:28-30).

In the Book of Revelation, Jesus' invitation is extended to a much larger group of people whom God has chosen to join Christ in this cosmic battle against the Prince of evil and his forces. These children of God were chosen to repeat His victory over Satan by means of their own purity of life (cleansed by the blood of the Lamb), by means of their own testimony for the truth of God, and by means of their own crucifixion or death. It is absolutely normal and reasonable to find that if they conquer as He has conquered, they will obtain from God the same reward, the same honor, and the same position of ruling that He has received. This promise is the perfect confirmation of all that we have read in the Gospels and in the rest of the New Testament about Jesus as the Example, the Pioneer, the Forerunner, and the First of many brethren who are chosen and called to the heavenly destiny of ruling and glory.

It would be very instructive for our study to step back at this time and to acquire a bird's eye view of the concept of rewards in the Book of Revelation. As we do just that, we will be struck by the frequent mention of "works," of the judgment based upon works, and of rewards for those works.

To begin with, five of the seven letters to the seven churches commence with these words spoken by Jesus: "I know your deeds" (Rev. 2:2, 19; 3:1, 8, 15). The other two, the letters to Smyrna and Pergamum, are actually no exception: the difference is that instead of "deeds," in these two letters, Jesus directly mentions their severe persecution and their faithfulness in the midst of it (2:9, 13).

Special attention is given again and again to the martyrs. In 6:11, they are given white robes and are told to "rest for a little while longer" until their time for action will come. In 11:11-12, the two witness-martyrs are given a special resurrection and are invited to go up into heaven. In the same chapter, at the sound of the seventh trumpet, the twenty-four elders declare: "and the time came for the dead to be judged, and the time to give their reward to Thy slaves the prophets and to the saints and to those who fear Thy name, the small and the great, and to destroy those who destroy the earth" (11:18).

In chapter fourteen, in the midst of the most dreadful slaughter of the Christians, the Holy Spirit proclaims that the ones who die in the Lord are blessed, because they will "rest from their labors" and because "their deeds follow with them" (14:13). Then, in chapter fifteen, the conquering martyrs are given the privilege of singing the song of Moses and of the Lamb proclaiming the coming of all the nations to worship God (15:2-4).

In the nineteenth chapter, when the marriage of the Lamb is announced and His bride is proclaimed ready, we read that "it was given to her to clothe herself in fine linen, bright and clean" (19:8a); thereupon, John explains that "the fine linen is the righteous acts (δικαιώματά) of the saints" (19:8b).

The following chapter tells us that the martyrs will be given a special resurrection in order to reign with Christ for a thousand years (20:3-5). A few verses further in the same chapter, we see the great white throne and the books opened, "and the dead were judged from the things which were written in the books, according to their deeds" (20:11-12). For the sake of emphasis, John describes the scene of the general resurrection one more time, and we read again that "they were judged, every one of them according to their deeds" (20:13).

At long last, in the twenty-first chapter, we see the newly created heaven and earth, the new creation without the evils of the present one. Now we see the nature of the reward given to the overcomers: "He who overcomes shall inherit these things, and I will be his God and he will be My son" (21:7). "These things" are in fact the entire new universe. From the beginning, men and women were created to be put in charge of and rule over (inherit) God's creation, and here we see the great and glorious fulfillment of the destiny of mankind. However, men and women must be qualified to inherit and to rule over the newly created cosmos; thus, they must be "overcomers."

The last chapter of the book presents a picture of "the throne of God and of the Lamb," and we read that "His slaves shall serve Him (22:3). We have already established the fact that the slaves in Revelation are the martyrs. Two verses later, the author explains the meaning and the content of the martyrs' service to God: it is precisely that "they shall reign forever and ever" (22:5). Finally, we hear the last heralding of the coming of Christ: "Behold, I am coming quickly, and My reward is with Me, to render to every man according to what he has done" (22:12).

Yes, indeed, a survey of what the Book of Revelation has to say about the "deeds" and consequent "rewards" of God's children is very impressive. For exactly this reason, it is quite disconcerting and sometimes even painful to discover that so many Protestant commentators take great pains to explain these teachings away, insisting that because salvation is by grace alone, these works are meant only to confirm the fact that one is truly saved.

It is certainly true that salvation is by grace alone. John allows no room for doubting the fact that it was Christ who, by His death on the cross, redeemed every man, woman, and child who is in the kingdom of heaven. Even after the last announcement that Christ is coming soon to reward His own for their works, John makes a final invitation to people to come and "wash their robes, that they may have the right to the tree of life" (22:14). However, the issue at stake here is not salvation! The issue is, rather, man's qualification to rule with Christ, to hold positions of authority or, in other words, to receive meaningful and responsible jobs in the newly created universe!

Starting from the Gospels and running through all the epistles and through the Book of Revelation, we are told that "works" are the duty of the children of God. Works matter because they are God's criteria according to which He will judge us and according to which He will assign to us different ranks and functions in His eternal kingdom. Again, these works are not meant to give us credit or to earn for us those positions of ruling. The basis of obtaining them is solely the goodness of the Father and His gracious decision before the foundation of the world to give us these things.

God is making and testing His children through various trials and tribulations. He has destined His children to rule with Christ; but first, He calls them to be partners with Him in tribulation, in endurance, in faithfulness, in witness to God's love through sufferings, and in death. Only partnership in suffering qualifies one to be a partner with Christ in ruling.

In closing, I should mention the fact that most Protestant theologians cannot accept the idea that people will not be equal in heaven. Of course, what follows from the premise of equality in heaven is the logical conclusion that a judgment according to one's works has no finality. However "democratic" or egalitarian we may want to be, Jesus nevertheless taught us plainly, clearly, and repeatedly that some would be great and some would be small in the kingdom of heaven. The rest of the New Testament simply continues to develop and expand this teaching of Christ. A judgment based on works has purpose and meaning only if it is followed by a commensurate distribution of rewards or degrees of authority in the eternal kingdom.

The real issue, however, is the "authority" itself. Rebellious spirits cannot submit to authority; for this reason, they should never be entrusted with authority, because if they cannot submit to it, they will not be capable of wielding it themselves. This quality of being able to handle authority is aptly illustrated in Revelation 4:9-10. In this vision, John sees the twenty-four elders prostrating themselves before the throne, casting down their crowns, and joining in the adoration of the One who lives forever and ever.

I once heard a famous American preacher commenting on this passage. He obviously did not believe in meaningful rewards in heaven, because he poked fun at the idea of being given crowns in heaven, saying that the crowns will be of no lasting significance there, since we shall only cast them all down at the feet of Jesus! This preacher clearly did not take this text seriously. Moreover, he sadly failed to see that this action on the part of the twenty-four elders is not an unrepeated, once and for all event; on the contrary, it is an integral and perpetual part of the eternal worship in heaven. Furthermore, the action of the elders is symbolic. The elders seated on the twenty-four thrones surrounding the great throne of God wear the royal crowns as symbols of their authority and positions of ruling. And, as Mounce points out, "in casting down their crowns before the throne the elders acknowledge that their authority is a delegated authority. The honor given them is freely returned to the One who alone is worthy of universal honor."[21] J. W. Mealy adds:

> the same may be said of the gesture of prostrating themselves (Rev. 4.10a), since in performing this act of worship, they must give up their places on the thrones. In fact, the elders are pictured as continuously receiving, yet continuously releasing both of these symbols of their authority. The paradoxical image evoked is of an uninterrupted reciprocation between divine giving and creaturely giving back of authority. No one in the scene (not even God) stakes a claim to autocratic rule.[22]

Only in difficulties and in tribulations do people really learn how to submit to authority and how to demonstrate their submission to authority. Only thus can they become qualified to handle authority themselves.

A short note on the resurrection of the martyrs will end this chapter. I shall not go into the "when" and the "how" of their resurrection, whether as depicted in Revelation 11:11-12 or as portrayed later in 20:4-5. If I did, it would involve us in the unending debate of the a-, pre-, and post-millennialists, and as the old English vicar said, this would be a "preposterous situation." It will be sufficient to say that, alongside many other commentators, I insist that the resurrection of 20:4-5 is one that is limited to the martyrs. Some would see two categories included there, one being the actual martyrs and the other being the "confessors," or those who went through the torture but were not actually put to death. The text might support such a distinction.

The main issue that I see in Revelation 20:4-5 is the *meaning* of the special resurrection given to the martyrs. I accept the interpretation of those who see it as the special reward given to the martyrs spoken about in the sixth chapter. The question asked by the martyrs in 6:10 ("How long, O Lord, holy and true, wilt Thou refrain from judging and avenging our blood on those who dwell on the earth?") is in fact answered in 20:4-5. I also adhere to the following interpretation expertly expressed by Mounce: "The essential truth of the passage is that the martyr's steadfastness will win for him the highest life in union with God and Christ. It is a commentary on the Lord's saying in Matthew 10:39, 'He who has lost his life for My sake shall find it.' "[23]

Chapter 11

The Holy Spirit and Martyrdom

Jesus trained His disciples to be His witnesses to all the world; that is, He trained them to spread His gospel to all the nations of the world. He knew very well that this task would bring upon them the violent reaction of the world, and thus He trained His disciples for martyrdom. An important element in this preparation was the promise given to the disciples that the Holy Spirit would be with them when they are arrested and taken before the authorities, and that they should not worry because *He* will speak through them (Matt. 10:18-20; Mk. 13:11; Lk. 12:11-12; 21:14-15).

The implications of this promise are enormous. First of all, it tells the disciples that they will not be alone in the battle; the Holy Spirit will be in them and with them. Secondly, it makes them aware that this battle is actually not their own; this is God's initiative and God's action and concern. They are His ambassadors, fully endowed with His authority and power. Thirdly, whatever they will achieve will be God's achievement, because God's Spirit has acted through them.

In the Gospel of John, in chapters fourteen through sixteen, we are given the last lesson in a series of teachings through which Jesus trained His disciples for their job as witnesses to a hostile world. The place of the Holy Spirit in the life of Jesus' agents became even more central and explicit in this lesson. Jesus began with these words: "I will ask the Father, and He will give you another Helper, that He may be with you forever" (John 14:16). Later in His instructions, Jesus told them that the Holy Spirit will be His main witness in the world (15:26). Next Jesus made it clear that the work of persuading and convicting the world was the task of the Spirit (16:8). The comforting thing for the disciples to know was that the Holy Spirit will guide them (16:13), and that He will take all that belongs to Jesus and will disclose these things to the disciples (16:15).

John also tells us that after His resurrection, Jesus first of all gave them His peace, and then He renewed their commission: "As the Father has sent Me, I also send you" (20:21). The most important thing here is to notice that immediately after this solemn sending of the disciples into a hostile world, Jesus "breathed on them and said to them, 'Receive the Holy Spirit' " (20:22). From the start of their training to the end of the process, Jesus made it absolutely clear to the disciples that they would not be alone; they will have God's Holy Spirit inside of them, and He will give them authority and power and guidance. He will speak and act through them, fulfilling God's purposes in and through them.

One more time, before He ascended into heaven, Jesus instructed His disciples to wait in Jerusalem for a few more days until they have received the Holy Spirit; and *then* they will be His witnesses "in Jerusalem, and in all Judea and Samaria, and even to the remotest part of the earth" (Acts 1:8b).

The role of the Holy Spirit in the life and ministry of a martyr is certainly a vast topic of study, and I want to point out here that an entire doctoral dissertation has been written solely on this subject.[1] For an analysis of all the biblical texts pertaining to this topic, and for a survey of the literature of the first two Christian centuries in which the Holy Spirit is mentioned in the context of persecution and martyrdom, I refer the reader to that dissertation.

In my own approach to the study of martyrdom, I purposed to discover the goals God desires to achieve *through the martyr in this world*, and the things He wants to achieve *in the martyr himself* through the martyrdom. The Holy Spirit is the Person of the Trinity who has been active throughout history and is active today, working to achieve the divine purposes in these two areas. Books that explain the role and the functions of the Holy Spirit in the world today are relevant also for explaining the functions of the Holy Spirit in the life and witness of the martyr.

For our present investigation, it is relevant to mention that the evangelical theologian Peter Wagner considers martyrdom to be a gift of the Holy Spirit. In his view, the thirteenth chapter of 1 Corinthians is located in the broader context of a discussion on spiritual gifts; therefore, the words "though I give my body to be burned" (1 Cor. 13:3) represent one item in Paul's list of spiritual gifts, and signify the gift of martyrdom. Wagner writes that the gift of martyrdom "is an attitude toward suffering and death that is quite unusual"; he defines it in these words: "The gift of martyrdom is a special ability that God has given to certain members of the Body of Christ to undergo suffering for faith even to death while consistently displaying a joyous and victorious attitude that brings glory to God."[2] As a further explanation, Wagner adds:

> When death is imminent, but it is possible to escape, the person having the gift of martyrdom may well choose to suffer and die. Christians who have other gifts and feel that God wants them to continue to use them, but do not have the gift of martyrdom, will usually choose to flee.[3]

I concur with the definition Wagner gives to the gift of martyrdom. However, the fact that martyrdom for the faith is a gift of the Holy Spirit must never be used as an excuse to escape death for the cause of Christ by saying that one does not have this particular gift. This type of reasoning would in fact be an attempt to save one's own life, an act which Jesus said would result in the loss of one's life (Matt. 16:25). No, Jesus Christ calls us all to stand up for Him and for His gospel whatever the cost. It is God who will decide whom He will call to literally give his or her life for Christ, thereby showing that he or she has been given this special gift of martyrdom. No one can determine beforehand that he has this gift and then decide to exercise it. Such an action would go against the teaching developed by the Church in the second century, maintaining that whoever provoked his own martyrdom was disqualified from that title, having instead committed a sort of suicide.

We need to be very clear on the fact that Jesus calls us to be faithful *to Himself and to His gospel*; He calls us to be His witnesses in the place in which we are now and in the places to which he sends us. We do not seek persecution and suffering and death; we seek *Christ and His cause*. We seek to be obedient to Him and to His commandments. We pursue His goal of spreading His gospel around the world. Our greatest desire is to be like Him. Our supreme goal is to honor Him and to glorify Him. It is for these purposes that the Holy

Spirit empowers us.

Furthermore, Jesus told us beforehand that these actions will attract the hatred of the world, putting our lives in danger. Nevertheless, Jesus promised us that when this will happen, the Holy Spirit will give us the necessary power, sustaining us and giving us the victory.

Chapter 12

Conclusions to the Survey of
the Scriptures

The main purpose of this research has been to enable us to put together a theology of martyrdom. Very early in the process, however, we found ourselves compelled to take into consideration the larger subject of suffering, as well. In addition, we discovered that in the Scriptures, the subject of suffering and self-sacrifice is intimately and organically related to the issue of rewards in heaven. Therefore, the three issues cannot be studied apart from each other. In fact, they form essentially one subject.

A further discovery that we made in the course of our investigation was the fact that suffering, martyrdom, and rewards are intrinsically and inseparably connected to the most important issue one could ever study, namely, God's ultimate plan with humanity. This plan is none other than man's ultimate purpose for existing and his final destiny for all eternity. We saw that God made man with the purpose of giving him dominion over His creation. Man was destined to become like Christ and to rule with Christ over God's created universe. For this final purpose, God intends to fashion free and responsible persons who will voluntarily submit to His authority and who will be trustworthy, reliable, and worthy of being entrusted with the authority to rule.

With this final end in mind, God has chosen to educate His children by means of the harshness of this present earthly history.

Because His goal is to form a Christlike character in each of them, the main character traits that God wants to develop in His children are the following: submission to God's authority, obedience to God's commands, total fidelity to God and total dependence upon God, the love of God and of other people, a servant's attitude, endurance of all tribulations, an attitude of self-sacrifice and of giving everything to God and to others, and a passion for holy living.

Through the many trials of this life, God also tests His children. By their reactions to God's commands and to the challenges of life, they reveal their worth, their faithfulness, and their trustworthiness. The most important moment for each child of God is the moment of his appearing before the judgment seat of Christ. All of his works, thoughts, intentions, words, and attitudes will be brought out into the light so that God can determine the worthiness of that person. God has to be pleased with what He sees in each of His children on that final day of reckoning. Finally, according to what is ascertained at that judgment, God will assign to each person a place, rank, and function in His eternal kingdom and over His new creation.

Before time began, God elected those who would be His children. He then determined to give them dominion over all His creation, and this was to be their inheritance from their Father. He also redeemed them, by the death of His only Begotten Son, because they fell. In the present, He gives them grace, power, and everything else they need in order to grow and be transformed into what God intends them to be.

God's children are not called to earn anything, because their heavenly Father has already determined from eternity to give them everything. Since God has given them all that they have, and since He has worked in them all that they have become, through the tribulations of life on earth, they can never boast that *they* have achieved or merited anything. Ultimately, He will give them the inheritance that was theirs from the very beginning, *if* they prove to be worthy of it. Therefore, the elect of God will always give Him all the glory and praise.

In the kingdom of heaven, God has prepared different functions or jobs for His children to do. He will give them different ranks or positions of lower or higher authority, depending on how they have performed their duties on earth, and depending on the outcome of the last judgment of Christ. This truth is most unpalatable for Christians who are used to a theology which insists that because *everything* is by grace alone, there are no obligations of any kind imposed upon the believer. This type of theology also provides them with the comfortable assurance that all the saints will enjoy equality in the eternal bliss of heaven. Notwithstanding, the Bible consistently speaks of good works and of a judgment according to works. God's Word also informs us repeatedly and insistently that it is necessary for each child of God to develop a holy character, and that there will be dreadful consequences for the ones who disobey His command.

Protestants have been deficient in putting together a reasonable and well-integrated theology of good works, of character development, and of the momentous judgment of every Christian according to his works. One of my basic conclusions thus far has been that such a theology, so badly needed, can be built only if we accept that the final purpose of God with man is to give him a position of ruling with His Son over all creation, and only if we accept that in God's kingdom, there will be a differentiation of function and position according to what the child of God has done and according to what he has proven himself to be during his life on earth.

Suffering and martyrdom are an integral part of the process by which God is educating and testing His children here on earth. God has two basic purposes to accomplish by means of the suffering and martyrdom to which He calls His children. The first purpose has to do with what He intends to work *in us* through suffering and martyrdom. The other consists of what He intends to achieve *in the world* through our suffering and martyrdom. His work in us and His work through us in the world are parallel and concomitant achievements. Hence, we should not disregard either one by concentrating mainly on one, while neglecting the other.

By now we know that what God desires to produce *in us* is a Christlike character. What He has purposed to accomplish *in the world* through us is, first of all, the spreading of the gospel to the ends of the earth (or the spreading of grace and of the salvation that is in Jesus Christ). Secondly, He has purposed to bring about the triumph of the truth of God and the defeat of Satan.

Before we attempt to construct a systematic theology of suffering, martyrdom, and rewards in heaven from the ideas that we have gleaned from our study of the books of the Bible, it is necessary to first conduct a survey of the various ways Christians in different times and different places have understood their own suffering and martyrdom. Rather than reinventing the wheel, we should try to build on what Christians have thought throughout the course of history. As we scan the history of Christianity for ideas about suffering and martyrdom, we shall also discover portions of Scripture that have particularly spoken to people in times of persecution, and we shall pay specific attention to the ways in which persecuted Christians have interpreted those Scriptures. In the process, we shall uncover numerous examples of extremely moving and deep biblical thinking; on the other hand, we shall also find mistakes and sometimes tragic errors that have had disastrous consequences for all subsequent Christian history.

After we have completed a thorough review of the Christian ideas on this subject, we shall then be able to start reasoning and judging for ourselves, in order to formulate a strictly scriptural theology of suffering, martyrdom, and rewards in heaven for our own time.

PART FOUR

A Survey of Christian Thought on Suffering, Martyrdom, and Rewards in Heaven

My aim has not been to write a history of martyrdom or to offer biographies of great martyrs. There are plenty of books which achieve this admirably. Rather, my aim has been to discover what Christians have thought about their own suffering and martyrdom, how they have interpreted their plight, and what meaning and value they have perceived therein. Hence, what follows is a survey of the Christian literature on this subject from several historical periods, by means of which we shall gather the ideas, concepts, and interpretations pertinent and important to our study of suffering, martyrdom, and rewards in heaven.

Chapter 13

Martyrdom in the First Centuries of the Christian Church

Ignatius

We shall begin our survey with Ignatius, the Bishop of Antioch, Syria. He lived at the beginning of the second century A.D. A contemporary of the Apostle John, Ignatius wrote his letters about twelve or thirteen years after John had penned the Book of Revelation. In A.D. 107 or 108, Ignatius was arrested and tried for his faith. After sentencing him to death, the authorities decided to send him to Rome to die by being thrown to the wild beasts in the Colosseum. Consequently, he was bound with ten chains to ten soldiers and was forced to walk in this manner through all of Syria and Asia Minor (present-day Turkey), finally being put on a ship from there to Rome.

In his painful walk through Asia Minor (they would not unbind him even during the night), as he passed through different cities, the Christians in each city would come to greet him and to encourage him. He took advantage of meeting these Christians, subsequently writing short letters to their churches. He also wrote a letter to Polycarp, the Bishop of Smyrna, and a letter to the church in Rome. Happily, these letters have been providentially preserved for us. From them we can understand something of what was going on in the mind of a Christian leader who was soon to be martyred for his faith and for his Lord.

What strikes us as extraordinary from the beginning of his correspondence is his intense desire to be martyred. Ignatius looked forward to being martyred; he was hungry and thirsty for it, and his only fear was that somehow the Christians in Rome might intervene for him in high places and might obtain his release, depriving him of the privilege and the joy of martyrdom. Therefore, he wrote to the Roman Christians, imploring them not to divert him from his way to death:

> I am writing to all the churches to tell them all that I am, with all my heart, to die for God—if only you do not prevent it. I beseech you not to indulge your benevolence at the wrong time. Please let me be thrown to the wild beasts; through them I can reach God. I am God's wheat; and let me be ground by the teeth of the wild beasts that I may end as the pure bread of Christ. If anything, coax the beasts on to become my sepulcher and to have nothing of my body undevoured so that, when I am dead, I may be no bother to anyone. I shall be really a disciple of Christ if and when the world can no longer see so much as my body. Make petition, then, to the Lord for me, so that by these means I may be made a sacrifice to God. Not like Peter and Paul do I issue any orders to you. They were Apostles, I am a convict, they were free, I am still a slave. Still, if I suffer, I shall be emancipated by Jesus Christ, and, in my resurrection, shall be free. But now in my chains I am learning to have no wishes of my own.[1]

A little further, he continued explaining his motivation to them: "For alive as I am at this moment of writing, my longing is for death. Desire within me has been nailed to the cross and no flame of material longing is left. Only the living water speaks within me saying: 'Hasten to the Father.'"[2]

Repeatedly Ignatius expressed his conviction that through martyrdom he would be "attaining to God" or "attaining to Jesus Christ." This did not mean, however, that he understood martyrdom as a means of obtaining salvation. Ignatius very clearly stated that salvation was procured for him by Christ through His death on the cross. Accordingly, he maintained that "of His most blessed passion we are the fruit; . . . I am well aware that you have been made perfect in unwavering faith, like men nailed, in body and spirit, to the Cross of our Lord Jesus Christ, and confirmed in love by the blood of Christ."[3] To the Ephesians, he declared: "My spirit is devoted to the Cross, which is a stumbling block to unbelievers but salvation and eternal life to us."[4]

What then did Ignatius believe that his martyrdom would achieve? Here is what he said to the Christians in Rome: "If you will say nothing on my behalf, I shall be a word of God. But if your love is for my body, I shall be once more a mere voice."[5]

It seems that here Ignatius had in mind the difference between Jesus—the Word that became flesh (John 1:14)—and John the Baptist, who was a voice crying in the wilderness (John 1:23). If Ignatius would die as a martyr, as his Savior had done, his life would speak to the world clearly, as Jesus spoke through His cross. This is why he implored the Romans: "Allow me to be a follower of the passion of my God."[6] If the Roman Christians would obtain his freedom, thus stopping him from becoming a martyr, his life would remain meaningless, like a cry in the wilderness. Ignatius continued to explain: "Nothing merely visible is good, for our God, Jesus Christ, is manifest the more now that he is hidden in God. Christianity is not a work of persuasion, but, whenever it is hated by the world, it is a work of power."[7]

In other words, by martyrdom the Christian becomes a revelation of God, as Jesus revealed the Father in the supreme way by crucifixion. Only after Ignatius had suffered for Christ, could he speak with authority on God's behalf. This is why, when he appealed to the Trallians for brotherly unity, he referred to the authority of his chains: "My bonds—which I bear about with me for the cause of Jesus Christ and as a petition that I may reach God—are my exhortations to you. Persevere in harmony with one another and in common prayer together."[8]

As Ignatius suffered, he was only drawing near to the sufferings of Christ, and this meant drawing near to God and attaining to God: "In fact, near the sword, near to God; among the beasts, along with God— provided only that, in the name of Jesus Christ, I suffer along with Him."[9]

Ignatius made the distinction between a "Christian," one who received this quality through the sacrifice of Christ ("For He suffered all these things for us that we might be saved;"[10]) and a "disciple," one who obtains this distinction by suffering and martyrdom. This is what he wrote to the Romans: "I shall be really a disciple of Christ if and when the world can no longer see so much as my body,"[11] and this is what he wrote to Polycarp: "If only through suffering I come to God, so that, by the help of your prayers, I may be reckoned a disciple."[12]

A Christian is one who gives himself totally to God and becomes a co-laborer with God: "A Christian is not his own master, since all his time belongs to God. When you have done this work, it will be God's and yours."[13] But true discipleship and true victory with God are obtained only through suffering. For this reason, he wrote to Polycarp: "Stand firm like an anvil under the hammer. A great boxer will take a beating and yet win through."[14]

Through this victory, Ignatius clearly expected to obtain the inheritance: "I shall know that the beginning is providential if, in the end, without hindrance, I am to obtain the inheritance."[15] But even this inheritance, which he understood to be a high position or rank, will not be based on his own merit: "If I reach God, I shall be someone only by His mercy."[16] Here is the amazing combination of factors contributing to Ignatius' final position: "However, your prayer to God will make me perfect, so that I may gain the inheritance that God's mercy has assigned me."[17]

The prayers of the other Christians helped him to reach the perfection by which he would gain the inheritance, but this inheritance had already been designated to him by the mercy of God. This is precisely the theology that we found to be ubiquitous in the New Testament.

Polycarp

The first detailed description we have of a martyrdom is that of Polycarp. He was already a bishop in Smyrna when Ignatius passed by on his way to Rome, but Polycarp's call to martyrdom came only fifty years later. From Irenaeus and Eusebius we learn that Polycarp was a disciple of the Apostle John in Ephesus. John had appointed him bishop in nearby Smyrna, where he continued to serve to an advanced old age.

Polycarp's epistle to the Philippians has been preserved for us, and from this letter, we learn the extent to which Polycarp's thinking was formed by the epistles of the Apostle Paul. It was from Paul's epistles that Polycarp drew his teaching about salvation through Christ, and just as Paul had done, Polycarp called Christians to suffering, to the imitation of Christ, and to the reward that is obtained through suffering and martyrdom:

> Let us persevere by our hope and by the guarantee of our righteousness, which is Jesus Christ who . . . but for our sake, that

we might live in Him, endured all things. Let us, then become imitators of His patient endurance, and if we suffer for His name, let us praise Him. For He gave us this example in His own person, and we have believed this. I exhort you all then to obey the word of justice and to practice all endurance as you saw with your own eyes in the blessed Ignatius and Zosimus and Rufus. This you saw also in others from your own group and in Paul himself and the other Apostles. Be convinced that all these "ran not in vain," but in faith and in righteousness, and that they are with the Lord, with whom they also suffered, in the place which they have deserved. For they loved not the present world, but Him who died for them and who was raised up by God for our sake.[18]

Polycarp was over 80 years old when a violent persecution broke out in Smyrna, sometime between A.D. 156 and 163. In the course of that persecution, Polycarp was burned at the stake. Soon after the event, somebody wrote a short record entitled "The Martyrdom of Polycarp." It is the first record of its kind, followed by many others, together known as *The Acts of the Martyrs* (*Acta Martyrum*). This collection, included by Eusebius in the *Historia Ecclesiastica*, will be one of the sources from which we shall gather the thinking of the first centuries about martyrdom.

One of the primary things that the author tells us about Polycarp's martyrdom is that it "happened in order that the Lord might show once again a martyrdom conformable to the gospel."[19] Here is how the author describes the true martyrs:

Those martyrs are blessed and noble, they, which take place according to the will of God, for we must be careful to ascribe to God the power over all occurrences. For everyone surely marvels at their nobility and patience and love of the Lord. For, when they were so torn by whips that the structure of their flesh was visible even to their inner veins and arteries, they endured so that even the bystanders pitied them and wept; while some of them attained such a degree of heroism that they neither groaned nor cried, thus showing all of us that at the time of their torture the noble martyrs of Christ were absent from the flesh, or rather that the Lord stood by and spoke to them.[20]

The author also explains the reason why the martyrs were able to bear such unspeakable tortures:

Because they kept in mind the grace of Christ, they despised the tortures of the world, thus purchasing eternal life at the price of a single hour. And the fire of their savage tortures was cool to them, for they kept before their eyes the escape from eternal and unquenchable fire, and with the eyes of their heart they looked up to the good things which are stored up for those who have persevered "which neither ear hath heard nor eye hath seen, nor hath it entered into the heart of man." This they were shown by the Lord, for they were no longer men, but already angels.[21]

Hence, the first essential element of a true martyrdom, distinguishing it from a false one, is that it necessarily originates in the will of God. Therefore, martyrdom must not be provoked by the Christian; he should not turn himself in to the authorities, as some were doing in order to be martyred. Polycarp's attitude is given here as the correct procedure. When the persecution erupted, he did not offer himself up for martyrdom, but "like the Lord, he waited to be betrayed."[22] Yet when the majority of the Christians begged him to leave the city, he refused to run away. He merely accepted to move to a nearby farm, sufficiently close to the city so that the authorities could find him if they so desired.[23] There at the farm, three days before being arrested, he fell into an ecstasy while praying and saw how the pillow underneath burned in flames. Then he turned to his friends and told them, "I must be burned alive."[24] Clearly, his martyrdom originated in the will of God; that is why it was revealed to him that he was going to die.

In contrast to Polycarp, a certain Quintus came before the authorities, telling them that he was a Christian, and he instructed others to do the same; but when he saw the wild beasts, he took fright.[25] This leads us to the second essential element that distinguishes a true martyrdom from its counterfeit: the one who suffers according to the will of God endures to the end, because God Himself, who has destined him for martyrdom, gives him the power to pass victoriously through the torture and the execution. However, God does not give His power to the one He has not chosen, to the one who initiates his own martyrdom. The author draws this conclusion: "For this reason, therefore, brethren, we do not approve those who give themselves up, because the gospel does not teach us this."[26]

A third characteristic of a genuine martyrdom, of one that is "according to the gospel," is that the suffering child of God does not think of himself; he thinks rather of the others, desiring to set them a good example and even suffering for their good. This is exactly what Polycarp did, "for he waited to be betrayed, just as the Lord did, to the end that we also might be imitators of him, 'not looking only to that which concerns ourselves, but also to that which concerns our neighbors.' For it is a mark of true and steadfast love for one not only to desire to be saved oneself, but all the brethren also."[27] The author refers to the fact that the arrest and execution of Polycarp seemed to have calmed the populace's anger against the Christians, because after his death, the persecution was stopped: "the blessed Polycarp, by his martyrdom, as by a seal, put an end to persecution."[28]

A few other elements of that early theology of martyrdom would be useful for us to know. One is the desire to imitate the Savior all the way to the end. This aim was undoubtedly illustrated in Polycarp's life. At the beginning of the account of his martyrdom, we are told that he waited to be betrayed "just as the Lord did." Furthermore, he was betrayed by one of the Christian slaves who revealed to the authorities where Polycarp was staying because he could not stand the torture.

The basic thing that the authorities asked Polycarp to do was to declare that "Caesar is Lord," and to offer incense on the altar of the emperor. This would be the pattern for all the interrogations of Christians in those early centuries. The Chief of Police asked Polycarp, "But what harm is there in saying 'Caesar is Lord' and in offering incense, and so forth, to be saved?"[29] This kind of advice, making the way of escape look easy and simple, has been a temptation for Christians under arrest not only in the first centuries but throughout the centuries to follow, even up to the present time.

The promise made to the future martyrs that they would see the heavens opened before they faced execution was fulfilled in Polycarp's experience, as well. He heard a voice from heaven saying, "Be brave, Polycarp, and act like a man."[30]

When the proconsul promised Polycarp to release him if he cursed Christ, he answered, "Eighty-six years I have served Him, and He never did me any wrong. How can I blaspheme my King who saved me?"[31] The author describes Polycarp being bound to the stake as a sacrifice prepared by God and accepted by Him: "like a noble ram out of a great flock ready for sacrifice, a burnt offering ready and acceptable to God."[32]

A fragment of Polycarp's final prayer at the stake gives us an even deeper look into the early conception of martyrdom:

> I bless Thee, for having made me worthy of this day and hour; I bless Thee, because many have a part, along with the martyrs, in the chalice of Thy Christ, unto resurrection in eternal life, resurrection both of soul and body in the incorruptibility of the

> Holy Spirit. May I be received today as a rich and acceptable
> sacrifice among those who are in Thy presence as Thou hast
> prepared and foretold and fulfilled, God who are faithful and
> true.[33]

When the author referred to Polycarp as a "burnt offering," by no
means did he consider Polycarp's sacrifice identical to the sacrifice of
Christ for the salvation of the world. Moreover, when Polycarp said
that he would be drinking the cup of Christ "unto resurrection in
eternal life," he did not mean that he would earn entry into heaven by
means of his martyrdom. The author makes these things perfectly clear
to us when he records the fact that the enemies of the Christians
refused to give them Polycarp's body for fear that the Christians "will
abandon the Crucified, and begin worshipping this one."[34] The author
then explains the nature of the believers' faith:

> For they did not know that we can never abandon the innocent
> Christ who suffered on behalf of sinners for the salvation of those
> in this world who have been saved, and we cannot worship any
> other. For we worship Him as the Son of God, while we love the
> martyrs as disciples and imitators of the Lord, for their
> insuperable affection for their own King and Teacher. With them
> may we also be made companions and fellow disciples.[35]

A fundamental idea that once again emerges plainly from this
document is that martyrdom must be God's choice. God is the One
who wills that someone should become a martyr. Furthermore, it is a
great honor for a Christian to be earmarked for martyrdom. Polycarp
thanked God because he had been deemed "worthy of this day and
hour, to take part in the number of the martyrs."[36] Polycarp also
believed that following his death, he would be rewarded by God with
an immediate resurrection and acceptance into the heavenly glory. We
see this from the way Polycarp also thanked God for the fact that he
had been found worthy to take part "in the chalice of Thy Christ, unto
resurrection in eternal life, resurrection both of soul and body in the
incorruptibility of the Holy Spirit. May I be received today as a rich
and acceptable sacrifice among those who are in Thy presence."[37] The
author then speaks about the evil one who hated to see "the greatness
of his martyrdom and his blameless life from the beginning, and how
he was crowned with the wreath of immortality and had borne away an
incontestable reward."[38] The belief in the immediate resurrection of
the martyrs became an established doctrine for the Christians of the
first centuries.

Another element characteristic of early martyrology was the preservation of the body or bones of the martyrs along with the other relics usually retained. These bones were used both in Christian celebrations and in the preparation of other Christians for martyrdom. Here is the very first indication we have about this practice: "So we later took up his bones, more precious than costly stones and more valuable than gold, and laid them away in a suitable place. There the Lord will permit us, so far as possible, to gather together in joy and gladness to celebrate the day of his martyrdom as a birthday, in memory of those athletes who have gone before, and to train and make ready those who are to come hereafter."[39]

This passage shows us that in those days, the church deliberately trained her members for martyrdom. It appears that new converts were taught the principles of martyrdom as soon as they enrolled in the baptismal class. This explains the fact that even young Christians demonstrated great readiness for martyrdom, as we shall see from the documents that we shall study next.

The Martyrs of Lyons

In the summer of A.D. 177, a fierce persecution was unleashed against the Christians in Lyons, France. The local authorities began spreading rumors that Christians ate their own children, that in the evenings they met in homes for banquets ending in sexual orgies, and that they committed numerous other such monstrous actions. The fury of the population became so intense that Christians were forbidden to appear in the marketplace, at the public baths, and in other public places. First, many Christian slaves were arrested, and then some of the poorer free people were taken, as well. They were submitted to the cruelest tortures and were forced to "testify" that such monstrous acts, repugnant to any human being, were indeed being committed by the Christians. These "confessions" only increased the fury of the population. Even those non-believers who had been their friends turned against the Christians. Mass arrests were made and all those taken were submitted to terrible tortures. Some Christians were strangled in prison, but most of them were brought out into the amphitheater to face the wild beasts, in order to delight the masses. Those who were not killed by the wild beasts were finally massacred by the gladiators.

Shortly after the popular anger burned itself out and the persecution was halted, a Christian who survived the ordeal wrote a letter to the churches of Asia Minor and Phrygia relating what had happened to the Christians of Lyons during that terrible summer. The letter subsequently fell into the hands of Eusebius, and he included it in the fifth book of his *Historia Ecclesiastica*.

Lucidly written with transparent sincerity and simplicity, but at the same time with great forcefulness and descriptive skill, this document is unequaled among the writings that have come down to us from ancient times. What is important for us is the fact that the author did not limit himself to merely relating the facts. He interpreted each event step by step as he recorded it; he sought to find the spiritual motivation and reason for the events taking place and for the consequences that they produced. In the course of his narration and explication, the theology of martyrdom that was to dominate in the coming centuries gradually takes shape. For this reason, we shall give it adequate space in our survey.

Right from the start, the author tells us that the dramatic events of that summer were in fact an attack of the devil against the servants of God: "For with all his might the Adversary has fallen upon us, already giving us a foretaste of his coming which is to take place without restraint, and he has tried in every way to practice and train his own against the servants of God."[40]

As the story progresses, the author frequently refers to the evil one as the instigator of the entire persecution. The devil was the active agent who organized and conducted the whole operation. He was behind the attitude of the authorities and that of the multitude. The hatred, the blasphemies, the tortures, and the abandonment of the faith that the torturers succeeded to provoke in some of the Christians were all originated by him. Even the kind words of the judges, trying to save the Christians from certain death, were considered the weapons of Satan. The purpose of the devil was not only to make the Christians "testify" that shameful acts happened among them but also to compel them to blaspheme Christ:

> Now, the devil, thinking that he had already consumed Biblias, also, one of those who denied, and wishing to condemn her by blasphemy likewise, brought her to torture, trying to force her to say impious things about us, as if she were already beaten and weak. But she recovered during the torture, recalling through temporal punishment the eternal torment of hell, and she

contradicted the blasphemers, saying: "How would such men eat children, when it is not even permitted them to eat blood even of irrational animals?" And after thus, she confessed herself a Christian and was added to the rank of martyrs. . . . the holy martyrs endured punishments beyond all description, as Satan strove to wring some blasphemy even from them.[41]

God fought against this massive attack of Satan upon the church through the martyrs. Instead of crushing His enemies with lightening or with other calamities, God raised against the evil one the patience, faithfulness, and self-sacrifice of the martyrs. It was indeed the grace of God that determined Him not to respond with force but with sacrifice: "But the grace of God led us and strengthened the weak and arrayed in opposition steadfast pillars of men able through patience to draw all the attack of the wicked one upon themselves, and they closed with the wicked one, enduring every kind of abuse and punishment."[42]

Due to the fact that God has invested His life and His grace in His children, the goal of the Adversary has always been to break their faithfulness, since this, in turn, would represent the defeat of God. If the devil could break the Christian's capacity to endure, he obtained a victory against God; hence the violence, the cruelty, and the persistence of the tortures. The devil has always been hard at work, attempting to break the endurance of Christians by any and all imaginable means.

On the other hand, the martyrs exactly through their endurance absorbed the attacks of the evil one and rendered the instruments of torture impotent. This is why in order to be chosen by God for martyrdom, one must first be found "worthy." The author tells us that "they who were worthy were arrested."[43] If the endurance of some people was broken it was because they "were manifestly unready and untrained and weak, unable to bear the strain of a mighty conflict"; for these reasons, they proved to be "abortions."[44]

Besides endurance, the martyrs had another weapon that defeated the evil one, and that was their testimony. What was at stake in the conflict between the Christians and the Roman Empire was the issue of sovereignty. The Roman Empire demanded from all its subjects the declaration that "Caesar is Lord." However, the Christians believed and affirmed categorically that "Jesus Christ is Lord." They took the word "Lord" in its absolute sense of exclusive sovereignty that cannot be shared with another. They knew that either "Caesar is Lord" or "Jesus Christ is Lord"; these statements cannot both be true. Once they had chosen Jesus Christ as their Lord, they could not also proclaim the sovereignty of Caesar. For precisely this reason, the Roman emperors could not tolerate the existence of the Christians; their existence was an affront to the emperor's sovereignty and an attack on his absolute authority. This is why it was enough for somebody to say "I am a Christian," to give sufficient reason for being condemned to a violent death.

The other confession that the authorities of Lyons tried to extract from the Christians, namely, that abominable acts took place in their midst, was meant only to ignite and fuel the fury of the population and to justify the destruction of the Christians.

Sovereignty by definition always demands submission. Moreover, one's submission must be expressed in public, by a solemn declaration in which one accepts and recognizes the other's sovereignty. Christians learned the importance of this public declaration or confession from their Lord who had taught them: "Everyone therefore who shall confess Me before men, I will also confess him before My Father who is in heaven. But whoever shall deny Me before men, I will also deny him before My Father who is in heaven" (Matt.10:32-33). The concept of a public recognition of one's sovereign Lord was powerfully imprinted in each new convert's mind by the fact that at his baptism, he was asked to publicly disown his former owner, Satan, and to publicly confess that "Jesus Christ is Lord."

The testimony (μαρτυρία) was, therefore, a vital element of a Christian's belief. His greatest concern when he was arrested was to make a clear and categorical testimony. In the document from Lyons, a special emphasis is placed on the act of witnessing. We are given the example of Sanctus who:

> nobly endured beyond all measure and human endurance all the ill-treatment of men. When the wicked hoped through persistence and the severity of the tortures that they would hear something from him which should not be said, he resisted them with such firmness that he did not even tell his own name or of what race or city he was, nor whether he was a slave or free, but to all their interrogators he answered in the Latin language: "I am a Christian." This he confessed for name and for city and for race and for everything in succession and the heathen heard no other word from him. Accordingly, there was great eagerness on the part of the Governor and the torturers to subdue him, so that, finally, when they had nothing more to do to him, they fastened plates of heated brass to the tenderest parts of his body. And these were

burning, but he himself remained unbending and unyielding, strong in his confession.[45]

It is remarkable that on the one hand, this man's testimony was the act that had provoked and brought on the tortures; on the other hand, the testimony itself became a source of power, of rest, and of liberation from pain. Similarly, we read this about the experience of Blandina: "But the blessed woman, like a noble champion, in confession regained her strength; and for her, to say 'I am a Christian, and with us no evil finds a place' was refreshment and rest and insensibility to her lot."[46]

The martyrs of Lyons were not afraid of the tortures. Their fear was that their testimony might not be clear enough, and that because of this, some of their brethren might stumble and fall. The intervention of the young Vettius Epagathus on the side of the Christians at the trial brings a special dimension to the notion of witness. Vettius was a man of high social status as well as a Christian with a life of moral purity. The author tells us that he was "one filled with love for God and for the neighbour, whose life was passed so strictly that although he was young, his reputation equaled that of the elder Zacharias. He had indeed walked in all the commandments and justifications of the Lord without blame, and was unwearied in all his ministrations to his neighbour, having much zeal for God and being fervent in spirit."[47]

Vettius asked the judge to let him speak on behalf of the ones unjustly accused. The judge asked him if he was a Christian and, after his answer in the positive, "he also attained to the inheritance of the martyrs."[48] The author adds this comment: "Called the Paraclete of the Christians, he had the Paraclete within him, the Spirit of Zacharias, which was made manifest through the fullness of love. For he consented to lay his own life on behalf of the defense of the brethren. For he was and is a genuine disciple of Christ, following the Lamb wherever he goes."[49]

The representation of this defender of the brethren as an agent who bore the Divine Advocate within him leads us to think of the heavenly, cosmic tribunal. The author had informed us from the beginning that the devil had incited the pagans to bring false charges against the Christians. Now the Holy Spirit entered the tribunal through Vettius as the Paraclete "whom the world cannot receive, because it does not behold Him or know Him" (John 14:17). Because of this, Vettius was not allowed to deliver his defense. Nevertheless, he "witnessed" that he was a Christian, and by this he engaged in the task of a witness-martyr. By his witness and martyrdom, Vettius condemned the devil and gave the victory to the Holy Spirit. Likewise, we are told that Blandina by her own death made the condemnation of the devil "irrevocable."[50]

The martyrs of Lyons were not exceptional beings, robust or strong or accustomed to suffering. To emphasize this point, he author repeatedly describes their fragile condition and physical weakness. For example, he tells us about Pothinus, the bishop of Lyons, who "was above ninety years of age, and very weak in body. He was scarcely breathing because of his bodily weakness which was laid upon him, but the earnest desire for martyrdom filled him with that renewed strength which a willing spirit supplies."[51] The author places the greatest stress on the description of the physical weakness of Blandina, a young woman who proved to be the greatest hero in that drama, despite the fact that no one had expected her to be able to make even the simplest confession. She was the one:

> through whom Christ pointed out that the things among men which appear mean and obscure and contemptible, with God are deemed worthy of great glory because of the love for Him shown in power and not in appearance. For, while we all feared and her mistress in the world, who was herself alone one of the contenders among the martyrs, was in distress, lest she be not able even to make her confession boldly because of the weakness of body, Blandina was filled with so much strength that . . . [she resisted tortures in relays for a whole day]. But the blessed woman, like a noble athlete, renewed her strength in the confession.[52]

How can we explain the strength of these people under such beastly tortures? What was the source of their strength? What enabled them to remain faithful and to continue in their testimony unto death? The author has clear answers to these questions. First of all, since the grace of God had raised these people to be bulwarks against the Adversary, then it is natural and reasonable that even the battle was not their battle, but Christ's. It was Christ who fought through the martyrs in order to conquer the forces of evil through suffering and dying. The author explains the endurance and the victory of Sanctus with this reasoning in mind: ". . . and Christ suffering in him manifested great glory, routing His Adversary, and for the example of the rest showing that there is nothing to be feared where there is love of the Father and nothing painful where there is Christ's glory."[53]

We are also told that Sanctus was "bedewed and strengthened by the heavenly fountain of the water of life which issues from the body of Christ."[54] The "water of life" represents the Holy Spirit (cf. John 7:37-39); if we interpret the metaphor in this way, we can begin to see that the strength of the suffering martyr came from the entire Trinity: "the love of the Father," the glory of Christ, and the refreshing presence of the Holy Spirit.[55]

Although fragile, young, and inexperienced, Blandina proved to be one of the greatest heroes of the faith. The author explains the reason why she demonstrated such unexpected strength: she "had put on Christ; . . . she, the small, the weak, the despised, who had put on Christ the great and invincible Athlete, and who in many rounds vanquished the Adversary."[56] The same explanation is given regarding the bishop Pothinus: "Although his body was weakened by old age and disease, his soul was kept in him that through it Christ might triumph."[57] About the terribly tortured Sanctus the author writes that in his "body Christ suffered and accomplished many wonders."[58] The sufferings of Blandina were extended so "that by conquering through more trials she might make the condemnation of the crooked Serpent irrevocable."[59]

The overall image we obtain from this document is that in this great battle, that had been instigated by the devil, God had raised His warriors from among His most humble and despised children, but in whom He was present and through whose endurance He obtained a glorious victory. In the author's own words, "the tyrant's torments had been brought to naught by Christ through the endurance of the blessed."[60]

The general impression we have from this letter is that a superior honor is bestowed upon those who are called to be martyrs and soldiers of God, so that God might win His great victory through them. With this in mind, we can understand the author's words describing Pothinus: "the earnest desire for martyrdom filled him with that renewed strength which a willing spirit supplies."[61]

Continuing his argument, the author next enumerates the sources of the martyrs' strength: "For the burden of the confessors was lightened by the joy of martyrdom, the hope of the promises, their love to Christ, and the Spirit of the Father."[62] The joy of martyrdom came, first of all, from the awareness that a great honor had been given to them to suffer for the Lord. Here is how this joy is described: "For they went forth with joy, great glory and grace blended on their countenances, so that even their *chains* hung around them like a *goodly* ornament, as a bride adorned *with golden fringes of divers colours*, perfumed the while with the *sweet savour of Christ*; hence some supposed that they had been anointed with earthly ointment as well."[63]

The martyrs' love for Christ takes the form of a deep desire to imitate Him in suffering as well as in dying:

> To such an extent were they emulators and imitators of Christ, "who being in the form of God, thought it not robbery to be equal with God," that, although they had attained such glory and not once or twice but many times had given testimony, and had been taken back from the beasts with burns and scars and wounds all over them, they neither proclaimed themselves martyrs nor did they permit us to address them with the name, but if ever anyone of us by letter or by word addressed them as martyrs, they rebuked sharply. For they gladly conceded the name of martyrdom to Christ, the faithful and true witness and first begotten of the dead and author of the life of God, and they recalled the martyrs who already passed on and said: "They are already witnesses, whom Christ has deemed worthy to be taken up at their confession, having sealed their martyrdom by their departure, but we are lowly and humble confessors," and with tears they besought the brethren, begging that earnest prayers be offered that they might be made perfect.[64]

The value and the beauty of this imitation of Christ in His passion is supremely illustrated by the suffering of Blandina:

> Blandina was hung on a stake and was offered as food for the wild beasts that were let in. Since she seemed to be hanging in the form of a cross, and by her firmly intoned prayer, she inspired the combatants with great zeal, as they looked on during the contest and with their outward eyes saw through their sister Him who was crucified for them, that He might persuade those who believe in Him that everyone who suffers for the glory of Christ always has fellowship with the living God.[65]

The extraordinary intimacy between God and the sufferer is another source of strength for Christians when they must endure the terrible tortures: "nothing is to be feared where the love of the Father is, nothing is painful where there is the glory of Christ."[66] The martyr Alexander was able to suffer all the tortures, without groaning or crying, because he "held converse with God in his heart."[67] And Blandina reached a point where "she had now lost all perception of what was happening, thanks to the hope she cherished, her grasp of the objects of her faith, and her communion with Christ."[68]

Still another source of strength mentioned by the author was "the hope of the promises," or in the case of Blandina, "the hope she cherished." The promises to which he was referring were, of course, the promises concerning the martyrs' rewards beyond martyrdom, as the consequences of their martyrdom. Even in the very beginning of his account, the author states that the martyrs "hastened to Christ, truly showing that the sufferings of this present time are not worthy to be compared with the glory which shall be revealed to us."[69]

In order to explain the martyrs' hope of a reward, he describes the sufferings and the death of the martyrs using this metaphor: "For having woven a single crown of divers colors and variegated flowers they offered it to the Father"; and then he adds, "And so it was fitting that the noble champions, after having endured a varied conflict and mightily conquered, should receive as their due the mighty crown of incorruptibility."[70] Writing about Marturus and Sanctus, the author says that during their repeated tortures, they had "already vanquished their antagonist in many rounds"; and now, as they faced martyrdom in the amphitheater, they "were . . . contending for the crown itself."[71]

He repeats the same pattern when writing about Blandina, "who in many rounds vanquished the Adversary and through conflict was crowned with the crown of incorruptibility."[72] Blandina was an inspiration to the other suffering Christians, and her courageous example determined many to stand strong for martyrdom. The author says that she "exhorted her children and sent them forth victorious to the King," and then she "traveled herself along the same path of conflicts as they did, and hastened to them, rejoicing and exulting in her departure, like one bidden to a marriage supper."[73] The following beautiful words depict what these Christians envisaged beyond the resurrection: "All who suffer for the glory of Christ have unbroken fellowship with the living God."[74]

It is significant to read that the pagan authorities knew that the hope of the Christians was the resurrection, and that it was because of this hope that they were "ready to go to their death and that too with joy."[75] Due to their knowledge of this hope, the authorities burned the remains of the martyrs and scattered the ashes in the river Rhone, in order to "deprive them of the regeneration."[76]

The author balances this doctrine of rewards for suffering and martyrdom with an emphasis on the grace of God, which gives Christians the power to be conquerors of the evil one.[77] He also accentuates the presence of Christ and of the Holy Spirit in the suffering believers.

There is another aspect of the story in Lyons that demands our attention, namely, the recuperation of the Christians who denied their Lord under torture. Normally, people who had denied Christ were released from jail immediately, but in Lyons, they were kept in prison awaiting further orders from Rome regarding their fate. During this time, the ones who had unwaveringly confessed their Lord through all the tortures were exuberant in their joy, while the ones who had denied the Lord were downcast, broken, and miserable. However, the joy and the victory of the confessors began working in the hearts of the ones who had denied Him. In the words of the author, this is what happened next:

> But the intervening time was not idle or fruitless for them, for by their patience the immeasurable mercy of Christ was made manifest. Through the living the dead were being made alive, and martyrs gave grace to those who failed to be martyrs, and there was great joy in the Virgin Mother, as she received back alive those who had been brought forth as dead. For, through them, most of those who had denied were restored again and were conceived again and were made alive again and learned to confess; now alive and strong, as God made them happy, who desires not the death of the sinner but is kind toward repentance, they approached the judgment seat in order that they might again be interrogated by the Governor. . . . And Christ was greatly glorified in those who, though they had formerly denied, now, contrary to the expectation of the heathen confessed. For they were examined privately as if, indeed, they were to be set free, but on confessing they were added to the rank of the martyrs.[78]

At the end of his letter, the author tells us that the greatest victory won by the martyrs against the devil was this recovery of the brethren:

> For this was their greatest struggle with him, because of the genuineness of their love, that the beast, on being choked, threw up alive those whom he at first thought to have swallowed down. For they did not take to boasting over the fallen, but that in which they abounded they supplied to those in need, having the compassion of a mother; and shedding many tears in their behalf to the Father, they asked for life, and He gave it to them; and they divided it among their neighbors, having departed to God in every respect victorious.[79]

Here we see the beginning of a doctrine and practice that would be developed by the church in the coming centuries with enormous consequences. Two significant things were said here about the martyrs. In the first place, the "martyrs gave grace to those who had failed to be martyrs."[80] Secondly, after the martyrs had asked the Father to give them life, their request was granted, and they gave this "life" to others, restoring those who had fallen.

For the sake of being as precise as possible, let us notice that the document does not say that the martyrs became the *owners* of a grace which they were then free and able to distribute to others. In addition, it does not say that their prayers had such a power on God that the prayers themselves determined the restoration of the apostates. In this letter, we do not find the martyrs having a special prerogative with God or a special mediatorial position with God. By reading the letter carefully, we can observe exactly where the author sees the true miracle and the true work of the recuperation of the fallen ones.

The letter makes it clear that the grace of God had sent the martyrs into battle. The Lord was present in the martyrs and was seen in them. He decided even the kind of death each one was to die. For example, the author tells us that some were strangled in prison: "as many as the Lord willed thus to depart."[81] In the same place we are told that Christ manifested His glory by the fact that some, "though tortured so cruelly that it seemed they could no longer live even with every attention, remained alive in the prison, destitute indeed of human care, but fortified afresh by the Lord and strengthened both in the body and soul, cheering on and encouraging the rest."[82]

The role of the martyrs in the restoration of the fallen ones was first of all in their position as fighters against the devil. Through their unbroken endurance, they gave the evil one such a terrible blow that it caused him to throw up the ones he had swallowed. Secondly, the martyrs had a love like that of a mother towards the fallen ones. Their love, joined by their example of endurance and their joy in victory, determined the ones who had denied the Lord to turn back, repent, and reappear before the judge in order to confess and die. The martyrs were the instruments through whom the grace of God acted and was manifested to others. But because Christ was the One who fought in the martyrs, it was Christ who manifested His power and glory through the martyrs both in their defeat of the devil and in the restoration of the apostates.

Although at the time this letter was written, the teaching about martyrdom had still been maintained very close to the New Testament writings, the idea that the martyrs "gave grace" to those who had failed, along with the notion that they possessed a special power of mediation, was soon to be developed in the third century into a completely unbiblical teaching.

Before leaving this document, we should also note that it reflects a belief held at that time that separated the martyrs into a detached and distinct class of Christians. Three times the author used the phrase κλῆρος τῶν μαρτύρων which can be translated as "the inheritance of the martyrs"; the context, however, shows that the author meant "the portion," the group, or the "clergy of martyrs." Thus we read that Biblias "was added to the κλῆρος of the martyrs."[83] She did not belong to it at first because she had denied the Lord under torture. But after she had changed her attitude, she was able to qualify for entrance into this new class or category. The martyrs were referred to as "the true disciples of Christ," as the ones who "follow the Lamb wherever He goes." This description of the martyrs in the words of Revelation 14:4 would be constantly applied to the martyrs in the literature of the following centuries. The designation was based on the fact that the martyrs were the ones who followed Jesus even in torture and death; they were the ones who fought to attain to the most exact imitation of Jesus that is humanly possible. And because they followed Jesus so closely in *this* life, for this reason, the martyrs will forever enjoy a unique fellowship with God in heaven.

It is also significant that at this stage in the history of martyrology, one was designated a martyr only if one had actually died. Those who had only passed through the tortures, however terrible, identified themselves merely as "humble confessors." Each of them had indeed made "the confession of witness" (ὁμολογία τῆς μαρτυρία), but in order to be "a perfected martyr," a person had to suffer death. Thus, from the Lyons' letter onwards, the death of a martyr came to be called "the perfection of the martyr."

As that hot summer in Lyons came to an end, some of the pagans asked the following question concerning the martyrs: "Where is their God and what good to them was their worship which they preferred beyond their lives?"[84] This question was to be repeated again and again throughout the bloody history of Christian martyrdom, by those who had witnessed it. However, this very question would be the beginning of their search for the secret of these strange people who were willing to die for what they believed. Many of the pagans happily found this secret, which is Jesus Christ, and in finding it, became

Christians themselves.

Clement of Alexandria

By the end of the second century, the desire for martyrdom among the Christians was burning like an all-consuming fire. There was one teacher, however, who dared to speak against the general trend and who, in a veiled and tactful way, tried to temper the spirits. This man was Clement of Alexandria. Here is what he wrote:

> Now some of the heretics who have misunderstood the Lord, love life in a manner which is at once impious and cowardly, saying that true martyrdom is Knowledge of God (which we also confess), and that a man who makes confession by death is a suicide and braggart. . . . But we too, say that those who rush to their death (for there are some, who are not ours, but merely share our name, who hasten to give themselves up, athletes of death out of hatred for the Creator), these we say depart from life not as martyrs, even though they are punished publicly. For they do not preserve the true mark of faithful martyrdom, because they do not know the real God, giving themselves up to a futile death like Indian fakirs in a senseless fire.[85]

Clement openly expressed his opinion that "to make a defense of our faith is not universally necessary."[86] For him, martyrdom was only the culminating act,[87] the rare climax of a life dominated by a love for God.[88] For him, true martyrdom was the emancipation of the self from the bodily passions: "Whoever follows out the commands of the Savior, bears witness (μαρτύρει) in each of his acts, by doing what He will, consistently naming the Lord's name, and being martyrs by deed to Him whom they trust, crucifying the flesh with its desires and passions."[89]

What Clement attempted to do was to replace martyrdom with asceticism. This tendency was to become the common and accepted dogma in the fourth century, when martyrdom was in fact replaced by monasticism, a self-induced suffering and self-sacrifice.

Carthage, A. D. 202

In the year 202 after Christ, the Emperor Severus issued an edict by which he forbid the conversion to Judaism or to Christianity. On the basis of this edict, six young people were arrested in Carthage, two women and four men. Most of them were young converts, still attending their church's baptismal class (catechesis); consequently, they were baptized after their arrest, in prison. One of the young women, Perpetua, came from a wealthy family and was highly educated. It appears that she recorded her thoughts, feelings, and visions while in prison. Among the six, there was also a Carthaginian priest named Saturus, and he also kept a diary in prison. Shortly after their martyrdom, someone collected their writings, edited them, and prefaced them with the historical account of the death of the six martyrs. Most likely, that editor was Tertullian, and the text that has been handed down to us is known as the *Passio Perpetuae*. This document represents another exceptional primary source from which we can learn a great deal about the thinking and the beliefs of the would-be martyrs. It offers us another excellent example of the Christians' fiery zeal for martyrdom at that time and of their burning desire to obtain the supreme title of *martyr*.

Of the greatest interest here is Perpetua, a young convert of only twenty-two years of age. Her father was a pagan, but the other members of her family had embraced the Christian faith. Hence, we are not dealing here with bishops or with other elderly Christians, long established in their Christian beliefs, but rather with young ones, still learning the tenets of their new faith. The pertinent question to ask is this: What had they taught these new converts in that baptismal class that had caused them to be not only fearless in the face of death but also intensely desirous of martyrdom? One thing is clear: the teaching that had been given to them had indeed prepared them well and had made them ready to die for Christ. By studying the *Passio Perpetuae*, we can discover some of the ideas that had been instilled in those young people even in their earliest Christian instruction.

Perpetua, one of the two young women in the group, was taken to prison with her baby whom she was still breast-feeding. Listen as Perpetua describes her first impressions in prison: "I was terrified; never before had I experienced such awful darkness. O dreadful day! The heat overpowering by reason of the crowd of prisoners, the extortions of the guard. Above all, I was torn with anxiety for my babe."[90] Two of the deacons of the church intervened on her behalf and obtained the concession that she should stay a few hours each day in a better room. From there she wrote: "Then I was suckling my babe, who was slowly wasting away. Nevertheless the prison was made to me a palace, where I would rather have been than anywhere else."[91]

Perpetua's greatest source of power was in her visions. Her account of them reveals to us the things these young people expected their martyrdom to achieve. In one vision, Perpetua saw a golden ladder with its upper end in heaven. At the top of the ladder stood the Good Shepherd in the midst of a beautiful garden; but at the bottom, surrounding the ladder, were the instruments of torture and a dragon who blocked the approach of the people who endeavored to reach the ladder. Because the ladder was narrow, only one person could climb on it at one time, and in order to do so, each one had to crush the head of the dragon first; only then could the victor hear the Good Shepherd saying: "Thou hast borne thee well, child." For Perpetua, the first "crushing" of the dragon's head took place when she was taken before the judge, where she was asked to sacrifice to the gods. Because she refused, she was condemned to death by being thrown to the wild beasts in the arena. We are told that after her sentencing, she returned "with joy in prison."[92]

In another vision, Perpetua saw her pagan brother Democrates who had died and was in hell. Perpetua interceded for him before the Lord, thus obtaining his transfer to heaven from hell. This is very significant because it is the first known instance of the belief that martyrs have a special prerogative of conversing with God and of interceding for the forgiveness and salvation of other people.

In her last vision, Perpetua saw her own martyrdom as a hand-to-hand combat with an Egyptian. The person who had taken Perpetua to the place of combat announced the possible outcomes: "If the Egyptian should conquer her, he shall kill her with the sword; if she should defeat the Egyptian, she shall receive this branch."[93] When Perpetua woke up from the vision, she realized that she was "going to fight not with the wild beasts but with the devil."[94]

The other young woman arrested with Perpetua was Felicitas. She was eight months pregnant. Her greatest fear was that, because she was with child, she might be excluded from the fight in the arena and sent home. For this reason, her "brother martyrs prayed with united groaning," causing her labor to begin:

And since from the natural difficulty of an eight-months' labour

she suffered much in child-birth, one of the warders said to her:
"You who so suffer now, what will you do when you are flung to
the beasts which, when you refused to sacrifice, you despised?"
And she answered: "Now I suffer what I suffer; but then Another
will be in me who will suffer for me, because I too am to suffer for
Him."[95]

The evening before their martyrdom, the young people held a
special celebration. They spoke of the day of their fight with the wild
beasts as their "day of victory:"

The day of their victory dawned, and they proceeded from the
prison to the amphitheater, as if they were on their way to heaven,
with gay and gracious looks; trembling, if at all, not with fear but
joy. Perpetua followed with shining steps, as the true wife of
Christ, as the darling of God, abashing with the high spirit in her
eyes the gaze of all; Felicitas also, rejoicing that she had brought
forth in safety that so she might fight the beasts, from blood to
blood, from midwife to gladiator, to find in her Second Baptism
her child-birth washing.[96]

Next we are told that Perpetua was singing psalms, because "she was
now treading down the Egyptian's head."[97]

The two women were put in nets that were hung in such a way as
to be exposed to the bull. When the bull gore Perpetua, her only
thought was to cover her body, because the bull tore her tunic: "she
then clasped up her hair for it did not become a martyr to suffer with
disheveled looks lest she should seem to be mourning in her glory."[98]
The ecstasy of the joy of martyrdom made Perpetua feel no pain, and
when she was taken out of the arena, she could not believe that she
was hurt. In the end, the two women were taken back to the arena,
where the gladiators finally killed them.

What comes out strongly in this writing is the martyrs' belief that
in their suffering, they were engaging in a battle with the evil one.
Even in the appeals of her father to have pity on her own child,
Perpetua saw the arguments of Satan. The dragon that was blocking
the passage of the Christian to the golden ladder and the Egyptian
with whom they had to fight in the arena were symbolic
representations of Satan. Moreover, it was the devil who had chosen
the wildest beast to attack the young Christian women in the arena.

In the *Passion of Perpetua*, we also find new beliefs, as in time, the
martyrs acquired new functions and prerogatives foreign to the
teachings of the Bible. In the first place, the Christian's way to heaven

was blocked by Satan, and it was the Christian alone who, by suffering and dying, had to break through to heaven. When the martyr was taken to the place of contest, the ensuing battle was between the devil and the martyr alone. Furthermore, this battle would decide the eternal destiny of the martyr, and the glory that the martyr would win by defeating the enemy would be his or her own glory. Evidently, the emphasis was no longer on Christ, as being present in the martyr, fighting and winning through the martyr. The emphasis was now on the heroism of the martyrs themselves, who acquired merit and glory through their martyrdom.

The merit of the martyrs was so great that it gave them special prerogatives. They now had the privileges of interceding efficaciously with God for sinners, of forgiving the sins of other people, of communicating directly with God, and of having special visions and revelations. These teachings, which appear in an incipient form in the *Passio Perpetuae,* would be further developed in similar writings during the third century. Stories of martyrdom became very popular in this century, and they became more and more exaggerated in the miraculous acts attributed to the martyrs. They may be interesting for the one who wants to observe to what extent the admiration of the martyrs grew at this time and the kind of high esteem that was given to them, but for the purpose of this dissertation, it is enough to simply mention that this phenomenon existed.

What is indeed worthy of study is the fact that in the third century A.D., martyrdom became a subject of theological discussion. Some of the greatest theologians of this century dedicated special works solely to this subject. Others discussed it in their theological works as a phenomenon that needed biblical and theological explication. We shall now delve into these writings in order to extract from them the most important ideas, theories, and explanations pertaining to our subject.

Tertullian

Tertullian was a lawyer, strongly influenced by the Stoic philosophy of his day. Intrigued by the fact that so many Christians accepted to die for their faith, marching to their death in the arena with gladness, he set his mind to discover their secret. In the course of his inquiry, he found Christ and became a Christian. Then, at the beginning of the third century, he started writing short pamphlets or articles on current issues. These were followed by extensive apologetic, theological, and practical works, representing three decades of creative activity.

In reaction to the worldly lifestyle of some of the priests, Tertullian embraced Montanism. Consequently, he became even stricter in his personal renunciation of the things of this world, and his rejection of the world's philosophy, entertainments, pleasures, and possessions became even more uncompromising. In spite of his adherence to Montanism, Tertullian's influence on the thinking of the Western church is strong and permanent. It is unfortunate, however, that his attitude of separation from worldly things gave birth to Donatism, one of the strongest opponents of the Catholic Church in the fourth century. The nonconformist Puritanism of the centuries after the Reformation also had its roots and could recognize itself in the writings of Tertullian.

Christian martyrdom was a theme that Tertullian addressed in practically all of his writings; however, he also wrote books specifically committed to this subject. For him, each Christian was a "soldier of Christ," from the moment when, at baptism, he took the oath in which he renounced his old master, the devil, declaring that from now on his master would be Christ. The life of a Christian, like that of a soldier, can only be one of obedience to the Master to whom he has sworn allegiance. Persecution comes to the Christian just like war comes to the soldier: not as something unexpected and accidental, but something to which he was called from the beginning and for which he was trained through severe and extended exercise. Many times in his writings, Tertullian described the whole Christian life as a preparation for martyrdom. The pleasures of this world, its entertainments, and its luxuries are all things that destroy the power of a Christian's faith and his strength for battle when the persecution comes. For these reasons, a Christian is under obligation to begin training for the day of testing immediately, and the renunciation of worldly things is simply part of the training for battle.

Since the Christian is a soldier who enters into his Master's service by taking an oath, the most important element in his life from that moment onward is obedience. How far will he go in obedience to his Lord? Persecution, torture, and death are the supreme tests in which the Christian is given the opportunity to demonstrate and prove his faithfulness and obedience to God. For Tertullian, the main purpose of persecution was to be the ultimate test of a Christian's faithfulness and obedience.

Tertullian discussed this issue in his work entitled *Flight in Time of Persecution.* He began his exploration of the subject by saying that first of all, one must determine the source of the persecution, "whether it comes from God or from the devil."[99] His immediate answer is that persecution is willed by God, for in and through it, God "puts the faith of His children to the test."[100] This is the conclusion of his argument:

In this sense, then, a persecution is a "judgment," and the verdict is either approval or condemnation. To be sure, to God alone it belongs to judge, and this is His winnowing fan which even now cleanses the Lord's threshing floor—His church, winnowing the mixed heap of the faithful and separating the wheat of the martyrs from the chaff of the cowards. This judgment, too, is the ladder of which Jacob dreamed, on which some are ascending on high, while others descend below.[101]

Whatever the outcome of the test might be, it will be for the glory of God. If the Christian proves worthy and comes out victorious, his victory glorifies God; if he proves unworthy, if he falls to the ground and is thrown out, God is still glorified by the fact that His threshing floor was cleansed of what was unworthy. "The essence, then, of a persecution is the glory of God, whether He approves or condemns, raises up or casts down. And whatever concerns the glory of God will certainly flow from the Will of God."[102]

As a secondary effect of persecution, Tertullian gave the fact that in a time of fear and danger, faith becomes stronger and more sincere. When a wave of persecution starts,

the church is mightily stirred; then the faithful are more careful in their preparations, greater attention is given to fasts and station days, to prayers and humility, to mutual charity and love, to holiness and temperance. Men have time for nothing but fear and hope. Therefore, it is clear that persecution, which works for the improvement of the servants of God, cannot be blamed on the devil.[103]

Now, in order for persecution to take place, hostile attitudes must be ignited, giving rise to violent actions taken against the children of God; in order for these to exist Satan must initiate and take part in the violence. Nonetheless, Satan only serves as God's instrument or agent in executing the testing of His servants: "The real cause of the persecution is the act of God's will, choosing that there be a trial of faith; then there follows evil on the part of the devil as the chosen instrument of persecution which is the proximate cause of the trial of faith."[104]

The injustice done to the believers is only an instrument placed in Satan's hands: "However, this instrument in the hands of the devil does not make him a master, but really a servant; it is the will of the Lord that chooses persecution as a means to the trial of faith, and the devil is only an instrument to be used so that persecution can take place."[105]

If the essence and purpose of martyrdom is to test the faithfulness and obedience of the Christian, we must discover what God's role is in this process of testing. Tertullian presents God in the position of a "superintendent" (ἀγωνοθέτες) over the fight of the gladiators. God calls for and institutes the fight, He supervises it in the capacity of referee and judge, and He decides the final result of the fight, proclaiming one combatant victorious and the other defeated and dishonored. The Holy Spirit is presented at first as the "trainer" of the Christians. In his work entitled *To the Martyrs*, Tertullian says to them: "You are about to enter a noble contest in which the living God acts the part of superintendent and the Holy Spirit is your trainer."[106]

Yet the Holy Spirit lives *in* the martyrs, and He is therefore present as their companion in prison as well as on the battlefield; moreover, if the martyrs are victorious, the Holy Spirit leads and escorts them until they reach the Lord: "In the first place, then, O blessed, do not grieve the Holy Spirit who has entered prison with you. For, if He had not accompanied you there in your present trial, you would not be there today. See to it, therefore, that He remain with you there and so lead you out of that place to the Lord."[107]

In another book, Tertullian makes the following clarification: even though the Holy Spirit goes into the battle with the martyrs, He does not engage in or share the suffering: "We are not able to suffer for God unless the Holy Spirit of God is in us, who even speaks through us those things which pertain to confession. Not that He Himself suffers, but He sees to it that we are capable of suffering."[108]

Regarding the presence of Jesus Christ in the martyr, Tertullian mentions it only once, in passing. Similar to the presence of the Holy Spirit, Jesus' presence in the martyr is detached and disengaged. In *Flight in Time of Persecution*, Tertullian rebukes the Christian who runs away from persecution with these words: "You have put on Christ, you have been baptized into Christ, yet you flee before the devil! You certainly make little of Christ who is in you when, as a fugitive, you hand yourself back to the devil!"[109]

Tertullian never tried to explain how it was possible for the believer to fail the test, losing the battle and being disqualified and rejected by God, when both Christ and the Holy Spirit are present in him. However, since he had adopted the thesis that the only reason for persecution was the testing of the faith of God's servant, a test whose outcome would decide his eternal salvation or eternal damnation, it was logical for Tertullian not to see an organic and indestructible unity between the believer and Christ and the Holy Spirit.

As a consequence of this, Tertullian saw the believer's preparation for battle as an enormous physical effort which was his responsibility to undertake, by submitting himself to exercises, to difficulties, and to all kinds of privations. When the real battle came, the personal power of the martyr, developed through his training, would enable him to remain stalwart and faithful. To the martyrs in prison, Tertullian wrote toward this end: "We who are to win an eternal [crown] recognize in prison our training ground, that we may be led forth to the actual contest before the seat of the presiding judge well practiced in all hardship, because strength is built in austerity, but destroyed by softness."[110]

He further advised them to make spiritual exercises an integral part of their training: "In spirit wander about, in spirit take a walk setting before yourselves not shady promenades along porticos but that path which leads to God. As often as you walk that path, you will not be in prison. The leg does not feel the fetter when the spirit is in heaven."[111]

The victory of the Christian in the testing of his faith also represents the defeat of Satan. So Tertullian writes that God permits persecution for one of two reasons: either to show that those who failed had, in fact, belonged to Satan from the outset, or to demonstrate "that the devil may be destroyed by the victory of the faith of the elect in overcoming temptation."[112] To the martyrs in prison he gives the following instructions:

> Indeed, the prison is the devil's house, too, where he keeps his household. But you have come to the prison for the very purpose of trampling upon him right in his own house. For you have engaged him in battle already outside the prison and trampled him underfoot. Let him, therefore, not say: "Now that they are in my domain, I will tempt them with base hatreds, with defections or dissensions among themselves." Let him flee from your presence, and let him, coiled and numb, like a snake that is driven out by

charms or smoke, hide away in the depths of his den. Do not allow him the good fortune in his own kingdom of setting you against one another, but let him find you fortified by the arms of peace among yourselves, because peace among yourselves means war with him.[113]

Regarding the reward that the martyr will receive for his endurance in suffering, Tertullian puts his explanation in words that practically describe salvation. Thus, to the martyrs to whom he had written that they would soon enter into the great contest, he adds that this is "a contest whose crown is eternity, whose prize is angelic nature, citizenship in heaven and glory for ever and ever."[114] Rebuking the Christian who fearfully shuns martyrdom, he writes: "O Christian, are you afraid of man? You whom angels should fear as their judge; you who should be feared by the demons, since you have received power over the devils, too; you who should be feared by the whole world, since the world will be judged by you, too."[115] Contrary to the position adhered to by most of his contemporaries, Tertullian apparently did not distinguish between the rewards of the martyrs and the rewards of other Christians.

Tertullian spoke vividly and emphatically about the impact of the martyrs' endurance and faithfulness in suffering upon the pagan world. Primarily, the curiosity of the pagans is at first stirred by the joy with which the Christians accept to go to prison; then by the fact that they enter the arena singing, fearless before the gladiators or the wild beasts. The Christians' incredible endurance under tortures, as well as their eager renunciation of wealth, family, and even life for their faith, also surprise the unbelievers who are watching. Their interest having been aroused, the pagans are then motivated to seek out the content of the faith that produces such people and such behavior. Their search most often leads them to Christ and to His kingdom. Tertullian summarized this in a memorable sentence which was to become the motto of Christian martyrs across the centuries: "the blood of the martyrs is seed";[116] it is the seed from which new Christians spring up, or, as the quote is usually rendered, "the blood of the martyrs is the seed of the church."

One other aspect of Tertullian's teaching on martyrdom should receive our attention in particular. We notice it in a remark he made to the martyrs in prison: "Some, not able to find this peace in the church, are accustomed to seek it from the martyrs in prison. For this reason, too, then, you ought to possess, cherish and preserve it among yourselves that you may perhaps be able to bestow it upon others also."[117]

This statement points to a phenomenon that was about to take center stage in the practice of the church in the coming decades, and we must explain it here. The martyrs were, by now, kept in the highest esteem by the churches; understandably, they were highly admired and revered by the other Christians. At this time, however, the church began attributing to the martyrs great powers and special functions from God, especially the power to forgive sins; in addition, one power that the martyrs were believed to possess exclusively was the power to forgive the greatest of all sins, the sin of apostasy.

During periods of persecution, which were usually of very short duration, hundreds of Christians would deny their faith and sacrifice to the pagan deities or to the emperor, in an effort to have their lives spared. But after the persecution had ended, and many times even before, many of the apostates would feel very sorry for what they had done and would want to come back to the church, asking for forgiveness and for restoration into the membership. But could the church receive them back? Should they be accepted once more in their midst?

The problem of how to deal with the apostates was one of the most difficult problems ever faced by the Christian church. The third and fourth centuries were marked by painful debates and splits in the churches on this issue. In the end, the entire church was divided by this great question, and the Donatist movement emerged as the rigorist wing, opposing the restoration of the ones who had apostatized.

In Tertullian's day, however, the practice was as follows: The one who had committed apostasy but now desired to be received back into the church was placed in the position of "penitent" for life. Only when he was close to death would he finally be given the forgiveness of the church and would be accepted to take part in Communion.

As these ideas developed, the unique powers of the martyrs were brought into play. The church appealed to the martyrs to solve this most difficult problem of apostasy, since the church held that it had been given to them to intercede with God for the forgiveness of the sins of others. The accepted position of the church was that after Christians had passed through the tortures, remaining faithful to their Lord, and after they had been sentenced to die in the arena and the date for it had been fixed, they already possessed all the rights and functions of martyrs, including the forgiveness of sins. The established practice was to bring the repentant apostates before the soon-to-be martyrs in prison; there the apostates would ask the future martyrs to forgive their sin.

It seems that Tertullian approved of this practice and gave the would-be martyrs the authority to give "peace" to the ones who could not find it in the church. We shall presently see the many serious problems that this practice would soon create for the church.

Origen

Origen was without doubt one of the greatest theologians of all time and one of the most prolific writers of his time. In A.D. 202, when a persecution broke out against the Christians in the city of Alexandria, in Egypt, Origen was seventeen years old. Even at this young age, Origen had the ardent desire to become a martyr. For this reason, when his father was arrested and sentenced to death, Origen devised a plan that when they would take his father to the place of execution, he would rush there, pleading with the executors to kill him alongside his father. Somehow Origen's mother detected his plan, and during the night before his father's execution, she took all the clothes out of the house. In the morning, Origen could not find anything to put on and was forced to stay in the house. This was how his mother spared his life.

The time of his own martyrdom actually came fifty years later. During the great persecution of Decius, Origen was arrested in Caesarea, Palestine, and was submitted to the cruelest of tortures in order to force him to deny his faith. He went victoriously through all the forms of torture applied to him, yet it was not given to him to die at the hand of the executioner. His body broken by the tortures, Origen was sent home, where he died shortly, in A.D. 254.

In A.D. 235, nearly twenty years before his own ordeal, Origen wrote a book entitled *Exhortation to Martyrdom*. The book was occasioned by the arrest of some of the leaders of the church in Caesarea. In this book, Origen brought together his immense knowledge of the Scriptures to show all that could be said about martyrdom from the Word of God. In what follows, I have tried to select from this text all that I consider necessary and useful for our own inventory of ideas about martyrdom.

According to Origen's theology, as articulated in his *Exhortation to Martyrdom* and in other works he dedicated to this subject, martyrs have a very special place in God's strategy. Origen believed that the divine Logos has always been the guide and instructor of the human race, acting through men such as Moses and the other Old Testament prophets, and then in the most supreme way through Jesus. After the Incarnation, the Logos was also active through the apostles, and He is now at work through the martyrs. In order to convince us that those who had been martyred now formed a special class of apostles, Origen begins his argument by pointing out that Jesus' "prophecies of martyrdom" were addressed not to the multitudes but only to the apostles. To support this claim, he refers to the Gospel of Matthew 10:5, 17-23; to Mark's Gospel 13:11-13; and to the Gospel of Luke 12:11-12; 21:14-19.[118] Then, he adds: "Also the following exhortation to martyrdom, found in Matthew, was spoken to no others but the twelve. We, too, should hear it, since by hearing it we shall be brothers of the apostles who heard: and shall be numbered with the apostles. This is the passage: Matt. 10:28."[119]

Origen believed that the martyrs had been elected by God for this function. To back up his statement that "nobody comes to the contest of martyrdom without providence," he quoted Matt. 10:29-33.[120] He also observed that the commandment given by Jesus about bearing fruit was not given to His slaves but to His friends.

At the present time, Jesus is continuing His own work through those who will accept to enter the contest of martyrdom. Addressing Ambrazius, his own bishop, Origen tells him: "You go in procession bearing the cross of Jesus and following Him when He brings you before governors and kings (Matt. 16:24; Mark 8:34, Luke 9:23). His purpose is to go with you and to give you speech and wisdom—and to you, Protoctebus, his fellow contestant, and to you others who suffer martyrdom with them and complete what is lacking in Christ's afflictions (Col. 1:24)."[121]

The martyr is the one who, by being arrested and taken before the authorities, has the possibility to witness for God: "We must recognize that the person who confesses the Son before man, commends, as far as it is his to do, Christianity and the Father of Christianity to those before whom he confesses."[122] Nonetheless, the One who speaks through the martyrs is the Spirit of God: "Through your eagerness for martyrdom you give place to the Spirit of your Father, which speaks in those who are arrested for their religion" (Mat. 10:20).[123]

By now we should be familiar with the idea, present in almost all the writings of this time, that the martyrs are engaged in a battle with the cosmic forces of evil, with evil spirits, and with the devil himself. Origen presented the same picture of the martyrs who in their march towards the place of execution celebrate their victory against the devil and his wicked angels. However, Origen also introduced the idea that the martyrs are athletes who fight before a cosmic audience, consisting not only of people, but also of angels, both good and evil. When the martyrs fight with courage, they are applauded by the good angels and by the whole cosmos. When they are defeated, hell rejoices and the devil with his evil spirits applaud. Here is Origen's description:

> A great multitude is assembled to watch you when you combat and are called to martyrdom. It is as if we said that thousands upon thousands gathered to watch a contest in which contestants of outstanding reputation are engaged. When you will be engaged in the conflict, you can say with Paul: "We were made a spectacle to the world and to the angels and to men" (1 Cor. 4:9). The whole world, therefore, all the angels on the right and on the left, all men, both those on the side of God and the others—all will hear us fighting the fight for Christianity.[124]

In order to explain how the martyrs defeat the devil, Origen gives us the example of Job. The devil had made the claim that if God would take away all of Job's possessions, Job would surely curse God. Yet, contrary to the devil's expectations, Job did not curse God; instead, he blessed Him, and by this "the devil was put to shame."[125] Even when Job was afflicted with terrible suffering, he still remained faithful to God: "the devil was conquered by the athlete of virtue and proved to be a liar. For though he suffered extreme hardships, Job endured, sinning in no way 'with his lips' before God (Job 2:10). Job wrestled and conquered twice."[126]

Due to the fact that the martyrs are a special class of people, having the function of the apostles and being the perpetuators of the work of Jesus on the earth, they will enjoy a special reward or position of ruling with Jesus in eternity: "Jesus once endured the cross, despising the shame, and therefore is seated at the right hand of God (Heb. 12:2; 8:1). Those who imitate Him by despising the shame will be seated with Him and will rule by His side in heaven (2 Tim. 2:12)."[127]

However, even among the martyrs there will be degrees of honor. The greater the wealth you renounced on earth or the more relatives you gave up in this life, the greater your position in heaven will be:

Therefore, just as it is right for those who have not been tested with tortures and sufferings to yield the first places to those who have demonstrated their endurance in instruments of torture, in different sorts of racks, and in fire, so also the argument suggests that we poor, even if we also become martyrs, should get out of the first seats for you who because of your love for God in Christ trample upon the deceitful fame most people seek, upon such great possessions, and upon affection for your children.[128]

We have already noted that Tertullian perceived martyrdom as a way of obtaining eternal life in heaven. Origen went even further in this direction. He considered martyrdom to be second only to baptism among the means of winning the remission of sins. In a sermon on Leviticus, he enumerates these means as: baptism, martyrdom, almsgiving, forgiveness of others, converting the sinners, manifestation of love, and ecclesiastical penance.[129]

Origen was also the first Christian theologian to argue that the death of the martyrs has the same function as the death of Jesus; in other words, a martyr's death also functions as an atonement for the sins of others. This was the most radical departure from the uniqueness and all-sufficiency of the sacrifice of Christ for the salvation of the world as presented in the Bible. Strangely enough, Origen argued it point by point using texts from the Bible. Due to the fact that this is a key issue in Christian theology and in the theology of martyrdom, I will cite Origen's discussion of it extensively.

He commences the argument by quoting Psalm 116:13: "I will take the cup of salvation and call on the name of the Lord"; then he declares:

Martyrdom is customarily called "the cup of salvation," as we find in the gospel. For when those who wish to sit on Jesus' right and left in His kingdom yearn for so great an honor, the Lord says to them, "Are you able to drink the cup that I am to drink?" (Mt. 20:22). He means by "cup" martyrdom; and the point is clear because of the verse, "Father, if it be possible, remove this cup from me; nevertheless, not as I will, but as you will" (Mk. 14:36; Mt. 26:39). We learn, moreover, that the person who drinks that cup which Jesus drank will sit with Him and rule and judge with the King of kings. Thus, this is "the cup of salvation"; and when someone takes it, he will "call on the name of the Lord." For whoever calls on the name of the Lord shall be saved (Joel 2:32; Acts 2:21; Rom. 10:13).[130]

After touching upon some issues of lesser significance, Origen resumes his central argument:

> At any rate, clearly "the cup of salvation" in Psalms is the death of
> the martyrs. That is why the verse "I will take the cup of salvation
> and call on the name of the Lord" is followed by "Precious in the
> sight of the Lord is the death of His saints" (Ps. 13:15). Therefore,
> death comes to us as "precious" if we are God's saints and worthy
> of dying not the common death, if I may call it that, but a special
> kind of death, Christian, religious, and holy.[131]

> . . . Let us also remember the sins we have committed, and that it
> is impossible to receive forgiveness of sins apart from baptism,
> that it is impossible according to the laws of the gospel to be
> baptized again with water and the Spirit for the forgiveness of
> sins, and that the baptism of martyrdom has been given to us. This
> is what it is called, as is evident from the fact that "Are you able
> to drink the cup that I drink?" is followed by "or to be baptized
> with the baptism with which I am baptized?" (Mk. 10:38). And in
> another place it is said, "I have a baptism to be baptized with, and
> how I am constrained until it is accomplished!" (Lk. 12:50). Note
> also that the baptism of martyrdom, as received by our Savior,
> atones for the world; so, too, when we receive it, it serves to atone
> for many. Just as they who assisted at the altar according to the
> law of Moses seemed to procure for the Jews remission for sins by
> the blood of goats and oxen (Cf. Lev. 16.3ff.; Ps. 49.13; Heb. 9.13,
> 10.4), so the souls of believers that *are beheaded for the testimony
> of Jesus* (Apoc. 20.4; cf. 6.9), do not assist in vain at the altar of
> heaven (1 Cor. 9.13), but procure for them that pray the remission
> of sins.[132]

At the end of this work, Origen concludes: "It may be that as we
have been purchased by *the precious blood* of Jesus who has received
a name above all names, so some will be ransomed by the precious
blood of martyrs."[133]

We have seen that Tertullian attributed to the martyrs the function
of interceding before God for the forgiveness of other people's sins.
Now we observe Origen taking a step further, arguing that a martyr's
death atones for sins in a similar fashion to the death of Jesus Christ
Himself. I doubt that it is necessary at this point to enter into a
dialogue with Tertullian and Origen, and to take the time to show that
their theology and their interpretation of the Bible were utterly wrong
in this respect. I assume that the doctrines of the uniqueness of Christ
as our Mediator and of the uniqueness and all-sufficiency of His death
for the atonement of the sins of mankind are among the most basic and

essential elements of Protestant theology. It is only necessary here to indicate the way in which the most disastrous ideas for the whole of Christian theology entered into Christian teaching in the third century, snowballing into a veritable catastrophe for the church in the decades and the century to follow.

The Crisis of the Confessors

It was the year 250, when the Emperor Decius launched a vast and cruel persecution against the Christians. This persecution came after a long period of peace for the churches. Prosperity and ease had started to soften the Christians, and it appears that most of them were not trained and prepared for suffering and sacrifice. This was the reason why in many places, thousands of Christians hurried to sacrifice to the gods rather than face confiscation of property, torture, and death. Many others used another way of escape: they bribed the local authorities into giving them a certificate stating that they had sacrificed to the gods, although they had not actually done it. On the other hand, many others did pass heroically through the cruel tortures. While some of them were put to death, many more were waiting in prison for the glorious day of their martyrdom in the arena. Then, unexpectedly, in A.D. 251, Decius died and the persecution was stopped. The confessors who had endured the tortures and had been waiting to seal their martyrdom in the arena were suddenly released from prison. Now, according to the standards of that time, the church maintained that these stalwart Christians were already in possession of all the rights and prerogatives of the martyrs despite the fact that they had been spared.

Then the confusion and the crisis came. When many of those who had sacrificed to the idols or had bought false certificates returned to the church, the church refused to receive them. Notwithstanding, there were now a significant number of confessors in the church who, according to popular belief, had the power to forgive sins; hence, those who had committed apostasy turned to them for forgiveness. However, in some places the confessors were more generous than in others, forgiving *all* the apostates. This action stirred anger and opposition among the Christians.

In his *Historia Ecclesiastica*, Eusebius included a letter which Bishop Dionysius of Alexandria wrote to Bishop Fabius of Antioch concerning this issue. The letter shows us the very high esteem in which the martyrs were kept at that time. Here is the passage that is of greatest interest to us:

> So the divine martyrs themselves among us, those who are now assessors of Christ, and share His kingdom, and take part in His judgments, and make decisions with Him, received some of the brethren who had fallen away and had become answerable to charges of sacrificing; and seeing their conversion and repentance, and thinking that it could be acceptable to Him who does not wish at all for the death of the sinner but for his repentance, received them back, and gathered them together, and met with them, and had fellowship with them in prayers and feasts. What then do you counsel us, brethren, regarding these men? What must we do?[134]

The greatest crisis of all seems to have been in Carthage. Cyprian, the Bishop of Carthage, dealt with this issue theologically in a paper he presented to the Synod of Carthage in A.D. 252. His work, entitled "About the Apostates," was well accepted by the Synod, and it became the basic source for a uniform approach to the apostasy issue in all of North Africa.

A few ideas formulated by Cyprian in this writing should be incorporated into our survey of ideas about martyrdom. In the first place, Cyprian establishes that there are differing degrees of guilt, and therefore, the punishments for the different forms of apostasy must be different, as well. Even so, all the apostates, even the ones who had only bought false certificates and had not actually sacrificed to idols, must be submitted to lengthy and severe penitential discipline in order to accomplish what Cyprian called "due atonement."

In the second place, Cyprian states his belief in the prerogative of the martyrs to intercede with God, but he believed that this intercession is not done in the present, neither by the ones who are still on the earth nor by the ones who are already in heaven. Their intercession will be effective only on the day of the last judgment, when the people of God will stand before the tribunal of Christ.

Cyprian offers examples of great men of God from the Bible, like Moses, Jeremiah, Noah, and Daniel, who interceded with God for other people but were not given what they asked for and sometimes were even told not to intercede anymore. From their stories, he draws the conclusion that the martyrs should not believe that they have the power to dictate something to the Supreme Judge; likewise, they should not suppose that their decision to forgive the apostates automatically obtains the approval of God. He warns the martyrs that they must not give the apostates a false hope and by this divert them from the true way of recovery.

Eusebius

At this point, it is appropriate to include a few words about Eusebius of Caesarea, the first historian of the Christian church (ca. A.D. 265-339). He is called "the father of Christian history" because he was the first man to bring together the various texts documenting the history of Christianity in its first centuries, and he was the first to write a history of the church. In this book, entitled *Historia Ecclesiastica*, we find both the best factual accounts and the main theological treatises written about the persecutions and martyrdoms of those times. As all historians inevitably do, Eusebius brought to the facts his own general conception of the world and of history, editorializing and commenting upon the facts according to his own personal world-view. His basic presuppositions, as well as the way these are reflected in his remarks, are of particular interest to us.

Central to his theology and philosophy of history was the belief that through the coming of Jesus Christ, the Eternal Word of God, into the world, through His atoning death and His glorious resurrection, and then through the apostles' work of spreading the gospel, a new nation was born, a nation whose people spread among all the other nations of the earth. It is true that God has always had His own people, in all the epochs of human history. But only now, through Jesus Christ, the people or nation of God was formed, "a nation which has been honored by all with the name of Christ."[135]

Yet the appearance of this new people stirred the hatred of all the nations dominated by the evil one, and as a result, the nations have launched attack after attack against the people of God. Some agents of the evil one have even infiltrated into the church with false teachings, thereby seeking its destruction from the inside. Some others, however, as furious and cruel as wild beasts, have risen with force against the children of God, thus seeking to destroy them physically. Amazingly, the sufferings of the people of God, and especially their deaths as martyrs, have become their supreme form of conquering the world. Even more astonishing is the ultimate purpose of God, that through the difficulties of this world, through suffering and martyrdom, special beings would be shaped and formed for His heavenly kingdom. The tortures are only the preliminary test, followed by the supreme proof that these people are fit for the heavenly kingdom: "the greatest soldiers of His kingdom had given sufficient proof of their training."[136]

Suffering and martyrdom are God's ways of testing us, but at the same time, they are also the instruments by which God completes His work of perfecting the saints and of bringing them to maturity. For this reason, in the third and fourth centuries, one did not say that a martyr was killed or executed; instead, the martyr was said to have been "perfected." Eusebius used this phrase frequently. Speaking about Origen's father, the historian says that he "had reached perfection through martyrdom."[137] In another place, he speaks about a group of Christians who "were captured and attained perfection by martyrdom."[138] About another one, he writes that he had "been perfected through fire."[139] Still another man "was perfected for martyrdom and was beheaded,"[140] and one more "was led away to death and was perfected."[141]

The general picture of Eusebius' conception of martyrdom can be ascertained from a passage in "The Martyrdom of Polycarp," praising the martyrs of Palestine:

> Oh, the blessed confessors of the kingdom of Christ, who like gold were tried in the excellency of their righteousness, and attained the heavenly life of the angels by the contest in which they stood fast, and obtained the promises of hidden good which is the prize of the high calling. "For eye hath not seen nor ear heard, neither hath entered into the heart of man that which God hath prepared for those that love Him."[142]

The Veneration of the Martyrs

The last great persecution of the early church took place between A.D. 306 and 313. The most extended in space and time, this wave of persecution exhibited the most cruelty of all the persecutions of the early church. In order to illustrate what torture meant at that time and to portray the courageous stand of the Christians, I refer to Eusebius' account of their situation. Eusebius, in turn, offers us the report of Phileas, the Bishop of Thmuis, a report in which Phileas informed his own people about the horrifying events that were taking place in Alexandria in A.D. 306:

What account would suffice to reckon up their bravery and courage under each torture: for when all who wished were given a free hand to insult them, some smote them with cudgels, others with rods, others with scourges; others, again, with straps, and others with ropes. And the spectacle of their tortures was a varied one with no lack of wickedness therein. Some with both hands bound behind them were suspended upon the gibbet, and with the aid of certain machines stretched out in every limb; then, as they lay in this plight, the torturers acting on orders began to lay on over their whole body, not only, as in the case of murderers, punishing their sides with the instruments of torture, but also their belly, legs and cheeks. Others were suspended from the porch by one hand and raised aloft; and in the tension of their joints and limbs experienced unequaled agony. Others were bound with their face towards pillars, their feet not touching the ground, and thus their bonds were drawn tight by the pressure upon them of the weight of the body."[143]

Here is the report given by Eusebius himself who was an eyewitness of the events occurring in the years 311 and 312, in Thebaid:

And we ourselves also beheld, when we were at these places, many all at once in a single day, some of whom suffered decapitation, others the punishment of fire; so that the murderous axe was dulled and, worn out, was broken in pieces, while the executioners themselves grew utterly weary and took it in turns to succeed one another. It was then that we observed a most marvelous eagerness and a truly divine power and zeal in those who had placed their faith in the Christ of God. Thus, as soon as sentence was given against the first, some from one quarter and others from another would leap up to the tribunal before the judge and confess themselves Christians; paying no heed when faced with terrors and the varied forms of tortures, but undismayedly and boldly speaking of the piety towards the God of the universe, and with joy and laughter and gladness receiving the final sentence of death; so that they sang and sent up hymns and thanksgivings to the God of the universe even to the very last breath.[144]

History tells us that this persecution ultimately led to the final victory of Christianity in the Roman Empire. We have seen again and again that one of the main purposes of martyrdom is to actualize the triumph of the truth. Lactantius, another great Christian historian and "Church Father" of that time, writing about the same persecution, gives us an extended explanation of God's reason for allowing the persecution as a means of opening the eyes of the unbelievers. Due to its clarity and depth, I will quote it here *in extenso*:

> There is also another reason why He allows persecution to be carried on against us. It is that the people of God might be increased, and it is not difficult to show how and why this is done. First, very many people are put to flight from the cults of the false gods by a hatred of cruelty. Who would not shrink from such sacrifices? Then, virtue and the faith itself are attractive to certain ones. Some suspect that not without cause is the worship of the gods thought to be evil by so many that they would prefer to die rather than do that which others do that they may live. Someone wishes to know what that good is which is defended even to death, which is preferred to all things that are pleasing or dear in this life, and from which neither loss of possession, nor of light, nor pain of body, nor torture of its members deter. These are very strong, but those causes have always increased our number. The people standing around hear them saying in the very midst of torments that they do not sacrifice to stone statues made by human hands, but to the living God who is in heaven. Many know that this is true and admit it in their hearts. Then, as is accustomed to happen in uncertain matters, while they question each other as to the cause of this perseverance, many things which pertain to religion, being noised abroad and caught in turn, are learned. Since these things are good, they must please them. Besides vengeance gained, as it always happens, strongly impels to belief. This is not a slight cause, either, the fact that unclean spirits of demons inhabit the bodies of many people, permission having been granted. When these have been ejected afterwards, all who have been cleansed adhere to the religion whose power they have felt. These many reasons, gathered together, marvelously gain a great multitude for God.[145]

At this point in the history of the Christian church, respect for the martyrs was transformed into the cult of the martyrs. The martyrs became "saints" to be revered, prayed to, and worshipped. From the moment that the martyrs were given the prerogative to intercede with God, and especially from the moment that their death was believed to be an atonement for other people's sins, the other steps leading to the formation of a cult of the martyr-saints were easily taken, being looked upon as merely natural, logical developments, and were met with almost no opposition. For, since the martyr was said to win by his death the capacity to forgive sins, it seemed reasonable and desirable to pray to this saint for the forgiveness of one's sins. In addition to this, all the other acts of veneration directed toward the martyrs, who were by now canonized as saints, seemed perfectly justified by the same reasoning.

We noted that this special respect paid to the martyrs originated in the second century A.D., in reaction to the martyrdom of Polycarp. At first, it was simply the commemoration of the day of Polycarp's martyrdom, as the day of the martyr's heavenly birth. Then, the church began meeting at the tomb of the martyr for an annual commemoration of his heavenly birth. A short time later in the third century, at such meetings, they started celebrating the Lord's Supper, as well, with Polycarp's tomb serving as an altar table. Another century passed and, with evident logic, they took a step further: instead of the whole church going to the tomb of the martyr, they took the bones of the martyr and placed them inside the altar of the church! By the fifth century, it was of utmost importance that every church should have the relics of a martyr inside its altar.

According to the rules established in the fourth and fifth centuries, there were seven specific honors that had to be paid to the martyrs:

1. The name of the martyr was inscribed in the catalogue of saints, and a public recognition of him/her was ordered.

2. His/her intercession was invoked in the public prayers of the church.

3. Churches were dedicated to God in his/her memory.

4. The Eucharist and the Divine Office were celebrated in his/her honor.

5. His/her festival was observed.

6. Pictorial representations of him/her were made in which he/she was surrounded by a heavenly and glorious light.

7. His/her relics were enclosed in precious vessels and were publicly honored.[146]

It is necessary to examine more closely the means by which the theologians of that time justified their veneration of the martyrs. In A.D. 396, Victricius, Bishop of Rouen, preached a sermon, which he would later develop into the ample treatise entitled *De Laude Sanctorum*. Eric Kemp gives us a summary of Victricius' arguments:

> Victricius begins by congratulating his people on their great good fortune. They have not been persecuted or tortured, or seen the sword drawn from its sheath, and yet they must multiply altars to receive the relics of martyrs. A great part of the heavenly host has

deigned to visit their city, and even in this life they now dwell in the company of the saints. The rest of the treatise is a long exposition of the theme of unity in spite of diversity. Starting from the doctrine of the Trinity, three in one, Victricius emphasizes the unity of the saints with the Godhead by adoption. As the sun lightens and fills all parts of the earth so the Holy Trinity shines through the saints and its splendor fills all the basilicas and churches, and the hearts of all the faithful. If God has called this spiritual vessel and members out of nothing, why should He not have transformed this living body, compact of the ferment of blood, into the substance of His own light? The blood therefore, as part of the body, partakes of the heavenly fire, and so we can say truly that the apostles and martyrs have come to us with their virtues. Even the smallest relics and particles of dust share the virtue of the whole. In them is found the completeness of the members because they contain a spiritual and sacred principle. Thus the power of healing resides in the parts no less than in the whole, and we hear of the same saints curing the sick in many places.

In effect in this treatise Victricius lays down the main lines on which the theology of the cult of the saints and of relics was to develop. The saints are to be venerated for their holiness which, through intimate union with the Godhead, enables them to become channels of grace to the faithful. Further, soul and body are so closely joined together that the relics of a saint, particles of his body, or objects which have been in contact with him, become as it were sacraments, material signs through which this grace is conveyed. This it would seem is the theological explanation and defense of the cult of relics.[147]

There were two eminent Christian theologians at this time who vehemently defended the veneration of the martyrs' remains, and one of them was Jerome. In A.D. 404, Jerome was informed that Vigilantius, a clergyman from Aquitania, had attacked the respect given to the remains of the martyrs, claiming that the practices linked with these remains were of pagan origin. In response, Jerome wrote a vitriolic work against him entitled *Contra Vigilantium*. The essence of the position that Jerome passionately defends is that the martyrs continue to pray for the church on earth even after their departure from this life. Furthermore, their prayers exercise a stronger power in heaven, because the martyrs now possess the merit of having conquered and of having won the contest by enduring torture and death.

Augustine was the other great theologian of the early church who strongly advocated the cult of the martyr-saints. By means of his many sermons and writings, he did much to justify this cult theologically in the eyes of the church. He delivered a great number of commemorative sermons on the days dedicated to the martyr-saints. In these sermons, he described the special favors obtained by Christians due to the intercession of the saints on their behalf. He also listed reasons why Christians should pray to the martyrs; here are some of them:

> The sanctification of the Martyrs is completed. In virtue of their sacrificial deaths they have reached the summit of perfection. For this reason, the church does not offer prayers on their behalf. She prays for the rest of the faithful, but not for the Martyrs; for they have departed from this world with such a high degree of perfection that instead of being in need of our assistance, they are actually in a position to assist us.[148]

In another sermon, Augustine said, "We ourselves are the fruit of their labor. While we admire them, they have compassion on us; we rejoice with them and in turn they pray for us."[149]

In order to justify the role of the martyr-saints as mediators, Augustine argued in the following manner:

> Their role as our advocates, however, is not based on their own personal power, but on the Person to Whom they adhere as perfect members are joined to their head. He is in truth the unique advocate who intercedes for us (1 John 2), seated at the right hand of the Father, but He is the unique Advocate in the same sense that He is unique Pastor. As He Himself said: "I must reunite those sheep who are not of this fold" (John 10.16). If Christ is shepherd, must we say that Peter is not a shepherd? Of course, Peter is a shepherd as the rest of them are shepherds indeed. If he be not a shepherd, how could our Lord have directed to him these words: "Feed my lambs." Yet it is He who feeds the sheep who is the true shepherd. That is why our Lord did not say to Peter: "Feed *thy* sheep" but rather "Feed my sheep."[150]

It can be clearly seen from their works that these theologians did, in fact, make an effort to limit the veneration of the saints to merely a form of respect and not of worship, since worship ought to be given only to God. Additionally, they attempted to define the saints' capacity for intercession as something derivative from their union with Christ the Mediator. Yet, in spite of their endeavors to fine-tune definitions and to establish specific boundaries, the phenomenon of the worship of the saints took on enormous proportions. Suddenly, it seemed that everybody was rushing madly in every direction, trying to find relics of the martyrs and other objects that had come in contact with their bodies. Every church took great pride in being the owner of such relics and other "sacred objects." Every individual yearned to possess a "chip from the cross of Jesus," or a hair of the Virgin Mary, or a tooth of St. Thomas. All these objects were considered to have healing, saving, and protective powers. Crosses and chapels dedicated to the martyrs were being erected everywhere. These soon attracted many who set out on pilgrimages, as a result of the fact that to all of them were attributed spectacular healings and other sensational miracles.

Moreover, each day of the Christian calendar was dedicated to a saint, or to a number of saints, and on each one, a special liturgy and other special ceremonies had to be performed. From the saints, people came to expect the forgiveness of sins, assistance in life, success in business, protection in travels, healing of sickness, and all the other blessings for which people had previously petitioned God. Praying to the saints became more important than praying to God, since prayers to them were believed to be more efficacious than petitions to God; the martyr-saints were considered more accessible, easier to convince, and more merciful and understanding of human weaknesses. Instead of one God, there were now thousands of saints that demanded the Christian's attention, and each saint had his or her own special favors that had to be carefully fulfilled. Hence, the situation in the church became not too different from the one existing in the pagan religions of that time, and for more than a thousand years, the Christian religion remained under the dark shadow of what was truly a tragic theological and spiritual catastrophe.

When the Protestant Reformation erupted in the sixteenth century, two of the main targets that they attacked were the aberrant prayers to the saints and the misguided veneration of their relics.

The True Martyr

Before we leave early church history, we need to touch on a few more ideas that are important for our survey. The first concept can be stated in the form of a question: What are the characteristics of a true martyr? In other words, what are the necessary and essential elements comprising a true Christian martyrdom? Augustine, who stood firmly against the Donatists, denying that those who had died for that heresy were true martyrs, wrote this:

> They who seek the glory of the martyrs would rightly claim to be true martyrs if they had suffered for the right cause. The Lord did not say those who suffer will be blessed, but rather, those who suffer for the Son of Man, who is Jesus Christ.
>
> True martyrs are those of whom the Lord spoke, saying, "Blessed are they who suffer persecution for justice's sake." Therefore, not they who suffer for an iniquitous purpose, for the sinful destruction of Christian unity, but rather those who suffer persecution for justice's sake, are to be accounted true martyrs.[151]

John Chrysostom contrasted the death of the martyrs with the death of evildoers in order to arrive at an undistorted definition of martyrdom:

> The bodies of robbers, those who desecrate sepulchers, and other evildoers, are severely afflicted, just as are the bodies of the martyrs. But although the suffering is the same, the purpose differs; hence, there is a great distinction to be made between those who suffer for their crimes and the martyrs. In the martyrs we do not look only to their sufferings; we consider first the intention, the cause, for which they suffer. We do not love them because they suffer, but rather because they suffer for Christ. On the contrary, we detest the robbers, not because they suffer, but because of the crimes for which they are punished.[152]

A much more comprehensive definition of genuine martyrdom was formulated by Gregory of Nazianzus:

> The law of martyrdom forbids us to ask voluntarily for martyrdom, for to act thus is temerarious and rash. . . . The purpose must also be considered; he who seeks primarily martyrdom acts sinfully, as did the Circumcelliones. The primary end must be the glory of God, the exaltation of the Faith, the confounding of the persecutor, the conversion of unbelievers, the wresting of peace for the church, or the strengthening of the faithful, etc. Finally, the effects of spontaneous confession are to be observed, for self-offering is illicit of neither the glory of God, nor the exaltation of the Faith, nor the promotion of the salvation of others is hoped therefrom, as when a Christian goes secretly, without witnesses, to present himself voluntarily to the tyrant for martyrdom, and is slain.[153]

The Martyr and the Monk

The concept of monastic life appeared in the Christian church at the beginning of the fourth century. One of the first monks was Anthony of Egypt, and he was made famous by the fact that Athanasius, the renowned Christian theologian of that time, justified and endorsed Anthony's action in his book *The Life of Anthony*. The portion of Scripture upon which Anthony based the idea of retreating into the desert and living there in austerity and seclusion was taken from Jesus' dialogue with the rich young ruler: "If you wish to be perfect (complete), go and sell your possessions and give to the poor, and you shall have treasure in heaven; and come, follow Me" (Matt. 19:21). This was understood as a call to completely renounce the world with its riches, pleasures, and corruptions, accompanied by a command to totally separate oneself from the world, by living a secluded life of asceticism and of prayer in the desert.

Understanding this new movement is important for our theology of martyrdom because, from its very beginnings, monasticism was associated with martyrdom. As an author from the seventh century remarked, "Monasticism arose from men's desire to become martyrs in will, that they might not miss the glory of them who were made perfect by blood."[154]

An accurate picture of the way in which the theologians of the fourth and following centuries assimilated the idea of martyrdom into the monastic movement will help us to understand and better define the concept of true martyrdom. In a study entitled "The Monk and the Martyr," E. E. Malone delineates the manner in which the word "witness" (μάρτυς) evolved and acquired its new meaning in the first centuries of Christian thought:

> From its broad meaning of the one who bears testimony to a certain truth, it narrowed its meaning to designate one who endures hardship, suffering and death for the gospel of Christ, and then it becomes even more restricted until it is used exclusively for those who die for their beliefs. On the other hand, the word "martyr" starts to enlarge its own meaning, so that by the third and the fourth century it is used to designate something else than death for the sake of the gospel. So, we read about "a martyrdom of virginity,"[1] of a daily martyrdom of subjecting one's mind to Christ,[2] of a martyrdom of will "perfect without suffering,"[3] of the martyrdom of resisting temptations by the spirit of fornication,[4]

and of the daily martyrdom of the ascetical life.[5]

[1] Ambrose, *De virginibus 1, 9 (Florilegium Patristicum 31, 22* Faller) See also Methodius, *Convivium, vel de virginitate 7, 3 (GCS* Methodius 74, 8-14 Bonwetsch); Cyprian, *De habitu virginum 21 (CSEL 3.I, 202* Hartel); Jerome, *Ad Demetriadem, Epistola 130, 5 (CSEL 56, 180, 10* Hilberg).

[2] Jerome, *Epitaphium Sanctae Paulae, Epistola 108, 31 (CSEL 55, 349, 12 f.* Hilberg).

[3] Tertullian, *Scorpiace 8 (CSEL 20. 161, 26-28* Reifferscheid-Wissowa).

[4] Ambrose, *Comm. in ps. 118, 47 (PL. 15, 1234^{C}).*

[5] Sulpicius Severus, *Epistola II ad Aurelium (CSEL 1, 143, 9 ff.* Halm).[155]

This broadening of the meaning of martyrdom eventually led to an almost complete identification of martyrdom with monasticism. The process began with Clement of Alexandria, when he attempted to tone down the believers' zeal for martyrdom by "spiritualizing" it. Let us take a closer look at what he wrote. Clement argued that the essence of martyrdom is not in the actual death for the faith; its essence is rather in the perfect love that is shown by that act: "We call martyrdom perfection, not because a man has reached the end of his life as others do but because he has displayed the perfect work of love."[156]

Then Clement distinguished between a "confession of the faith," which is the call and duty of every Christian, and a "defense of the faith," which is the call that God gives only to a few since it demands that one accept to die for the faith:

If it is expedient it will be given to some to make a defense that both by their martyrdom and by their defense all may be benefited - those in the church being strengthened, and of the heathens those who were concerned about salvation, wondering and being led to the faith, and the rest of the heathen being seized with amazement. Therefore, confession is absolutely necessary, for that is in our power, but to make a defense of our faith is not absolutely necessary, for that is not in our power.[157]

Clement enlarged the meaning of "bearing witness" to Christ to include even the keeping of the commandments of Christ as a testimony to Him, calling this a martyrdom, as well: "If therefore confession before God is a martyrdom, every soul that has lived purely in the knowledge of God, that is, that has obeyed His commandments is, in whatsoever manner it be released from its body, a martyr both in life and in word, pouring out its faith like blood, throughout its whole life even to the end."[158]

Origen took this process of extending the concept of martyrdom a step further. While Origen made it very clear that a person can be classified as a martyr only if he/she was killed for Christ, at the same time, he had "a tendency to place other forms of bearing witness to Christ on a footing almost equal to that of martyrdom."[159] Thus he wrote that some people can be martyrs by "the testimony of their conscience": "I doubt not that in this assembly, too, there are some, known only to Him, who are already martyrs by the testimony of their conscience, ready if anyone were to ask it of them, to shed their blood for the name of the Lord."[160]

Origen summoned Christians to a complete abnegation of the world and to a life of self-sacrifice and total obedience to the demands of Scripture:

> But these things are written for you, for you too believe in God, but unless you perform the works of faith, unless you observe all the precepts, even the more difficult ones, unless you offer sacrifice, and demonstrate that you do not prefer your father, nor your mother, nor your children, to God, you do not show that you fear God, nor can it be said of you, "Now I know that thou fearest God." . . . And now they say these things for our improvement, (namely) "Now I know that thou fearest God." For example, I have the will to become a martyr, but not for this reason will the angel be able to say of me, "Now I know that thou fearest God," for the proposal of the mind is known to God alone. If however, I approach the contest and bear a firm testimony, if I bear with constancy whatever is imposed upon me, then the angel can say, "Now I know that thou fearest God" as if confirming and corroborating my confession.[161]

To buttress his insistence upon the importance of the believer's renunciation of the world, Origen repeatedly quoted Matthew 19:21, a text that would later become the justification for martyrdom. He himself writes: "Nor can there be any doubt that he is made perfect who sells all his possessions as we have said and distributes them to the poor."[162] Origen's ideal was a life characterized by self-denial, a life lived totally for Christ:

> Thus also on the other hand, he who does not deny himself confesses himself, but denies Christ, and just like one who denied

Christ, he will pay the penalty of "and I also will deny him." Therefore, let all our thinking, and understanding, all our speech and action, breathe denial of ourselves, but Christ-inspired testimony and confession of Christ.[163]

Origen intended that this kind of life should be lived both *in* the church and *in* society-at-large. Unfortunately, the monks interpreted self-denial as a *separation from* both society ("the world") and the church, in order to lead a life of solitary asceticism in the desert. They considered that by this way of life, they could continue the contest of the martyrs, thereby obtaining the martyrs' glory in the hereafter. For this reason, the monks attributed to themselves all the functions and privileges that in the previous centuries had been credited only to the martyrs. It is very instructive to read Malone's summary of this historic phenomenon:

In early monastic literature the monk now becomes the "athlete of Christ," as the martyr had once been.[35] The monk, the virgin, and the ascetic are now pictured as contending in the arena for imperishable crowns as the martyr had once been pictured.[36] Monastic life becomes a *militia spiritualis,* a spiritual warfare, or spiritual military service; the monk is now the soldier of Christ who goes forth to give battle for Christ against the evil spirits and the enemies of Christ in the world.[37] Because the death of the martyr, the act by which he consummated his offering of himself to God, had been thought of and spoken of as a second baptism, a second washing,[38] the act by which the monk makes an irrevocable offering of himself to God, his monastic profession, becomes also a second baptism.[39] The very ritual of monastic profession becomes a thinly veiled and frank imitation of that of baptism, and some of the Fathers, on rather tenuous grounds perhaps, begin to claim for monastic profession the same effects that are produced by baptism.[40]

[35] Eusebius, *Hist. Eccl.* 5. pr. 1, 4 (GCS Euseb. 2.1.400, 13-23 Schwartz).

[36] Cf. E. Budge, *The Paradise, or Garden of the Holy Fathers,* (Eng. Tr. from the Syriac text of Anan-Isho, by E. A. W. Budge, London, 1907) 2, 36, n. 164.

[37] *S. Isaiac Abbatis orationes 17 (PG 40, 937 B)*. Ambrose, *Expositio evangelii secundum Lucam 4, 14 (CSEL 32, 146* Schenkl-Petschenig). Jerome, *Ep. 22, 39 (CSEL 54, 206* Hilberg). Macarius, *Homiliae 26 (PG 34, 684 B). Ibid. (PG 34,*

469 B). S. Arsenius, *Doctrina et exhortatio (PG 66, 1617* A).

[38] *Passio SS. Perpetuae et Felicitatis 18, 3 (42* van Beek).
Tertullian, *De baptismo 16 (CSEL 20.215, 14-16* Reifferscheid-
Wissowa). *De pudicitia 22 (CSEL 20.272, 24* Reifferscheid-
Wissowa). Melito of Sardis. *Fragmenta (Corp. apol. 9.418*
Otto). Justin, *Dialogus cum Tryphone 46, 7 (1, 212*
Archambault).

[39] *De ecclesiastica hierarchia 6, 3 (PG 3, 533* A-B).

[40] Cf. Malone, *The Monk and the Martyr 6* (Catholic
University Press, Washington, D. C., 1950) p. 121, n. 32. [164]

There are several texts, passed down to us from the fourth century
A.D., which show how the sufferings of the martyrs were assimilated
to those of the monks. The *Vita Pachomii*, written by a Greek monk,
states the following:

> For those of the Gentiles who believed in Christ, *considering the
> sufferings of the martyrs, and their sincere desire for confessing
> in Christ,* also began through the grace of the Lord to follow the
> life and manner of living of the saints, and to be of this institution
> (i.e., the monastic institute) so that this saying of the Apostle may
> be applied to them: "They wandered about in sheepskins, in
> goatskins, being in want, distressed, afflicted, of whom the world
> was not worthy, wandering in deserts and mountains, in dens and
> caves of the earth . . ." For having put away all worldly affairs,
> while still dwelling in the body, they have imitated the sanctity of
> the angels, through which, scaling the lofty heights of virtues, they
> have distinguished themselves beyond the admiration of mortals,
> so that they were absolutely in no way inferior to the ancient
> Fathers; *also equaling the merits of those who for the name of
> Christ Jesus the Lord, have striven unto blood,* destroying the
> attacks of invisible enemies, of whom the Apostle says: "For our
> wrestling is not against flesh and blood, but against principalities
> and powers, against the rulers of the world of this darkness,
> against the spirits of wickedness in high places."[165]

In the *Liber de Libertate Mentis,* written towards the end of the
fourth century, we read this illuminating explanation:

> The martyrs, as it were, after encountering torments and evincing
> patient endurance even unto the endurance of death, thus were
> made worthy to receive crowns of glory, and just as the glory and
> the intimacy they achieved with God was in proportion to the
> multitude and the severity of the labors they underwent, in
> precisely the same manner souls given over to afflictions of

various kinds, be it that they are afflicted externally by men, or proceed from foul thoughts arising from the mind itself, or spring from diseases of the body; if such souls persevere patiently unto death, *they will receive the same crowns as the martyrs and acquire the same intimacy.* For the martyrdom of afflictions which the former suffered at the hands of men, these have endured from the evil spirits attacking them; the more afflictions they too had to bear from their adversary, the greater also will be the glory which they shall receive, not only in the world to come from God; but already in this world, will they be vouchsafed the consolations of the good spirit.[166]

Written at approximately the same time, the *Doctrina ad Monachos* tells us that:

The martyrs were often consummated in a battle that lasted for only a moment; but *the monastic institute obtains a martyrdom* by means of a daily struggle. We are struggling not with flesh and blood, but against the principalities and powers, against the spiritual forces of evil, continuing the struggle until the last breath.[167]

And, lastly, in *The Constitutiones Monasticae*, a piece inserted into the works of Basil, we read:

It is becoming first of all for him who enters on [the monastic] life to have a firm, stable, and immovable spirit, and a purpose which the evil spirits cannot assail or change, and to show by his firmness of spirit even unto death the constancy of the martyrs, clinging to the commandments of God and obeying his masters.[168]

Regarding this interpretation of the monk as martyr, let us remember that in "The Martyrdom of Polycarp," the author insisted on the fact that "a martyrdom according to the gospel" is a martyrdom which has not been provoked. Individuals cannot initiate their own martyrdom. It was a firm belief all the way through the first three centuries that martyrdom could only be initiated by God. He is the One who has the sole prerogative to elect and to call somebody for this special function. On the other hand, if monasticism is interpreted as a martyrdom, then evidently, this kind of martyrdom is not only *self-provoked* but *self-inflicted*, as well. Therefore, according to the earliest teaching of the church, such a martyrdom is not "according to the gospel."

Getting to the heart of the matter, however, the most essential element in the teaching of Jesus concerning His "witnesses" was that suffering and death should only come as a consequence of preaching the gospel to hostile peoples. This is the fundamental meaning of Jesus' call to lose our lives for His sake and for the sake of the gospel (Mk. 8:35). By running *from* the world into the desert, the monks were running away precisely from fulfilling Jesus' command to go *into* the world with His gospel and to work for the salvation of the world by being *in* it (while, at the same time, not *of* it). The solitary suffering of the monk in the desert, however heroic this suffering might be, is not the suffering to which the New Testament invites us.

Chapter 14

Martyrdom in the
Protestant Reformation

Developments in the Middle Ages

In the Middle Ages, the saints became a central part of popular religious life. As new saints were continually being added to the established ranks, they were increasingly invested with new mythological dimensions and magical powers, elements that were pagan both in origin and in nature. The saints came to be seen as carriers of blessings and of power from heaven to earth; as such, they were the mediators between heaven and earth. Regarding the role of the saint in medieval society, Robert Kolb writes:

> The saint, on the basis of his or her holiness, was thought to command the power to meet the needs of the people who encountered signs of their own helplessness and impotence at every turn. Peasants and townspeople looked to cunning men, soothsayers, and witches, but above all to the saints, to provide for their physical well-being and for vengeance, love, and reassurance about death. . . . The saints had taken their place near the very heart of the medieval faith.[1]

The most popular medieval collection of stories of such saints was *The Golden Legend*, compiled in the thirteenth century by Jacob

Voragine. Published in Latin as *Legenda Aurea*, it was translated into English, German, French, Dutch, and Italian, and it was printed and re-printed numerous times in each country.[2]

All the sixteenth-century Protestant writers who dealt with the issue of martyrdom took a position against the *Legenda Aurea*. Martin Luther, with his typical bluntness, writes: "In the papacy there is a book containing the legends or accounts of the saints. I hate it intensely, solely for the reason that it tells of revolting forms of worship and silly miracles performed by idle people."[3]

John Foxe attacked it in 1570, writing in the dedication of his own *Book of Martyrs* to Queen Elisabeth that the Catholics offered "feigned fables, lying miracles, false visions . . . and almost no true tale in all their 'lives and festivals.' " Foxe remarked that even the Christians of the first centuries preserved the relics of the martyrs with "admiration, almost superstition," and he demanded that Protestants should have a different kind of admiration for the martyrs' remains.[4]

A return to biblical Christianity by necessity had to repudiate all the pagan developments that had led to the veneration of the saints. Martin Luther defined these practices as "things which are against the service of God, against faith and the chief commandments—such as their running about on pilgrimages, the perverse worship of the saints, the lying saints' legends, the various ways of trusting in works and ceremonies and practicing them."[5] Luther especially condemned the prayers addressed to the saints: "The invocation of the saints is one of these antichristian abuses. It conflicts with the chief article of the faith [justification through faith in the merits of Christ] and blots out the recognition of Christ. It is neither commanded nor suggested in Scripture and has no basis there at all."[6]

Robert Kolb, in his recent book *For All the Saints: Changing Perceptions of Martyrdom and Sainthood in the Lutheran Reformation*, gives us a comprehensive analysis of the process by which the reformers purged the concept of martyrdom and sainthood of its pagan accretions. For our purposes, the introduction to his study summarizes this important process very well:

> The Protestants repudiated this dehistoricizing of the heroic and the holy associated with these pagan accretions, and they strove to revive the early Christian sense of history. They reclaimed providential power over daily human life for God alone, and they insisted that mediation with Him is provided by Jesus Christ alone. This meant that holy people could no longer function as

intercessors or workers of magic.[7]

Kolb's conclusion also provides us with a felicitous elucidation:

Sixteen-century Lutheranism, like every other Protestant movement, had to deal with the medieval beliefs and practices surrounding the veneration of the saints. Luther and his followers attacked that veneration on the basis of their belief in the providence of God and in the sufficiency of Christ's mediating work on behalf of sinners. The Lutheran Reformation turned all believers into saints and emphasized that saints serve God by hearing and proclaiming his Word and by carrying out their divinely-assigned callings in daily life, within their households, their political communities, and their churches.

The focus on God's providence, Christ's intercession, and the believers' callings in daily life came to be common among Calvinists, Puritans, and Lutherans alike. On the basis of these doctrinal foundations, all three Protestant confessions criticized the medieval veneration of the saints and sought to replace the old reliance upon the saints with new conceptual frameworks for faith and discipleship. Each confession used a variety of polemical and pedagogical tools to accomplish this, among them the martyrology.[8]

The essence of the Reformation was Martin Luther's understanding that the forgiveness of sins does not come by means of good works and acts of penance but by the atoning sacrifice of Christ alone, by grace alone, and by faith alone. The idea that the saints can forgive sins because of their own death as martyrs was evidently destroying the uniqueness and all-sufficiency of the death of Christ for the redemption of the world. Exactly for this reason, the Protestant Reformation completely rejected all the beliefs and practices related to the saints and their intercessory prayers on our behalf.

However, we should remember that all these repudiated beliefs and practices had arisen as a result of the first three centuries' Christian teaching about martyrdom. Was it possible to jettison all the dogmas about the saints, and yet preserve a biblical view of martyrdom? The Protestants necessarily asked this question since they faced martyrdom themselves, right from the start. Hence, they needed a healthy, positive theology of martyrdom, avoiding all the nonbiblical augmentations of the third and fourth centuries and thereafter. Did the reformers succeed in formulating such a teaching? Did they develop a coherent and comprehensive Protestant theology of martyrdom?

In order to discover the answers to these questions, we shall now turn to an examination of the main sources of the Protestant Reformation, in order to glean the relevant concepts that are crucial for our investigation.

Martin Luther

When Martin Luther nailed his ninety-five theses to the door of the Wittenberg Cathedral on 31 October 1517, he was certainly aware that it might not be long before the Pope's men would nail him to the stake and burn him alive for his stand against the papal indulgences. Practically speaking, from that moment onward, for the rest of his life, Luther was a candidate for martyrdom. Consequently, he meditated a great deal on the subject of martyrdom, writing prolifically and especially preaching about it.

Shortly after 1520, two Protestant Christians were martyred in Holland. Luther was very moved by this event, and it prompted him to write an emotional letter to the brethren in Holland, in which he expressed his thoughts and feelings about this historic moment. In the letter, he exclaims: "God be praised and blessed forever that we who have hitherto canonized and worshipped so many false saints have lived to see and hear true saints and real martyrs!"[9]

For Luther, the fact that Protestantism had begun giving martyrs was a sign that the life of God was present in this movement and that it was an authentic expression of the kingdom of God: "Let us, moreover, thank Him for the great signs and wonders He has begun to do among us. By these martyrdoms He has provided us with fresh and new examples of His own life. Now it is time that the kingdom of God shall be not in word but in power (1 Cor. 4:20)."[10]

Luther's letter conveys not only his very real joy that martyrdom had appeared in Protestantism but also his envy that believers in another country had been given the honor of martyrdom before those in Germany could have had this privilege. "We in Upper Germany have to date not been worthy of becoming so precious and worthy an offering to Christ, though many of our members have not been, and still are not, without persecution."[11]

Luther envied the believers in Holland for two reasons. First, the fact that some of their brethren had been martyred showed that the church in Holland had reached a Christian maturity that had made them worthy of the high calling of martyrdom. Second, Luther was envious of the great honor these martyrs now enjoyed in heaven:

> And now you have grown so strong and full of fruit that you confirmed and watered the cause with your own blood. For among you those two precious jewels of Christ, Henry and John at Brussels, have held their life of no account, so that Christ with His Word might be praised. Oh, how miserably were those two souls executed! But how gloriously and with eternal joy will they return with Christ and pronounce a just judgment on those by whom they were now unjustly condemned! Ah, what a trifling matter it is for those to be dishonored and killed by the world who know that their blood is precious and their death dear in the eyes of God, as the Psalms say (9:13; 116:15)! What is the world compared with God? With what joy and delight have all the angels of heaven looked at these two souls! How glad they were to have the fire help them from this sinful life to eternity, from this ignominy to glory everlasting![12]

On many occasions, Luther expressed the desire to lay down his own life for the truth of the gospel. Thus, in 1520, commenting on the fact that John Huss had been burned at the stake for his articles of faith, Luther exclaimed: "Ah, would to God I, too, were worthy most disgracefully to be burned, torn to pieces, and exiled because of articles such as these . . . and that their defense would cost me a thousand necks! They would all have to suffer."[13] At another time, in 1539, Luther declared: "I would be honored by death ten times, nay, a hundred times, if God considered me worthy of suffering for the sake of His Word."[14]

Luther understood the reality that Christians are continually and deeply involved in the conflict between God and Satan. The fact that the world hates them is nothing other than a sign that they are genuine disciples of Christ. Baptism is, therefore, not only the beginning of the Christian life, but also its primary symbol. The whole Christian life is a constant dying and being raised with Christ; it is the union with Christ in the battle against the devil. Just as Christ has conquered by the cross, so the Christian is called to conquer by suffering. Hence, in martyrdom, the Christian becomes like Christ. Following Christ's example, the believer puts off the self, taking on the form of a servant. He gives up the pride, glory, and honor of the world, accepting to enter the sufferings of Christ. In this way, the disciple becomes like his Master.

According to Luther's ecclesiology, the true church is a church of martyrs. The new mankind that Christ aims to create is a suffering church. A true church will follow Him wherever He goes, especially into suffering and martyrdom. In his book, *Of the Councils of the Church*, written in 1539, Luther lists the seven marks of a genuine and authentic church. The seventh mark is "the holy possession of the sacred cross."[15]

Furthermore, the battle between God and the devil is fought in the children of God. The devil does not attack God directly. He assails His children here on earth. For this reason, when Christians are being attacked, they must receive the attack as a confirmation of their status as children of God and must be joyful because God is in them; *He* is assaulted in them. *God suffers* in His children, and *He* certainly conquers in and through them:

> Observe this for your comfort: here these enemies are never called our enemies, or those of Christendom, but enemies of the Lord Christ. "Thine enemies," he says, although they really attack Christendom and Christians must suffer and be plagued by them, as it actually happens. For Christ, who sits above at the right hand of the Father, cannot be attacked; they cannot hurt one hair on His head, much less drag Him down from His throne. Still they are properly called His enemies, not ours. For the world and the devil do not attack and plague us because of secular matters or because we have merited or caused it. The only reason for it is that we believe this Lord and confess His Word. Otherwise they would be in agreement with us, and we would be at peace with them. For this reason He must deal with them as enemies who attack His Person. Everything that happens to the individual Christian, whether it comes from the devil or from the world—such as the terrors of sin, anxiety and grief of the heart, torture, or death—He regards as though it happened to Him. Thus He also says through the prophet Zechariah (Zech. 2:8): "He who touches you touches the apple of My eye." And in Matt. 25:40 we read: "As you did it to one of the least of these My brethren, you did it to Me." And to Paul, while he traveled from Damascus in order to bind Christians and hand them over to the tribunal, Christ speaks from heaven (Acts 9:4): "Saul, Saul, why do you persecute Me?" Again (Acts 9:5): "I am Jesus, whom you are persecuting."[16]

As a man who strongly believed in the sovereignty of God, Luther clearly saw how God uses even His enemies for the fulfillment of His own plans. Thus the persecutions and the martyrdoms are simply the various means by which the interests of God and the interests of the children of God are promoted:

It is ever characteristic of God's mastership most successfully to carry out His will through the instrumentality of His enemies. By their very raging to exterminate the Word and the people of God they exterminate themselves and must only further the cause of God's Word and His people. Therefore for the sake of the faith and the Word of God, it is a very good, advantageous, and wholesome thing to have enemies and persecutors. Incalculable consolation and benefits are derived from them.[17]

Persecution leads to the propagation of the gospel, while at the same time, it purifies and perfects the Christians:

To this day it happens that when tyrants rage against the Gospel, they do no more than blow into the ashes. Then the fire becomes greater, and the ashes fly into their eyes. This is the success which their tyranny is to meet. When they shed innocent blood, this blood of the Christians is to act as a fertilizer on the field, making it rich and productive. For through persecution Christendom grows; conversely, Christians become lazy and lax when conditions are peaceful and quiet.[18]

Although all the devils, the world, our neighbors, and our own people are our enemies, revile and slander us, pound and plague us, we should consider this nothing but a shovelful of manure dumped around the vine to fertilize it well, or as a cutting away of useless, wild branches, or as a taking away of a little excess and hindering foliage. Therefore when they think they have done us great harm and have well avenged themselves, they do but teach us more patience and humility and stronger faith in Christ.[19]

In addition to all the great things that persecution achieves here on earth, persecution brings great rewards in heaven:

For whatever your injury and loss of temporal possessions may be, they are, in these circumstances, sacrifices offered to Christ Himself. They have turned into something very holy, into heavenly jewels which grace and beautify Christ Himself. One penny has become of more value than ten thousand gulden. Oh, how well your possessions are invested, because you invested them in the Lord Himself![20]

Having such a high view of the role of suffering and martyrdom, it is no surprise that Luther arrived at the following conclusion: "We should not fear harsh treatment (*Gewalt*), but prosperity and good days we should fear. These may harm us more than fear and persecution."[21]

John Foxe's *Book of Martyrs*

In England, the Protestant Reformation began during the reign of Henry VIII, and it was later deepened and extended under the rule of Edward VI. After the premature death of Edward, the throne of England went to the next Tudor in line, the Roman Catholic Mary. She immediately proceeded to return the country to Catholicism, bringing it back under the authority of the Pope. The leaders of the English Reformation, Bishops Cranmer, Ridley, and Latimer were immediately arrested and cruelly tortured in order to force them to recant their new faith and to return to Catholicism. Eventually they were burned at the stake in Oxford. Many other bishops, pastors, and preachers, as well as numerous lay men and women, were arrested, tortured, and martyred. In the five years of Queen Mary's bloody reign, approximately 275 men and women were burned at the stake or beheaded. Subsequent to Mary's death, her half-sister Elisabeth took the throne in 1559, and restored the English Reformation essentially to what it had been under Edward VI.

Just as the martyrs of the first three centuries found a chronicler in Eusebius of Caesarea, the martyrs of England discovered their chronicler in John Foxe. Educated at the University of Oxford, he was preoccupied by the events of his time and tried hard to understand them in light of the meaning of the whole history of mankind. During the time of persecution under Queen Mary, Foxe took refuge, together with many others, on the continent of Europe. He lived for a time in Strasbourg, then in Frankfurt, and finally in Basel. In the meantime, he was busy collecting information about the people who had been martyred. Eventually he published his great work entitled *Acts and Monuments*, better known as *Foxe's Book of Martyrs*. The book immediately enjoyed an extraordinary success in England. The English authorities gave the order that this book should be placed near the Bible in every cathedral and church, as well as in other public places, so that everyone could have access to it. A century later, only *The Pilgrim's Progress*, authored by John Bunyan, would experience the same kind of popularity.

John Foxe's influential work begins with the words of Jesus addressed to Peter: "You are Peter, and upon this rock I will build My church; and the gates of Hades shall not overpower it" (Matt. 16:18). Then, Foxe highlights three things that were revealed in this declaration of the Lord:

First, that Christ will have a church in this world. Secondly, that the same church should mightily be impugned, not only by the world, but also by the uttermost strength and powers of all hell. And, thirdly, that the same church, notwithstanding the uttermost of the devil and all his malice, should continue.[22]

All history thereafter, said Foxe, has been a demonstration of the truth of Jesus' statement. Therefore, Foxe wrote his history in order to show "the wonderful works of God in His church," so that the readers might draw from it lessons for their own lives.

Foxe did not limit himself to simply presenting the accounts of the martyrs in England during the reign of Queen Mary; he also tried to present a comprehensive history of the martyrs from the apostles onwards, using the *Ecclesiastical History* of Eusebius as his source for the first three centuries. Then, for his culminating conclusion, he related the stories of the martyrs of his own day who had felt convicted to return to the Holy Scriptures, turning away from the Roman Catholic superstitions.

Foxe shared Eusebius' philosophy of history, a philosophy that had also been developed by Augustine in his *City of God*. Their view was that human history is nothing other than the story of the conflict between the world and the kingdom of Christ, the world consisting "of all such as be without or against Christ," and the kingdom of Christ consisting "of all which belong to the faith of Christ, and these take His part in this world against the world."[23]

For the Protestant Christians under Queen Mary, the situation was complicated by the fact that their oppressors were people who also called themselves Christians, and they persecuted and killed the reformers in the name of the church and of God. The Catholics' reason for persecuting their dissenting brethren was because the latter had repudiated the Roman Catholic Church. However, after having studied the Scriptures thoroughly, and after having discovered in them the revealed truth of God, the reformers had seen how far this Church had strayed away from the Bible. Hence, they decided to come out of the Roman Catholic Church and to start their own churches, based only on the truths they had discovered in the Word of God. For them, there were now two churches: a true church and a false church. The persecuted Christians in the time of Queen Mary perceived themselves to be fighting in a war on three levels; Foxe tells us that the first level was between Christ and the Antichrist, the second between the church and the world, and the third between the true church and the false church.

If we understand this general picture, then we can see that Foxe's work is not a collection of unrelated stories about a series of cruel persecutions that had randomly taken place in different parts of the world. On the contrary, his book is a coherent whole, presenting us with an image of a continuing spiritual war in which every new episode is but a new phase of the same phenomenon.

The main challenge confronting the Protestant believers in the sixteenth century was in determining the true Christian faith and in proving this to the Church that they had just left. As we have already remarked, central to the persecution and the martyrdoms of this time was the reformers' belief that in the Holy Scriptures, they had found the revealed truth of God; having found this truth, they were now called to confess this truth and to seal their testimonies with their own lives. The Truth Himself had chosen them for precisely this purpose and task; and the very fact that they had been chosen for persecution and for martyrdom was a confirmation to them that they were among the "elect." This certainty gave them the power to endure the tortures that otherwise would have been beyond all human powers of endurance. Some of the testimonies of those who were martyred under Bloody Mary will illustrate this point.

Walter Mill, an eighty-two year old preacher from Edinburgh, spoke these words from the stake upon which he was to burn:

> The cause why I suffer this day is not for any crime, (though I acknowledge myself a miserable sinner) but only for the defense of the truth as it is in Jesus Christ; and I praise God who hath called me, by His mercy, to seal the truth with my life; which, as I received it from Him, so I willingly and joyfully offer it up to His glory. Therefore, as you would escape eternal death, be no longer seduced by the lies of the seat of Antichrist: but depend solely on Jesus Christ, and His mercy, that you may be delivered from condemnation.[24]

About Bishop Hooker, Foxe writes, "The place of his martyrdom being fixed at Gloucester, he rejoiced very much, lifting up his eyes and hands to heaven, and praising God that he saw it good to send him among the people over whom he was pastor, there to confirm with his death the truth which he had before taught them."[25] And concerning William Hunter we are told that "he yielded up his life for the truth, sealing it with his blood to the praise of God."[26]

Similarly, the martyrs on the European continent who gave up their lives during this same period of time had the identical belief that they had been called by God to fight for the truth and to defend it with their lives. Thus, Foxe presents the Count of Rugenia on the stake speaking to the people who were watching his execution: "I am better pleased at the sentence of death, than if the emperor had given me life; for I find that it pleases God to have His truth defended, not by our swords, but by our blood."[27]

Due to the fact that these people knew that they had been elected by God for a special mission, they looked forward to their day of martyrdom with exuberant joy, as to a glorious celebration. Their extraordinary joy was vividly and poignantly expressed in a letter written by three soon-to-be martyrs from Antwerp, addressing their Protestant brethren:

> Since it is the will of the Almighty that we should suffer for His name, and be persecuted for the sake of His Gospel, we patiently submit, and are joyful upon the occasion; though the flesh may rebel against the spirit, and hearken to the council of the old serpent, yet the truths of the Gospel shall prevent such advice from being taken, and Christ shall bruise the serpent's head. We are not comfortless in confinement, for we have faith; we fear not affliction, for we have hope; and we forgive our enemies, for we have charity. Be not under apprehensions for us, we are happy in confinement through the promises of God, glory in our bonds, and exult in being thought worthy to suffer for the sake of Christ. We desire not to be released, but to be blessed with fortitude; we ask not liberty, but the power of perseverance; and wish for no change in our condition, but that which places a crown of martyrdom upon our heads.[28]

As Foxe relates the martyrdom of Dr. Taylor, we get a glimpse of the exceeding joy of a future martyr, going to the stake as to a holiday feast:

> All the way Dr. Taylor was joyful and merry, as one that accounted himself going to a most pleasant banquet or bridal. He spake many notable things to the sheriff and yeomen of the guard that conducted him, and often moved them to weep, through his much earnest calling upon them to repent, and to amend their evil and wicked living. Oftentimes also he caused them to wonder and rejoice, to see him so constant and steadfast, void of all fear, joyful in heart, and glad to die. When he had prayed, he went to the stake and kissed it."[29]

This sublime act of a martyr kissing the stake upon which he or she would be burned alive was repeated many times; but why did they do this? Simply because they did not see a stake there but the cross upon which Christ their Beloved Lord was crucified, and they considered it a privilege to share literally in His death and resurrection. Thus, we are told that Mrs. Cicely Ormes, upon reaching the place of execution, "laid her hand on the stake, and said, 'Welcome, thou cross of Christ.' Her hand was sooted in doing this, (for it was the same stake at which Miller and Cooper were burnt,) and she at first wiped it; but directly after again welcomed and embraced it as the 'sweet cross of Christ.' "[30] Even more moving was the scene at Coventry, where "Mr. Saunders then slowly moved towards the fire, sank to the earth and prayed; he then rose up, embraced the stake, and frequently said, 'Welcome, thou cross of Christ! Welcome everlasting life!' "[31]

Foxe also presents each of the martyrs as a sacrifice, with the stake as the altar for the sacrifice. We are told of Rawlins White, that "being come to the altar of his sacrifice, in going toward the stake, he fell down upon his knees, and kissed the ground."[32] Anne Askew was another Christian heroine who "being compassed in with flames of fire, as a blessed sacrifice unto God, slept in the Lord."[33]

Frequently representing the martyrs as lambs of sacrifice, Foxe says about Cranmer: "and the lamb about to suffer was torn from his stand to the place of slaughter."[34] About two others, he writes, "They both ended this moral life, July 12, 1555, like two lambs, without any alteration of their countenances, hoping to obtain that prize they had long run for."[35]

Once again, this time in Foxe's England, we find that the heavenly reward, the prize of the course, the crown of victory, and the special position of the martyrs in heaven were among the essential elements of the concept of martyrdom. By keeping their eyes fixed upon the reward, the martyrs received the necessary power during the tortures, and then as they faced the stake, the fear of the fire disappeared from their hearts when they contemplated the glorious hope before them. Foxe relates this about Mr. Cardmaker and Mr. Warne: "Both had passed through the fire to the pleased rest and peace among God's holy saints and martyrs, to enjoy the crown of triumph and victory prepared for the elect soldiers and warriors of Christ Jesus in His pleasant Kingdom, to whom be glory and majesty forever."[36]

Concerning the bliss of another martyr, Foxe writes: "And he now reigneth, I doubt not, as a blessed martyr in the joys of heaven, prepared for the faithful in Christ before the foundations of the world; for whose constancy all Christians are bound to praise God."[37] And concerning yet another, the author reports: "On December 18, 1555, perished this illustrious martyr, reverenced by man, and glorified in heaven!"[38]

Foxe was aware that all of human history is in fact a fierce war, a war between the people of God and the forces of hell let loose against them. God is fighting this war through His elect, through their suffering and sacrifice and death. At the same time, in the course of this war, God is testing His children, and by their endurance and faithfulness in sufferings, they are showing themselves qualified for ruling with Christ in glory. The evil ones are also being tested and proved worthy of damnation. Foxe fittingly concluded his book with a prayer asking that the days of the kingdom of Satan might be shortened and that the coming of the kingdom of Christ upon the earth would take place soon.

It seems appropriate to supplement what John Foxe has said with two statements made by John Bradford in his letters from prison. They are significant because Bradford emphasizes the fact that through suffering, one becomes like Christ in the life to come; thus, Bradford writes, "Now do I begin to be Christ's disciple; now I begin to be fashioned like to my master in suffering, that so I may be in reigning. . . . Then doubtless, the greater the crosses, the greater comforts we shall feel: and, the more sharp and heavy they be, the more like we shall be unto Christ in this life, and so in eternal life."[39]

English writers continued to produce works about martyrdom after Foxe's death. The separatists and then the nonconformists of the second half of the sixteenth century and the seventeenth century were heavily persecuted. They, too, had to face martyrdom and, as a result, wrote about their beliefs and experiences in the midst of persecution. However, even though these great men of God penned wonderful things about suffering and martyrdom, they did not add any new concepts to our theology. Nevertheless, for the sake of their beauty and depth, I will include one statement by John Milton and two by John Bunyan pertaining to our study.

In his essay entitled *"On Reformation in England,"* Milton described the basic achievement of the Reformation in his own inimitable way: "Then was the Sacred BIBLE sought out of the dusty corners where prophane Falsehood and Neglect had throwne it, the . . .

Martyrs, with the unresistible *might of Weaknesse,* shaking the *Powers* of *Darknesse,* and scorning the *fiery rage* of the old *red Dragon.*"[40]

John Bunyan also painted striking portraits of Christians suffering for Christ. The following excerpt was taken from his book entitled *Seasonable Counsel:* "A man when he suffereth for Christ, is set upon an *Hill,* upon a *Stage,* as in a *Theatre,* to play a part for God in the World."[41]

Perhaps the greatest expression of a man's trust in God, even when God seemed absent and brought no comfort or consolation whatsoever, was put into words by Bunyan, when he found himself in this very situation. Bunyan declared, "[If God] doth not come in, I will leap off the Ladder even blindfold into Eternitie, sink or swim, come heaven, come hell; Lord Jesus, if thou wilt catch me, do; if not, I will venture for thy Name."[42]

Chapter 15

The Anabaptists and Martyrdom

In many Swiss cities in the early 1520s, groups of Christians were gathering to search the Scriptures for the true Christian faith. Between A.D. 1523 and 1524, one of these groups near Zurich came to the conclusion that infant baptism was not according to the Bible. They came to see that baptism had to be preceded by personal faith and repentance. Acting upon their new understanding of the Scriptures, a leader of the group baptized himself and then baptized all the others who had made a personal profession of faith. Because these believers were re-baptized, they came to be known as the ana-baptists (re-baptizers).

This most radical form of the Reformation spread quickly from Zurich to many other parts of Europe. The Roman Catholic Church had the same treatment for them as for the other Reformers: the fire and the sword. However, not only the Roman Catholics were against them. Even the other Reformed denominations considered the Anabaptists so dangerous that they also determined to use force to exterminate the latter group as quickly as possible.

The violent reaction against the Anabaptists was due to the ecclesiastical and political consequences of a baptism based on personal choice. As long as infants were baptized, every individual born in a certain area was automatically incorporated into the church of that territory. The city-state, which was the form of government and economic structure in many places at that time, considered religion to be a concern of the state. The government decided the religion of its subjects, and infant baptism was one form of securing the total conformity of all the citizens of that state. If every person asserted his/her right to choose his/her own faith, and concommitantly, the right to be or not to be baptized as he/she chose, then the state would lose all control over the religion of its subjects! The church itself would cease to be a territorial church (parish). Instead, the church would become the voluntary assembly of persons who have chosen that particular faith and have been baptized accordingly.

As a consequence of their belief in a baptism based on personal faith and individual choice, the Anabaptists were the first people in history to plead for the freedom of conscience. They were the first to say that each individual should be free to choose whether he wanted to be a Christian, a Jew, a Moslem, or an atheist. However, such an idea seemed preposterous at that time. It meant taking away from the leader or leaders of the state the right to determine the religion of the land. It was a political threat, considered fatally dangerous by all the heads of state. Hence, the Anabaptists came to be classified as anarchists and anti-state rebels.

For this very reason, all the cruelty of the medieval authorities turned against them with no mercy and no pity. Upon their arrest, the Anabaptists were dreadfully tortured in order to force them to give up their "heresy." If torture did not prevail, they were then beheaded, drowned in lakes or rivers, or burned at the stake. In other places, all the men, women, and children were either butchered or whole communities were forced into exile.

This cruel and deadly persecution against the Anabaptists lasted almost a century and a half, a time in which many thousands of them gave their lives for their faith and many others endured numerous other forms of unspeakable suffering. Due to the fact that their persecution lasted for an unusually long period of time, the Anabaptists had ample time to think about their suffering and martyrdom, constantly searching the Scriptures for God's explanation and rationale for them. Thus, they were able to develop their own theology of suffering and martyrdom.

Before we go straight to their writings on these issues, we should also be aware of the fact that the various groups of Anabaptists throughout Europe tended to be referred to by different names; specifically, they were most often named after their founder in each particular country. For example, in Germany, the Anabaptist leader was Hutter, and so they were called Hutterites. In Holland, they were named Mennonites, after Menno Simons. Most of their descendants live today in the United States and Canada.

The starting point for the Anabaptist faith was a personal encounter with Jesus Christ and a personal union with Him expressed publicly in the act of baptism. The Anabaptists expected to see this personal union with Christ demonstrated in a genuine, visible transformation of that person's life. They demanded an external manifestation of the internal experience. An individual's repentance of a past way of life had to be proven by a radical change in behavior. One's entire life had to be brought, sternly and uncompromisingly, under the Lordship of Christ and then one's entire life had to be lived in obedience to Christ. Not surprisingly, the word "obedience" was a key word in the theology of the Anabaptists. The other key word was "following"; the Christian was called to follow Jesus, that is, to live as Jesus had lived on the earth and to obey the commandments of Jesus. The Anabaptists were often heard declaring that "nobody can truly know Christ but if he follows Him in life."

According to the Anabaptist teaching, following Jesus, or being His disciple, means imitating Him in every area, especially in the area of suffering—in the bearing of the cross. Jesus Himself was perceived as a martyr and as the Head of all Christian martyrs. Here is how Thielemann J. van Braght presented Him:

> To Jesus Christ, the Son of God, we have accorded the first place among the martyrs of the new covenant; not in the order of time, for herein John was before, and preceded with his death; but on account of the worthiness of the person, because He is the head of all the holy martyrs, through whom they all must be saved.[1]

Menno Simons also described Jesus in this way: "The eternal Glory was dishonored, eternal Righteousness was persecuted, eternal Truth blasphemed, . . . eternal Life was made to suffer a shameful death."[2]

The martyrdom of the Son of God was a victory of God in apparent weakness, because the evil one was defeated exactly by this supreme manifestation of God's power. Accepting death, the Son of God defeated death and thus procured the salvation of the world. But the fact that Jesus suffered for the salvation of the world does not mean that all suffering has ended, and that no one has to suffer anymore. On the contrary, the fight is not yet over, the evil forces have not yet been eternally conquered, and Christ still has to suffer through His disciples. This is how Conrad Grebel, one of the founders of the first Anabaptist group in Zurich, Switzerland, expressed this fundamental truth in 1524:

> True Christian believers are sheep among wolves, sheep for the slaughter. They must be baptized in anguish and affliction, tribulation, persecution, suffering and death. They must be tried with fire. . . . And if you must suffer for it, you know well that it cannot be otherwise. Christ must suffer still more in his members.[3]

The Anabaptists saw their suffering and self-sacrifice first of all as a participation in the sufferings of Christ and a fellowship with Christ in the work of His cross; the sacrifice of the disciple is a co-sacrifice for the triumph of the truth. For the Anabaptists the purpose of salvation is the transformation of the saved person into the image of Christ. However, this transformation is possible only through the suffering of Christ in the believer. Suffering purifies the believer and transforms him into the image of Christ, bringing him closer to God in a special way.

Besides the fact that suffering is a cleansing and a means of transformation for believers, suffering is also the test and the proof that they are indeed genuine believers. The following excerpt is the testimony of an Anabaptist believer who had been savagely tortured for his faith and was sentenced to death; from prison, Jan Van Kuyck writes to his little daughter:

> Yes, I have joy in my heart, that the Lord has counted me, poor man, worthy to suffer so much reproach, and contempt, and so many threats and stripes. Herewith the Lord proves me, even as He proved His dearest chosen ones, as to whether I fear Him, sincerely, trust Him in the greatest distress and love Him from the heart. My heart leaped up in my body, as it seems to me, for joy, because we have such a good dear God. I thought that I loved Him, but now that my skin is touched, He proves this best Himself. Job 2:4, 5. But, my chosen, be not dismayed on this account; this vile flesh has merited yet much more, but the Lord chastens us according to His mercy. Thus my faith is tried as gold in the furnace; now all the glorious promises of the Lord belong to me; henceforth there is laid up for me the crown of eternal life; yea, our King, Christ Jesus, will honor me Himself. Luke 12:37. Oh, alas! oh this I know myself that I am unworthy; but our Lord has obtained it from His heavenly Father, that He may do this to us, that our joy may be full, and that we should console ourselves with

His promises in our tribulation.[4]

Through experiences such as this one, the Anabaptists learned that an "untested faith" is not a genuine faith. Just as gold has to be tested in the fire, so faith has to be tested in suffering. One of the Anabaptists' favorite texts was 1 Peter 1:7; however, they were also fond of Ecclesiasticus 2:5: "For in fire gold is tested, and those God favors, in the crucible of humiliation."

Significantly, baptism and the Lord's Supper were interpreted as symbols of suffering and were taught in such a way that they became acts of preparation for suffering. The use of baptism as a symbol of suffering was inspired from the fact that Jesus Himself used baptism in the same manner when He stated: "I have a baptism to undergo, and how distressed I am until it is accomplished" (Lk. 12:50). On another occasion, Jesus used both "baptism" and "the cup" as symbols of His death, asking two of His disciples: "Are you able to drink the cup that I drink and to be baptized with the baptism with which I am baptized?" (Mk. 10:38).

Anna of Rotterdam, on the morning of 24 January 1539, a few hours before she went to die "for the name and the testimony of Jesus," wrote a testament addressed to her son; in her testament, she made use of this likeness between martyrdom and baptism that she had learned from Jesus:

> My son, hear the instruction of your mother; open your ears to hear the words of my mouth. Prov. 1:8. Behold, I go today the way of the prophets, apostles and martyrs, and drink of the cup of which they all have drank. Matt. 20:23. I go, I say, the way which Christ Jesus, the eternal Word of the Father, full of grace and truth, the Shepherd of the sheep, who is the Life, Himself went, and who went this way, and not another, and who had to drink of this cup, even as He said: "I have a cup to drink of, and a baptism to be baptized with; and how am I straitened till it be accomplished!" Having passed through, He calls His sheep, and His sheep hear His voice, and follow Him whithersoever He goes; for this is the way to the true fountain, John 10:27; 4:14. This way was traveled by the royal priests who came from the rising of the sun, as we read in Revelation, and entered into the ages of eternity, and had to drink of this cup. 1 Peter 2:9.[5]

For the Anabaptists, baptism was not so much a symbol of a past experience as a covenant, a pledge made with one's whole being that one will follow Him wherever He goes. Baptism was understood as an oath of discipleship, similar to a monastic oath, and as a seal that indicates a new life.[6] In this sense, Pilgram Marpeck writes that "baptism is the sealing of the new life," and Hans Hut says that "baptism is a sign, a covenant, a parable, and a reminder of the consent, bringing to mind what such a person has to expect through right baptism (namely suffering)."[7]

In Anabaptist theology, it was very strongly emphasized that baptism stood at the beginning of a road whose end was martyrdom. This was resolutely stated by Balthasar Hubmaier, who took the example of Jesus and showed that each believer was called to imitate Jesus and to follow Him on the same road; most certainly, if one had been baptized and was now actively witnessing to the truth, "tribulation, temptation, persecution, and the cross will follow and all the trials such that man has no comfort and support whatsoever but the Word of God as it happened to Christ after his baptism (Mt. 3)."[8]

Similarly, in *The Martyrs' Mirror*, we read that "Prosperus, in his Epigrams, puts the martyrs and the candidates for baptism on an equal footing, when he says: 'Sanctify, baptism will indeed; But the martyr's crown doth all complete.' "[9] The author comments that Prosperus "means to say that those who were then baptized had to expect martyrdom."[10] Conrad Grebel, in a similar vein, wrote to Thomas Muntzer that "true Christian believers are sheep among wolves . . . and must be baptized in anguish and affliction, tribulation, persecution, suffering and death."[11] Huns Hutt also shared this conviction that "baptism always means suffering."[12]

At that time, it was simply a fact of life that whoever accepted to be baptized as an adult had to be ready to be persecuted and killed. This fact in itself created the need for a very serious preparation for baptism. Indeed, preparation for baptism meant preparation for death: for death to the world and death to sin, but at the same time, for almost certain death by torture and fire or sword. As a consequence of this, for the Anabaptists, baptism was loaded with many more and far deeper meanings than it is for believers in the West today. I refer to "the West," because in my own country, adult baptism even today, in the late 1990s, signifies a preparation for ostracism, ridicule, and persecution.

It is significant that the Lord's Supper to them was also a practical lesson in suffering, training the Christians for the suffering that lay ahead of them. Hans Neder describes a celebration of the Lord's Supper in an Anabaptist meeting:

Then we celebrated the Lord's Supper at Augsburg in 1527, the Lord's wine and bread. With the bread the unity among brethren is symbolized. Where there are many small kernels of grain to be combined into one loaf there is need first to grind them and to make them into one flour . . . which can be achieved only through suffering. Just as Christ, our dear Lord, went before us, so too we want to follow him in like manner. And the bread symbolizes the unity of the brotherhood.

Likewise with the wine: many small grapes come together to make the one wine. That happens by means of the press, understood here as suffering. And thus also the wine indicates suffering. Hence, whoever wants to be in brotherly union, has to drink from the cup of the Lord, for this cup symbolizes suffering.[13]

In order to better understand the Anabaptist theology of martyrdom, we must understand the way they interpreted their own world and the way they interpreted history. The Anabaptists returned to the earlier Christian concept of the two worlds or two kingdoms in conflict. One kingdom is this "world," which is governed by "the prince of this world," that is, Satan; this kingdom consists of people separated from Christ, without the life of God. The other is the "kingdom of God," whose citizens are people born from above and united with Christ. The two worlds interpenetrate and coexist, although they have different laws, principles, and goals. These two worlds, the kingdom of darkness and the kingdom of light, are engaged in a life and death war; this war is also a cosmic battle in which every individual born on this earth is a participant, having no choice but to choose a side and fight accordingly. The victory of the kingdom of God is certain, but it cannot be accomplished without the suffering and martyrdom of its members. With this world-view in mind, the Anabaptists recognized that they had a great responsibility in this cosmic and historic war.

I refer to this war as "historic" because the Anabaptists saw all of human history as the history of the war between the kingdom of light and the kingdom of darkness. This image of history as a colossal stage upon which the conflict between the two worlds takes place is reflected in the title T. J. van Braght gave to his record of the history of Anabaptist martyrdom: *The Bloody Theater or Martyrs' Mirror of the Defenseless Christians Who Baptized Only Upon Confession of Faith and Who Suffered and Died for the Testimony of Jesus, Their Savior, From the Time of Christ to the Year A. D. 1660.*

In the introduction to his massive book, van Braght writes:

> Yea, the whole volume of holy Scriptures seems to be nothing else than a book of martyrs, replete with numerous, according to the flesh, sorrowful, but according to the spirit, happy, examples of the holy and steadfast martyrs, whose sufferings, conflicts and triumphs have been recorded in as holy and worthy manner as it is possible to imagine. However, they are variously spoken of, according to the importance of their merits. Some of them suffered and fought much, but not unto blood, nor unto death; their victory and their honor are, therefore, not represented as of the highest degree. Others, however, suffered and fought not only unto blood and death, for the Lord's name, but even to the greatest pain and most bitter death.[14]

This division of the world into two camps in continuous conflict with each other does not contain merely two different types of people or two different nations; even in the church there is this separation between the ones who belong to the darkness and the ones who belong to God. In fact, there have always been two churches, not only at the present time, but from the very beginning of the history of mankind. Van Braght explained it like this:

> As there are two different peoples, two different congregations and churches, the one of God and from heaven, the other of Satan and from the earth; so there is also a different succession and progress belonging to each of them.
>
> We shall first speak of the divine and heavenly church, and then of the last mentioned one.
>
> The divine and heavenly church, which is the separated holy flock and people of God, originated upon earth at the beginning of the world; has existed through all the ages up to the present time; and will continue to the end of the world.[15]

But what is the reason for the conflict between these two kingdoms? What do they fight for? What do they aim to achieve? What is the nature of the victory at the end of this conflict? For the one who fights on the side of the kingdom of God, the answer to all of these questions is found in one word: the Truth.

Soon after its beginning, the world fell pray to the lie. The devil, the prince of this world, "is a liar and the father of lies. . . . [He] does not stand in the truth, because there is no truth in him" (John 8:44). All who have fallen under his power and dominion have him as their father. Therefore, they are under the power and dominion of the lie and of all that is false, illusory, and dark. Christ is the truth (John 14:6), and He came into this world to bear witness to the truth (John

18:37). But in a world that hates the truth and rejects it by all means, in a world that fights the truth through sophisticated arguments as well as through bitter hate and brutal force, the only way in which the truth can penetrate and shine, thereby making a devastating impact upon the lie, is by self-sacrifice. The truth cannot manifest itself as truth any other way but by remaining true to itself even unto death. The truth must express itself, it must witness to itself, and it must proclaim its own content; then it must confirm that it is the truth by dying, by sealing its testimony with blood. Van Braght succinctly conveys this reality with these words:

> Martyrdoms are effectual sermons, which touch the heart, and awaken the slumbering eyes. . . . The plain and pure truth, confirmed by an innocent life, is the means to overcome error and falsehood; they who depart from this to carnal weapons, betray themselves, and disclose their injustice and impotence; for, since they cannot prevail against the truth, they endeavor, by exterminating and crushing the persons, also to exterminate and crush the truth.[16]

From the very beginning, the history of mankind has been a clash between the truth on one side and the lie on the other. Human history in its entirety is a series of battles fought by the true ones, culminating in their martyrdom. The Captain of their faith is Christ, who Himself "had to enter into His glory through much derision, ignominy and suffering, and ultimately through the most shameful death of the cross."[17] These fighters are appropriately called "soldiers under the bloody banner of Christ"; they all march under His banner, since "the cross is also the ensign of those who serve and follow Jesus Christ, the Captain of the faith."[18]

The result of the sufferings and martyrdom of these courageous warriors is that the light of truth shines powerfully through them:

> However, all this [persecution], instead of obscuring the truth, tended only to illuminate and glorify it the more, just as gold when contrasted with copper, the mountain's height with the deep valley, and the light of day with the darkness of night, can be distinguished the more plainly; also the praiseworthy commended, and the contemptible condemned. This was the case at that time, not only with the assailed truth, but also with those who defended it, as shall be related and proven in the sequel.[19]

One element repeated again and again in the testimonies of the Anabaptist martyrs was the fact that they have been called to bear witness to the truth and then to seal this witness with their own lives. Thus Conrad Grebel wrote to his brother-in-law Vadian: "If God permits, I shall testify the truth unto death."[20] And Joss Kindt wrote from prison:

> I have heard that I am to be severely tortured; for they think to obtain from me all the particulars; but I trust the Lord, that He will keep my lips. Hence, pray the Lord for me, that He will succor me, for they thirst for much blood; but they can do no more than the Lord permits them. Therefore I commend myself into the hands of the Lord; and anything you may hear which is not in this letter, regard as lies. In token of the truth, I hope to seal this letter with my blood.[21]

In the last letter he penned before being martyred, Kindt came to the conclusion that verbal arguments were of no use and that only martyrdom would confirm his testimony: "Know, that I am of such good cheer, that it would be impossible for me to describe the joy or gladness I have, and I hope that the seal of this letter will be the putting off of my body."[22]

Another martyr, Hendrick Alewijns, wrote: "It is now done, and I must and will now disengage myself, and prepare to die, as I think, in four days. And, behold, my dear children, I rejoice in this, and am of good cheer in the Lord, and trust not to spare my body for the truth, but to present it in worship as a living sacrifice, holy and acceptable unto God."[23]

Braght himself, commenting on these letters written by martyrs shortly before they went to their death, says: "We find in their writings many devout lessons, edifying teachings and comforting admonitions written in dark prisons, hurriedly and negligently indeed, on account of inconvenience and with poor materials, but sealed with the most glorious mark, their own blood. Then the words have power and weight, when their truth is confirmed and attested by the deed."[24]

For the Anabaptists, as we have just seen, this world was the theater of a war between the kingdom of light and the kingdom of darkness. In this war, the martyr is "the true soldier of God." The concept is the same as in the first centuries of the Christian Church, only the language and the images of warfare have been changed, reflecting life in medieval times. Stauffer explains this change in vocabulary:

> In the place of the "athlete" in the Greek and the Roman "agon" comes now the knight on his charger, and in place of the arena the

tournament or the battlefield. In this sense the Anabaptists speak of "life on earth as an incessant warfare," a "warfare of the Cross," as Menno Simons calls it, which must be carried out to its very end. Martyrdom is, of course, never an affair of weakness but rather of strength. "Only a hero is able to walk the path of martyrdom."[25]

Having gone through such a long period of sufferings and having given so many of their ranks to martyrdom, the Anabaptists were able to observe its impact on both the people of the world and on the members of the church. Menno Simons, in his book entitled *The Cross of the Saints*, a systematization of the Anabaptist teaching on suffering and martyrdom, arrived at this judicious formulation of their effects:

> You see, my worthy brethren, if you conduct yourselves after this manner in your oppression and trials, if you drink with patience the cup of the Lord, give testimony to Christ Jesus and His holy Word in word and deed, if you allow yourselves as meek lambs for the testimony of Christ to be led with perfect constancy to the slaughter, then in you the name of God will be praised and made holy and glorious, the name of the saints will be revealed, the kingdom of heaven extended, the Word of God made known, and your poor weak brethren in the Lord will be strengthened and taught by your courage.[26]

Van Braght describes even more extensively the effects of the martyrs' deaths on both the brethren and the unconverted:

> They were endowed with such strength that even cruel and inhuman torture could not extort from them the names of their fellow brethren so that, filled with divine and brotherly love, they sacrificed their bodies for their fellow believers. The brotherhood in general was thereby so enkindled with zeal and love, that each, despising the earthly and regarding the heavenly, prepared his heart for the sufferings to which his brethren were subjected, and by which he himself was daily threatened. They shunned no danger, in the way of sheltering their fellow believers, visiting them in prison, calling boldly to them in the place of execution, and comforting and strengthening them with words of Scripture. The tyrants found themselves deceived in their design; they thought they could cause these Christians to apostatize; they put them into assurance of their salvation; they supposed they could destroy and extirpate those who opposed them, but, on the contrary, they raised up more opponents; for many of the spectators, at the said spectacle of killing people, who were

harmless and of good name and report, yea, who would rather die
than do ought by which they supposed to offend God, were thereby
brought to reflection, and thus to investigation, and ultimately to
conversion.[27]

This impact of the martyrs' deaths on the masses was perceived
even by the persecuting officials. In 1529, the Burggraf of Altzey in
the Palatinate came to despair, exclaiming: "What shall I do? The
more I sentence and have executed, the more numerous they
become."[28]

At this point we must ask ourselves: What had made these
Christians so courageous, ready for suffering, and strong under
tortures and in death? The Anabaptists themselves gave us the answer:
they had discovered in the Scriptures the greatness of the rewards in
heaven for those who accept to walk the way of the cross—the way of
suffering and death. The Anabaptists had collected these texts from the
Holy Scriptures, had learned them by heart, and had founded their
entire existence upon them. Thus we read that Hans Hut testified at his
trial in Augsburg on 4 November 1527, that he had "assembled his
views out of the Scripture *for the consolation of those who are
persecuted so that they may perceive the reward that is bound to come
to them in the next world.*"[29]

I have already quoted liberally from T. J. van Braght's book, *The
Martyrs' Mirror*, a huge text that holds an enormous collection of
letters from prison, written by Anabaptists a few days or hours before
they went to their execution. These letters were addressed to the wife
or to the husband, to parents or to son or daughter, or to the church.
What impresses us in these letters is that almost all of them are mainly
composed of quotations from the Bible. Sometimes entire pages are
filled with verse after verse of Scripture speaking about the way we
must follow Jesus to crucifixion and speaking about the rewards
awaiting the ones who follow Him in this way. Van Braght uses a
similar style in his introduction when he tells us that the persecutions
and the tortures:

> were to them sweet pleasure and recreations in the Lord, for they
> knew that this would afterwards be turned into joy to them, since
> it is written; "Blessed are ye that weep now: for ye shall laugh."
> Luke 6:21. Again: "That we must through much tribulation, enter
> into the kingdom of God." Acts 14:22. And, in another place: "If
> we suffer, we shall also reign with him." 2 Tim. 2:12. This caused
> them to say with the apostle: "For our light affliction, which is but

for a moment, worketh for us a far more exceeding and eternal weight of glory." 2 Cor. 4:17. "For I reckon that the sufferings of this present time are not worthy to be compared with the glory which shall be revealed in us." Rom. 8:18. "For whether we live, we live unto the Lord; and whether we die, we die unto the Lord: whether we live therefore or die, we are the Lord's." Rom. 14:8, etc.[30]

And then van Braght tells us that the Anabaptists' meditation on the portions of Scripture that speak of the future things "begat in their souls a longing for the future riches, so that they were enabled to esteem the present ones as of little worth and forget them"; consequently, "their souls were kindled into a flame far more intense than were their bodies through physical fire though these were reduced to ashes."[31]

Heaven was conceived by the Anabaptists as a territory that had to be won by conquest. Persecution, torture, and martyrdom were but the final assault on the citadel. Van Braght writes: "They have taken by force the blessed Fatherland, the Canaan rich with milk, the true promised land which flows with honey.[32] He elaborates on this theme, saying:

> The place which they stormed, was the city filled with all good things, or the new and heavenly Jerusalem, whose foundations are all manner of precious stones, the gates of pearls, the streets of gold, like transparent glass. Her they took by force, to possess forever; . . . The honor which they obtained for their victory, is an everlasting honor; their joy a perpetual joy; the triumphal crowns which were given them, are eternal and heavenly crowns. Here no earthly tombs, pyramids, or obelisks need be mentioned, to honor their dead bodies; since their souls were honored with God, and obtained rest under the altar of God, the place of all the blessed martyrs.[33]

Jan Van Kuyck, from whose letter we quoted earlier, ended his message from prison with these superb and triumphant words: "Adieu, my only daughter; your beloved father shall be crowned a king by our dear Lord. Hence be resigned and be an obedient daughter, and diligently read the Holy Scripture. Live according to them, and we shall meet again and rejoice forever, without end. Amen."[34]

One other way in which the Anabaptists trained and prepared their members for suffering and martyrdom was through hymns. Stauffer expresses the value of the Anabaptist hymns in these words:

> The majority of all the hymns are martyr's hymns, that is they are either composed by the martyrs themselves shortly before their execution, or they deal with the last hours of the martyrs or with the manifold persecutions of the church at large. Also the great witnesses of faith of the past, above all of Jesus Christ himself, are the subject of many hymns. By using these hymnals year for year, the church became strongly aware of being surrounded by a host of great martyrs and of living in an atmosphere of witnessing.[35]

In conclusion, the Anabaptists fostered and nourished in themselves not only an attitude of readiness but also a passion for martyrdom by means of the following practices: by their study of the Bible, seen as a history of martyrdom; by their special preparation for baptism, understood as a preparation for suffering and death; by their celebration of the Lord's Supper, interpreted as a symbol of suffering and martyrdom; and by their singing of hymns written by the martyrs or about them.

With great respect and admiration, we hear van Braght exclaiming, "Ah, how often did I wish to have been a partaker with them!"[36] With these words, van Braght was expressing the fervent desire, which he shared with all of the Anabaptists, to be found worthy of the greatest honor of suffering and dying for Christ.

The events of history following the great Anabaptist persecution are aptly summarized by the Hefleys in the following excerpt:

> By the end of the seventeenth century the violent persecution of the Protestants ended in most of the Western European countries. As things quieted down for them, their interest in martyrdom and its interpretation also faded out. Protestant theologians have not been interested to integrate a theology of martyrdom in their theological system ever since.
>
> In the nineteenth century, as the modern missionary movement started to develop, some missionaries were martyred here or there. Native Christians started to be persecuted and martyred. While there are some books that record such martyrdoms, there is no new theological thinking in them.
>
> The twentieth century exploded in persecutions almost on all continents. Not only individual martyrdoms but mass killings of Christians and enormous labor camps designed for their extermination appeared in many places of this planet. By 1964, the statement was made that this century gave more Christian martyrs than all the other nineteen centuries taken together.[37]

The carnage is still going on. Even now, there are persecutions, unspeakable sufferings, and numerous heroic martyrdoms taking place in many countries around the globe. Yet we still do not have a systematic teaching on the meaning, value, purpose, and final outcome of suffering and martyrdom. Jesus expressly trained His disciples for martyrdom, and that is why He produced such strong disciples. We do not train our new converts for martyrdom, and that is why we produce such weak Christians.

The study represented here was initiated both because I myself had to face martyrdom and because the Christian Church today has a great need for the systematic consideration of this crucial subject. Now that we have seen what the Bible has to say about it and we have also examined what Christians across the centuries have believed and experienced, we are now in a position to draw our own conclusions. Based on this survey of ideas, I shall endeavor to put together what I consider to be a biblical theology of suffering, martyrdom, and rewards in heaven.

Chapter 16

Rewards in Protestant Theology

Side by side with their theology of sainthood, the Roman Catholics developed a theology of merit and of meritorious works on the basis of which special positions in heaven were said to be given. A few centuries later, when the Protestants developed their theology of salvation by grace alone, they believed that they had to completely exclude the idea of merit and of meritorious works. As they did this, some Protestant theologians argued that they should also exclude the concept of rewards in heaven. They thought that they could not speak of rewards without implying that the rewards had been given as a recompense or payment for the work done and thus as something that had been earned. However, if the notion of rewards is rejected, then one also has to show that in heaven, all the saved will be equal in rank and in glory. This is exactly what these Protestant theologians have tried to do. Typical of this kind of position were the authors Jean Veron, in *The Overthrow of the Justification of Works and the Vain Doctrine of the Merits of Men* (1561) and John Cameron, in *Praelectiones* (1632). According to Emma Disley, Cameron quotes "fifteen arguments in favour of heavenly degrees of glory, each of which he carefully refutes, and twelve arguments against, which he defends, concluding that the elect in heaven are equal in glory."[1]

A theology of rewards in heaven and punishments in hell was perceived by these theologians as a deadly threat to Christian disinterestedness. William Tyndale wrote that with all our works we "may not seek our own profit, neither in this world nor in the world to come"; particularly, we should not seek "an higher place in heaven," because such a presumption would send us "down far beneath the bottom of hell."[2] For Tyndale, the new birth was of such a nature that it determined the person who experienced it to do good works for the sheer love of God, not for the attainment of future rewards. Once the bad tree was changed into a good one, it would make good fruit "naturally, . . . freely, . . . even of his own nature, . . . [and] of his own accord, . . . not for heaven's sake."[3]

The attitude of total rejection toward the concept of rewards, coupled by the desire to eradicate all thought of rewards from the moral life, were radicalized by Kant in his "categorical imperative." In his rigorous view of morality as a "duty," Kant considered the notion of rewards as "an inferior eudaemonism, that defaces the purity of true morality."[4]

Nevertheless, other Protestants theologians have defended the concept of rewards as a proper motivation for good works and for a moral life in general. For example, William Forbes, in *Considerationes modestae et pacisicae controversiarum de Justificatione* (1658), "insisted that Protestants, 'even the more rigid,' had never denied that it is lawful to do good works with a view to eternal wages, and cites in his favour Bucer, Davenant, and the Remonstrants. . . . He adds that it is neither slavish nor mercenary that we should be moved by the same arguments which God uses throughout the Scriptures to move and to persuade."[5]

The Protestant theologians who do admit that there are distinctions and degrees of glory in heaven, attribute them not to the merit of the elect, but to the generosity of God and to His freedom to do whatever He wants with His gifts. Thus, William Tyndale, in 1532, commenting on Matthew 5:12, "your reward is great in heaven," wrote:

> though God, when he promises to bless our works, do bind us to work if we will obtain the blessing or promise, yet must we beware of this pharisaical pestilence, to think that our works did deserve the promises . . . [which] cometh of the pure mercy of God. . . . The promise cometh of the promiser, and not of the deserving of those works, of which God hath no need.[6]

Veron also admits that some special people like the Virgin Mary, the apostles, and the martyrs might have "higher glory" in heaven; but if that were the case, it would be entirely due to the "unsearchable judgments of God": for "if in the lyfe to come any do excell other in glori, it is not by reason of their workes merites in deservinges, but the same doeth altogether come of the mere mercye, grace and goodnesse of God, who doth most liberallye crowne in them hys owne gyftes."[7]

Disley underscores the fact that these theologians shift the debate "from the rewarded to the rewarder," emphasizing "that rewards originate with the giver, rather than the receiver," quoting the words of Tyndale that the rewards are "given freely of the goodness of the giver, and not of the deservings of the receiver."[8]

Another argument advanced by some Protestant theologians is that the rewards given by God are so much greater that the works for which they were given, that the rewards cannot be said to have been merited. Because the rewards are manifoldly and disproportionally greater than the works performed, the rewards can justly be said to be given solely by grace. Here is how John Buckeridge (1628) explained this:

> Brass or copper money may be made current by the King's proclamation, but still it is but brass and copper and wants of the true value of gold and silver; and good works   . . . may go for current by God's promise, and receive a reward out of justice but justice with mercy. For there is *justitia in reddendo,* "justice in giving" the crown of glory according to his promise; but there is *misericordia in promittendo,* "mercy" that triumpheth over justice, "in promising" to give an infinite reward to a finite work, as heaven for a cup of cold water, or bread, or drink, or clothes, and the like, and between the kingdom of heaven and the crown of glory and eternal life which is infinite, and a few crumbs, or drops or rags which are scant so much as finite, there is no equality. *Inter finitum at infinitum nulla est proportio,* "There is no proportion between that which is finite and that which is infinite." So that as much as infinite doeth exceed that which is finite, so much do God's infinite rewards exceed the best finite works of the best man. And the rule of the school in this is true: God punishes *citra condignum,* "less than we deserve"—so there is mercy in God's justice and punishments; and God rewards *ultra meritum,* "beyond our merit or desert," and so eternal life is the grace and free gift of God.[9]

Several seventeenth-century theologians used the concept of the covenant of promise and the concept of inheritance to prove that the rewards given by God do not imply merit. William Perkins wrote that "in this covenant we do not so much offer, or promise any great matter to God, as in a manner only receive: even as the last will and testament of a man is not for the testators, but for the heir's commodity."[10]

Bullinger also made use of the notion of inheritance and argued that the rewards, being already prepared for the children of God, precede the good works, and therefore cannot be earned.[11] The reasoning behind this belief, that the inheritance cannot be earned, is given by Fulke: "In the testimony of St. Paul, the word of 'inheritance' following immediately after the word of 'reward' or 'retribution' excludeth merits: for the inheritance depends on God's free adoption, by which he maketh us his sons, that he may give us that inheritance which we can never deserve."[12]

Another idea worthy of mention is that heavenly rewards follow as a *natural consequence* of good works and of holiness. Protestants have borrowed a phrase to this effect from Bernard de Clairvaux; he said that works are the *"via regni, non causa regnandi."* Downame translates it like this: works are "the way which leadeth to the kingdome, not the cause of our coming unto it."[13]

The concept of reward as the natural consequence of ethical living was expanded by Davenant (1631) in this way: "habitual grace itself is a *disposition,* not a *merit,* as regards future glorification: so the works of grace, wrought by the children of God, are *means,* not *merits; prerequisites,* not *causes,* of the reward received."[14]

Other theologians have made the distinction between justification, that was by faith, and sanctification, that results in rewards in heaven. Here is the formula Hugh Latimer used many times in his preaching:

> We must first hear the word of God and know it; and afterward we must believe the same; then we must wrestle and strive with sin and wickedness, as much as it is possible for us, and so live well and godly, and do all manner of good works which God has commanded us in his holy laws; and then *we shall be rewarded in everlasting life, but not with everlasting life,* for that everlasting life is a gift of God, a free gift given freely unto men through Christ.[15]

Melanchthon also made this distinction when he explained the position of works in Lutheran theology. He even retained the concept of merit by this reasoning:

> We teach that good works are meritorious—not for the forgiveness of sins, grace, or justification (for we obtain these only by faith) but for other physical and spiritual rewards in this life and in that which is to come, as Paul says (1 Cor. 3:8), "Each shall receive his wages according to his labour." *Therefore there will be different*

rewards for different labours. . . . There will be distinctions in the glory of the saints.[16]

Emma Disley observes that "although he used the term 'merit,' Melanchthon insists that eternal life is a gift of God (cf. Rom. 6:23) and quotes Augustine's maxim that 'God crowns his gifts in us' to this effect; he argues that the concept of condign merit is a misinterpretation of the word 'reward'—which thereby does 'violence not only to Scripture but also to the very usage of language.' "[17]

Some time later in the sixteenth century, Richard Hooker interpreted "meriting" as "obtaining," justifying the use of the word in the Wittenberg Confession in this way: "The ancient [Fathers] use *meriting* for *obtaining*, and in that sense they of Wittenberg have it in their Confession: 'We teach that good works commanded of God are necessarily to be done, and that by the free kindness of God they *merit* their certain rewards.' "[18] John Buckeridge also supported the idea that the Fathers of the Church used the word "merit" in the sense of *via obtiendi*, "the way and means of obtaining."[19]

M. Amyraut explained that the kind of life we live here as children of God determines our capacity for receiving that which God wants to give us in heaven. He used the analogy of the vases of unequal sizes that are each filled to capacity by water. One vase cannot complain that she has received less than others, because they have all been filled according to their own volume.[20]

In summary, some of the theologians of the Protestant Reformation rejected the idea of rewards altogether, and taught equal rank and status for all the elect in heaven. The majority, however, admitted that the Bible teaches that there will be rewards in heaven and therefore ranks or degrees of glory in heaven. But these theologians were very careful to exclude the idea that these rewards would be given on the basis of the merit of the one who received them. They found the solution to this problem by attributing the degrees of glory not to the merit of the good works performed but to the great generosity and mercy of God. They also taught that the rewards, that is, the degrees of glory, will result naturally and automatically from the good works.[21]

It is fair to say that Protestant theologians in the twentieth century have not advanced a considerable distance from these positions. On the one hand, we still find some Protestants who cannot accept any concept of rewards, insisting on the equality of all the saved in heaven.[22] On the other hand, the ones who do admit that God rewards the good deeds of His children, still do not offer us a clear picture of what this means in concrete terms. For a summary of two modern formulations of the biblical teaching on rewards, I will limit myself to quoting the conclusion of the articles on μισθός in *The New International Dictionary of New Testament Theology* and *The Theological Dictionary of the New Testament*. In the first place, P. C. Bottger writes:

> According to the witnesses of the Old Testament and the New Testament, the fulfillment of life's meaning is not something that lies within our capacity. It is a gift that comes from outside ourselves. It comes from God himself who, as our judge, pronounces us righteous despite ourselves. All rewards lie in God's gift. This excludes the idea of God having to bestow an equivalent reward for our meritorious action. And yet there is a connection between the anticipated reward and our conduct. But the relationship is not one of direct cause and effect. We see it, when we realize that all goodness comes from God and that the reward is yet one further token of the free grace of God which enabled us to act in the first place. The New Testament statements about rewards are thus opposed to the diametrically opposite ideas that man can deserve salvation and that justification by faith makes unimportant what we do with our lives.[23]

Our second example comes from the concluding ideas in Herbert Preisker's article, from which we may gather that the gift is the kingdom, and that this gift "is so uniquely and incomparably great that it can only be given by God and no man can merit it, so that all reward is simply God's generous love."[24] It is God's initiative to adopt someone in His kingdom and to endow him with His Spirit, while "the incomparable greatness of this gift frees man completely of calculating on rewards from men."[25] Therefore, the incentive for moral action should be "the power of faith, the omnipotence of God, and the possession of the Spirit"; the experience of these blessings should put man in a state in which "there neither can nor should be any thought or talk of reward."[26]

It is evident from these articles that neither author mentions ranks or degrees of glory in heaven, nor do we find a doctrinal formulation of the importance of good works and of their consequences. We are simply shown the great generosity of God, who initiates and achieves His glorious purposes in men and women. This is good, as far as it goes, but it is not the whole biblical picture of God's purposes and methods with His children.

However, I did come across one article by G. De Ru, entitled "The

Conception of Reward in the Teaching of Jesus," whose ideas were very helpful for my thesis.[27] In reaction to Kant and to moral idealism, De Ru remarks that this philosophy "has for centuries distorted Christian preaching and given rise to an unbiblical moral rigidity." He goes on to lucidly explain why:

> Man has always had the desire to be "more moral" than God. This unbiblical hubris, which makes of man an autonomous being who creates his own norms and whose purpose lies in the development of his personality in full creative freedom, means nothing more nor less than the elevation of man to the throne of God. He therefore has no need of a reward or other fulfillment, since he is busy projecting his life into the future as freedom in complete independence.[28]

Further on, De Ru writes these very important comments for our study:

> In sounds ever so disinterested and morally pure, one says that man must love God (or the Highest Good) simply and only for Himself, and not because of a possible reward or any favorable results. Peter's question, "See, we have left everything and followed you. What then shall we have?" (Matt. 19:27) is then far below the mark. It seems in fact inferior and the Christian promises of future blessedness in the Kingdom of Heaven then merely disturb true moral disposition and behavior. However, it might be possible that behind this seeming disinterestedness and self-denial lurks the old lying pride that will not admit man's dependence as a creature, but will have us like God, who has need of no one and possesses life in Himself (Acts 17:25). This proud independence (hubris) is as old as mankind, and has put in an appearance in each successive "modern" philosophy. But it has nothing to do with Christian faith.[29]

The basic idea that we should pick up from De Ru is that we must see Jesus' teaching on rewards in the greater framework of the relationship between God and man, which is a relationship between master and slave, not between employer and hired laborer. As De Ru affirms, the slave is the property of the master, so that:

> his master has the right to make every demand on him and his work (Lk. 17:7-10). He lays an unconditional and unlimited claim on his entire time and capacity. He can entrust his money and goods to him (Matt. 25:14-16), and ask them back (Matt. 18:23-25). The slave has neither freedom nor any say in his master's

> affairs. The house, land and the vineyard are not his, and the
> service to which he is bound is not his to choose or judge. He
> simply has to do as he is told. . . . It is the slave's duty to be
> faithful to the strange and often incomprehensible wishes of his
> lord, his master.[30]

This means that the slaves can never *claim* wages or rewards. After they have done everything their owner has commanded, they can only say: "We are unworthy slaves; we have only done our duty" (Lk. 17:10). The master is in no way *obligated* by the work done by his slaves. However, he is free to "reward" his slaves, and whatever he gives them comes truly as a "reward" and not as "wages." It comes from his *generosity* not from his *obligation*. This is what we mean when we say that the rewards are an act of grace. As De Ru states, in the teaching of Jesus, the reward "can never be intended as a return on the part of God for any action of man's, but is simply a manifestation of his sovereign grace and undeserved kindness."[31]

The other important idea that I want to highlight in De Ru's article regards what he calls "the nature of the reward," and what I previously referred to as "the content of the reward." De Ru believes that the reward is a "closer communion with God." He explains this notion as follows: "If we try to define this communion more precisely, it then appears to be nothing other than the service itself *sub specie aeternitatis*. . . . [The reward] is, in reality, a promotion of the servant: to him is entrusted a more responsible post."[32] He quotes the rabbinical saying that " 'The reward for the fulfillment of one's duty is more duties.' "[33] De Ru continues with the following useful clarification: "Heavenly bliss is not to be regarded as 'blessed idleness,' but as a heavenly 'liturgy' in which the redeemed serve God and the Son as 'angels' or as 'cultic powers.' "[34]

Pointing then to the parable of the talents in Matthew 25:14-30, he states that:

> The "reward" of the first two servants consists in an
> intensification of their communion with their master, in that they
> are given more responsibility. There is no difference in the
> reward; both are told, "You have been faithful over a little, I will
> set you over much; enter into the joy of your master.' "[35]

Of the greatest interest for me, however, is what De Ru adds in a footnote:

> In the parallel at Luke 19:11-27 it is just the same. The difference

in the "reward" found there (ten cities and five cities) indicates no difference in the value that the master attaches to what the two servants have accomplished. It is merely a wise decision of the master who knows the capabilities of his servants and in his goodness gives each what he will be able to manage.[36]

Thus far I have argued that the "capabilities" of the slaves are developed in the process of their faithful fulfillment of the duties given to them by God on earth. Therefore, this inner development of the slaves *is* the true connection between the work and the reward.

De Ru appends this meaningful remark after discussing the heavenly existence of the children of God:

> In God's kingdom there is no uniformity. Among the children of God there will be differences of place and rank, and also in the duties entrusted to them (Matt. 11:11). It is clear from a number of passages that the reward Jesus promises his followers is progress in the heavenly "liturgy" to a higher place, which will mean a complete change from their earthly situation and a closer relationship with God. Progress in heavenly glory seems sometimes to be the obvious result of humiliation on earth. But this consequence is not to be thought merely automatic, since obedience to God, and not the quality of the "human personality," is the most important requirement for the "reward.". . . There is a hidden continuity between "being persecuted for Christ's sake" and "being glorified with him," between "poverty in spirit" and "inheritance in the kingdom."[37]

Again, I differ from the above by believing that obedience to God is what *produces* the quality of the human personality. I also insist that the joyful acceptance of being persecuted for Christ's sake actually *results in* our qualification for being glorified with Him; similarly, a person's poverty in spirit *produces* the inner qualities required for obtaining the inheritance, or for being put in charge over God's possessions.

At this time, it is fitting to say a few words about the much debated parable of the workers in the vineyard (Matt. 20:1-16). This parable of Jesus has been used many times to "prove" that in the end, everybody will receive the same pay, meaning that everybody will be equal in heaven. This conclusion is reached despite the parable's obvious context, which shows that Jesus told this parable specifically to affirm that "many who are first will be last, and many who are last will be first" (19:30; 20:16, NIV).

Let us start by looking at the event that occasioned this parable. The rich young ruler had just walked away in frustration because he had considered it too great a price to sell all his possessions and to give them to the poor in order to be accepted into Jesus' school. Peter then realized that they, the apostles, had done exactly what the young man had refused to do, and so he asked Jesus what *their* gain would be as a result of the price they had accepted to pay. Jesus answered that "at the renewal of all things," the twelve will sit on twelve thrones and will judge the twelve tribes of Israel; He added that "everyone who has left houses or brothers or sisters or father or mother or children or fields for My sake will receive a hundred times as much and will inherit eternal life. But many who are first will be last, and many who are last will be first" (19:29-30, NIV). After having said all this, Jesus narrated the parable of the workers in the vineyard, concluding it with these words, "So the last will be first, and the first will be last" (20:16, NIV).

Jesus was in effect telling Peter that the reward the disciples will receive for their service to God will not be equal pay for equal service; rather, the reward or the payment will be a hundred times greater than the service done. I submit that the real purpose of this parable was to illustrate and to explain this very principle. Jesus wanted Peter to see himself not as the first worker, who had been hired for a previously confirmed wage, but as the one who works in the vineyard, leaving the matter of payment to the generosity and good will of the owner. By means of this parable, Jesus assured Peter that God, the Owner, is not only free to do whatever He pleases with His own goods, but He is also extremely generous and will give enormous riches to the ones who have served Him sacrificially. God will still pay the one who has worked for a fixed price, because He is just. Yet He is not only just; He is free and large-hearted. In the final reckoning, His way of assessing the work of each laborer will result in the fact that the ones who seemed to be first will be last and the ones who seemed to be last will be first.

The first purpose of the parable was to tell us that the sovereign Father can do whatever He wants with His goods; at the same time, He is so generous towards His slaves that His "rewards" will by far exceed what they have accomplished in His service. The other purpose of the parable was to teach us not to view ourselves as hirelings, working for an agreed wage. Let us recall that De Ru described the context of the teaching of the Gospels on rewards as a relationship between a master and his slaves.

However, I now want to show that this master-slave relationship is not the complete picture. The Master of the slaves is also the Father of those slaves. It is characteristic of the Bible to treat children as the slaves of their father. This is why in the twelfth chapter of Luke, Jesus' teaching about treasures in heaven and about slaves being faithful in the things entrusted to them is preceded by the statement, "Do not be afraid, little flock, for your Father has been pleased to give you the kingdom" (Lk. 12:32, NIV). Likewise, the one who will reward you for giving help to the poor, for praying in secret, and for fasting is "your Father" (Matt. 6:4, 6, 18). Only when we combine these two relationships, the master-slave and the father-child, can we understand the actual nature of the rewards spoken about in the Scriptures. The rewards are the positions of responsibility that the Father wants to give to His children at the end of their growing and training process. The rewards are "all His possessions" (Matt. 24:47; Lk. 12:44) or, in the language of the epistles, "the inheritance." The time of their training, in which the children-slaves have to demonstrate their faithfulness and reliability, is not for the purpose of earning the rewards, since the rewards originate in the generosity of the Father and in His desire and determination to see His children become mature partners in the administration of His kingdom. The training process is meant to produce in His children the ability to handle authority and the capacity to administrate wisely, thereby proving them reliable.

With respect to the issue of our motivation, God places before us His goal for our lives and commands us to be motivated by it. All that we do in this life has to be directed toward the achievement of God's purpose for our lives. Saying that we serve God simply out of our love for Him and not for the eternal rewards indicates that we have continually misunderstood God's ways and purposes, and that we have stubbornly refused to obey God. It means that we have tragically missed His target for us.

Chapter 17

General Conclusions: Toward a Modern Protestant Theology of Martyrdom

The Westminster Catechism asks the question: "What is the purpose of man?" The answer given is this: "To glorify God and enjoy Him forever." I believe that while this answer is good, a much more important question needs to be asked: What is *God's* purpose with man? In other words, why did God create man? What is God's final purpose with him and how is that purpose achieved? These are the most important questions that we can ask today.

The Bible gives us a clear answer to the question of why God created mankind. God created man in His own image with the purpose of giving him dominion over all creation. This purpose of God has never been changed or thwarted or abandoned. The fall of man did create a problem, but that problem was solved in the cross of Christ. However, a strange thing has happened in Protestant theology: the redemption of man through the cross of Christ has been made so central that for many, it has become the primary purpose of human history. This is equal to saying that God created man in order to save him. This simple reformulation shows us by just how far our theology has missed the mark.

The central purpose of God in human history has always been to make for Himself a people "conformed to the image of His Son," so that Christ would be "the first-born among many brethren" (Rom.

8:29), ultimately, "bringing many sons to glory" (Heb. 2:10). God's final purpose with these "sons" is to "put [them] in charge of all his possessions" (Matt. 24:47; Lk. 12:44). Throughout the course of earthly history, God has been at work shaping His children, forming their character, preparing them for ruling, and testing their faithfulness and reliability. He does this by giving them tasks and responsibilities, by confronting them with difficulties and challenges, and by testing their allegiance to Himself and their obedience to His rules and commandments. Moreover, God will continue this work until the end of history. The Bible refers to the realization of God's final purpose with man in several ways: at times, it is called obtaining the inheritance; at other times, reigning with Christ or being glorified with Christ; and it is also referred to as having treasures in heaven, or simply, as having rewards in heaven.

One of the basic arguments of this dissertation has been that we must see suffering and martyrdom as an integral part of this ultimate purpose of God with man. More exactly, suffering and martyrdom should be perceived as two of the best means by which God achieves His purposes with man. Both suffering and self-sacrifice in the service of Christ produce the character traits that will bring a child of God to the closest likeness of Christ. This should be *our* goal because a Christlike character is the essential qualification for reigning with Christ.

Another basic affirmation of this dissertation has been that the character which a person develops here on earth will remain a part of that person after death and will become a main issue for investigation at the judgment seat of Christ. The goal toward which we must aim in our earthly life is to develop a character that will be found blameless on that future day. God has to be pleased with what He sees in the configuration or the structure of our character. The works of each one of us will be judged there, but those works will simply reveal the character we developed in our lifetime on earth. In the end, our works and our character will both determine the verdict of the Judge: the place and rank He will assign to us in the kingdom of heaven. In fact, God's decision will reflect whether or not each one of us has fulfilled the goal for which God created man from the beginning.

A third basic thesis of this dissertation has been that man has not been called to *earn* his place and rank in heaven. It is God who has predestined him for a specific place and rank. God has redeemed that individual and has given him the Holy Spirit. It is the Holy Spirit, then, who produces Christlikeness (2 Cor. 3:18) and a godly character (the fruit of the Spirit) in him. God's enabling grace makes one capable to do the good works that God has prepared for him to do. Meanwhile, God, in His goodness and generosity, has determined to give all His possessions to His children. Due to all these divine investments, the possibility of merit is utterly excluded, leaving no reasons whatsoever for man to boast. At the same time, however, all the things that the Holy Spirit is said to be doing in a person are also that person's own responsibility and obligation. In this way, the activity of God and the responsibility of man go hand in hand throughout the entire training process.

Suffering and martyrdom have to be seen as part of God's plan; they are His instruments by which He achieves His purposes in history and by which He will accomplish His final purpose with man. As we look at them from God's standpoint, we are able to see that they act in two directions. In the first place, by means of the suffering and martyrdom of His children, God is working certain things in society and in history. In the second place, by means of the same suffering and self-sacrifice, God is working something in that child, in his inner structure or character. This is a very important differentiation, and we shall now look at suffering and martyrdom under these two headings: suffering and martyrdom as part of God's strategy in the world; and, suffering and martyrdom as God's methods for forming and shaping the character of His children.

Suffering and Martyrdom: God's Strategy in the World

Jesus Christ, as King of kings and Lord of lords, calls people to Himself and demands from them total allegiance to Himself. Nothing of this world, not father or mother, husband or wife, son or daughter, or material goods, ought to stand between Him and His children. Jesus expects them to learn from Him and to become like Him. Then Jesus sends them into the world as His Father sent Him into the world, to spread His message and to be His witnesses. He knows that the world will hate His witnesses and will turn against them with merciless violence. Nonetheless, He expects them to meet that hatred with love, and to face that violence with glad acceptance, following His example by suffering and dying for the lost world. Their suffering and martyrdom are prompted by their allegiance to His own Person and are endured for the purpose of spreading His gospel. Christ's disciples do not seek these things for their own sake, and they do not inflict these on themselves. Their goal is not to suffer and to die; on the contrary, their goal is Christ's Person and Christ's cause in the world, the spreading of His gospel.

Suffering for Christ is not only the suffering of persecution. It begins when one leaves close relatives for the service of Christ. For some, it means selling their possessions and giving them to the poor, which often means giving them for the propagation of the gospel. For others, suffering for Christ may mean agonizing in prayer for the cause of Christ, or agonizing and toiling for the building up of the body of Christ and the perfecting of the saints. Again, to clarify this concept, suffering for Christ is not a self-inflicted suffering. The disciple of Christ seeks to do the will of Christ and to promote the cause of Christ. However, suffering for Christ does mean that the disciple will *voluntarily* involve himself in suffering and in sacrificial living for Christ and His gospel.

Furthermore, a disciple of Christ thinks as a slave of Christ: he is totally at the disposition of the Master. It is the Master who decides what kind of service this particular disciple should perform. The first duty of the disciple is, therefore, to discover the will of his Master and to do it with joy and passion. If and only if the disciple does his duty, can he be certain that his Master is always with him, living in and through him to accomplish His own purposes.

Martyrdom is the function God gives to some of His elect to literally die for the sake of Christ and His gospel. From what the Scriptures intimate, it is apparent that there is a fixed number of God's children who have been predestined by God for this supreme sacrifice. For some, martyrdom might be a quick event, like being shot or beheaded, but for others it could also be preceded by torture. God may have in His plan a long martyrdom of toiling in a labor camp or the misery and pain of a long imprisonment. In such a situation, even if the Christian is released after some time and the actual death occurs at home because of his health having been shattered by the long detention and suffering, I believe that God still reckons his death as a martyrdom. In our more sophisticated age, martyrdom might also take the shape of an imprisonment in a psychiatric hospital—a modern form of torture that is possibly the most cruel form of martyrdom—where one's mental health and even one's personality are utterly ruined by means of drugs and other psychological torture.

God does everything with a purpose. If He chooses to call His children to suffering and self-sacrifice, He must have very important purposes to achieve through them. Hence, it is the duty of the children to obey their Father even if they do not understand the purpose or rationale behind the Father's command. But the Father wants His children to understand Him, because He wants them to develop a mind like His. Therefore, He has revealed His mind, His purposes, and His methods to His children in His written Word and in His Incarnate Word.

God entered into history by sending His Incarnate Son as a suffering slave who would end His own earthly life enduring torture and martyrdom. In this event, God revealed to us that suffering and self-sacrifice are His specific methods for tackling the problems of rebellion, of evil, and of the sin of mankind. Self-sacrifice is the only method consistent with His own nature. For instance, God cannot respond to hate with hate, because if He did, he would borrow not only the method but also the nature of the one who is the originator of hate, the evil one. God can only respond with love, because He *is* love, and by suffering and sacrificing Himself for the ones who hate Him, He expresses the essence of His own nature.

Now, the ones who are born of God have become partakers of the nature of God (2 Peter 1:4). Therefore, the children of God are called to tackle the problems of this world with the same *agape*-love which is the nature of God (1 John 4:4-21). More than this, Christ united Himself with His brethren in a union that is comparable to His union with the Father (John 17:21-26). Christ lives in them and continues His work in the world through them. But He has not changed the strategy He used when He was in the world. His method is still the method of the cross. With this in mind, Christ told His disciples that He would send them into the world just as His Father had sent Him into the world; in other words, He sent them to be in the same position and to conquer by the same method, namely, the method of the cross. For precisely this reason, Jesus asked them to take up their own crosses and to follow His example by going into all the world to preach the gospel (to witness), to serve others, and to die for others. Their crosses represent their voluntary sacrificial involvement in the fulfillment of their Father's purposes with mankind.

Three basic things are achieved by the deaths of the martyrs, and we shall take a closer look at them below:

1. The triumph of God's truth;

2. The defeat of Satan; and,
3. The glory of God.

Martyrdom and the Triumph of God's Truth

The unredeemed world lives in spiritual darkness. The eyes of unbelievers have been darkened by Satan, resulting in their hatred of the light of truth. For people who have lived a long time in darkness, a bright light that suddenly shines upon them produces pain. They cannot stand the light. They hate the light, and they do their best to put it out. Jesus explained the world's reaction to His own coming into the world in these terms (John 3:19-20), and He told His disciples to expect exactly the same kind of treatment.

Speaking in modern terms, each group of people on this planet considers its own religion to be one of its most precious treasures. Thus, telling them that their faith is wrong or untrue becomes an unforgivable offense and insult against them. The attempt to change their religion is perceived as an attack on their "national identity." This is why Christian missionaries are met with hostility and violence in every place to which they carry the gospel. For his part, the missionary must be convinced that the population to which he takes the Word lives in the lie of Satan and is damned to hell as a result of it. If the missionary is not convinced of this, he will not risk his life to kindle the light in their midst.

However, when the ambassador of Christ speaks the truth in love, and meets death with joy, a strange miracle occurs: the eyes of unbelievers are opened, they are enabled to see the truth of God, and this leads them to believe in the gospel. Ever since the centurion's eyes were opened at Calvary, ever since he believed that Jesus was the Son of God *because* he had seen *the manner of His death* (Mk. 15:39), thousands and thousands of Christian martyrdoms over the centuries have produced the same results. Moreover, this was precisely what Tertullian had in mind when he wrote that the blood of the martyrs is the seed out of which new Christians are born. Many, many groups of people on this planet have testified that the darkness which had been over them was dissipated only when a missionary was killed there. However, countless areas and peoples of the world today still experience a darkness that will be vanquished only when enough Christians have given up their lives in martyrdom among them.

Martyrdom and the Defeat of Satan

Jesus saw His own coming into this world as an invasion of the strong man's house in order to spoil his goods (Matt. 12:29). He saw the Prince of this world being cast out at His own death (John 12:31-33), and as a result of the ministry of His own disciples (Lk. 10:17-19). Jesus taught them not to be afraid of the ones who can kill only the body, and He charged them to bravely lose their lives in order to gain the victory (Matt. 10:26-39). Hence, John was simply following the teaching of his Lord when he depicted the casting out of Satan and his defeat through the deaths of the martyrs in Revelation 12:9-11.

Satan has two instruments with which he keeps humans in bondage and slavery. His first instrument is sin. The sins of people are Satan's "certificate of ownership." But this document was nailed to the cross of Calvary and was canceled by the death of Christ (Col. 2:14-15). Satan's second instrument is the fear of dying (Heb. 2:14-15). Again, by His own death, Jesus liberated His own from the fear of death. When the martyrs meet their death without fear, Satan's last instrument is rendered powerless, and he is crushed and defeated.

As the deceiver of the nations, Satan maintains their enslavement by keeping them in the darkness of his deception. When the martyrs cause the truth of God to shine brightly among the nations, those who were formerly in the bondage of darkness respond by turning back to God. The death of the martyrs opens the eyes of unbelievers, and when they see the light, Satan's power over them is gone. We have further proof of this reality in the Book of Revelation, where we see the knowledge of God coming to all the nations as a result of the deaths of the martyrs (Rev. 11:1-19; 14:1-12; 15:2-4). The martyrs are shown to defeat Satan by bringing all the nations to God through their witness and death.

The story of Job shows us another aspect of Satan's defeat by the faithfulness in suffering of God's people. Job's refusal to curse God demonstrated to the whole population of heaven that God had genuine worshippers on the earth, thus proving Satan wrong. The suffering of Job was watched by the hosts of heaven as an extraordinary spectacle. It appears that Paul had the experience of Job in mind when, speaking of the suffering of the apostles, he said that they "have become a spectacle to the world, both to angels and to men" (1 Cor. 4:9).

Writing from prison about his own ministry, Paul told the Ephesians that "the rulers and the authorities in the heavenly places" now have the opportunity of knowing God's "manifold wisdom" as it is being manifested in the church (Eph. 3:10). Paul was talking about the same wisdom of God that he had earlier described in 1 Cor. 1:17-31. This is the wisdom of God which the world considers utter foolishness: that He sent His only Son to die on the cross. However, the manifestation of God's wisdom in this world did not end with Jesus on the cross; it is continued in His children when they obey God's commission to go into the world and to sacrifice themselves for the cause of Christ. As they conquer by dying, God's children demonstrate His wisdom to the whole cosmos. Moreover, by their witness and death, Satan is discredited and defeated.

Martyrdom and the Glory of God

Jesus described the outcome of His crucifixion as both His own glorification and as the glorification of God (John 12:27-32; 13:31-32). Yet death by crucifixion was one of the most shameful and barbaric modes of execution; how could *that* be considered an act glorifying to God? The answer becomes clear when one sees what that act has revealed to the world. In Christ's voluntary suffering for the salvation of mankind, the true nature of God was revealed. His essence was shown to be perfect love, utterly and unconditionally giving itself to others, even enduring pain and death for them. The glory of God shines through the beauty and splendor of self-sacrifice as nowhere else, and most importantly, this glory of God, the glory of His self-sacrificing love, shines out in each martyrdom. For this reason, John referred to the martyrdom of Peter as "the kind of death by which Peter would glorify God" (John 21:19, NIV). It was also the reason why Paul was so determined to glorify Christ by his own dying (Phil. 1:20, NASB).

Martyrdom has the power of revealing the love of God to those in darkness. Herein lies its power to convince and to persuade: people see the love of God in the death of the martyr and are compelled to believe in God's love and sacrifice for them. Paul expressed the same idea in the concept of reflecting the image of Christ or the glory of God to other people through our suffering and our loving self-sacrifice for others (2 Cor. 3:18; 4:1-15). As the knowledge of Christ and the grace of God is spread to more and more people through the sacrifice of the children of God, there is more and more thanksgiving, praise, and glory given to God.

Suffering and Martyrdom: Forming the Character of the One Who Accepts Them

God achieves great things in the world through the one who accepts His way of suffering and self-sacrifice. In the end, however, it turns out that the greatest things are achieved in the sufferer himself. The one who sacrificially accepts to be a blessing for others discovers that, in the final analysis, he is the one who has harvested the greatest blessings.

In all the literature that we have studied, from the Book of Isaiah to the Book of Revelation, from the Books of the Maccabees to *The Martyrs' Mirror*, we have seen the following truth clearly expressed and taught: the ones who suffer and die for their faith will have special rewards and will enjoy special privileges in heaven. As we investigated this issue, we saw that there were two main questions to answer. The first one was this: What is the nature or the content of these rewards? Or, worded in a slightly different way, what are the things that are promised to us as our future rewards in heaven? The second question we then asked was the following: Upon what criteria will the distribution of these rewards be based? The latter is an especially acute question if one seriously believes that God in His sovereignty has destined everything for His children, and that He bestows everything on His children by grace.

I have already indicated, at the beginning of these concluding remarks, that the answers to these questions are found when one understands the final purpose of God with man. We have seen that God created man so that he would ultimately be a partner with His only begotten Son in the ruling of the affairs of the created universe. Now, we have to focus in on a few aspects of this final purpose of God with mankind.

To begin with, God created the man and the woman in His own image. The creation of humanity "in His image" is interpreted here to include both a structural and a relational sense. In the structural sense, man was created as a responsible person, with the capacity to reason, to feel emotion, and to will freely. In the relational sense, God made man with the capacity to enter into relationships; from the beginning, God put the first man in relationship with Himself, with his wife, with the created universe, and later on with other human beings. I used the word *capacity* in both areas because in both, man must learn and grow. While the image of God in man was damaged by the fall of man, it was not destroyed. The basic damage was resolved by Christ's redemption and by the new birth; yet the need to grow into that image or to develop it to full maturity is still there (cf. 2 Cor. 3:18; Eph. 4:22-24; Col. 3:9-10).

A very important aspect of "the image of God" in us is character. A person's character is made up of all the things that a person does "by habit," or that "are his custom to do." They are the things that have been practiced so much that they have became part of the inner structure or makeup of that person. These "habits" come to be recognized as the "way of being" of a certain person. Jesus expressed this concept with His analogy of the "good tree" and the "bad tree." Each tree produces its kind of fruit naturally. Jesus made it very clear that we shall be judged according to what "our tree" produces (Matt. 7:16-20; 12:33-37: Lk. 6:43-45). However, it is very important for us to see that Jesus not only commanded us to *bring forth* good fruit, but He commanded *us* to "*make the tree* good" (Matt. 12:33, italics mine). Jesus also referred to this inner structure as "the heart" of a person (Matt. 15:19-20; Mk. 7:20-23; Lk. 6:45). And again, Jesus made people directly responsible for the inner content of their lives, since it is out of "the heart" that the outer behavior flows (Lk. 11:39-41). Of course, this emphasis on *our* duty to change our own character does not mean that we can do it in our own power, but it does mean that we are responsible for using or not using the resources God has placed at our disposal.

There are three fundamental character traits that God aims to produce in us, and they are the most basic for our growth in Christlikeness. The first and most important is the willingness and the capacity to live under the authority of God. The attitude of submission and obedience to God, manifested by the fervent desire and diligent struggle to do things according to His commandments, is the basic trait that makes one fit to live harmoniously in the kingdom of God. God desires to have children who are free and capable of determining and choosing "the good" themselves, and who, in that freedom, always choose to do what the Sovereign Father and Lord wants them to do. They would never presume that there might be a better way than God's way of doing things. Since they are convinced that God's ways are always perfect and because they have the inner pleasure of doing the will of the Father, they will always fully obey Him and will gladly submit to His commands.

The second most important character trait of a perfected child of God is *agape*-love. This love is the essence of the relationships in the Holy Trinity, in which each Person gives everything to the others and does everything for the others, to the honor and glory of the others. This is the love that produces a servant attitude even to the point of self-sacrifice. It makes service to others and self-sacrifice for others not a grudging obligation but a happy privilege.

The third character trait of a perfected child of God is wisdom. This is the capacity to apply the commandments of the Father and the ways of the Father in the most diverse and complex situations. It leads to combinations like "speaking the truth in love" (Eph. 4:15) and other such Godlike attitudes and actions. Furthermore, a child of God displays wisdom when, possessing the freedom to choose between right and wrong, he always enjoys being totally obedient to the Father.

God did not desire robots that would automatically execute the tasks for which they had been previously programmed. He wanted free persons, capable of fellowship and partnership with Him. But in order for this to happen, free persons need to have their character developed to this end in conditions and situations conducive to such growth. God, in His wisdom, decided that our present life on earth, with all its difficulties and challenges, is the kind of environment necessary for this purpose.

Suffering is a key aspect of the environment designed by God for the formation of His children's character. Christ Himself was made "perfect through suffering" (Heb. 2:10, NIV). We are told that this meant, at least in part, that "He learned obedience from the things which He suffered" (Heb. 5:8, NASB), and that "because He Himself suffered when He was tempted, He is able to help those who are being tempted" (2:18, NIV). The Book of Hebrews, in the twelfth chapter, applies this principle to all the children of God. As His "sons," we are commanded to "endure hardship as discipline" (12:7), since "God disciplines us for our good, that we may share His holiness" (12:10). "Those who have been trained by it," discover on that final day that their suffering has produced in them "a harvest of righteousness and peace" (12:11). Both the Apostles Paul and James develop the idea that trials, afflictions, and temptations "produce" in our character the qualities that will make us fit for our final destiny (Rom. 5:1-5; James 1:2-12).

The suffering of Christ's messengers, when they are violently and brutally treated by the very people they are trying to reach with the truth, is an integral part of this process of Christlike character formation. As God's chosen ones suffer the arrests, tortures, and martyrdoms, special qualities are inscribed deep within their character, bringing them in the closest possible way to Christlikeness. This biblical teaching was well applied by Christians in the second and third centuries in their practice of calling the day when a Christian was martyred, the day of "his perfection." In addition, they recognized that Christians were not to pursue or to seek after these sufferings, inflicting them on themselves; they must pursue only Christ and Christ's ministry in the world. It is the Lord who chooses if and what kind of sufferings and tribulations will come to them.

Alongside God's purpose of *training* His children through suffering and martyrdom stands His equally important purpose of *testing* them. Again, this is a concept that is constantly taught in the Bible, both in the Old and the New Testaments. To summarize what was previously shown in the above study in greater detail, let us review the main points of Jesus' teaching on this subject, bringing in the concepts of δόκιμος and ἀδόκιμος used by Paul, James, and Peter.

On four different occasions, Jesus used the analogy of a king who entrusted his affairs to his slaves, and then went away, leaving them on their own for a long time. When the king came back, he gave rewards to his slaves according to the faithfulness they had demonstrated in the administration of what he had entrusted to them (Matt. 24:45-51; 25:14-30; Lk. 12:35-48; 19:11-27). When He had finished telling them this parable, Jesus gave them His conclusions, as well as His practical applications for this analogy, in the form of another parable: the story of the shrewd steward (Lk. 16:1-13).

1. If one is faithful in the administration of little things, he will be faithful in the administration of big things (Lk. 16:10). Accordingly, the awarding of smaller or greater positions of responsibility in the kingdom of heaven will correspond to the degree of faithfulness demonstrated by the "slave" in the management of the things entrusted to him in this world (Lk. 19:11-27).

2. The riches of this world are not "true" riches: they are merely temporary things. Nonetheless, if one is not faithful in their administration, one will not be given the "true," eternal riches in heaven (Lk. 16:11).

3. The things we have in this world are not ours. We are "slaves,"

and slaves do not have ownership of anything. On the other hand, we are also God's children, and God has destined us for the possession of everything He has: the whole created universe has been designated as our inheritance. There is a catch, however. Although it is God's bountiful generosity to give us everything He has, He will not entrust us with what is our own, if we were not faithful in managing the things of this world, of which we were not owners but simply stewards (Lk. 16:12). At the same time, we are not called to "earn" the inheritance by the things we do in the service of God in this life; rather, we are called to do these "works" in order to prove ourselves reliable and trustworthy.

Therefore, the tasks we were given to do on earth, the trials and sufferings we endure, and the sacrifices we make, are both *training* us, that is, they are producing in us the character or the capability for responsibilities in heaven, and they are *testing* us, that is, they are giving us the possibility to demonstrate our faithfulness to the One who is so generous that He wants to give us all that He has.

At the end of the production line in every factory is the "quality control," the person who has the job of checking each product, making sure that it meets the standards of the maker and that it is fit to be launched on the market. The judgment seat of Christ is where we will face our own "quality control." The verdict, in the words of Jesus, will be either "Well done, good and faithful slave, . . . you are worthy," or "You wicked, lazy slave!" In the words of the Apostle Paul, the verdict will be either "δόκιμος," that is, "tested and approved" as fit for ruling with Christ, or "ἀδόκιμος," that is, "tested and rejected" as unfit for positions of responsibility.

Paul depicted the lamentable situation of a person who has been saved, that is, has been accepted in heaven, but who has no reward there. Although he is in heaven, he cannot be entrusted with any responsibility, because he is not capable of handling the authority to rule. The analogy of the vessels of different sizes is very useful at this point. All the "vessels" in heaven will be filled to the brim. Each one will be filled to its full capacity. For this reason, not one of them can complain that it has not been given enough or that it should have been given more. Most significantly, we have learned from the above investigation that the capacity of each vessel is developed here on earth in the faithful service that each renders to the King.

Additionally, the Bible makes it clear that although a child of God may be submitted to the harshness of life in order to be tested for

reliability, it is God Himself who will provide that child with all the
necessary resources for success. As a result, his final victory does not
provide him with any reasons for boasting; knowing this to be true,
God's child will say with all his being: "All that we have
accomplished you have done for us" (Isaiah 26:12, NIV). The concept
of personal merit cannot have any place in the thinking of a child of
God who has learned that God gives to each one of His children both
the willing and the achieving (Phil. 2:13).

It is very important for Christians living in affluent countries to
understand the test of earthly riches. God wants us to keep for
ourselves and for our family that which we truly need and to invest
everything else in the promotion of His kingdom. The great temptation
is to keep it all for ourselves, and the more we accumulate, the greater
our desire to acquire even more. Our heart becomes tied to our riches,
and they become our "treasure." Sadly, we do not realize that this is
the essence of the test to which we are being submitted: God wants to
see whether we obey Him or we follow our own appetites for more
riches, hoarding them all to ourselves. Meanwhile, we are tragically
unaware that, in this manner, our riches on earth become our poverty
in heaven.

The following question may be asked: How much should we keep
and how much should we give? This very question is part of the test.
God has given us sufficient wisdom to know how much we need, and
He gives us sufficient guidance to know what He expects from us in
each situation. There will be no room for excuses at the judgment seat
of Christ. There will only be the verdict, "good slave" or "bad slave";
we will only hear, "tested and approved" or "tested and rejected." It is
in this light that we have to understand what Jesus taught us about
"the deceitfulness of wealth" (Matt. 13:22, NIV), symbolized by the
thorns that choke the Word so that it never comes to fruition in an
individual's life.

As vital as the test of earthly riches is for our eternal destiny, the
supreme test is nonetheless in the form of suffering and martyrdom for
Christ and His gospel. In these situations of extreme pain and agony,
the endurance, perseverance, and faithfulness of the child of God is
tested to the maximum. It was in Gethsemane and on Calvary that God
tested His Son in the ultimate way, and it was because of His
obedience in those situations that God gave Him the highest position
of honor and glory (Phil. 2:5-11; Heb. 2:9). This is why God has
reserved the greatest honor and glory for those of His children who go

through sufferings, tortures, and martyrdom.

As we can see from the main body of this study and from the conclusions stated above, suffering and martyrdom have an extremely important role in God's strategy in human history. They express the essence of God's nature—His self-sacrificial love—and they point to the method of God's own involvement in the world. Furthermore, suffering and martyrdom play an essential part in God's way of transforming man into His own image.

For untold numbers of Christians passing through terrible sufferings and persecutions in many countries around the world today, the understanding of this biblical teaching may come as a life-changing revelation, revolutionizing their lives. As a consequence, their sufferings will suddenly "make sense." They will not see the trials and afflictions that have come over them as unfortunate calamities, but as the greatest gift and privilege they could ever have received from their Lord. Furthermore, this teaching may revolutionize not only the lives of persecuted Christians but also the lives of Christians living in freedom and affluence. In fact, these rich Christians may be in a greater danger than their brethren suffering trials and tribulations, because the testing of the former may be even more severe; having been given riches and freedom, they must now choose whether they will be Christlike and self-sacrificing or selfish and indulgent.

Jesus Christ is not a Santa Claus with the task of distributing goodies and pampering our feelings. He is the King of kings and Lord of lords who calls all of us to submit to Him and to do our part in carrying out His own program in this world. Of course, His program entails sacrificial living on our part, and when He comes again on that Last Day, He will judge us and assess us according to our obedience to His royal commands. He wants to make us kings just as He is King, but He will only entrust such positions to those who have obeyed Him as He Himself obeyed His Father.

It is possible that if confronted with it, most Christians today will reject this teaching, because it is too demanding. It is much more comfortable to live with a theology that offers only blessings and no demands. But wise people do not ask which theology is the most convenient; instead, they ask which teaching is true or, even better, which one comes from God.

My endeavor has been to capture the mind of God as it has been revealed to us in His inerrant Word and as it was understood by people who were challenged by the harsh realities of persecution, suffering, and martyrdom throughout history. This study has changed my own approach to life, and I pray that it will do the same for many others. However hard this teaching may seem, through it we come to understand that from the start of this difficult and exacting pilgrimage, all the way to its triumphant finish in our heavenly home, it is God who works His own extraordinary purposes in us, and it is He who will always merit all the praise and all the glory.

Notes

Introduction

1. This paper was recently printed in Dr. Beyerhaus's book, *Kingdom of God and Utopian Error* (Wheaton, Ill.: Crossway Books, 1993).

PART ONE: Suffering, Witness, and Martyrdom in the Old Testament

1. All Scripture references hereafter unless otherwise indicated shall be from the New American Standard Bible.

Chapter One: Isaiah

1. Allan A. MacRae, *The Gospel of Isaiah* (Chicago: Moody Press, 1977): 31.
2. J. Muilenberg, *The Book of Isaiah: Chapters 40-66* (New York: The Interpreter's Bible, 1956), 486.
3. Allison A. Trites, *The New Testament Concept of Witness* (Cambridge: Cambridge University Press, 1977), 44.
4. Alec J. Motyer, *The Prophecy of Isaiah: An Introduction & Commentary* (Downers Grove, Ill.: InterVarsity Press, 1993), 476.
5. Claus Westermann, *Isaiah 40-66: A Commentary* (Philadelphia: Westminster Press, 1969), 425.
6. Ibid.
7. Ibid., 426.

Chapter Four: The Intertestamental Literature

1. 1 Macc. 2:29-30, in Jonathan A. Goldstein, trans. and ed., *1 Maccabees* (Garden City, N.Y.: Doubleday, 1976).
2. Assump. of Moses 9:1-7, in H. F. D. Sparks, ed. *The Apocryphal Old Testament* (Oxford: Clarendon Press, 1984). All further citations from the Assump. of Moses are from this translation.
3. 2 Macc. 6:11.
4. 1 Macc. 2:50-61, (Goldstein).

5. 4 Macc. 18:10-19, in Moses Hadas, trans. and ed., *The Third and Fourth Books of Maccabees* (New York: Harper & Bros. Publishers, 1953).

6. Assump. of Moses 9:6-7.

7. 2 Macc. 7:6.

8. For the use of Isaiah by these authors see George W. E. Nickelsburg, *Resurrection, Immortality, and Eternal Life* (Cambridge: Harvard University Press, 1972), 17-33, 40-42, 58-84.

9. E.g., Ascension of Isaiah 2:15-16; 5:1-16, in Sparks, *Apocryphal Old Testament*. All further citations from the Ascension of Isaiah are from this translation.

10. 2 Macc. 7:31-36, in Solomon Zeitlin, ed., *The Second Book of Maccabees*, trans. Sidney Tedesche (New York: Harper & Bros. Publishers, 1954).

11. Ibid., 7:18, (Goldstein).

12. Ibid., 7:32-36, (Goldstein).

13. Wisd. of Sol. 3:4-5, in David Winston, trans. and ed., *The Wisdom of Solomon* (Garden City, N.Y.: Doubleday, 1979). All further citations from the Wisd. of Sol. are from this translation.

14. 4 Macc. 6:12-16, (Hadas).

15. 2 Macc. 7:38, (Goldstein).

16. 4 Macc. 17:20, (Hadas).

17. Ibid., 18:4.

18. X:1.

19. 1 QpHab 9.

20. 1 QS 8.3, et seq.

21. 4 Macc. 1:11, (Hadas).

22. Ibid., 17:21-22.

23. 1 Enoch 47:1, 4; italics mine, in Sparks, *Apocryphal Old Testament*.

24. Ecclus. 2:2-5, in Sparks, *Apocryphal Old Testament*.

25. Wisd. of Sol. 3:5-6.

26. 2 Macc. 7:19, (Zeitlin).

27. 4 Macc. 16:14, (Hadas).

28. Ibid., 9:23.

29. Ibid., 11:20.

30. Ibid., 6:9.

31. Ascension of Isaiah 4:2.

32. Ibid., 5:1.

33. Ibid., 5:10.

34. Ibid., 5:13.

35. Ibid., 5:14.
36. 2 Macc. 7:36-37, (Goldstein).
37. 4 Macc. 16:16, (Hadas).
38. J. S. Pobee, "Persecution and Martyrdom in the Theology of Paul " (Ph.D. diss., University of Cambridge, n.d.), published in *The Journal for the Study of the New Testament* Supplement Series 6 (Sheffield: JSOT Press, The University of Sheffield, 1985).
39. Cf. Nickelsburg, *Resurrection*, 18.
40. 2 Macc. 7:9, (Zeitlin).
41. Ibid., 7:14.
42. Ibid., 7:22-23.
43. Ibid., 7:29.
44. 4 Macc. 7:3, (Hadas).
45. Ibid., 9:4.
46. Ibid., 13:14-17.
47. Assump. of Moses 10:1-10.
48. Jubilees 23:29-31, (Sparks).
49. Testament of Judah 25:1-4, (Sparks).
50. Wisd. of Sol. 2:10.
51. Ibid., 2:16.
52. Ibid., 2:19, 20.
53. Ibid., 2:22.
54. Ibid., 2:20-23.
55. Ibid., 3:1-8.
56. Ibid., 3:13.
57. Ibid., 3:14.
58. Ibid., 3:15.
59. Ibid., 5:4.
60. Ibid., 5:15-16.

Chapter Five: Jesus and Martyrdom

1. R. T. France, *Jesus and the Old Testament* (Downers Grove, Ill: InterVarsity Press, 1971), 110-148.
2. The New International Version has been used for all subsequent quotations from John 17 in this section.
3. H. Strathmann, "μάρτυς," in *The Theological Dictionary of the New Testament,* ed. G. Kittel, trans. and ed. G. W. Bromiley, vol. 4 (Grand Rapids: W. B. Eerdmans, 1979), 509.

Notes to Chapter Five

4. C. E. B. Cranfield, *The Gospel According to Saint Mark* (Cambridge: Cambridge University Press, 1972), 397-398.

5. C. K. Barrett, *The Gospel According to St. John* (London: S. P. C. K., 1955), n.p., quoted in Trites, *New Testament Concept of Witness*, 80.

6. Trites, *New Testament Concept of Witness*, 89.

7. Ibid., 114.

8. T. M. Lindsay, *The Gospel According to St. Mark* (Edinburgh: T. & T. Clark, 1883; reprint, Minneapolis: Augsburg Publishers, 1964), 153 (page citations are to the reprint edition).

9. H. B. Brascomb, *The Gospel of Mark* (New York: Harper & Bros. Publishers, n.d.), on 8:34.

10. D. E. Nineham, *The Gospel of St. Mark* (Baltimore: Penguin Books, 1963), on 8:34.

11. Alan Menzies, *The Earliest Gospel* (London: Macmillan, 1901), 172, on 8:34.

12. Vincent Taylor, *The Gospel According to St. Mark* (London: Macmillan, 1953), on 8:34.

13. C. F. D. Moule, *The Gospel According to Mark* (Cambridge: Cambridge University Press, 1965), on 8:34.

14. A. E. J. Rawlingson, *St. Mark* (London: Methuen, 1925), on 8:34.

15. Plutarch *De Sera* 9.55.4b, quoted in Morna D. Hooker, *The Gospel According to Saint Mark* (Peabody, Mass.: Hendrikson Publishers, 1991), on 8:34.

16. Norval Geldenhuys, *Commentary on the Gospel of Luke* (Grand Rapids: W. B. Eerdmans, 1957), on 9:23.

17. Leon Morris, *Luke* (Grand Rapids: W. B. Eerdmans, 1974), 186.

18. K. S. Wuest, *Mark* (Grand Rapids: W. B. Eerdmans, 1952), on 8:34.

19. H. A. Ironside, *Expository Notes on the Gospel of Matthew* (New York: Loizeaux Bros., 1945), on 16:24.

20. J. W. McGarvey, *Matthew and Mark* (Cincinnati: Chase & Hall, 1876), on Matt. 16:24.

21. Ralph Earle, *The Gospel According to Mark* (Grand Rapids: Zondervan Publishing House, 1957), on 8:34.

22. J. C. Ryle, *Mark* (Wheaton, Ill.: Crossway Books, 1993), on 8:34.

23. W. C. Allen, *A Critical and Exegetical Commentary on the Gospel According to St. Matthew* (New York: Scribner's, 1907), on 10:38 and 16:24.

24. Ibid.

25. R. V. G. Tasker, *The Gospel According to St. Matthew* (Grand Rapids: W. B. Eerdmans, 1961), on 10:38.

26. Cranfield, *Saint Mark*, on 8:34.

27. Alexander Maclaren, *The Gospel of St. Matthew*, vol. 2 (London: Hodder & Stoughton, 1898), on 10:24.

28. William Manson, *The Gospel of Luke* (London: Hodder & Stoughton, 1930), 111, on 9:23.

29. W. R. Bowie, *The Compassionate Christ: Reflections on the Gospel of Luke* (New York: Abingdon Press, 1965), on 9:23.

30. M. F. Sadler, *The Gospel According to Matthew* (London: George Bell, 1897), on 16:24.

31. J. H. Thornwell, *Collected Writings*, vol. 2 (1875; reprint, Edinburgh: Banner of Truth Trust, 1974), 437.

32. Giving to the poor should not be understood simply as providing material help, such as food, clothing, or shelter. In view of Matt. 11:5, "and the poor have the gospel preached to them," we should understand "the poor" to be all those who do not know the gospel. This means that all our giving to "missionaries," that is, to the spreading of the gospel, is equivalent to giving to the poor.

Chapter Six: Suffering and Martyrdom in the Book of Acts

1. Trites, *New Testament Concept of Witness*, 128.

2. Eusebius *Ecclesiastical History*, trans. and ed. Roy J. Deferrari (New York: Fathers of the Church, 1953), 2.23.

3. Ibid.

4. E. Harrison, *Acts: The Expanding Church* (Chicago: Moody Press, 1975), 127.

5. Ibid.

6. Ibid.

7. Ibid.

8. Trites, *New Testament Concept of Witness*, 132.

9. Joseph Parker, *Apostolic Life As Revealed in the Acts of the Apostles*, vol. 1 (London: R. Clarke, 1883), 175.

10. Ibid., 176.

11. Miles W. Smith, *On Whom The Spirit Came: A Study of the Acts of the Apostles* (Philadelphia: Judson Press, 1948), 3.

Chapter Seven: The Teaching of the Apostle Paul

1.   J. S. Pobee, "Persecution and Martyrdom in the Theology of Paul" (Ph.D. diss., University of Cambridge, n.d.), published in *The Journal for the Study of the New Testament*, Supplement Series 6 (Sheffield: JSOT Press, The University of Sheffield, 1985).

2.   Ibid., 93-107.

3.   Ibid., 107-119.

4.   Sam K. Williams, *Jesus' Death As a Saving Event: The Background and Origin of a Concept* (Missoula, Mont.: Scholars Press, 1975).

5.   Pobee, "Persecution and Martyrdom in the Theology of Paul," 113-115.

6.   D. E. Hiebert, *The Thessalonian Epistles: A Call to Readiness* (Chicago: Moody Press, 1971), 194.

7.   Gordon D. Fee, *The First Epistle to the Corinthians* (Grand Rapids: W. B. Eerdmans, 1987), 172.

8.   W. Michaelis, "πάσχω," in *The Theological Dictionary of the New Testament*, ed. G. Kittel, trans. and ed. G. W. Bromiley, vol. 5 (Grand Rapids: W. B. Eerdmans, 1979), 922.

9.   Ibid., 925.

10.   Ibid., 926.

11.   Ibid., 932.

12.   Ibid., 932-33.

13.   Ibid., 920.

14.   Quoted in John R. W. Stott, *The Cross of Christ* (Downers Grove, Ill.: InterVarsity Press, 1986), 330-331.

15.   Quoted in Paul S. Fiddes, *The Creative Suffering of God* (Oxford: Clarendon Press, 1992), 2.

16.   H. Wheeler Robinson, *Suffering: Human and Divine* (London: SCM, 1940).

17.   Abraham Heschel, *The Prophets* (New York: Harper & Row, 1962).

18.   Terrence E. Fretheim, *The Suffering of God: An Old Testament Perspective* (Philadelphia: Fortress Press, 1984).

19.   Jürgen Moltmann, *The Crucified God* (London: SCM, 1974); idem, *The Future of Creation* (London: SCM, 1979); idem, *God in Creation* (London: SCM, 1985).

20.   Paul S. Fiddes, *The Creative Suffering of God* (Oxford: Clarendon Press, 1992).

21. Kazoh Kitanori, *The Theology of the Pain of God* (London: SCM, 1946)

22. Stott, *Cross of Christ*, 329-337.

23. Ibid., 335.

24. Victor P. Furnish, *2 Corinthians* (Garden City, N.Y.: Doubleday, 1984), 187.

25. Philip E. Hughes, *Paul's Second Epistle to the Corinthians* (Grand Rapids: W. B. Eerdmans, 1962), 77-78.

26. W. L. Knox, *St. Paul and the Church of the Gentiles* (Cambridge: Cambridge University Press, 1939), 131-133.

27. W. C. van Unnik, *The New Testament: Its History and Message* (New York: Harper & Row, 1964), 167.

28. Fee, *First Corinthians*, 174.

29. Gerard Kittel, ed., *The Theological Dictionary of the New Testament*, vol. 3 (Grand Rapids: W. B. Eerdmans, 1979), 43.

30. Ibid., 179.

31. F. F. Bruce, *1 and 2 Corinthians* (Grand Rapids: W. B. Eerdmans, 1980), 50-51.

32. C. K. Barrett, *The Second Epistle to the Corinthians* (New York: Harper & Row, 1973), 112, 113.

33. Quoted in Hughes, *Second Corinthians*, 423.

34. F. Godet, *Commentary on St. Paul's First Epistle to the Corinthians*, trans. A. Cousin (Edinburgh: Clark, 1886), 388.

35. Spiros Zodhiates, *Conquering the Fear of Death: An Exposition of 1 Corinthians 15* (Grand Rapids: W. B. Eerdmans, 1970), 505-506.

36. C. R. Bowen, "I Fought with the Beasts at Ephesus," *Journal of Biblical Literature* 42 (1923): 59-68.

37. Quoted in Hughes, *Second Corinthians*, 439.

38. Ibid.

39. C. K. Barrett, *The First Epistle to the Corinthians* (New York: Harper & Row, 1968), 216.

40. John Murray, *The Epistle to the Romans* (Grand Rapids: W. B. Eerdmans, 1959), 164.

41. John R. W. Stott, *Romans: God's Good News for the World* (Downers Grove, Ill.: InterVarsity Press, 1994), 141-142.

42. Hughes, *Second Corinthians*, 180.

43. Ibid., 181.

44. Barrett, *Second Corinthians*, 161.

45. Stott, *Romans*, 184.

46. Barrett, *Second Corinthians*, 132.

444

Notes to Chapter Seven

47. Stott, *Romans*, 185.
48. Ibid., 186.
49. Ibid., 52.
50. Ibid.
51. Quoted in F. W. Beare, *A Commentary on the Epistle to the Philippians* (London: Adam & Charles Black, 1973), 53.
52. See James L. Blevins, "Introduction to Philippians," *Review and Expositor* 77 (1980): 311-325.
53. Gordon D. Fee, *Paul's Letter to the Philippians* (Grand Rapids: W. B. Eerdmans, 1995), 332.
54. Ibid., 336.
55. Merrill C. Proudfoot, "Imitation or Realistic Participation? A Study of Paul's Concept of 'Suffering with Christ,' " *Interpretation* 17 (1963): 140.
56. Albert Schweitzer, *The Mysticism of Paul the Apostle*, trans. William Montgomery (New York: Henry Holt, 1931), 141.
57. Proudfoot, "Imitation or Realistic Participation?" 147.
58. Merrill C. Proudfoot, *Suffering: A Christian Understanding* (Philadelphia: Westminster Press, 1964), 22-23.
59. Fee, *Philippians*, 332-333.
60. Hugh J. Michael, *The Epistle of Paul to the Philippians* (Garden City, N.Y.: Doubleday, 1929), 151-152.
61. Moises Silva, *Philippians* (Grand Rapids: Baker Book House, 1992), 190-192.
62. Peter T. O'Brian, *Colossians & Philemon* (Waco, Tex.: Word Books, 1982), on Col. 1:24; and Robert W. Wall, *Colossians & Philemon* (Downers Grove, Ill.: InterVarsity Press, 1993), on Col. 1:24.
63. William Hendriksen, *Exposition of Colossians and Philemon* (Grand Rapids: Baker Book House, 1964), 87.
64. W. L. Knox, *St. Paul and the Church of the Gentiles* (Cambridge: Cambridge University Press, 1939), 166.
65. Hendriksen, *Colossians and Philemon*, 87.
66. Ibid.
67. J. B. Lightfoot, *Saint Paul's Epistles to the Colossians and Philemon* (London: Macmillan, 1892), 164.
68. C. F. D. Moule, *The Sacrifice of Christ* (Philadelphia: Fortress Press, 1964).
69. Morna D. Hooker, ed., *Suffering and Martyrdom in the New Testament* (Cambridge: Cambridge University Press, 1981), 81.
70. E. P. Sanders, *Paul and Palestinian Judaism: A Comparison of Patterns of Religion* (Philadelphia: Fortress Press, 1977), 455.

71. Lightfoot, *Colossians and Philemon,* 166.

72. Fee, *Philippians*, 91.

73. Ibid., 177.

74. Ibid., 175.

75. Ibid.

76. Silva, *Philippians*, 99.

77. Roy W. Hoover, "The HARPAGMOS Enigma: A Philological Solution," *The Harvard Theological Review* 64 (1971): 110.

78. Ibid., 118.

79. C. F. D. Moule, "Further Reflections on Philippians 2:5-11," in *Apostolic History and the Gospel*, ed. W. Ward Gasque and Ralph P. Martin (Grand Rapids: W. B. Eerdmans, 1970), 271.

80. Ibid., 272.

81. Ibid.

82. Fee, *Philippians*, 208.

83. Ibid., 211.

84. Silva, *Philippians*, 118.

85. Fee, *Philippians*, 197.

86. Gerald F. Hawthorne, *Philippians* (Waco, Tex.: Word Books, 1983), 91.

87. Beare, *Philippians,* 187.

88. Hawthorne, *Philippians*, 90.

89. Ibid.

90. Ibid.

91. Silva, *Philippians,* 127.

92. Ralph P. Martin, *Carmen Cristi: Philippians 2:5-11* (Cambridge: Cambridge University Press, 1967), 231.

93. Ibid.

94. Ibid., 232.

95. Ibid.

96. Ibid.

97. Martin, *Carmen Cristi*, 232, quoting Rudolf Bultmann, *Jesus and the Word: The Will of God—Insistence on Obedience* (New York: Scribner's, 1958).

98. Martin, *Carmen Cristi*, 232.

99. Ibid.

100. Arthur C. McGill, *Suffering: A Test of Theological Method* (Philadelphia: Westminster Press, 1982), 75-76.

101. Ibid., 82.

102. Ibid.

103. Fee, *Philippians*, 217.

104. Quoted in Peter T. O'Brian, *The Epistle to the Philippians: A Commentary on the Greek Text* (Grand Rapids: W. B. Eerdmans, 1991), 256; see also 253-262.

105. Ibid.

106. Martin, *Carmen Cristi*, 288n2.

107. Fee, *Philippians*, 229.

108. Ibid., 227 (author's italics).

109. Ibid., 228 (author's italics).

110. Quoted in Silva, *Philippians*, 138.

111. Beare, *Philippians*, 90.

112. For a comprehensive survey of this alternative in the New Testament, see O'Brian, *Philippians*, 285-286.

113. Appraisal by Moises Silva, quoted in John Murray, *Redemption: Accomplished and Applied* (London: Banner of Truth Trust, 1961), 148-149.

114. O'Brian, *Philippians*, 293.

115. Ibid.

116. Beare, *Philippians*, 92.

117. Hawthorne, *Philippians*, 101.

118. F. F. Bruce, *Philippians* (Peabody, Mass.: Hendrickson Publishers, 1983), 88 (author's italics and bold).

119. Hawthorne, *Philippians*, 105.

120. Silva, *Philippians*, 150.

121. Bruce, *Philippians*, 88-89.

122. Andrew T. Lincoln, *Ephesians* (Dallas: Word Books, 1990), 192.

123. William Hendriksen, *Exposition of Philippians* (Grand Rapids: Baker Book House, 1962), 165.

124. Quoted in Beare, *Philippians*, 116.

125. O'Brian, *Philippians*, 393.

126. Hendriksen, *Philippians*, 169.

127. Ibid.

128. J. H. Bernard, *The Pastoral Epistles* (Grand Rapids: Baker Book House, 1980), iv.

129. C. K. Barrett, *The Pastoral Epistles* (Oxford: Clarendon Press, 1963), 86. He mentions it as a "suggested reference" only to dismiss it.

130. Quoted in Anthony T. Hanson, *The Pastoral Epistles* (Grand Rapids: W. B. Eerdmans, 1982), 111.

131. Ibid.

132. Barrett, *Pastoral Epistles*, 102n7.

447

Notes to Chapter Nine

133. Ibid., 104.
134. John R. W. Stott, *The Message of 2 Timothy* (Downers Grove, Ill.: InterVarsity Press, 1973), 63-64.
135. Bernard, *Pastoral Epistles*, 121.
136. Stott, *2 Timothy*, 169.
137. Leon Morris, *The Biblical Doctrine of Judgment* (Grand Rapids: W. B. Eerdmans, 1960), 66.
138. Ibid., 67.
139. Ibid.
140. Ibid., 66-67.

Chapter Eight: Hebrews: The Final Destiny of Man

1. Spicq, quoted by F. F. Bruce, *The Epistle to the Hebrews*, rev. ed. (Grand Rapids: W. B. Eerdmans, 1990), 59.
2. Translation by Bruce, *Hebrews*, 44.
3. Ibid., 80.
4. Ibid.
5. Ibid.
6. Ibid., 130n67.
7. Ibid., 131.
8. Millard J. Erickson, *Christian Theology* (Grand Rapids: Baker Book House, 1985), 969.
9. Bruce, *Hebrews*, 101n68.
10. Ibid., 325.
11. 2 Macc. 7:1-41; 4 Macc. 8:1-24.
12. William J. Fuller, "I Will Not Erase His Name from the Book of Life (Revelation 3:5)," *Journal of the Evangelical Theological Society* 26 (1983): 299.
13. Bruce, *Hebrews*, 333.
14. Ignatius *Magnesians* 8.2.
15. Bruce, *Hebrews*, 333.

Chapter Nine: 1 Peter: The True Grace of God

1. J. N. D. Kelly, *A Commentary on the Epistles of Peter and Jude* (Grand Rapids: Baker Book House, 1969), 5-12.

448

2. Peter H. Davids, *The First Epistle of Peter* (Grand Rapids: W. B. Eerdmans, 1990), 200.

3. Davids, *First Peter*, 200n7, citing N. Brox, *Der erste Petrusbrief* (Zurich, 1986), 244-45.

4. Ibid., 200.

5. Kelly, *Epistles of Peter and Jude*, 116.

6. Ibid., 118.

7. Davids, *First Peter*, 107.

8. Ibid., 108.

9. Ernst H. Reisenfeld, "παρά," in *The Theological Dictionary of the New Testament*, ed. G. Kittel, trans. and ed. G. W. Bromiley, vol. 3 (Grand Rapids: W. B. Eerdmans, 1979), 733.

10. Ibid.

11. Davids, *First Peter*, 108-109.

12. Ibid., 195.

13. Ibid., 196.

Chapter Ten: Revelation: The Contours of a Theology of Martyrdom

1. Quoted in Robert H. Mounce, *The Book of Revelation* (Grand Rapids: W. B. Eerdmans, 1977), 43.

2. Ibid.

3. Ibid., 318.

4. William Barclay, *The Revelation of John*, vol. 2 (Philadelphia: Westminster Press, 1959), 88.

5. Fuller, "I Will Not Erase His Name from the Book of Life (Revelation 3:5)," 299.

6. Quoted in Mounce, *Revelation*, 90.

7. Ibid.

8. G. B. Caird, *A Commentary on the Revelation of St. John the Divine* (London: Adam & Charles Black, 1966), 46.

9. R. H. Charles, *The Revelation of St. John* (Edinburgh: Clark, 1920), 67.

10. Martin Kiddle, *Revelation* (New York: Harper & Bros. Publishers, 1940), 35.

11. Colin J. Hemer, *The Letters to the Seven Churches of Asia in Their Local Setting* (Sheffield: JSOT Press, 1986), 102-103.

12. Ibid.

13. W. Siegbert Becker, *Revelation: The Distant Song of Triumph* (Milwaukee, Wis.: Northwestern Publishing House, 1985), 56.

14. Hemer, *Letters to the Seven Churches*, 147.

15. Caird, *Revelation*, 86.

16. Fuller, "I Will Not Erase His Name," 304.

17. Ibid., 305-306.

18. Kiddle, *Revelation*, 46.

19. Caird, *Revelation*, 50.

20. Mounce, *Revelation*, 114.

21. Ibid., 139.

22. J. Webb Mealy, *After the Thousand Years: Resurrection and Judgment in Revelation 20* (Sheffield: JSOT Press, 1992), 103-104.

23. Mounce, *Revelation,* 359.

Chapter Eleven: The Holy Spirit and Martyrdom

1. William C. Weinrich, *Spirit and Martyrdom: A Study of the Work of the Holy Spirit in the Contexts of Persecution and Martyrdom in the New Testament and Early Literature* (Washington, D.C.: University Press of America, 1981).

2. C. Peter Wagner, *Your Spiritual Gifts Can Help Your Church Grow*, rev. ed. (Ventura, Calif.: Regal Books, 1994), 60-61.

3. Ibid.

Chapter Thirteen: Martyrdom in the First Centuries of the Christian Church

1. Ignatius *To the Romans* 2.4, in Gerald G. Walsh, trans., "Ignatius of Antioch," in *The Apostolic Fathers*, trans. and ed. Francis X. Glimm, Joseph M. F. Marique, and Gerald G. Walsh (New York: Christian Heritage, 1947).

2. Ibid., 7, (Walsh).

3. Ignatius *To the Smyrnaens* 1, (Walsh).

4. Ignatius, *To the Ephesians* 18.1, in Robert M. Grant, trans. and ed., "Ignatius of Antioch," in *The Apostolic Fathers*, vol. 4 (London: Thomas Nelson Publishers, 1966).

5. Ignatius *To the Romans* 2, (Walsh).

6. Ibid., 6.

7. Ibid., 3.
8. Ignatius *To the Trallians* 12, (Walsh).
9. Ignatius *To the Smyrnaens* 4, (Walsh).
10. Ibid., 2.
11. Ignatius *To the Romans* 4, (Walsh).
12. Ignatius *To Polycarp* 7, (Walsh).
13. Ibid.
14. Ibid., 3.
15. Ignatius *To the Romans* 1, (Walsh).
16. Ibid., 9.
17. Ignatius *To the Philippians* 5, (Walsh).
18. Polycarp *To the Philippians* 8-9, in Francis X. Glimm, trans., "Polycarp," in *The Apostolic Fathers*, trans. and ed. Francis X. Glimm, Joseph M. F. Marique, and Gerald G. Walsh (New York: Christian Heritage, 1947).
19. "The Martyrdom of Polycarp" 1.1, in Glimm, *The Apostolic Fathers*.
20. Ibid., 2.1-3.
21. Ibid.
22. Ibid., 1.1.
23. Ibid., 5.1.
24. Ibid., 5.2.
25. Ibid., 4.1.
26. Ibid.
27. Ibid., 1.2.
28. Ibid., 1.1.
29. Ibid., 8.2.
30. Ibid., 9.1.
31. Ibid., 9.3.
32. Ibid., 14.1, in Cyril Richardson, trans. and ed., *Early Christian Fathers* (New York: Macmillan, 1970).
33. Ibid., 14.2, in Glimm, *The Apostolic Fathers*.
34. Ibid., 17.2.
35. Ibid., 17.2-3.
36. Ibid., 14.2, in Richardson, *Early Christian Fathers*.
37. Ibid., 14.2.
38. Ibid., 17.1.
39. Ibid., 11.2-3.
40. Eusebius *Ecclesiastical History* 5.1.
41. Ibid.

42. Ibid.
43. Ibid., 5.13.
44. Ibid., 5.11.
45. Ibid., 5.20-22.
46. Ibid., 5.1.
47. Ibid., 5.9.
48. Ibid., 5.10.
49. Ibid.
50. Ibid., 5.1.
51. Ibid., 5.29.
52. Ibid., 5.1.
53. Ibid.
54. Ibid., 5.22.
55. Ibid., 5.23.
56. Ibid., 5.43.
57. Ibid., 5.29.
58. Ibid., 5.23.
59. Ibid., 5.42.
60. Ibid., 5.27.
61. Ibid., 5.29.
62. Ibid., 5.34.
63. Ibid., 5.1.
64. Ibid.
65. Ibid., 5.41.
66. Ibid., 5.23.
67. Ibid., 5.51.
68. Ibid., 5.56.
69. Ibid., 5.6.
70. Ibid., 5.36.
71. Ibid., 5.38.
72. Ibid., 5.42.
73. Ibid., 5.55.
74. Ibid., 5.41.
75. Ibid., 5.63.
76. Ibid.
77. Ibid., 5.6, 24.
78. Ibid., 5.45, 48.
79. Ibid., 5.49.
80. Ibid.

81. Ibid., 5.27.

82. Ibid., 5.27-28.

83. Ibid., 5.26.

84. Ibid., 5.60.

85. Clement of Alexandria *Stromata* 4.17-18, in John Ernest Oulton and Chadwick Henry, trans. and eds., *Alexandrian Christianity: Selected Translations from Clement and Origen* (Philadelphia: Westminster Press, 1954).

86. Ibid., 4.9.73.

87. Ibid., 4.14.3.

88. Ibid., 4.43.2.

89. Ibid., 4.7.43.

90. *Passio Perpetuae* 3.30, in E. C. E. Owen, *Some Authentic Acts of the Early Martyrs* (Oxford: Clarendon Press, 1927), 74-93.

91. Ibid., 3.45.

92. Ibid.

93. Ibid., 10.9.

94. Ibid.

95. Ibid., 17.5.

96. Ibid., 18.1.

97. Ibid., 17.29.

98. Ibid., 20.30.

99. Tertullian *Flight in Time of Persecution* 2, in *Disciplinary, Moral, and Ascetical Works,* trans. Rudolph Arbesmann (New York: Fathers of the Church, 1959).

100. Ibid., 3.

101. Ibid., 4.

102. Ibid., 5.

103. Ibid., 6.

104. Ibid., 11.1.

105. Ibid., 11.2.

106. Tertullian *To the Martyrs* 3.4, in *Ascetical Works.*

107. Ibid., 1.3.

108. Tertullian *Adversus Praxeas* 29.7, in *Ascetical Works.*

109. Tertullian *Flight* 10.2.

110. Tertullian *To the Martyrs* 3.5.

111. Ibid., 2.8-9.

112. Tertullian *Flight* 1.2.

113. Tertullian *To the Martyrs* 5.3.

453

Notes to Chapter Thirteen

114. Ibid., 3.3.
115. Tertullian *Flight* 10.2.
116. Tertullian *Apology* 50.13, in *Apology & De Spectaculis*, trans. T. R. Glover (London: William Heinemann, 1931).
117. Tertullian *To the Martyrs* 1.6.
118. Origen *Exhortation to Martyrdom* 34, in *On Prayer & Exhortation to Martyrdom*, trans. John J. O'Meara (New York: Newman Press, 1954).
119. Ibid.
120. Ibid.
121. Ibid., 36.
122. Ibid., 35.
123. Ibid., 39.
124. Ibid., 18.
125. Origen *On Prayer* 30.2, in *On Prayer & Exhortation to Martyrdom*.
126. Ibid.
127. Origen *Exhortation to Martyrdom* 37.
128. Ibid., 15.
129. W. H. C. Frend, *Martyrdom and Persecution in the Early Church: A Study of a Conflict from the Maccabees to Donatus* (Grand Rapids: Baker Book House, 1965), 395, quoting Origen, Homily on Levit. 2.4.
130. Origen *Exhortation to Martyrdom* 29-30.
131. Ibid., 30.
132. Ibid., 29-30.
133. Ibid., 50.
134. Eusebius *Ecclesiastical History* 6.42.
135. Ibid., 1.4.2.
136. Ibid., 10.4.15.
137. Ibid., 6.2.
138. Ibid., 6.3.
139. Ibid., 6.4.
140. Ibid., 6.11.
141. Ibid., 6.15.
142. Ibid., 4.15.
143. Ibid., 8.10.4-5.
144. Ibid., 8.9.4-5.
145. Lactantius *The Divine Institutes, Books 1-8*, trans. Mary McDonald (Washington, D.C.: The Catholic University of America Press, 1964), 8.5.

454

Notes to Chapter Fourteen

146. Eric W. Kemp, *Canonization and Authority in the Western Church* (London: Oxford University Press, 1948), 2.

147. Ibid., 4-5.

148. Paolo Molinari, *Saints: Their Place in the Church* (New York: Shedd & Ward, 1965), 114, quoting Augustine, Sermon 285.5.

149. Molinari, *Saints*, 114, quoting Augustine *In Natali Martyrum Perpetuae et Felicitatis*, Sermon 280. 6.6.215.

150. Ibid., 115-116.

151. Quoted in James E. Sherman, *The Nature of Martyrdom: A Dogmatic and Moral Analysis According to the Teaching of St. Thomas Aquinas* (Paterson, NJ: St. Anthony Guild Press, 1942), 61.

152. Ibid.

153. Ibid., 125.

154. Frend, *Martyrdom and Persecution*, 547, quoting from "Barlaam and Joasaph."

155. Edward E. Malone, "The Monk and the Martyr," *Studia Anselmiana* 38 (1956): 201.

156. Malone, "Monk and Martyr," quoting Clement of Alexandria *Stromata* 4.4.

157. Ibid., *Stromata* 4.9.

158. Ibid., *Stromata* 4.4.

159. Malone, "Monk and Martyr," 206.

160. Ibid., quoting Origen *In Num. hom.* 10.2.

161. Ibid., quoting Origen *In Genes. hom.* 8.8-10.

162. Ibid., quoting Origen *Com. in Matt. Ser.* 15.19.

163. Ibid., quoting Origen *In Matt. hom.* 12.24.

164. Malone, "Monk and Martyr," 211.

165. Ibid., 223.

166. Ibid., 225.

167. Ibid., 226.

168. Ibid.

Chapter Fourteen: Martyrdom in the Protestant Reformation

1.   Robert Kolb, *For All the Saints: Changing Perceptions of Martyrdom and Sainthood in the Lutheran Reformation* (Grand Rapids: Baker Book House, 1986), 3-4.

2.   See Sherry L. Reames, *The "Legenda Aurea": A Reexamination of its Paradoxical History* (Madison: University of Wisconsin Press, 1985).

3. Quoted in Kolb, *For All the Saints*, 14.

4. Quoted in John R. Knott, *Discourses of Martyrdom in English Literature, 1563-1694* (Cambridge: Cambridge University Press, 1993), 40.

5. Quoted in Kolb, *For All the Saints*, 12.

6. Ibid., 13.

7. Ibid., 4.

8. Ibid., 156.

9. Martin Luther, *What Luther Says: An Anthology*, compiled by Ewald M. Press, vol. 2 (St. Louis, Mo.: Concordia Publishing House, 1959). 1036.

10. Ibid.

11. Ibid.

12. Ibid., 1035-1036.

13. Ibid., 1037.

14. Ibid.

15. Ibid.

16. Ibid., 1040-1041.

17. Ibid., 1040.

18. Ibid.

19. Ibid., 1038.

20. Ibid., 1038-1039.

21. Ibid., 1039.

22. John Foxe, *Foxe's Book of Martyrs: A History of the Lives, Sufferings, and Deaths of the Early Christian and Protestant Martyrs* (1563; reprint, ed. W. B. Forbush, Grand Rapids: Zondervan Publishing House, 1926 and 1982), 1 (page citations are to the 1982 reprint edition).

23. Ibid.

24. Ibid., 205.

25. Ibid., 214.

26. Ibid., 220.

27. Ibid., 156.

28. Ibid., 174-175.

29. Ibid., 218-219.

30. Ibid., 264-265.

31. Ibid., 212.

32. Ibid., 222.

33. Ibid., 228.

34. Ibid., 249.

35. Ibid., 229.

36. Ibid., 226.
37. Ibid., 215.
38. Ibid., 240.
39. Quoted in Knott, *Discourses of Martyrdom*, 96.
40. Ibid., 153.
41. Ibid., 179.
42. Ibid., 195.

Chapter Fifteen: The Anabaptists and Martyrdom

1. Thielemann J. van Braght, *The Bloody Theater or Martyrs' Mirror of the Defenseless Christians,* trans. J. F. Sohm (1660; reprint, Scottdale, Pa.: Herald Press, 1979).
2. Quoted in Ethelbert Stauffer, "The Anabaptist Theology of Martyrdom," *The Mennonite Quarterly Review* 19, no. 3 (1945): 191.
3. Quoted in Robert Friedmann, *The Theology of Anabaptism* (Scottdale, Pa.: Herald Press, 1973), 131.
4. Van Braght, *Martyrs' Mirror,* 910.
5. Ibid., 453.
6. Friedmann, *Theology of Anabaptism,* 135.
7. Quoted in Friedmann, *Theology of Anabaptism,* 135.
8. Quoted in Stauffer, "Anabaptist Theology," 207.
9. Van Braght, *Martyrs' Mirror,* 190.
10. Ibid., 198.
11. Quoted in Stauffer, "Anabaptist Theology," 184.
12. Quoted in Friedmann, *Theology of Anabaptism,* 137.
13. Ibid., 140-141.
14. Van Braght, *Martyrs' Mirror,* 12.
15. Ibid., 21.
16. Ibid., 360.
17. Ibid., 357.
18. Ibid.
19. Ibid., 364.
20. Quoted in Stauffer, "Anabaptist Theology," 209.
21. Van Braght, *Martyrs' Mirror,* 543.
22. Ibid., 546.
23. Ibid., 757.
24. Ibid., 356.

25. Stauffer, "Anabaptist Theology," 200.

26. Menno Simons, *The Cross of the Saints,* in *The Complete Writings,* trans. L. Verduin, ed. J. C. Wenger (Scottdale, Pa.: Herald Press, 1966), 620.

27. Van Braght, *Martyrs' Mirror,* 355-356.

28. Stauffer, "Anabaptist Theology," 200.

29. Quoted in Friedmann, *Theology of Anabaptism,* 107, (italics mine).

30. Van Braght, *Martyrs' Mirror,* 7.

31. Ibid.

32. Ibid., 7.

33. Ibid., 353.

34. Ibid., 911.

35. Stauffer, "Anabaptist Theology," 165.

36. Van Braght, *Martyrs' Mirror,* 5.

37. James Hefley and Marti Hefley, *By Their Blood: Christian Martyrs of the 20th Century* (Milford, Mich.: Mott Media, 1979), 589.

Chapter Sixteen: Rewards in Protestant Theology

1. Emma Disley, "Degrees of Glory: Protestant Doctrine and the Concept of Rewards Hereafter," *Journal of Theological Studies* 42, part 1 (April 1991): 87. I am indebted to E. Disley for the information on the Protestant theologians of the sixteenth and seventeenth centuries.

2. Disley, "Degrees of Glory," 97, quoting W. Tyndale, *Wicked Mammon* (1527), *P. S. Works* i. 62, 98, 117.

3. Ibid.

4. G. De Ru, "The Conception of Reward in the Teaching of Jesus," *Novum Testamentum* 8 (1966): 220.

5. Disley, "Degrees of Glory," 98.

6. Ibid., 90, quoting Tyndale, *An Exposition upon the V., VI., VII. Chapters of Matthew* (1532).

7. Ibid., quoting Veron, *Overthrow,* 72. The words "God crowns in them his own gifts" are a quote from Augustine *De Gratia et Libero Arbitro,* c.15.

8. Ibid.

9. Ibid., 93, quoting John Buckeridge, funeral sermon for Lancelot Andrewes (1628), in Andrewes, *Ninety-six Sermons,* vol. 5 (Library of Anglo-Catholic Theology, 1843), 282-3.

10. Ibid., 92, quoting W. Perkins, *Works,* i. 70b.

11. Ibid., quoting Bullinger, *Sermonum Decades,* 159 (in Latin).

458

12. Ibid., quoting Fulke, *A Defense of the Serene and True Translation of the Holy Scriptures into the English Tongue against the Cavils of Gregory Martin* (1583), 370.

13. Ibid., 98-9, quoting Bernard of Clairvaux *De Gratia et Libero Arbitro, XIV*, 51; Downame, *A Treatise of Justification* (1639) lib. 2, c. VI, xii, 79.

14. Ibid., 99, quoting John Davenant, *Disputatio* ii, trans. J. Alport, (1846), 85.

15. Ibid., 101, quoting Hugh Latimer, "Lincolnshire Sermon," (1552), P. S. *II Latimer* (1845), 74.

16. Ibid., quoting Philipp Melanchthon, *Apology of the Augsburg Confession*, iv. (1531), 193-4.

17. Ibid., 102.

18. Ibid., quoting Richard Hooker, "A learned discourse of justification, works, and how the foundation of faith is overthrown," (preached, 1586; published 1612); cf. *Works*, iii, (1830), 396.

19. Ibid.

20. Ibid., 103, quoting Amyraut, *Discours de l'estat des Fideles apres la mort*, 230. The writer of *The Glory and Happiness of the Saints in Heaven* (1692) employs the same analogy.

21. Ibid., 105.

22. James E. Rosscup, "The Overcomer of the Apocalypse," *Grace Theological Journal* 3, no. 2 (1982): 261-286.

23. P. C. Bottger, "μισθός," in *The New International Dictionary of New Testament Theology*, ed. Colin Brown, vol. 3 (Grand Rapids: Zondervan Publishing House, 1971), 144.

24. H. Preisker, "μισθός," in *The Theological Dictionary of the New Testament*, ed. G. Kittel, trans. and ed. G. W. Bromiley, vol. 4 (Grand Rapids: W. B. Eerdmans, 1979), 728.

25. Ibid.

26. Ibid.

27. De Ru, "The Conception of Reward in the Teaching of Jesus," 202-222.

28. Ibid., 221.

29. Ibid., 221-222.

30. Ibid., 211-212.

31. Ibid., 213.

32. Ibid., 218.

33. Ibid., quoting Pirqe Abot, from T. W. Manson, *The Sayings of Jesus*, 247.

34. Ibid.
35. Ibid.
36. Ibid.
37. Ibid., 219.

Bibliography

Abedi, Mehdi, and Gary Legenhausen, eds. *Jihad and Shahadat: Struggle and Martyrdom in Islam.* Houston: IRIS, 1986.

Agus, Aharon (Ronald E.). *The Binding of Isaac and Messiah: Law, Martyrdom and Deliverance in Early Rabbinic Religiosity.* New York: State University of New York Press, 1988.

Alexander, Donald L., ed. *Christian Spirituality.* Downers Grove, Ill.: InterVarsity Press, 1988.

Allen, Willoughby C. *A Critical and Exegetical Commentary on the Gospel According to St. Matthew.* New York: Scribner's, 1907.

Ante-Nicene Fathers. *Translations of The Writings of the Fathers down to A.D. 325.* Edited by Alexander Roberts and James Donaldson. Grand Rapids: W. B. Eerdmans, 1969.

Applebury, T. R. *Studies in First Corinthians.* Joplin, Mo.: College Press, 1963.

Arndt, William. *Bible Commentary: The Gospel According to St. Luke.* St. Louis, Mo.: Concordia Publishing House, 1956.

Arnold, Duane W. H. *Prayers of the Martyrs.* Grand Rapids: Zondervan Publishing House, 1991.

_____. *Praying With the Martyrs.* Grand Rapids: Zondervan Publishing House, 1990.

Arnold, Eberhard. *The Early Christians.* Grand Rapids: Baker Book House, 1970.

Atkinson, David J., ed. *New Dictionary of Christian Ethics and Pastoral Theology.* Downers Grove, Ill.: InterVarsity Press, 1995.

Barclay, William. *The Gospel of Luke.* Philadelphia: Westminster Press, 1975.

_____. *The Revelation of John.* Vol. 2. Philadelphia: Westminster Press, 1959.

Barrett, C. K. *The First Epistle to the Corinthians.* New York: Harper & Row, 1968.

_____. *The Gospel According to St. John: An Introduction With Commentary and Notes on the Greek Text.* London: S. P. C. K., 1955.

_____. *The Pastoral Epistles.* Oxford: Clarendon Press, 1963.

_____. *The Second Epistle to the Corinthians.* New York: Harper & Row, 1973.

Bassler, Jouette M., ed. *Pauline Theology: Thessalonians, Philippians, Galatians, Philemon.* Vol. 1. Minneapolis: Fortress Press, 1994.

Bauckham, Richard. *New Testament Theology: The Theology of the Book of Revelation.* Cambridge: Cambridge University Press, 1993.

Beare, F. W. *A Commentary on the Epistle to the Philippians.* London: Adam & Charles Black, 1973.

Becker, O. "μισθός." In *The Theological Dictionary of the New Testament,* edited by Gerhard Kittel, translated and edited by Geoffrey W. Bromiley, vol. 3, 138-145. Grand Rapids: W. B. Eerdmans, 1979.

Becker, W. Siegbert. *Revelation: The Distant Song of Triumph.* Milwaukee, Wis.: Northwestern Publishing House, 1985.

Ben Sirah, *The Wisdom of Ben Sirah.* Translation with notes by Patrick W. Skehan. Introduction and commentary by Alexander A. Di Lella. Garden City, N.Y.: Doubleday, 1987.

Bernard, J. H. *The Pastoral Epistles.* Grand Rapids: Baker Book House, 1980.

Best, Ernest. *A Commentary on the First and Second Epistles to the Thessalonians.* New York: Harper & Row, 1972.

Bilheimer, Paul E. *Adventure in Adversity.* Wheaton, Ill.: Tyndale House Publishers, 1984.

_____. *Destined for the Throne: A New Look at the Bridge of Christ.* Ft. Washington, Pa.: Christian Literature Crusade, 1975.

_____. *Destined to Overcome: The Technique of Spiritual Warfare.* Minneapolis: Bethany House Publishers, 1982.

_____. *Don't Waste Your Sorrows.* Wheaton, Ill.: Tyndale House Publishers, 1982.

Black, Matthew, ed. *The Scrolls and Christianity: Historical and Theological Significance.* London: S. P. C. K., 1969.

Blevins, James L. "Introduction to Philippians." *Review and Expositor* 77 (1980): 311-325.

Bong, Rin Ro, ed. *Christian Suffering in Asia: "The Blood of the Martyrs is the Seed of the Church."* Taiwan: Evangelical Fellowship of Asia, 1989.

Bornkamm, Gunther. *Jesus of Nazareth: The Will of God.* New York: Harper & Row, 1960.

Bottger, P. C. "μισθός." In *The New International Dictionary of New Testament Theology,* edited by Colin Brown, vol. 3, 138-144. Grand Rapids: Zondervan Publishing House, 1971.

Bouttier, Michel. *Christianity According to Paul.* Translated by Frank Clarke. London: SCM Press, 1966.

Bowen, Clayton R. "I Fought with the Beasts at Ephesus." *Journal of Biblical Literature* 42 (1923): 59-68.

Bowie, W. R. *The Compassionate Christ: Reflections on the Gospel of Luke.* New York: Abingdon Press, 1965.

Braght, Thielemann J. van. *The Bloody Theater or Martyrs' Mirror of the Defenseless Christians.* Translated by Joseph F. Sohm. 1660. Reprint, Scottdale, Pa.: Herald Press, 1979.

Brascomb, Harvie B. *The Gospel of Mark.* New York: Harper & Bros. Publishers, 1937.

Braumann, G. "μορφή." In *The New International Dictionary of New Testament Theology,* edited by Colin Brown, vol. 1. 705-708. Grand Rapids: Zondervan Publishing House, 1971.

Brown, Colin. *New Testament Theology.* 3 vols. Vol. 2. Grand Rapids: Zondervan Publishing House, 1978.

Brown, Raymond E. *The Gospel According to John (1-12).* Garden City, N.Y.: Doubleday, 1966.

Brownlee, William H. *The Midrash Pesher of Habakkuk.* Missoula, Mont.: Scholars Press, 1979.

Bruce, A. B. *The Training of the Twelve.* Grand Rapids: Kregel Publications, 1971.

Bruce, F. F. *1 and 2 Corinthians.* Grand Rapids: W. B. Eerdmans, 1980.

_____. *The Epistle to the Colossians, to Philemon, and to the Ephesians.* Grand Rapids: W. B. Eerdmans, 1984.

_____. *The Epistle to the Hebrews.* Rev. ed. Grand Rapids: W. B. Eerdmans, 1990.

_____. *Philippians.* Peabody, Mass.: Hendrickson Publishers, 1983.

_____. *Second Thoughts on the Dead Sea Scrolls.* Grand Rapids: W. B. Eerdmans, 1956.

Bultmann, Rudolf. *Jesus and the Word: The Will of God—Insistence on Obedience.* New York: Scribner's, 1958.

Caird, G. B. *A Commentary on the Revelation of St. John the Divine.* London: Adam & Charles Black, 1966.

Caird, J. B. *The Gospel of Luke.* Baltimore: Penguin Books, 1963.

Carr, A. *The Gospel According to St. Matthew.* Cambridge: Cambridge University Press, 1884.

Carrington, Philip. *According to Mark.* Cambridge: Cambridge University Press, 1960.

Charles, R. H. *The Revelation of St. John.* Edinburgh: Clark, 1920.

Chilton, David. *Paradise Restored: A Biblical Theology of Dominion.* Tyler, Tex.: Reconstruction Press, 1985.

Clarke, O. Fielding. *God and Suffering: An Essay in Theodicy. The Justification of God in the Face of Evil.* Derby: Peter Smith, n.d.

Clarckson, Margaret. *Destined for Glory: The Meaning of Suffering.* Grand Rapids: W. B. Eerdmans, 1983.

Colclasure, Chuck. *The Overcomers: The Unveiling of Hope, Comfort, and Encouragement in the Book of Revelation.* Nashville: Thomas Nelson Publishers, 1981.

Cole, R. A. *The Gospel According to St. Mark.* Grand Rapids: W. B. Eerdmans, 1961.

Coleman, Robert E. *Songs of Heaven: A Book of Praise From the Author of The Master Plan of Evangelism.* Old Tappan, N.J.: Fleming H. Revell, 1980.

Conyers, A. J. *The Eclipse of Heaven: Rediscovering the Hope of a World Beyond.* Downers Grove, Ill.: InterVarsity Press, 1992.

Conzelmann, Hans. *A Commentary on the First Epistle to the Corinthians.* Translated by James W. Leitch. Philadelphia: Fortress Press, 1975.

Coxe, A. Cleveland. *The Apostolic Fathers with Justin Martyr and Irenaeus.* Vol. 1. Grand Rapids: W. B. Eerdmans, 1969.

Cranfield, C. E. B. *The Gospel According to Saint Mark: An Introduction and Commentary.* Cambridge: Cambridge University Press, 1972.

Criswell W. A., and Paige Patterson. *Heaven.* Wheaton, Ill.: Tyndale House Publishers, 1991.

Cullmann, Oscar. *Immortality of the Soul or Resurrection of the Dead? The Witness of   the New Testament.* London: Epworth Press, 1958.

Dante Alighieri. *The Divine Comedy: Paradiso.* Translated with a commentary by Charles S. Singleton, Italian Text and Translation. Princeton, N.J.: Princeton University Press, 1982.

Davids, Peter H. *The First Epistle of Peter.* Grand Rapids: W. B. Eerdmans, 1990.

Davies, P. O. "Did Jesus Die a Martyr-Prophet?" *Biblical Research* 2 (1957): 19-34.

De Haan, M. R. *Studies in I Corinthians: Messages on Practical Christian Living.* Grand Rapids: Zondervan Publishing House, 1957.

Depoortere, Kristiaan. *A Different God: A Christian View of Suffering.* Grand Rapids: W. B. Eerdmans, 1995.

De Ru, G. "The Conception of Reward in the Teaching of Jesus." *Novum Testamentum* 8 (1966): 202-222.

Dillow, Joseph C. *The Reign of the Servant Kings: A Study of Eternal Security and the Final Significance of Man.* Miami Springs, Fla.: Schoettle Publishing Company, 1992.

Disley, Emma. "Degrees of Glory: Protestant Doctrine and the Concept of Rewards Hereafter." *Journal of Theological Studies* 42, part 1 (April 1991): 77-105.

Downing, John. "Jesus and Martyrdom." *Journal of Theological Studies* 14 (1963): 279-293.

Dumbrell, W. J. "The Judgment of the Nations." In *Alive To God: Studies in Spirituality,* ed. J. I. Packer & Loren Wilkinson, 72-82. Downers Grove, Ill.: InterVarsity Press, 1992.

Duncan, George B. *Studies in the Epistle to the Philippians: The Life of Continual Rejoicing.* Chicago: Moody Press, 1965.

Eadie, John. *A Commentary on the Greek Text of the Epistle of Paul to the Colossians.* Edinburgh: Clark, 1884. Reprint, Grand Rapids: Baker Book House, 1979.

Earle, Ralph. *The Gospel According to Mark.* Grand Rapids: Zondervan Publishing House, 1957.

Edelman, John T. "Suffering and the Will of God." *Faith and Philosophy* 10 (July 1993): 380-388.

Ellis, Earle E. *The Gospel of Luke.* Camden, N.Y.: Nelson, 1966.

English, Schuyber E. *Studies in the Gospel According to Mark.* New York: "Our Hope" Publication Office, 1943.

Erdman, Charles R. *The Gospel of Matthew: An Exposition.* Philadelphia: Westminster Press, 1940.

Erickson, Millard J. *Christian Theology.* Grand Rapids: Baker Book House, 1985.

Estep, William R. *The Anabaptist Story*. Grand Rapids: W. B. Eerdmans, 1963.

Eusebius *Ecclesiastical History, Books 1-5*. Translated and edited by Roy J. Deferrari. New York: Fathers of the Church, 1953.

_____ *Ecclesiastical History, Books 6-10*. Translated and edited by Roy J. Deferrari. New York: Fathers of the Church, 1955.

Fairbairn, Patrick. *Commentary on the Pastoral Epistles*. Grand Rapids: Zondervan Publishing House, 1956.

Fee, Gordon D. *The First Epistle to the Corinthians*. Grand Rapids: W. B. Eerdmans, 1987.

_____. *Paul's Letter to the Philippians*. Grand Rapids: W. B. Eerdmans, 1995.

Fenton, J. C. *The Gospel of St. Matthew*. Baltimore: Penguin Books, 1963.

Fiddes, Paul S. *The Creative Suffering of God*. Oxford: Clarendon Press, 1992.

Filson, Floyd V. *A Commentary on the Gospel According to St. Matthew*. New York: Harper & Bros. Publishers, 1960.

_____. "Partakers With Christ: Suffering in First Peter." *Interpretation* 8 (1955): 400-412.

Flemington, W. F. "On the Interpretation of Colossians 1:23." In *Suffering and Martyrdom in The New Testament*, ed. William Horbury and Brian McNeil. Cambridge: Cambridge University Press, 1979.

Foxe, John. *Foxe's Book of Martyrs: A History of the Lives, Sufferings, and Deaths of the Early Christian and Protestant Martyrs*. 1563. Reprint, edited by William Byron Forbush, Grand Rapids: Zondervan Publishing House, 1926 and 1982.

France, R. T. *Jesus and the Old Testament*. Downers Grove, Ill.: InterVarsity Press, 1971.

Frend, W. H. C. *Martyrdom and Persecution in the Early Church: A Study of a Conflict from the Maccabees to Donatus*. Grand Rapids: Baker Book House, 1965.

Fretheim, Terrence E. *The Suffering of God: An Old Testament Perspective*. Philadelphia: Fortress Press, 1984.

Friedmann, Robert. *The Theology of Anabaptism*. Scottdale, Pa.: Herald Press, 1973.

Fuller, William J. "I Will Not Erase His Name from the Book of Life (Revelation 3:5)." *Journal of the Evangelical Theological Society* 26 (1983): 299-304.

Furnish, Victor Paul. *2 Corinthians*. Garden City, N.Y.: Doubleday, 1984.

Gadler, M. F. *The Gospel According to Matthew: With Notes Critical and Practical*. London: George Bell, 1895.

Gaffin, Richard B. *The Centrality of the Resurrection: A Study in Paul's Soteriology*. Grand Rapids: Baker Book House, 1978.

Gartner, B. "πάσχω." In *The New International Dictionary of New Testament Theology*, edited by Colin Brown, vol. 3, 719-725. Grand Rapids: Zondervan Publishing House, 1971.

Geldenhuys, Norval. *Commentary on the Gospel of Luke*. Grand Rapids: W. B. Eerdmans, 1957.

Gerstenberger, Erhard S., and Wolfgang Schrage. *Suffering*. Translated by John E. Steely. Nashville: Abingdon Press, 1980.

Ginsberg, L. M. "The Oldest Interpretation of the Suffering Servant." *Vetus Testamentum* 3 (1953): 400-404.

Glimm, Francis X., Joseph M. F. Marique, and Gerald G. Walsh, trans. and eds. *The Apostolic Fathers*. New York: Christian Heritage, 1947.

Godet, F. *Commentary on St. Paul's First Epistle to the Corinthians*. Translated from the French by A. Cousin. Edinburgh: Clark, 1886.

Goldstein, Jonathan A., trans. and ed. *1 Maccabees*. Garden City, N.Y.: Doubleday, 1976.

_____. *2 Maccabees*. Garden City, N.Y.: Doubleday, 1983.

Gooding, David. *According to Luke*. Grand Rapids: InterVarsity Press, 1987.

Grant, Robert M., trans. "Ignatius of Antioch." In *The Apostolic Fathers*, vol. 4. London: Thomas Nelson Publishers, 1966.

Grayston, Kenneth. *Dying, We Live: A New Inquiry into the Death of Christ in the New Testament*. New York: Oxford University Press, 1990.

Green, Benedict H. *The Gospel According to Matthew*. Oxford: Oxford University Press, 1975.

Grudem, Wayne. *1 Peter*. Grand Rapids: W. B. Eerdmans, 1988.

Grundmann, Walter. "δόκιμος." In *The Theological Dictionary of the New Testament*, edited by Gerhard Kittel, translated and edited by Geoffrey W. Bromiley, vol. 2, 255-261. Grand Rapids: W. B. Eerdmans, 1979.

Gundry, Robert H. *Mark: A Commentary on His Apology for the Cross*. Grand Rapids: W. B. Eerdmans, 1993.

Guthrie, Donald. *Hebrews*. Grand Rapids: W. B. Eerdmans, 1983.

_____. *The Pastoral Epistles*. Grand Rapids: W. B. Eerdmans, 1989.

Guyon, Jeanne. *Final Steps in Christian Maturity.* Gardiner, Maine: Christian Books Publishing House, 1985.

Hadas, Moses, trans. and ed. *The Third and Fourth Books of Maccabees.* New York: Harper & Bros. Publishers, 1953.

Haller, William. *The Elect Nation: The Meaning and Relevance of "Foxe's Book of Martyrs."* New York: Harper & Row, 1963.

Hanson, Anthony Tyrrell. *The Pastoral Epistles.* Grand Rapids: W. B. Eerdmans, 1982.

_____. *The Pastoral Letters: Commentary on the First and Second Letters to Timothy and the Letter to Titus.* Cambridge: Cambridge University Press, 1966.

Hargreaves, John. *A Guide to St. Mark's Gospel.* Valley Forge, Pa.: Judson Press, 1965.

Harris, Murray J. *Colossians & Philemon.* Grand Rapids: W. B. Eerdmans, 1991.

_____. *From Grave to Glory: Resurrection in the New Testament, Including a Response to Norman L. Geisler.* Grand Rapids: Zondervan Publishing House, Academie Books, 1990.

_____. *Raised Immortal: Resurrection Immortality in the New Testament.* Grand Rapids: W. B. Eerdmans, 1985.

Harrison, E. *Acts: The Expanding Church.* Chicago: Moody Press, 1975.

Hartman, Louis F. *The Book of Daniel.* A new translation with notes and commentary on chapters 1-9, introduction and commentary on chapters 10-12 by Alexander A. Di Lella. Garden City, N.Y.: Doubleday, 1978.

Hauerwas, Stanley. *Character and the Christian Life: A Study in Theological Ethics.* Notre Dame, Ind.: University of Notre Dame Press, 1994.

_____. *A Community of Character: Toward a Constructive Christian Social Ethic.* Notre Dame, Ind.: University of Notre Dame, 1981.

Hawthorne, Gerald F. *Philippians.* Waco, Tex.: Word Books, 1983.

Hay, David M., ed. *1 & 2 Corinthians.* Vol. 2 of *Pauline Theology.* Minneapolis: Fortress Press, 1993.

Hefley, James, and Marti Hefley. *By Their Blood: Christian Martyrs of the 20th Century.* Milford, Mich.: Mott Media, 1979.

Hemer, Colin J. *The Letters to the Seven Churches of Asia in Their Local Setting.* Sheffield: JSOT Press, 1986.

Hendriksen, William. *Exposition of Colossians and Philemon.* Grand Rapids: Baker Book House, 1964.

_____. *Exposition of Ephesians.* Grand Rapids: Baker Book House, 1967.

_____. *Exposition of the Gospel According to Luke.* Grand Rapids: Baker Book House, 1978.

_____. *Exposition of the Pastoral Epistles.* Grand Rapids: Baker Book House, 1957.

_____. *Exposition of Philippians.* Grand Rapids: Baker Book House, 1962.

_____. *Exposition of Thessalonians, Timothy and Titus.* Grand Rapids: Baker Book House, 1979.

_____. *More than Conquerors: An Interpretation of the Book of Revelation.* Grand Rapids: Baker Book House, 1940.

Heschel, Abraham. *The Prophets.* New York: Harper & Row, 1962.

Hiebert, D. Edmond. *The Thessalonian Epistles: A Call to Readiness.* Chicago: Moody Press, 1971.

Hodge, Charles. *An Exposition of the Second Epistle to the Corinthians.* 1891. Reprint, Grand Rapids: W. B. Eerdmans, 1995.

Hodges, Zane C. *The Gospel Under Siege: A Study on Faith and Works.* Dallas: Redencion Viva, 1981.

_____. *Grace in Eclipse: A Study on Eternal Rewards.* Dallas: Redencion Viva, 1985.

Hoekema, Anthony A. *Created in God's Image.* Grand Rapids: W. B. Eerdmans, 1986.

Hooker, Morna D. *From Adam to Christ: Essays on Paul.* Cambridge: Cambridge University Press, 1990.

_____. *The Gospel According to Saint Mark.* Peabody, Mass.: Hendrikson Publishers, 1991.

_____. *Jesus and the Servant.* London: S. P. C. K., 1959.

_____, ed. *Suffering and Martyrdom in the New Testament.* Cambridge: Cambridge University Press, 1981.

Hoover, Roy W. "The HARPAGMOS Enigma: A Philological Solution." *The Harvard Theological Review* 64 (1971): 95-119.

Horbury, William, and Brian McNeil, eds. *Suffering and Martyrdom in the New Testament.* Studies presented to G. M. Styler by the Cambridge New Testament Seminar. Cambridge: Cambridge University Press, 1979.

Hughes, Philip Edgcombe. *Paul's Second Epistle to the Corinthians: The English Text with Introduction, Exposition and Notes.* Grand Rapids: W. B. Eerdmans, 1962.

_____. *The True Image: The Origin and Destiny of Man in Christ.* Grand Rapids: W. B. Eerdmans, 1989.

Hunt, Dave. *Whatever Happened to Heaven?* Eugene, Ore.: Harvest House, 1988.

Hurtado, Larry W. *Mark.* Cambridge: Harper & Row, 1983.

Ironside, H. A. *Expository Notes on the Gospel of Matthew.* New York: Loizeaux Bros., 1945.

Johnson, Sherman E. *A Commentary on the Gospel According to St. Mark.* New York: Harper & Row, 1960.

Johnston, George. "Christ as ARCHEGOS." *New Testament Studies* 6 (1959-1960): 381-385.

Jones, Stanley E. *Christ and Human Suffering.* London: Hodder & Stoughton, 1933.

Kelly, Geffrey, ed. *Karl Rahner: Theologian of the Graced Search for Meaning.* Minneapolis: Fortress Press, 1992.

Kelly, J. N. D. *A Commentary on the Epistles of Peter and Jude.* Grand Rapids: Baker Book House, 1969.

Kemp, Eric Waldram. *Canonization and Authority in the Western Church.* London: Oxford University Press, 1948.

Kennedy. James D. *The Overcomers: The Unveiling of Hope, Comfort, and Encouragement in the Book of Revelation.* Nashville: Thomas Nelson Publishers, 1981.

Kepler, Thomas S. *Dreams of the Future.* London: Lutherworth Press; New York: Abingdon Press, 1963.

Kiddle, Martin. *The Moffatt Commentary: Revelation.* New York: Harper & Bros. Publishers, 1940.

Kirk, Albert, and Robert E. Obach. *A Commentary on the Gospel of Matthew.* New York: Paulist Press, 1978.

Kistemaker, Simon J. *Hebrews*. Grand Rapids: Baker Book House, 1984.

Kitanori, Kazoh. *The Theology of the Pain of God*. London: SCM Press, 1946.

Kleist, James A. *The Epistles of St. Clement of Rome and St. Ignatius of Antioch*. New York: Newman Press, 1946.

Knight, George W. *The Faithful Sayings in the Pastoral Letters*. Grand Rapids: Baker Book House, 1979.

_____. *The Pastoral Epistles: A Commentary on the Greek Text*. Grand Rapids: W. B. Eerdmans, 1992.

Knott, John R. *Discourses of Martyrdom in English Literature, 1563-1694*. Cambridge: Cambridge University Press, 1993.

Knox, W. L. *St. Paul and the Church of the Gentiles*. Cambridge: Cambridge University Press, 1939.

Kolb, Robert. *For All the Saints: Changing Perceptions of Martyrdom and Sainthood in the Lutheran Reformation*. Grand Rapids: Baker Book House, 1986.

Kreeft, Peter. *Everything You Ever Wanted to Know about Heaven, But Never Dreamed of Asking*. First complete edition. San Francisco: Ignatius Press, 1990.

_____. *Making Sense Out of Suffering*. Ann Arbor, Mich.: Servant Books, 1986.

Kuzmic, Peter. *The Church and the Kingdom of God: A Theological Reflection*. Grand Rapids: Baker Book House, 1986.

Lactantius. *The Divine Institutes, Books I-VIII*. Translated by Mary McDonald. Washington, D.C.: The Catholic University of America Press, 1964.

_____. *The Minor Works.* Translated by Mary McDonald. Washington, D.C.: The Catholic University of America Press, 1965.

Ladd, George Eldon. *A Commentary on the Revelation of John.* Grand Rapids: W. B. Eerdmans, 1972.

Lane, William L. *The Gospel According to Mark.* Grand Rapids: W. B. Eerdmans, 1974.

Larson, Bruce. *The Communicator's Commentary: Luke.* Waco, Tex.: Word Books, 1983.

LaVerdiere, Eugene. *Luke.* Wilmington, Del.: Michael Glazier, 1980.

Leaney, A. R. C. *A Commentary on the Gospel According to St. Luke.* London: Adam & Charles Black, 1958.

_____. "The Eschatological Significance of Human Suffering in the Old Testament and the Dead Sea Scrolls." *Scottish Journal of Theology* 16 (1963): 286-296.

Lee, Jung Young. *God Suffers for Us: A Systematic Inquiry into a Concept of Divine Passibility.* The Hague: Martinus Nijhoff, 1974.

Lenski, R. C. H. *The Interpretation of the Acts of the Apostles.* Columbus, Ohio: Wartburg Press, 1944.

_____. *The Interpretation of St. Luke's Gospel.* Columbus, Ohio: Wartburg Press, 1946.

_____. *The Interpretation of St. Mark's Gospel.* Minneapolis: Augsburg Publishers, 1964.

_____. *The Interpretation of St. Matthew's Gospel.* Columbus, Ohio: Wartburg Press, 1943.

_____. *The Interpretation of St. Paul's First and Second Epistles to the Corinthians.* Minneapolis: Augsburg Publishers, 1935.

Lightfoot, J. B. *Saint Paul's Epistles to the Colossians and Philemon.* London: Macmillan, 1892.

_____. *Saint Paul's Epistle to the Philippians.* Reprint, Grand Rapids: Zondervan Publishing House, 1963.

Lincoln, Andrew T. *Ephesians.* Dallas: Word Books, 1990.

_____. *Paradise Now and Not Yet: Studies in the Role of the Heavenly Dimension in Paul's Thought with Special Reference to His Eschatology.* Grand Rapids: Baker Book House, 1991.

Lindsay, Thomas M. *The Gospel According to St. Mark: With Introduction, Notes, and Maps.* Edinburgh: T. & T. Clark, 1883. Reprint, Minneapolis: Augsburg Publishers, 1964.

Lockyer, Herbert. *Last Words of Saints and Sinners.* Grand Rapids: Kregel Publications, 1969.

Lossky, Nicholas, et al, eds. *Dictionary of the Ecumenical Movement: Martyrdom.* Geneva: WCC Publications; Grand Rapids: W. B. Eerdmans, 1991.

Luther, Martin. *What Luther Says: An Anthology.* Compiled by Ewald M. Plass. Vol. 2. St. Louis, Mo.: Concordia Publishing House, 1959.

Maclaren, Alexander. *The Gospel of St. Matthew.* Vol. 2. London: Hodder & Stoughton, 1898.

MacRae, Allan A. *The Gospel of Isaiah.* Chicago: Moody Press, 1977.

Malone, Edward E. "The Monk and the Martyr." *Studia Anselmiana* 38 (1956): 201-228.

Manson, T. W. "Martyrs and Martyrdom." *Bulletin of John Rylands Library* 39 (1957): 463-84.

Manson, William. *The Gospel of Luke.* London: Hodder & Stoughton, 1930.

Martin, Ralph P. *Carmen Christi: Philippians 2:5-11.* Cambridge: Cambridge University Press, 1967.

_____. *Colossians: The Church's Lord and the Christian's Liberty.* Grand Rapids: Zondervan Publishing House, 1973.

_____. *2 Corinthians.* Waco, Tex.: Word Books, 1986.

McDannell, Colleen, and Bernhard Lang. *Heaven: A History.* New Haven: Yale University Press, 1988.

McGarvey, J. W. *Matthew and Mark.* Cincinnati: Chase & Hall, 1876.

McGill, Arthur C. *Suffering: A Test of Theological Method.* Philadelphia: Westminster Press, 1982.

McGrath, Alister E. *The Mystery of the Cross.* Grand Rapids: Zondervan Publishing House, Academie Books, 1988.

Mealy, J. Webb. *After the Thousand Years: Resurrection and Judgment in Revelation 20.* Sheffield: JSOT Press, 1992.

Meier, John P. *Matthew.* Wilmington, Del.: Michael Glazier, 1980.

Melick, Richard R. *Philippians, Colossians, Philemon.* Vol. 32 of *The New American Commentary: An Exegetical and Theological Exposition of Holy Scripture.* Nashville: Broadman Press, 1991.

Menzies, Alan. *The Earliest Gospel: A Historical Study of the Gospel According to Mark.* London: Macmillan, 1901.

Meyer, Heinrich August Wilhelm. *Biblical and Exegetical Hand-Book to the Epistles to the Corinthians.* Translated from the fifth edition of the German by Douglas Bannerman. New York: Funk & Wagnalls Publishers, 1884.

Michael, Hugh J. *The Epistle of Paul to the Philippians.* Garden City, N.Y.: Doubleday, 1929.

Michaelis, Wilhelm. "πάσχω." In *The Theological Dictionary of the New Testament,* edited by Gerhard Kittel, translated and edited by Geoffrey W. Bromiley, vol. 5, 904-939. Grand Rapids: W. B. Eerdmans, 1979.

Michelson, A. Berkley. *Daniel & Revelation: Riddles or Realities?* Nashville: Thomas Nelson Publishers, 1984.

M'Neile, Alan Hugh. *The Gospel According to St. Matthew.* London: Macmillan, 1915.

Molinari, Paolo. *Saints: Their Place in the Church.* New York: Shedd & Ward, 1965.

Moltmann, Jürgen. *The Crucified God.* London: SCM Press, 1974.

_____. *The Future of Creation.* London: SCM Press, 1979.

_____. *God in Creation.* London: SCM Press, 1985.

_____. *History and the Triune God: Contribution to Trinitarian Theology.* London: SCM Press, 1991.

_____. *Jesus Christ for Today's World.* London: SCM Press, 1994.

_____. *The Way of Jesus Christ: Christology in Messianic Dimensions.* Minneapolis: Fortress Press, 1993.

Montague, George T. *Growth in Christ: A Study in Saint Paul's Theology of Progress.* Kirkwood, Mont.: Maryhurst Press; Friebourg, Switzerland: St. Paul's Press or Regina Mundi, 1961.

Morgan, Campbell G. *The Corinthian Letters of Paul: An Exposition of I and II Corinthians.* New York: Fleming H. Revell, 1946.

Morison, James. *A Practical Commentary on the Gospel According to St. Matthew.* London: Hodder & Staughton, 1890.

Morris, Leon. *The Biblical Doctrine of Judgment.* Grand Rapids: W. B. Eerdmans, 1960.

_____. *The First Epistle of Paul to the Corinthians: An Introduction and Commentary.* Grand Rapids: W. B. Eerdmans, 1958.

_____. *Luke: An Introduction and Commentary.* Grand Rapids: W. B. Eerdmans, 1974.

Morris, M. Henry. *The Revelation Record: A Scientific and Devotional Commentary on the Book of Revelation.* Wheaton, Ill.: Tyndale House Publishers, 1983.

Motyer, Alec J. *The Message of Philippians.* Downers Grove, Ill.: InterVarsity Press, 1984.

_____. *The Prophecy of Isaiah: An Introduction & Commentary.* Downers Grove, Ill.: InterVarsity Press, 1993.

Moule, C. F. D. "Further Reflections on Philippians 2:5-11." In *Apostolic History and the Gospel: Biblical and Historical Essays,* edited by W. Ward Gasque and Ralph P. Martin, 264-276. Grand Rapids: W. B. Eerdmans, 1970.

_____. *The Gospel According to Mark.* Cambridge: Cambridge University Press, 1965.

_____. *The Sacrifice of Christ.* Philadelphia: Fortress Press, 1964.

Moule, H. C. G. *Studies in II Timothy.* Grand Rapids: Kregel Publications, 1977.

Mounce, Robert H. *The Book of Revelation.* Grand Rapids: W. B. Eerdmans, 1977.

_____. *Matthew.* San Francisco: Harper & Row, 1985.

Muilenburg, J. *The Book of Isaiah: Chapters 40-66.* New York: The Interpreter's Bible, 1956.

Murphree, Jon Tal. *A Loving God & A Suffering World: A New Look at an Old Problem.* Downers Grove, Ill.: InterVarsity Press, 1981.

Murphy-O'Connor, Jerome, ed. *Paul and Qumran: Studies in New Testament Exegesis.* Chicago: The Priory Press, 1968.

_____. *The Theology of the Second Letter to the Corinthians.* Cambridge: Cambridge University Press, 1991.

Murray, John. *The Epistle to the Romans.* Grand Rapids: W. B. Eerdmans, 1959.

_____. *Redemption: Accomplished and Applied.* London: Banner of Truth Trust, 1961.

Nickelsburg, George W. E. *Resurrection, Immortality and Eternal Life.* Cambridge: Harvard University Press, 1972.

_____. "Studies on *The Testament of Moses.*" *Society of Biblical Literature*, Septuagint and Cognate Studies, 4 (1973): n.p.

Nineham, D. E. *The Gospel of St. Mark.* Baltimore: Penguin Books, 1963.

O'Brian, Peter T. *Colossians & Philemon.* Waco, Tex.: Word Books, 1982.

_____. *The Epistle to the Philippians: A Commentary on the Greek Text.* Grand Rapids: W. B. Eerdmans, 1991.

O'Donoval, Oliver. *Resurrection and Moral Order: An Outline for Evangelical Ethics.* Grand Rapids: W. B. Eerdmans, 1994.

Origen. *On Prayer & Exhortation to Martyrdom.* Translated by John J. O'Meara. New York: Newman Press, 1954.

Osborn, Eric. *The Emergence of Christian Theology: Martyrdom and Askesis.* Cambridge: Cambridge University Press, 1993.

Oulton, John Ernest and Chadwick Henry, trans. and eds. *Alexandrian Christianity: Selected Translations from Clement and Origen.* Philadelphia: Westminster Press, 1954.

Owen, E. C. E. *Some Authentic Acts of the Early Martyrs.* Oxford: Clarendon Press, 1927.

Packer, James Innell. "Richard Baxter on Heaven, Hope, and Holiness." In *Alive to God: Studies in Spirituality,* edited by J. I. Packer and Loren Wilkinson, 161-174. Downers Grove, Ill.: InterVarsity Press, 1992.

Pain, Timothy. *Glory in Sacrifice.* Eastbourne: Kingsway Publications, 1989.

Parker, Joseph. *Apostolic Life As Revealed in the Acts of the Apostles.* Vol. 1. London: R. Clarke, 1883.

Parry, R. St. John., ed. *The First Epistle of Paul the Apostle to the Corinthians.* Cambridge: Cambridge University Press, 1916.

Pelonbet, F. N. *The Teachers' Commentary on the Gospel According to St. Matthew.* New York: Oxford University Press, 1901.

Peterson, David. *Hebrews and Perfection: An Examination of the Concept of Perfection in the Epistle to the Hebrews.* Cambridge: Cambridge University Press, 1982.

Plummer, Alfred. *An Exegetical Commentary on the Gospel According to St. Matthew.* London: Robert Scott, 1909.

Pobee, John S. "Persecution and Martyrdom in the Theology of Paul." Ph.D. diss., University of Cambridge, n.d. Published in *The Journal for the Study of the New Testament* Supplement Series 6. Sheffield: JSOT Press, The University of Sheffield, 1985.

Preisker, Herbert. "μισθός." In *The Theological Dictionary of the New Testament,* edited by Gerhard Kittel, translated and edited by Geoffrey W. Bromiley, vol. 4, 695-728. Grand Rapids: W. B. Eerdmans, 1979.

Proudfoot, Merrill C. "Imitation or Realistic Participation: A Study of Paul's Concept of 'Suffering With Christ.' " *Interpretation* 17 (1963): 140-160.

_____. *Suffering: A Christian Understanding.* Philadelphia: Westminster Press, 1964.

Rawlingson, A. E. J. *St. Mark.* London: Methuen, 1925.

Reames, Sherry L. *The "Legenda Aurea": A Reexamination of its Paradoxical History.* Madison, Wis.: University of Wisconsin Press, 1985.

Redpath, Alan. *The Royal Route to Heaven: Studies in First Corinthians.* New York: Fleming H. Revell, 1960.

Reisenfeld, Ernst H. "παρά." In *The Theological Dictionary of the New Testament,* edited by Gerhard Kittel, translated and edited by Geoffrey W. Bromiley, vol. 3, 727-736. Grand Rapids: W. B. Eerdmans, 1979.

Rice, Edwin W. *People's Commentary on the Gospel According to Matthew.* Philadelphia: The American Sunday School Union, 1987.

Rice, John R. *The King of the Jews: A Commentary of the Gospel According to Matthew.* Wheaton, Ill.: Sword of the Lord Publishers, 1955.

Richard, Lucien. *What Are They Saying About the Theology of Suffering?* New York: Paulist Press, 1992.

Richard, Ramesh P. *The Population of Heaven.* Chicago: Moody Press, 1994.

Richardson, Cyril, trans. and ed. *Early Christian Fathers.* New York: Macmillan, 1970.

Ridderbos, Herman. *Paul: An Outline of His Theology.* Translated by John Richard de Witt. Grand Rapids: W. B. Eerdmans, 1975.

Robinson, H. Wheeler. *Suffering: Human and Divine.* London: SCM, 1940.

Robinson, Theodore H. *The Gospel of Matthew.* London: Hodder & Staughton, 1928.

Rosscup, James E. "The Overcomer of the Apocalypse." *Grace Theological Journal* 3, no. 2 (1982): 261-286.

Roth, Cecil. *Dead Sea Scrolls: A New Historical Approach.* New York: Norton, 1966.

Rowan, Crews D. "Martyrdom." In *The Dictionary of the Ecumenical Movement,* edited by N. Lossky, et al., 658-661. Geneva: WCC Publications; Grand Rapids: W. B. Eerdmans, 1991.

Russell, D. S. *The Method & Message of Jewish Apocalyptic: 200 B.C.—A.D. 100.* Philadelphia: Westminster Press, 1964.

Ryle, J. C. *Mark: Expository Thoughts on the Gospel.* Wheaton, Ill.: Crossway Books, 1993.

_____. *Matthew: Expository Thoughts on the Gospel.* Wheaton, Ill.: Crossway Books, 1993.

Sadler, M. F. *The Gospel According to Matthew.* London: George Bell, 1897.

Sanders, E. P. *Paul and Palestinian Judaism: A Comparison of Patterns of Religion.* Philadelphia: Fortress Press, 1977.

Scharlemann, Martin H. *Qumran & Corinth: The Theology & Life of the Dead Sea Community.* N.p.: N. C. U. P., Masterworks of Literature Series, 1962.

Schippers, R. "θλίψις." In *The New International Dictionary of New Testament Theology*, edited by Colin Brown, vol. 2, 807-809. Grand Rapids: Zondervan Publishing House, 1971.

Schneider, W. "πειρασμός." In *The New International Dictionary of New Testament Theology*, edited by Colin Brown, vol. 3, 798-808. Grand Rapids: Zondervan Publishing House, 1971.

Schweitzer, Albert. *The Mysticism of Paul the Apostle*. Translated into English by William Montgomery. New York: Henry Holt, 1931.

Seeley, David. *The Noble Death: Graeco-Roman Martyrology and Paul's Concept of Salvation*. Sheffield: JSOT Press, 1990.

Shelley, Bruce. *The Cross and the Flame: Chapters in the History of Martyrdom*. Grand Rapids: W. B. Eerdmans, 1967.

Sherman, James Edward. *The Nature of Martyrdom: A Dogmatic and Moral Analysis According to the Teaching of St. Thomas Aquinas*. Paterson, N.J.: St. Anthony Guild Press, 1942.

Shires, Henry M. *The Eschatology of Paul in the Light of Modern Scholarship*. Philadelphia: Westminster Press, 1966.

Silva, Moises. "Perfection and Eschatology in Hebrews." *The Westminster Theological Journal* 39 (Fall 1976–Spring 1977): 60-71.

_____. *Philippians*. Grand Rapids: Baker Book House, 1992.

Simons, Menno. *The Complete Writings*. Translated from the Dutch by Leonard Verduin. Edited by John Christian Wenger, with a bibliography by Harold S. Bender. Scottdale, Pa.: Herald Press, 1966.

Smith, Miles W. *On Whom the Spirit Came: A Study of the Acts of the Apostles*. Philadelphia: Judson Press, 1948.

Smith, Wilbur M. *The Biblical Doctrine of Heaven*. Chicago: Moody Press, 1968.

Sparks, H. F. D., ed. *The Apocryphal Old Testament*. Oxford: Clarendon Press, 1984.

Springsted, Eric O. *Simone Weil & The Suffering of Love*. Cambridge, Ma.: Cowley Publications, 1986.

Stanley, Glen J. *Pastoral Problems in First Corinthians*. Philadelphia: Westminster Press, 1964.

Staton, Weitbrecht. *The Gospel According to St. Matthew*. New York: S. P. C. K., 1919.

Stauffer, Ethelbert. "The Anabaptist Theology of Martyrdom." *The Mennonite Quarterly Review* 19, no. 3 (1945): 179-194.

_____. *New Testament Theology*. Translated by John Marsh. New York: Macmillan, 1956.

Stern, Harry Joshua. *Martyrdom and Miracle: A Collection of Addresses*. New York: Bloch Publishing Company, 1950.

Stevenson, J., ed. *A New Eusebius: Documents Illustrative of the History of the Church to A.D. 337*. London: S. P. C. K., 1960.

Stott, John R. W. *The Cross of Christ*. Downers Grove, Ill.: InterVarsity Press, 1986.

_____. *The Message of 2 Timothy*. Downers Grove, Ill.: InterVarsity Press, 1973.

_____. *Romans: God's Good News for the World*. Downers Grove, Ill.: InterVarsity Press, 1994.

Strathmann, Herbert, "μάρτυς." In *The Theological Dictionary of the New Testament*, edited by Gerhard Kittel, translated and edited by Geoffrey W. Bromiley, vol. 4, 474-514. Grand Rapids: W. B. Eerdmans, 1979.

Swete, H. B. *The Gospel According to St. Mark.* London: Macmillan, 1913.

Tasker, R. V. G. *The Gospel According to St. Matthew.* Grand Rapids: W. B. Eerdmans, 1961.

Taylor, Vincent. *The Gospel According to St. Mark.* London: Macmillan, 1953.

Tertullian. *Apology & De Spectaculis.* Translated by T. R. Glover. London: William Heinemann, 1931.

_____. *Disciplinary, Moral, and Ascetical Works.* Translated by Rudolph Arbesmann. New York: Fathers of the Church, 1959.

Thomson, E. T. *The Gospel According to Mark.* Richmond, Va.: John Knox Press, 1954.

Thomson, G. H. P. *The Gospel According to Luke.* Oxford: Clarendon Press, 1972.

Thornwell, James Henley. *Collected Writings.* Vol. 2. 1875. Reprint, Edinburgh: Banner of Truth Trust, 1974.

Tinsley, E. J. *The Gospel According to Luke.* Cambridge: Cambridge University Press, 1965.

Toon, Peter. *Heaven and Hell: A Biblical and Theological Overview.* Nashville, Tenn.: Thomas Nelson Publishers, 1986.

Towner, Philip H. *1 and 2 Timothy & Titus.* Downers Grove, Ill.: InterVarsity Press, 1994.

Trites, Allison A. *The New Testament Concept of Witness.* Cambridge: Cambridge University Press, 1977.

Tugwell, Simon. *Human Immortality and the Redemption of Death.* London: Darton, Longman & Todd, 1990.

Turner, James. *The Shrouds of Glory: Six Studies in Martyrdom.* London: Cassell, n.d.

Unnik, Willem Cornelis van. *The New Testament: Its History and Message.* New York: Harper & Row, 1964.

Vine, W. E. *Expository Dictionary of New Testament Words.* Grand Rapids: Zondervan Publishing House, 1952.

Wagner, C. Peter. *Your Spiritual Gifts Can Help Your Church Grow.* Rev. ed. Ventura, Calif.: Regal Books, 1994.

Wall, Robert W. *Colossians & Philemon.* Downers Grove, Ill.: InterVarsity Press, 1993.

Walle, A. R. van de. *From Darkness to the Dawn: How Belief in the Afterlife Affects Living.* Mystic, Conn.: Twenty-Third Publications, 1985.

Walsh, Gerald G., trans. "Ignatius of Antioch." In *The Apostolic Fathers,* translated by Frances X. Glimm, Joseph M. F. Marique, and Gerald G. Walsh. New York: Christian Heritage, 1947.

Weiner, Eugene, and Anita Weiner. *The Martyr's Conviction: A Sociological Analysis.* Atlanta: Scholars Press, 1990.

Weinrich, William C. *Spirit and Martyrdom: A Study of the Work of the Holy Spirit in the Contexts of Persecution and Martyrdom in the New Testament and Early Literature.* Washington, D.C.: University Press of America, 1981.

Weinstein, Donal, and Rudolph M. Bell. *Saints & Society: The Two Worlds of Western Christendom, 1000-1700.* Chicago: University of Chicago Press, 1982.

Westermann, Claus. *Isaiah 40-66: A Commentary.* Philadelphia: Westminster Press, 1969.

Wiersbe, Warren W., ed. *Classic Sermons on Suffering.* Grand Rapids: Kregel Publications, 1984.

Wilcock, Michael. *The Message of Revelation: I Saw Heaven Opened.* Downers Grove, Ill.: InterVarsity Press, 1975.

Wiles, M. F. *The Divine Apostle: The Interpretation of St. Paul's Epistles in the Early Church.* Cambridge: Cambridge University Press, 1967.

Williams, Sam K. *Jesus' Death as a Saving Event: The Background and Origin of a Concept.* Missoula, Mont.: Scholars Press, 1975.

Winston, David, trans. and ed. *The Wisdom of Solomon.* Garden City, N.Y.: Doubleday, 1979.

Wirgren, Allen. "Patterns of Perfection in the Epistle to the Hebrews." *New Testament Studies* 27 (1981): 159-167.

Wood, Diana, ed. *Studies in Church History: Martyrs and Martyrologies.* Vol. 30. Oxford: Blackwell Publishers, 1993.

Workman, B. Herbert. *Persecution in the Early Church.* Oxford: Oxford University Press, 1980.

Wuest, K. S. *Mark.* Grand Rapids: W. B. Eerdmans, 1952.

Young, Edward J. *The Book of Isaiah: Chapters 40-66.* The English text with introduction, exposition, and notes. Vol. 3. Grand Rapids: W. B. Eerdmans, 1972.

Youngblood, Ronald F. *The Book of Isaiah: An Introductory Commentary.* 2d ed. Grand Rapids: Baker Books, 1993.

Zeitlin, Solomon, ed. *The Second Book of Maccabees.* Translated by Sidney Tedesche. New York: Harper & Bros. Publishers, 1954.

Ziesler, John A. *Pauline Christianity.* Rev. ed. Oxford: Oxford University Press, 1983.

Zimmerli, W., and Jeremias J. Zimmerli. *The Servant of God.* Naperville, Ill.: Alec R. Allenson, 1952.

Zodhiates, Spiros. *Conquering the Fear of Death: An Exposition of 1 Corinthian 15*. Grand Rapids: W. B. Eerdmans, 1970.

Scripture Index

500

Scripture Index

Scripture Index

Name and Subject Index

of life, 339; martyrdom as a
gift of the, 317
Hooker, Richard, 413
humility, 101, 104, 191, 194, 200,
235, 263, 265, 267, 351; of
Christ, 101, 140, 174, 187,
195, 210-11
Huss, John, 383
Hutterites, 395
idealist interpretation of the Book
of Revelation, 270
Ignatius, Bishop of Antioch, 148-
49, 207, 254, 325-29
image of God: as damaged by the
fall of man, 230, 430;
character as an important
aspect of the, 430; God's
work of transforming man
into the, 168, 175, 200-201,
210, 217, 229-30, 237, 430,
435; mankind created in the,
29, 60, 216, 421, 429
imitation of Christ, 176, 201, 215;
by the remnant of Israel, 8; in
suffering, 128, 135-36, 138,
150-52, 156, 166, 179, 202,
328-32, 340, 344, 358, 383,
391, 395, 398
immortality, 57; man created for,
60; of the soul, 58, 61
inheritance, the heavenly, xviii,
35, 96, 99-100, 115, 131,
158-62, 166-68, 176-77, 197,
212, 216, 228, 232, 236, 238-
39, 248, 250-51, 254-55, 261-
65, 268, 302, 304-5, 311, 320,
337, 344, 411-412, 417, 419,
422, 433; obtained by God's
mercy, 328
intellectual blindness: as a result
of man's alienation from God,
8-9, 12; produced by Satan's
deception, 12

intertestamental period: 47-61;
literature of the, xv, 33, 47,
49-61, 125-26, 429
Irenaeus, 328
Israel: in the Book of Revelation,
279, 289, 298; as joined by
the survivors from the
nations, 18, 19; as pattern and
type, 66; as servant(s) of God,
10, 14-17, 19, 73; calling of,
to suffering, 14-16, 19, 26;
disobedience of, 3, 161, 202,
234, 251; exaltation of all, 59;
exiled nation of, 7, 25, 66-68,
96, 102, 113, 115, 127-28,
155, 162, 249-51; revelation
of God through the people of,
10; history of, 9, 10, 67;
mission of, as a witness, 9-11,
14-17, 19-20, 73; failure of, to
fulfill her mission, 20, 68,
202; remnant of, 8; restoration
of, 57-58
Jason (high priest), 48
Jerome, 368
Jesus Christ. *See* Christ
joy, 130, 140, 232, 238, 333, 391;
in doing God's will, 424; in
suffering and martyrdom,
116-17, 128, 164, 185-89,
190-91, 202, 206-7, 215, 217,
247, 260, 262-63, 317, 326,
339, 341-43, 347-49, 354,
365, 382-84, 388-89, 396, 426
judgment, the last, 59, 71-72, 99-
100, 121, 140, 159, 165, 214,
271, 290, 299; based upon
works, 57, 61, 167-68, 227,
232, 237-38, 299-300, 310,
312, 320-21, 422, 430, 435; of
the enemies of God's people,
59
judgment seat of Christ, xi, xiii,
133, 164-67, 176, 202-3, 205-

215, 237-38, 243, 300, 312,
406, 409-11, 413
Protestant theology: Christ's work
of redemption as central in,
421; of grace, xiii; of
martyrdom, 381
Protestantism, 182, 382
Protestants, 76, 181, 214, 225,
259, 300, 312, 321, 380-82,
387-89, 406
providence of God, 381
purification: of the believer
through suffering, 32-34, 36,
54-55, 385, 396
Puritanism, 350
Puritans, 381
purposes of God: as fulfilled and
accomplished through
suffering, 5, 13, 14, 16, 17,
19, 129, 197, 215, 268, 422-3,
425; as fulfilled by His
enemies, 60, 129, 273, 296,
298, 384; in creating
mankind, 95, 104, 168, 229,
319; the final, with mankind,
xiii, 32, 99, 143, 174, 168,
216, 229, 319, 321, 421-22,
429; with His witnesses, 77,
80-81, 90, 100, 108, 112, 129,
141, 174-75, 229, 247, 263,
267-68, 291, 316; with the
twelve disciples, 68, 70, 73,
75, 84-86, 91
punishment: suffering as, for sin
and disobedience, 3, 13, 26,
33, 39, 53, 60, 284
Reformation. *See* Protestant
Reformation, the
Reformed theologians, 196
Reformers, the, 380, 387-88;
purging the concept of
martyrdom, xiv; ignoring the
subject of martyrdom, xiv

relics: cult of, 368, 370; powers
of, 368; preservation of, 333,
367, 380
resurrection, 23; a "better," 215,
252-53; day of, 34-35;
intertestamental belief in the,
57-61; of believers, 232, 306,
326, 331, 341, 390; of Christ,
74, 85, 88, 105, 111-12, 150,
178-80, 208-9, 212, 217, 261,
266, 272, 316, 363; of the
body, 57, 59, 79, 156; of the
dead, 36, 94, 129, 153-56,
178, 214, 271, 299, 311; of
the just, 57; of the Servant of
the Lord, 57; special, of the
martyrs, 59-60, 214-15, 252-
53, 283, 285, 289-90, 299,
310-11, 313-14, 332; the first,
215
rewards in heaven, 409-419; as
given by grace, 99, 103, 133-
34, 168, 200, 228, 255, 261,
411, 414, 416; as greater
intimacy with God, 376-77; as
motivation for good works,
410, 419; as unbroken
fellowship with God, 341;
attained at the resurrection,
34; content of, xiv, 95, 168,
197, 228, 390, 416-419, 429;
criteria for distribution of,
429; for faithful obedience,
57, 61, 75-76, 91-92, 95-6,
99-100, 156, 237-39; in the
teaching of Jesus, 74-76, 78,
91-92, 95-96, 99-100, 103;
nature of, 429; of the apostles,
96; Paul's teaching on, 157-
168; receiving no, 433. *See
also* motivation for suffering
and martyrdom
riches, earthly: deceitfulness of,
434; need wisdom to deal

Printed in the United States
17536LVS00004B/28-204